Teaching Students with Mental Retardation

A Life Goal Curriculum Planning Approach

Glen E. Thomas
Brigham Young University

Merrill,
an imprint of Prentice Hall
Englewood Cliffs, New Jersey   *Columbus, Ohio*

Library of Congress Cataloging-in-Publication Data

Thomas, Glen E.

Teaching students with mental retardation : a life goal curriculum planning approach / Glen E. Thomas.

p. cm.

Includes bibliographical references and indexes.

ISBN 0-02-420240-1

1. Mentally handicapped children—Education—United States. 2. Curriculum planning—United States. 3. Life skills—Study and Teaching—United States. I. Title.

LC4631.T56   1996

371.92'0973—dc20

95-46387

CIP

Cover art: David Kost/Arc South Workshop, Columbus, Ohio, Franklin County Board of Mental Retardation/Developmental Disabilities

Editor: Ann Castel Davis

Production Editor: Linda Hillis Bayma

Copy Editor: Linda Poderski

Photo Editor: Anne Vega

Design Coordinator: Julia Zonneveld Van Hook

Text Designer: STELLARViSIONs

Cover Designer: Brian Deep

Production Manager: Pamela D. Bennett

Electronic Text Management: Marilyn Wilson Phelps, Matthew Williams, Karen L. Bretz, Tracey Ward

This book was set in Transitional 511 by Prentice Hall and was printed and bound by Quebecor Printing/Book Press. The cover was printed by Phoenix Color Corp.

Photo credits: pp. 93, 117, 129, 149, 197, 230, 352, Scott Cunningham/Merrill/Prentice Hall; pp. 223, 255, 447, Barbara Schwartz/Merrill/Prentice Hall; pp. 16, 27, 45, 63, 159, 272, 321, 337, 382, 423, 440, Glen Thomas; pp. 3, 57, 183, 283, 347, 397, 406, 454, Anne Vega/Merrill/Prentice Hall; pp. 99, 314, Tom Watson/Merrill/Prentice Hall; p. 373, Todd Yarrington/Merrill/Prentice Hall.

Printed in the United States of America

10 9 8 7 6 5 4 3 2 1

ISBN: 0-02-420240-1

Prentice-Hall International (UK) Limited, *London*
Prentice-Hall of Australia Pty. Limited, *Sydney*
Prentice-Hall of Canada, Inc., *Toronto*
Prentice-Hall Hispanoamericana, S. A., *Mexico*
Prentice-Hall of India Private Limited, *New Delhi*
Prentice-Hall of Japan, Inc., *Tokyo*
Simon & Schuster Asia Pte. Ltd., *Singapore*
Editora Prentice-Hall do Brasil, Ltda., *Rio de Janeiro*

TO

OLIVER P. KOLSTOE

WHOSE DEDICATION
AND SCHOLARLY
EXAMPLE HAVE BEEN A
GREAT INSPIRATION TO
COUNTLESS STUDENTS
AND OTHER
PROFESSIONALS WHO
TOUCH THE LIVES OF
INDIVIDUALS WITH
MENTAL RETARDATION

I suppose I have been writing this book for more than 30 years. After college, I taught mathematics for many years. One of my first assignments was teaching remedial arithmetic classes that included a number of students who were mentally retarded, but none of them were so identified. It was a frustrating experience because they just couldn't keep up, and I had neither the time nor the resources to help them. Later, I was assigned to teach special classes that included only students with mental retardation. This gave me more time to pay attention to the individual differences of the students, but there were still no suitable workbooks or texts for them. The only reading, arithmetic, and other materials they could master were designed for younger children and they used childish examples, which meant that my students were leaving high school with a second or third grade education—at best. Materials designed expressly for them were, in truth, "watered down" college prep content—highly impractical, theoretical, and unmotivating. I had to either adapt materials designed for normal or gifted students or produce my own.

Adapting grade-level materials was discouraging, for although the available materials were essentially chronological-age appropriate, they were much too difficult for the students no matter how much help I gave them. Over a period of time, I came to appreciate the tremendous heterogeneity among my students. Even though they all had mild or moderate mental retardation, some of them in a given class had achieved (albeit low) levels by ninth grade that others could never attain no matter how long they stayed in school.

Producing my own materials was more promising, but with my huge class loads and my training in secondary education, I struggled to meet the needs of an extremely diverse population. Further, it gradually dawned on me that while my teacher-made materials seemed to be effective, I was still not focusing my efforts on helping my students achieve maximum success in adult life.

Later, I served for many years as principal of a school for students whose mental retardation was severe and profound. There, the teachers and I concluded that we essentially were teaching the three R's in an unstructured round of units and activities to groups of children rather than concentrating on their real, individual needs. What we needed were procedures to identify each student's potential or probable life goals, prioritize those goals, and faithfully evaluate each child's progress toward them. The procedures must focus primarily on what the teacher must do to organize and sequence the tasks for the students.

Recently, I have come to appreciate the plight of regular classroom teachers in inclusion programs, who—with little or no special training—have students with mental retardation assigned to their classes, usually with no compensating reduction of class loads. Thus, the instructional procedures must meet the needs of each student with mental retardation whether the student is in regular or special classes.

This book is designed to fill all of these requirements. It begins with a brief introduction to mental retardation. The introduction emphasizes the practical aspects of mental retardation that are particularly important in curriculum planning and teaching. Then it provides an uncomplicated, systematized method of identifying and prioritizing each student's life goals. It shows teachers and others how to locate and track a student's attainment of those goals. It emphasizes the roles of parents, who—with the imperative support of an effective individualized educational program (IEP) team—must assume the major responsibility for planning and conducting the curriculum.

The book demonstrates how to plan with specificity day-by-day activities for each student that are consistent with both the needs of each student and the available time and other resources of the teacher. It shows regular and special class teachers how to train parents, teaching assistants, volunteers, and peer tutors to monitor and conduct the teacher-planned learning increments under the teacher's supervision. Thus, students with mental retardation in inclusion programs can take advantage of potential social, communication, and other skills of the regular class while their curriculum can be adapted to meet their life goals as completely as possible.

A persistent theme of the book is that all school programs must enable each student with mental retardation to be as successful as possible in adult life. Thus, it emphasizes the preparation for independent living, transition, and work experience at every age level.

Therefore, the book is designed primarily as a text for an advanced undergraduate or beginning graduate-level curriculum planning and methods course in mental retardation and other severe disabilities. It will serve well in those situations where only one course in mental retardation is offered. It is also designed to meet the needs of regular and special class teachers, special consultants, parents, administrators, and others who serve and teach students with mental retardation.

Acknowledgments

I would like to thank my wife, Thelma, and our children, whose social lives suffered immensely during the writing of this book but without whose patience it would never have been completed. I am also indebted to many regular and special class teachers and graduate and undergraduate students from whom I learned an incredible amount about mental retardation. Many of the students assisted in the preparation of the manuscript.

I would like to thank the following reviewers for their helpful comments during the preparation of the manuscript: Charlotte Erickson, University of Wisconsin at LaCrosse; Barbara L. Fox, James Madison University, Harrisonburg, Virginia; Pamela Gent, Clarion University of Pennsylvania; Meredith Jamieson, Ashland University; Phillip J. McLoughlin, University of Georgia; and Robert Michael, State University of New York at New Paltz.

Special thanks to Ann Davis, administrative editor, Linda Bayma, production editor; and Linda Poderski, copy editor, for their assistance in making this text a reality.

CONTENTS

II Life Goal Planning for Individuals and Groups   55

Chapter 3 • Life Goal Curriculum Planning   57

Chapter 4 • **Working with Parents**   93

III Diagnostic/Prescriptive/ Evaluative Teaching   147

Chapter 7 • **Goal Instruction Analysis**   **183**

IV Scope, Sequence, and Content of Curriculum   253

Chapter 9 • Curriculum Planning for Students with Severe/Profound Mental Retardation and Multiple Disabilities   255

Chapter 16 • Leisure, Recreation, Motor, Art, and Music Skills   447

Epilogue   463

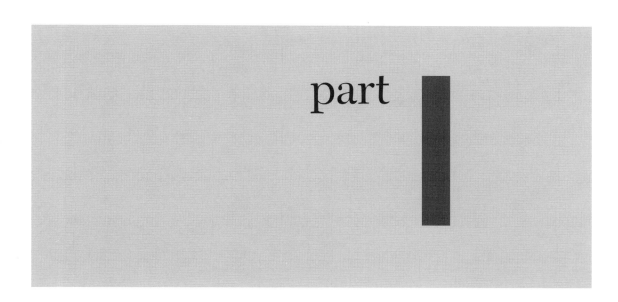

part I

An Overview of Mental Retardation

CHAPTER 1

Introducing Mental Retardation

Points to Study and Ponder

1. How is mental retardation defined?
2. What other terms are used to describe the condition of mental retardation?
3. What part does (and should) IQ play in defining mental retardation?
4. What is adaptive behavior, and what does adaptive behavior have to do with defining mental retardation?
5. Are any other terms used in place of *adaptive behavior*?
6. What specific areas of curriculum are mentioned by name in the 1992 AAMR definition of mental retardation?
7. What is regional variation, and what does it have to do with defining and discussing mental retardation?
8. Is your home state a low-identification or high-identification state?
9. What effect does regional variation have in planning curriculum and teaching students with mild/moderate mental retardation?
10. Who are the slow learners, and why are they important in planning programs in mental retardation? Do slow learners have mental retardation?
11. What is conceptual distance, and what does it have to do with curriculum planning and teaching in mental retardation?
12. What are multicultural considerations, and what effect do they have on curriculum planning and teaching in mental retardation?
13. What is heterogeneity, and what does it have to do specifically with mental retardation?

This book will help teachers, parents, and others enable students with mental retardation to achieve maximum success in adult life by using a twofold approach to curriculum planning and teaching: (a) prioritized, individual life goal planning and (b) a carefully designed diagnostic-prescriptive instructional approach to assessing each student's current progress with respect to these life goals and to helping each student achieve goals having the highest priority and practicality.

In the first two chapters, I discuss the basic nature of mental retardation and demonstrate why students with mental retardation must be given special consideration in curriculum planning and instruction. Mental retardation imposes a wide range of critical conditions and limitations on an individual, and these are discussed in some detail. In the remaining chapters, I demonstrate how to diagnose these limitations and how to identify the individual's remaining abilities on which his or her educational programs are constructed.

A considerable part of this chapter covers two fundamental but little known principles of mental retardation: *regional variation* and *conceptual distance*. These two principles have been largely overlooked in the literature, yet they have momentous implications in curriculum planning and in providing instruction and services to students with mental retardation. In this chapter, I review the great difficulty the profession has experienced in defining mental retardation. I also reveal the tremendous confusion in applying the terms *mild, moderate, severe,* and *profound* and discuss why throughout the book I use *mild/moderate* and *severe/profound* in describing the degrees of mental retardation.

TERMINOLOGY AND PUBLIC LAW 101–476

In 1990, Congress passed Public Law 101–476, the Individuals with Disabilities Education Act (the IDEA), which strengthens and augments Public Law 94–142 (1975) without substantially weakening any part of it. In effect, P.L. 101–476 supersedes P.L. 94–142, so it is proper to refer to both laws as P.L. 101–476. Throughout this book, I follow this format, except where specific reference to the IDEA is necessary.

Historically, the terminology of special education has undergone constant change in the United States and elsewhere (Corbett, 1994). The IDEA uses the term *disability*, rather than *handicap*, as in P.L. 94–142. *Disability* is probably an unfortunate choice of terms because it conflicts with current philosophy in special education and with the intent of the IDEA by focusing on a person's lack of ability. In fact, most dictionaries define disability as simply the lack of ability or as inability. *Handicap* suggests that an individual has an impairment that may be overcome or compensated for (often with difficulty), whereas *disability* somehow suggests a more permanent condition. *Disability* is used here with the reservation that even though mental retardation imposes a predictable and wide array of inabilities on a person, it is important to help such persons compensate for these inabilities and to use their remaining abilities as effectively as possible.

For many reasons, the terminology of mental retardation has been particularly transitional. *Mental retardation* seems to be the dominant expression in the field and is the one used primarily in this book. Currently, mental retardation has a number of euphemisms, such as intellectual disabilities and developmental disabilities. Few of these designations, however, appear in the titles of professional journal articles. Furthermore, a person using one of these substitute terms will almost invariably use *mental retardation* when asked for clarification. *Mental retardation* is also the term used by the IDEA and the Office of Special Education and Rehabilitation Services (OSERS) in official publications. Thus, *mental retardation* is a harsh-sounding but "official" term that describes a serious condition. With apologies to those who understandably prefer other terms, it is the one used throughout this book.

A related consideration has to do with "people first" language. In recent years, it has become increasingly popular, in referring to people with disabilities, to use language that emphasizes the person, rather than any disability he or she may have (Henderson, 1993; Tyler, 1990). For example, it is preferable to use *person with a disability* or *person who is disabled* rather than *disabled person*. In mental retardation, people-first language uses *person, student, or individual with mental retardation* or one who has mental retardation, rather than *mentally retarded person, student, or individual*. Such terms as the *retarded, the mentally retarded,* and *retardate, retard,* or *MR* are particularly offensive because they refer only to the disability without mention of the person. Not only are these references demeaning, but they also are often used deliberately as terms of derision and should never be included in either oral or written expression.

DEFINITIONS OF MENTAL RETARDATION

One reason students with mental retardation need careful individualized curriculum planning is that mental retardation has proven difficult to define. Many years ago, Cartwright and Cartwright (1978) reported that at least 31 different definitions of mental retardation were used in state codes, professional books, textbooks, and journals. Taylor (1980) reported that almost half of the articles in his review of the literature used either incorrect or indefinite terminology. The use of various terminology to refer to the same phenomenon or condition creates confusion. Without a practical, accurate, and uniformly accepted definition, it is difficult to determine specifically which students have mental retardation and how each can be identified and properly served.

The particular definition used also has a significant impact on the number of individuals identified and served. For example, more stringent definitions and identification procedures tend to identify fewer students, and in practice, such procedures tend to identify individuals with more severe forms of mental retardation (Forness, 1985; MacMillan, 1982). An examination of early sources shows that mental retardation has been traditionally defined in very strict terms (Benda, 1954; Doll, 1941; Tredgold, 1937). According to these early definitions, an individual with mental retardation had extremely limited abilities and probably needed to be institutionalized. Experience eventually showed that most individuals with mental retardation exhibit a somewhat greater capability than those early definitions suggested.

AAMD (AAMR) Definitions

The early definitions justifiably came under increasing criticism until officers of the American Association on Mental Deficiency (AAMD; now American Association on Mental Retardation, AAMR) formed a committee to examine the field of mental retardation, review the literature, and develop a more accurate and workable definition. In 1961, the committee proposed the following definition:

> Mental retardation refers to subaverage general intellectual functioning which originates during the developmental period and is associated with impairments in adaptive behavior. (Heber, 1961, p. 3)

The AAMR definition was slightly revised in 1973, 1977, and 1983, although the revisions retained most of the original terminology. Since publication, these definitions have been widely used but have resulted in much confusion and criticism, just as the earlier ones did (Clausen, 1972; Kidd, 1979; Taylor, 1980).

In 1992, the AAMR published another, more explicit definition:

> Mental retardation refers to substantial limitations in present functioning. It is characterized by significantly subaverage intellectual functioning, existing concurrently with related limitations in two or more of the following applicable adaptive skill areas: communication, self-care, home living, social skills, community use, self-direction, health and safety, functional academics, leisure, and work. Mental retardation manifests before age 18. (Luckasson et al., 1992, p. 5)

This was the first of the AAMR definitions that consisted of more than a single sentence. This definition introduced some newer, functional terminology but also retained some of the old. In addition to the definition itself, the AAMR published some guidelines to be used in applying the definition:

> Valid assessment considers cultural and linguistic diversity, and differences in communication and behavioral factors.
> The existence of limitations in adaptive skills occurs within the context of community environments typical of the individual's age peers and is indexed to the person's individualized needs support.
> Specific adaptive limitations often co-exist with strengths in adaptive skills or other personal capabilities.
> With appropriate supports over a sustained period, the life functioning of the person with mental retardation will generally improve. (Luckasson et al., 1992, p. 5)

The major improvement of the 1992 AAMR definition was the identification of the major and specific areas of endeavor in which a student with mental retardation may be deficient. These areas—communication, self-care, home living, social skills, community use, self-direction, health and safety, functional academics, leisure, and work—are all strongly emphasized in later chapters of this book. Substantial deficits in any two or more of these areas qualify the person to be identified and served as having mental retardation. Further, these areas constitute an excellent base on which to build a curriculum for a student with mental retardation.

AAMR Definitions

Probably no other academic field has been so hampered by the inability to agree on basic definitions. The AAMR definitions—even the 1992 version—have been extremely vague and difficult to put into practice, largely because of the committee's persistent use of ambiguous terminology. Apparently, in their efforts to be scholarly and brief, the committee members sacrificed some precision and practicality. As a result, even the recent AAMR definitions have been subject to persistent confusion and criticism (Blatt, 1961; Smith, 1994). Also, for a pervasive historical review of Blatt's article and the continuing controversy surrounding the AAMR definitions, see Boggs, Dybwad, and Taylor (1994).

General Intellectual Functioning

The AAMR committees' persistent retention of the term *subaverage (general) intellectual functioning* has caused immense confusion. The committees considered *intellectual functioning* to be synonymous with intelligence or intelligence quotient (IQ), a traditional measure or indication of a person's ability to learn (Anastasi, 1988). Although the intention of each committee was to set an IQ ceiling, it would probably have been better simply to specify an approximate IQ in the definition itself. *Subaverage* refers either to IQs below a point of 100 or a range based on the number of standard deviations below the mean. Because this concept has not been universally understood, it has always left the upper IQ limit of mental retardation in doubt in the minds of many people, including educators. For example, the 1961 definition was based on an upper limit of one standard deviation below the mean—or an IQ of 85. Beginning with the 1973 version, subsequent AAMR definitions reduced the upper IQ limit to two standard deviations below the mean—an IQ of 70 or below. This action was highly significant. The normal distribution curve suggests that 13.59% of a typical school population are likely to have IQs between 70 and 85. Thus, if IQs and the normal curve are assumed to be accurate and meaningful concepts, the AAMR committees, with a stroke of a pen, automatically reduced by 84% the number of individuals who could be identified as having mental retardation (Patton & Jones, 1994). Although the AAMR committees (since 1973) retained essentially the same wording in the definition itself, the full committee reports allow some flexibility in the upper IQ limit. As a result, considerable uncertainty remains over how the definition should be used to identify mental retardation.

Professionals have differing opinions on the part IQ should play in identifying individuals with mental retardation. On the one hand, Mercer (1973) suggested that the use of IQ scores in identifying students with mental retardation should be either greatly reduced or eliminated altogether. Greenspan and Granfield (1992) proposed that definitions be based on social skills and adequacy, rather than on IQ. On the other hand, Clausen (1972) also proposed to use IQ scores exclusively but disregarded adaptive behavior as being too indefinite and too hard to define. Zigler, Balla, and Hodapp (1984) suggested that mental retardation be defined essentially as an IQ of less than 70, with no consideration of adaptive behavior.

A reasonable compromise between these two opposing positions is probably best represented by Huberty, Koller, and Ten Brink (1980) and Barnett (1986), who suggested that IQ scores and some consideration of adaptive behavior are both necessary in a workable definition. Without the use of IQ scores, it is difficult to distinguish students with mental retardation (who lack the basic ability to learn) from other students (who have most of the essential abilities but do not achieve well for other reasons). Although admitting that intelligence testing may be subject to inaccuracies and inconsistencies, Berk, Bridges, and Shih (1981) identified IQ as the most critical component in the placement process of students with mental retardation. MacMillan, Gresham, and Siperstein (1993), however, pointed out that continued reference to both IQ and adaptive behavior was troublesome because neither suggested the level of needed services. Dever (1990) suggested that mental retardation should be defined in terms of the specific skill training needed for the person to become as independent as possible. Likewise, Chadsy-Rusch (1992) recommended that definitions be based on a student's social and employment abilities.

An IQ is a rough numerical attempt to compare an individual's present level of mental functioning with that of other individuals (Anastasi, 1988). It is possible to draw misleading and impractical inferences from the use of IQs. For example, an IQ of 75 does not equal a learning rate that is 75% of normal. Dunn (1963) stated that children with IQs ranging from 50 to 75 "have difficulty in school because their intellectual development is only about one-half to three-fourths of that of the average child" (p. 71). Although Dunn, in this early work, possibly did not mean to imply that learning rate and IQ are equivalent or interchangeable values, his chart (Dunn's Figure 2.2, p. 63) suggests that a child with an IQ of 50 will learn approximately half as much as a child with an IQ of 100, and so on. It has become increasingly popular to make this erroneous assumption. Although IQ scores seem to have considerable predictive value, they do not operate in a strictly linear fashion (see Figure 1.1 and the discussion of conceptual distance, discussed later in this chapter).

Adaptive Behavior

Adaptive behavior in the pre-1992 AAMR definitions included (a) maturation, (b) *learning*, and (c) social adjustment; but these are specified only in the follow-up manuals. Translating *adaptive behavior* into practical terms has proven difficult for the profession (Barnett, 1986; Hodapp & Zigler, 1986; Leland, 1972; Zigler et al., 1984). Utley, Lowitzer, and Baumeister (1987) reported that only 61% of the states emphasized adaptive behavior in identifying mental retardation, with only 10% of the states specifying measurement techniques, procedures, and cutoff points. However, there may be some light at the end of this definitional tunnel. The 1992 AAMR definition uses the term *adaptive skill areas* in place of *adaptive behavior.* This definition offers considerable clarification by spelling out 10 specific adaptive skill areas that might have been considered adaptive behavior in applying the earlier versions. Perhaps a greater number of states will include reference to adaptive behavior or adaptive skill areas in identifying mental retardation among their student populations. The difficulty in determining the measurement techniques, procedures, and cutoff points in the 10 adaptive skill areas of the 1992 definition (Utley et al., 1987) is likely to persist. At this writing, prominent members of the AAMR are to be commended for the workshops they are conducting throughout the country. These workshops are intended to promote clarification and adoption of the 1992 definition, and they place a heavy emphasis on the 10 adaptive skill areas.

Most people identify sociological skills and concepts as predictable weaknesses for individuals with mental retardation but rarely think of learning in their interpretations of the AAMR definitions. Certainly, poor sociological skills (e.g., inability to cope with new or complicated social situations) have long been recognized as serious problems for people with mental retardation, but their most serious problem is their inability to learn efficiently. If not for a wide array of pervasive learning deficiencies, the problems encountered by students with mental retardation could be overcome with education.

Developmental Period

Persistent reference to the developmental period has also been impractical and largely unproductive. Mental retardation does not disappear when an individual with mental retardation passes any particular birthday. Mental retardation imposes many of the same limitations on youths and adults in employment and other adult life goals as it does in school programs (Clark & Kolstoe, 1990; Edgerton; 1967; Foss & Peterson, 1981). Whether needed postschool services are to be provided by the public schools or other agencies is another matter. Some early AAMR committees insisted that mental retardation begins during the *developmental period,* which begins at birth but logically includes the prenatal period because some causes of mental retardation (e.g., Down syndrome) can be traced to chromosomal aberrations that occur at the time of conception. The AAMR committees eventually raised the upper age limit of the developmental period from 16 to 18, but the resulting age span still does not include adults or students with mental retardation who may remain in school through age 21. In most instances, mental retardation manifests itself prior to age 16 or 18, but it makes little sense to define it in a way that disinherits these young adults. The definition should include adults with mental retardation and in need of vocational, independent living, and other survival services even if they have not been so identified while they were in school. Certainly, adults not yet identified as having mental retardation should be included in the definition.

Implications of Definitions

Most states employ some variation of a two-factor process to define and identify mental retardation: learning potential (usually IQ) and adaptive behavior (or learning performance). To be considered initially as having mental retardation, a student must be certified to have extremely limited learning ability. The student must then consistently fail to meet the minimum social, behavioral, and educational standards of other individuals. In practice, to be identified as having mental retardation, a student must perform considerably below grade level. This dual approach to identifying students with mental retardation leaves little doubt as to their need for intensely special consideration in achieving even their most modest life goals. The requirement of having a student demonstrate persistent failure may be essential in diagnosing mental retardation but is, obviously, unfortunate. Any student subjected to repeated failure loses self-confidence and may even drop out of school.

In fairness to the AAMR committee members, many of the issues and problems of the definitions were addressed in the full committee reports. Largely unforeseen by the committee members, however, the full reports were not widely circulated. The limited distribution of the reports and manuals has been unfortunate because, without these reports and manuals, virtually all important decisions about individuals with mental retardation are being made by reference only to the definitions (Affleck, 1980; Cegelka, 1978; Sluyter, 1982; Stile & Pettibone, 1980). Wolraich and Siperstein (1986) pointed out that even most of the professionals who make significant decisions affecting the lives of people with mental retardation are not trained in mental retardation. Having untrained people making important decisions means that several generations of teachers, parents, and others have had only a scholarly, single-sentence definition of mental retardation—a definition that stresses social problems but makes no direct reference to the affected person's inability to learn.

Thus, one can begin to see why people with mental retardation have such a difficult time getting an appropriate, functional education. Educators not only have great difficulty agreeing on basic definitions but also can't even identify with certainty the terms to be defined. As to the disability itself, the definitions are being formulated and discussed exclusively by persons not directly affected. Do any other fields of endeavor have these problems? It has always been difficult to describe the condition of mental retardation to parents, regular educators, and others whose training and experience are outside the field. The task is made considerably more difficult, however, as the terminology of mental retardation changes about every decade.

REGIONAL VARIATION IN THE IDENTIFICATION OF MENTAL RETARDATION

Not only has the profession had difficulty in defining mental retardation, but great variation also exists in the ways and the extent to which the existing definitions are implemented. The definitions used have changed over the years and have been subject to numerous regional and situational interpretations (Hallahan, Keller, & Ball, 1986; MacMillan, 1982). This concept of regional or state-by-state variation is vital to one's understanding of mental retardation. Regional variation in definition and identification is possibly the most compelling rationale for giving special consideration and assistance in life goal planning, instruction, and service delivery to students with mental retardation. Without an understanding of the various ways mental retardation is perceived and defined in different parts of the country, one can never fully comprehend the problems individuals with mental retardation have in gaining an appropriate and realistic education and how difficult it is for their teachers and individualized educational program (IEP) teams to identify and prioritize their life goals.

MacMillan (1982), using data the states report to OSERS, made some revealing state-by-state comparisons of the numbers of students identified as having mental retardation. He reported that some states routinely identified students with mental retardation from among their school-age populations at rates many times higher than other states. By using MacMillan's procedure, the data in Table 1.1 were compiled from

TABLE 1.1   A State-by-State Comparison of the Rates at Which Students with Mental Retardation Were Identified During Two School Years 14 Years Apart

State	A 1978-79 Overall Percentage	B 1978-79 Percentage Over IQ of 50	C 1992-93 Overall Percentage	D 1992-93 Percentage Over IQ of 50
Alabama	3.08	2.68	2.51	2.11
Alaska	0.50	0.10	0.36	None
Arizona	1.00	0.60	0.60	0.20
Arkansas	2.46	2.06	1.75	1.35
California	0.59	0.19	0.38	None
Colorado	0.64	0.24	0.35	None
Connecticut	0.88	0.48	0.55	0.15
Delaware	1.08	0.68	0.96	0.56
Dist. of Columbia	0.26	None	1.09***	0.69
Florida	1.22	0.82	1.04	0.64
Georgia	1.97	1.57	1.49	1.09
Hawaii	0.72	0.32	0.55	0.15
Idaho	1.37	0.97	0.92	0.52
Illinois	1.18	0.78	0.91	0.51
Indiana	1.52	1.12	1.44	1.04
Iowa	1.43	1.03	1.63***	1.23
Kansas	1.17	0.77	0.89	0.49
Kentucky	2.13	1.73	1.98	1.58
Louisiana	1.53	1.13	1.03	0.63
Maine	1.42	1.02	0.59	0.19
Maryland	0.81	0.41	0.51	0.11
Massachusetts	1.41	1.01	1.12	0.72
Michigan	0.78	0.38	0.84***	0.44
Minnesota	1.16	0.76	0.94	0.54
Mississippi	2.33	1.93	1.04	0.64
Missouri	1.59	1.19	1.03	0.63

the *Seventh* (1985) and *Sixteenth Annual Report to Congress on the Implementation of the Individuals with Disabilities Education Act* (1994). Table 1.1 shows the rates at which each state identified students with mental retardation from among its school-age populations for two school years, 1978–79 and 1992–93.

Column A of Table 1.1 shows the rates at which each state identified its students with all levels of mental retardation—mild to profound—from among its total school population during the 1978–79 school year. The percentages in Column A were derived

TABLE 1.1 Continued

State	A 1978-79 Overall Percentage	B 1978-79 Percentage Over IQ of 50	C 1992-93 Overall Percentage	D 1992-93 Percentage Over IQ of 50
Montana	0.82	0.42	0.60	0.20
Nebraska	2.11	1.71	1.17	0.77
Nevada	0.70	0.30	0.47	0.07
New Hampshire	0.76	0.36	0.35	None
New Jersey	0.85	0.45	0.30	None
New Mexico	0.97	0.57	0.48	0.08
New York	0.82	0.42	0.48	0.08
North Carolina	2.64	2.24	1.38	0.48
North Dakota	0.90	0.50	0.84	0.44
Ohio	1.72	1.32	1.75***	1.35
Oklahoma	1.59	1.19	1.50	1.10
Oregon	0.56	0.16	0.59***	0.19
Pennsylvania	1.38	0.98	1.13	0.73
Rhode Island	0.66	0.26	0.50	0.10
South Carolina	2.94	2.54	1.64	1.24
South Dakota	0.54	0.14	0.78***	0.38
Tennessee	1.88	1.48	1.11	0.71
Texas	0.73	0.33	0.54	0.14
Utah	0.72	0.32	0.57	0.17
Vermont	0.51	0.11	1.01***	0.61
Virginia	1.22	0.82	0.90	0.50
Washington	0.89	0.49	0.63	0.23
West Virginia	2.13	1.73	1.76	1.36
Wisconsin	1.01	0.61	0.37	None
Wyoming	0.68	0.28	0.49	0.09
National Average	1.24*	0.84*	0.90**	0.50**

* 7th Annual Report **16th Annual Report ***Represents an increase over 1978-79.

Sources: Seventh Annual Report to Congress on the Implementation of the Individuals with Disabilities Education Act (1985); Sixteenth Annual Report to Congress on the Implementation of the Individuals with Disabilities Education Act (1994).

by simply dividing the number of students identified as having mental retardation by the total number of school children in that state. Column C shows the same type of information for the 1992–93 school year. Comparing the percentages in Columns A and C shows the trend in each state's overall identification rates during the two school years 14 years apart. But a comparison also shows the tremendous variation in identification rates among the states. For example, Column C shows the identification rate in 1992–93 was 0.30% in New Jersey, compared with 2.51%—over 8 times as high—in Alabama. Similarly, the identification rate in Ohio (1.75%) was over 4 times greater than in nearby Wisconsin (0.37%). These data mean that only 1 in 4 students identified as having mental retardation in Ohio would be so identified in Wisconsin.

Comparing the data in Column A with those in Column C illustrates the identification trend for each state during the 14 years. This comparison shows that all but seven states had made moderate to substantial reductions in the percentage of students identified as having mental retardation. During that time, the identification rates for the nation as a whole decreased from 1.24% to 0.90%.

Percentage of Children Identified with Mild/Moderate Mental Retardation

The regional variation in defining mild and moderate mental retardation separately is even more dramatic than in all categories of mental retardation considered as a whole. Columns B and D of Table 1.1 show the estimated identification rates for students with mild/moderate mental retardation or those with IQs over 50 for each of the two school years. These columns were generated as follows: MacMillan (1982) assumed that every state would logically identify most of its students whose mental retardation was most obvious and severe. He further assumed that an IQ of 50 divides severe/profound from mild/moderate mental retardation. Thus, severe/profound mental retardation is assumed to correspond roughly to an IQ of 50 and below, and mild/moderate mental retardation to IQs over 50. MacMillan agreed with Abramowicz and Richardson (1975), who hypothesized that an IQ of 50 correlates approximately with an identification rate of 0.40%. In other words, 0.40% of U.S. school children presumably have severe/profound mental retardation (or IQs of 50 and below). The identification rate for students with mild/moderate mental retardation was obtained by subtracting 0.4% from each state's overall percentage (in Columns A and C). With this procedure, Columns B and D provide an estimated state-by-state comparison of the rates at which students with mild and moderate mental retardation were identified. In Ohio, for example, 1.75% minus 0.4% equals 1.35%, which is the approximate percentage of students who have mental retardation with IQs over 50 identified in that state. Thus, the mental retardation identification rate for students with IQs over 50 in Ohio (1.75%) is over 8 times the rate in Arizona (0.20%) and over 20 times higher than in New York (0.08%). This procedure indicates that some states presumably are identifying no students who have mental retardation with IQs over 50.

Implications of Regional Variation

Minor differences in the way the data in Table 1.1 were collected and reported by the states are reason for some concern (Haring, Farron-Davis, Goets, Karasoff, & Sailor, 1992). Nevertheless, MacMillan's (1982) pervasive analysis and Table 1.1 suggest several implications and raise some disturbing concerns:

Extent of Regional Variation Generally

The first concern addresses the variation in the identification rates among the states themselves. If one assumes a general uniformity in the U.S. school population, Column C of Table 1.1 shows that, in 1992–93, a school-age child was almost 5 times more likely to be identified as having mental retardation in Alabama or Ohio than in six other states (Alaska, California, Colorado, New Hampshire, New Jersey, Wisconsin). This means that only 1 of 5 students with mental retardation in Alabama or Ohio would be so identified in these other states.

Regional Variation and Mild/Moderate Mental Retardation

The second concern is the extremely low identification rates for students with mild/moderate mental retardation. Zetlin and Murtaugh (1990) asked what is happening to those students with IQs from 50 to 70 or 75 who are not being identified in low-identification states. Only three alternatives seem possible: (a) They are served in other categories of special education, (b) they exist in regular elementary and secondary classes with no special help, or (c) they drop out of school. Several later chapters cover in greater detail the consequences of these possibilities.

Data in Column D of Table 1.1 suggest that some states are identifying virtually none of their students with IQs over 50 as having mental retardation. This inference means that the chance of a student with mild or moderate mental retardation obtaining service in a high-identification state is infinitely greater than in the lowest identification states, where they appear to have little or no chance at all. Because the percentages reported to OSERS include the students with mental retardation being served in all service delivery patterns, low-identification states apparently have great numbers of students with IQs from 50 to 75 and many other students with IQs considerably under 50 who are not receiving any special education services. It is difficult to envision such a student surviving (much less preparing for successful adult life) in regular classes without any kind of special assistance. Michaelis (1981) reported that, under current identification and service procedures, many parents complain they cannot get the help they need for their children with mental retardation.

Forness (1985) described how California's current use of lower IQ cutoff points and other criteria has resulted in "declassifying" many students who would previously have been classified as having mental retardation. He also pointed out that, as a result, many school districts identify and serve only their children and youths whose mental retarda-

The major purpose of education in mental retardation is to prepare individuals for successful adult life.

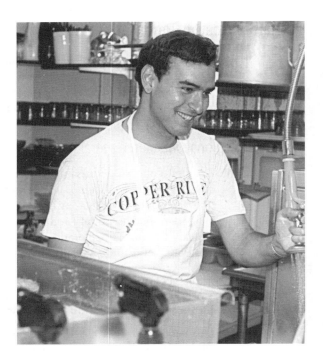

tion is most severe. Polloway and Smith (1983) suggested that this practice has resulted in a lack of interest and enthusiasm in identifying students with mental retardation and in making placements appropriate to their unique needs. With the increasing popularity of inclusion programs, educators might be understandably reluctant to expend time, money, and other limited resources to identify individuals with mental retardation if official policy insists that students so identified are to be treated no differently than their classmates.

Loss of Services

A third concern involves the loss of services to students who are badly in need of assistance. To some, the failure to identify a student with mental retardation may not seem like a misfortune, but identification is an essential prerequisite to service. *Service* refers to all inclusion (or integrated programs), as well as segregated, service delivery patterns and placements for students identified with mental retardation. It includes residential institutions, special schools, special classes on regular school campuses, regular class placement, regular-resource combinations, regular classes with consulting assistance, and regular classes with no special help. Service also includes all students who are not in any of these special placements but who may be receiving any type of auxiliary services, such as adaptive physical education, counseling, therapy, or other special services, if they are identified as having mental retardation. Failure to identify usually means that the student is not being served in any of these facilities—unless the student is being served but not reported.

Regional Variation, Research, and Discussions of Mental Retardation

A fourth concern involves research, as well as the way mental retardation is perceived by the public in general. The concept of regional variation has some additional implications for any discussion of mental retardation—including formal research. The concept of regional variation points out that a condition considered to be mild or moderate mental retardation in one geographical location may be severe or profound mental retardation in another. Thus, any discussion or research of any aspect or characteristic of mental retardation should make careful reference to regional variation and the particular individual or group to which reference is made.

These inconsistencies further demonstrate the need for individual consideration in identifying or providing educational or other services to students with mental retardation. Kidd (1979) and Spitz (1983) reported considerable variation in diagnosing mental retardation because some IQ tests yield higher scores than others. It is also essential to consider the way and the vigor with which parents, teachers, and others are likely to pursue the matter of identification and diagnosis in individual cases. Ysseldyke and Algozzine (1982) pointed out that many students now being served in some states would not qualify for any services in other states. Frankenberger and Fronzaglio (1991) reported that the procedures and qualifying criteria for identifying mental retardation vary greatly from one geographical location to another. Finally, in addition to regional variation, variation in definition and identification are related to gender, race, culture, economics, and other conditions. For example, boys are much more likely than girls to be placed in special education programs, to commit suicide, and to participate in other self-destructive behaviors (Bushweller, 1994).

Multicultural Variations

A fifth concern is the effect regional variation has on multicultural variations. The multicultural variations alone add particular and substantial challenges in providing an individually functional curriculum for each student with mental retardation (Brady, Lineham, Campbell, & Nielsen, 1992). Successful programs must meet these challenges. Harry, Torguson, Katkavich, and Guerrero (1993) and Morrison, Laughlin, Smith, Ollansky, and Moore (1992) pointed out that multicultural concerns vary tremendously from one location to another and that they must be a major consideration in curriculum planning. Garcia and Malkin (1993) pointed out that successful programs for students from divergent cultural and language backgrounds must be commensurate with their unique needs. The concept of regional variation suggests that about the only way to effectively meet these challenges is to rely heavily on the judgment of a well-trained IEP team. These teams must enlist the cooperation of all other teachers (Dean, Salend, & Taylor, 1993). Further, Voltz and Damiano-Lantz (1993) maintained that a sense of "ownership" of the school's programs must be established among the students themselves. Only such a team—that necessarily includes the student's parents or guardians—can assess local conditions and formulate a curriculum that best meets each student's unique needs. The team must also evaluate the extent to which minority and multicultural components are involved and select and design the student's educational program accordingly (Browder, 1991; Lim & Browder, 1994). The organization, training, and duties of the IEP team are discussed in several later chapters.

Prevalence and Incidence of Mental Retardation

Finally, regional variation has a significant effect on the prevalence and incidence of mental retardation. *Prevalence* is usually defined as the total number of cases of a condition that exist at a specified point in time; *incidence* refers to the number of new cases that occur over a specified period of time, such as a year (Marozas, May, & Lehman, 1980; Morton & Hebel, 1978). These studies were concerned primarily with the prevalence of mental retardation, but only among individuals of school age. It is difficult—and can be misleading—to discuss either the prevalence or the incidence of mental retardation for the United States as a whole. The foregoing discussion of regional variation suggests that both the total number of students reported as having mental retardation and the number being identified each year are largely a matter of individual state interpretation, ranging in 1992–93 from a high of 2.51% in Alabama to a low of 0.30% in New Jersey.

IDENTIFICATION AND OTHER AREAS OF SPECIAL EDUCATION

Compared with other major areas of special education, the identification of mental retardation has decreased rapidly. For most of the states and for the country as a whole, the overall percentage of students with mental retardation who are identified from the nation's pool of school-age children has dropped sharply. Table 1.2 shows that the overall identification rate has dropped from 2.16% in 1976–77, to 1.92% in 1982–83, to 0.90% in 1992–93 (*Sixteenth Annual Report to Congress*, 1994).

Richardson (1989) pointed out that, in practice, the decreasing identification rate translates into loss of vitally needed services. Table 1.2 shows the percentage of students (ages 6 to 21) served in the various categories of disability during a 16-year span. From the data in Table 1.2, it is clear that the United States identifies fewer than half as many students with mental retardation as 10 years ago. These figures are assumed to be reasonably accurate because every state provides funds to its school districts for students with disabilities at a higher rate than for other students, so there is a strong financial incentive to report all special education students. Tables 1.1 and 1.2 and the definitions of mental retardation point out that, to qualify for special education services in mental retardation, a student must be thoroughly evaluated and must place roughly in the bottom 1% of whatever criteria are used in a given state to identify mental retardation.

Some have speculated that many students with mild/moderate mental retardation are being identified and served in other categories of special education—the most logical category being learning disabilities. Hallahan et al. (1986) suggested that learning disabilities has always been an attractive euphemism for mental retardation. But the educational programs and curricula for students with learning disabilities are rarely appropriate for those with mental retardation. Moreover, students with mental retarda-

TABLE 1.2   Percentage of Children Age 6 to 21 Served in Programs for Students with Disabilities by Disability During 4 School Years 16 Years Apart

Condition	1976-77	1982-83	1990-91	1992-93
Learning Disability	1.79	4.40	3.75	4.09
Mental Retardation	2.16	1.92	0.97	0.90
Speech Impairment	2.84	2.96	1.73	1.73
Emotional Disturbance	0.64	0.89	0.69	0.70
Other Health Impairment	0.32	0.13	0.10	0.11
Multiple Disabilities	NR*	0.07	0.17	0.18
Hard of Hearing, Deaf	0.20	0.18	0.10	0.10
Orthopedic Disabilities	0.20	0.14	0.09	0.09
Visual Disabilities	0.09	0.07	0.04	0.04
Deaf-Blind	NR*	0.01	0.00**	0.00**
Totals	8.33	10.76	7.44	7.98

*Not Reported   **Some—but less than 0.01%

Source: Sixteenth Annual Report to Congress on the Implementation of the Individuals with Disabilities Education Act (1994).

tion are unable to qualify in most states because the criteria for learning disabilities usually require an extensive discrepancy between academic potential and achievement—often 40% to 50%. Students with mental retardation cannot meet these stipulations because their potential and achievement levels are both low.

Shepard, Smith, and Vojir (1983) reported that more than half of students with learning disabilities being served did not meet the criteria for such a placement. Only a small fraction of the students being served, however, would have qualified for services under any other category of special education, and virtually none had mental retardation. Some students who would have been identified earlier as having mental retardation are now classified as having multiple disabilities. The total number and percentages of students so identified, however, have never been significant (0.07% in 1982–83, and 0.18% in 1992–93). Thus, it appears unlikely that any appreciable number of students with mental retardation are being served as having either a learning disability or multiple disabilities.

Classification in Mental Retardation

Once an individual is identified as having mental retardation, the next logical step is to determine the severity. Classification is a process that attempts to categorize students with mental retardation into groups on the basis of ability and/or achievement. Teachers in particular need to recognize the extent of a student's general learning limitations (and potential) because, in practice, they will be primarily responsible for the design and conduct of that student's educational program. Regional variation suggests that attempts to classify students with mental retardation in this manner are extremely

TABLE 1.3   Traditional Classification System

IQ Limits	Description
71-80 or 85	Slow Learner (No Mental Retardation)
51-70	Educable Mental Retardation (EMR)
30-50	Trainable Mental Retardation (TMR)
Below 30	Profound Mental Retardation (PMR)

indefinite and possibly impractical. The severity of the mental retardation, however, is important in life goal planning procedures and in the needed diagnostic/prescriptive teaching process. Students with mental retardation are likely to be classified and educated in different school district settings or programs according to the relative severity of their learning deficiencies. Also, most states use some type of classification system, and it may be helpful to at least be aware that various systems exist and to become familiar with classification procedures.

Traditionally, students with mental retardation have been classified by IQ in school and other settings. Traits, abilities, and attributes other than IQ should probably be given greater emphasis in defining, classifying, and serving students with mental retardation. Most school districts do make considerable use of some non-IQ abilities, such as performance and achievement levels, in determining placements and planning curriculum, but these abilities are difficult to translate into concrete data and to deal with statistically. Finally, classification in mental retardation must be carefully considered in light of regional variation, regardless of the criteria used. Two classification systems, both based on IQ, are presented in Table 1.3 to demonstrate the relative severity of mental retardation.

Table 1.3 is a traditional classification system, and though considered outdated by some, it is probably in wider use today than any other. This system was used by all early AAMR committees. Early definitions and classification schemes often referred to profound mental retardation (PMR) as custodial mental retardation (CMR), a term suggesting that a person so identified may need full-time custodial or institutional care.

Table 1.4 illustrates a more recent, four-level AAMR classification scheme that allows some needed flexibility in assigning an individual to a particular classification level. It is widely cited in the mental retardation literature and is used throughout this book. Utley et al. (1987), however, reported that although 74% of the states use some type of classification, only 14% use this particular system.

These two classification systems are merely representative. It is important for teachers, parents, and other IEP team members to understand the particular system used to classify students with mental retardation in their school district—whether or not it is either of these. In both Tables 1.3 and 1.4, profound and often severe mental retardation often include persons with multiple disabilities.

Classification by Intensity of Needed Support

The 1994 AAMR definition classifies mental retardation from a different perspective. The new system bypasses direct consideration of IQ and classifies individuals by the

TABLE 1.4   More Recent Classification System

IQ Limits	Description
70-75 to 80 or 85	Slow Learner (No mental retardation)
50-55 to 70-75	Mild Mental Retardation
35-40 to 50-55	Moderate Mental Retardation
20-25 to 35-40	Severe Mental Retardation
Below 20-25	Profound Mental Retardation

Source: Based on Luckasson et al., 1992.

level or intensity of support their disabilities require. The levels of support from most to least intensive and direct are (a) pervasive, (b) extensive, (c) limited, and (d) intermittent. *Pervasive* and *extensive* supports are characterized by ongoing, highly intrusive and intense services that may extend beyond school to home and work environments. *Limited* and *intermittent* supports provide less intensive services and require fewer staff members. The obvious intent of the new scheme is to organize and provide whatever supports are necessary and to the extent they are needed. The major strength of the system is that it places the primary responsibility for the individual's education on his or her IEP team members, who are in a position to investigate and evaluate the quality and availability of local educational placements and services.

Slow Learners

Slow learners are listed in both Tables 1.3 and 1.4 even though they are not included in the classification systems of recent AAMR committees. Students classified as slow learners were not considered to have mental retardation by any of the committees, yet they are included here because their existence is important in curriculum planning and in providing services for students with mental retardation; they are also discussed in several later chapters. Basically. however, the concept of regional variation suggests that students identified and served as having mental retardation in one location may be considered slow learners in another. If, at any time, such a borderline student is not educated in programs designed specifically for students with mental retardation, he or she will be placed in whatever programs the school or school district has designed for slow learners. Current inclusion service delivery patterns typically place students with mental retardation part- or full-time in programs intended for slow learners. Therefore, the educational programs available to slow learners are of vital concern to persons planning such programs for students with mental retardation.

Implications of Classification

The terms *mild, moderate, severe,* and *profound* are subject to greatly varying interpretations and cannot be used as though they are discrete categories. For this reason, *mild/moderate* in this book refers to individuals whose mental retardation falls roughly into the first two categories and *severe/profound* includes those in either the severe or profound category. The widely varying interpretations also make it misleading and impractical to ascribe learning and other characteristics to individuals in these four cate-gories. Rather, the characteristics must be identified, diagnosed, and considered individ-ually in planning IEPs and curricula for students with mental retardation. To assist in this process, in the next chapter I discuss learning characteristics as they apply to mental retardation. Also, Appendix A lists some major considerations relating to classification and the severity of mental retardation. The list is long, but each entry has one or more serious implications for IEP and curriculum planning. For example, the more severe the mental retardation, the more slowly a student will learn and progress toward his or her life goals; the more detailed the student's program must be regardless of the programs employed; and the more extensively the student's program must include intensive train-ing in employment, independent living, communication, social, and other transitional skills and concepts not offered to students with average and gifted cognitive abilities.

Conceptual Distance versus Available Resources

Figure 1.1 introduces and illustrates conceptual distance, a fundamental key to under-standing the basic nature of mental retardation. *Conceptual distance* is the composite of the skills and concepts to be mastered by a student during a specified period of time, and it must always be considered in view of the time, money, effort, and other resources necessary to cover the specified distance or to master the indicated skills and concepts.

Figure 1.1 compares achievement of students with mental retardation with the per-formance typical of slow learners, gifted students, and those with average ability. The heavy line in Figure 1.1 illustrates this definition by showing the approximate relation-ship between average achievement level and chronological age. An "average" student does fifth-grade work while in fifth grade with a chronological age (CA) of 10 or 11, ninth-grade work while in ninth grade, and so on. At any point, some individuals achieve at a faster or slower rate than average and will be above or below grade level.

The upper line of Figure 1.1 represents students who are gifted and talented, those who achieve substantially faster than average. Other students, represented as *slow learners* in Figure 1.1, learn more slowly than average. These students could possibly remain in school for an additional year or two, but few of them do so, and most of them graduate at about the same age as their classmates. The achievement lines representing the slow-learning students and those with mental retardation are curved downward and do not extend to the 12th-grade level. Most of those who are very far below grade level will never be able to achieve at the same levels as their average and gifted class-mates, regardless of the additional time they remain in school. If this were not so, every student—including those with mental retardation—could eventually earn a doctoral degree by simply remaining in school for an extended period of time.

The bottom line in Figure 1.1 represents students with mental retardation who achieve at the lowest levels and rates. This is not merely an assumption, but rather it reflects the definitions of mental retardation that require both extremely low learning potential and persistent and prohibitive performance deficiencies. The achievement levels shown by the lines of Figure 1.1 are merely representative, however, and are not intended to be exact.

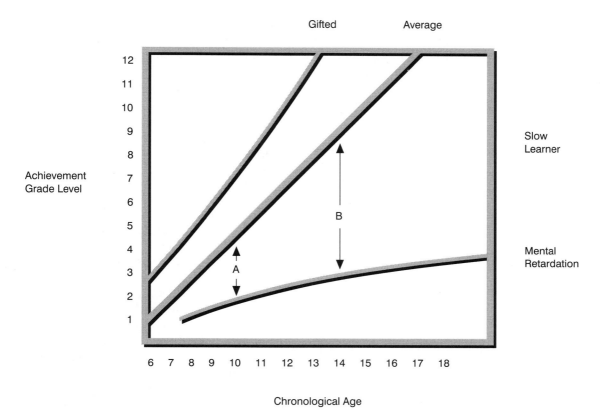

FIGURE 1.1   Achievement and Chronological Age

Implications and Applications of Conceptual Distance

Conceptual distance demonstrates the need for special, intensive consideration in mental retardation. Conceptual distance shows that as students with mental retardation continue through school, they fall progressively behind their classmates (Deneau, 1985; Ellis & Dulaney, 1991; Retish, 1982). The vertical (conceptual) distance between the learning curve of students with mental retardation and that of their age-mates increases with the passage of time. Thus, if a student with mental retardation achieves 2 to 3 years below grade level in fourth grade (Point A in Figure 1.1), he or she will probably be 4 to 6—or even more—years behind (Point B) in ninth grade.

To progress from one level to another, the individual must master a wide array of skills and concepts. In this sense, conceptual distance is the space between a student's current level of mastery and the level projected by all or part of the student's individualized educational program (IEP) or individualized transitional plan (ITP). In mental retardation, the consideration of time, effort, and other resources necessary for a student to achieve the goals is much more important than the consideration of the actual distance to be covered. Other students lagging behind their classmates—even those with other disabilities—can often make a year or more of measurable progress for each year in which they receive intensive, special education services. But the limitations imposed by mental retardation prevent an individual from doing so—even with the best teachers and programs. As discussed earlier, students in the area in Figure 1.1 between *mental retardation* and *slow learner* are likely to be identified as having mental retardation in one location and not in another.

Heterogeneity and Students with Mental Retardation

Conceptual distance also points to the great heterogeneity that exists in mental retardation. During the early school years, the circumstance of a student without disabilities achieving at a level somewhat below his or her classmates is not ordinarily cause for undue concern. Even if the conceptual distance between the achievement level of one nondisabled or gifted student and that of another is quite pronounced, remedial action is usually minimal. Often, the lagging students will recognize the problem and catch up on their own.

Ordinarily, conceptual distance is more difficult to recognize among younger than older students. The magnitude of measurable achievement levels within groups of younger students is never great—a condition that can be deceiving. In other words, how far below grade level can a student be in third or fourth grade? Thus, it is understandable for any elementary teacher to underestimate the plight of a student who has mental retardation and whose performance is only a few grade levels below normal. When a student with mental retardation falls only slightly below a projected level of achievement, careful planning and prioritizing of curriculum are necessary. This is so because students with mental retardation require much instructional time, effort, and other resources to close the conceptual distance separating achievement and potential or desired levels. It is too easy to assume that a student with mental retardation who appears to be only slightly deficient on some skill or concept will catch up at a later date or in another class as other students do. This attitude overlooks the fact that this student may require months of instruction to cover as much conceptual distance as other students accomplish in days or weeks. Thus, if the difference between the achievement levels of a student with mental retardation and the levels of a CA peer is not great, it may appear to be a relatively simple matter to close the gap—until one considers the extremely slow rate of learning imposed by mental retardation. The concept of conceptual distance suggests that grouping students with mental retardation for instruction must be done carefully because, in a practical sense, the ability levels of any two such students are likely to be much more divergent than they would at first appear.

Conceptual distance also suggests that a common curriculum for such students— even those in the same school class—may not be appropriate. Therefore, each student with mental retardation needs an individually designed curriculum to make the transition from school to life as an adult.

Many students with mental retardation may never master either academic or "functional" skills and concepts at the same level as another student with mental retardation regardless of the time each remains in school. It is not unusual to find two such students in the same school class and even with similar CAs. Although the observable levels of achievement of two such students may appear to be relatively slight, conceptual distance helps IEP teams in focusing on the practical and greatly divergent needs of the two students.

In U.S. society, even among professionals, frequent reference is made to people with disabilities as if they constitute a homogeneous group. For example, students with mild or moderate mental retardation and those with severe or profound mental retardation are often lumped together even though each combined group is extremely diverse. Because of regional variation and the great heterogeneity of mental retardation, in this book I refer to students with severe/profound mental retardation and students whose mental retardation is severe/profound. *Severe or profound* mental retardation seems to imply that these are two separate and distinct groups.

Other examples of apparently assuming unwarranted homogeneity can be found in both P.L. 94–142 and P.L. 101–476 (the IDEA), some parts of which seem to treat all disabilities as a single entity. Although all people with and without disabilities have many needs and characteristics in common, each disability invariably imposes some significant and different limitations (Hallahan & Kaufman, 1986; Kirk & Gallagher, 1993; Swanson & Willis, 1979). Thus, the needs and limitations imposed by each disabling condition are likely to be unique in their effect on each individual.

SUMMARY

Mental retardation has been very difficult to define. Obviously, a discipline that cannot be defined in widely accepted terms is destined to incur some controversy. Mental retardation, however, is a serious disability no matter how it is defined.

Regardless of the definition used, to be identified as having mental retardation, an individual must have not only a serious deficiency in his or her ability to learn but also a record of repeated failure in academic activities. Mental retardation is subject to significant regional and situational variation, a circumstance that makes meaningful discussions and research difficult to apply in any given instance. Regional variation means that a student with mental retardation identified and served in one state or school district under a particular ability classification may be identified under a different classification (or may not be identified and served at all) in another state or school district.

Mental retardation imposes severe and persistent learning difficulties on an individual in all areas of human endeavor. Students with mental retardation tend to fall significantly and progressively behind their age-mates as they proceed through school. Nevertheless, mental retardation is an extremely heterogeneous disability that makes individual life goal curriculum planning extremely vital.

CHAPTER 2

Mental Retardation in Perspective

Points to Study and Ponder

1. What is proactivity, and what does it have to do with curriculum planning and teaching in mental retardation?
2. What is an IEP team, and what are its purpose and composition?
3. What three general procedures have been used to study the learning characteristics of mental retardation?
4. Which of these procedures are used today and why?
5. What are some significant learning characteristics of mental retardation, and what implications do they have for curriculum planning and teaching students with mental retardation?
6. How can these learning characteristics—that always seem to be negative—be used in positive planning and teaching procedures?
7. What are stereotypes, and how can their negative effects be overcome?
8. How do learning characteristics interact with each other, and what is likely to be the result?
9. Do you think society will find a cure for mental retardation during your lifetime? In your opinion, is mental retardation primarily a result of hereditary or environmental factors?
10. Can you discern any significant general or specific differences between mental retardation and other disabilities, such as learning disabilities, emotional/behavioral, visual, or auditory problems? What implications (if any) do these differences have in curriculum planning and teaching students with these problems?

n academic settings, students with mental retardation must often compete along-side students with disabilities other than mental retardation, as well as alongside those with no disabilities. This competition continues into adult life, where all of these former students vie in employment, living arrangements, and other sociolog-ical situations. The primary purpose of this chapter is to help parents, teachers, and others in designing and conducting educational programs that will enable individu-als with mental retardation to become responsible, successful adults. In this chapter, I accomplish this by placing mental retardation in perspective with other disabilities and no disabilities and by discussing the significant learning and other characteristics that mental retardation imposes on a person. Throughout the chapter, I continually remind the reader that all individuals have some ability in every area of human endeavor and that these abilities must be evaluated on an individual basis. Despite inherited and other tendencies, a student with mental retardation is generally amenable to instruc-tion based on his or her individual evaluation. The only purpose of studying learning characteristics is to assist parents, teachers, and others in evaluating the remaining abil-ities of each student with mental retardation. For the purposes of this chapter, learning characteristics include all learning traits, abilities, disabilities, deficiencies, and perfor-mance levels on various tasks and activities.

In this chapter, I also introduce a key concept called *proactivity*. This concept is par-ticularly helpful in life goal curriculum planning and teaching students with mental retar-dation. Proactivity is discussed in several later chapters as it applies to a particular topic.

POSITIVE CONSIDERATIONS

Although mental retardation is a severe disability, a number of positive considerations exist. The ultimate success of an educational program for students with mental retarda-tion should be determined by long-term results—the extent to which the students suc-ceed as adults (Wehman et al., 1985). Despite serious learning limitations, students with mental retardation can be quite successful in life through well-planned and appro-priate educational programs (Cronis, Smith, Garnett, & Forgnone, 1986; Fox, 1989; Martin, 1994; Williams & Ewing, 1991).

Furthermore, teaching students with mental retardation can be a very positive experi-ence. The professional job market for teachers of students with mental retardation is criti-cal in almost every part of the country (Green, 1994). Most students with mental retarda-tion seem to love school and tend to be greatly disappointed by unexpected disruptions, such as early school dismissal. Also, without doubt, the students will make little progress toward their life goals without the guidance of a well-trained, professional teacher. Sellin (1979) observed that most people with mental retardation have a generally positive out-look on life. Kregel, Wehman, Seyfarth, and Marshall (1986) reported that a group of 300 adults with mild to severe mental retardation appeared to be making a good adjustment to adult life several years after leaving school. Stancliff (1995) noted that older persons with mental retardation (CA = 19–61) indicated that they were allowed to make signifi-cantly more of their personal decisions than did a variety of staff members.

LEARNING CHARACTERISTICS

A careful study of the learning characteristics of mental retardation is a vital prerequisite to any discussion of curriculum or program planning. In Chapter 1, I discussed the great difficulties the profession has had in even defining mental retardation. I further pointed out that educational planners cannot rely on any of the current classification systems. The designations *mild, moderate, severe,* and *profound* refer to individuals whose abilities vary greatly from one state to another. Likewise, the terms *educable* and *trainable*—still used in many locations—are applied to students with widely divergent cognitive and other abilities.

Therefore, a major reason to discuss the learning characteristics imposed by mental retardation is to assist in the identification of students who need help in achieving success in adult life; that is, mental retardation can be diagnosed by identifying individuals who have the learning deficits discussed here. A further reason for such a discussion is more obvious—the learning strengths and weaknesses of any student greatly influence the success that student will experience in any instructional program or activity. Diagnosing a student's mental retardation would probably not be necessary if special educators could learn to adequately design that student's educational programs in a manner that is truly commensurate with his or her needs and abilities.

People with mental retardation have the same human traits as others. They do not have a separate set of learning characteristics. They all have some aptitude in memory, cognition, reasoning, and all other human abilities, but they invariably have serious *deficiencies* in all or most of these areas (Parmar, Cawley, & Miller, 1994). One advantage that most other individuals have over those with mental retardation is a normal IQ. Thus, any realistic investigation of mental retardation—as with other disabilities— tends to be rather negative.

STEREOTYPES

Stereotypes can be a real obstacle in discussing people who have disabilities—especially mental retardation. By definition, any disability sets the affected person at some disadvantage. For this reason, the person's disability must be considered in helping him or her plan for the future. Those who help the person plan can gain valuable insights by reviewing past research done on individuals with that disability. Everyone falters from time to time, however, and therefore an individual's poor performance on a given task cannot necessarily be attributed to that individual's disability. Similarly, research with only two or three subjects tends to be unreliable because the results may be unduly influenced by chance or extraneous factors, such as unequal abilities or more extensive experience at the outset. Thus, other things being equal, research credibility is improved by comparing the performance of larger groups of participants (Vockell & Asher, 1995). But discussing the collective traits of groups of people can lead to stereotyping or unjustifiably ascribing all or selected attributes of the group to each member.

Every attempt is made or intended here to discourage the establishment or persistence of stereotypes as characteristics are discussed that seem to be common to groups of individuals with mental retardation.

Stereotyped Parent

One possible stereotype to be avoided is the use of the term *parent*. A great many children do not live in a traditional family with both biological parents. As used throughout the book, *parent* refers to one or both biological, foster, surrogate, or other substitute parents or guardians, male or female. Some of the foregoing individuals will have temporary custody of and/or responsibility for the child; that of others will be more permanent. In any event, P.L. 101–476 (the IDEA) and good practice assign to one or more of these adults the primary responsibility for overseeing the education of each student with a disability. Throughout this book I assume this responsibility to be indispensable and insist that *parents* be given the chief decision-making role in the design and conduct of their child's education—and that educators have an added role to train the parent where necessary. I assume that the responsibility and authority of some of these *parents* may continue beyond the child's graduation, but of course, this may or may not be the case—even with the biological parents. Experience demonstrates that some of the *parents* may choose to participate in the child's education, whereas others do not. In fact, in Chapter 4 I point out that parents must be given the opportunity to participate in their child's educational program to the extent that they choose. The obligation to train and encourage parental participation continues—although it diminishes greatly or may terminate at the child's graduation from school.

NEGATIVE CONSIDERATIONS

To work effectively with any group of students having severe learning problems, one must be prepared to deal with some inevitable negative attributes and limitations. Mental retardation is a severe disability primarily because its very nature involves a diminished intelligence or ability to learn. This disability affects all of the person's faculties and, therefore, every task he or she performs. It is unfair and unethical to place arbitrary limitations on any person. It is equally unfair and ineffective, however, to assume that a student has abilities he or she does not possess. Determining a person's limitations and abilities becomes particularly difficult in mental retardation because these individuals tend to fall increasingly behind their peers in any kind of program (Clark & Kolstoe, 1990; Retish, 1982).

The "negativeness" of mental retardation also lies in the fact that the learning characteristics of students with mental retardation inevitably emerge as learning deficiencies. One reason for the seeming emphasis on the negative aspects of mental retardation is that learning characteristics are almost always reported in the literature as deficiencies. A great many articles, however, stress that students with mental retardation do learn and develop to some extent despite any particular deficiency and that they almost always respond to well-planned educational programs. The deficiency approach is used to identify specific learning characteristics, but programs are built or based on residual abilities or strengths. Further, as pointed out in Chapter 1, labels and classifications are unreliable indicators of either need or ability. Therefore, IEPs can and should be planned and conducted without undue restraint from classifications, such as mild, moderate, severe, or profound—which the concept of regional variation suggests should serve only as general references. All later chapters include how this can be done.

Mental retardation is a particularly negative disability because it currently requires a student to be in the bottom 1% to 2% of observed and tested ability and performance levels among that student's age-mates. But the extent to which mental retardation imposes these learning deficiencies varies greatly with the individual. Thus, in designing educational programs, each student's IEP team must evaluate each characteristic as it applies to that individual (Retish, 1982). The IEP team must make two basic assumptions: (a) Each individual has some ability, with respect to each trait or characteristic, that will enable him or her to learn, and (b) each individual has some ability to improve, with respect to that particular trait or characteristic.

Finally, both P.L. 94–142 and P.L. 101–476 (the IDEA) require that an IEP be prepared for every student who has a disability as defined by these laws—including students with mental retardation. Further, these laws require that the IEP list the student's individual weaknesses and strengths. These weaknesses are the primary justifications for placing the student in special education in the first place; that is, without significant weaknesses there would be no need for either special education or an IEP, regardless of the student's strengths. Thus, the requirement to identify the student's strengths implies or asks, Given the weaknesses that qualified this student for special education, what residual strengths does the student have on which the IEP can be formulated? In evaluating these characteristics, do not become discouraged. In fact, many students with mental retardation are capable of becoming responsible and self-supporting adults, but they must have a great deal of special assistance to do so (Edgerton, Bollinger, & Herr, 1984; Hasazi et al., 1985).

STUDYING THE LEARNING CHARACTERISTICS OF MENTAL RETARDATION

The learning characteristics of individuals with mental retardation have been studied in three basic ways: (a) comparing groups of students with and without mental retardation who have similar chronological ages, (b) comparing one group of students whose mental retardation was known or strongly suspected with another group whose mental retardation had no known cause, and (c) comparing groups of students with and without mental retardation who are of similar mental ages.

Studies Based on Chronological Age (CA)

Early research investigated the learning abilities of students with mental retardation by comparing their IQ test results with the academic achievement test results for students of similar chronological age (CA). At first, this was done by computing the degree of correlation between the group scores of IQ and achievement tests administered to large numbers of randomly selected students (Lennon, 1950; Turney, 1931). These correlations were always consistently high. Frandsen (1950) reported strong, positive correlations (.69–.76), with the differences depending mainly on the specific tests that were used. In other words, students with very low IQ scores also had predictably low achievement scores.

Later researchers actually identified students with mental retardation and compared their abilities directly with those of normal and gifted students (see Blackman & Heintz, 1966; Kirk, 1964). These studies immediately and consistently demonstrated that the performance of students with mental retardation lags significantly behind that of their CA peers, regardless of the task or ability selected. In fact, the predictably poor performance of the groups with mental retardation became so firmly established that the CA-equated studies were largely discontinued. Abandonment of the CA-equated studies was unfortunate because they were producing valuable (albeit predictable) information that could not be obtained by any other means.

Exogenous-Endogenous Studies

The deserted CA-equated research of students with mental retardation was temporarily replaced by studies based on etiological (or pathological) considerations. These studies were referred to as the exogenous-endogenous studies (Frazeur & Hoakley, 1947; Kelly, 1949). *Exogenous mental retardation* was generally defined as having been imposed by the child's external environment; *endogenous mental retardation* was assumed to have been present at birth. Both the exogenous and endogenous students were identified by low IQ and achievement test scores, but the endogenous students usually manifested pathological conditions or outward appearance that could logically account for their mental retardation. Examples of endogenous mental retardation include Down syndrome, rubella, hydrocephalus, and phenylketonuria (PKU).

Most "causes" of mental retardation, however, are unpredictable and sometimes difficult to diagnose with certainty. For example, having or being exposed to rubella and hydrocephalus do not always result in mental retardation, as is usually the case with Down syndrome. Thus, a researcher could not always be certain that the mental retardation of a child with one of these pathological conditions was necessarily the result of the condition. Therefore, children with Down syndrome became increasingly popular as representatives of the endogenous group. The exogenous-endogenous studies soon evolved into investigations in which groups of children with Down syndrome were compared empirically with other groups of students with mental retardation who had no identifiable pathological condition.

The exogenous-endogenous studies were generally inconclusive and have lost popularity presumably because any identifiable differences in learning characteristics or abilities were quite artificial, often the result of definition and selection of subjects (Doll, 1946; Dunn & Capobianco, 1956). The exogenous-endogenous studies were beneficial to some extent because they tended to focus attention on teaching methods for students with mental retardation. Hewes, Holt, Meranski, and Snell (1924) also noted that all of the students with mental retardation were achieving several years below grade level. These studies called attention to the special help needed by these students and seemed to enhance the popularity of special, self-contained classes for students with mental retardation. The publicity regarding the causes of mental retardation had both positive and negative effects. On the positive side, the exogenous-endogenous studies resulted in increased efforts to identify and eliminate these causes, thereby reducing the incidence of mental retardation. On the negative side, publicizing the causes of mental retardation seems to have encouraged the mistaken but popular notion that mental retardation can usually be identified by a person's outward appearance and that all mental retardation is a result of Down syndrome. Currently, exogenous-endogenous studies have largely fallen into disuse, although one appears occasionally (Burack & Zigler, 1990; Kavale & Forness, 1985).

Studies Based on Mental Age (MA)

While some researchers were still experimenting with exogenous-endogenous studies, others discovered that students with mental retardation could compete favorably with students of similar *mental ages* (MA) (Groff & Linden, 1982). The MA establishes standards that would be met by a majority of children of a given CA, failed by younger children, and exceeded by older children. MA-equated studies have older students with mental retardation compete against chronologically younger children who have normal or even above-average IQs.

The control groups for MA-equated studies are easily selected because they usually consist of already identified groups or classes of students with mental retardation. The IQs (and, hence, the MAs) of the students in these groups are readily available, and each group's mean MA is easily computed. The comparison groups are younger children without mental retardation, and each group's IQ mean is near 100. The MAs of the comparison groups can be adjusted upward by adding students with higher IQs or downward by dismissing students with the higher IQs. This process can be continued until the mean MAs of the overall groups are exactly equal. Then the groups can be compared empirically on one or more learning tasks, abilities, or other characteristics.

Figure 2.1 gives an example of an MA-equated study of this nature. It compares groups of 14-year-old students with mental retardation (mean IQs of 50) with groups of 7-year-olds with mean IQs of 100. Notice that the MAs of the two groups are equal even though the IQs and CAs are unequal. This relationship can be demonstrated by using the traditional ratio IQ formula.

This comparison procedure is widely accepted and currently used. The ratio IQ formula illustrates the relationship involved but is no longer used in many IQ tests. When

FIGURE 2.1 Equating Studies on Mental Age (MA)

$$IQ = \frac{MA \times 100}{CA} \qquad \text{or—solving for MA} \qquad MA = \frac{IQ \times CA}{100}$$

Students without Mental Retardation

$$MA = \frac{IQ \times CA}{100}$$

$$MA = \frac{100 \times 7}{100}$$

$$MA = 7$$

Students with Mental Retardation

$$MA = \frac{IQ \times CA}{100}$$

$$MA = \frac{50 \times 14}{100}$$

$$MA = 7$$

MA-equated studies are used, students with mental retardation no longer demonstrate predictable inferiority. Their group deficits are not necessarily a foregone conclusion, as they were with the CA-equated studies. In fact, some studies have actually found groups of students with mental retardation to be superior to their younger MA peers on a variety of tasks (Ezell & Goldstein, 1991; Kamhi, 1981).

Problems with MA-Equated Studies

Although they are still widely used, MA-equated studies result in much less practical information than one might expect and can actually be misleading and potentially damaging to students with mental retardation. These studies tend to greatly overestimate the learning abilities of students with mental retardation. In the hypothetical example shown in Figure 2.1, the students with mental retardation would logically be in eighth or ninth grade and may have as few as 3 or 4 years of school remaining. It would not be unusual for them, however, to achieve on only a second-grade level or even lower. The students without mental retardation would typically *be* in second grade and have almost their entire school careers ahead of them. The students with mental retardation would have had up to 7 or 8 more years of reading and other instruction than the students without mental retardation. To claim or imply that students with mental retardation learn as other students do, on the basis of this type of study, is misleading and impractical (Ezell & Goldstein, 1991; Kamhi, 1981; Taylor, 1980).

Learning Rate

It makes little sense to conclude that a junior high school student with mental retardation performs on the same level as an average first or second grader. Significantly, a junior high school student typically has fewer than half of his or her school years remaining, whereas the younger child has an entire school career yet to come. No one would suggest placing this teenager with mental retardation in a first- or second-grade class and rightly so. Furthermore, a follow-up study would logically find that the children without mental retardation gain approximately 1 year of achievement level per year of instruction—a nearly impossible task for students with mental retardation. Instead of demonstrating that students with mental retardation learn as students without mental retardation do, the MA-equated studies show just the opposite. In fact, students with mental retardation do *not* learn as others do; they learn much more slowly (Kail, 1992; Vicari, Albertini, & Caltagirone, 1992). They also forget more rapidly (Burack & Zigler, 1990) and show significant deficits in every area of learning (Bray, Turner, & Hersch, 1985; Forness & Kavale, 1993; Tomporowski & Tinsley, 1994). The fact that they must be compared with much younger children in order to identify those with whom they can compete successfully illustrates these points (Gottlieb, 1981; Gresham, 1982).

Misuse of Results

It is ironic and unfortunate that educators rely on empirical research comparing students who have mental retardation with their *MA* peers to investigate how well they learn but then place them in regular classes with their *CA* peers with whom they do not compete successfully. If students with mental retardation are to be placed in classrooms and other facilities with classmates of equal CA but without mental retardation, it is essential to compare their abilities with this group, rather than with their MA peers. This does not mean that they cannot be mainstreamed when it proves advisable or when the parents insist. Before mainstreaming students with mental retardation, however, their IEP expectations must be compatible with their true abilities.

How MA Studies Can Help

Despite their inherent problems, properly interpreted MA-equated studies can be of some help in curriculum planning for students with mental retardation. In a practical sense, a study showing that older students with mental retardation are performing on the same level as their younger, less experienced MA peers actually indicates that students with mental retardation lag behind their CA peers, with whom they are typically placed. MA is rarely a consideration for anything outside school and after leaving school because students with mental retardation must compete with their CA peers. Moreover, MA-equated studies usually identify one or more learning characteristics that are deficiencies among students with mental retardation. These characteristics can then be diagnosed to identify the individual's level of mastery on that particular skill or concept; that diagnosis, in turn, suggests the type and level of instruction he or she needs. If a student who is thought to have mental retardation does demonstrate a normal or near-normal achievement level with respect to any task or characteristic, parents and teachers should simply initiate the student's educational program at that level. Both MA- and CA-equated studies can be valuable in suggesting typical group traits and abilities to be investigated further with individual students. The essential questions are how much ability a student has in a particular area and how the student's IEP team can capitalize on this ability in designing a program that will help the student in achieving optimum success as an adult.

Regional Variation and Learning Characteristics

Every statement made about any individual with mental retardation must be considered in light of regional variation. Students in low-identification states tend to manifest each learning deficiency to a greater extent than those in high-identification states. A greater percentage of students with mental retardation from high-identification states can be expected to respond more favorably to mainstreaming and inclusion programs, whereas those from low-identification states are more likely to need more concentrated, specialized services.

Conceptual Distance and Learning Characteristics

A study of the learning deficiencies imposed by mental retardation helps one understand conceptual distance, an indication that the learning distance to be traversed by a student with mental retardation is much greater than it may appear. Because of the limitations imposed by mental retardation, much more instructional time and effort than with other students are required to overcome any distance that exists between such a student's present and projected levels of mastery.

SOME SIGNIFICANT LEARNING CHARACTERISTICS

Learning characteristics themselves are often difficult to define, and it is sometimes difficult to determine whether a stated characteristic is really a characteristic per se or simply a component of another one. In fact, learning characteristics are so interrelated that there seems to be no logical order for their presentation. For example, the poor auditory processing ability of a student with mental retardation may be a consequence of poor reading ability, poor memory, failure to pay adequate attention, lack of experience, or a combination of these. Each characteristic or component, however, must be carefully assessed before formulating the educational prescription. Only the more significant deficiencies that are typical (or characteristic) of students with mental retardation are presented below as entities to be individually assessed, together with some citations that confirm their existence and that offer avenues for further investigation.

Intelligence, Cognition, and General Learning Ability

No matter how intelligence is defined, the most significant learning characteristic of students with mental retardation is *diminished intelligence,* or the predictable and generally poor ability to learn (Baumeister & Brooks, 1981; Kail, 1992; Rosenzweig, 1981). This is the primary attribute that makes mental retardation a more serious educational disability than others. Although intelligence may not be synonymous with the ability to learn, a person with mental retardation—by definition—lacks both. Vicari et al. (1992)

demonstrated that cognitive ability is highly correlated with IQ. They also found that the nature of cognitive deficits is not necessarily uniform among individuals with mental retardation. The authors concluded that mental retardation is much more complicated than simply a low IQ and can only be understood by investigating cognitive deficits on an individual basis.

It is unfortunate and, somehow, incomprehensible that none of the AAMR definitions specifically mention the term *learning*. If students with mental retardation could learn as others do, planning their educational programs would be simple. Regardless of any particular deficiency, their teachers could help them catch up to age-mates by identifying areas of weakness and by providing a good developmental or remedial program. Low intelligence and poor learning ability, however, cause students with mental retardation to fall increasingly behind their peers (Ellis et al., 1982; Ellis & Dulaney, 1991). One reason is that they typically perform more slowly even those tasks they can complete successfully (Cuvo & Riva, 1980; Lanier & Chesnut, 1990; Merrill, 1985; Mosley, 1985). In an educational setting, a person is not considered to be disabled unless the impairment diminishes his or her ability to perform needed or expected school tasks. The limited cognitive ability of a student who has mental retardation prevents him or her from performing tasks on a normal level in almost all areas (Cummins & Das, 1980). This fact is of particular consequence in the classroom because nearly everything done in this setting requires intelligence. Thus, with diminished or deficient intellect, a student with mental retardation approaches every classroom task poorly equipped and primed for failure.

Even though students with mental retardation may have other traits or abilities that fall in or near the normal range, their responses typically lack the purpose and meaning expected from individuals with normal intelligence. This situation has at least two significant implications: (a) Any advantage they would otherwise gain by having traits or abilities in the normal range is blunted by their low intelligence or learning ability, and (b) it is sometimes difficult to determine whether their poor performance is because of faulty sensory input or their diminished intelligence. For example, Watkins, Boyd, and Cavalier (1982) compared students with profound, severe, and moderate mental retardation on learning, memory, and transfer of training (discussed below) and found that all three characteristics were positively correlated with IQ. However, they were encouraged by their findings that showed that the performance of the students at all IQ levels could be improved somewhat with intensive training.

Memory

Generally, people who learn more slowly than others also tend to forget more rapidly (Ellis & Allison, 1988; Forness & Kavale, 1993; Hornstein & Mosley, 1987). Hutt and Gibby (1979), in an early but extensive review of the literature, concluded that students with mental retardation suffer both long- and short-term memory deficits. Burack and Zigler (1990) compared students who had exogenous and endogenous mental retardation with those who had no mental retardation and reported that the latter were superior on a memory task. Drew, Logan, and Hardman (1992) and MacMillan (1982) declared the research in this area to be somewhat inconclusive. Because virtually all of the research of the past two or three decades, however, has been of the MA-equated variety, the deficiencies appear to be less pronounced than they really are (McCartney, 1987; Whiteley, Zaparniuk, & Asmundson, 1987). These studies tend to agree that students with mental retardation not only have some abilities in both long- and short-term memory but also are likely to respond to some extent to programs designed to increase memory span (Forness & Kavale, 1993; Mosley, 1985). Carney, Levin, and Levin (1993) reported that various mnemonic devices help improve the memories of students with other disabilities and may help those with mental retardation as well.

Thinking, Reasoning, and Concept Formation

Predictably, students with mental retardation also suffer deficiencies in *metacognition,* the ability to use their cognitive abilities to perform well in language and other learning processes and activities (Berger & Reid, 1989; Ellis & Dulaney, 1991). The most noticeable of these processes is the inability to think and reason effectively (Baroody, 1987; Schultz, 1983; Zetlin & Bilsky, 1980). Mosley (1985) reported that these students process written and oral stimuli poorly and slowly. Stephens and McLaughlin (1974) found students without mental retardation to be superior to those with mental retardation on Piagetian tasks of both reasoning and memory. Bray, Saarnio, and Hawk (1994) suggested that students with mental retardation do not seem to develop reasoning and strategies necessary for effective problem solving. Further, Wehmeyer (1994) found these students to hold unrealistic awareness of causality and excessive general perceptions of control. The learning and curriculum-planning problems associated with metacognition are discussed in greater detail in Part IV of this book.

Physical and Mental Abilities

A common myth says that individuals with mental retardation may not learn very rapidly, but they work well with their hands. Research does not justify this statement; they typically lag behind their age-mates in this respect too. This myth does have some foundation in fact, however, and can be used to illustrate an important principle. Realistically, no task or skill can be classified as purely mental or purely physical. Students with mental retardation, however, compare more favorably with both their CA and MA peers on tasks that require relatively more motor activity or physical exertion than reasoning and higher thought processes. Although such an individual may achieve at a higher level than another who has no disability, studies done on a group basis almost invariably show that students with mental retardation do more poorly on tests of physical ability or endurance (Bruininks, 1974; Holland, 1987; Moon & Renzaglia, 1982; Stein, 1963). The general health and well-being of students with mental retardation are generally poorer than those of their peers (Asberg, 1989; Dunne, Asher, & Rivara, 1993) and are discussed in Chapter 16.

Decision Making and Independence

Undoubtedly as a result of a number of other learning deficiencies, students with mental retardation typically have difficulty making appropriate decisions and tend to be dependent on those around them. For example, many of their basic sociological decisions, such as their right to marry and have children, are made or challenged by other persons as consequences of their disabilities. Like other characteristics, the decision-making abilities of students with mental retardation vary greatly and each individual's ability must be carefully diagnosed. Teaching independent living and decision-making skills is important in their curriculum (Clark & Kolstoe, 1990; Langone & Burton, 1987; Luchow, Crowl, & Kahn, 1985).

Generalization, Transfer, and Incidental Learning

Students with mental retardation exhibit poor generalization skills and have classic difficulty with transfer of training (Hayes & Taplin, 1993). *Generalization* is the ability to draw conclusions or to make inferences from rules, ideas, or experiences. Typically, a person with mental retardation not only fails to generalize and to arrive at conclusions supported by adequate evidence but also jumps to unwarranted conclusions prematurely (Ellis et al., 1982). Ferguson and McDonnell (1991) and Tirapelle and Cipani (1992) agreed that difficulty in making generalizations is a typical problem for students with mental retardation, but one that can be overcome to some extent with well-designed instruction. Horner, Williams, and Stevely (1987) demonstrated that students with moderate to severe mental retardation could generalize intensive telephone training to nontrained situations.

Transfer of training is the ability to apply acquired skills and concepts in practical situations—or even in other classroom settings. For example, a teacher may report to the mother of a student that the child has learned how to set a table for a meal. The mother then assigns the child to demonstrate the table-setting skills for a meal in the home. She is likely to discover that the child demonstrates considerable confusion and is unable to set the table without help. Aside from the possible embarrassment of being "on stage," the child's deficit in transfer of training may make this a nearly impossible task without additional, specific instruction. The tables may be different sizes or shapes, the utensils and napkins may be different, or the glasses may be a different color. Therefore, the IEPs of students with mental retardation must provide extensive opportunities to apply learned skills and concepts in a variety of settings.

Individuals with mental retardation also have difficulty with incidental learning (Gast, Doyle, Wolery, Ault, & Farmer, 1991). Incidental learning is closely related to generalization and transfer of training in that it may occur unintentionally or while some other skill or concept is being taught. For example, two students are taught different colors but in the same setting and at the same time. Incidental learning is the extent to which each student learns the colors presented to the other student. Generally, students without mental retardation learn quite readily from the observed or recounted experiences of others, but those with mental retardation do not. Moreover, students with mental retardation typically have difficulty learning from their own misfortunes and accomplishments. Because of the difficulties these students have with incidental learning, their lessons must be carefully prescribed to move directly toward their life goals because they have difficulty applying what they learn to real life situations without assistance (Gast, Doyle, Wolery, Ault, & Baklatz, 1991; Greeson & Vane, 1986).

Fear of Failure

Bialer and Cromwell (1965), Cummins and Das (1980), Schloss, Alper, and Jayne (1994), and Zigler (1973) reported that people with mental retardation have a greater fear of failure and risk taking than those without mental retardation. Wehmeyer (1991) found that students with both mental retardation and learning disabilities scored more poorly on the Career Decision Diagnostic Assessment (Bansberg & Sklare, 1986) than students with no disabilities. The significant components on which they performed poorly included decision anxiety, authority orientation, and luck and fate orientation. Wehmeyer concluded that the students' lack of self-determination is one contributor to poor employment potential. He also postulated that the students' lack of self-determination was partly because of their being repeatedly subjected to failure. Perske (1972) pointed out that freedom from fear of failure and the willingness and ability to take increasingly meaningful and considered risks are important prerequisites to independent living and vocational success. As such, risk taking should be an ongoing part of the curriculum for students with mental retardation. Examples include attempting a difficult assignment, looking for employment, and going to an unfamiliar social engagement.

Creativity and Initiative

Students with mental retardation typically lack the creativity and ability to design and initiate their own learning strategies (Bridges, 1986; Greeson & Vane, 1986). They tend to be much less innovative than other persons in all respects. Students with mental retardation are also less likely to originate appropriate action that is not directed by other people. Dulaney and Ellis (1994) reported that individuals with mental retardation persist longer than others on repetitive tasks—a tendency they found to increase with age. These students can learn to be creative to varying degrees, however, but they require a great deal more instruction, support, advice, and supervision than most other students. Creativity, initiative, and independent actions also seem to be inhibited by a fear of failure (Cummins & Das, 1980; Kreitler & Kreitler, 1990). Wasserman (1992), however, contended that creativity can be developed or at least encouraged by an absence of fear of failure and by allowing children considerable freedom to select play activities. Similarly, in later chapters of this book, I point out how absence of fear of failure and teaching students with mental retardation to make their own choices and decisions can also foster optimum self-determination, independent living, and a modicum of creativity.

Teachability and Gullibility

A good example of a trait that can have either positive or negative effects is the extent to which an individual can be influenced by other people. On the one hand, students with mental retardation tend to be quite teachable because they view most adults as authority figures. This does not mean that they learn readily or that they are necessarily obedient, but they rarely question their educational placements or the teacher's motives for presenting particular skills and concepts. They can also be taught to follow the good examples of peer tutors and other responsible citizens (Webster, 1987).

On the other hand, students with mental retardation tend to be gullible and can often be persuaded by older, more experienced people to perform socially unacceptable or foolhardy acts that they would not do by themselves (Collins, Schuster, & Nelson, 1992). They often are influenced by statements, the falsity of which is obvious to others. A person with mental retardation often has great difficulty in discerning good-natured pleasantry and serious advice from taunting or teasing. Encouraging teachability and overcoming gullibility are worthy goals that students with mental retardation can achieve with good instruction and examples (Kreitler & Kreitler, 1990).

Judgment and Common Sense

Partly because of their gullibility, the actions of people with mental retardation often appear to be the result of poor judgment and a lack of common sense. Such students are likely to make unwarranted assumptions and conclusions that would be more appropriate for younger individuals. They often become frustrated and discouraged when they observe another person performing tasks they cannot perform. They are also likely to become understandably angry when they are criticized or teased for doing inappropriate things. Gargiulio and Sulick (1978) reported that the ability to take responsibility for one's actions is positively related to IQ. Further, it is difficult for individuals with mental retardation to determine which of their actions are inappropriate. Morris, Niederbuhl, and Mahr (1993) pointed out that school programs for students with mental retardation must be designed to teach, inform, and test the student's ability to make judgments. Teachers and others must find a balance between self-determination and exposing the person to danger.

Dealing with Abstract Concepts

Another prominent learning problem associated with mental retardation is the inability to deal effectively with abstract concepts and ideas (Nelson, Cummings, & Boltman, 1991; Soraci, Deckner, Baumeister, & Carlin, 1990). Terman (1916) defined intelligence largely as the ability to deal effectively with abstractions. One reason the abstract-concrete consideration is so important is that it is involved in every aspect of a student's education. In teaching students with mental retardation, the teacher must remember that every spoken or written word is an abstraction. Every lesson must be taught with a proper balance between abstract concepts (oral or written descriptions), semi-abstractions (pictures, maps, diagrams), and concrete materials (the objects themselves). Scott and Greenfield (1992) found students with learning disabilities and those without to be superior to students with mild mental retardation on several taxonomic information tasks. The tasks included describing exemplars of categories and describing the similarities and differences among those exemplars.

Attention Span and Distractibility

The limited attention span of students with mental retardation and their inclination to be distractible has been recognized and documented (Distefano & Brunt, 1982; Lerner, Lowenthal, & Lerner, 1995; Nugent & Mosley, 1987; Zeaman & House, 1963). Tomporowski and Tinsley (1994) reported that individuals with mental retardation have greater deficiencies in both memory and attention span than those without mental retardation. The authors hypothesized that these two deficiencies are closely dependent on each other. It is a mistake to assume, however, that all students with mental retardation are highly distractible or that their lessons must be presented in extremely small increments. They experience a great range of attention span that must be carefully diagnosed, with lesson length designed to fit the attending ability of each individual. Tomporowski and Allison (1988) investigated the attention spans of 23 young adults with mild mental retardation and without mental retardation. The authors reported that the attention span problems of those with mental retardation seemed to center on tasks that included heavy memory demands. Kelly and Heffner (1988) emphasized attention span as a primary element in helping students with severe or profound mental retardation successfully overcome serious social problems.

The problems of attention span and distractibility appear to be closely related. That individuals with mental retardation are generally distractible has been well established (Crosby, 1972; Krupski, 1972; Merrill & Peacock, 1993). Individuals with mental retardation have particular difficulty in directing their attention to significant details and events (Melnyk & Das, 1992). Merrill and Peacock (1993) found that problems of attention span seemed to be related to the inability of students with mental retardation to allocate attention commensurate to problem difficulty. In a fascinating experiment, Stoffregen, Baldwin, and Flynn (1993) drew the attention of adults with and without mental retardation to a videotaped basketball game. The authors reported that those with mental retardation were significantly less likely to notice a lady with an open umbrella passing through the game.

Social Adjustment

Much has been written about the social problems of people with mental retardation. Most current definitions of mental retardation either state or imply that individuals cannot be classified having mental retardation unless they have significant social and other adaptive behavioral problems. Simply stated, students with mental retardation are likely to have serious, persistent deficiencies in most if not all social skill areas (Kopp, Baker, & Brown, 1992; McKinney & Forman, 1982). These problems are discussed in greater detail in Chapter 12.

Communication

Learning to effectively communicate is one of the most complex tasks any person has to master and is particularly difficult for persons with mental retardation. *Communication* is the total process of giving and receiving information. Such an exchange can be written or oral and can actually use most of the other senses. Considering the many things that can go wrong, one might marvel that any child learns to communicate at all. Individuals with mental retardation are likely to suffer mild to severe deficits in every facet of the communication process (Grieve, 1982; Kennedy, 1930; Mire & Chisholm, 1990). Warren and Abbeduto (1992) concluded that deficiencies in communication skills set people with mental retardation apart from others more consistently than any other cognitive skills. Individuals with mental retardation have understandable difficulty in dealing with humor, innuendo, and the subtleties of language (Short, Basili, & Schatschneider, 1993). Scudder and Tremain (1992) also found that such individuals have greater difficulty following up and clarifying their statements that are misunderstood by others.

Not only is evaluating a student's language ability vital in teaching him or her to communicate effectively with others, but the teacher must also present each student's lessons in every area of learning at a language level appropriate to that student. All instructions given must be simple enough that each student can understand and respond, but challenging enough to encourage language improvement. A considerable part of communication for students with mental retardation is following written and oral instructions, with which they also have great difficulty (Hornstein, 1986; Merrill & Mar, 1987).

Academic Ability

Students with mental retardation are likely to suffer significant difficulties in every area of academic ability or classroom task. They have particular problems in the more formal aspects of education, such as reading, writing, spelling, and arithmetic (Bilsky & Judd, 1986; Cummins & Das, 1980; Porter, 1993). They have less severe but still serious difficulties with the less formal, non-academic curriculum elements, such as physical education, independent living, personal grooming, work experience, and transition. All "academics" in the curriculum of students with mental retardation must be highly practical in nature and carefully designed in order to be beneficial (Ezell & Goldstein, 1991; Gottardo & Rubin, 1991). Several later chapters cover specific academic and other areas of curriculum and the learning characteristics associated therewith.

INTERACTION AMONG LEARNING CHARACTERISTICS

Not only are the learning deficiencies of students with mental retardation consistent and relatively severe, they also interact with each other to aggravate and compound an already serious situation. For example, a student with mental retardation is likely to have a poor memory, which in itself is a severe disability. But if this were the only learning problem, the educational and vocational prognoses would not be poor. Such students could be taught to compensate for this problem to some extent if they did not also have other limitations, such as distractibility, poor reading skills, and a generally slow rate of learning. The addition of each deficiency makes it more difficult for a student with mental retardation to overcome the consequences of the other deficiencies. In this sense, having mental retardation is having multiple disabilities because every inability or weakness must be treated through diminished cognitive ability or intelligence and a wide array of other deficits.

PROACTIVITY

Students with mental retardation have particular difficulty with problem solving (Bilsky & Judd, 1986; Spitz & Semchuck, 1979), transfer of training, and generalization (Hayes & Taplin, 1993). **Proactivity** is the ability of a student (especially one with mental retardation) to recognize when a practical, life problem is at hand, to set up the problem, solve it, and use the solution appropriately—and do so without the help of a teacher or an instructional assistant. Instruction and experience in proactivity help motivate students with mental retardation and enhance their ability to actively solve their practical life problems. There is little value in any skill acquired in school or elsewhere if the student fails to master the practical application of that skill. For example, in teaching arithmetic and reading skills to students with mental retardation, one must go considerably beyond the mastery of the fundamentals.

The concept of proactivity has wide application in planning and conducting all classroom activities, many of which tend to be highly academic and often difficult to relate to real-life situations. Making classroom experiences relate to adult life is particularly

Individuals with mental retardation must learn to be proactive in solving even seemingly simple life problems.

difficult with students who have mental retardation. The two-pronged definition of mental retardation (low learning potential and poor classroom performance) virtually ensures that their performance lags behind that of their peers. This lag usually means that they are much older than other students before (and if) they acquire a modest sight vocabulary and master rudimentary concepts such as simple addition and subtraction. Understandably, this age difference usually causes their parents and teachers to redouble their efforts to teach the rudimentary concepts.

Deficiencies in arithmetic problem solving and reading comprehension are particularly significant because they are the most practical aspects of these two important areas of learning. In arithmetic, for example, many older students with mental retardation in both regular and special classes have a common fear of "story problems" and are quite content to spend their time with mathematical computation. They frequently expect the teacher to identify the operation required to complete each problem. In reading, many students with mental retardation can identify sight words and "read" sentences far beyond their abilities to comprehend what they are reading. With repeated exposure to the same sight words and stories at home and at school, students with mental retardation can often convince their teacher and parent that they are much better readers than they are. There is questionable value in a person's being able to identify words—even a sequence of words—if the person cannot use that ability to gain information from printed material. Likewise, there is little utility in being able to perform rudimentary—even complicated—mathematical operations if one can't use these skills to solve practical, life problems. The basic steps of proactivity require the person to

1. Recognize that he or she is confronted with a problem (in the classroom, home, job, or social situation)
2. Recognize the given information
3. Set up the problem
4. Solve the problem
5. Understand the information produced by the solution (e.g., cents, dollars and cents, total cost, amount of the tax, the proper social or employment action to take, the moral of the story)
6. Use the obtained information in practical situations

In arithmetic, as well as in other areas of learning, a good teaching technique is to have the student *estimate* a reasonable solution to a problem. In solving a social dilemma or problem, the student should be trained to perceive and describe what he or she considers to be a reasonable—often a compromise—procedure to follow. Without an acceptable solution as a goal, it is unlikely the student will solve the problem.

MENTAL RETARDATION: UNLIKE OTHER DISABILITIES

People with mental retardation are like others in that they share most of the needs of all other members of society. The learning deficiencies of mental retardation, however, point out that these individuals also have some unique needs that must be carefully investigated. Of course, many learning characteristics not discussed here must also be accounted for. Even a cursory review of these learning characteristics suggests that curriculum, programs, services, and service delivery patterns designed for students with other disabilities are not necessarily appropriate for students with mental retardation.

Equating Unequals

On the whole, people with disabilities are an extremely heterogeneous group, but a particularly broad range of ability and achievement exists among students with mental retardation (Baroody, 1986). Karen, Austin-Smith, and Creasy (1985) reported an extreme range of ability on even a simple task, such as using the telephone. This range is particularly significant in consideration of *conceptual distance*, a concept that emphasizes the time, effort, and other resources represented by the range. Despite this fact, many professional educators attempt to equate some elements of disability that are not necessarily equal. For example, students with all types of disabilities are often classified according to level of severity. This practice often lumps students together in mild, moderate, or severe categories without regard for the type of disability involved (Storey & Mank, 1989). This practice seems to work reasonably well if a student's "mild" or "moderate" disability is an emotional disturbance, behavioral disorder, learning disability, speech or language disorder, or a visual impairment. These students can often be educated satisfactorily in a regular class—with limited special education services. Although the teacher may need to consult with a specialist about the student's problems, the student with a mild or moderate disability may not even qualify for special education unless he or she needs to spend time in direct contact with the special educator during the school day. In other words, the terms *mild* and *moderate* with respect to these disabilities really mean of lesser consequence or not excessive, but these terms imply more severe deficiencies in mental retardation.

From an educational standpoint, students with only mild or moderate mental retardation have a devastating disability. These are the students whose general and specific learning abilities rank them in the bottom 1% or 2% of the student population as a whole. The ability and achievement levels of students with severe or profound mental retardation are even lower. All students with mental retardation—mild/moderate and severe/profound—have a wide array of severe limitations that their gifted, nondisabled, or otherwise-disabled classmates do not have. Furthermore, an appropriate curriculum for students with mental retardation must include a great many tasks and skills not formally taught to other students. Later chapters deal with these formal and informal aspects of curriculum planning and content.

People with mental retardation also have great difficulty gaining admission to trade schools, technical colleges, and other post-high school programs, except when the program is designed especially for them—for example, a sheltered workshop. They rarely qualify for admission to specialty schools operated by businesses or industries, but if they are fortunate enough to find employment with firms that offer this type of post-high school education, they typically encounter little success. This general situation must be applied on an individual basis, however, and each person should be encouraged and enabled to take advantage of these opportunities wherever possible and to succeed as well as he or she can. Consideration of the typical situation should serve mainly as a reminder that public school experiences must be thorough, functional, and well-planned because they are usually terminal.

Incorrect Diagnosis

Of course, it is possible to incorrectly diagnose an individual as having mental retardation (Myers, 1989; Reiss, Levitan, & Szyszko, 1980; Taylor, 1980). The mass media frequently report incidents in which an individual (often in a residential institution for those with severe and profound mental retardation) has been found to have some disability other than mental retardation. In almost every case, it is considered newsworthy that the individual was found to have a "lesser" disability. Ordinarily, it would take a severe disability (e.g., deafness, which is sometimes mistaken for mental retardation) to cause such a gross error in diagnosis. Often, parents, on hearing from professionals that their child may have mental retardation, recall these published accounts and express the possibility that a similar mistake is being made in their child's case. Unfortunately, even some professionals have been reluctant to place an individual who really has mental retardation into an appropriate program or facility because of the slight possibility that the individual may not actually have mental retardation.

Educational Profiles of Students with Mental Retardation

A phenomenon that becomes increasingly obvious as one works with individuals with mental retardation is that they typically have low, flat educational profiles (Kirk & Gallagher, 1993). This profile configuration means that they compare unfavorably with their peers on nearly every ability and characteristic—except CA, weight, and height. Thus, unlike many other disabled students, those with mental retardation do not typically excel in any area of endeavor. By definition, students with other disabilities have normal or gifted IQs, which give them a tremendous advantage over students with mental retardation. Thus, the educational strategies and programs designed for those students with other disabilities are not necessarily appropriate for students with mental retardation.

Relative Permanence of Mental Retardation

Compared with other disabling conditions, mental retardation seems to be relatively permanent. This is particularly significant because such a small and decreasing percentage of U.S. school children are being identified as having mental retardation (*Sixteenth Annual Report to Congress*, 1994). Doll (1946) received a great deal of criticism for his suggestion that mental retardation was essentially incurable. In the years since Doll made this unpopular declaration, however, little appreciable progress has been made toward the elimination of mental retardation. Insofar as IQ can be used as a determiner of mental retardation, Booney, Blixt, and Ellis (1981) pointed out that scores of the WISC-III (Wechsler, 1991) are relatively stable over time. The pioneering works of Kirk (1958), Skodak and Skeels (1949), and Spitz (1945) demonstrated that IQs of individuals can be raised somewhat with intensive educational and sociological programs. Even if such programs could raise by 5 IQ points the IQ of every student with mental retardation, the students would still have substantial learning deficiencies.

After an extensive review of the literature, Pruess, Fewell, and Bennett (1989) discovered that vitamin therapy had no effect on the IQs of children with Down syndrome, and Weathers (1983) had similar findings on other nutritional supplements. Likewise, Rosenzweig (1981) reported that no drug lessens the effects of mental retardation. Because mental retardation by its very nature causes a student to fall increasingly behind his or her peers, the student typically does not completely outgrow the need for various types of assistance. Despite the possibility of an incorrect diagnosis and the sincere assertions of well-meaning relatives (and, on occasion, a pediatrician or an enthusiastic advocate), mental retardation does not simply disappear (a) as a person grows older, (b) by failure to identify it, (c) by switching labels, (d) by switching educational placements, (e) by moving from a high-identification area to a low-identification area, or (f) by graduating or dropping out. My major intent in this section is not to debate whether mental retardation is curable, but rather to point out that it is not justifiable to avoid one's responsibility to teach a student by anticipating a cure for the student's condition. Moreover, reasonably effective diagnostic/prescriptive teaching techniques used by a competent teacher should properly identify a student who is only suspected as having mental retardation.

Mental Retardation and Self-Criticism

Students with mental retardation typically have limited (but variable) ability to offer valuable criticism to improve their educational and other programs. Sigelman, Budd, Spanhel, and Schoenrock (1981) identified a strong tendency for students with mental retardation to give an almost automatic yes response to questions. They challenged the validity of using questionnaires and other questioning techniques, particularly those requiring only yes-or-no answers, to gain information from people with mental retardation.

Questionnaires that require more sophisticated responses complicate the matter even further. Wood (1981) attempted to identify problems that were of general concern to students with learning disabilities, behavioral disorders, and mental retardation. He proposed to investigate how the students' concerns correlated among the disability groups and among their parents and teachers. He found that students with mental retardation (unlike the other students in his study) were unable to respond effectively to a simple questionnaire. Although some could read the items on the questionnaire, they were unable to evaluate the simple concepts involved and to make even minimal suggestions for program improvement. As a result, they and their parents and teachers had to be dropped from the study.

Students with mental retardation do have preferences and opinions, and several later chapters cover how they can be taught to make increasingly significant decisions that affect their lives. Stanovich and Stanovich (1979) and Dudley (1987) suggested that people with mental retardation can speak for themselves to some extent but that they need to be taught and encouraged to do so. Because people with mental retardation are generally unable to speak effectively for themselves and do not join or organize advocacy groups, their educational and other programs are almost always organized and operated by people who do not have mental retardation. The question of how well students with mental retardation are able to speak for themselves and to make their own decisions is a reminder that their teachers must be particularly well-educated because they typically play the major role in designing and implementing curriculum for these students. Students with mental retardation can be taught to monitor and evaluate their own activities to varying degrees, however, and their educational programs should be designed to help them do so (Agran, Fodor-Davis, Moore, & Deer, 1989; Baer, 1990; Zohn & Bornstein, 1980).

Mental Retardation and In-Group Champions

Another difference between people with mental retardation and those with other disabilities is that mental retardation rarely produces "champions" from within the ranks of the group. Other groups of people with disabilities occasionally (and sometimes routinely) produce exemplars whose accomplishments are widely publicized. The failure of mental retardation to produce this type of outstanding individual places people with mental retardation at a distinct disadvantage in several respects.

No one from within the group is likely to become highly successful and set an example for individuals with or without mental retardation.

Individuals with mental retardation do not typically become teachers, counselors, or advocates and come back to help others with similar afflictions.

People with mental retardation do not usually organize committees or serve in organizations designed to help other people with mental retardation.

Mental Retardation and Remediation

Unlike other disabilities, the basic learning ability of a person with mental retardation cannot be improved or compensated for in any practical sense by mechanical or electronic devices, corrective lenses, corrective surgery, drug therapy, or other external means. Typical remediation programs are also inappropriate. Generally, *remediation* suggests procedures designed to heal, cure, or help a student "catch up" to others. In education, the term has also come to describe methods, materials, and techniques that help a faltering student return to grade level. Admission to remedial education programs usually requires a student to achieve considerably below grade level while having a high potential for learning (normal or above average IQ). The chances for success of a program are greatest with students having high IQs coupled with low achievement. This is a major reason why students with mental retardation cannot legally qualify for programs for students with learning disabilities in most states (Berger & Reid, 1989; Parmar, Cawley, & Miller, 1994). Further, these programs tend to be highly academic, often focused on reading and mathematics, rather than on preparation for adult life. Lindsey and Armstrong (1984) reported that students with mild mental retardation had significant deficiencies on the Brigance Diagnostic Comprehensive Inventory of Basic Skills (Brigance, 1983), the Peabody Individual Achievement Test (PIAT; Dunn & Markwardt, 1970), and the Wide Range Achievement Test (WRAT; Jastak & Jastak, 1965), compared with their CA peers who had learning disabilities. The group with learning disabilities was nearly 1.5 years younger than the group with mental retardation, which makes the results even more significant.

Mental Retardation and Simulation

Mental retardation is almost unique among the various disabilities in that it cannot be simulated. Therefore, it is difficult for people without mental retardation to be aware of the serious limitations of this disability. People without a disability can learn to appreciate at least one type of physical impairment by participating in a game of wheelchair basketball. Disabilities such as visual and auditory impairments, and even learning disabilities, can be temporarily induced by frustrating sensory input or by other external means. All people experience anxiety and frustration from time to time; this experience helps them in understanding the feelings of a person with an emotional disability. It is impossible for a person without mental retardation to fully appreciate the problems facing a person with mental retardation, however, because this condition cannot be simulated. Working with students with mental retardation is probably the closest one can come to experiencing mental retardation firsthand, but even this type of experience is vicarious in nature.

LOOKING AHEAD TO CURRICULUM PLANNING

A few final but important introductory notes are necessary before I begin a direct deliberation of curriculum planning. The primary purpose of this chapter and Chapter 1 is to identify and establish perspective for the population usually referred to as having mental retardation. In Chapter 1, I pointed out that not all states use the term *mental retardation*, though a majority do so. In this chapter, I identified some of the learning characteristics usually associated with mental retardation. The major purpose in doing this was not only to describe mental retardation but also to help IEP teams in planning curriculum for students who have these characteristics—even though a number of other terms are currently used instead of *mental retardation*. That is, students having the learning characteristics discussed in this chapter need special consideration in curriculum planning whether or not they are identified as having mental retardation.

The Individualized Educational Program (IEP) Team

The many variations in definitions, identification procedures, classification systems, and learning characteristics considered in light of broader issues, such as curriculum and program quality and availability, make functional curriculum appear extremely complicated. Gallivan-Fenlon (1994) suggested that a multidisciplinary team is vital in planning the educational programs of students with severe disabilities. I strongly support the proposal that a well-trained and dedicated IEP team is the best—if not the only—solution to these problems (Orelove & Sobsey, 1991; Vandercook, York, & Forest, 1989). In Chapter 5, I outline the duties of the student evaluation and IEP teams and charge their memberships to assess local conditions in formulating the educational program and identifying special services for each student with mental retardation. For example, nationwide issues, such as the dropout problem and the availability of transitional and work experience programs, are essentially beyond the power of the team to rectify. Awareness of these issues serves only as a reminder to consider how they apply locally and to the individual for whom the teams are responsible. The questions that team members must resolve are as follows:

What are the learning characteristics and capabilities of the student for whom they are responsible?
What is the nature and quality of local programs available to this individual?
Do large numbers of the students in these programs drop out of school before graduation?
Which, if any, programs offer needed work experience?

Similarly, the team must evaluate multicultural considerations on a local level and determine the extent to which they bear on the individual's quest to achieve optimum success as an adult.

Multicultural Considerations

In discussing regional variation in Chapter 1, I made a brief reference to multicultural considerations as one of several significant ways in which some students with mental retardation may differ from each other and from other students. The high correlation between ethnic group membership and mental retardation has been investigated with increasing intensity during the past decade (Lim & Browder, 1994). Historically, students from minority groups have been overrepresented in classes for students with mental retardation (Artiles & Trent, 1994; Epstein, Polloway, Patton, & Foley, 1989). Ford (1992) surveyed African American students in gifted, above average, and average academic programs. Underachievement behaviors were noted among students in all academic programs. The students considered psychological factors to be the most significant causes of underachievement. Cultural considerations have also revealed the close relationship of mental retardation to poverty and malnutrition (McDermott &

Altekruse, 1994). Weber and Stoneman (1986) found that parents from minority groups had lower than average incomes, had more single-parent families, and were less likely to participate in planning their children's educational programs. Lee (1993) reported that less advantaged families had less access to information needed to help in planning their children's education.

Single parenthood has also been shown to contribute to poor academic achievement (Featherstone, Cundick, & Jensen, 1992; Zimiles & Lee, 1991). Lee, Burkham, Zimiles, and Ladewski (1994) reported that serious behavioral problems were two to four times as likely to occur in single or stepfamilies as in intact families. Other significant elements among disadvantaged children include poor general health (Galston, 1993), ineffective communication with minority families (Harry, 1992; Lee, 1993), and malnutrition (Gupta, 1990). Scrimshaw (1993) pointed out that correcting early malnutrition has a significant, positive effect on children later in their lives. Dubow and Luster (1990) reported a strong relationship between poverty and the incidence of behavioral and academic problems of children born to teenage mothers. Schmitz (1992) reported a strong relationship between simply living in public housing and poor academic performance. In Chapter 4, I discuss family problems in greater detail and define families to include group home and foster parents, as well as guardians who may or may not be blood relatives. Obviously, these variations affect each individual in dissimilar ways and to different degrees. Further, some are beyond the control of the IEP team members, who must often seek the assistance of other individuals and agencies.

SUMMARY

In this chapter, I placed mental retardation in perspective with other disabilities by discussing some of the more significant learning characteristics and limitations that typically plague students with mental retardation. In working with people with mental retardation, it is important to avoid stereotyping, imposing unwarranted limitations on students with mental retardation, or assuming that they have talents and abilities they do not have or cannot demonsrate.

I pointed out that individuals with mental retardation typically have deficiencies in every trait or ability that is essential for effective learning. Therefore, the teacher and other IEP team members must diagnose carefully and take nothing in the students' education for granted.

Because of the students' constant need to communicate with others, the teacher must diagnose communication problems with particular care. I also stressed that programs for students with mental retardation must stress proactivity, independence, and decision making—concepts emphasized throughout the book.

The diversity imposed or aggravated by the learning characteristics of mental retardation—discussed in this chapter—provides further evidence that educational programs for students with mental retardation must be carefully planned and executed by a well-trained IEP team.

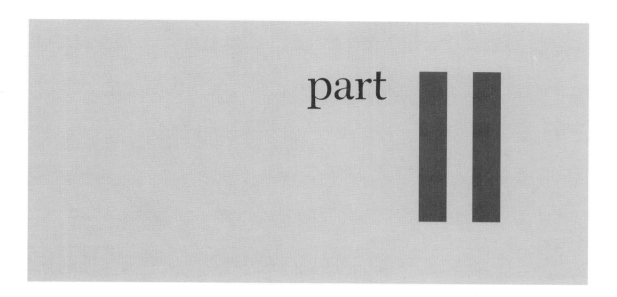

Life Goal Planning for Individuals and Groups

CHAPTER 3

Life Goal Curriculum Planning

Points to Study and Ponder

1. What is your definition of curriculum? Does your definition agree or disagree with the definition in this chapter?
2. Should curriculum be any different for students with mental retardation than for other children?
3. Why should the skills and concepts of curriculum be prioritized for students with mental retardation?
4. What is terminal education, and how does it apply to students with mental retardation?
5. What are Area A, B, and C skills? Why might a given Area C skill for one student be an Area B skill for another?
6. What is an IEP, and how is it related to life goal curriculum planning?
7. How do long-term goals differ from annual goals, according to this chapter?
8. What is level-to-level program planning?
9. What are entry-level skills, and what do they have to do with life goal curriculum planning?
10. Why is the secondary level so important in the life goal curriculum planning process?
11. What does prioritizing have to do with life goal curriculum planning?

n this book, I emphasize two major themes in teaching students with mental retardation: (a) functional, life goal curriculum planning, discussed in this chapter, and (b) diagnostic/prescriptive teaching, discussed in Chapters 6 and 7. These three chapters are closely related and must be considered together. In this chapter, I outline the first of these themes and begin by defining curriculum and showing how curriculum has been planned in traditional programs, as well as in those intended for students with disability. I discuss the reasons why students with mental retardation need special consideration in curriculum planning and describe the curricular improvements and adaptations necessary to accommodate the unique needs of these students.

Since the passage of P.L. 94–142 in 1975, the individualized educational program (IEP) has been the basis for curriculum planning for all students with disabilities. In this chapter, I discuss the formulation of IEPs, specifically for students who have mental retardation. I also show how IEPs lead to general curriculum planning for these students, for individuals, for groups, and for classes.

I focus on IEPs and general life goal curriculum planning for students with mental retardation by using an invaluable procedure referred to as the *age 25 projection*. I also emphasize long-term IEP and curriculum planning that spans the entire time a student with mental retardation is likely to remain in school. In later chapters, I show how to select and prioritize the specific goals and content of each student's IEP and curriculum and outline strategies, techniques, and methods to help the student in achieving those goals.

Curriculum planning for students with mental retardation concentrates on five basic components, all of which must be designed to enable the student to achieve optimum success in adult life:

1. Teaching the student fundamental-to-advanced skills and concepts, or developmental learning
2. Helping the student acquire learning strategies and abilities so that he or she can learn with increasing independence
3. Teaching the student necessary life skills and concepts while he or she is acquiring the competencies necessary to learn additional skills with increasing independence
4. Teaching the student how to compensate for the skills and concepts he or she is unable to master and how to adapt as well as possible to adult life without such mastery
5. Planning for the student within his or her limitations and potentials imposed and enhanced by the student's cultural background and other individual differences.

Common sense, P.L. 94–142, P.L. 101–476 (the IDEA), and the court cases that resulted in the passage of these far-reaching laws require that educational programs for students with disabilities be based on their individual needs and abilities. According to the law, each student with a disability is entitled to a thorough, and sometimes expensive, evaluation that determines the extent of his or her unique educational weaknesses and strengths.

The educational program (the placement and the curriculum) for each such student must be carefully based on the individual assessment, and it must undergo periodic review.

The key to successful curriculum planning for students with mental retardation lies with a well-trained, strongly motivated IEP team. Because students with mental retardation tend to be quite dependent on others, they must rely on those others to plan their educational programs. The chapters of Part I covered the difficulties encountered in defining mental retardation and the limitations it imposes on an individual.

Educational programs for all students, with or without mental retardation, should be commensurate with each student's needs and abilities. Ideally, every student's education should be designed to ensure maximum achievement and readiness for a successful adult life (Smith & Dowdy, 1992). Unfortunately, this type of intensive, individualized planning is not usually available to all students. The large enrollments in regular education classes make an individually planned education difficult, if not impossible, to achieve. But a major advantage of special education is smaller class sizes, which allow for much more intensive and individualized planning.

Mental retardation imposes the most severe educational limitations of any disability, and students with mental retardation have great difficulty achieving success under even the most ideal conditions. To meet the unique needs of a student with mental retardation, it is necessary to design a curriculum that is likely to be different from that of his or her peers. The unique and serious learning problems of students with mental retardation suggest that they are essentially the only students in the schools who need a distinctive curriculum. Most other students with a disability (those with learning disability or with speech, emotional, behavioral, physical, and sensory problems) may need specially trained teachers and a variety of helping and intervention techniques, but they follow essentially the same basic curriculum as their peers. A teenager with mental retardation must also be taught many of the skills and concepts needed by all teenagers before that student is able to read and learn about those skills and concepts for him- or herself. In this chapter, I summarize some of the reasons why students with mental retardation need special consideration in curriculum planning. I show how to design their individual programs and demonstrate how to combine the individual programs into a total class curriculum.

CURRICULUM DEFINED

The fact that the term *curriculum* has been defined and used in a great many ways perhaps precludes any real agreement on the matter. This uncertainty may be why many authors who write on education and teaching use the term without defining it. *Curriculum* has traditionally been used as a general term that included all of the classes taught by the faculty of a particular school. In this sense, curriculum applies to large groups of students. Each student may or may not be expected to take all of the classes offered, but the curriculum must be sufficiently extensive to meet the needs of all students. Ellis, Mackey, and Glenn (1988) described curriculum as "the sum total of all that is studied, taught and learned in school" (p. 192).

HOW CURRICULUM APPLIES TO DIFFERENT INDIVIDUALS AND GROUPS

Curriculum also applies to a course of study or the list of classes that an individual student is expected to take. Because of the severe limitations and the wide range of abilities of mental retardation, this application is particularly important in planning curriculum for students with mental retardation. And because the life goals of students with mental retardation parallel those of other students, it is important to at least briefly discuss regular curriculum and how it relates to curriculum development for students with mental retardation.

Curriculum must be developed for three groups: (a) students without a disability, (b) students with a disability but not mental retardation, and (c) students with mental retardation. Many student with mental retardation never have the opportunity to study a curriculum designed especially for their needs. Because curriculum means different things to different people, it may be helpful to discuss some principles and practices that have shaped curriculum in the past, particularly as they apply to these three groups.

Regular Class Curriculum

Many forces determine what curriculum is taught in a school. Although a full discussion of these influences is beyond the scope of this book, they include customs or traditions, special interest or pressure groups, colleges and universities, and popular or special needs. The decision whether or not a particular topic should be included in the regular class curriculum is usually made on the basis of how that topic is likely to affect great numbers of students in large geographical areas. Such decisions are essentially beyond the jurisdiction of the individual teacher or even a school faculty.

This assertion does not imply nationwide agreement on the content of curriculum, but the general skills and concepts to be taught, as well as the sequence for teaching them, are quite similar. From time to time, new skills must be added to the regular class curriculum, and they generally take several years to gain wide adoption. For example, the past few years have demonstrated the need for students to be computer literate. The value of computer-related skills is largely unchallenged, but adoption has been slow in some areas, partly because of expense. The current issue involves not so much the need for such instruction, but rather how it can be provided in a particular school or district. But the decision to vary the curriculum to include skills such as computer literacy takes place on the state, district, or school level. Individual teachers typically have little choice whether they will include these in their curricula. Having been adopted, the new elements of curriculum are usually offered at the same grade level or in the same classes in a particular state or school district. This practice helps ensure that all students receive the appropriate instruction and are not penalized by changing schools.

Curriculum for Students with Disabilities Other than Mental Retardation

Teacher preparation programs often provide separate pre-service curriculum courses for teachers of students with visual and hearing impairments and those with learning, emotional, and behavioral disabilities. Such courses have recently come under increasing criticism (Cobb, Elliott, Powers, & Voltz, 1989). Critics point out the inadequate justification for offering separate curriculum courses for teachers of students with these disabilities, and perhaps their complaints have some validity. After all, students with disabilities follow essentially the same curriculum as their nondisabled age-mates—unless the disability is mental retardation.

A close examination of the courses and textbooks for these teachers reveals few real changes to curriculum. The textbooks usually suggest special procedures, methods, techniques, and materials that have been found effective in dealing with a particular disability. But ordinarily, the content of the curriculum is about the same as for nondisabled students. Schools must provide additional academic support (e.g., resource rooms and teachers, remedial education or consultative assistance) for these students, but the procedures and facilities are largely designed to help students with disabilities keep up with their studies in regular classes. Thus, "curriculum" for students with disabilities other than mental retardation is essentially a matter of using different techniques, technology, and methods to teach the same skills and concepts that nondisabled students are taught.

If any learning problem is primarily attributable to low IQ, the student is usually classified as having mental retardation. Definitions of other disabilities usually include a disclaimer that the learning problem is not primarily because of a low IQ or mental retardation (Myers, 1989; Reiss et al., 1980). Obviously, to be classified educationally as having a disability other than mental retardation, a person must have intelligence in the normal and gifted ranges. Only students with mental retardation have very low IQs and—because intelligence is unquestionably the most important requisite for learning—this places them at a significant disadvantage. The educational problems of any other disability (even total blindness or deafness) can be overcome or circumvented to a great extent if the individual has adequate intelligence. All other disability groups can and often do include individuals who are intellectually gifted, as long as they have a disability that qualifies them for special education services.

Mental Retardation and Curriculum

Smith and Hilton (1994) pointed out that the curriculum for students with mental retardation should be driven by the individual needs of the students, rather than by clinical labels, philosophical issues, or the regular education initiative. They maintain that the program should be responsive to curricular differentiation, life skills, community-based instruction, and planning for the individual's future. In addition, Chapters 1 and 2 in this book added the need to consider the individual's unique learning characteristics and abilities and emphasized the need to select and train an effective IEP team to be responsible for the student's program—within legal parameters. To adequately consider the individual's unique learning characteristics and to train an effective IEP team to plan and main-

Because of the limitations imposed by mental retardation, the elements of curriculum must be carefully prioritized.

tain an effective and functional curriculum for students with mental retardation, these individuals need a number of special considerations in IEP and curriculum planning.

Prioritized Curriculum

The content of the curriculum for students with mental retardation must be carefully prioritized. Because of the limitations imposed on students by mental retardation, they cannot achieve as much as students with other disabilities or students who have no disabilities. Skills and concepts within the grasp of these other students are not necessarily appropriate for students with mental retardation. Therefore, their teachers and IEP teams must carefully prioritize the skills and concepts to be taught. Most other teachers are essentially consumers or implementers of curricula whose scope and sequence have been established primarily by others. Essentially, only the teachers of students with mental retardation need to be skilled in the design of ongoing curriculum. Designing curriculum for a student with mental retardation requires the IEP team to determine not only what is to be taught but also why.

MacMillan (1982) put it this way:

Mentally retarded children pose a unique problem to education, one not presented by any other exceptionality. While the blind, deaf, or learning disabled require modifications in the way they are taught, students who are mentally retarded require educators to decide what they should be taught. Since their limited intellectual ability slows down the learning process, one must consider the most efficient use of the time available for instruction and determine what is going to be emphasized. (p. 468)

Most teachers, if asked why they are teaching a certain topic (e.g., long division, the multiplication of fractions), will point out that they must comply with well-established areas of curriculum. If long division is typically taught at a particular grade level in a school district, every teacher at that level is expected to follow suit. A teacher of students with mental retardation, however, should be able to show how each student's daily activities relate to that student's life goals.

Individualized Curriculum

Individualizing IEPs and curriculum must go considerably beyond prioritizing, which emphasizes the differences among the IEPs of students with and without mental retardation. Because of the great heterogeneity of mental retardation, the eventual life status of the students will range from full employment and independent living to lifelong dependence on other people. Some students will ultimately achieve on a much higher level than their classmates even though all of them have mental retardation. Individualizing for students with greatly divergent life goals means they do not necessarily have IEP and curriculum skills and concepts in common with each other.

Individualizing IEPs and curriculum is further necessitated and intensified by regional variation in the rates with which mental retardation is identified by geographical area. Although proper IEP formulation should presumably be uniform throughout the country, the effects of regional variation must be carefully considered. Planning the overall curriculum for a group of the higher functioning students in a high-identification state is quite a different matter from planning the same in a low-identification state. For example, even the highest functioning students in a low-identification state are likely to have severe degrees of mental retardation.

Truly Long-Term Curriculum Planning

IEP and curriculum planning for students with mental retardation must be done on a long-term basis. Special education programs for students with disabilities who do not have mental retardation are usually limited to relatively brief encounters, part-time special services, or placements of short duration. The services are usually provided for only a few hours per week and are intended to last only a year or two. Furthermore, most of these students are expected to need less special support as they go through school. Students with mental retardation, however, tend to fall increasingly behind their CA peers as they continue through school, regardless of the educational program. Therefore, the needs of a student with mental retardation for special assistance and programs are likely to increase, rather than decrease, as he or she proceeds through school. As a result, the teacher must often plan a program spanning several years because the student will ordinarily remain for some time in a given service delivery pattern or class.

Broad Curriculum

Curriculum planning for students with mental retardation must be broader in scope than for other school children. Regardless of the extent to which a student with mental retardation is mainstreamed or included in regular classes, that student is likely to spend a larger portion of his or her school experience in some type of special education than any other student. This measure means that his or her special education teachers will be responsible for a wider range of the student's IEP and curriculum goals. Special class teachers must usually teach—or be involved in—most of the student's classroom activities. Because a student with mental retardation is likely to remain longer in special education, his or her teachers also must be prepared to plan, teach, or assist with each topic or activity for several years.

Terminal Education

IEP and curriculum planning must provide a terminal education that is as complete as possible when the student leaves school. Students with mental retardation are about the only ones in U.S. schools whose education is necessarily terminated when they leave the public school system. This termination means they must be as well prepared for adult life as possible when they leave the public schools. All others (even other individuals with disabilities) have a good chance to qualify for additional schooling in public or private institutions, trade or technical schools, community colleges, universities, and schools operated by business and industry after they finish high school (Jones & Moe, 1980).

Because a student with mental retardation typically does not attend college or other educational programs beyond age 21, his or her education must be planned to assume termination with the education of the public schools. The principle of proactivity calls for a functional curriculum that prepares the student as well as possible for adult life. Proactivity reminds teachers and other IEP team members that the student must be able to apply classroom skills and concepts to practical life situations. Some excellent sheltered workshops and other facilities are designed especially for people with mental retardation. But these programs typically admit only the students whose mental retardation is most severe, and it is difficult to obtain the funding necessary to maintain the students in these programs after they are out of school.

Carefully Planned Instructional Pace

The curriculum must be planned to proceed at each student's unique learning rate. The principle of conceptual distance warns each student's IEP team that even though the difference in the performance levels between two students may appear to be slight, those levels must be carefully considered in view of the amount of instructional time and resources that separate the students. Even more important is the amount of instructional time and resources necessary for an individual student to progress from his or her present performance level to that projected by the IEP. For a student without mental retardation, approximately 1 year of achievement can be anticipated from each year of instruction. However, this is usually an unrealistic expectation for a student with mental retardation. The evaluations that diagnose mental retardation place a student in the bottom 1% or 2% of that student's age-group on whatever criteria are considered necessary for academic success in the student's home state or school district. Thus, the IEP and the curriculum must be essentially unique for each individual, although efficient instruction may be executed individually and in groups. In the chapters in Parts III and IV of this book, I show how this goal can be accomplished.

PLANNING CURRICULUM FOR STUDENTS WITH MENTAL RETARDATION

Not only do students with mental retardation learn much more slowly and retain less than their age-mates, but also their educational programs must include a number of skills and concepts that other children tend to learn incidentally. Moreover, there are so few students with mental retardation, compared with the total student population, that they often find themselves in learning environments designed for other students with far greater learning capacities. Usually, these environments do not offer instruction in the kinds of practical skills that students with mental retardation need to succeed in life.

As if these were not sufficient challenges for their teachers, students with mental retardation constitute such a diverse group that no single curriculum guide is suitable for all students with mental retardation. Consequently, no single approach, strategy, or technique will accommodate all students with mental retardation. Clearly, the curriculum for an individual with mental retardation can be formulated only after a thorough evaluation of his or her life needs. These needs are referred to as *life goals* because they suggest some curricular activities not ordinarily included in the program for other students. For example, most schools hesitate to admit children to a regular kindergarten until they are toilet trained. Such training of children with severe/profound mental retardation, however, is often a significant part of their school programs that may take years to complete. Furthermore, relatively few students in regular classes experience the specific job training that should be central to the curriculum for students with mental retardation. To individualize the education for such a student, a teacher must first carefully consider the learning characteristics of the group as a whole and then of each student individually (Abbeduto & Nuccio, 1991; Scudder & Tremain, 1992).

The Sequence of IEP and Curriculum Planning and Service Delivery

Good practice and the IDEA require that the first task after a student is found to have mental retardation is to formulate the student's IEP. It is not possible to plan an effective IEP for such a student without having a thorough understanding of the complete process of teaching students with mental retardation. It is also imperative that the parents, teachers, and other members of the IEP team understand curriculum planning as thoroughly as possible so that they can include the most essential elements of curriculum in the student's IEP. The team must then prioritize those elements and sequence them in the student's IEP and total curriculum plan so that he or she may become as successful and independent as possible in adult life (Brolin, 1992; Nickles, Cronis, Justen, & Smith, 1992).

The content of every IEP in mental retardation has several component parts, each of which plays a vital role throughout the formulation of the IEP. Therefore, the following components are not necessarily mastered by teachers in the same order they will be used in the classroom:

1. The group learning characteristics of mental retardation (already discussed) that are likely to be present in the student whose IEP is being developed.
2. The extent to which each of these learning characteristics is deficient and present in that individual. It is essential to determine as accurately as possible the residual abilities the student has with respect to each characteristic. The IDEA refers to these deficiencies and abilities as the student's weaknesses and strengths.
3. The scope and sequence of general curriculum planning.
4. The content of curriculum that is likely to be appropriate for the student in question.
5. IEP requirements and procedures generally.
6. Service delivery patterns and placement. Although these are among the last components to be instituted, they must be considered. For example, some needed services may not be available, but listing them on the IEP may obligate the district to provide them and result in a difficult lawsuit.
7. Knowledge and experience in teaching students with mental retardation. A large part of most teacher training programs is devoted to the science and art of teaching, both of which provide valuable insights for the content and procedures to be followed by the IEP.

Members of the IEP team will, of course, vary in their expertise or experience on each of these components. Each team member is expected to contribute according to his or her particular training and experience. The teacher, however, should have training and either pre-service or in-service experience in all component areas. In practice, the teacher is usually the one primarily responsible for the specific lesson plans that result from the IEP, as well as for the actual teaching of the skills and concepts the IEP specifies (Burton, 1981). Before planning the curriculum for a student with mental retardation or for an entire class, the teacher must thoroughly understand the complete process from general curriculum planning to almost minute-by-minute instruction for each learner. The major purpose of general curriculum planning is to provide overall, appropriate learning activities for each learner. But it is the minute-by-minute activities that must fill in the general curriculum plan. All remaining chapters of this book are devoted to effectively planning, conducting, and evaluating each student's progress on his or her IEPs and curriculum.

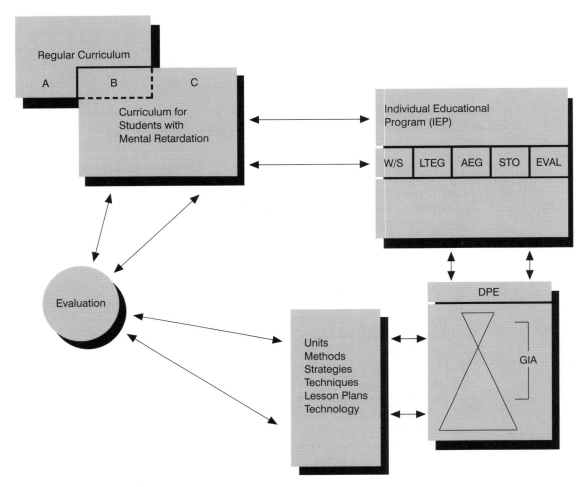

W/S   = Weaknesses and Strengths
LTEG = Long-Term Educational Goals
AEG = Annual Educational Goals
STO = Short-Term Objectives
EVAL = Evaluation
DPE = Diagnosis/Prescription/Evaluation (Chapter 6)
GIA   = Goal Instruction Analysis (Chapter 7)

FIGURE 3.1 Schematic Curriculum Planning Flow Chart

Schematic Model or Flow Chart

Figure 3.1 represents a model or schematic chart that illustrates how the curriculum should be planned for students with mental retardation. The concepts illustrated in Figure 3.1 are discussed throughout this chapter, and parts of Figure 3.1 are reproduced in this and other chapters. Area A skills and concepts in Figure 3.1 are those from the regular curriculum that are beyond the mastery of a student with mental retardation and are not included in his or her programs. Area B skills and concepts represent those that might be mastered by a student with mental retardation, depending on that student's ability levels. Area C skills and concepts are essentially unique to students with mental retardation.

Areas A and B represent all of the skills, concepts, activities, and experiences (or total curriculum) a school offers to all students without mental retardation. This curriculum must be broad enough to accommodate the brightest student but sufficiently flexible to provide a good education to the less able. For example, it would include all classes and subject areas from those appropriate for the slowest students to advanced placement classes for those planning to attend college. If students with mental retardation could learn as others do, their curriculum would include all Area A and B skills and concepts, but this is not possible. Therefore, the IEP team must carefully choose the skills and concepts to teach them.

Areas B and C of Figure 3.1 represent the skills and concepts that might appropriately be taught to a student with mental retardation. The dotted line separating these areas suggests that the needs and abilities of individuals with mental retardation vary considerably. For example, the curriculum of a more capable student with mental retardation will typically call for more Area B skills than that of a student whose mental retardation is more severe.

Area A, B, and C Skills and Placement

The IEP team must carefully consider, prioritize, and select the skills and concepts of Areas A, B, and C if the resulting curriculum is to be effective in preparing the student for life as a successful adult. However, the student's IEP team must soon (almost simultaneously) consider possible placements and determine how the curriculum elements could be delivered in the service delivery patterns available to the student. For example, a good work experience program may be available in one school but not in another (McCrea, 1993). One advantage of an inclusion-type program is the ready availability of Area A and B skills and concepts. A definite challenge of an inclusion placement is the difficulty of providing Area C skills (those that need to be taught only to students with mental retardation) that are usually of highest priority until they are mastered (Brolin, 1992; Clark, 1994). The major focus of Area A skills and concepts must be on regular curriculum. Discriminating among the skills and concepts of Areas A, B, and C is crucial because it is easy to simply assemble a watered-down array of Area A and B skills and concepts and label them as the curriculum for students with mental retardation (Fettgather, 1989). Designing lesson material in this way does not necessarily make it appropriate for students with mental retardation. In other words, just because a student with mental retardation can master a skill or concept is not sufficient reason to include it in that student's curriculum.

Area B skills and concepts (those that under appropriate circumstances might be taught to students with or without mental retardation) may be incorporated in two ways into the curriculum for students with mental retardation. First, the IEP team may place a student with mental retardation directly in a specified regular class where those skills are taught. Ordinarily, the student must take such a class in its entirety because it is difficult to adapt such a class to that particular student's unique needs. He or she must usually use the same textbooks and take the same examinations as other class members.

Area B skills and concepts may also be incorporated into the curriculum by teaching them in a resource room, a self-contained class, or a facility appropriate for students with mental retardation. Whenever Area B skills and concepts are taught to students with mental retardation, they must be adapted to the needs and ability levels of each student. For example, all students need instruction on keeping the body healthy. But such instruction must be carefully adjusted to the language and reading comprehension levels and learning rates of those with mental retardation. Watered-down grade-level work has little practical value. It takes a skillful, well-trained teacher to teach adolescent skills to a teenage student who reads at a second- or third-grade level. Such a student must learn how to read as well as possible, to solve everyday math problems, to obtain and hold a job, and to take care of his or her money. He or she must be taught the lessons with materials and methods that are chronological age appropriate. Other examples of skills and concepts of Area B are basic arithmetic, English, civic responsibilities, basic science, and physical education.

Area C skills and activities make up the bulk of the curriculum in self-contained classes for students with mental retardation. Area C skills and concepts include, but are not necessarily limited to, self-help skills, survival words and phrases, telling time and using time concepts, work responsibilities, and social skills. Most regular students learn these skills before entering school or at least much earlier in life. Thus, these skills are not usually considered a part of the school's responsibility.

Although some Area C skills and concepts (those that need to be taught only to students with mental retardation) might be described with the same terminology as those in Area B (those that under appropriate circumstances might be taught to students with or without mental retardation), great differences usually exist between the performance levels being discussed. For example, the titles of the skills and concepts used to exemplify Area B (basic arithmetic, English, civic responsibilities, health, science, and physical education) could also be used in Area C. In fact, many students with mental retardation have life goals that require experience in these areas. The main difference is that Area C skills must be taught on a more basic level.

THE INDIVIDUALIZED EDUCATIONAL PROGRAM (IEP)

After an evaluation of the student's individual weaknesses and strengths and after gaining an understanding of the general principles of curriculum content and planning, the IEP team is ready to determine the specific skills and activities to be taught to the student. This determination, required under the IDEA, is referred to as an IEP. Practically all Area A and Area B skills have advocates who insist that every student—including those with mental retardation—must complete 1 or more years of whatever the advocate is teaching. The IEP team—including the parents—must make the final decisions about which skills and concepts are taught to their student. The team must also prioritize the skills and concepts so that the student can become as independent and self-sustaining as possible. Therefore, the student must also participate on the team to the extent that it is appropriate.

Multicultural Considerations

Another major responsibility of the IEP team is to determine how each of the Area A, B, and C skills and concepts accommodates the student's cultural and ethnic background. The team must find an acceptable balance between the important elements of the student's culture and the student's need to be assimilated into the larger culture. A well-trained IEP team should be in the best position to make the necessary decisions and to prioritize those decisions in the student's IEP. The full participation of the parents is crucial in finding the necessary balance and priorities.

Elements of an Acceptable IEP

Federal regulation 34CFR300.346 that implements the IEP specifications of the IDEA requires six elements for an acceptable IEP. These elements are listed below, followed by a brief discussion that describes each and shows how they fit into the overall IEP:

1. Present levels of performance
2. Annual goals
3. Short-term objectives
4. Specific special education and related services to be provided and the amount of time in regular education
5. Projected dates for initiation and anticipated duration of services
6. Criteria and schedules for determining goal achievement

Because IEPs must be constructed on an individual basis, each IEP begins with the information necessary to identify a particular student. This information usually includes the student's name, birthdate, address, school, and the names of the parents. For privacy reasons, as well as for brevity, it is important to omit information not essential in planning the student's educational program.

Present Levels of Performance

Figure 3.2 is a simplified diagram of the IEP format in general use. Figure 3.3 shows an improved IEP format especially for students with mental retardation. Figure 3.1 illustrates how the IEP relates to the overall curriculum planning process for students with mental retardation. The IEP is based on the student's weaknesses and strengths (W/S in Figures 3.1, 3.2, and 3.3). The weaknesses are the specific reasons for the student's being in special education. To qualify the student for special education services, the

FIGURE 3.2   Current IEP Format

Identifying Data and Services to Be Provided			
W/S	AEG	STO	EVAL

W/S = Weaknesses and Strengths
AEG = Annual Educational Goals
STO = Short-Term Objectives
EVAL = Evaluation

weaknesses must have a generally adverse affect on the student's ability to succeed in school. The qualifying weaknesses for students with mental retardation, as well as for students with other disabilities, are carefully and extensively specified in federal and state regulations, which are subject to frequent change. A copy of these regulations can be obtained from each state education agency (they are referred to as SEAs in the IDEA). The regulations also identify the specific tests and other criterion measures to be used in assessing the student's weaknesses.

The strengths are the student's residual abilities that make the goals and objectives of the IEP achievable for that student. Only the student's most significant weaknesses and strengths need to be included on the IEP, and these may be summarized. The strengths are the composite of the type, quality, and extent of the educational capabilities with which the student attacks each skill and concept of his or her IEP. The student's strengths must be compared with the entry-level skills required to master a given task. In the chapters of Part III of this book, I describe how this is done.

Annual Educational Goals

The IEP must include a list of annual educational goals (AEG in Figure 3.2) for each student. Annual educational goals are goals projected to be mastered during the next 12 months. It is necessary to formulate the student's initial IEP before he or she begins receiving special education services. Thereafter, the annual educational goals are reviewed and evaluated, and new goals are identified during each school year. Annual educational goals project the general direction the student's education will take. According to the IDEA, the identification of annual education goals is to be the combined efforts of the child's parents or guardians and whatever professional educators and others might logically make valuable contributions. But, in practice, some of the strict provisions of the law tend to be overlooked, and many special education teachers find themselves largely responsible for providing the content of the IEP, including the annual educational goals. Often, the teacher formulates the IEP and presents it to the parents and other members of the team for their approval.

Short-Term Objectives

Short-term IEP objectives (STO in Figure 3.2) are subdivisions of the student's annual goals and should be completed by the next annual IEP evaluation. Each annual educational goal (which is usually quite general) is broken down into a number of short-term objectives (which are more specific). The exact number of short-term objectives for each annual educational goal is not specified, but three or more are usually required in practice. It is assumed that if an annual educational goal is worthy of being included on the IEP, the goal should be sufficiently viable and obvious to be broken down into a reasonable number of component parts.

Short-term objectives must be measurable. A functional annual goal for many students with mental retardation might be stated in general terms, such as "Follows directions." A short-term objective for this goal must specify how it is to be measured and the level of anticipated performance. For example, such a short-term objective might be "Given oral (or written) directions for finding a designated schoolroom or office, the student will do so consistently and without assistance." This objective suggests a variety of related activities or tasks that contribute to the accomplishment of the annual educational goal. These activities and tasks can be included in teaching units, lesson plans, and teaching procedures and need not be stated as individual short-term objectives.

Evaluation and Achievement

Once an IEP is in operation, the regulations that implement the IDEA specify that it must be evaluated within the next 12 months. The law requires that the evaluation be done periodically, which in practice has evolved to an annual review. After the first evaluation, some schools review the IEP and formulate a new one on the 12th anniversary of the first one. To avoid having to complete all of the IEPs for a group in the same month, it is permissible to formulate succeeding IEPs during each student's birth month and annually thereafter. It is also possible to distribute the IEP meetings evenly throughout the school year in any other way—as long as they are performed at least annually.

The major purpose of the annual IEP evaluation (EVAL in Figure 3.2) is to determine the extent to which the student has progressed toward his or her projected goals. At the evaluation meeting, the annual educational goals and the short-term objectives are reviewed and the student's performance is compared to the anticipated levels. The comparisons are then used to revise and reformulate the IEP for the coming year. The formality of the annual reviews and evaluations will vary greatly with the situation. They were intended to involve all or most members of the student's IEP team, but they often involve only the teacher, with varying participation by parents and other team members. The teacher is required to participate except in unusual circumstances, and in practice the annual review is often a parent-teacher conference.

The IDEA rules and regulations of most states call for a more extensive, thorough evaluation of the student's IEP, although this may vary considerably with individual states. These evaluations usually occur every 3 to 5 years. At this time, it is customary to retest each student in the program, rejustify the student's placement and qualification for special education services, and reevaluate his or her progress toward the stated IEP goals. IQ and appropriate achievement tests are readministered, and the data are updated. It is intended that most of the student's IEP team members participate in the 3-year evaluations. In practice, the formality and extent of participation of team members range from the type of full participation of the student's initial IEP to the less formal annual evaluations.

NEEDED IMPROVEMENTS TO THE PRESENT IEP FORMAT

Figure 3.3 shows some substantive changes that should be made to the IEP format currently in use. The changes are necessary because the current format does not provide for genuine long-range planning and evaluation. Annual educational goals project a student's needs only a year into the future and therefore provide no plan beyond that period of time (Frank, 1983). A series of 1-year IEPs may work reasonably well with learners with disabilities without mental retardation because their exposure to special education is usually part-time and of short duration. Students with mental retardation, however, do not usually outgrow their need for special education services.

Long-Term Educational Goals

The central component of the proposed IEP format is to create a category of long-term educational goals (LTEG in Figure 3.3) in the IEPs for students with mental retardation. Smith and Dowdy (1992) pointed out that students with mental retardation need truly long-term goals that satisfy future needs. The proposed improvement would be beneficial for all students with disabilities but is particularly essential for students with mental retardation. The current IEP format provides for a statement of the anticipated

FIGURE 3.3   Proposed IEP Format

Identifying Data and Services to Be Provided				
W/S	LTEG	AEG	STO	EVAL

W/S   = Weaknesses and Strengths
LTEG = Long-Term Educational Goals
AEG = Annual Educational Goals
STO = Short-Term Objectives
EVAL = Evaluation

duration of needed services but does not require any consideration of what the services are expected to accomplish beyond the planned year of the IEP. This additional category anticipates all the life goals a student with mental retardation is likely to master while he or she is in special education. For most students with mental retardation, long-term planning should be available for their entire school careers. In rare instances, a student with mental retardation may reach a point at which he or she no longer needs any special services, but this is highly unusual.

For many students with other disabilities, an appropriate long-term educational goal may be to bring them up to grade level in one or more academic areas. This is an unrealistic goal for most students with mental retardation because they tend to fall steadily farther behind their age-mates regardless of the services provided. Another long-term educational goal might be to help a student with disabilities gain full-time placement in regular classes. This goal is also more difficult to achieve for most students with mental retardation than it is for those with other disabilities. If the IEP team anticipates the placement of a student with mental retardation into a mainstreamed or inclusion program, this should be listed as a long-term educational goal, together with the projected or target date for attainment. In fact, the future termination of any special education services that may be no longer needed (e.g., speech therapy) should be projected as a long-term educational goal with an anticipated target date. Likewise, any service, such as recreational therapy, career education, or vocational preparation, not currently in the program but anticipated at some time in the future should also be projected and a target date identified. Target dates are considered tentative and are subject to ongoing review and appropriate adjustment.

Annual Educational Goals, Short-Term Objectives, and Evaluation

Each long-term educational goal is converted into annual educational goals showing the yearly progress necessary for the long-term educational goal to be realized. For example, a long-term educational goal to discontinue one or more of a student's special education services is subdivided into annual educational goals. Each annual educational goal describes the progress toward the long-term educational goal that must be made during each school year remaining until the target date is reached. Likewise, long-term educational goals calling for a special service to be initiated must specify any preparation or entry-level skills the student will need at the target date the service is to begin.

Each annual educational goal is subdivided into short-term objectives as usual. The student's progress toward this annual educational goal is then evaluated and noted each year. In this manner, the preparation of a student with mental retardation for such a move can be built into short-term goals and carefully implemented or discontinued at the proper time. The annual educational goals and short-term objectives should also specify the criteria and conditions to be used in assessing the student's yearly progress toward the long-term educational goal.

As the participating IEP team members evaluate the annual educational goals, they adjust the expectations of long-term educational goals upward or downward, as the student's progress indicates. For example, the student's preparation for a needed change may have been either more or less rapid than projected. An annual evaluation may show that the student is not as well prepared for participation in an integrated setting as the long-term and annual IEP goals predicted. In this case, the new IEP should provide for either more time or more intensive instruction to master the criteria.

To be functional, short-term goals may also require ongoing adjustment, clarification, and expansion. Major adjustments may require reconvening the IEP team, or they may be made at the annual evaluation meeting when the IEP for the next year is formulated. However, less significant changes can be made by the teacher, often by consulting only the parent.

The proposed long-term educational goal component goes beyond the requirements of the IDEA, but it can be instituted at any level—local, state, or federal. The IEP team of any student or the faculty of any school might incorporate this type of long-term planning in the programs of even their students with mental retardation.

Elements Not Required in an IEP

An examination of federal regulation 34CFR300.346 that implements the IEP specifications of the IDEA shows that several elements are frequently included on IEPs but are not actually required. These elements may be advisable—even required by higher authority—but they needlessly complicate the IEP, which was intended to be a general statement of the student's needs and the program required to meet those needs. Some of the elements not required by the IDEA are lesson plans; teaching methods; textbooks to be used; specific computer programs or software to be used; specific reading, math, or other program; home visits made; phone calls made to the home; daily reports; any suggestion or indication that the educational goals of the IEP constitute a contract binding on the district; and specific length of the IEP.

It is important that the IEP not be confused with the complete curriculum, teaching units, teaching procedures, lesson plans, or lesson materials. Doing so has resulted in IEPs being unnecessarily long, complicated, and time-consuming. Some of the elements listed above are simply good practice and may be required by the IDEA, but they can be entered on other forms that do not require action by the full IEP team. Also, nothing in either P.L. 94–142 or the IDEA sets the length of the IEP. In fact, one of the original provisions of the IEP was to maintain small IEP meetings so as to encourage parents to participate and not be intimidated. Some team members can participate by submitting written reports and by being available for consultation. Implementing the plan remains the primary responsibility of the student's teacher, with assistance from others where appropriate. Parents are not expected to participate in either the writing or execution of daily, weekly, or other lesson plans. In fact, they are not actually required to assist in meeting the goals of the IEP, but of course most do so.

Schools and districts that employ a 20- or 30-page IEP would have a difficult time convincing anyone that the parents participated in every provision of such a large document. IEPs can be completed in outline form only, because there is no need for extensive explanations or paragraphs. IEPs that exceed a reasonable limit contribute to the "paperwork blizzard" that has plagued special education teachers since the passage of P.L. 94–142 in 1975. As much detailed information as possible should be reserved for lesson plans. Paperwork that is not necessary for improving the educational programs for students obviously detracts from the teacher's primary task of teaching. School officials at every level should seek to relieve teachers from unnecessary paperwork so that the teachers can devote as much of their energies and resources as possible to working directly with the students. Paperwork that a teacher might complete should be expected to pass the following test:

* Is it necessary?
* Is it required by higher authority?
* Will it likely result in program improvements?
* If it is necessary, how extensive must it be? Could it be done in outline form?
* If it is necessary, could it be done by someone else?
* Who will review it and for what purpose?
* Could it be eliminated or reduced in size?

CURRICULUM PLANNING AND LIFE GOALS

Life goals for most students are those goals they plan to achieve during their lifetimes. For our purposes, the life goals of students with mental retardation are the IEP teams' projections of the goals these students might reasonably achieve during their lifetimes. The IEP team typically makes these projections on behalf of the student with mental retardation. Furthermore, the more severe the mental retardation, the less the student is able to participate. Certainly, a student's IEP team must consult the student in every possible way, but a person with mental retardation is less able to participate in making his or her own life decisions than others, including individuals who have other disabilities (Downing, 1987; Wood, 1981). Dudley (1987), however, correctly pointed out that most students with mental retardation can be taught to make increasingly significant decisions in their own lives and that such instruction is a legitimate long-term goal. Stanovich and Stanovich (1979) demonstrated that such instruction is both appropriate and beneficial.

Given the fact that students with mental retardation will be unable to master all the skills and concepts of the regular curriculum, the IEP team must make some serious curriculum decisions. The team must decide each student's potential and design a program to help him or her reach that potential. The primary responsibility of the IEP team is to identify the most important skills and concepts and to include them in the individual's curriculum. Because of the inherent limitations of mental retardation, the IEP team must also identify many skills, concepts, and activities that are beyond the individual's level of mastery. These cannot be included in the curriculum. Understandably, accommodating these limitations may seem like a formidable task, but it can and must be done. Students with mental retardation are basically dependent on those around them to make these important decisions.

Life Goal Planning for Students Without Disabilities

If it were possible to somehow predict the eventual situation and status in life of each student in the schools, educators could do a better job of planning his or her education. While insisting on a fairly well rounded education for students, schools could provide invaluable assistance by helping them specialize and by emphasizing those skills and concepts the students would most desperately need in order to achieve their life goals.

But, in the schools, little individual program and curriculum planning takes place for those whose future does not include post-high school academic work. In most instances, staff merely lump all other students together in common programs as though they had common goals. One reason is because, in either public or private schools, sufficient money is seldom available to cover all desirable parts of even the basic curriculum. Also, it is simply not possible for a teacher to do much individual program planning when he or she has 25 or 30 young students to teach and plan for in each class. Teachers at the secondary level have even more students and less time to spend with each one. Then staff may not know whether a student will seek and qualify for college. Generally, parents and teachers have few indications of what the eventual status of their students will be and cannot plan accordingly. Finally, teachers must operate their curricula within the regulations of state and district bodies that maintain extensive control over curriculum specifications.

Life Goal Planning for Students with Disabilities

The IDEA requires life goal planning to some extent for all students with disabilities. In practice, this requirement is referred to as the *individualized transitional plan* (ITP). This long-needed plan may start as early as age 14 but must be in place by age 16. Its purpose is to provide a smooth transition from school to adult life; it stresses career education, job preparation, and employment (Repetto, White, & Snauwaert, 1990). Edgar (1988) pointed out that future employment should be a primary goal in the curriculum of every student with a disability. A major weakness of the welcome ITP is that it does not start soon enough. To be effective, transitional skills must begin early. Elementary schools serve more than 5 times as many students with disabilities per year as the secondary schools (*Thirteenth Annual Report to Congress*, 1991). By the time the ITP takes effect, the majority of the students are no longer in special education or have dropped out of school altogether (Walker et al., 1988; Ward & Halloran, 1989).

Life Goal Planning for Students with Mental Retardation

Considering all these problems, it is easy to see why educators do so little life goal planning for individuals whose future does not include college. In working with students with mental retardation, however, there are fewer excuses. The classes for these students tend to be relatively small; thus teachers have more time available to spend with individual students. Although there is no surplus of financial resources, there is certainly adequate opportunity to do much more individual planning than is often being done.

No one can predict with absolute accuracy the eventual life situations of a student with mental retardation, but one can make reasonably accurate projections over a period of time. As the teachers of a student with mental retardation diagnose, prescribe, teach, and evaluate that student's programs and work with him or her in transitional and vocational programs, they get an increasingly clear picture of his or her future family, social, and employment possibilities. The mental retardation of some students is so severe that even at an early age their future in a sheltered work environment with close personal supervision appears likely. But others, especially if given an appropriate educational program, may become quite independent. This possibility usually becomes increasingly apparent as they proceed toward graduation.

AGE 25 PROJECTION AND LIFE GOAL PLANNING

An effective way to perceive and structure long-term life goal planning is a procedure referred to as the **age 25 projection.** Age 25 is used because it allows the student a few years to adjust to adult life. The age at which the student graduates or leaves school is even more significant in long-term planning because, in effect, it marks the end of the school's influence. Figure 3.4 illustrates this important principle of planning a curriculum for students with mental retardation. At each annual evaluation, the IEP team uses the age 25 projection to estimate as accurately as possible the student's social, family, vocational, and other status at age 25. At each evaluation, the IEP team adjusts this estimate upward or downward, depending on the individual's progress since the last evaluation. If

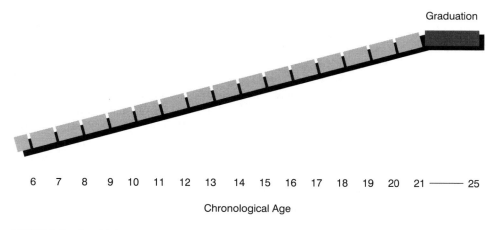

FIGURE 3.4   Age 25 Projection

the student's rate of achievement has exceeded the rate projected by the team, the estimate of that student's eventual life status is raised and the IEP is adjusted accordingly. If the student's performance has fallen short of the projections, the estimate of the student's life goal status is lowered. In practice, the changes in the estimates are not great in any single evaluation. Persistent use of the age 25 projection, however, yields increasingly accurate predictions of what and how the student will perform in adult life.

One important side benefit of the age 25 projection is that it helps students reach their full potential and helps prevent the assumption of unwarranted abilities or disabilities. One major purpose of a student's initial evaluation is to determine whether the student needs special services and to predict how well the student will do in school programs once the services are provided. The age 25 projection provides a means of direct observation and evaluation of the student's performance in the programs themselves. Students whose abilities are superior to the projections of the initial evaluation can be screened out of special programs and services and returned to more integrated settings. Those whose performance rates and levels are inferior to the estimates can be given the additional help and curriculum considerations they need.

Age 25 Projection and Different Service Delivery Patterns

Figure 3.5(A) is an age 25 projection for Jerry, a 16-year-old male with severe mental retardation. He is in a special school for students with mental retardation. Jerry's IEP committee estimates that, if Jerry remains in his present special education program, he will graduate from school at age 21, or in 5 more years. This means that in each of the remaining 5 years, Jerry must master approximately one fifth of the skills and concepts he needs to function at his long-term goal levels. Of course, he may make some additional progress after he leaves school, but this is largely beyond the influence of the school. Therefore, Jerry's IEP team must concentrate on his ability to function at the time of his graduation.

An important provision of the IDEA is that a student like Jerry, who has a severe disability, can remain in school until he or she is 21 years of age. It is increasingly apparent, however, that students in mainstream or inclusion programs tend to graduate or leave school at earlier ages than those who remain in special classes (Joekel, 1986; Walker et al., 1988; Ward & Halloran, 1989). For example, students with mental retardation in full inclusion programs are likely to graduate with their classmates at about 17 or 18 years of age. These students may remain legally in school through their 21st birthdays, but most do not. Figure 3.5(B) shows what Jerry's situation would likely be if he were in regular classes or possibly in a special class within a regular school. In either event, Jerry's placement is such that he will graduate at about age 18. Thus, he has only 2 years of school remaining, which means that during each remaining year he must master half of the skills and concepts necessary for him to function at his projected life goal level. By understanding the program a student is in, the IEP team can anticipate with some accuracy the age at which that student will complete his or her education.

Jerry's projected status at age 25 allows him a little time to adjust to his postschool environment. Some important considerations for this time period include his probable employment, living arrangements, lifestyle, leisure skills, and any family relationships.

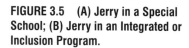

FIGURE 3.5 (A) Jerry in a Special School; (B) Jerry in an Integrated or Inclusion Program.

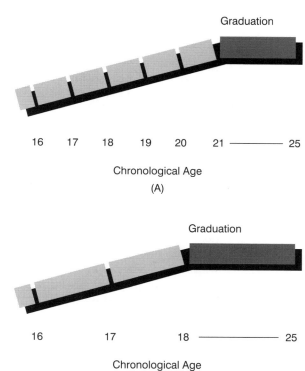

In planning Jerry's program, his teachers and other IEP team members must carefully prioritize his long-term and annual goals, and include those goals considered to be most crucial to Jerry's success as an adult. Moreover, it may be advisable to assign higher priority to those goals and objectives they estimate he can complete before graduation. Unless some assurance is given that Jerry will subsequently receive continued and correlated instruction from his parents or in a group home or other program, it is highly likely that a given skill may not be developed to the point of usefulness by the time he leaves school. If an activity, skill, or concept will take longer than the time remaining before Jerry's graduation, it may be best to drop it and instead choose another that he can complete. Of course, some long-term goals are continuous (e.g., developing communication and socialization skills, as well as good work habits), and Jerry might profit regardless of the limited instructional time available.

Curriculum Planning Courage

Curriculum planning for students with mental retardation usually involves some agonizing decisions. Sometimes the most difficult decisions in prioritizing such a student's long-term goals involve what to omit from the curriculum. Selecting the highest priority skills and concepts for a student with mental retardation automatically means eliminating other goals that have lower priority but are nonetheless valuable. It takes a particular type of courage to omit any skill from the curriculum of a student with mental retardation, knowing that the student might have mastered the skill had it remained in his or her program. Also, some skills and concepts must be eliminated because the student's evaluation clearly indicates that he or she cannot master them. Many teachers find it particularly difficult to omit subjects from a student's curriculum that they enjoy personally. Most people enjoy teaching skills and concepts they use frequently, although these skills and concepts may not be crucial—or even high priority—for a student with mental retardation to master.

Age 25 Projection and Younger Children with Mental Retardation

The benefits of the age 25 principle are quite apparent in planning curriculum for students with only 4 or 5 years of school remaining. However, it is also necessary and helpful in planning programs for younger students. For example, it is the younger students with mental retardation for whom long-term planning is most likely to include projections of the time they are to remain in special education programs. Admittedly, a younger student's eventual life status is not as clear as it becomes later. For this reason, adjustments to the projections in the life status of a younger student with mental retardation tend to be less accurate and possibly less crucial than the changes made later. But if the program is to prepare the student for maximum success in adult life, the student's IEP team must begin to evaluate the student's abilities and performance and to carefully plan the student's program when he or she enters school. If the IEP teams for students with mental retardation cooperatively and consistently apply the age 25 projection every year, by the time their students approach graduation, estimates of the students' performance levels become increasingly accurate. The chapters of Part III cover how this is done; the chapters of Part IV cover how to plan curriculum in specific content areas.

Lesson Plans

Although other IEP team members may make helpful suggestions, the teacher (or, in some cases, the therapist) bears the ultimate responsibility for the formation of lesson plans. The teacher must convert and expand the goals and objectives of each student's IEP into component parts and incorporate the parts into lesson plans. Teaching students with mental retardation adds a dimension to lesson planning—the need to track individual students more carefully, rather than groups or whole classes as most other teachers do. One of the most difficult decisions in lesson planning is the amount of detail and specificity to build into the plans. Some teachers perform best with rather limited lesson plans; others feel more comfortable with extensive and detailed plans.

A good rule to follow in lesson planning is simply to note how well one's plans are serving. On the one hand, if at times during the school day a student's next activity or objective is unclear, more detailed plans may be in order. On the other hand, if there is often little need to refer to the detailed portions of the lesson plans, perhaps less specificity would be permissible. Actually writing the details helps one commit them to memory, so the recommendation is to err on the side of more complete, rather than less complete, plans.

Many teachers prefer to do their lesson plans in outline form. The following is a general format for lesson planning:

1. **Lesson objectives** are either short-term objectives or subdivisions of the short-term objectives from the student's IEP. In formulating lesson objectives, the teacher must consider why the objective is being taught, why it is being taught at this time, and how it relates to the student's long-term and annual goals.
2. **Materials** needed to teach the lesson objectives are listed so that they can be ordered, collected, and organized before the lessons begin.
3. **Procedures** identify anticipated individual and group activities to be used in teaching the lessons. Procedures include field trips, films, videos, and integration with other classes. Lesson planning procedures for students with mental retardation must be planned in greater detail than those for other students by showing what each student is to do during each block of time, as well as whether and how two or more students are to be taught together.
4. **Evaluation** must not be overlooked. Initial lesson plans should project how the student's progress is to be measured and recorded. Because of the prioritization needed in curriculum planning for students with mental retardation, their teachers must consider each student's readiness and project the level of mastery each student needs to justify teaching the lesson objectives. (Chapter 6 covers the diagnostic/prescriptive/evaluative (DPE) approach and how this is accomplished.)

Common advice on the specificity of lesson plans suggests that a reasonably well qualified substitute teacher could take one's plans and, given the necessary materials and a reasonable amount of time to prepare, effectively teach the group of students with mental retardation for which the plans were designed. This is probably good advice, but it may result in excessive paperwork. Most teachers miss so few days of school that it is inefficient to add unnecessary detail to accommodate a seldom-used substitute teacher. Most often, the teacher is making lesson plans primarily for his or her own use. Therefore, a copy of each student's IEP and a brief description of each student should suffice.

GENERAL CURRICULUM PLANNING

Figure 3.6 is a curriculum planning chart to use in planning either an educational program for one student or a total school program. It outlines the educational programs from school entry to graduation for all students with mental retardation in a program. In a sense, it is the composite of all the students' long-term and annual life goals, as reflected by their IEPs. It also covers all subject areas for which the school is responsible. In fact, one primary purpose of the curriculum planning chart is to ensure that no part of a student's curriculum (or that of a group of students) is overlooked. The column

	Communication	Social	Transitional & Vocational	Home & Family Living	Leisure	Arithmetic
Preprimary						
Primary						
Intermediate						
Prevocational						
Vocational						

FIGURE 3.6   Curriculum Planning Chart

headings show the clusters of subject areas and are grouped for convenience into six general headings. The number of headings is quite arbitrary, and any convenient number of columns could be used. Regardless of the number of columns used, it is necessary to combine several skill areas under a heading that may not appear to be the most appropriate. The curriculum planning chart is diagrammatic and may be of any convenient size with any number of supporting documents.

The major purposes of the curriculum planning chart are as follows:

- To show the interrelationship among the various elements of curriculum for students with mental retardation
- To visually display the scope and sequence of a special curriculum available to students with mental retardation in a school or school district
- To define teacher responsibilities at each age level
- To ensure that no important experiences in the curriculum are overlooked
- To facilitate consistent planning from one age level to another

Chart Columns

It is important to notice that there is no intention or suggestion that the clusters of subject areas in each column are to be taught as separate subject areas or classes. These clusters are interrelated, and efficient instruction necessitates combining elements of several clusters in each lesson or activity. Each composite life goal of each student with mental retardation is placed in the appropriate column and at the proper age and ability level. This must be done at the district or school level because of the many variations in definition, identification, and placement of students who are mentally retarded. If a skill or activity does not fit exactly into any column, it should simply be placed in the column that seems most appropriate. In fact, many skills and activities can be listed in more than one column.

The column headings can be altered to fit a particular situation. However, all of the column headings should be used. For example, the tendency may be to downgrade the need for vocational activities for younger students, but including the vocational heading on the chart provides a reminder that these skills need to be introduced in the curriculum sometime and that the chart will help with the timing. Also, vocational entry-level skills (e.g., following instructions, establishing good work habits, developing a variety of social and communication skills) should be presented at the preprimary and primary levels. Noting these on the chart suggests that they can be incorporated into the activities of other columns. For example, a younger student can listen to stories on these topics. Later, as the student learns to read, his or her reading material should center around these types of practical skills and concepts that contribute as directly as possible to that student's long-term life goals.

The arrangement of subtopics for each column of the Curriculum Planning Chart used throughout the book is as follows:

Communication	Language concept development, listening, speaking, reading, writing, speech alternatives
Social	Personality development, personal appearance, self-help, good manners, social awareness, grooming
Transitional and Vocational	Following instructions, work habits, career education, work experience, industrial arts, transportation
Home and Family Living	Decision making, domestic arts, safety, independent living, sanitation, hygiene, sex education
Leisure	Recreation, physical education, motor activities, endurance, health, art, music, ambulation, body movements
Arithmetic	Basic operations, measurement, money, time, consumer education, numbers, counting

Horizontal Curriculum Planning

The chart is designed to show how the clusters of subject areas relate to each other. In several other chapters, I demonstrate how to combine specific subject areas. Some skills or activities might logically fit in more than one column because each skill and concept relates to many others at the same age and ability level. In fact, it is difficult to conceive of an activity that does not relate to those in other columns. For example, suppose the selection of wholesome foods for a balanced diet is identified as an intermediate health skill. **Horizontal curriculum planning** correlates concepts from several other columns. The skills and concepts from the other areas of curriculum are diagnosed and taught in a single cohesive unit:

Communication	Listening, reading, reporting, discussing foods
Arithmetic	Counting, measuring, weighing foods
Vocational	How foods are grown and prepared for market (what jobs are available in the food industry)
Social Studies	How people work together to provide food, where foods come from
Safety	Keeping foods safe and avoiding contamination
Home Arts	Preparing and serving food, table setting, nutritional values of various foods
Recreation	Selecting food for recreational activities
Fine Arts	Comparing pictures of foods, drawing pictures of food items

One should not place too much emphasis on the column headings. A rigidly departmentalized approach to curriculum planning for students with mental retardation is not the recommended action or intent, although the chart may appear to do so. But there are communication, arithmetic, social, and other skills that IEP teams at every level need to include in their students' programs. How these skills are taught is the responsibility of the individual teacher. But planning the curriculum must be coordinated among teachers so that students receive a well-articulated, complete education.

The chart is intended to demonstrate the scope, sequence, and organization of curriculum planning. Some teachers may want to use separate pages for additional notes to the columns, but single descriptive words and short phrases are more time efficient.

Chart Rows (Age and Ability Groups)

The age and ability groups listed down the left side of the curriculum planning chart (Figure 3.6) were arbitrarily selected for the purpose of illustration only. In practice, they should reflect the actual service delivery pattern and placement structure of the school district in which they are used. The age and ability groups do not imply or favor any particular service delivery pattern or placement. The rows are necessary to show *horizontal curriculum planning,* or how the prescriptions from two or more of the curriculum planning columns may be combined for efficient teaching. Horizontal curriculum planning is covered in several later chapters.

Entry-Level Skills

Usually, skills or concepts should be introduced at an early level and developed at succeeding levels. After a given skill is placed in its position on the chart, plot the entry-level skills that the students should or need to have before they begin learning that skill. Then these entry-level skills should be placed in the columns and at the levels where each should logically be introduced. For example, a teacher decides to introduce telling time as an arithmetic skill at the intermediate level. The chart suggests that the entry-level skills of time awareness and counting by 5s need to be placed earlier on the chart so that the student will be prepared to learn to tell time.

Sometimes the teacher will compare the entry-level skills for a particular activity with the abilities, needs, and experience of his or her students. Then that teacher will want to change the level at which he or she initially plans to teach the activity itself. Every entry should be considered tentatively and adjusted as necessary when monitoring the success level each student achieves. (Entry level skills are discussed in greater detail in the chapters of Part III.)

As students are evaluated with the age 25 projection and the succession of their IEPs, it will become apparent that they usually accomplish a little more or less than anticipated. When this happens, the teacher may want to add or omit some activities, as well as adjust the level at which they are taught. The activities and skills presented at each level relate to those of every other level; this relationship, in turn, may involve other teachers in the school and other schools the students might later attend.

LEVEL-TO-LEVEL PROGRAM PLANNING

Level-to-level program planning is a vital part of curriculum planning for students with mental retardation, but it is often overlooked. *Level-to-level program planning* refers primarily to planning that must be done between grades or years in school. It is particularly important where the student with mental retardation will change schools, for example, from the elementary to secondary level. It is absolutely crucial as the student prepares to enter senior high school (McKenzie & Houk, 1993). Level-to-level program planning is closely related to horizontal and vertical curriculum planning, both of which are discussed in the chapters of Part IV.

Much of the overall curriculum planning for students without disabilities has been done largely outside the classroom and has required the participation of parents and many professionals. That is, individual teachers are involved essentially in adapting the curriculum prescribed by state and local legislative bodies. Likewise, curriculum planning for students with mental retardation is also a cooperative activity, but is best done by each student's IEP team. The curriculum planning chart itself suggests that all teachers of students with mental retardation in a school or school district should plan curriculum cooperatively. The teachers have a composite responsibility to all students who will progress through their classes. If students with mental retardation are to receive an appropriate, well-rounded education, their curriculum must be an overall school or district plan that takes them from preschool through graduation. It is not sufficient for each teacher to plan individually or merely be aware of what the other teachers are doing. All teachers responsible for the education of a student with mental retardation must plan together carefully to ensure that all parts of the student's education fit together as a complete whole.

	Communication	Social	Transitional & Vocational	Home & Family Living	Leisure	Arithmetic
Preprimary						
Primary						
Intermediate						
Prevocational						
Vocational						

FIGURE 3.7 Level-To-Level Curriculum Planning Chart

To prepare for the level-to-level planning session with the other teachers who have had or who will have the same students with mental retardation in their classes, each teacher sketches out a curriculum planning chart that covers the age/ability group for which he or she is responsible. However, each must plan the curriculum in greater detail at his or her age and ability level than for other levels. Figure 3.7 is a diagram that suggests how this is done.

For example, the curriculum of a prevocational teacher is represented by Figure 3.7. This teacher has his or her curriculum plotted in some detail, even though it may be tentative at this point. The area cells on the prevocational row are expanded to signify that each teacher describes his or her curriculum in greater detail. This teacher must also have a good idea about the curriculum that his or her students have studied at all previous levels, particularly the intermediate level, where the students were most recently. As each student advances to the next class, the transition should be as smooth as possible. This prevocational teacher also needs to know what academic and other skills the teachers stress at the vocational level, as well as the achievement levels they expect of their typical graduates. In deciding whether or not to teach a particular skill or concept, it is a good idea to consult with the teacher who teaches the next older group.

The levels of achievement will vary with each student. So, at the level-to-level planning meeting, the abilities and performance of each student should be discussed. It is good for each participant to bring all of his or her students' IEPs. If insufficient time is available for discussion of all the IEPs, it is helpful for each teacher to present his or her highest and lowest functioning students' IEPs. In this manner, each teacher can see how his or her curriculum fits into the overall curriculum the students with mental retardation will follow. He or she can also learn about the unique needs of incoming students that must be considered and accommodated. Each teacher is also made aware of the general expectations of each student's teacher at the next higher level. Some students are not as ready for advancement as others, but their ages and other circumstances may suggest they should move on. One of the anticipated outcomes of such a planning meeting is the negotiation of the curriculum "borders" between each teacher's expectations and the expectations of his or her colleagues.

Suppose, for example, the teacher at the primary level proposes to teach a beginning level of arithmetic that introduces one-to-one correspondence and counting from 1 to 10. In a planning session, the preprimary colleague reports that those concepts appear to be too difficult for most of the students who will be advancing from her class. Knowing that he or she must accommodate these students in his or her curriculum, the primary teacher must make the required adjustments on both a group and an individual basis.

In another example, the intermediate teacher intends to begin teaching reading. As he or she compares the communication curriculum with that of her primary colleague, it becomes apparent that the incoming students (or at least some of them) will not be ready for the beginning reading activity. These "borders" between age and ability levels must be discussed and reconciled in order to develop a complete, consistent, and well-correlated curriculum.

For students with mental retardation who are *included* into regular classes, level-to-level planning is particularly crucial, yet even more difficult to accomplish. The major difficulties of planning in this setting are that more teachers are involved, including many teachers who are not trained in special education and who really don't have the time necessary to plan extensively for individual students.

Proactivity, Conceptual Distance, and Level-to-Level Curriculum Planning

The principle of proactivity is particularly valuable in level-to-level planning. In the planning meetings, it is advisable that each teacher be prepared to demonstrate the quality of practical problems each of his or her students can identify, set up, and solve. The real abilities of students with mental retardation can be very deceiving. As the students progress through school, their abilities to perform mechanical and rudimentary reading and mathematical tasks often divert attention from their poor problem-solving skills. Awareness of a student's proactivity skills is especially helpful at the secondary level, where the curriculum has an emphasis on practical problem-solving, vocational, and transitional skills and concepts.

It is also helpful to consider the principle of conceptual distance. This concept reminds the IEP team members and the level-to-level planning participants that students with mental retardation need more time and effort to complete tasks and master skills that others do more quickly and easily. For example, it is particularly difficult for a student with mental retardation to learn how to recognize and solve practical problems even after mastering the skills, concepts, and operations necessary to do so.

Curriculum Planning at the Secondary Level

Level-to-level curriculum planning must continue through all age/ability levels. Such planning offers some particular challenges at the secondary level (Clark & Kolstoe, 1990; Hasazi et al., 1985; McCrea, 1990). The differences in curricula and teacher expectations are likely to be most diverse as the student makes the difficult transition from the elementary to the secondary school level. Entering the secondary level for most students with mental retardation involves changing schools. In some instances, the student must even change school districts because districts in some states operate elementary or secondary schools, but not both. Secondary schools in a given district usually have much larger enrollments. They also tend to be more departmentalized, so curriculum planning involves a greater number of teachers for each student.

With the continuing national trend to identify only the students whose mental retardation is most severe, the general level of ability of students arriving at the secondary levels is decreasing every year (*Sixteenth Annual Report to Congress*, 1994). As a result, many teachers at the secondary level have unrealistic expectations of incoming students; these make level-to-level curriculum planning particularly crucial.

Another challenge is that elementary and secondary schools follow different pre-service preparation programs and operate under different philosophies and procedures. Understandably, the general emphasis of curriculum at the secondary level has always tended to be highly academic and, thus, less functional and practical (Cronis et al., 1986; Meyen, 1968). This philosophy tends to influence the operation of a school's special education programs, often making these programs unreasonably rigorous and academic. The secondary level is the final step in the transition of a student with mental retardation from the schools to the world of work. Therefore, their curricula must strongly emphasize the practical aspects of work experience, parenting, transition, independent living skills, and other practical and vocational aspects of adult life (Bruininks, Thurlow, & Ysseldyke, 1992; Ward & Halloran, 1989).

SUMMARY

I began this chapter by comparing and contrasting curriculum planning as it applies to regular and special education teachers. Regular class teachers generally do not have enough time to plan an individual curriculum for each of their students, as must be done with students with mental retardation. Naturally, geographical and philosophical differences in education preclude nationwide agreement on the content of curricula, but generally the same basic concepts are taught in every school.

Curriculum planning as it applies to teachers of students with disabilities but not mental retardation was discussed. Because much of special education is designed to help students who are otherwise disabled keep up with their regular classwork, their teachers are also limited in the extent to which they are permitted to alter the basic content of regular class curriculum.

I presented additional support for individual curriculum planning for students with mental retardation by restating some of their most significant learning characteristics and by relating these characteristics to curriculum planning. The educational program of every student with a disability must be commensurate with his or her individual needs and abilities.

I also showed how to design IEPs based on the life goals of each student and how to correlate the IEPs in planning the total curriculum for a class. I also introduced the age 25 projection, which is a way to select and prioritize the most important life goals for each student with mental retardation and relate these goals to the student's IEP.

I showed how the curriculum for students with mental retardation needs to be based on their individual life goals. A curriculum planning chart helps in planning and correlating the skills, concepts, and activities needed by the students.

Finally, I strongly stressed level-to-level curriculum planning. Such curriculum planning requires that teachers of students with mental retardation must become fully informed on curriculum planning at all levels of instruction and at all age groups—not just the age and ability group a particular teacher is teaching.

CHAPTER 4

Working with Parents

Points to Study and Ponder

1. From an educational standpoint, who are parents, in addition to the biological parents?
2. Why is parental cooperation desirable in planning educational programs for students with mental retardation? Is such parental cooperation and participation required by law?
3. What reactions would you expect parents to experience as they discover that their child has mental retardation?
4. Would you expect these reactions to vary from one family to another? Why or why not?
5. What reactions would you expect other family members—particularly brothers and sisters—to experience as they learn they are closely related to a person with mental retardation?
6. Do any of your personal experiences cause you to agree or disagree with the family reactions discussed in this chapter?
7. What was the Baby Doe incident, and what issues did it raise? Do you tend to agree or disagree with the action that was taken?
8. Can you identify any possible positive effects of having a person with mental retardation in a family?
9. If, during your lifetime, you anticipate adopting a child, would you consider one with mental retardation?

As explained in Chapters 1 and 2, mental retardation is a severe disability, unlike other disabilities in several important ways. Nowhere is this importance more evident than in working with parents. To work effectively with parents, educators must recognize not only the extent of the problems of a child with mental retardation but also the varied effects this disability will have on the child's family. *Parent* always includes foster parent, surrogate parent, relative, or any person who acts in the place of the parent in representing the educational interests of a student with mental retardation.

A positive relationship between home and school is probably the most significant component in the educational success of any individual with mental retardation (Michaelis, 1981; Richardson, Koller, & Katz, 1985). Not only is this vital working relationship between parent and teacher mandated by P.L. 101–476 (IDEA), but it also makes good practical sense. Regardless of the competence or compassion of the teacher, parents bear the ultimate responsibility for their child, and their influence will be strongest and probably the most lasting in that child's continued attitude and accomplishments. The legal authority and responsibility of foster parents and other parent surrogates, however, often terminate when the individual graduates from school or reaches his or her majority—usually age 18 to 21. Even the rights of biological parents terminate at that age but usually continue in the absence of a legal challenge (Yudof, Kirp, & Levin, 1992).

Having any disability results in serious effects on a person, as well as on the members of his or her family. Dyson and Fewell (1986) found stress to be much more evident among parents of children with disabilities. Blacher, Nihira, and Meyers (1987) and Eden-Piercy, Blacher, and Eyman (1986) reported that the stress to family members seems to increase with the severity of the disability. Mental retardation characteristically has a much greater debilitating effect on parents, siblings, and other relatives than do most other disabilities.

In this book, I identify a considerable number of limitations that mental retardation imposes on an individual. Although these limitations are neither absolute nor uniform, they are real and each presents significant challenges that must be dealt with. One major emphasis of this book is that these challenges can and must be met by the best IEP team that can be assembled. If such teams are to be successful, they must be well-trained and must work smoothly and effectively together. They must not only share information with each other on their student with mental retardation but also train each other.

I offer suggestions for developing a positive, comfortable working relationship with parents to extend knowledge and training into the child's home. I also show ways that teachers can work effectively with other educators and professionals in a team effort to provide for the child the most effective, practical education possible. I stress the need to train the parents and help prepare them to assist their child to become as successful as possible in adult life. In practice, much of the task of assisting parents falls on the special education teacher (Foxx & Foxx, 1986). Further, the IEP team must assess the stress factors as they apply to individual parents—regardless of the extent to which they affect other parents (Kirkham, 1993). For example, in some instances, mental retardation may cause varying degrees of stress on one or more family members, but little if any stress in other instances. Likewise, I point out that some parents choose to participate in the planning and conduct of their child's education, whereas others do not. The IEP team should be prepared to deal with these variations wherever they occur.

POSITION OF THE PARENTS

No teacher effort or school program is likely to succeed long range without the cooperation and support of the parents, in light of the proportion of time a child spends under the influence of the family. From birth until the 18th birthday, less than 10% of a child's time is spent in all school-sponsored activities combined, even when school attendance is 100% in grades K–12. Percentages are only slightly higher for a child whose educational disability allows participation in additional school programs. For example, if the child attends 2 years of half-day preschool and 10 years of half-day summer school, the increase is only to about 10.5%. If the student remains in school until age 21, the additional 3 years of school ironically decrease the percentage, setting it back to just under 10%. Even during the time of greatest school concentration—a specific week when school is in session—the child spends less than 18% of his or her time with teachers. Admittedly, these simple examples overlook the fact that the child spends about a third of his or her time sleeping, but the parents must supervise and protect the child during this time as well. The point is that the school's ability to influence ends abruptly after age 18 to 21, when the child becomes the full-time moral and legal responsibility of the parents. In any event, the total time the child spends in school is both limited and crucial.

Because of the overriding influence of the family and the negative effects of mental retardation, the school can often have its greatest impact working through that family. Teachers, IEP team members, and other professionals trained and experienced in mental retardation must establish and conduct an ongoing, persistent program to educate parents about mental retardation. The program should persist from level to level and must be particularly active and effective as the child advances into junior and senior high school. There is no single procedure for effective training, and not all parents and other family members will agree to participate. In fact, Allen and Hudd (1987) pointed out that parents are not required to participate in their child's education programs if they choose not to do so and that the purpose of their participation should not be to relieve professionals of their responsibilities. Further, parents of children with disabilities can be expected to vary considerably in the extent to which they participate in their children's school programs and expect services from the school (D'Amato & Yoshida, 1991; Hilton & Henderson, 1993). D'Amato and Yoshida (1991) reported that, for all practical purposes, the parents of students with disabilities need basically the same type of information as other parents do. The IEP team must carefully, tactfully, and persistently evaluate the willingness of family members to participate in their child's education as well as the strengths they have to offer (Ronnau & Poertner, 1993). This chapter contains my explanation of why persistence is necessary and why the family education program is likely to be effective over time, as parents usually become increasingly accepting of their child with mental retardation.

Initially, the educational program should identify and explain the parents' rights and the programs and services available to assist their child. The IEP team members and other professionals should also help the parents select the programs and services that are likely to be most appropriate for that child. Later, the program tactfully should inform the parents of the basic nature of their child's learning deficiencies and how these deficiencies relate to their child's future and to the parents' responsibilities. It also should encourage the participation of the parents and other family members both at school and in the home. Thus, efforts to help parents improve their effectiveness in working with their children with mental retardation are among the most significant contributions teachers can make (Seifer, Clark, & Sameroff, 1991).

Certainly, any cooperative venture requires the support of all participants, but the initial move toward establishing a good working relationship between home and school must usually come from the classroom teacher. By law and in practice, the teacher has the major responsibility to enlist the parents in developing and carrying out the child's educational program. Other professionals will be involved, but their participation is ordinarily more limited and less personal than that of the child's teacher.

This chapter is based on several premises and assumptions:

- If teachers and parents understand each other, they will be in a better position to build a positive relationship resulting in a unified team effort.
- Parents should make the final decisions in the educational program for their son or daughter with mental retardation, with exceptions only when circumstances are extreme. A teacher should offer counsel and persistent, gentle persuasion in helping the parents make wise choices and deal effectively with their child.
- School officials, including the teacher, should be careful that virtually everything planned for a student either has the approval of the child's parents or would most likely receive such approval if it were sought.
- Although parental approval is most significant in major decisions, such approval should also be sought for most of the seemingly less important details and procedures even though these have traditionally been the responsibility of the professional faculty.

PARENTAL RIGHTS AND RESPONSIBILITIES

Society makes parents the principal agents in rearing and caring for their children, including children with mental retardation. Accordingly, P.L. 94–142 and the IDEA protect parents' rights regarding the placement and educational programs of their children with disabilities. On the one hand, under these acts, parents have more *rights* than parents had at any time in the past. But these laws say very little about parental *responsibilities,* particularly in the day-to-day aspects of the child's school experience. On the other hand, both laws, as well as the clarifying rules and regulations of federal and state agencies, impose specific responsibilities on school personnel but say very little about their rights. Thus, although parents have the privilege of making the final decisions, the schools must provide the options and context in which those decisions must be made.

Because of the imbalance of parental rights and parental responsibilities, parents cannot be forced to accept a placement or educational program for their child with disability, except in rare circumstances. They cannot be forced to participate in the planning or maintenance of the child's education if they choose not to. Thus, although parents are the most important decision makers on their child's IEP team, they do not have to follow through on the plan. When major disagreements arise, the IDEA gives school officials and parents roughly equal access to the civil courts in resolving their disputes. But in practice, educators rarely resort to court action because it is both unpopular and expensive. Parents, then, possess an effective overriding veto power. With this situation of juxtaposed parental rights and teacher responsibilities, it is to the advantage of teacher, parent, and child to establish effective bonds of communication and cooperation between school and home.

SEEKING PARENTAL COOPERATION

Working closely with the parents of students with mental retardation can be one of the most rewarding experiences in teaching. Ironically, however, it can be one of the most difficult tasks that teachers face. Most parents of children with mental retardation are like parents of other children: cooperative, supportive, and grateful for whatever help educators and other professionals can provide for their child. A study by Yanok and Derubertis (1989) found little difference in the extent to which parents of children in regular and special education classes participated in school programs. Some parents of children with mental retardation, however, are neither supportive nor cooperative. Because these parents will present challenges, it is important to anticipate these challenges as parent-teacher relationships are discussed. Although effective cooperation requires the support of all participants, by law and in practice the teacher has the major responsibility in developing and conducting a child's educational program. Likewise in practice, the initial steps in establishing a good working relationship between parents and school are essentially the teacher's responsibility.

One potential barrier the teacher must consider in establishing this working relationship is feelings of inferiority that parents may experience. Parents tend to see themselves working with a teacher who is knowledgeable and educated in the mental retardation area, whereas they themselves may have no academic training. Hilton and Henderson (1993) suggested that parents often express the feeling that professionals tend to treat them as patients, rather than as responsible adults. Whatever procedures teachers use, they must be aware of parent sensitivities and be tactful, avoiding patronizing or arrogant attitudes. It is important to avoid insulting or offending parents, even those who are uncooperative; they may be uncooperative because they are uninformed or insecure.

It is important to remember that parents tend to react more strongly and more negatively to this disability than to others because mental retardation usually imposes substantially more limitations on an individual than any other disability (Farber, 1959; Herr, 1984; Lawlis & Roesel, 1983). One reason is that they experience heavy personal demands, in addition to the normal stresses of marriage and raising a family that other parents face. Another reason is that mental retardation may be viewed as being caused by either hereditary or environmental factors; from either theory of causality, the parents feel a degree of responsibility for their child's disability. It is important for teachers and other members of the IEP team to consider the parents' adjustment to their child's disability. With work, pressure, and the possibility of self-inflicted guilt, most families find that having a member with mental retardation is more difficult than having a member with another disability; thus, parents need special consideration and support from the schools (Erickson & Upshur, 1989; Westling, 1986).

STAGES OF PARENTAL REACTION TO MENTAL RETARDATION

Parents and other members of the IEP team have unique insights about mental retardation—the parents regarding their own child, and the other members of the team regarding mental retardation in general. To be successful, it is essential that they share their knowledge and skills with each other. One major reason for discussing the stages of reaction to mental retardation through which parents typically pass is to help each member visualize the training process. It is essential that other members understand and empathize with the parents' emotions and state of affairs at each point in their child's life. The members must be aware of the reaction that parents of a child with mental retardation are likely to have and must be patient with them as they pass through any stages that might materialize. Moreover, the other team members must not be condescending; they must treat the parents as full participants. Many parents do not choose to cooperate, and often training and working with them is not easy; however,

The teacher must be prepared to work with single parents, surrogate parents, and guardians who may represent the parents.

the team must persist. Powers, Singer, Stevens, and Sowers (1992) cited a unique situation in which three such mothers themselves had mental retardation. Their children had serious learning and behavioral problems. These mothers were taught child management techniques and how to plan appropriate activities.

Any feelings, fears, and accompanying resentments must be worked through so that parents can accept their child's limitations and begin to cooperate with educators in providing for the child's education. Parents seem to go through a series of loosely defined but identifiable stages when they find that they have given birth to a child with mental retardation (Batshaw, Perret, & Trachenberg, 1992; Rosen, 1955). The basic pattern is to progress from shock or rejection of the child to acceptance and finally to a realistic attitude toward the child's future. As Eden-Piercy et al. (1986) pointed out, these stages can be defined in many ways. Some parents may bypass one or more of the stages; others may be offended at the suggestion that they have ever had a negative feeling toward their child. For some parents, acceptance may occur in a matter of weeks. For others, the process may take years. A few parents never seem to fully accept the fact that their child will always have severe limitations. Others may become convinced that their child has no talent or ability of consequence. Moreover, these variations often occur within a family in which the parents do not agree on their child's potential. It is easy for teachers to prejudge or stereotype parents or to assume that negative reactions are inevitable. But it is extremely important to avoid doing so.

The stages that parents seem to experience when they become aware that their child has mental retardation refer primarily to the child's biological parents. As theses stages are discussed, it is well to ponder the implications the stages may have for nontraditional parents. The effects a child with mental retardation may have on surrogate parents is not well researched. The IEP team may find it necessary to train and work with a succession of temporary foster parents whose information regarding mental retardation may or may not have come from reliable sources. The team may interact with a single parent who may work during the schoolday or otherwise be unavailable to participate in meetings and conferences. Often, no father lives in the home, and far more children live with single mothers (including surrogate mothers) than with single fathers. Experience shows that mothers are much more likely to participate in the child's education. Nevertheless, the legal guardian may be a single father or other male who should be invited and trained to participate in the child's education wherever possible.

Denial

"Nothing could be wrong with *my* child." If mental retardation is apparent soon after the child's birth, denial may begin at that time. Parents want to assume that their child is normal, and as Ehlers, Krishef, and Prothero (1977) pointed out, unless the child also has a physical impairment or deformity, they may continue to do so even though it may be apparent to everyone outside the family that the child has serious problems. Denial may be prolonged by well-meaning relatives or even physicians who assure the parents that the child will outgrow the difficulty.

Elements of the denial stage are likely to recur even after parents have gone through the other stages and finally accepted and committed to work with their child's disability. For example, they may attempt to hide evidence of their child's learning problem or distort accounts of their child's accomplishments at home. A striking example occurred at a workshop in which parents of children with mental retardation were given instruction in setting up trust funds and making other arrangements for their children's future economic security. The father of a teenage girl whose mental retardation was severe/profound—and obvious—prefaced a question to the speaker with this comment: "My daughter is not really mentally retarded, but does have some difficulty in keeping up with her classmates." He then asked a question about his daughter's legal status after she would leave school, despite the reality that the girl would undoubtedly need lifelong assistance and constant supervision. On the basis of the parent's misleading and glowing description of his child, the speaker erroneously assumed that, in adult life, the child would be essentially independent, and he gave advice to the parent regarding marriage, managing a home, and other roles that were completely unrealistic.

Recognition

"Something does seem to be wrong with my child." The stage at which parents recognize a mental retardation problem is difficult to place sequentially because recognition may come gradually, intermingled with some of the other conditions. The recognition may or may not follow a phase of active denial. A child whose mental retardation is relatively mild or moderate often appears normal and functions normally in the usual family and neighborhood activities. If the parents' expectations for the child are modest, the retardation may not be detected until the child begins school. As the child's condition becomes more evident, in addition to dealing with the needs of the child, the teacher may have to deal with the parents' growing recognition that something is wrong with their son or daughter and that the condition is not going away.

Shock and Disbelief

"This can't be true!" "This can't be happening!" Many parents go through a stage of shock or disbelief when they are forced to recognize that their son or daughter may have mental retardation. Several factors have been found to affect the stress level in this stage. Dyson and Fewell (1986) reported that families with a member with disability attract more external support than those in which no members have disabilities and that families with the greatest support seemed to suffer less stress. A valuable but underused form of support is *respite care,* which offers periodic care by trained individuals to provide relief for family members who can easily become exhausted or discouraged by the needs of the child with a disability. Respite care may be provided through a variety of agencies, including placement agencies, group day care, existing community residences, state residential facilities, and funding providers (Russell, 1984). Gaventa (1990) suggested that religious groups and individuals should become more heavily involved in respite care. Diamond (1994) provided a reminder that the trend to place students with severe disabilities in regular classes and community-based programs implies that these teachers and supervisors need to be aware of respite care and to make it available to parents. Salisbury (1990) reported that mothers of children with mental retardation—either severe/profound or mild/moderate—made little use of respite care; usage did not increase among the mothers whose children had more severe retardation. An important contribution that teachers can make to families in this stage of adjustment is to recommend respite care as a means of dealing with accompanying stress.

Another contributing factor in adjustment that teachers can urge for the families of children with mental retardation is more equivalent participation between the parents. Houser and Seligman (1991) found that fathers of children with mental retardation did not experience more stress than fathers of children without the disability. But when Wood and Flynt (1991) surveyed 35 mothers of children with mental retardation, they found that the mothers who recalled the least stress were those whose husbands had been present during the initial diagnosis and during the sessions in which physicians offered positive suggestions. Teachers and other school personnel who work with children with mental retardation need to encourage and sometimes engineer all of the external and internal support a family can obtain (Krauss, 1993). Lillie (1993), in a review of literature, concluded that fathers of children with disabilities seem to be more interested in the special needs of their children than previously thought. Lillie theorized that some fathers tend to be discouraged or even intimidated by the dominant role of the mother and the nature of their child's program. Likewise, Dudley (1991) suggested that those who work with divorced parents pay increased attention to fathers—who may have justifiable reasons for their lack of attention to their children. The fathers ($N = 84$) in his study seemed to fall into four categories: (a) those whose conflict with their former spouses was particularly severe, (b) those who had a variety of personal problems, (c) some who lived great distances away, and (d) those whose teenage children had busy lives.

Search for a Cure

"What can be done about this?" Once they have recognized that their child has a serious problem, parents often follow one of two patterns. They may recognize the child's potentials, along with the problems, and realize that with a positive, loving home life and an appropriate educational program the child will be able to live an enjoyable and productive life. They may detour to this acceptance, however, through another phase—a search for some type of miraculous cure (Drash & Raver, 1987; Robinson & Robinson, 1976; Warren, 1987). They have been known to visit uranium mines; place their child in schools that claim a "cure" for mental retardation; experiment with various nutrients, minerals, and vitamins; persuade doctors to prescribe medications; and even try out electronic gadgets. They seem to reason that a condition as severe as mental retardation certainly must have a cause and that a cause should imply a cure. On a more positive note, a search for a "cure" may also include looking for appropriate educational programs.

Unfortunately, parents in this stage are particularly vulnerable to questionable advice. For example, the parents of a boy whose mental retardation was obvious and profound were told by a physician in Mexico that their child's retardation would be alleviated if they limited his consumption of water. The IEP team was skeptical about this advice and consulted several pediatricians, who confirmed its absurdity. But in the meantime, the boy would often get so thirsty that he would break away from his teacher to get a drink of water from any source he could find—including the toilet bowl.

Self-Pity

"Why did this have to happen to us?" Many parents react with self-pity when they recognize that their child has mental retardation and that the condition cannot be cured by denial or treatment. They tend to focus inward, concentrating on their own feelings, rather than on their child's needs. In such circumstances, the educator can do little except wait patiently and realize that attempting to help the parents move through the stages quickly will have serious or lasting effects on the child—and on the parents as well.

Depression

"My child will never progress very far." At some point, parents of a child with mental retardation often experience feelings of depression, despair, or chronic sorrow (Wikler, 1981). Kirkham (1993) conducted a 2-year follow-up of mothers of children with disabilities and reported a high incidence of stress, depression, and an inability to cope with their child. These feelings may never disappear completely, and at every stage of the child's life the parents may long for achievements beyond those the child is capable of. Like feelings of shock or self-pity, such reactions may surface periodically; however, occasional periods of depression will not necessarily prevent a parent from being very cooperative and effective in the education of the child. All parents at times have become upset or depressed over the failures and mistakes of their children—even when a child is gifted or talented. Most parents eventually adjust—at least somewhat—to the levels at which their children function, or possibly to their perception of these levels. The difference in the parents of children with mental retardation is that they must constantly observe ways in which other children, even those who are much younger, outperform their child.

Resentment or Rejection

"I can't stand to be around my own child." Relatively few parents seem to resent the existence of their son or daughter with mental retardation, but a few do, and that resentment may be bitter or prolonged. Recently publicized incidents—such as the Baby Doe, Phillip Becker, and Bowen cases—remind us that parents who harbor resentment may go to the extreme of starving a child to death or withholding treatments necessary to sustain the child's life. The parents, as well as others involved in these cases, were no doubt motivated by their perception of an extremely complex matter. At issue were the rights of the parents, the right of public agencies to interfere, as well as the right to life and quality of life (Tiemann, 1991).

Resentments that are suppressed and do not result in injury to the child may still result in deep pain for a parent. During an IEP conference, the father of a teenager with profound mental retardation expressed the hopes and dreams that had once centered on the boy, his only son. With tears in his eyes, he confessed that at times he thought he could have killed the boy. Every few moments, he would flinch as his wife kicked him under the table. Those present knew that this man could never have committed such an act, but they understood his pain. Teachers and administrators involved with the parents of children with mental retardation need to be aware of such feelings so that they can react with compassion, not with alarm.

Guilt Feelings and Blame Fixing

"What could I have done wrong?" "What did we do to deserve this?" Some parents attempt to absorb the blame for their child's mental retardation themselves (Nixon & Singer, 1993). Others blame each other, assuming that the condition must have been inherited from the *other* side of the family. Teachers need to be sure that no careless comment on their part could be misinterpreted and allowed to fuel either side's destructive attempt to place blame.

Acceptance

Many parents demonstrate some degree of acceptance of their son's or daughter's mental retardation soon after the child's birth. They realize that, despite serious problems, the child has potentials that can be developed through warmth, acceptance, patience, and time commitment in the home, supplemented by an exemplary school program tailored to meet the child's individual needs. These parents are able and eager to participate in designing such a program. It is easy and rewarding for teachers and administrators to work with them. However, many parents must progress through the early, largely negative stages before they arrive at the point of acceptance where they are ready to work cooperatively with school personnel in choosing and adapting a program for their child (Gardner, 1988).

The teacher's immediate goal is for the parents to cooperate and participate in designing and conducting their child's educational program. Once parents have reached an acceptance level on which they become actively involved in the education of their child, many will reach out to help other children with disabilities and their parents. Through participating with a parent group such as the Association for Retarded Citizens (ARC), they are reassured in the early stages of their own acceptance through contacts with others who have struggled with the same problems and learned to manage them. As they continue participation, they often find comfort and satisfaction in assisting others.

EFFECTS OF PARENTAL REACTIONS

The varying stages of parents' reactions to their child's mental retardation affect the nature of their cooperation and the extent of their participation in the child's school experience. Awareness of the stages a parent is likely to experience should help the teacher and other members of the IEP team empathize with parents and other family members in planning long-term programs and curriculum for the child. In any event, however, the actual effects of these reactions may be more apparent and helpful than the reactions themselves. Under the law, the major responsibility for establishing a beneficial school-home relationship falls on the school. If teachers understand both the nature and the normalcy of the adjustment stages that parents go through, they should be able to accept and work in situations that could otherwise present major barriers to essential cooperative effort.

Unwarranted Criticism

In an effort to diffuse blame for their child's failures and disabilities, some parents tend to become unduly critical of the child's past and present teachers. Because having more than one child with mental retardation in a family is relatively rare, most of these parents have seen their other children pass through the first few years of school without unusual problems. If they are in a denial or a blame-fixing stage, they want to assume that any problems with this child are due to faulty instruction. It is particularly frustrating to observe the progress of a younger family member surpassing that of an older child, as often happens with mental retardation. Teachers need to recognize that parents may have a tendency to misplace blame or to give undeserved criticism; otherwise, statements or implications that the child would be better off in another setting can be devastating to a teacher trying very hard to meet the child's needs.

An example of unwarranted criticism occurred in a family that had two daughters 3 years apart, both with severe/profound mental retardation. The parents had great difficulty acknowledging that their daughters' problems went beyond simple developmental difficulties they would eventually outgrow, even when the girls were in their late teens. Both girls attended a special program where their educational programs were carefully designed and monitored by trained special education personnel. When the older daughter was 17, the family moved to another state for a year and managed to convince the local school authorities to enroll the girls in regular high school classes. At the end of the year, the older sister graduated from high school. When they returned to their home community, the parents flaunted the older girl's graduation, claiming that the schools in the other state were more capable in dealing with students with disabilities than the specialized program their daughters had attended most of their lives. But ironically, they immediately applied to re-enroll both girls in the same program, making no effort to have either of them placed in regular classes. As an additional irony, the older girl was ineligible for public school services because she had graduated from high school.

A teacher is placed in a particularly difficult situation when parents of a student with mental retardation complain about the skills of another teacher. Taking sides with a parent against a colleague is generally unprofessional and is likely to result in embarrassment. On the one hand, it rarely helps in solving any problem, and it often increases the intensity of the problem and postpones the parents' acceptance of their child's disability. On the other hand, the teacher being addressed may not know the teacher whose skills are being challenged or may not know enough about that teacher's ability to vouch for the quality of instruction the child has received. Realizing the vulnerability of parents to denial, cure seeking, and blame-fixing behavior, teachers must understand the necessity of taking a neutral stance when parents attempt to involve them in criticism of others.

Overprotection

Some parents become overly concerned about the treatment a child with mental retardation will receive. Teachers can help such parents realize that all children—with or without mental disabilities—are subject to teasing and ridicule and that children with disabilities are really quite durable, especially if they receive positive treatment in the home. Children with mental retardation usually need more, rather than less, exposure to social situations than their parents are inclined to give them; for example, the child must be taken more often to the grocery store, the park, and other public places. Another way teachers can help is through class discussions to help all children realize the damage name-calling can do. The teacher can also help the child with a disability learn ways to resist internalizing the teasing that will be received.

Overexposure

In attempting to avoid overprotection, some parents overcompensate and subject their child to more frequent and complex social situations than the child is equipped to handle. For example, a child with mental retardation can and should attend church services and other social events with the family, but the child shouldn't be forced to recite scriptures in public or sing in the choir. Overexposure is relatively rare among parents of children with mental retardation, but it does occur (Blumberg, 1991) and can be damaging.

The overprotection-overexposure continuum demonstrates the importance of the teacher and other team members knowing parents and counseling with them individually, rather than in groups. For example, if parents who are already overexposing their son or daughter hear a lecture on the dangers of overprotection, they may insist on having their child perform in the school play. On the other extreme, overprotective parents may hear the following week's presentation about the frustrations that can occur with overexposure and decide that a birthday party would result in too much social interaction for their child.

Shopping Behavior

When parents arrive at the stage at which they are able to acknowledge the limitations of their child with mental retardation and to recognize the worth and potential of that child, they will begin looking at the options available for the child's education and development. Because most parents have no way of diagnosing their son's or daughter's condition specifically, they may place the child in one program after another, only to be frustrated as the child continues to fall behind other children of the same age. Keirn (1971) and MacMillan (1982) referred to this situation as "shopping" behavior.

The parents' confusion is understandable, considering the variety of advice that most parents of a child with mental retardation receive from every quarter—even from those in the special education profession—concerning their child's education. As those within the profession continue to debate the relative merits of the least restrictive environment (LRE) and the resource room, parents trying to follow the debate from a lay person's perspective become more and more confused. Many of the negative and unhelpful suggestions can be recognized as such when the parent is willing to engage in intelligent inquiry. According to Kanner (1948), parents reach the final stage when they face the actuality of the child's limitations in a mature way. This acceptance usually leads to the parents' taking the initiative to begin long-range planning and working to improve their personal attitudes.

When parents are at this stage of realistic acceptance and planning, the most helpful contribution the teacher can make is to help the parents understand the options available to them, demonstrate the benefits of each, and indicate availability for counseling with the parents individually when possible. Seligman (1993) reported that group counseling with parents of children with disabilities is very popular. The parents should also be encouraged to cooperate in their child's educational program—both at school and in the home. Having the parents participate regularly in the age 25 projection, in parent-teacher conferences, and in IEP team activities helps the parents in understanding their child's abilities and prepares the parents for their future responsibilities.

Persistence at One Stage

The severity of the retardation seems to be a catalyst in the parents' reactions. Some parents seem unable to escape from a particular stage, such as denial or depression; most, however, experience several stages at the same time. If the mental retardation is severe/profound, some parents experience severe forms of rejection (Herr, 1984) and move quickly toward institutionalization (Bradley & Agosta, 1985). In contrast, the severity of some cases seems to assist the parents in realistically accepting their child. If the retardation is mild, denial may be facilitated, and the parents often have difficulty moving beyond their refusal to recognize their child's disability.

Recognizing that early stages are often negative and highly emotional, IEP team members can help parents realize that their emotions are normal and will likely change. Sometimes parental problems become so intense during these stages that irreparable family disruptions occur, and even subsequent healthy acceptance of the child's condition cannot repair the relationship. Parents—mothers as well as fathers—who were divorced at a stressful early stage have frequently expressed the feeling that divorce or other breakdown in the family structure would not have happened if they had endured a little longer until the initial stress, blame, or self-pity had been allowed to pass.

It is tempting for educators to try to help parents move through the reaction stages quickly so that acceptance of the child and constructive planning can take place. Attempts to do this, however, may have serious or lasting effects on the parents and the child. Educators must recognize the stages and continue to work with the parents, not in opposition to their feelings and behavior. When parents do reach acceptance, they often express gratitude to professionals and other parents who have persisted in offering support to them and opportunities to their child, even when their feelings and reactions caused them to be unappreciative and uncooperative at times. Often, a special education teacher will be the first knowledgeable and responsible adult whose friendship and expertise have been offered. Additional specific suggestions for teachers are listed at the end of this chapter.

EFFECTS ON FAMILIES

The individual stages of adjustment to a child with mental retardation are not as significant as the final cumulative effects. The effects vary greatly among families because of the many factors that influence the presence, nature, duration, and intensity of each stage. Thus, each family situation must be evaluated differently. Team members can anticipate some general patterns of reaction that may influence the way they choose to work with the child in the context of the family unit.

Negative Effects on Other Family Members

It is important for everyone involved with the family of a child with mental retardation to remember that the child's siblings experience all the tensions and frustrations of growing up that other children do—in addition to problems caused specifically by the brother or sister with the disability. Lindsey and Stewart (1989) suggested that teachers and others consider training the child's siblings, as well as the parents.

Peer pressure, either real or imaginary, is a powerful factor in the life of any child. Thus, other children in the family may sometimes experience as much or more tension over the child with the disability than the parents do. Wilson, Blacher, and Baker (1989) found that siblings of children with severe disabilities held generally positive attitudes, but reported they felt a heavy weight of responsibility. Siblings are often embarrassed by having to explain why their brother or sister looks different from other children or may be unable to participate in some of the neighborhood activities. Siblings are sometimes teased or victimized by thoughtless remarks. In addition, an empathic sibling may experience pain and indignation at a peer's unkind treatment of the brother or sister with the disability.

The necessity of competing for the parents' interest or attention may further complicate the sibling's life. A family member with mental retardation may get more than what seems a fair share of the parents' time and focus, and justified or not, the siblings may become resentful or unduly critical of the child with the disability. Often, the child with mental retardation is treated as the youngest member of the family regardless of the actual birth order; this treatment can cause problems for all of the children in the family. For example, if the child with mental retardation is considered "too young"—mentally—to be expected to help with household chores, discontent among the other children, especially the younger ones, is likely to result.

Most problems of the overall family are caused by more than one factor—often by a complex of influences that family members themselves are unable to identify. Therefore, it is not likely that family problems, such as divorce, marital stress, unhappy or unstable home life, or other family dysfunctions, can be attributed solely to having a family member with mental retardation. These problems do seem to be more prevalent, however, in families that have a child with mental retardation. Having a child with the disability does put additional stress on an already troubled home. Significantly, though, Blacher et al. (1987) compared family relationships when children had different degrees of mental retardation and found that although more severe forms of mental retardation had more negative effects on families overall, they did not seem to make a difference in impact on marital adjustment. Likewise, Roesel and Lawlis (1983) investigated divorce among parents ($N = 113$) of children with mental retardation and found a divorce rate significantly lower than in the general population. They also reported that young parents of first-born males with disabilities and older mothers of first-born children were at a higher risk of divorce.

Positive Effects on the Family

Although the initial stages of parental reaction to the child with mental retardation are often intense and negative and day-to-day living with the child may cause stressful situations, many parents and other family members affirm that having a person with mental retardation in the family is ultimately not a negative experience. Many parents and other family members who have had a child with mental retardation born or adopted into the family have shown neutral and often positive effects on family life. Herman and Thompson (1995) found that most parents of children with developmental disabilities perceived their basic resources to be at least adequate but reported the special needs of their child consumed an inordinate amount of time and financial resources.

Historically, adoptive and foster placements for children with any disability have been difficult to find. Adoption agencies report they have particular difficulty when mental retardation is the handicap (Drydyk, Mendeville, & Bender, 1980). Once children with mental retardation or other disabilities have been placed, however, the reports have been encouraging. When Rosenthal, Groze, and Aguilar (1991) surveyed 800 families that had adopted children with a variety of disabilities, most reported positive family relationships. Few negative experiences were mentioned, and the families thought the presence of a disability, including mental retardation, did not seem to be a significant factor in their family situation. In a study focused more specifically on retardation, McHale, Sloan, and Simeonsson (1986) interviewed 90 children, ages 6 through 15, with adopted siblings, some with mental retardation or autism and some without any disability. When the children were asked about their sibling relationships, except for slightly more cohesive family relations, children with nondisabled brothers and sisters did not differ from children with brothers and sisters with disabilities. Glidden, Valliere, and Herbert (1988) found that many families reported having had positive experiences with adoptive children with mental retardation. Some family members have thought that having a child with a disability in the family and learning to appreciate the positive attributes of that child caused them to search more diligently for positive characteristics in all people. Some parents have reported that having a family member with a disability provided a common, uniting family goal—often discovered only in retrospect.

The information on the basic nature of mental retardation given in Chapters 1 and 2 should also be beneficial to educators as they help parents of children with mental retardation understand the limitations and potentials of their children. Parents and teachers must work together to find and nourish the abilities and potentials these children possess. Because the formal education provided by the school and the informal and pervasive education provided by the home are complementary and interactive, an effective home-school partnership is essential in bringing out the fullest potential of each individual child.

DEGREES OF PARENTAL SUPPORT

In addition to the parents' overall attitude and behavior toward their child and their ability to make the family interrelationships positive, the stages of adjustment to a child's mental retardation also affect the extent to which parents are willing to cooperate with educators in support of their child's educational program. These degrees are easy to identify and are discussed here in the sequence from most to least desirable.

Active Cooperation

When parents enthusiastically participate in all aspects of their child's programs, active participation results. In the early stages, they are active in assessing the child's abilities and designing the IEP. They learn enough about the services and programs available to the child that they may disagree, sometimes strongly, with administrator and teacher recommendations, and they make their positions known. Supportive beyond just the special services, they typically go the extra mile in cooperating and assisting with the activities of the total class and school, often serving as room parents or volunteering as drivers or chaperons for field trips. They are aware of the educational goals that have been set for their child, and they support and actively pursue these goals at home; thus, the child experiences continuity between significant places and persons in his or her life. Often, they reach beyond their own child to offer counsel and assistance to other parents who think, fear, or deny that their child may have mental retardation. These parents often join and actively participate in support groups and are of great assistance to other parents of children with mental retardation.

Passive Support

A passive support position is characterized by fairly consistent cooperation regarding the parents' own child, but less actively involved with the class or school in general and less desire to work with parents of other children with mental retardation. Occasional participation in whole-class activities or with other parents of children with disabilities may be solicited by the teacher, but response is less eager and less consistent than it is with actively cooperative parents. These parents usually participate in forming the child's IEP and can be depended on to carry out school programs with their child at home on a fairly consistent basis.

Strong Approval

Strong approval involves less personal participation by parents than the active cooperation and passive support patterns. Parents showing this degree of support may attend their child's IEP meetings, but they tend to rely largely on the proposals of other members of the IEP team, rather than learn of options and participate in the decision-making process. They show fairly strong approval of the adopted programs but do not become involved in applying them in the school setting. They work occasionally with their child at home but cannot be depended on to do so on a regular or consistent basis.

Reluctant Approval or Acquiescence

Some parents show limited commitment to their child's education but are usually content to let educators work out most of the decisions and difficulties. They may or may not participate in forming the child's IEP, but they do not tend to be critical. When they do participate, they may hesitate to approve suggestions of other team members but usually do not have strong proposals of their own. Sometimes this acquiescence is evidence that they are not convinced their child has serious problems or is in need of a special program.

Passive Disapproval

Passive disapproval is the reaction of parents who are critical of any educational program that may be recommended for their child but still permit it to be carried out. They may attend IEP meetings but would prefer not to be bothered. They express disapproval but reluctantly permit their child to remain in school or in a particular program. Although such parents may resist coming to the school, they are often receptive to a home visit by teachers or other school personnel.

Active Disapproval

Like other negative parental attitudes, active disapproval is rare, but frustrating to teachers and others when it does occur. Parents with this attitude often assume that their child's problems stem from faulty instruction and/or inadequate or inappropriate services. Some may resort to court action to enforce their preferences. Moreover, they may prevail. In such an instance, the team must accept the decision of the court and continue to work cooperatively with the parents. Educators must not assume that parents who sue the schools are unjustified or uninterested in their child's education. Often, it is school personnel who propose inappropriate or inadequate programs, and filing a lawsuit is the only logical course for parents to pursue. Currently, some parents are suing to gain a placement in an inclusion program; others are suing to avoid such a placement for their child. Lawsuits may occur even though school officials have considered the parents' objections and proposals carefully and have explained tactfully why they are not reasonable within the facilities and capacities of the school or are contrary to the best interests of the child.

Both active and passive disapproval are extremely difficult for a teacher to deal with because they often represent lack of knowledge or understanding of available options, unrealistic expectations of the school and of the child, and either denial or lack of genuine concern for the strengths and weaknesses of the child. Without support from the parents, little education is likely to occur. Thus, educators must continue to work with both parents and student even though a solution seems almost impossible to obtain.

PRESSURES RESULTING IN NEGATIVE RESPONSE

Educators may find it easy to pass negative judgments on parents who respond negatively to the realization that their child has mental retardation or who struggle against a special education program that has been prepared for the child. It is important for teachers and administrators to recognize some factors that may cause parents to be troubled, uncertain, or uncooperative where their child with mental retardation is concerned. Some parents may resist supporting a specialized educational program because they are not really aware of the needs of the child. Because parents are not likely to make extensive intellectual demands on a preschooler, the slow progress of a young child with mental retardation may not be noticed until the child begins to have repeated failures in school. Only as failures become more and more frequent and pronounced do schools initiate testing or make formal and serious comparisons between "slow" children and their age-mates. Even when testing is administered, it is not particularly accurate before the second or third grade. For example, on the second-grade version of an achievement test, a student could hand in a blank test paper and score only 1 or 2 years below grade level. Thus, a student may be labeled merely "at risk" until repeated attempts to teach a skill such as reading result in failure and considerable frustration for teacher and child. Thus, the teacher may be the one to convince the parents their child has a serious learning problem that necessitates some type of special support.

Even when a child's disability is recognized and acknowledged, parents may be unable to actively cooperate because they are acting from limited sources of information and experience. Not understanding the dysfunction, parents—as well as others—may conclude that the child with mental retardation is just lazy or happens to be a late bloomer.

Another contributing factor to the parental support level may be the personal threat that many parents feel in admitting that their child has mental retardation and needs special services. Parents of children with learning disability, emotional disturbance, or behavioral disability are much more inclined to actively seek programs that provide special education support than are parents of children with mental retardation. Not only are parents of children with retardation less likely to seek special placement, but they are also more likely to resist such help when it is offered (Brady, McDougall, & Dennis, 1989; Scandary, 1981). This is particularly ironic because the educational disabilities of a child with mental retardation are more serious than those of children with other disabilities; thus, special services are more necessary to prevent failure, yet these services are less likely to be sought, approved, and supported. Educators must be aware of the prevalence of parental problems and the reasons behind them in order to work with, not against, parents who lack adequate knowledge, recognition, or acceptance of the needs and educational options involved with their child.

PARENT-TEACHER PARTNERSHIP

P.L. 94–142, the IDEA, and their subsequent clarifying legislation have had many positive effects on the education of students with mental retardation and other disabilities. These laws have also had a few negative effects, however, one of which is a tendency to place teachers and parents in adversarial relationships.

Many court cases involving educational law are initiated by parents, naming teachers as defendants or co-defendants. Unfortunately, a large portion of the litigation in education involves something a teacher allegedly did or did not do in the classroom. Even if the target of the complaint is an administrative move, attorneys prefer to name a teacher as the defendant whenever possible because they have wider latitude in interrogating defendants than they do with witnesses. It is important for teachers to be aware of their legal rights and for administrators to be aware of the importance of legal and interpersonal support because the prospect of being a defendant in a lawsuit or even a respondent at a due process hearing will probably be more threatening to the child's teacher than to anyone else.

Although personal trauma is likely to be severe, monetary costs of litigation can be overwhelming as well. Ordinarily, school budgets have no provision to cover such costs, and in most states all funds used to defend school programs against lawsuits are taken out of much-needed educational budgets. Thus, everybody suffers from legal action, not just those who are called to defend or testify.

Few parents actually resort to court litigation or due process action when an educator takes the initiative to help them understand their rights and their position as part of their child's educational team and thus makes a genuine effort to assist them in teaching and caring for the child with the disability. IEP team members must encourage parents to exhaust all remedies and avenues of relief before resorting to the extreme measure of legal action, and they must educate parents as to what those alternatives are.

Parents are usually supportive when they are aware of the reasoning behind a school policy or procedure, particularly when they understand how the procedure is in the best interests of the child. So, teachers and administrators must take time to explain. Also, parents are not likely to complain, especially to the point of bringing lawsuits, against programs they have helped design; thus, educators must make an effort to get parents involved in every aspect of the child's program development. Teachers can gain confidence from the fact that parents have much more to gain from the parent-educator partnership than the teachers do. Thus, relationships should be approached in a mood of goodwill and cooperation whenever possible.

PARENT-TEACHER CONFERENCES

Parent-teacher conferences provide an opportunity for establishing good relationships with parents and for initiating important home-school cooperation. When conferences are held at the school, they allow parents to experience the school environment even though they may not be able to participate regularly in the child's classroom. During the conference, the teacher should report the child's progress, reviewing specific performance records with the parents and answering any questions they might have. If teachers are well prepared to discuss the child's progress and needs, these conferences are usually rewarding experiences, where communication can be opened and cooperation can be arranged.

If parents are unable or unwilling to come to the school, home visits may be appropriate. If a teacher takes along the child's school records and representative work, the home visit can follow the same procedure as the in-school conference. Although home visits may consume more time, they do have some advantages. Some parents are more comfortable and thus more likely to be responsive and cooperative in their own homes. Also, home visits can allow the teacher to observe the child's home environment.

SUMMARY

Although most parents respond well to conferences and visits with their child's teacher, occasionally encounters with parents present special challenges. In this section, I present a summary and suggest implications from the first three chapters of the book—particularly as they apply to parents and surrogate parents of children with mental retardation.

- Be aware of the stages and phases that parents are thought to experience as they learn that the child born (or assigned) to them has mental retardation. In individual circumstances, however, assume that the stages, at best, offer only potential guidelines that may or may not apply.

- Be aware that even in instances where the stages do exist, parents usually progress through them. Therefore, patiently but persistently strive with the parents at all levels of their child's education. Law and good practice require parental participation at every level of education no matter how reluctant the parent may have been to participate in the past.

- Defer to the wishes of parents in educating their child with mental retardation. The experience of the parents in mental retardation generally is likely to be limited, but according to law and custom, they are held primarily responsible for the care and upbringing of their child—except under unusual circumstances.

- Be keenly aware that not all children with mental retardation (in some areas, fewer than half) live with both biological parents in a traditional family. Single parents, foster parents, surrogate parents, and others often have little or no background in mental retardation. Even if they do, they usually approach the child's education with widely diverse backgrounds and possibly even have more problems and questions about the child's education than the child's biological parents.

- Seriously consider your professional obligation to help train the parents in their duties—particularly as they pertain to the child's education—as well as other persons (discussed in the next chapter). Bear in mind that generally the more closely and extensively parents and others work with their child, the more accurate perceptions they will have regarding the limitations—and particularly the potential—the child has to prepare for life as an adult. Tactfully, ask the parents and others what they perceive the individual will be doing at age 25.

Appendix B is an additional, more complete list of do's and don'ts I have compiled and taught to students and others over many years of working with individuals with mental retardation and their parents. None of these were consciously taken from any published source, yet probably none are completely unique. Therefore, official credit is hereby given to all persons living or dead who have worked in mental retardation during the last 100 years or so.

CHAPTER 5

Working with IEP Team Members and Others

Points to Study and Ponder

1. Who are the significant others in the life of a student with mental retardation?
2. Why do significant others make decisions for individuals with mental retardation that other individuals usually make for themselves?
3. Which significant others are likely to actually serve on a student's IEP team or the team that decides whether or not the student has mental retardation?
4. Which significant others have strong backgrounds in education? special education? mental retardation?
5. Why does a teacher have a particular responsibility to train educational assistants (aides), classroom volunteers, and peer tutors?
6. How can teachers and other members of the IEP team help the significant others better understand mental retardation?
7. What are mainstreaming, integration, and inclusion?
8. What does it mean to educate a student with mental retardation in the least restrictive environment?
9. What does it mean to ensure that a student's educational program is commensurate with the student's individual needs and abilities?
10. How can IEP teams evaluate regular and special educational programs available to their student?
11. Who are slow learners, and why are they and the programs designed for them important to the IEP team when the slow learners do not have mental retardation and do not qualify for special education?
12. Are the local educational programs designed for slow learners likely to be appropriate for students with mental retardation? Why or why not?

Typically, students with mental retardation do not speak well in their own behalf, and many, if not most of them, will not eventually develop the reasoning and communicative capabilities to effectively do so. Sigelman et al. (1981) reported from their studies that students with mental retardation have a strong tendency to routinely answer yes in response to most verbal questions. Even as adults, most of them have fewer opportunities than others to make their own decisions (Kishi, Teelucksingh, Zollers, Park-Lee, & Meyer, 1988).

Despite limitations, however, every student with mental retardation has some ability to speak for him- or herself and has the right to learn to do so to the extent of his or her capability (Dudley, 1987; Sigelman, Winer, & Schoenrock, 1982). IEP team members must realize that such instruction should be an integral part of each student's training. But as students with mental retardation are learning to make decisions and express themselves, many of their life decisions must be made and are typically made by those adults responsible for maintaining the students' rights and acting in their best interests; Cooley (1962) refers to these individuals as **significant others.**

This chapter continues the theme of IEP team members not only working together but also training each other as well. Many significant others do not serve on the IEP team and may not work directly with the student—at least on a day-to-day basis. Thus, they must pass their expertise on to others—mainly the parents and teachers. In this chapter, I discuss contributions each may make. For example, the major contribution of special education teachers is to help other team members understand mental retardation and the impact it has on an individual. The major contribution of the parents is to share information about their child in particular.

Special education teachers—probably to a greater extent than any other educators—work extensively with colleagues and others with whom they do not share common backgrounds and training. Virtually all significant others in the lives of students with mental retardation graduated from the public schools, where they experienced a wide array of regular elementary and secondary classes and interacted with those teachers. Very few of them were educated in special classes, however, and it is highly unlikely that any were in programs for students with mental retardation.

Thus, teachers of students with mental retardation must learn to function in a setting that is essentially unique. They are often the only persons—including IEP team members—with any specific education and/or experience in mental retardation. Moreover, they, like some others, may serve for several years on an individual's IEP team. As such, they must not only deal with the largely untrained significant others but also help them understand the basic nature of mental retardation and how it affects a person. They must also help each one see how his or her decisions can contribute to that person's becoming as successful as possible as an adult. In effect, they must train each of these people in duties each is uninformed about—a formidable task. The task is difficult because many of these significant others have strong opinions about mental retardation regardless of their training or lack thereof and because many of them have meager to extensive backgrounds in mental retardation. This educational task is easier if the special education teachers understand the backgrounds that are typical of the significant others, as well as the nature of the decisions they typically make. In many instances, the teacher may never actually meet or have opportunity to train or share experience with the person, but must deal with that person's decisions nonetheless. Significantly, relatively few significant others actually serve on a student's IEP team.

SOME GENERALIZATIONS

It is important for teachers and other IEP team members to realize that many of the people who make serious decisions on behalf of persons with mental retardation are largely unqualified to do so (Cegelka, 1978; Wolraich & Siperstein, 1986). Although these people may be legally and morally responsible for the child, many of them are not well informed on the limitations involved with mental retardation or on the training, procedures, or support systems that will be necessary to help students with mental retardation ultimately achieve optimum independence and success when they are adults. But it is unrealistic to expect appropriate decisions to be made by those who lack specific training and experience. The relative helplessness of individuals with mental retardation makes them particularly vulnerable. This situation of inadequately informed decisions being made for a very dependent population has contributed to what Baumeister and Brooks (1981) identified as program instability and erratic shifts in public policy regarding those with mental retardation.

The only solution to the problems of inadequately trained persons delivering services to students with mental retardation is to place the responsibility for their significant decisions in the hands of a well-informed IEP team (Rosen, 1994). Further, if the team members are to achieve maximum efficiency in the foreseeable future, they must train each other. Every team should include one or more members who can assist the other members as they steer an appropriate course through a diverse sea of individual needs and multicultural considerations. Hartshorne and Boomer (1993) suggested that the team must also learn to respect confidences and to avoid any invasion of privacy. Doing so is further complicated by the student—the key figure involved—who isn't usually in a position to insist on his or her rights.

An important contribution of the teacher educated in dealing with mental retardation is to tactfully provide to significant others necessary background information on the child's condition, limitations, potentials, and available options so that sound, well-informed decisions can be made. The teacher should feel confident in assuming this role. In addition to recognizing the knowledge that may be lacking in significant others, the teacher must identify the important potential contributions that each will be able to make to the welfare and progress of the child. Cooperative team efforts must involve the participation of all persons who, by personal or professional interest, are in a position to offer assistance. It is important for the teacher to be aware of the specific contributions that family members and various professionals will make and to work tactfully and respectfully with them so that individual efforts are brought together into a unified program.

Diverse backgrounds and philosophies can be an advantage because different fields of expertise can offer services for the child's varying needs. If the teacher, who may be the only team member with specialized training in mental retardation, works from a genuine appreciation of the knowledge and experience that others may have gained through specialized training in other fields, cooperative working arrangements can usually be made. Gentle, persistent persuasion directed toward decisions on which the teacher is most qualified should be combined with deference when the decision requires medical or administrative skills beyond the teacher's knowledge or responsibility. Background information on the position, influence, and information base of many of these significant others may help the teacher in assessing potential contributions and employing necessary tact.

ASSOCIATES FROM THE FIELD OF EDUCATION

Many IEP team members and significant others who make highly significant decisions in the lives of individuals with mental retardation are trained and/or employed in education. Associates trained directly in the field of education include regular class teachers and administrators, including superintendents and principals. In instances where a student with mental retardation is placed in regular classes for all or part of the school day, these professionals make important decisions—and have a tremendous influence—in the lives of the students. The training of many other specialists, such as adaptive physical education teachers, physical therapists, recreation therapists, speech/language specialists, and audiologists, may include some education course work and/or experience, but this training is usually not in colleges of education. Given the significant responsibilities of these specialists, however, they generally have extremely limited backgrounds in any area of special education, but especially in mental retardation.

Regular Class Teachers

Although most students with mental retardation begin their education in regular classes and many remain there either full- or part-time until their education is completed, most regular class teachers have little training in mental retardation or any other type of disability. This is particularly true at the secondary school level (Sluyter, 1982). With the need to keep abreast of rapidly expanding technology and troublesome social problems, it is little wonder that regular educators receive little more formal education in mental retardation than they did several decades ago. Because inclusion programs are now so prevalent, education for these teachers is necessary, and the special education teacher may need to provide much of it through participation and shared experience.

To work appropriately with regular class teachers, the special education teacher must understand the perspectives from which they work. Because of their position in the overall school program, they are understandably oriented toward grade level and subject matter considerations. Hanrahan, Goodman, and Rapagna (1990) reported that the curriculum priorities of regular class teachers are much more oriented to formal academics than special class teachers. Regular class teachers are used to teaching in large groups. Society demands that they teach mostly from standard textbooks, with curriculum largely devoted to preparing their students to enter college. Their perspective is further limited by the fact that they have little opportunity to follow the progress of a student with mental retardation from one grade level to another, particularly between elementary and secondary schools. Further, they have neither the time nor the expertise to do life goal planning with a person with mental retardation. This lack of opportunity to see their position in the child's educational sequence often results in poor planning and uncoordinated programs for the child.

In addition to a perspective that does not easily accommodate the child with mental retardation, most regular class teachers have little time and few resources to devote to such children. Any learner with a disability must be worked in around the needs of a large class, and the child with mental retardation is one of the most difficult to work in. Thus, the teacher with specific training in mental retardation can contribute significantly by helping regular class teachers learn methods and techniques for meeting the needs of students with mental retardation. Regular classes may need some reorganizing, and programs may need restructuring. Materials may need to be adapted or created. Trained special education teachers can offer guidance to regular class teachers in all of these areas.

School Administrators

In a public school setting, administrators—such as the building principal or vice principal—will usually be in charge of placement committees and IEP teams. Most of their backgrounds, however, are similar to those of regular class teachers as far as special education issues are concerned. Most of them obtain a regular teaching certificate and then add administrative degrees or credentials by completing administrative course work. Their advanced studies typically include neither course work nor practical experience in working with students with disabilities. After surveying all 50 states and the District of Columbia, Stile and Pettibone (1980) reported that whereas 26 states offered a specific credential in special education administration, only 12 required any special education course work for a general administrative credential, the certification held by most superintendents and principals. Obviously, it would be unfair and unrealistic to require administrators to be certified in every area over which they preside.

Some districts employ directors of special education on the level of district administrator. Their backgrounds are usually more closely aligned to special education than those of other administrators; however, even they do not necessarily have strong backgrounds in special education studies, and many have little or no formal training or direct experience with students with mental retardation. Again, the special education teacher may need to find tactful ways to share the knowledge and background necessary for these individuals to create policies and make informed decisions in matters where the education and future of students with mental retardation are at stake.

Professionals from Fields Related to Education

Several classes of professional workers may have training partly or primarily in education but typically not in special education. These persons include adaptive physical education teachers, physical therapists, recreation therapists, speech/language specialists, and audiologists. The IDEA greatly enhances the possibility of having them work with students with mental retardation, as well as other disabilities. These specialists may serve as members of the IEP team or, in some cases, may offer consulting advice. In most instances, these people have no formal training in mental retardation. Nevertheless, they are often called on to assist the IEP team and may render invaluable service.

APPOINTED STATE OFFICIALS

State officials—directors of special education, program specialists, auditors, and others—significantly affect the lives of individuals with mental retardation at every age level. As they review and evaluate programs for students with mental retardation, they are often in a position to approve or disapprove those programs and to grant, reduce, or withhold the necessary funding. Although they are empowered to make decisions that will drastically affect the education and future opportunities of students with disabilities, many of them have little or no training or direct experience in special education. Because their positions often do not require teaching or administrative certification, many do not have backgrounds in education at all. Most, however, are dedicated, well-educated professionals who will listen to the concerns of special education teachers and parents of children with mental retardation. Both groups should be aware of the services these professionals can provide and of avenues for making the needs of students with mental retardation known.

In working with this group of significant others, teachers and parents need to be aware of the relationship of these administrators to their programs. A well-recognized principle of administration states that important decisions should be made by persons who must later live with the consequences of those decisions (Hoy & Miskel, 1991; Lunenburg & Ornstein, 1991). These state administrators regularly make decisions that will significantly affect students with mental retardation, the work of their teachers and parents, and the nature of the programs. But because of the appointive nature of their positions, they may not have to deal with the results of those decisions. If local educators and state officials disagree on the merits of a particular program, the state administrators usually have the final word. Local teachers and administrators may then be left to conduct a program they neither designed nor approved and to try to answer the criticism of offended parents.

SPECIALISTS FROM THE FIELD OF PSYCHOLOGY

Many IEP team members and significant others, including school psychologists, school counselors, and school psychometrists, are trained and have experience in psychology. The preparation programs of these specialists—like those of school administrators—are likely to require a teaching credential as a prerequisite, but these credentials are not usually in special education.

School Psychologists

Hired into school districts to work with students who have serious problems in adjustment, personality, or behavior, school psychologists typically have strong backgrounds in psychology, with varying degrees of training and experience in education. Often, their training is more clinical than educational. Usually, they have little background in special education, particularly in working with students with mental retardation. Wodrich and Barry (1991) found that school psychologists use a wide variety of practices and procedures to identify students with mental retardation. When these students have personality or behavioral disorders, however, the school psychologist, working cooperatively with the teacher, can usually offer counseling and help develop specialized programs for the child.

School Counselors

School counselors are more likely to have more specialized training and experience in the field of education than school psychologists, and their backgrounds probably will be less clinical. Both school counselors and school psychologists are likely to be qualified and certified to administer and interpret standardized tests legally required in formally evaluating and identifying students with mental retardation. Although their professional preparation usually emphasizes psychology, many will have served internships in schools where they will have dealt with many kinds of student problems and participated in offering a variety of services. Their broad knowledge of student needs and program options is valuable in making decisions and plans for the student with mental retardation.

School Psychometrists

Psychometry is the study of various types of tests; school psychometrists usually have some training and experience in both education and psychology, but they specialize in administering, scoring, and reporting the results of various educational tests. Teachers of students with disabilities work closely with these psychometrists in identifying, classifying, and discerning individual needs of students who appear to have varying degrees of mental retardation.

A school district may employ a number of professionals with strong backgrounds in psychology as guidance, career, vocational, or family counselors. Titles and job descriptions in these specialty areas may become indistinct: For example, a "school counselor" may deal with personal conflicts, vocational testing, and family dysfunctions. It is wise for a teacher dealing with students with mental retardation to become personally acquainted with these specialists and to determine each individual's areas of expertise, rather than to assume skills and interests the person may not have. Although most of them have training outside the fields of education and special education, most of these specialists can be very helpful in working with students with mental retardation. Their insights and experiences are often very helpful in counseling parents, especially when acceptance of the disability and involvement in educational programs are sought.

School counselors and psychologists are often placed in charge of special education programs or asked to function as "captain" of an IEP team for special education, including evaluation, placement, curriculum, and/or IEP formulation. Because many of these persons may not be adequately trained in special education, it is fortunate that the parents do have final authority in making serious decisions regarding the welfare or education of their child. Team members are asked to contribute their own expertise and experience within areas of decision they are qualified to advise. Well-informed teachers can be influential in understanding the potential contributions of different personnel and in assisting parents in assessing and acting on their ideas.

SPECIALISTS FROM THE FIELD OF SOCIOLOGY

Some significant others have training and backgrounds in sociology. The discussion of these specialists includes social workers and vocational rehabilitation counselors. These professionals may render invaluable service to students with mental retardation, parents, and teachers, but their preparation typically lies outside education, special education, and mental retardation.

Social Workers

Although rarely trained in education or special education and not usually employed in school districts, social workers serve students with disabilities and their parents in a variety of ways. Because of their knowledge and frequent interaction with other service groups and agencies, they can collect information and enlist additional assistance when the child and the family have needs beyond those the school can meet. Social workers often assist the family with problems, such as budgeting and child care. They may also serve as advocates of the parents in dealing with school difficulties.

Vocational Rehabilitation Counselors

Students whose mental retardation is mild enough to permit them to eventually be employed need guidance in making a positive transition from school to the world of adult life and work. Vocational rehabilitation counselors typically offer such help to people who have been unemployable because of accident, illness, or disability. They have financial resources available to temporarily assist their clients and to pay employers to provide necessary job training for them. Chapter 14 has strong emphasis on a procedure called *supported employment.* Briefly, this procedure provides partial or full financial employment support for a student with mental retardation. Vocational rehabilitation counselors are in a position to provide much of this support, roughly 80% of which is provided by federal funds and the rest from state sources. Although these counselors usually work only with adults, they often accept older students with mental retardation who are nearing graduation. It has been a common practice in recent years to assign to certain counselors students with mental retardation and other disabilities. The IEP team should be in constant association with the local "voc rehab counselor."

SPECIALISTS FROM THE FIELD OF MEDICINE

The field of medicine contributes in significant ways to students with mental retardation. The discussion of these specialists includes physicians, nurses, and usually occupational therapists.

Physicians

Before a child reaches school age, physicians such as the family internist, obstetrician, or pediatrician are often the parents' primary source of information about mental retardation (Smith, 1981). These specialists from the field of medicine provide a wide variety of invaluable services and advice to others in mental retardation. But the information physicians give is often inadequate, misleading, or unnecessarily discouraging. Rosen (1994) suggested that physicians have wielded tremendous influence and that decision-making power should be vested in the hands of those who work directly with students with mental retardation.

Physicians typically receive training oriented only to the medical and clinical aspects of mental retardation. They usually receive no instruction or experience in recognizing and dealing with mental retardation as a social or educational phenomenon. Few, if any, medical schools provide experience in working with patients with mental retardation; a physician's background rarely includes psychological testing, educational programming, or counseling with parents of a child with the disability. Only 64% of physicians surveyed by McDonald, Carlson, Palmer, and Slay (1983) were even aware of the existence of P.L. 94–142, although most indicated an interest in receiving information about it and learning more about educational programs for children with disabilities. Most physicians would like to provide more information about such programs to their patients, but unfortunately, though understandably, they are unable to do so.

Not having a knowledge of available programs and potential progress for children with mental retardation, many physicians unintentionally cause unnecessary discouragement for the parents. Less stress has been reported among parents whose physicians made positive suggestions at the time the child was diagnosed than among those whose doctors were less optimistic (Wood & Flynt, 1991), but many physicians do not have positive suggestions to make. In their studies of the knowledge and attitudes of a number of professionals toward mental retardation, Wolraich and Siperstein (1983) found that medical doctors have lower expectations than either educators or social workers for the general abilities of children with mental retardation and more pessimism about the future abilities of these children to live independently and to make their own decisions. Although Wolraich and Siperstein (1986) applauded the advice and services of many physicians, they found an overall tendency to make pessimistic prognoses about the future abilities of infants and young patients with mental retardation. In a later study, Siperstein, Wolraich, and Reed (1994) reported that medical doctors had significantly lower expectations of students with mental retardation than professionals from psychology and social work.

Unfortunately, lack of knowledge does not prevent physicians from offering their advice. Of all the significant others, they seem to be the most likely to enjoy credibility they haven't earned in making and influencing decisions on behalf of people with mental retardation (Lynch & Staloch, 1988). Sadly, their advice is usually given early in the child's life, when the parents are particularly vulnerable. There have been tragic reports of pediatricians and even obstetricians advising parents of infants with Down syndrome or other conditions associated with mental retardation to place such a child in an institution, pretend the birth never occurred, or even allow the child to die, as in the well-publicized case of *Baby Doe* (Affleck, 1980; Herr, 1984; Smith, 1981; Smith, 1989; Vitello, 1978). Because of the confidence that parents have in their child's physician, the misinformation and poor advice are often very difficult for teachers and other informed personnel to correct.

Even though physicians' informed or uninformed advice to parents can influence decisions they make regarding the education of their child, physicians do not usually serve on a child's school evaluation, placement, or IEP team; thus, they are not able to see the child's eventual progress. Although their recommendations may be responsible for difficulties in a child's program, they do not have to answer to the parents who are dissatisfied with the result; educators do.

Teachers can usually do little to prevent flawed advice by physicians, yet they are sometimes in a position to recommend a physician to help parents with a specific problem of a child with mental retardation. Because of the tremendous credibility of physicians, together with their tendency to emphasize the inabilities of individuals with mental retardation, the responsibility of IEP team members to orient and train them is particularly important. Team members—including parents—have a great deal of information that can help a physician gain a realistic perception of an individual with mental retardation. Team members can also become aware of physicians who are most informed and reasonable and make appropriate recommendations whenever possible.

School Nurses

Although nurses are yet another example of significant others whose training is unlikely to include mental retardation, all special educators should form a cooperative working relationship with the school nurse (Steadham, 1993). Currently, students with multiple and severe disabilities can be found in practically any classroom. Some of these students require health services, including special catheters and feeding procedures that exceed the qualifications of virtually all teachers. Also, teachers everywhere are currently expected to administer powerful medications, a task for which they lack qualifications. Having been trained in mental retardation or not, a school nurse to supervise these procedures can be of great comfort to the teacher.

Occupational Therapists

Under the direction of physicians, occupational therapists select and direct activities to help individuals with physical and mental disabilities overcome their limitations and develop their potential as fully as they can. Often, the activities are focused to develop movement and muscular capabilities that will help the patient in achieving optimum vocational or occupational success. The training of these therapists may include some experience in working with individuals of all ages who have mental retardation. Although they are not usually employed full-time in school districts, their services may be contracted for special cases. Parents of a child having mental retardation and approaching the age to be leaving school and seeking employment should be made aware of occupational therapy services.

SPECIALISTS FROM THE LEGAL PROFESSION

Currently, attorneys and judges also have a great deal of influence in mental retardation, as well as in the rest of the field of special education (McCarthy, 1981). Specialists from the field of law include judges, magistrates, and attorneys.

Attorneys

Although they may specialize in assisting individuals with disabilities, most attorneys have no specific training or background in special education. Their professional education prepares them to serve a wide variety of individuals with a focus on legally defensible rights. Given this background, it is understandable that they emphasize their clients' rights, rather than their clients' responsibilities, but often this focus results in action that is legal but not necessarily best for the child. For example, a parent who was overly concerned about his son's safety at school consulted with the family attorney, who wrote a letter to the school, threatening a lawsuit over alleged unsafe devices and practices in the school. Such threats were probably within the legal rights of the parents, but in practice the teachers were literally afraid to let the boy out of the classroom, which was more detrimental to his development than any minor bumps and scrapes he might have received on the playground. Had they countered with legal action of their own, the school administration would probably have won. But like most school officials, they were reluctant to spend precious educational funds for legal action with no guarantee of success. This typical reluctance creates an imbalance of power that often works against the real needs and interests of the child with mental retardation. Teachers need to recognize this reluctance and be prepared to help parents, fellow teachers, or teacher trainers recognize how the law can protect the needs of children without becoming a stumbling block to the school. They also need to know how to avoid lawsuits in conducting their school affairs. Finally, teachers and others must recognize that attorneys—like all significant others—are primarily performing the functions for which they are trained.

The significant other of an individual with mental retardation may or may not be a member of the person's IEP team.

Judges and Magistrates

Like attorneys, judges and magistrates usually have little knowledge of the nature of mental retardation or the issues involved with the needs, rights, and education of individuals with the disability. Nevertheless, a judge in a juvenile, divorce, or other civil hearing may declare that an involved child with mental retardation should be cared for and educated in a state residential institution. Appropriate or not, the child automatically bypasses all admission tests, interviews, and other procedures—including purposefully mandated waiting periods—and is quickly assigned to the institution. In some instances, the law permits the court to remove legal custody of children with mental retardation from their natural parents and grant it to the director of the institution.

Although educators can do little to change the law, if they are aware of decisions that can be made and the uncertain bases on which they may be made, they can serve as a tactful information source both to parents and to professionals. For example, Everington and Luckasson (1989) pointed out that special educators can be of great assistance in helping attorneys and judges understand mental retardation—especially for individuals who find themselves in the criminal justice system. Often, if an educator will respect the professional's position and authority, the professional will, in turn, respect the educator's experience and be open to information on the true needs of the child that an educator will be able to give.

It is not feasible to require that course work in special education be included in the professional training of medical and legal personnel. Yet, having individuals who know little or nothing about mental retardation make significant decisions affecting the lives of students with mental retardation is a matter of serious concern for those who work with such students on a daily basis. Specialists in the field of mental retardation need to be alert to all possible opportunities to educate and inform significant others whose decisions and actions may determine the outcome of a child's life.

AIDES AND ASSISTANTS

Some persons—often with little or no training—are currently employed in school districts to work directly with students with mental retardation. In most instances, these helpers are under the direct supervision of classroom teachers and must be carefully trained.

Paraprofessionals

Because students with mental retardation often have great difficulty working independently, outside assistance is often needed. To alleviate this problem, many schools employ paraprofessional personnel, including instructional assistants, aides, monitors, teaching assistants, and tutors. These individuals are not usually involved in major decisions, such as making placements or formulating IEPs, but they are available to assist in the daily school routines and usually serve the entire time the child is in school. When properly trained, they can provide consistent, competent support for the child. Their service can be adapted beyond normal classroom use. For example, Cooley, Singer, and Irvin (1989) reported success in using volunteer paraprofessionals on a one-on-one basis with children with developmental disabilities for weekend instructional and recreational activities.

Cautions do need to be exercised in using paraprofessionals with children with mental retardation. Occasionally, administrators will employ a disproportionate number of aides and assistants, diverting funds that could be used more profitably to hire credentialed teachers. Sometimes students with mental retardation are assigned almost exclusively to instructional assistants, rather than to qualified teachers. Teachers and administrators must remember that students with learning deficiencies need the highest quality of instruction. Assistants can provide valuable help to a regular or special education teacher, but it is the well-prepared, credentialed teacher who must train the assistant and assume ownership and responsibility for the education of the child.

Adult Volunteers and Peer Tutors

Many teachers find an additional source of individual help for students with mental retardation through volunteer programs. Special education is more widely publicized than ever before, and as more people become aware of the needs of individuals with disabilities, many are volunteering their assistance (Kohl & Stettner-Eaton, 1985). Many public and private schools regularly use volunteers recruited from women's clubs, church groups, service organizations, parents, interested lay persons, and even elementary and secondary students. Although they are valuable in any classroom, these people are especially helpful in working one-on-one with students with mental retardation. As early as 1972, Fredericks, Baldwin, Hanson, and Fontana reviewed several studies of programs in which volunteers from a community assisted in special education classrooms. They reported that most of these programs rated as very successful. These researchers agreed with Hyde (1990), however, and cautioned that volunteers must be carefully trained. Maheady, Sacca, and Harper (1987) indicated that peer tutors have a positive effect on the academic performance of students with mental retardation—especially in mathematics. Goldstein and Mousetis (1989) found that peer tutors can be especially effective in providing good language models. Staub and Hunt (1993) pointed out that peer tutors are much more effective when they are well trained. The researchers gave social interaction training to same-age peers and found them much more effective in encouraging the initiation of social interactions among students with severe disabilities than nontrained peers. One major advantage of inclusion programs is the exposure of students with mental retardation to their peers. For those in special classes, peer tutors can provide similar service in those classes. In addition to planning for appropriate training of volunteers, teachers need to handle scheduling carefully so that part-time volunteer help can be used as fully as possible.

Parents and Other Family Members as Classroom Assistants

Family members are the most likely of the significant others to feel the real impact of the mental retardation of a child. Where they are responsible for the child's welfare before and after school and for significant decisions affecting the child during school, they are likely to volunteer to assist in the classroom as well.

Parents may be particularly desirable as classroom helpers. They are the only members of the IEP team who do not get released. As parents become more involved in planning and monitoring their child's educational programs, they are often eager to participate actively, and some are willing to give entire days, sometimes several days a week. They bring with them the maturity that comes from daily association with the child and the dedication that results from carrying the ultimate responsibility for the child's future. A fundamental aspect of educating a child with mental retardation is to help the parents continue that education in the home. What better way to accomplish this goal than to teach the child and the parent together, right in the classroom? As parents learn to diagnose their child's abilities and to supervise their child in mastering skills, they gain capabilities essential in helping the child continue to master and use those skills outside the school setting.

This mastery of skills causes concern for a large percentage of parents. Brotherson et al. (1988) reported that the greatest needs expressed by parents are for help in preparing their child with skills necessary for socialization, employment, and future independent living. Self-help skills, grooming, independent travel, and supermarket shopping were skills implemented into a home intervention program by Patterson (1984), which provided effective preparation for individuals with mental retardation. Such skills could easily be instructed by the teacher and supervised by the parent right in the classroom.

As parents participate in teaching their child, the personal relationship is also enhanced. Richardson et al. (1985) reported that parenting style was more significant than neurological impairment in later behavioral disturbance of children with mental retardation. They suggested that cooperative efforts between parents and teacher can produce very positive results in creating that effective parenting style. When parents are willing to develop and refine their style of interaction with their child under the teacher's guidance at the school, this process has maximum chances for success.

Working with a parent in the classroom requires understanding and tact. Experience with one or two children with mental retardation, even one's own, does not qualify a person as an authority on the disability. But teachers and school officials must avoid contradicting or devaluing a parent's knowledge. In comparing the perceptions of parents and teachers of the levels in self-help and socialization skills and the presence of behavioral problems in children with developmental delays, Handen, Feldman, and Honigman (1987) found only a 68% agreement. This difference should not be interpreted to suggest that either the teachers or the parents had superior knowledge of the child, but rather that because perceptions will be so different, teachers and parents need to be tactful and cooperative in considering each other's ideas. Teachers may need to be gently persistent in helping parents understand their child's needs as they evaluate appropriate placement and curriculum. Differences in perception can often be handled by carefully monitoring and documenting the child's performance.

Occasionally, a parent's presence in the classroom may cause a significant change in the child's behavior. If the change is positive, the learning environment will improve and the situation should be encouraged. But negative behavior from the child causes special challenges for both the teacher and the parent. The child's behavior may allow the teacher to assess strengths and weaknesses in the parent-child relationship, and cooperative effort to strengthen the relationship will be well worth the investment of time and energy (Allen & Hudd, 1987; Seyfarth, Hill, Orelove, McMillan, & Wehman, 1987). Because occasionally a parent's presence in a classroom is unreasonably disruptive to the class as a whole and because a parent's work may not be satisfactory, it is best to agree at the outset that either the parent or the teacher may terminate the arrangement.

HELPING OTHERS UNDERSTAND MENTAL RETARDATION

Each significant other has a specific role in serving students with mental retardation. The role of each is unique in the cooperative effort to assist the student; thus, each will have a different perspective and a different contribution. Ironically, some significant others who are professionally trained may not have ongoing contact with the student, whereas some with less special education instruction, such as the classroom teacher, may be involved with the child on a daily basis. Some who have input into the student's IEP and educational placement may have little or no direct contact with the student thereafter, never observing the results of the decisions they made. Because of this diversity of backgrounds, perspectives, rights, and responsibilities, the special education teacher or other specialist with specific training and experience in mental retardation can make an important contribution by helping the others understand both the limitations and potentials of people with mental retardation in general and those of the individual child whose program is being addressed.

In addition to providing basic background understanding for those involved in making decisions, the teacher who is informed about mental retardation will need to give more direct and extensive instruction to those who will be working in the classroom with the child. Because teachers in inclusion programs tend to have less time to work directly with students with mental retardation, their need to train volunteers, instructional assistants, peer tutors, and others is particularly compelling. The life goal curriculum planning and diagnostic/prescriptive techniques of this book are a good example of the needed instruction. In these situations, the teacher can spend whatever time he or she can in diagnosing the abilities of a student with mental retardation, and once the prescription is outlined, these paraprofessionals can perform much of the instruction—under the teacher's supervision. Older students with mental retardation have also been successfully used as tutors for younger children. Blackbourn and Blackbourn (1993) trained adolescents with moderate mental retardation to tutor a 7-year-old in arithmetic.

Parents should be urged to participate as fully as possible in the education of their child with mental retardation, including classroom involvement if possible. The relationship between parents and teacher is sensitive, and the teacher needs to train and encourage the parents with full respect for their perspective and rights as parents of the child. During the time they are participating together in the classroom, however, the teacher is legally in charge (Yudof et al., 1992). If parents are unable or unwilling to assist at school, the teacher can arrange to provide help and guidance through home visits and through regular parent-teacher conferences at the school.

When paraprofessionals and volunteers are given meaningful tasks, they become more personally involved, are more valuable to the child, and as a result stay longer and may come more often. Most of them are willing to perform some routine, non-teaching tasks, such as keeping records, counting lunch money, running errands, and grading papers. Some may even enjoy the safety of perfunctory involvement. Most will have a more meaningful experience, however, and thus will remain longer if involved in working directly with the children. Of course, the longer these helpers remain, the more they will be able to contribute and the less time the teacher will need to spend on orienting and training new aides and volunteers.

All classroom helpers—parents, paid employees, and volunteers—must be oriented to their responsibilities and status in the classroom. Following are some guidelines that may be shared with classroom participants during the orientation process. Because every situation will be different, the general principles may be applied, adapted, or not applicable to any specific personnel.

- **Volunteers and paraprofessionals must discuss a student's shortcomings only with the teacher, in private.** Mentioning a student's weakness, or even perceived preferences, in a student's presence can result in damaged self-confidence, and an inaccurate judgment may become a self-fulfilling prophecy.
- **Be dependable.** Whether or not an assistant is paid, the individual must meet time commitments reliably. It is difficult for a teacher to set aside important activities that require the participation of an undependable assistant. Eventually, an unreliable volunteer will have to be excluded from significant plans.
- **Support the teacher.** If an assistant does not fully support the teacher in the classroom, his or her presence will not be a help and may be a detriment. Even something as simple as laughing at a behavior the teacher is trying to discourage can be damaging. If an assistant questions the purpose of an activity or experience or has a criticism of a student's program, such matters should be discussed in private interviews, never in the presence of students, parents, participants, or outsiders.
- **Reinforce the students as the teacher does.** All classroom helpers must look to the teacher for discipline and reinforcement cues. All classroom praise and discipline must be consistent. For example, if a teacher is trying to encourage any kind of verbal expression from a child with mental retardation and ignores the fact that the child usually does not raise a hand before speaking, it would be damaging for an assistant to scold the child for forgetting the hand-raising rule. Inconsistent praise can also be confusing to a child. Many classroom volunteers have a tendency to issue an oral "Good job!" every few minutes whether or not the child is working to capability level.
- **Allow the students to do their own work.** Too much assistance may create a dependency in a child with mental retardation, and the child soon learns to manipulate an overly eager assistant. A volunteer must be patient with the slow progress of the student and avoid the temptation to hurry things by giving too much help or by completing part of the student's work.
- **Respect confidences.** No one should discuss the progress or behavior of a student with those who have no right to the information. When instructional assistants gain access to sensitive material, either from a teacher or from the students' records, such information should be considered confidential. All team members should realize the importance of the students' and parents' right to privacy.
- **Treat each student with respect.** Sensitive or derogatory terms—even the term *mentally retarded*—should not be used in the presence of parents or child.
- **Use the appropriate language level for each student.** Even experienced teachers find it difficult to instruct each student with mental retardation at that student's unique language and general information level. It is particularly difficult for paraprofessionals and other classroom helpers to develop the ability to sense the correct language and style for each child. Guidance and modeling must be given.
- **Follow the teacher's program.** The child's IEP and the teacher's detailed program will often include elements that instructional assistants and volunteers will not understand. It is essential that they follow the program even though they may not agree with all aspects. For example, if the teacher selects a particular procedure as a corrective device for a student, the classroom helper should not sympathize with or console the child when the penalty must be applied (or avoid applying it if the teacher has left the room).

SERVICE DELIVERY PATTERNS AND PLACEMENT

One of the most important decisions the IEP team has to make is selecting the services needed to accomplish the student's life goals. Once the student's IEP has been formulated and the student's current achievement status on his or her IEP goals identified, the next task is to determine how the goals are to be met. Meeting the IEP goals ordinarily requires one or more special services. The IEP team must also decide where the services will be provided to the student—in other words, determine the educational placement. The placement can be in either regular and special classes. Most other possibilities are variations of these two settings. In this book, I try to avoid taking sides in the controversy over relative efficacy of various educational placements for students with mental retardation. The rationale for this is twofold: (a) The student with mental retardation is very likely to need continuing, long-term support and services whether he or she is in regular or special classes, and (b) IEP teams for these students must ordinarily select and/or adapt potential placements available to their student locally and are not usually free to develop an ideal program—at least in time to accommodate their student.

Many students with mental retardation attend regular classes, sometimes with and sometimes without auxiliary services. Regional variation (see Chapter 1) indicates that some students—whose mental retardation would have been identified a decade or so ago—also attend regular classes. Regular class-resource room combinations have been very popular, especially with students whose disabilities are mild/moderate. Students in these combination classrooms, however, usually spend most of their school day in regular classes. Cooperative or team teaching places two or more traditional classes under the care of two or more teachers, one of whom may be certified in special education, but a class member with mental retardation would still spend most of his or her school day in regular classes. *Collaborative consultation* may go by different titles but has the student with mental retardation in regular classes where the regular class teachers get supportive help from one or more consultants trained in special education. The team—often with the assistance of additional specialists—may serve as a teacher assistance team (TAT). A TAT may also provide support for special class teachers.

Special classes are usually those that require a teacher with a special education teaching credential. Such placements as special schools, special classes on regular school campuses, resource rooms, and consulting teachers ordinarily require special education credentials. Inclusion programs typically have the student spend some time in one or more of these classes in addition to regular classes. Currently, most of the settings are in public schools, but private facilities may be used under specified circumstances.

Special Classes versus Regular Classes

Mental retardation—by its very nature—imposes predictable and serious learning limitations on individuals. These limitations cause the individuals to fall farther and farther behind their age-mates regardless of the educational efforts and resources expended in their behalf. Therefore, it is understandable that both their teachers and their educational programs would be subject to severe—and often undeserved—criticism. For several decades, a controversy has raged over the relative efficacy of special and regular classes for students with mental retardation. Critics of both special and regular classes tend to forget that students with mental retardation usually do poorly in any educational setting—particularly those that emphasize formal academics. The IEP team must, however, not lose sight of the fact that all children can learn and have a right to do so to the best of their abilities.

Discussion of this controversy here is not intended to decide the issues on a national scale, but rather to help the team members—especially the parents—select the most appropriate school setting and services for their child. Law and good practice require that needed services, including the educational setting, for each student with a disability be selected on an individual basis (Storey, 1993).

The controversy has not been well handled, at least in mental retardation. One major problem was that advocates on both sides argue the issues as though all regular classes are inherently superior to all special classes or vice versa. Such arguments assume that mental retardation is a homogeneous disorder that affects all afflicted persons alike. Another problem is that people on both sides tend to assume that the second (or later) of two placements is totally responsible for all the progress and present status of an individual with mental retardation.

Special Classes

Comparative research has traditionally been kind to special, self-contained classes for students with mental retardation. Most studies showed that students with mental retardation did as well or better in special classes than students with mental retardation in regular classes. The superiority was demonstrated in academic achievement, as well as in sociological performance (Cassidy & Stanton, 1959; Cowen, 1938; Goldstein, Moss, & Jordan, 1965; see also the comprehensive review by Ottenbacher and Cooper, 1982). Further, all of these studies done prior to 1965 suffered from selective factors that made the regular class group inherently superior to the students in special classes. Moreover, all of the studies used standardized achievement tests as criterion measures that gave a tremendous advantage to the regular class groups. Although these studies are old, they are significant in that most included students with IQs as high as 85 with group means of 70–75, much higher than today's upper IQ limits.

Regular Classes

The professional literature on students with mental retardation in regular classes is difficult to classify. Comparative studies comparing inclusion practices with other procedures are nonexistent. Most of the research on regular and special classes in the past several decades has been preferential, mostly the result of polls, questionnaires, and philosophical statements. The predominance of the studies, however, strongly favors regular class arrangements as being the least restrictive environment, and most of these studies either state or imply that the preference was over special classes. Such a preference for inclusion programs can be regarded as generally disfavoring special education classes.

Mainstreaming, Integration, and Inclusion

The purpose of discussing mainstreaming, integration, and inclusion here is solely to show teachers and other IEP team members how the curriculum planning and diagnostic/prescriptive teaching procedures of this book can be used in situations in which students with mental retardation are educated in regular classes and educational programs. Each IEP team has the responsibility to assess the quality and availability of local programs available to the student in their charge. Their collective preferences are not likely to have an appreciable effect on national trends, particularly during the lifetime of their student. Their task is to enable the student to become as independent and as self-sufficient as possible in adult life, and they accomplish that by providing the best possible educational program for that student.

The terminology associated with the movement to return students with disabilities—particularly those with mental retardation—to regular classes has gone through an interesting transition. Historically, *mainstreaming* (Atterbury, 1984; Childs, 1983; Gottlieb, 1981; Gresham, 1982; Hanrahan et al., 1990; Huefner, 1994; Powers, 1979; Wilczenski, 1994) and *integration* (Affleck, Madge, Adams, & Lowenbraun, 1988; Gottlieb, Gampel, & Budoff, 1975; Hamre-Nietupski, Krajewski et al., 1992; Link, 1991; Mosley, 1978; York, Vandercook, Macdonald, Heise-Neff, & Caughey, 1991) have been used almost interchangeably in the literature to describe this movement. These two terms are still in current use. More recently, *inclusion* has become increasingly accepted to describe the procedures that tend to place students with mental retardation in regular classes (Browder & Cooper, 1994; Carr, 1993; Clark, 1994; Craft, 1994; Martin, 1994; Pearman, Barnhart, Huang, & Mellboom, 1992). Even though these three expressions are used more or less interchangeably, there are significant differences, having mainly to do with the basic responsibility for the student's education. Under mainstreaming, a student with mental retardation might be placed in one or more regular classes, but the primary responsibility for the student's education—including the IEP—remains with special educators. Integration assumes the student's education to be a shared responsibility; inclusion generally shifts this responsibility to regular education—with or without advice, consultation, and/or assistance from special educators (Turnbull, Turnbull, Shank, & Leal, 1995; Vandercook, York, & Forest, 1989).

The literature on inclusion can be divided roughly into three categories: (a) strongly favoring, (b) favoring on condition that recommended procedures be followed, and (c) critical to varying degrees. None of the studies on either side of the issue, however, offered any hard evidence. Nearly 100 studies fell into the first category. Studies that reviewed historical development are represented by Snell and Drake (1994), preschool by Hanline (1993), case studies by Kozleski and Jackson (1993), one school's efforts and challenge by Eichinger and Woltman (1993), and full inclusion—without even "pull out" programs—by Haas (1993) and Vandercook et al. (1989). Behrmann (1993) reviewed the most recent inclusion-related legal cases and declared that all five favored general education environments, but reminded that the IDEA mandates delivering individualized, specially designed instruction to every child.

Almost 20 studies in the second classification generally declared that inclusion was not working very well but included assurance that it would do so if school personnel and—presumably—IEP teams would incorporate their specific recommendations for improvement. Friend and Cook (1993) described the inclusion movement, explaining what inclusive education is and is not, how to make it work, why it sometimes fails, and how teachers feel about it. Other, similar points of view were represented with respect to preschool (Stafford & Green, 1993) and total inclusion (Wisniewski & Alper, 1994).

Authors of about a dozen studies expressed more serious and permanent misgivings about the status and direction of inclusion programs. This research might be particularly helpful to an IEP team in assessing local services and facilities. The most serious reservations were expressed by Edwin Martin (1994), former Director of the U.S. Bureau of Education for the Handicapped (1969–1981). He reaffirmed that the IDEA encourages inclusion but only if doing so is appropriate. He further insisted that inclusion be employed on an individual basis. He reasoned that improvement of educational services for students with disabilities must be linked to the measurement of outcomes. Martin also repudiated attempts to replace special education with improved regular education and pointed out that it is difficult to provide needed auxiliary services in integrated or inclusion settings (that are widely dispersed), especially at the secondary level. Other investigators have expressed additional reservations, including emphasizing inclusion, rather than instruction (Billingsley, 1993); losing sight of goals and perspective (Fuchs & Fuchs, 1994); lack of services, such as social and recreational programs, counseling, guidance, and job skill training—particularly at the secondary level (Edgar, 1992); lack of concern for the progress of the special needs students and their teachers (Pudlas, 1993); and the continuing lack of training in special education for regular class teachers (Carr, 1993). The undocumented assumption is all effects on nondisabled students are positive (Idstein, 1993). Klassen (1994) reported that the literature does not wholeheartedly support *mainstreaming* as practiced in Canada.

INDIVIDUAL NEEDS AND ABILITIES AND LEAST RESTRICTIVE ENVIRONMENT

One major provision of both P.L. 94–142 and the IDEA decrees that education for these students must be conducted in the least restrictive environment (LRE). The *LRE* was defined as the educational setting where the students with disabilities would have maximum contact with other students who have no disabilities. The controversy occurred partly because the same law directed that the education for students with disabilities must be commensurate with each student's individual needs and abilities. *LRE* refers primarily to sociological conditions, whereas *individual needs* pertains to all the skills and concepts needed by a student with disabilities in order to be as successful as possible. *Individual abilities* are the talent and aptitude the individual has to apply toward the mastery and achievement of his or her individual needs.

In strictly sociological terms, the LRE in any school system is regular classes designed to serve the needs of students with normal and gifted learning abilities. Thus, P.L. 94–142, later reinforced by the IDEA, appeared to create the controversy by mandating two seemingly opposing legal provisions—LRE on the one hand and basing a student's educational programs on his or her individual needs and abilities on the other.

DUTIES AND POSITION OF THE IEP TEAM

Congress, as well as the profession, appears to have been very serious about the education of each student with a disability being commensurate with that student's needs and abilities. According to the laws themselves and the rules and regulations of the executive departments of the federal and state governments, a highly individualized IEP is required for every student with a qualifying disability. These same agencies and regulations require the student's education to be planned and monitored by a special IEP team comprised of the child's parents and a team of professional specialists. By law and by practice, parents of the student are not only members of the team but also occupy a predominant position if they wish to do so. The parents are included on the IEP team because they are presumed to know the child best; teachers, counselors, therapists, and other specialists participate because they are the most knowledgeable about the facilities, personnel, and services available to the student. The IEP team supervises the IEP and ensures that its provisions are followed, evaluated, and improved where necessary.

Members of the IEP team should be as conversant with national trends as possible. Without this knowledge, they would be unable to make the best decision for the student for which they are responsible. Within legal parameters, however, they must concentrate on local conditions and how they can be used to meet that student's needs. Finally, these local conditions and available programs must be subject to careful scrutiny and evaluation (Beck, Broers, Hogue, Shipstead, & Knowlton, 1994). In selecting, training, and charging the IEP team with their duties, it is proposed that

- Greater responsibility and authority be given to the IEP team whose members are the most likely to understand the student's individual needs and how these needs can be achieved with the services and placements available locally.
- The IEP team and responsible others select or design the student's placement only after knowledgeable and objective consideration of the available options.
- Placements be made only after a careful consideration of a student's long-term life goals.
- The team be charged with the responsibility to find an optimum balance between the concept of LRE and the student's individual needs and abilities.
- Both auxiliary services and especially placements be considered and tried on a tentative basis while they are carefully evaluated.

EVALUATING SERVICE DELIVERY PATTERNS

This section provides IEP teams a rating scale and some advice in evaluating local regular and special classes and other special services and programs. Including students with mental retardation in regular classes has been a strong trend ever since the passage of P.L. 94–142 in 1975. Because inclusion programs are the prevailing trend, regular class placement is examined with particular care. In much of this section, I discuss and document the regular-special class controversy and describe general conditions that prevail across the United States. Acting within necessary fiscal, legal, and other

Evaluative Criteria	Setting or Program	
	Special Classes	Regular Classes
Curriculum Quality, Quantity of Instruction, and Individualization		
Specially designed curriculum		
Practical, life goal-oriented curriculum		
Controlled school and class atmosphere		
Tracking and evaluation—Life goal planning		
Tracking—Level-to-level (e.g., elem. to sec.)		
Appropriate physical facilities		
Greater academic gains		
Better academic role models		
More homogeneous grouping		
More individual attention		
Effect on classmates		
More years of education		
Age 22		
Dropout or graduate		
Shorter bus ride		
Potential for Transition and Independent Living Services		
Better role models – Transitional		
Greater practical academic gains		
More opportunity for transition programs		

FIGURE 5.1   Service Delivery Pattern Rating Scale

guidelines and restraints, a conscientious team that includes the parents is logically in the best position to discern the extent to which each condition applies locally.

It is very likely that both regular classes and special classes are necessary and will be available to IEP teams in most communities in the foreseeable future. Stainback and Stainback (1987) reviewed the literature, including pertinent court cases, and acknowledged that special classes and special schools will continue to operate for some time. Likewise, common sense and even a casual review of the literature show that inclusion programs will continue to use regular classes for students with mental retardation for a long time to come. Thus, the task for the IEP teams is to select the best placement—or best combination of placements—necessary to enable an individual with mental retardation to achieve as many of his or her high priority life goals as possible. Perhaps the most promising arrangement for accomplishing these goals for many, if not most, such

Evaluative Criteria	Setting or Program	
	Special Classes	Regular Classes
Specially designed vocational programs		
Preparation for independent living		
Availability of community-based education		
Sociological Considerations		
Attendance with neighborhood peers		
Better role models—Social		
Lasting friendships		
Better sociological adjustment		
Exposure to: Substance abuse		
Delinquency		
Dropout		
Unwanted pregnancy		
Concentration of Needed Professional Services		
Specially trained teachers		
Physical therapists		
School psychologists		
Speech and language specialists		
Assistance from paraprofessionals		
Assistance from nondisabled peers		
PARENT PREFERENCE ! ! ! !		

FIGURE 5.1   Continued

students is an inclusion (or cooperative) program in a regular school. This type of cooperative program has the potential to take advantage of the strengths of both the more restrictive and less restrictive arrangements.

Figure 5.1 is a sample rating scale an IEP team might use in evaluating the strengths and weaknesses of various locally available programs. It lists evaluative criteria that should be used to evaluate the community's educational placements. The major purpose of Figure 5.1 is to help the IEP team in deciding whether each criterion could best serve its student with mental retardation in the community's more or less restrictive educational settings. The rating scale assumes a wide array of service delivery patterns, some of which may not be available. The availability, as well as the suitability, of specific programs, however, must be evaluated locally.

Most items on the rating scale are self-explanatory, although a few are discussed in general terms. The IEP team rates each of the student's high-priority, long-term (IEP) goals with the appropriate evaluative criteria of Figure 5.1. Ratings are made as to the availability and quality of *local* facilities and services. Awareness and understanding of these conditions help the IEP team members in determining how they apply to each student. Each rating involves a judgment whether a given student's goal can best be achieved in a regular or special educational setting. Occasionally, a less inclusive setting is needed or favored because it offers the services of a particular teacher or specialist. Sometimes a more inclusive arrangement is thought best because it offers an outstanding feature or service not available elsewhere. It is usually easier to provide occupational and physical therapists and other specialists essential to a student's transitional needs in special facilities. An additional advantage is that special education classes are usually smaller. Although paraprofessionals, such as instructional assistants and peer tutors, are often used in special education classes, important instruction for a student with mental retardation is more likely to be provided or closely supervised by a qualified special teacher than adaptations that might be made for the student in a regular class. For a number of reasons, including these advantages, special schools and classes are likely to continue into the foreseeable future (Stainback & Stainback, 1992). Finally, the evaluative criteria of Figure 5.1 do not merit equal weight and must be appraised accordingly. Except in extreme circumstances, final team decisions must defer considerably to the preferences of the parents—often temporarily while team members continue to investigate and reevaluate the decision.

QUALITY OF CURRICULUM, INSTRUCTION, AND INDIVIDUALIZATION

Most criteria in the first segment of Figure 5.1 are discussed throughout the book. Some of its main features, however, refer to the general and specific benefits of regular and special classes and curricula. For example, special classes offer skills, concepts, and activities designed specially for students with mental retardation. These are difficult to provide or even adapt within regular class curriculum and often must be overlooked and compensated for with other benefits. Fletcher and Abood (1988) pointed out that the team must select regular class teachers whose subject matter has at least some relevance to the student's life goals. The teacher must also have the necessary skills, time, and willingness to help the student accomplish one or more of those goals. Simply having a student with mental retardation sit in a class that is beyond his or her comprehension is difficult to justify educationally. Carlson (1985) provided a reminder that independence is still the major goal for students with mental retardation.

Some high school programs offer work experience and other transitional services to all interested students; other programs do not. Students with mental retardation tend to have the same type of difficulty in these programs as they do in academic programs, though often to a lesser extent. Again, however, the team can evaluate such programs and provide much of the needed, additional assistance. Using the evaluative criteria of Figure 5.1 and a few related general considerations, the IEP team is in a position to make the best possible placement decision.

Attitude of the Regular Class Teacher

Equally important to selecting the regular classes for a student with mental retardation to attend is the attitude of the regular class teacher. Other school personnel, such as administrators and counselors, must also be well trained and oriented to the inclusion process (Edgar, 1992). Without a willing and capable regular class teacher, however, no such placement can be successful. At the elementary level, the team can usually choose from among two or more grade-level teachers. At the secondary level, the team must select from among those teachers whose expertise and subject matter are the most relevant to the student with mental retardation. The special education teacher and other team members must remember their duty to train regular class teachers and help them understand mental retardation in general and the needs and abilities of their student with mental retardation in particular (Lombard & Hazelkorn, 1993).

Many regular class teachers privately reveal their misgivings about having students with mental retardation in their classes. They express serious concerns about the long-term value of their course work for the student with mental retardation, as well as the impact the student has on the other students. Many are concerned about the student's obvious need for individual attention they are unable to provide. Some also express misgivings about why this student—who comes from classes where 6 to 10 students constitute a realistic teaching load for a specially trained teacher and one or more adult aides—is placed in their classes with no teaching load reduction. Many teachers—especially, but not exclusively, at the secondary level—express doubts about the sociological benefits that are simply presumed to accrue by having students with mental retardation audit their classes. Still others wonder why so many responsible professionals and parents seem to assume that placement in regular classes is naturally beneficial and appropriate and requires little if any evaluation. Wilczenski (1994) reported that the attitudes of student teachers toward inclusion became more positive during professional preparation but declined after student teaching. After selecting the best qualified teacher willing to participate, the team must pledge their best efforts to work with him or her and make the placement work.

Slow Learners

It is particularly important for the IEP team to evaluate the educational programs locally available to slow learners. *Slow learner* is loosely defined as a student who has trouble learning but does not have mental retardation and typically does not qualify for any special education services. Therefore, no IEPs are prepared for them. Members of this group are characterized by low IQs and poor academic performance and are unlikely to qualify for college entrance. Some districts specify an upper IQ limit (e.g., 80–85). The lower IQ limit also varies greatly from one geographical area to another, but it usually extends downward to the upper limit of mental retardation; that is, going up the IQ scale, the slow learner designation begins where mental retardation ends. This means that, in borderline cases, an IEP team or placement committee of significant others must determine whether the individual will be served in special education programs for students with mental retardation or in programs designed for slow learners. Further, the concept of regional variation serves as a reminder that huge numbers of students identified and served as having mental retardation in some states would not so qualify in other states and would, therefore, be identified and served in whatever programs are locally available to slow learners.

Slow learners may be identified by other designations, and some school districts have no particular category for them. Slow learner is an apt description of this group of students. For many reasons—known and unidentified—members of this group simply learn very slowly. They typically fall increasingly behind their peers—as do students with mental retardation—but to a lesser extent. This classification is particularly significant to the IEP team (or placement committee) at the secondary level because when a student with mental retardation is placed in regular classes, the placement is almost invariably in those programs that are locally designed for slow learners. One major task for the IEP team is to evaluate the track record of the educational programs designed to meet the needs of this group. Classes and programs that prove to be successful for slow learners may be at least considered for a student with mental retardation. Otherwise, they are open to serious challenge; that is, if the slow-learner programs are not meeting the needs of students with IQs as high as 80–85, they are questionable for students with IQs in the mental retardation range.

Historically, to be identified as having mental retardation, a student's cognitive or intellectual levels must be carefully assessed with IQ tests and other means. Beyond that, he or she ordinarily must fail repeatedly in regular classes before the identification can be made and a special class considered. Finally, the concept of regional variation indicates that virtually every state is identifying a progressively smaller percentage of their school children as having mental retardation. In practice, this means identifying primarily those school-age children whose mental retardation is most severe and obvious and whose abilities are subject to the greatest limitations. Whereas the reasons a slow learner performs poorly are largely unidentified, the low achievement of a student with mental retardation is carefully documented.

The Dropout Problem

The local dropout rate is probably the most important consideration of all for the placement committee or IEP team. Both the suitability and the availability of regular classes go for naught to the extent that they lack holding power. Lanier and Chesnut (1990) suggested that higher dropout rates for students with mental retardation are much more likely to occur in regular classes. The National Center for Educational Statistics (NCES) in 1988 estimated that the current dropout rate is about 25% for the nation as a whole, although the rates for most urban areas are much higher (e.g., 55% in Los Angeles). Moreover, the dropout rates usually cited are computed only on the secondary level and are based on the number of students still in high school on the cutoff date for the state financial aid head count—typically sometime in November. The dropout rate is usually calculated by dividing the number of "official" dropouts by the total number of potential graduates. The rate for a given school is never distributed uniformly through the student body. Assuming an overall rate of 25%, the rate for those with the highest academic standing would be much lower (Cuellar & Cuellar, 1991). Thus, if the rate for the top scholars is 5%, that of those at the lower end of the scale could be as high as 90% to 95%.

Although the dropout statistics are discouraging, in reality they tend to be low estimates, at best (Fine, 1991; Orfield & Ashkinaze, 1991). Many students drop out of school before they reach high school age and never enroll in high school at all. Other students not counted in the official dropout rates include those who enroll in high school but drop out before the officially designated average daily attendance (ADA) cutoff date. These dates vary from state to state but typically fall in October or November. Some states designate the sophomore year as the first in which students can be counted as dropouts. Often, students are not counted as dropouts if they obtain work permits, and many schools allow failing or dissatisfied students to officially withdraw from school, usually with the permission of the parents.

The dropout problem is a complex one with many causes and no simple solutions. A number of fairly recent studies, however, identify students with mental retardation as prime dropout candidates, especially in regular classes at the secondary level. Peng and Takai (1983), and Ekstrom, Goertz, Pollack, and Rock (1986) identified several predictors of dropouts, the most reliable of which are poor achievement and low grade point averages (GPAs)—in junior and senior high school. It is well known that students with low IQs are more likely than others to achieve on lower levels, to earn lower GPAs, and to drop out of school. Joekel (1986) reported that students with IQs below 90 are particularly vulnerable in this respect. He also disclosed that the graduating class of 1986 holds (or held at the time) a number of dubious records, which included the following:

More suicides than any other class in history
More unwanted pregnancies—about a million
    (Almost 5,000 abortions)
    (2 million teenage "parents")
More involvement with illicit drugs
More involvement with alcohol
More violence with other students
More violence against teachers
More reports of carrying weapons
More delinquency and violence of all other kinds

Perhaps this discussion of the dropout and other sociological problems can serve as a reminder that neither my purpose nor that of the IEP team is to criticize or second-guess others who make decisions and establish policies they deem necessary. The purpose is to evaluate that part of the local school program being considered as a placement for their student with mental retardation.

A PROPOSED EXERCISE

The following exercise is proposed to aid IEP team members in gaining a clearer perception of the task of evaluating the potential merits of *local* regular and special classes for particular students with mental retardation.

1. Consider the case of any school-age student with mental retardation.
2. Identify and list any specific skills and concepts the student will need to be successful in adult life. (You may want to consult Appendixes A through J.)
3. Eliminate any skills and concepts that are clearly or likely to be either too rudimentary or too advanced for the student.
4. Make a tentative decision whether the student with mental retardation is most likely to master each skill or concept in a typical regular or special class.
5. Consider each skill and concept with respect to the Service Delivery Pattern Rating Scale (Figure 5.1) and record the *available* regular or special class or program in which the student is likely to master each skill and concept.
6. Select the program or combination of programs that are most likely to result in optimum self-sufficiency, independent living, and overall success in adult life.

SUMMARY

In this chapter, I discussed the need for a well-trained IEP team to be in charge of the educational programs for students with mental retardation. I also discussed the probability that, in most communities, members of local IEP teams are likely to have weak backgrounds in mental retardation. Members of the team should train each other—sharing insights and expertise.

The training of instructional assistants, aides, volunteers, and peer tutors was also outlined. I also pointed out the advantages of having parents serve with their child's teacher.

I also outlined some of the problems IEP teams may have in identifying suitable services and placements for their student with mental retardation. A means of evaluating these services and programs was provided.

part

III

Diagnostic/Prescriptive/
Evaluative Teaching

CHAPTER 6

Diagnosis, Prescription, and Evaluation

Points to Study and Ponder

1. How do you define *diagnosis, prescription,* and *evaluation*?
2. How are diagnosis and prescription related to curriculum?
3. What is *age appropriateness,* and how does it apply to teaching students with mental retardation? Is age appropriateness any different for these students than for those without mental retardation?
4. What are *validity* and *reliability*? Why are these concepts particularly significant in curriculum planning for students with mental retardation?
5. What do *level* and *rate* have to do with *prescription*?
6. What are *basal* and *ceiling ages,* and what do they have to do with educational diagnosis and prescription?
7. What is *subjectivity*? Is subjective testing of any value in mental retardation?
8. What are the similarities and differences between *standardized* and *criterion-referenced* testing—particularly in mental retardation?
9. What are the advantages and disadvantages of standardized and criterion-referenced tests for students with mental retardation?
10. How can videotaping be used for diagnostic and prescriptive purposes? Is such videotaping essentially objective or subjective?
11. How can the age 25 projection aid in prioritizing the life goals of students with mental retardation?
12. What are *evaluation outcomes,* and how do they relate to ongoing diagnosis and prescription?
13. What is *compensation* in curriculum planning? Is it ever justified?
14. How can oral questioning be used in diagnosis and prescription?

Helping students with mental retardation achieve maximum success and independence in adult life can be accomplished through two primary procedures: individual life goal curriculum planning and diagnostic/prescriptive/evaluative (DPE) teaching. The planning procedure—which includes identifying, evaluating, and prioritizing the life goals that appear to be most significant for a student—has been described in previous chapters. Procedures for including annual and long-term life goals, as well as short-term objectives, in the curriculum for a student's IEP have been developed, and the roles and responsibilities of significant participants have been discussed. In this chapter, I introduce the second procedure, DPE, a methodology that helps one prioritize the life goals and examine the student's current status and progress toward achieving them. I also demonstrate how to compare the student's abilities and limitations with current achievement levels and how to determine the sequence in which the goals should be addressed. Strategies for reevaluating and adjusting the student's life goal projections are included as well.

IMPORTANCE OF A DPE APPROACH

Mental retardation imposes varied and severe limitations on the skills and concepts a student is able to master (Dever, 1990). Because of the nature and variety of limitations imposed by mental retardation and the wide range of skills and concepts to be taught to each student, an approach that adapts to the specific situation of each student and student family is necessary. DPE methods provide this important flexibility.

Student Needs

Generally, the student with mental retardation achieves only a fraction of the knowledge and skills developed by students without disabilities—or by those with other disabilities. Although the reality of limitation is consistent, individual limitations vary considerably. Teachers, parents, and other members of the IEP team must carefully assess the potential of each student, prioritize the skills and concepts they anticipate the student will be able to learn, and continually evaluate the student's progress, rearranging the priorities when abilities and disabilities become more apparent as the student moves through the program. On the one hand, those who plan curriculum must be careful not to oversimplify a student's wide array of serious learning deficiencies and attempt to teach academic and other formal concepts the student is unable to master or eventually use. On the other hand, they must avoid being intimidated by the student's predictable and persistent learning problems so that they restrict the student to learning activities appropriate for much younger children.

The DPE approach uses a form of curriculum-based assessment focused on the unique curriculum of an individual student with mental retardation. Yanok (1988) and Blankenship (1986) pointed out that the diagnostic/prescriptive approach is effective if it is performed on an individual basis; it has the potential to be particularly effective in special education (see also Collins & Cheek, 1984; Wixson, 1991). Diversity occurs among students with any disability, but particular diversity occurs among those with mental retardation. Teaching effectively requires a thorough knowledge of each student's current ability and performance levels. When the approach is used in conjunction with life goal curriculum planning on a highly individualized basis, DPE enables the student's IEP team to make decisions tailored to life goals, needs, abilities, limitations, and learning characteristics of each individual (Wesson, 1992). To design accurate IEPs and curriculum, assessments must be thorough yet not unduly time-consuming (Giek, 1992). In this chapter, I show how this is to be done.

Parental Involvement

Mental retardation forces an individual to depend on other people. For this reason, a well-organized, competent IEP team must take responsibility for planning such an individual's program and for providing necessary scaffolding and support. Administrators, counselors, therapists, and even teachers typically serve only a year or two on an individual's IEP team and leave the team as the student becomes older. Parents are usually the only members of the IEP team who serve throughout the student's school career. One important responsibility for the "professional" team participants is to assist the parents in understanding and carrying out their roles in planning, implementing, and facilitating their child's educational program.

Some parents choose to participate very little in their child's education, leaving the burden on other members of the team. Teachers and other team participants must continually solicit the parents' cooperation. Their participation is particularly critical in selecting the child's life goals and in monitoring the child's progress. Even if parents elect not to participate, they must be continually informed so that they are as well prepared as possible to assume the full responsibility for their child when he or she is no longer eligible for school.

THE PROCESS OF DIAGNOSTIC/PRESCRIPTIVE TEACHING

The terms *diagnosis* and *prescription* have been borrowed from the medical profession. During the past several decades, they have become part of the vernacular for those who work with any children with special needs (Kilpatrick, 1987). The application of the terms to children with mental retardation, however, is incomplete. A physician generally writes a prescription only when something is "wrong" with a person. The prescription is based on a diagnosis and specifies a remedy to make the person whole or well.

Applied to students with mental retardation, something (mental retardation) is wrong with the person, and the educational prescription identifies previously unmastered skills or concepts necessary to bring a student up to a desired level. It is based on a diagnosis of the student's level or lack of mastery in the designated area. Although many educational prescriptions are designed to return a student to grade-level achievement, typically the student with mental retardation is unable to progress to this extent. Thus, the diagnosis focuses on the person's weaknesses and strengths, and the prescription is designed to help the person do as well as possible. Once a tentative curriculum has been prescribed, the teacher, like a conscientious physician, constantly monitors the individual's condition, making necessary adjustments as the child progresses toward the ultimate goal of successful living.

Steps in DPE

DPE teaching, like development of the IEP, is an ongoing process, but the DPE process is usually much more detailed. The process can be applied for lesson planning in any degree of specificity—from general curriculum suggestions to minute-by-minute procedures. Four interrelated processes are involved: diagnosing, prescribing, teaching, and evaluating. The DPE diagnoses the student's abilities, recognizing achievement of some goals and designating realistic additional goals. The purpose of diagnosis is to generate an accurate, functional prescription by considering a student's weaknesses and strengths with respect to one or more high-priority life goals. Ordinarily, neither the weaknesses/strengths nor the suitability of the selected life goal will be initially apparent. The DPE collects and refines data on the student until a prescription emerges that is both precise and easy to evaluate. This teaching plan prioritizes the broadly stated skills and concepts; it identifies goals to be taught immediately, breaking them down into teachable segments and lesson plans. After the prescription is taught, the student's progress is evaluated, and new skills and concepts are added to the student's IEP. These phases are recursive and interactive; they must not be viewed as separate, although at times one aspect may be emphasized more than others. Teachers may need to teach the DPE procedure to other members of the IEP team, particularly parents, instructional assistants, peer tutors, and volunteers assigned to assist in the instructional process.

The DPE prescription must not be confused with the student's IEP as required by the IDEA. The DPE procedure is a means for accomplishing the goals of the IEP, one of many processes that will be involved in its implementation and accomplishment.

Phases of Diagnosis

Figure 6.1 is a diagram of the DPE process. For convenience in discussion, diagnosis is divided into four phases, but in reality there are no distinct dividing lines: The phases overlap and intermesh. The student's *educational frontier*—discussed below and in the next chapter—lies between diagnosis and prescription. The skills and concepts above the frontier have been shown by diagnostic assessment to have been mastered, and the skills and concepts below have not yet been achieved but have been determined to be within the student's present (and future) capacity.

FIGURE 6.1 The DPE Model

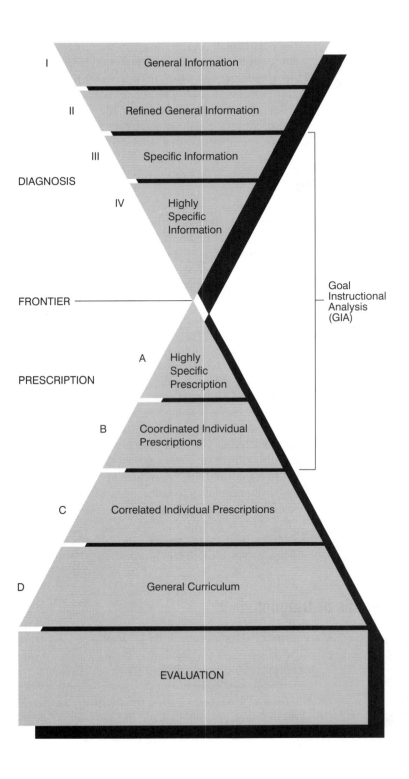

Diagnosis I: General Information

This phase includes relevant data already known, easily inferred, or readily obtained. Such information begins with personal and learning characteristics—strengths and weaknesses—that have been discerned during the IEP procedures. Because further refinement and validation follows, Diagnosis I may also include unverified information. Although the information gathered in Diagnosis I is usually too general to form the basis of educational programming, it is useful in becoming acquainted with the student and in gaining some sense of direction for further investigation and assessment.

Diagnosis II: Refined General Information

The second phase begins to evaluate, validate, and refine the information gathered in Diagnosis I. Norm-referenced tests may be used in identifying overall strong and weak areas. The student's specific needs and deficiencies may be pinpointed by administering the sections of tests that correspond to the general weaknesses; potentially compensating strengths are noted at this phase.

Diagnosis III: Specific Information

The emphasis in Diagnosis III shifts away from the deficiencies stressed in Diagnoses I and II and focuses on the student's strengths and ultimate potential. DPE considers the student's annual IEP goals and short-term objectives and then assesses the entry-level skills needed to master relevant specific skills and concepts. Teacher-made tests investigate areas of concern that have not been sufficiently represented in formal tests and earlier procedures. A checkpointing procedure called goal instructional analysis (GIA), described in detail in the next chapter, accurately locates the student's educational frontier, specifying both present performance level and assistance needed for the progress desired.

Diagnosis IV: Highly Specific Information

The final diagnostic phase uses the information that has been refined and validated in Diagnoses I to III to identify further procedures to assess the individual's knowledge, skill, and achievement in a targeted area. A highly specific teacher-made test, a GIA, or a demonstration of student performance is used to discern the individual's educational frontier so that the IEP team can select and prioritize the subskills, subconcepts, and subtasks for the student's educational prescription.

Sources of Diagnostic Information

Many sources of diagnostic information are commonly known and readily available to teachers. Cumulative or school record folders, parent and former teacher observations, and older IEPs should not be overlooked. Although most of these sources do produce subjective data, they can be adapted and refined.

Members of an IEP team are responsible for developing an educational program to prepare a student for life as an adult; obviously, they must have access to all pertinent information about that student. Although the requirements of IEPs should make the necessity self-evident, the notion still persists that some information about a student that may be shared with other school personnel must be withheld from teachers so that their treatment of a student will not be affected by knowledge of his or her background or disability. Except in rare instances, such a policy is unacceptable. In *Ferraro v. Board of Education* (221 N.Y. 2d 279, 1961), a school principal was sued and held to be negligent when he failed to warn other school personnel about a student's tendency for violent actions. That Ferraro was a substitute rather than a regular teacher did not alter the decision. This case also suggests that a teacher could be negligent for failure to warn other teachers or instructional assistants of such a problem student. All such information must be handled in a professional manner and not communicated to anyone not directly involved or responsible for the student. It is particularly important to deal carefully with information about the personal lives of students and their families. In addition to personal and interpersonal information, necessary cultural data should be provided by the parents.

From Prescription to Curriculum

Thus, an individual prescription for each student is formed. Often, prescriptions in different areas are combined: for example, prescriptions in communications, social skills, and family living frequently overlap and are compatible at many points. Sometimes individual prescriptions of two or more students are similar enough to be combined for teaching efficiency. Finally, on the basis of compatibility of prescriptions, a general curriculum is outlined for an entire group or class.

PARAMETERS OR DIMENSIONS OF DPE

As DPE procedures help in organizing curriculum planning and instruction, they practically ensure efficient use of both student and teacher time. Efficient planning and instruction are crucial in working with students with mental retardation: With their limited abilities, they continue to fall farther and farther behind their classmates. The prioritization and sequencing of life goals and the ongoing evaluation and adjustment prevent the teacher from wasting time with lessons and activities that will be ineffective or distracting. To promote efficiency, DPE is organized, maintained, and evaluated in terms of three dimensions: level, rate, and functionality.

Level

Level is the dimension most likely to be considered, as it is widely recognized in all areas of education. A major purpose for giving standardized tests is to determine the level at which instruction for a student should begin. Generally, three levels (frustration, achieved, and instructional) must be considered.

Frustration-level work is too difficult for the student. This level is discouraging for all students; for students with mental retardation, it can be devastating. Because these students progress slowly, skills and concepts that are only slightly too difficult can have a debilitating effect.

Achieved-level instruction may not produce negative effects that are readily apparent; however, in the long run it can be just as detrimental to the student. Teaching at the achieved level is inefficient but comfortable. A struggling student often seeks relief from the discomfort of performing difficult tasks. For example, a student with mental retardation tends to prefer arithmetic computation, rather than problem solving, and oral reading, rather than reading comprehension. Similarly, it can be more comfortable for a teacher to assign material the student has already mastered, thereby reducing the likelihood of motivational and behavioral difficulties. Administrators and supervisors are also comfortable with students at the achieved level because the classroom is orderly and the students appear to be learning—although they may be only busy. Students with mental retardation are less likely than others to complain of boredom. Even on previously mastered material, their performance will not excite their teachers into providing more difficult assignments.

Instructional level, which lies somewhere between a student's frustration and achieved levels, must be identified by teachers and parents. To progress, even a student with mental retardation must experience some of the discomfort and struggle involved with learning. Each individual must experience moderate educational challenges in the curriculum, challenges not so severe that the student becomes discouraged but sufficiently difficult that the student is not simply repeating material but is making steady progress toward the attainment of reasonable goals.

Rate

Unfortunately, a student with mental retardation cannot learn as rapidly as parents, teachers, and other IEP team members often hope and anticipate. Because the learning rate for the student with mental retardation will not exceed that established by the teacher or parent, setting an appropriate rate is as important as discerning an accurate level. Obviously, a prescription at the optimum level will not be effective if the instruction is presented at an incorrect rate. If a prescription begins at the correct level but moves too slowly, inefficient learning will inevitably result. But if the prescription moves too rapidly, the child is soon operating at frustration level.

Rate is usually assessed in terms of estimated time frames and dates projected by each prescription. In diagnosis, the IEP team considers the student's individual learning characteristics alongside the highest priority goals and objectives and then estimates the approximate time the student needs for sufficient mastery. A period must be designated to assess whether selected goals and objectives are attainable and to ensure that the sequence is appropriate. In the next chapter, I show how these projected time frames and dates are incorporated into the prescription and how they are used in ongoing evaluation.

Functionality

As each prescription begins at the proper level and continues at an appropriate rate, it must also be designed to ensure positive movement toward the student's optimum success in adult life. A prescription must link the skills and concepts being taught to one or more of the student's high-priority life goals. The progress does not need to be spectacular; indeed, for students with mental retardation, advancement is typically quite gradual. But progress should be ongoing and purposeful. Functionality is closely related to proactivity; that is, for a skill or concept to be functional or practical, the student must be able and motivated to recognize a problem in real life, set up the problem, and solve it by using the skill or concept without being shown how it applies or being assisted or prompted. Functionality also includes compensation (discussed later in this chapter). Briefly, functionality often requires the individual to recognize the point at which he or she lacks the ability to meet the challenge and to know how to and where to summon reliable help.

IEP team members must stress functional skills and concepts that promote transition from school to successful adult life. Functionality is also necessary in helping teachers avoid teaching splinter skills—skills or activities taught as separate entities that are not an integral part of the child's sequence of individual life goals. Maintaining appropriate level, rate, and functionality is a particular challenge when the student with mental retardation is in an inclusion situation, competing with age-mates who have different life goals and superior abilities. One potential advantage that the IEP team must identify and develop in inclusion programs, however, is having practical, life problems modeled by those classmates with superior abilities.

CONSIDERING AGE APPROPRIATENESS

One overriding principle of curriculum planning for students with mental retardation is **age appropriateness** (Hanline & Fox, 1993). Farley (1986) suggested that the interests of most individuals with mental retardation lie closer to their CA than their MA. Evans, Hodapp, and Zigler (1995), however, reported that the interests of students whose mental retardation was more severe generally tended to be more closely related to those of their MA peers. The extent to which this is true intensifies the problems of teaching a student with mental retardation—whose CA always exceeds his or her MA by a substantial margin. It also increases the need for individual diagnosis and curriculum planning and presents a particular challenge in inclusion programs. Brown et al. (1979) used the term *age appropriateness* in criticizing the practice of bottom-up curriculum planning for students with mental retardation. They acknowledged the difficult decision in abandoning activities appropriate to such a student's MA and stressing experiences based on the student's CA. They insisted, however, that the decision must be made—certainly by the approach of adolescence. They recommended an emphasis on self-help and other prerequisites to optimum independent living, recreational, and employment skills. Age appropriateness is a vital part of functionality. Both diagnostic

The age 25 projection helps the IEP team in determining the type and level of work the individual is likely to do in adult life.

and prescriptive procedures must emphasize skills and concepts suited to the future needs of the student. Because the IEP team should plan to teach whatever a diagnosis suggests, they should diagnose only in those areas in which we plan to teach. For example, diagnosing preprimer reading is not appropriate for a teenager with mental retardation—even though the student may be functioning at that level. Age appropriateness presents a particular problem for students whose mental retardation is severe/profound. Gardner, Taber-Brown, and Wissick (1992) pointed out that it is extremely difficult to find learning materials appropriate for teenagers with MAs of 6 years or less. These teens do not enjoy being treated as little children and should not be treated as such. The challenge is to locate or develop diagnostic and prescriptive materials with low language and cognitive levels but with themes appropriate to and pictures of older boys and girls as well as adults.

AGE 25 PROJECTION IN DPE

The age 25 projection, introduced in Chapter 3, is based on level, rate, and functionality, the parameters of DPE. The age 25 projection reminds the IEP team of the number of probable years the student has left in school and the proportion of the student's goals that must be accomplished during each of the remaining years. The age 25 projection can also help the IEP team in selecting skills and concepts age appropriate to students with mental retardation.

Prioritizing Life Goals

The age 25 projection enables the IEP team to prioritize a student's life goals into a workable, individualized curriculum. Except in very rare instances, the life goals of an individual with mental retardation must be achieved during the school experience. Such individuals rarely qualify for post-high school education, but even if they were to participate in such programs, it is unlikely the program would continue to develop the goals outlined in the school IEP. Parents who have remained active in their child's practical education may choose to continue working on some of the IEP life goals; this continuation is a major purpose of training and incorporating parents throughout the school years. But from a practical perspective, the school's financial and other participation is effectively over on the child's graduation.

The IEP team chooses and prioritizes the student's life goals and objectives and organizes the sequence in which they will be presented to the student (Lim & Browder, 1994). Highest priorities are assigned the achievable life goals necessary for the student to become as independent as possible in adult life. Through careful diagnosis and prescription of the individual needs and abilities of the student, the team arranges the skills and concepts in the sequence necessary to meet those goals and objectives (Browder, 1991). Evaluation procedures show how well the overall program is working and reveal places where alterations are needed to meet projected goals by the student's graduation date. Evaluation procedures are also designed to show the effectiveness of level-to-level program planning.

Assessing Learning Characteristics

DPE teaching is based on the assumption that every student, despite varying degrees of mental retardation, has some potential to progress in the areas a competent IEP team has included in his or her educational program. Mental retardation, however, makes grade-level achievement impossible. The team must engage in ongoing evaluation of the student's learning characteristics and design that student's educational program within his or her individual limitations. Because of time limitations and the importance of prioritization, team members must recognize that the ability of a student to achieve a goal is not sufficient reason to include that goal in the student's IEP. Figure 6.2 provides a way to visualize the student's ability on any specific characteristic.

Figure 6.2 shows how the age 25 projection can be used to estimate an individual's status on a particular learning characteristic. To assess that status on any increment of learning, the area is considered a tentative part of the student's overall age 25 projection. The broken line in Figure 6.2 represents the ability relevant to a particular learning characteristic the student is not likely to attain while he or she is in school. Therefore, that student's program must be designed to increase his or her ability in that area of deficiency to help the student achieve his or her life goals within those limitations. In this manner, the student should become a more efficient learner over time even

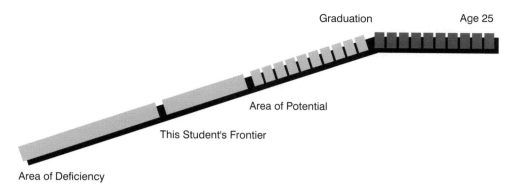

FIGURE 6.2   Age 25 Projection and a Student's Individual Learning Characteristics

though progress may be slow. Figure 6.2 involves no preset or standard increments to measure progress; thus, plotting or estimating performance level is left entirely to the teacher's judgment.

A specific area of deficiency that often prevents a student with mental retardation from becoming an efficient learner is the ability to deal with concrete objects/abstract ideas. Figure 6.3 is an example of a way to visualize a student's needs in this area and to plan a prescription accordingly. From Figure 6.3, one can infer that this student's concrete-abstract abilities might be improved somewhat in the time remaining but that the student's educational program cannot be delayed until substantial improvements are made. This student's other prescriptions must be planned and conducted so that the student makes optimum achievement despite limitations of potential in concrete/abstract ability.

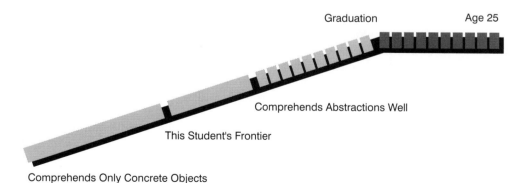

FIGURE 6.3   Age 25 Projection and Concrete/Abstract Ability

STATISTICAL CONCEPTS RELEVANT TO DPE

To effectively teach students with mental retardation, teachers must design and direct a variety of diagnostic procedures. The following statistical and testing concepts are significant in the DPE process.

Basal Age

Basal age refers to the level at which diagnosis or assessment should begin for a specific student. The purpose of determining basal age is to avoid administering items that are so easy that they provide no challenge for the individual. When items on a standardized test are arranged in order of increasing difficulty, the person administering the test can estimate the point to begin testing in terms of previous observations of the student. When the student fails his or her first test item, the administrator tests the preceding item. If the student responds correctly, the preceding item is administered and then the next until a specified number of consecutive correct answers has been reached. The student receives credit for all items below the basal age—even for items not administered.

Ceiling Age

Ceiling age is the diagnostic level at which the student is no longer successful—usually determined by a specified number or percentage of missed consecutive items. The student receives no credit for any correct items above his or her ceiling age.

Effective Test Range and Instructional Level

In a testing situation, *effective test range* refers to test items between the student's basal and ceiling ages. These are the items a given individual has a reasonable chance of completing correctly. They are neither so easy that they present no challenge nor so difficult that their challenge is too great. As a result, these items produce the most valuable information about a student, and results will be different for each individual. In prescription or instruction, the student's effective test range becomes his or her instructional level.

Basal and ceiling ages are particularly significant in administering DPE procedures. Testing or teaching items the student has already mastered or items that are too difficult for the individual wastes time. In the next chapter, I discuss *educational frontier*, a concept that marks the point at which diagnosis ends and prescription begins. A student's educational frontier lies somewhere between his or her basal and ceiling ages on a specified goal or objective.

Subjectivity and Objectivity

Subjectivity involves the influence of emotions or personal prejudices. For a subjective testing measure, the rating or score depends on the opinions of the rater. In contrast, an objective testing measure produces data largely or completely independent of rater opinion, preference, or emotion. On the surface, it is easy to assume that objectivity is good and that subjectivity is bad. Popularly, the phrase "not being objective" is used to indicate that a decision or judgment is not fair or does not adequately consider the views of others. From this perspective, subjective testing measures are assumed by some to be untrustworthy and inherently inferior to objective measures.

Beyond the classroom, however, most evaluations of personal performance are subjective, particularly where people with mental retardation are concerned. Job performance, independent living, ability to get along with others, self-help, dressing and grooming, honesty, and most other requirements for successful adult life are all judged in highly subjective ways—and so are their prerequisite skills and concepts. Therefore, teachers of students with mental retardation must be prepared to deal extensively with subjective diagnostic and evaluation procedures. Certainly, some true-false, multiple choice, and matching test items might be used in DPE analysis, particularly if such items are read to younger students and to students whose mental retardation is severe/profound. Yet, these items are most effective in providing factual data and are generally most useful when administered in conjunction with subjective procedures that allow the student to actually demonstrate skills and concepts that have been mastered.

Validity

The *validity* of a test refers to the degree to which the test really measures what it purports to measure. Teachers of students with mental retardation must personally design and administer many, if not most, tests used for diagnosing and assessing their students. Therefore, they are responsible for the validity of those tests that they design. They must consider conditions and elements that might interfere with the validity of their testing and teaching procedures. For example, if a reading achievement test includes arithmetic concepts, one might question whether reading ability is really the major factor influencing the results of a comprehension measure. Similarly, if the problems of an arithmetic achievement test are written at a reading level higher than that of most of the population being tested, the instrument would be considered of questionable validity for an arithmetic test because students' reading skills would influence test outcomes as much or more than arithmetic ability.

For a number of reasons, the validity of standardized tests is questionable in assessing the ability and achievement levels of students with mental retardation. Waterman (1994) pointed out that the value of such test results diminishes, depending on the extent to which the child is unlike the norm group. One reason most popular educational tests are not valid for assessing the performance of students with mental retardation is that they were not represented on the original normative samples for those instruments. Further, these tests tend to be highly academic and do not measure well the functional life goals of students with mental retardation. Also, the advanced reading and language levels of the tests almost always make them unsuitable (although by law, tests used to determine placement must be individually administered). The language level can impair the performance of a student with mental retardation even when the test is individually administered. Salvia and Ysseldyke (1991) pointed out that standardized tests are not only questionable for use with students with mental retardation but also deficient in testing members of minority groups. Thus, students with mental retardation—or those being tested to identify mental retardation—are doubly disadvantaged.

When subjective assessment is being performed, external factors may influence testing validity. A student's personal appearance, for example, is often a major influence in the way he or she is rated. For example, two students with mental retardation in a secondary science class may have identical abilities and achievement levels; one has Down syndrome, and the other's mental retardation is unidentified. Neither student completes any of the assignments, projects, or examinations required for class credit, but the student whose appearance reflects mental retardation is likely to be judged as not performing because he or she is not capable; the student whose appearance does not show a disability may easily be judged as not performing because of a poor attitude—or a myriad of other reasons. Other attributes that have been found to influence evaluations include gender, willingness to cooperate, supportiveness of parents, general patterns of behavior, past performance, and minority status. Leinbach and Fagot (1991), Elovitz and Salvia (1982), and Ross and Salvia (1975) found personal attractiveness to be a significant, distracting element in diagnosing the achievement levels of students with mental retardation.

Fuchs, Fuchs, Dailey, and Power (1985) reported that an examiner's professional experience and personal familiarity with the student may also have a significant effect on ratings of the student's abilities. Thus, a teacher might apply the criterion-related validity concept by periodically asking a colleague to observe and assist in evaluating a student. Such validation is important because continuous exposure to the same group of students with mental retardation may cause a teacher to overestimate or underestimate the progress of the students.

Reliability

The *reliability* of a test refers to its consistency over time. Theoretically, successive administrations of a reliable test yield similar results—or increasing scores if learning is taking place. But in practice, reliability is difficult to establish with precision. Elements other than learning, such as practice effect, tend to increase scores on the same or similar tests. Also, scores on successive administrations of a test may either increase or decrease with changes in testing conditions, excessive assistance, or improper scoring or evaluation. Forgetting or disuse of skills is the major cause of decrease in test scores over time. These factors must be considered in assessing the reliability of any evaluation. Both reliability and validity can be improved by having a colleague participate in a student's evaluation.

Gronlund (1990) suggested that reliability is a condition or subdivision of validity. He contended that a test cannot provide valid information if it is wholly unreliable. There are advantages, however, in considering the concepts of validity and reliability separately. Although these two terms are related, a test could conceivably be reliable but not valid because it could meet all the reliability criteria and still not measure what it purports to measure. In other words, a test could possibly be consistently—even accurately—measuring other than what was intended. As an extreme example, at the conclusion of an arithmetic unit, a teacher might decide to measure the students' achievement by having them run the 50-meter dash. Retesting would undoubtedly show the test to be highly reliable because the students' scores would be nearly identical on a number of successive days. The test would be obviously invalid, however, because a child's ability to run bears little or no relationship to his or her achievement in math.

USE OF STANDARDIZED TESTS

Simply defined, a *standardized* (or *norm-referenced*) *test* is one that yields a standard score: a score such as a percentile or a grade level that compares a student's score with that of others taking the same test. A test is standardized or "normed" when it is administered to a large number of subjects and the results are tabulated, usually by subjects' ages and scores. The result is a series of tables that indicate comparative or standard scores.

Potential Weaknesses of Standardized Tests

The use of standardized tests in evaluating the performance of students with mental retardation has a number of significant strengths and weaknesses; a full discussion of these factors is beyond the scope of this book. Because standardized testing is so widespread, however, some of the most basic strengths and weaknesses are reviewed. Individually administered tests are generally more accurate than group tests. But because neither variety included students with mental retardation in their normative samples, their validity for use with these students is questionable. The weaknesses are relative, and a given weakness may be partly overcome in many instances and with some students.

Lack of precision is perhaps the greatest limitation in using standardized tests with students with mental retardation. Because a test covering a general area may be extensive, the conceptual distance between items on a specific topic has to be great; otherwise, the test would not be useful for students with normal or gifted IQs. And any test measures less accurately at both its high and low extremes (Spitz, 1981; Waterman, 1994).

Because students with mental retardation function so far below age level, it is difficult to find a test that is not invalidated by the age-grade discrepancy. For example, if a teenager with mental retardation reads at a second-grade level, neither the ninth- nor the second-grade level of a test is appropriate. Besides being too difficult and thus frustrating for the student, the ninth-grade test may inaccurately assess the student's ability at fourth or fifth grade because its tables do not extend lower than that level. With some secondary-level achievement tests, a subject may score at the fourth- or fifth-grade level by simply handing in an empty paper.

With increasing numbers of students with mental retardation being educated in regular classes, teachers and others should be aware of the possible effects of guessing on standardized tests. Because of regional variation (Chapter 1), a student may be many times more likely to be identified as having mental retardation in one state than in another. Whether a student's mental retardation is recognized or not, he or she is increasingly likely to take standardized tests. The guess factor may cause significant variations in test results, particularly in a group testing situation. Guessing may either inflate or deflate a standardized test score for any student. Earlier, the seeming reluctance of students with mental retardation to take risks was discussed. Because of this reluctance, one might assume that such students would hesitate to guess on a test, but Gronlund (1990) pointed out that the instructions for some tests encourage guessing. In other instances (e.g., when asked by other testwise students), some test administrators also encourage students to guess. For students with mental retardation, the problem takes on an added dimension because the items for which they actually know or can figure out correct answers will be within the lower extremes of any test. Thus, students with mental retardation have an opportunity to guess at a greater number of items than others do, and correct guesses may account for a larger percentage of their score. On a test in a multiple-choice format, a student with mental retardation can get every fourth or fifth item correct by chance alone—even if the items are considerably beyond the student's effective test range. Such a student will obviously receive a much higher score than a student who recognizes his or her limitations and stops answering at the point at which items become too difficult. The situation in which guessing offers a student with mental retardation a possibility of a greatly inflated test score, coupled with the question of whether or not he or she does guess, poses serious questions about that test's reliability and validity for that student.

Potential Strengths of Standardized Tests

Despite many potential weaknesses, use of standardized tests for students with mental retardation has a number of potential strengths.

- They reveal largely raw, unrefined (Diagnosis II and Diagnosis III) data that can be used to determine whether particular subject matter is age appropriate and otherwise suitable for the student.
- They are often routinely administered and may be readily available.
- They may provide useful comparisons with peers even though a student's achievement levels may be greatly inflated or depressed. The results of such tests may help in documenting the futility of teaching skills and concepts that lack age appropriateness or other functionality.
- They are usually comprehensive and may suggest areas that could be easily overlooked.
- The test items are almost always sequenced in order of increasing difficulty, an organization that helps the teacher or parent in arranging materials.

- Standardized tests may serve as models to incorporate validity and reliability into other evaluative procedures. Although these tests may not be highly reliable or valid, the standardization process should increase both the reliability and validity.
- Learning to administer standardized tests can help teachers and other IEP team members in learning to administer other testing materials.

Adaptation of Standardized Tests

Adaptations may be necessary to make optimal use of standardized tests. A test may be imprecise, but its data can be refined and validated to formulate accurate and appropriate prescriptions. Selected parts may be given if not all areas measured by the test are needed for placement or other purposes. A teacher may read the test to a student with mental retardation and use teacher-made materials to investigate conceptual gaps.

USE OF CRITERION-REFERENCED TESTS

A *criterion-referenced test* typically focuses on subject matter or content, rather than on comparisons among groups of people (Anastasi, 1988; Salvia & Ysseldyke, 1991). Such tests are designed to measure a student's aptitude or achievement on a wide variety of skills, concepts, and topics. Examples include how to identify and deal with adverse behavior, how to remediate specific speech problems, and how to diagnose and teach survival and life skills. These tests are not standardized and thus yield no normative data, although some intersubject comparisons are possible. Teacher-made tests are examples of criterion-referenced tests, but not all criterion-referenced tests are teacher-made. Criterion-referenced tests are increasingly available on computer programs.

Teacher-Made Tests

Most teachers of students with mental retardation find that they need to design or personally adapt much, if not most, of their own diagnostic and evaluative materials. A teacher ordinarily uses a combination of standardized or norm-referenced tests and teacher-made tests.

The advantages of using teacher-made tests should not be overlooked when planning diagnostic procedures for a student with mental retardation. Teacher-made tests are generally the most precise way of assessing a student. They are versatile because they can be either written or oral and can be designed or adapted to be given to students individually or in a group. This type of test may also be used with nonverbal students who can successfully point to a picture on cue if unable to identify or describe it. Teacher-made tests can be created anytime they are needed in a student's program. Because they are personally designed, a teacher can be sure they are thorough but do not require an excessive amount of time.

The following advantages should be considered as the use of teacher-made testing is being planned.

* Teacher-made tests are highly individualized.
* They provide many insights about the attitudes and personalities of the students that go beyond their actual performance.
* They are usually more appropriate than other forms of testing in terms of learning rate and achievement level.
* In most cases, no other tests are available that measure the life goal skills and concepts that are vitally needed.
* Teacher-made tests can be designed to measure proactivity, which no other type of test can measure effectively.
* They can be designed to measure self-help, independent living, vocational, and transitional skills on an individual basis.
* They are less expensive than most other forms of testing.
* They do not have to be in a written format, so they can be especially designed or adapted for use with nonverbal students.
* They can be made age appropriate—a critical advantage with older students with mental retardation; these students read and achieve considerably below their CAs.
* They can be designed or adapted to meet multicultural needs.
* A given test can be adjusted quickly to meet the needs of students with varying levels of maturity and sophistication.
* A given test can be easily adjusted if an earlier test failed to include the student's effective test range.

Every classroom activity should be a learning experience, and tests should be designed with the needs of the specific student(s) in mind. The range of difficulty between the easiest and most difficult items on a teacher-made test should be sufficiently broad to locate the student's basal, ceiling, and effective test range. Further, these tests should include many items in the student's effective test range so that they can be used to expand, refine, and validate the results of earlier tests. Placing a few quite challenging items or activities on a test can initiate discussion and encourage a student to study harder, but too many difficult items can result in frustration for the student. A few already-mastered items should also be included to encourage review or discussion and to build a student's self-confidence before he or she attempts the more challenging parts of the test. But including many items or activities that are below a student's current ability level can be a waste of time.

Videotaping

Probably the most effective and practical means of diagnosing the abilities and performance of students with mental retardation is videotaping. This procedure is exciting for the student, as well as informative for the teacher. Even though diagnosis by videotape is subjective, it can be extremely precise. Viewing a tape of a student's performance can reveal small increments of learning that cannot be measured or demonstrated in any other way, increments that may not be noticed in the complexity of the daily classroom situation. The videotape can also reveal an unrecognized inability to progress in an area. An observer with a student day after day may think the student is making progress when the observer is really making accommodation for the student's needs and weaknesses.

It is important to make tapes that are satisfactory without editing; the editing process takes considerable time and additional resources. Merely viewing the activities takes the same amount of time that it took to tape them.

The most effective diagnostic procedure seems to be to tape a student often and in short segments separated by approximately equal time intervals, an adaptation of the principle of time-lapse photography. One or two sequences of 10 to 20 seconds taken every week or during alternate weeks is usually sufficient. The student should already be performing the target behavior when the taping begins. Irrelevant activities taped at the end of the short session can be erased or taped over, but when off-target actions are taped at the beginning, the tapes must be redone or edited. If the video camera and other equipment are in place well before the scheduled taping, the students can become accustomed to its presence and will be more at ease. If this is not possible, however, the students will adjust with a little experience and will not perform differently or object to being on camera.

The tapes can be played back to the students to show them where they have improved and where more improvement is desired. Usually, it is necessary to use a different tape for each student to preserve confidentiality.

Care must be taken to avoid violating laws or school regulations or invading a student's or family's privacy. Videotapes are excellent documentation for parent and IEP team meetings, but the members of a given team should not view the performance of any other student. Teams and students will vary, and comparisons should not be made. Also, because the individual tapings are intended to record a student's weaknesses and strengths, they may include aberrant or otherwise sensitive behavior. Because errors and technicalities can easily occur, it is wise to have parental release forms that cover all eventualities, including a situation in which a student is inadvertently included on another student's film. Tapes of an entire class engaged in a field trip or other class activity can usually be used for instructional purposes, but legal and ethical questions may be raised, depending on the audience to whom the tapes are to be shown; care must be taken to assess each individual situation.

Demonstration or Performance Tests

Although often overlooked, one of the most valuable methods of testing is to have the student demonstrate mastery of a skill or concept in a practical setting. Although evaluating a demonstration is quite subjective, the demonstration test does represent the ultimate test of many achievements and skills. A student may be able to pass extensive written or oral examinations about a task but be unable to perform the task itself. This is often the only type of testing procedure possible for students whose mental retardation is severe/profound.

A demonstration procedure may be either incidental or contrived. An *incidental demonstration* occurs as the student's performance is observed in one area as he or she is being tested or taught in another. For example, an individual first learns to carry out cleanup procedures under supervision, and then later a parent or teacher observes the student's cleanup performance at the conclusion of an activity: the later observation could be considered an incidental performance test. A *contrived demonstration* is deliberately set up as a demonstration. In such a performance assessment, an employer who has already agreed to accept a student on a work experience placement may conduct an interview with the student to provide the student an opportunity to demonstrate interview skills. The student may or may not know that acceptance has already occurred.

A sequence of demonstrations may be necessary to test some skill areas. For example, all safety procedures (e.g., safely crossing a street) must be mastered at the 100% level. Demonstration assessment works equally well in classroom or community-based settings. The procedure can be taped if desired.

Written Tests

Most students with mental retardation do not mind taking tests in areas in which they are capable unless the test items are too difficult. A teacher should experiment with the individual students to determine what kinds of adjustments need to be made. If a student reads poorly but the test items are not otherwise too difficult, the test may be read to the student. The items of written tests can often be incorporated into later discussion: for example, "many people find jobs through friends and relatives" or "most people keep their money in banks" could be worked into a discussion if questions about finding jobs or saving money were missed on a written test.

True-false items have many advantages over other types of objective items that can be included on a written test for students with mental retardation. A true-false item can be short and clear. One question can focus on a variety of points one at a time so that the student can deal with them separately. A teacher does need to be aware that some students with mental retardation will mark all or most items either true or false regardless of the content. The research of Sigelman et al. (1981) found a predictable preference for yes responses to questionnaire items. A teacher should know the students well enough to detect this kind of inclination.

Multiple-choice tests are usually difficult for students with mental retardation; however, multiple-choice items can be used in some circumstances if they are clear and concise. These items are relatively difficult to prepare but easy to score. Incorrect choices should appear plausible to the student so that correct answers are not obvious. It is not uncommon for a multiple-choice item to contain only one or two really plausible responses, thereby increasing to 50% the student's chances of guessing correctly. Multiple-choice items, like other written test questions, may be used to encourage discussion afterward and to help students in discerning the finer points of vital issues or procedures. For example, a discussion might easily grow from a multiple-choice question asking students to identify the conditions under which it is safe, honest, or otherwise permissible to take a certain action.

Essay testing is improbable for most students with mental retardation but may be appropriate for some older, more mature students in some circumstances. Those capable of written responses should be taught to write their ideas and encouraged to do so. Short answer essay questions can be used to test a student's recall of the information in a story or an instructional session. The short essay item ordinarily requires a higher degree of recall than multiple-choice or true-false items. In contrast to multiple-choice and true-false items, essay examinations are usually constructed quickly and easily, but they are more difficult and time-consuming to score than most other types of tests. Ironically, although they leave more room for student individuality, they may in some cases be even more objective than right-wrong response questions. However, they often have low reliability and validity.

The *cloze procedure* is a fill-in-the-blank type of short answer essay test that employs a verbatim or paraphrased statement from a story or instructional segment. In the statement, the teacher replaces every Nth word with a blank to be completed by the student. The tests may be more effective if the teacher selects key words to be replaced with blanks, rather than places the blanks regularly according to a specified formula.

QUESTIONS TO ASK WHEN DIAGNOSING A STUDENT AND WRITING A PRESCRIPTION

The following questions might be helpful in designing a diagnosis for a student with mental retardation:

* Is the goal to be diagnosed one of highest priority?
* Will mastery of the goal by the student contribute substantially to a high-priority long-term goal?
* Does the student appear to have the abilities necessary to master the goal sufficiently? general learning ability? memory? physical maturity?
* Is the student likely to master the goal sufficiently before leaving school?
* Can this goal be taught at a rate and level appropriate for the student?
* Is the student likely to be able to master the goal sufficiently to use it in daily living and other transitional skills?
* Can the goal be adequately taught in the designated setting and by those available to teach it?
* Did the student participate optimally in selecting the goal?
* Can the anticipated prescription for this goal be combined with other prescriptions for this student? with prescriptions of other students?

PRESCRIPTION MODEL

After the diagnosis has been completed, the prescription should follow logically. In general, the more specific the diagnosis, the more obvious and specific the prescription will be. A teacher need not be unduly concerned about the precision of the prescription at this point because there is ample opportunity to make adjustments once teaching begins. Every phase of the prescriptive process is somewhat tentative. This helps ensure continual reevaluation and increased precision. All phases of prescription involve some evaluation. It is essential to be alert at every point for clues to how well the prescription fits the learning style, level, and rate of the individual for whom it was designed.

Figure 6.4 is a model for the prescriptive portion of the DPE teaching approach. For discussion, the model is divided into four phases: Prescriptions A through D. Like the four aspects of diagnosis, the procedures have general guidelines, rather than distinct or mutually exclusive stages.

Prescription A: Highly Specific Prescription

Prescription A includes a single prescription in one specific part of one area of learning for one specific learner. When instruction begins, however, other students undoubtedly will be present. In the actual teaching, it is usually inefficient and unnecessary to teach each prescription on a one-to-one basis.

Prescription B: Coordinated Individual Prescriptions

In Prescription B, all prescriptions for an individual in two or more subjects and areas of learning are combined. Eventually, all of the individual's prescriptions will be included in this total, well-articulated learning/teaching package. For example, a prescription that teaches personal decision making can be combined with one involving independent living arrangements; gradually, other transitional goals can be added as well. Some of these goals or tasks might have been diagnosed formally; others may have been identified quite incidentally while other prescriptions were being taught. Each individual may be working on one or more prescriptions in arithmetic, one or more in language and communication, social skills, vocational skills, and so on, but as the teacher gains experience, it is not imperative that each prescription be committed to writing. Because all prescriptions involve some communication, memory, instruction following, eye-hand coordination, and small or large muscle motor activity, more and more can be brought into the unified plan. It is important to remember that all instruction must be given at the student's communication level, which though diagnosed separately, has become an integral part of each prescription or prescription unit.

In the next chapter, I discuss goal instruction analysis (GIA), a valuable tool in the DPE teaching procedure that helps in showing the relationship between diagnostic and prescriptive processes. Whether a GIA is to be written or the GIA process is merely considered, it is initiated at this point.

Prescription C: Correlated Individual Prescriptions

The DPE procedure offers students the advantages of highly individualized educational prescriptions but does not necessarily require one-on-one instruction. Highly

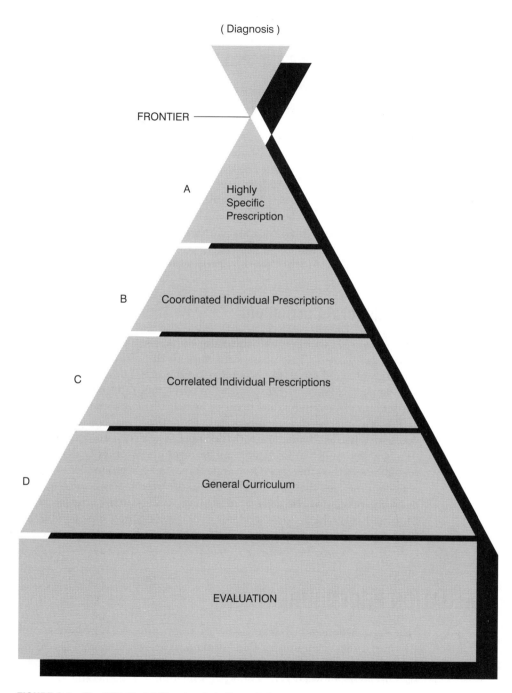

FIGURE 6.4   The DPE Model Showing Only Prescription

173

specific skills and concepts can be taught on an individual basis if doing so is feasible. The Prescription C phase, however, increases teaching efficiency by combining and correlating individual prescriptions for two or more students, so the students can be taught as a group.

As the teacher becomes increasingly familiar with the needs and abilities of each student, the students can be organized into small groups consisting of several students working on similar tasks or levels. The essential consideration is that the teacher recognizes each student's learning levels and rates and needs so that students will not be unduly pressured or bored by being assigned to an inappropriate group.

Another way to approach Prescription C is to provide a common activity in which several students can participate even though each may be achieving on a different level. For example, the teacher can diagnose, prescribe, and teach listening comprehension by reading a short passage or story to a small group of students, pausing periodically, and asking questions about the story. Having acquired a general idea of the abilities of each individual, the teacher varies the questions asked of each student according to that student's own comprehension level.

Prescription D: General Curriculum

Prescription D combines and correlates the individual prescriptions for all students in a class in all areas. This phase considers all the subject matter, skills, concepts, and activities planned for all class members at the time of diagnosis and in the near future. The major challenge of Prescription D is relating the learning activities and the total curriculum of each individual to his or her life goals as well as possible.

Prescriptions for class members can be correlated and combined even though the students may be functioning on varied competence levels. For example, a field trip to the produce section of a grocery store might meet prescriptions for each student in a group, though not in the same way. One student may only begin to identify the produce in very general terms. Another may be able to add descriptive terms, such as number, size, color, or utility; others may be capable of naming produce items or even classifying them into fruits and vegetables. Some students in the same group may be able to identify dishes that might include a particular vegetable—or possibly even name its nutritional benefits.

EVALUATION PROCEDURES

In a sense, when an IEP team achieves Prescription D, they have completed the tentative curriculum planning for their student. However, the team is responsible for future alterations to that student's total curriculum; in practice, curriculum planning is simply part of the ongoing DPE procedure. Evaluation is also ongoing, but periodically a more definite or formal evaluation is conducted by the student's teacher or other members of the IEP team.

As an integral part of the DPE procedure, evaluation is closely related to diagnosis. Diagnosis, however, focuses primarily on the student, whereas evaluation centers on the prescription. Evaluation concentrates on the appropriateness of a student's prescriptions in terms of level, rate, and proactivity or direction. This close relationship means that many diagnostic techniques and procedures are also used in evaluation because the student's performance is assessed at both phases. Evaluation techniques include videotaping, performance demonstrations, and traditional testing, all procedures that are part of the diagnosis as well. Validity and reliability in both diagnosis and evaluation can be improved by enlisting the aid of a third party, such as a colleague. A number of other techniques are used primarily in evaluation.

Evaluation and Age 25 Projection

The age 25 projection, discussed earlier in this chapter, provides the basis on which curriculum decisions are made and prescriptions are formulated. The prescriptions for each student are selected from that student's life goals as prioritized in diagnosis. The prioritized life goals are held somewhat in abeyance during Diagnoses I to III, in which the teacher compares those goals to the student's ability levels and rate of learning to determine the emphasis each goal should receive. All goals that pass this screening are included in the student's program. The age 25 projection helps in prioritizing the goals to be prescribed by suggesting how each goal is likely to contribute to the student's success in adult life.

The projection also displays the number of years the student is likely to remain in school and the percentage of that student's goals that must be accomplished during each remaining school year. Consideration of the number of school years remaining for a student requires participation by a number of teachers and other members of the IEP team. Evaluation must consider how well level-to-level program planning (discussed in Chapter 3) is working. Without adequate level-to-level program planning, most prescriptions—no matter how effective—are likely to have few long-lasting benefits to the student with mental retardation.

Evaluation and Projected Achievement Dates

During evaluation, the IEP team compares the projected goals with the student's actual performance and suggests any necessary alterations to the program. The best way to anticipate alterations is to predict the date by which the student can be expected to arrive at a specified point in his or her progression toward a desired goal. The precision of this technique is dependent on the precision of the prescription. If the student's prescription is stated in general terms, the evaluation can suggest only a general expectation. GIA, described in the next chapter, introduces a method to describe the prescription with great precision so that corresponding improvements can be made in the evaluation of the prescription.

Self-Evaluation

Because students with mental retardation are necessarily dependent on others for so many aspects of their lives, it is easy to overlook the fact that teaching them to be as independent as possible is one of the highest priority goals in their education. Although many of them will be able to do little in self-evaluating their educational progress, whenever feasible their participation must be sought. Teachers should train their students in as many evaluation procedures as the students are capable of carrying through. In fact, the IDEA requires that students participate in evaluation wherever appropriate.

Chapter 8 presents an outline of a program designed to help students with mental retardation learn how to make their own choices, including evaluative decisions, to become increasingly independent. That program begins early in a student's educational experience and makes the individual increasingly accountable for his or her own behavior. The student is given opportunities to choose activities and to evaluate the results of those choices, becoming increasingly responsible for the consequences of decisions. According to this program, the student participates in setting his or her own goals even if the goals must be approved or supervised by significant others. The student records or charts his or her own performance, grading the work with decreasing supervision.

EVALUATION OUTCOMES

Evaluation requires a number of important decisions. As the student's performances on the prescription emerge, several courses are available for the IEP team to pursue: (a) continuation, adaptation, or adjustment; (b) continuation in a related area; and (c) discontinuation. The course to be followed depends on the evaluation; obviously, any evaluation is no better than the improvements that result.

Continuation, Adaptation, or Adjustment

If the student is found to be progressing on the prescription basically as anticipated, the decision may be to continue. The evaluation should include an indication of whether the rate of instruction is still appropriate. There is no need for concern if a student's progress is somewhat slower than anticipated and if the prescription is otherwise satisfactory. If progress is considerably slower, the decision may be to continue but at a slower pace. If the student has made faster progress than anticipated, the IEP team might decide to continue with the goal but quicken the pace of the instruction.

In deciding whether to continue with a prescription, it may be necessary to reevaluate the goal. If the student is moving slowly and continues to fall farther and farther behind schedule, perhaps the anticipated level of mastery or the method of instruction on that particular goal is beyond the capability of the student. Perhaps an annual goal is no longer appropriate because the long-term goal from which it was taken has changed.

Continuation in a Related Area

Sometimes after a goal has been reached either the original diagnosis or the ongoing evaluation suggests continuing the instruction or activity but in a related area. For example, a social goal that has been mastered in the classroom setting might be expanded to application in the workplace. Or perhaps a student who has mastered basic dressing skills will focus similar efforts and processes on practicing other aspects of grooming.

Discontinuation

Sometimes evaluation will reveal that a particular goal should be discontinued, temporarily or permanently. That particular goal may be shown to have lower priority than other goals. For example, as an individual approaches adolescence, many high-priority goals emerge that were not under consideration earlier, and these goals may supersede some of the goals undertaken in earlier childhood. Or the student may have satisfactorily achieved the goal at the level deemed to be appropriate for his or her abilities and needs. A student, for instance, may have learned all the colors that seem to be necessary for his or her projected level of adult function.

APPROACHES TO EDUCATION FOR STUDENTS WITH MENTAL RETARDATION

In planning curriculum and constructing IEPs, three broad approaches to education are significant in dealing with students with mental retardation.

Basic Education

Basic education is ordinarily defined as the educational programs, procedures, and materials that teachers may appropriately use with most school-age students. For students with mental retardation, basic education includes the skills and concepts that are taught to all or most students in a particular group or class, the core of activities and experiences taught on a developmental, ongoing basis. The chapters in Part IV contain guidelines to aid IEP teams in developing the content designated as basic education for a student with mental retardation.

Remediation

Remedial education, or *remediation,* is defined as education offered outside the regular classroom that is intended to reteach specific skills not mastered in the basic education program (Roberts & Samuels, 1993). Historically, remediation has been limited to relatively few students, those who have extreme achievement deficits in the basic school subjects (Ekwall, 1989; Otto, McMenemy, & Smith, 1973). Remedial education has been criticized for its emphasis on highly academic areas, but the concept can be applied to self-help, socialization, and other transitional skills. Remediation sometimes includes speech therapy, counseling, and other supportive services.

Traditionally, remedial education has been offered to students who are achieving considerably below grade level but who have the potential to achieve at or above the appropriate grade level. These students usually include those with normal to high intelligence and specific learning disabilities. The basic intent of such programs is to use a district's limited resources with those students likely to make the greatest gains. This approach generally excludes students with mental retardation because they lack the potential needed to catch up with their classmates and because they usually fall increasingly behind as they continue through school. The notion of helping a student with mental retardation keep up with his or her classmates academically or catch up with them after falling behind is, in most cases, unrealistic.

Although a remedial approach may help some students with mental retardation, it often causes an individual to leave school with only a patchwork education, essentially on a low elementary level. Many remedial programs, however, offer materials and techniques that are age appropriate for adolescents with mental retardation and otherwise suitable to teach independent living and other transitional skills. If these materials are carefully adapted for the individual, they can be profitably used.

Compensation

Compensation is an approach that attempts to prepare an individual to succeed as well as possible in the adult world without thoroughly mastering the skills or concepts needed by most citizens. As the student with mental retardation progresses toward graduation, the age 25 projection helps the IEP team in determining which skills and concepts are likely to be mastered sufficiently to serve the student in adult life and which must be compensated for. Team members must make their decisions based on the services and education that will be available to the student after graduation. Because these services are usually limited or nonexistent, compensation must receive serious consideration.

The parents must be closely involved in all decisions regarding compensation because they must provide and/or manage most of the limited support that is available. For example, as the student approaches graduation, the IEP team must decide whether the remaining school time could be more profitably spent in a developmental program designed to increase the achievement level or in a program that helps the student make a good transition to life as an adult without a high level of achievement. The team must also diagnose the extent to which a student must master (and be allowed to use) any type of compensatory device. Such devices include communication boards, signing, computers, calculators, maps, and illustrated or animated directions. These devices are considered in appropriate chapters. Another important aspect of compensation involves teaching the student to recognize the point where assistance is needed and to know where to obtain the necessary help.

USE OF ORAL QUESTIONING AND OTHER INSTRUCTIONAL TECHNIQUES

Diagnosis and prescription are not separate entities, but rather are parts of a coordinated instructional procedure. One of the best illustrations of this concept occurs with class discussions. A creative teacher can evaluate students' performance and teach them simultaneously. The DPE approach to teaching is heavily based on oral techniques because so many skills can be involved and diagnosis can occur naturally without the discussion seeming to be artificial or contrived.

Oral questioning works effectively in diagnosing, as well as in teaching. For diagnosis, oral questions differ from written test items not only in format but also in their public nature. Written responses are privileged or private communication between teacher and pupil, whereas oral responses require students to respond in the presence of others. Therefore, oral questioning techniques must be used firmly and purposefully, but at the same time with tact, politeness, and consideration.

Every classroom must provide a nonthreatening learning environment in which each student feels free to offer opinions and respond to questions without fear of ridicule or embarrassment. Every individual needs to learn to communicate with others and to be tolerant of others' views. Teachers must ensure that students' answers are accepted and considered with dignity and respect.

Traditionally, the questioning procedures used in classrooms are limited to teacher asks–student answers situations, sometimes a necessary technique, but a practice that is weak in encouraging creativity, critical thinking, or reasoning on the part of the student. Several questioning techniques can be effectively adapted for use with students with mental retardation.

Rephrasing provides an opportunity for the questioner to clarify what the question really asks. If a question is not clear to a particular student, it should be restated at the student's own level of sophistication. If a student asks a question that is unclear to some of the other students in class, the teacher should rephrase the question until all participants can understand what was asked. For example, a teacher might say to the questioner, "You are asking what happens if you do not get to work but have a good excuse, right?" Or the teacher might directly ask, "Are you asking how we can be sure we get the best value for our money?"

Redirecting a question can be used to encourage creative thinking, discussion, opinion, or tolerance of others' views—while conveying information. Redirection restates a question by asking another question. The discussion leader rephrases and clarifies the questions and responses of students and redirects the responses as questions to the group. Sometimes the teacher starts a discussion by asking an introductory question.

Then he or she redirects by asking another question that involves a part of the original question or a related question likely to lead to the eventual answer. In using this technique, the teacher must be careful not to discourage the student seeking information by constantly asking that student to answer his or her own question. The teacher can praise the student for the question and then rephrase it—for example, "That is a good question: why *do* we need police officers?"

Pausing after a question encourages the students to reconsider shallow or cursory responses. The pause indicates that a quick, obvious answer will not suffice and that further thought is necessary. Questions such as the following might promote quick answers but really deserve more thoughtful consideration: "Why do we need class rules?" or "What is the purpose of getting a job?" or "What caused the trouble at lunch today?" Increasing the waiting time for an answer to such a question often increases the quality of the responses, as well as encourages wider participation among the students.

Most group discussions are dominated by a few individuals, and class discussions—even among students with mental retardation—are no exception. Unfortunately, a lively discussion carried on by two or three members of a group can convince the teacher that all are having a fine learning experience, but this may not be the case. Ideally, each student should have an equal opportunity to respond, but many students are hesitant to volunteer. Following are some procedures to encourage participation by nonvolunteers:

* Make it a practice to call on each class member occasionally, even when the individual does not volunteer.
* Whenever possible, allow students to speak without raising their hands.
* Praise frequently but make sure the praise is appropriate. Although younger students may seek praise, adolescents often cringe when praised, particularly if the praise seems artificial or contrived.
* Be positive and encouraging when a student makes an inappropriate or incorrect response.
* Encourage class members to disagree tactfully and politely when it is necessary; avoid direct confrontations such as "No" or "No, that's not right."
* Try taking the blame yourself for an incorrect response to a question, particularly at first. For example, it is nonconfrontive to say, "I didn't ask that quite right," or, "Let me try it again." Another way to imply you are accepting the blame is to simply rephrase the question by using more obvious hints or by giving additional information.
* Be cautious in referring a student's question to someone else. Doing so may promote resentment or discouragement by implying that the first student never knows the correct answer but that another student does. A puzzled student may be asked to choose someone to help.
* Prompt the extremely shy student in advance. Cover part of the material in private before the discussion. Be careful not to embarrass the student by making this obvious.
* Reemphasize and summarize by asking review questions of those who did not respond the first time.
* Be careful not to embarrass a student by waiting too long for a response. Restate or rephrase the question. Ask the student or a classmate a clarifying question, but don't let the student "lose face" in front of his or her classmates.

* Use oral questions to teach and promote discussion, rather than to demonstrate a student's lack of preparation. If the student is embarrassed by an oral question, he or she is less likely to respond in the future.

Oral questioning procedures can be effective and flexible in combining diagnosis and prescription and thus provide immediate feedback to the teacher. They can yield a great deal of precise data and provide additional insights about a learner that are not available from any other source. The teacher can locate the effective test range for each participant quickly and then create easier or more difficult questions as necessary. This type of questioning also works well with students who have poor writing skills. From a diagnostic standpoint, these procedures are highly subjective, but then so are most other evaluative procedures that are appropriate with students with mental retardation.

QUESTIONS FOR PRESCRIPTION EVALUATION

In evaluating a prescription, it is well to consider the questions posed at the time of the initial diagnosis, plus the following—adapted to fit the individual situation.

* Is the prescription generally meeting the student's needs?
* Is the prescription proceeding at the optimal rate? How well are the anticipated time lines or completion dates being met? Is the student working at a level already achieved?
* Is the student working at a frustration level that is too difficult even though it may have been on the appropriate level initially?
* Does it appear that the student has the entry-level skills that were assumed or anticipated?
* Is the student generally performing at the anticipated level and rate? If not, should the prescription be discontinued? Should it be taught at a faster or slower rate?
* Does the prescription fit the unique learning characteristics of the student: memory, distractibility, and so forth?
* Is another prescription (goal) now of higher priority?
* Is the prescription helping the student become a more efficient learner?
* Has the prescription been combined with others for this student and with the prescriptions of other students for efficient teaching?
* Could the prescription be more adequately taught in a different setting? more restrictive? less restrictive?
* Are additional, unanticipated services needed?
* Is the student (particularly one who is older) proactive in demonstrating practical mastery of the skills and concepts of the prescription? Was the student given an adequate opportunity to demonstrate practical proactive mastery? in a contrived situation? in an actual situation?
* Was the prescription written in sufficient/insufficient detail?

- Did teaching the prescription require an unreasonable amount of time? Could this time (or part of the time) have been better spent teaching more significant skills or concepts? Are the prescriptions of several children being correlated with each other for maximum teaching efficiency?
- Could more aspects of the prescription be entrusted to an aide or volunteer without serious negative effects?
- How adequate is the level-to-level program planning for this student on this prescription and others? What is likely to happen to this and to his or her other prescriptions in future years?

SUMMARY

In this chapter, I introduced DPE teaching. I discussed the relationship between standardized and teacher-made tests and showed how both can contribute to the practical education needed by a student with mental retardation. I reviewed some statistical concepts, including validity and reliability, that are needed in all three components of the DPE procedure. DPE is a highly specific procedure that produces detailed activity, and the elements of DPE should be written out only when necessary and in the detail required by the situation.

I also stressed evaluation and showed how to monitor a student's progress on his or her life goals as they are being taught with periodic adjustments to those goals as necessary.

Some differences between basic education, remediation, and compensation were pointed out as educational planning procedures for students with mental retardation. Compensation, an often overlooked principle that teaches an individual with mental retardation to be as successful as possible in adult life without having mastered all the lower priority skills and concepts that might have been achieved by others, was emphasized.

CHAPTER 7

Goal Instruction Analysis

Points to Study and Ponder

1. How is goal instructional analysis (GIA) related to task analysis, and how do they differ?
2. What is a target task, and how is it related to a long-term or annual life goal from the student's IEP?
3. What is a subtask, and how is it related to a target task or short-term objective from the student's IEP?
4. What is the difference between a graded-sequential goal and a procedural-sequential goal?
5. What is a GIA component, and why must a component be manipulatable? What does *manipulatable* mean?
6. What is a task segment, and why are task segments arranged in order of increasing difficulty?
7. What is a student's educational frontier?
8. What is checkpointing, and how does it help in diagnosing a student's abilities?
9. What is self-management, and how is it related to proactivity and independence?
10. What is a reversion point, and why does a student need assistance (and a slight change in the GIA) to get past a reversion?

n this chapter, I discuss **goal instructional analysis (GIA),** which is an integral part of diagnostic/prescriptive/evaluative (DPE) teaching. GIA helps in diagnosing the strengths and weaknesses of a student and in formulating, evaluating, and teaching the student's educational prescriptions. I discuss GIA as an important tool in analyzing the achievement level and learning rate of students with mental retardation and then explain how the data can be used in designing individualized educational prescriptions and in planning the student's overall curriculum. GIA can also provide a written plan for aides, volunteers, and parents.

I begin by outlining the steps necessary in performing GIA and by defining and discussing some important terms. Some terms refer to acts the student performs; other terms describe what the teacher, parent, or therapist must do. GIA focuses on the activities of the teacher or other person who has the direct responsibility to teach the goal taken from the student's IEP. Next, I outline and explain the steps necessary to learn GIA and then show how to use GIA in the classroom and at home. Finally, I include a worked example GIA. It may be necessary to read the entire chapter, including the outlined steps and the worked example, before the definitions will make sense.

GIA is a basic teaching tool or procedure that can be used to enhance any other method or technique. It is a stepwise procedure that uses basal and ceiling techniques borrowed from standardized testing and discussed in the preceding chapter. Its main assets are great precision and teaching efficiency, both of which can be increased almost without limit. With practice, GIA is essentially committed to memory, but initially it should be charted out. The charts are simple, and chart notations require only single words or symbols, such as plus (+) and minus (–) signs and arrows to indicate the planned increase or decrease of GIA components. Occasionally, an experienced teacher will need to resort to a detailed written GIA at those inevitable moments when one simply "runs dry" and needs to reexamine a particular student's strengths and weaknesses and reaffirm the general direction for that student's instruction. A written GIA may also be desirable or necessary when the teacher must report or demonstrate a student's learning level and rate to a parent, supervisor, or instructional assistant. Worked examples in this and several later chapters show how this is done.

Plotting out a GIA serves as a systematic, persistent reminder to keep instruction for the student on his or her educational frontier. For example, aides and volunteers, as well as classroom teachers, are prone to offer an enthusiastic "Good job!" at the conclusion of even the most minute increment of instruction. This comment is often given whether the quality of the work was the student's best or not. Moreover, everyone is likely to overlook the fact that, in real life, someone is not always available to applaud the individual's efforts. For example, encouragement, prompting, or a particular reward must be reduced or eliminated when the GIA so indicates. The effects are then observed and discontinued permanently or reinstated occasionally as needed.

LEARNING TO USE BASIC GIA PROCEDURES

Learning how to perform a GIA is different from actually doing one in the classroom. As in any theory-practice relationship, in a hypothetical or practice GIA, no student is actually involved; thus, procedures are more distinct and separate, and sequencing is more predictable. For convenience, the theory (learning) steps of GIA are numbered the same as the practice (applying) steps.

The steps in formulating and teaching a GIA are as follows:

1. Identify the primary or target task.
2. Identify subtasks of the target task if needed.
3. Identify and evaluate the student's entry-level skills.
4. Treat the entry-level skills if necessary.
5. Identify and list the appropriate GIA components to be used.
6. Create and list the appropriate checkpoints.
7. Diagnose the student's achievement level on the target or subtask.
8. Recheck the GIA components and the student's entry-level skills.
9. Formulate the detailed GIA segments.
10. Project completion dates for each checkpoint used in the prescription.

The steps are discussed in greater detail below. In the theory (learning) GIA procedures, Steps 4 and 8 are omitted if no actual student is involved; however, entry-level skills that would be appropriate for the particular target task should be considered. Likewise, in Step 8 if no student is involved, there are no student's entry-level skills to be rechecked. Step 7 requires an assumption of performance that represents the student's achievement level, or *educational frontier*—the point where the diagnosis ends and the prescription and teaching can begin.

TERMS RELATED TO THE TASK TO BE TAUGHT

GIA involves some simple terminology. For convenience, terms related to the tasks to be diagnosed and taught are presented first. Then terms related to the procedures that teachers use in teaching the tasks are discussed. The following terms define the tasks to be diagnosed and prescribed. Essentially, they describe what the student will do. The actions of the teacher or therapist are discussed below.

Target Task

The term *target task* refers to the overall achievement projected for the student on the section of curriculum being diagnosed and taught. Typically, this projection includes all or part of an annual or short-term goal that has been designated on the student's IEP. Target tasks may be as specific as counting to 10 or as broad as learning to succeed in independent living or competitive employment.

When a target task is difficult or time-consuming for a student, it is subdivided into *subtasks* so that instruction can be more efficient and convenient. For example, if the target task is to learn expressive language, one subtask might be to have the student develop the ability to point to body parts, classmates, or objects on command. Gradually, more subtasks can be added so that the student can advance to more complex and practical applications. No specific time restrictions can be designated for all target tasks or all subtasks: Length must be appropriate to instruction and will vary with each child, teacher, task, and situation.

The subtask can be evaluated as an entity to assess the student's readiness to complete the next subtask or to advance to an additional target task. If evaluation indicates that the subtask is too difficult or otherwise inappropriate for the student, time need not be wasted doing in-depth instructional planning that will be above the child's potential achievement level.

Types of Tasks

Tasks can be classified according to a number of criteria. For example, they could be viewed as verbal or nonverbal, motor or nonmotor, physical or mental, or combinations of these. For the purposes of GIA, however, tasks are usually classified according to the relationship of subtasks: graded-sequential, procedural-sequential, or nonsequential.

Graded-Sequential Tasks

When most tasks are broken into subtasks, the steps need to be accomplished in a specific order. A graded-sequential task requires that a given sequence be carefully followed because success with each step is contingent on skills or concepts acquired during previous steps. Accordingly, both the effort required and the achievement level reached increase with each step. For example, in learning to walk a beam, a child will begin with a wide beam and progress toward a narrow one, begin with a short beam and move toward a long beam, begin with a low beam and progress toward a high one. Children with mental retardation learn first to perform under close guidance of their parents and teachers and then move sequentially toward more independent function.

Procedural-Sequential Tasks

Like graded-sequential tasks, procedural-sequential tasks require order or sequence; the difference is that proficiency is less dependent on increasing difficulty or prerequisite skill and more contingent on procedure or practice. With a graded-sequential task, an individual cannot accomplish Step 4 without mastering Steps 1 to 3. With a procedural-sequential task, an individual will not perform Step 4 without Steps 1 to 3 because nothing would be accomplished by doing so. For example, building a campfire is a procedural-sequential task. No segment of the task is really any more difficult than another, nor does one need to have the skill of gathering wood before one can learn to strike a match. Nothing would be gained, however, by striking a match if fuel had not been previously arranged. Another procedural-sequential task is opening a combination lock, such as on a school locker.

It is important that students with mental retardation understand that some tasks cannot be completed successfully unless a sequence is carefully followed. A student completing a cut-and-paste project could conceivably paste before cutting, but the procedure would be inconvenient and would probably result in an inefficient and unskillful product. Similarly, the words in a sentence could be pronounced in reverse order, but they are usually only meaningful when pronounced in the sequence in which they are written. If an individual were to perform in an incorrect or illogical order the steps involved in catching a bus, a frustrating and quite possibly dangerous situation could result. Because procedural-sequence tasks are involved in most competitive employment jobs, students with mental retardation must gain an understanding of the importance that sequencing has on task performance.

Procedural-sequential tasks are further classified by the necessity or nonnecessity of the student's eventually mastering the skill. High-priority tasks might include preparing for a Special Olympics event, washing dishes, performing most self-help skills (e.g., brushing teeth, dressing, feeding, toileting), finding a number in a telephone book, and catching a bus. Less urgent tasks—such as doing math problems, baking a cake, riding a bike, watering plants, sweeping floors, cleaning a room, cutting and pasting, producing low-frequency speech sound, writing complete sentences, reading, or preparing a meal—are generally assigned lower priorities. The priority of all tasks, including those in this section, however, will vary in individual circumstances and must be determined by the teacher or the IEP team.

Nonsequential Tasks

Some tasks do not require a specific sequence: Easier steps do not need to be mastered first, and steps do not have to come in a particular order for the desired outcome to occur. A purely nonsequential task is relatively rare, however, because some nonsequential tasks become sequential when learning becomes more complex. For example, if a teacher is helping a student recognize common colors by using color cards, the cards can be presented in almost any order. Red is not inherently more difficult to recognize than green, and a student does not need to recognize red in order to be able to recognize green. Thus, learning color cards could be considered nonsequential. Similarly, if a teacher is working with the skill of recognizing consonant sounds from visual cues, the various consonants could be presented in any order; however, most teachers will note the order of consonants in the students' reading material and sequence the presentation to support that order.

DEFINITIONS RELATED TO THE TEACHING OF A TASK

The following definitions describe things the teacher or therapist must do, as opposed to what the student will do.

GIA Segments

The GIA is broken into segments, each consisting of components from previous segments that have been manipulated or adapted for use at the specified stage of the learning process. *Manipulating* a component means increasing, decreasing, discontinuing, or otherwise changing the component so that the resulting segment is slightly more demanding than the preceding segment. Occasionally, a previously discontinued component may be reinstated. This procedure is described below. A segment is more than a simple step: To describe it requires identification of the student's projected performance level, as well as the circumstances and efforts the teacher will use to attain the desired performance. Procedures for identifying and manipulating components to be grouped within the segment are described below.

GIA Components

GIA components are the basic elements of the GIA process. When tasks are broken into components, these components can be selected and manipulated for maximum efficiency in controlling the student's level of mastery and the rate at which the task can be taught. If a student is being taught to float, "shallow water" might be one of the GIA components included with other aspects of the task in the early segments. In later segments, that component might be changed to "deeper water" (indicated by a simple plus sign) so that these later segments are more demanding and produce a higher level of skill. As components are initiated, increased, decreased, terminated, and restated in the sequential GIA segments, positive movement and direction are given to the learning experience.

This chapter includes procedures for selecting and using GIA components in both hypothetical and real situations; later chapters include how to apply these processes to formulate practical teaching strategies. Although hypothetical GIAs are structured to include a wide range of possible components to demonstrate the power of the GIA procedure and the range of options that should be considered in using it, constructing the actual GIAs for classroom use involve a more limited number and range, including only those components that relate to the particular target task. Every GIA requires a different combination of components; however, in identifying and selecting the components for a given GIA, a teacher should at least consider those discussed in this chapter.

ARRANGING THE TASK SEGMENTS IN ORDER

Good teaching for any child with a disability might be defined as presenting that student with a well-organized sequence of learning tasks and segments that require increasing skill and understanding until the student is able to function as a responsible adult. Because the GIA is used throughout the DPE teaching process, a teacher must give thoughtful consideration to sequencing task segments and tasks themselves in view of helping the child reach his or her fullest potential. This sequencing is done by arranging the task segments in order of increasing student achievement or difficulty. In a later section, I explain how this is done.

The close relationship between prioritizing a student's life goals and arranging the task segments in order of increasing difficulty are obvious. In both diagnosis and prescription, segments and tasks must be arranged in order of gradually increasing difficulty (or increasing student performance) so that each succeeding segment results in a higher achievement level and the student moves steadily from simpler to more complex accomplishments; thus, understanding and skill increase in a logical fashion.

Arranging the task segments in order of increasing difficulty also enables the teacher to assess more quickly and accurately the performance level at which the student is beginning a task. Accurate assessment helps the teacher avoid rehashing previously learned material or presenting material on a level too difficult for the student, either of which decreases learning efficiency. One initial purpose of GIA is to help in determining whether the student will be able to master the high-priority goal the IEP team has selected. Diagnosis compares the requirements needed to master the goal with the student's abilities and interests. In many instances, the diagnosis will show that the goal is too difficult for the student—at least for the time being. Also, in some instances, the diagnosis will show that the goal has already been mastered and need only be reviewed and applied.

Once beginning performance level for a particular task has been assessed, the teacher manipulates GIA components to provide optimum ease and convenience for the specific student. As the student's skills increase, components that offer direct assistance, such as hand-on-hand, are gradually replaced by components that provide guidance that is less direct. Eventually, direct teacher guidance can be eased out of the GIA for a given skill as instruction is gradually turned over to an instructional assistant. Components are manipulated within skills, and skills are manipulated within the overall sequential plan so that tasks become gradually but continually more demanding as the student continues to progress.

The Educational Frontier

The purposeful arrangement of GIA segments makes it easier for a teacher to locate an individual student's educational frontier. *Educational frontier* is defined as the point between the skills and concepts a student has already mastered (diagnosis) and those he or she will learn next (prescription). The DPE process is designed to ensure that each student is working as closely as possible to the appropriate level and rate for his or her needs and capabilities. Because GIA is one of the most reliable ways to locate the educational frontiers for each student, it is important for teachers to sequence segments carefully so that the child's individual educational prescriptions can begin appropriately at his or her frontier.

Learning to Learn

If GIA segments are arranged in order of increasing difficulty, the student's ability to learn will also be increased. The student with mental retardation learns very slowly, so it is essential to make learning as efficient as possible. As a student repeatedly learns skills from a basic order of simple to complex, he or she becomes accustomed to the process, as well as to mastering the individual skills. So, the particular sequence of segments for any particular skill should be designed from the perspective of subsequent skills and accomplishments that will be expected of the student.

Chaining

A learning sequence in which individual parts or steps, such as GIA segments, lead to a single goal is referred to as *chaining* (Griffen, Wolery, & Schuster, 1992). For a procedural-sequential task such as putting on a sock, washing dishes, or setting a table, the contributing parts of the skill are performed in a sequence leading to a completed whole. Thus, the student learns to immerse the dish in soapy water, wash with an appropriate pattern of motion until the dish appears clean, rinse the dish in clear water, and place it appropriately to dry; all segments must be performed in sequence for an individual segment to accomplish its purpose. In most instructional planning, contributing parts of a skill are presented first and then are shown in relation to the final product. This process is referred to as *forward chaining* (Wright & Schuster, 1994). Interestingly, however, Wright and Schuster found greater success in allowing the student to perform a chained task in any functional order, rather than a tightly specified sequence. Generally, graded-sequential tasks are best presented with forward chaining because each step is built upon skills and concepts mastered in previous steps. Arithmetic, reading, and most academic tasks are usually presented with forward chaining because more complex operations must be built upon simpler ones. A student must know the sounds of the individual letters before blending them in short, simple patterns to form syllables and then in longer groupings to form words.

Some tasks, however, are taught more efficiently with *backward* or *reverse chaining* (McDonnell & Laughlin, 1989). The whole is presented first, and then the parts are broken down for mastery. Teachers often find that procedural-sequential tasks are easier to teach in this manner. For example, in teaching reading comprehension, the teacher may demonstrate the total task by having a student read an entire selection or by reading the selection to a student or the class before breaking down any of the parts for discussion. In such an approach, the teacher first asks general questions about the purpose or moral of the story to enable students to see the overall purpose behind the reading—or writing—of the story and then deal later with specific words and sentences.

Many procedural tasks, especially those involving survival or self-care skills, must be completed regularly long before the person is able to do them independently. In this type of task, the student participates partially at first, gradually increasing participation as independence is achieved (Ferguson & Baumgart, 1991; Karen et al., 1985; Snell, Lewis, & Houghton, 1989). Other examples of essential tasks often taught with reverse chaining include eating, brushing teeth, and dressing. Both forward and backward chaining have been used successfully with students with mental retardation, the choice being determined by the nature of the specific task (McDonnell & Laughlin, 1989), the student's performance (Ault, Gast, Wolery, & Doyle, 1992), and the procedures used (Schoen & Sivil, 1989). Westling and Fox (1995) maintained that the concept of partial participation can be extended to include situations in which the student is taught and encouraged to participate in activities that he or she may not be capable of mastering completely. They suggested merit in merely taking part in the activities of other children. The IEP team must recognize and prescribe the extent of this type of partial participation. In a sense, their proposal is akin to training such a student to be a helper, rather than a more independent worker (see Chapter 14). No doubt, it is best in most instances to train the person to be as independent as possible, but some may be able only to assist others who make the important decisions and provide the necessary supervision.

Checkpointing

Checkpointing is a procedure based on the concepts of basal and ceiling ages. A *checkpoint* is nothing more than a designated segment and is used in both diagnosis and prescription, although it has a different purpose in each. Checkpointing is discussed in greater detail below, and a worked example is included. In diagnosis, checkpointing helps in locating the student's educational frontier.

NONCOMPONENTS OF GIA

GIA assumes a reasonable level of teaching ability on the part of parents, teachers, and others. Therefore, such details as the specific instructions to be given to the student and the student's anticipated responses are not ordinarily planned in advance—or written into a GIA. An exception may be needed, however, in working with a student with severe or multiple disabilities. For such a student, a basic body movement or a specific response can be a major goal or target task.

Specific Body Movements

Basic body movements, such as "shift weight from left foot to right foot," "bend elbow slightly," and "pick up pencil" usually do not need to be listed as components on a GIA. Although these elements may be necessary for a student to perform a task and will definitely vary with the specific task, they should be obvious to the teacher. Not only does writing down the obvious take unnecessary time, but also listing obvious motions on the GIA may obscure more essential but easily overlooked items, such as the type and amount of assistance that must be provided. Viewing body movements as components can be misleading because they cannot be easily manipulated. For example, the component "familiar material" can be manipulated to make a task easier or more demanding for a student, whereas "shifting weight from left foot to right foot" cannot be changed according to the student's current performance level.

Dialogue

Specific oral or written instructions given to a student and responses anticipated from the student likewise should not be listed as components. As with body movements, the dialogue between teacher and student is necessary and will vary with the situation, but it will come naturally, and writing it down unnecessarily complicates the analysis of skills and concepts. For efficiency, dialogue can be classified under a more general heading—for example, detailed instructions, repeated instructions, written instructions, or verbal instructions. The degree of assistance planned for these instruction components can then be reduced into such components as "less complete," "no repeat," or "verbal only." If quality of anticipated response needs to be represented, such terms as *fluency* or *graceful performance* can be used. But the actual dialogue is often counterproductive if included in the GIA.

Number of Trials

Students with mental retardation need considerably more practice than other students to master even a simple task. Other things being equal, their performance improves with repeated trials (Lehr, 1985). Because repetition and practice are time-consuming, they must be carefully evaluated to ensure that the task is not too difficult, poorly planned, or already mastered. If the task is appropriate and the segment has the correct combination of components, however, a student may be given several trials before a teacher needs to make changes in the GIA. Repeated trials are not considered to be separate segments. If a student remains unusually long on one segment, however, a teacher needs to ask whether the component(s) of the segment were manipulated in a way that made the GIA progress too rapidly.

SPECIFIC COMPONENTS OF GIA

To prepare each GIA, a teacher must create an appropriate combination of components, manipulating them to gradually increase segment difficulty. It is not necessary, however, to begin each GIA as a completely new entity. Figure 7.1 lists classes of components that can provide a starting point for creating segments of a variety of tasks. The order of presentation is not significant. Some sequences for applying the components are also suggested. For example, the Materials section includes size and suggests

MATERIALS
size (small then large, large
  then small, etc.)
color (red, green, blue, etc.)
Large type then small type
number (few then more)
height (low to high, etc.)
weight (light to heavy)
depth (shallow then deep)
similar then not similar
familiar then unfamiliar
simple then increasingly
  complex

MASTERY
whole then parts or parts then
  whole
imitates then freehand
performs on command then
  initiates
simple to increasingly difficult
  instructions
makes simple, increasingly
  meaningful choices,
  decisions
makes movement
answers questions
working knowledge
gives examples
draws conclusions
draws implications
makes predictions
performs independently
performs gracefully
performs fluently
performs as others do
performs task independently
performs task repeatedly
self-monitor
initiative
Proactivity

AID (ASSISTANCE)
teacher-taught progressing to
  aide- or volunteer-taught
complete instructions to only
  needed brief instructions
repeated instructions
explained instructions
student repeats back instructions to teacher
advising
modeling
guiding
prompting
encouraging
supervising
monitoring
walk-through
multisensory approach
choral
unison

Direct Assistance
• carry
• hand-on-hand
• gentle push
• gentle pressure
Supporting Devices
• crutch
• wheelchair
• life jacket
• template
• calculator
• computer
• checklist
• copying
• dot-to-dot
• handrail
• puppets
• walker
Proactivity

*Listed in more than one category

TIME CONSIDERATIONS
allotted to task
allotted to segment
allotted to each trial
allotted to each example
allotted to each demonstration
from instruction to beginning
between completion and
  reward

MEMORY
long-term
short-term
recall
identification*
discrimination*
repetition

GOAL OR TASK
simple
complex
requires courage
Stages
• single/multistage
• number
• related/unrelated
• familiar/unfamiliar location

MONITOR/SUPERVISE
one-on-one
small group
larger group
total class

REWARDS
tangible/intangible
fixed/variable
negative/positive
extrinsic/intrinsic
immediate/delayed
Proactivity

FIGURE 7.1   Classes of Components of GIA

sequences related to size that might increase the achievement level or difficulty, depending on the task. Logically, lifting weights would begin with light weights and progress to heavier, and penmanship would begin with a large pencil and progress to a smaller one. In formulating a GIA, the component column lists the easier or less demanding of these, and the GIA procedures progress to the more demanding, depending on the nature of the task.

Amount and Type of External Assistance

To become a successful adult, any student should learn to complete important tasks without assistance, advice, or supporting devices provided by others. But for many tasks, students with mental retardation are likely to need direct assistance and close supervision throughout their lives. This need presents a dilemma for their teachers, parents, and others who are responsible for them. Students must be encouraged to become as independent as possible, yet they must be given assistance in areas in which they cannot reasonably be expected to perform adequately on their own. Relaxing supervision usually relaxes the student's performance level and raises the possibility of failure; however, overly persistent monitoring and assistance encourages helplessness, dependence, and loss of self-esteem. If the student is ever to be employable, he or she must be able to stay on a task and perform to capacity without constant supervision.

Accordingly, a critical element of the GIA procedure is diagnosis and prescription of the process by which surveillance and help will be purposefully diminished with each succeeding task or GIA segment. The GIA must indicate the order in which the elements of assistance will be lessened and eventually discontinued but with provision for monitoring to guard against excessive or repeated failure and discouragement. The student's prescription must be carefully followed by instructional assistants, volunteers, and peer tutors, as well as by the teachers themselves. Koury and Browder (1986) taught peer tutors how to use time delay in teaching sight words to students with mental retardation. When a student is not reaching the projected level of success, the most recently manipulated components will need to be reconsidered and altered to give greater support. The GIA must be continually adapted to ensure that the student is receiving adequate opportunity to experience controlled increments of independence and responsibility.

Type and Extent of Instructions/Directions

Because students with mental retardation must learn to perform with a minimum of instructions, the GIA diagnoses and prescribes a wide variety of instructional techniques that decrease gradually to guide the student toward greater independence. Instructions should be focused toward the student's educational frontier. The GIA indicates who should give the instructions, how they should be given, how extensive they need to be, how often they should be repeated, and how the student should be prompted. Initially, the GIA might indicate that the student should repeat the instructions to keep the student attentive and on task and to confirm that instructions have been communicated adequately. This technique, however, should be faded out as soon as possible. At first, the teacher is the logical one to give instructions, but gradually instructional assistants, volunteers, peer tutors, and others on the instructional team should participate so that the student will learn to work with a variety of people. The student's individual circumstances and capabilities should determine whether instructions are oral or written.

Videotapes are an effective means of rehearsing or previewing tasks that will be taught, particularly when the task is sequential and involves following directions. For example, a videotaped sequence showing the tasks involved in a work experience can help the student in making a successful transition to a new placement. On a simpler level, Thinesen and Bryan (1981) and Cuvo and Klatt (1992) used sequential pictures in teaching grooming skills. A visual series can help students in recognizing objects, furniture, and cupboards in a classroom, and later rooms and buildings on school grounds or in the community. Commercial videotapes, available on numerous subjects, are useful in many phases of teaching and learning. Teachers are encouraged to make their own videotapes so that they can focus on members of the class in familiar surroundings and on appropriately selected tasks. Such tapes are now inexpensive and relatively easy to produce.

Time Delay, Prompting, Encouraging, and Modeling

The four elements of this section are discussed together because they are often used in combination with each other in research and in practice (Ault et al., 1992). Ault et al. used a time-delay procedure and a variety of prompts to develop a graphing technique to coordinate, systematize, and pre-plan the combination of assisting and encouraging elements to be used. The graph can also be used to demonstrate student progress. Time delay provides for a small segment of instruction and a prompt that ensures success to be presented simultaneously. After the student has correctly responded a specified number of times, a time delay is introduced; that is, the prompt follows the instructional segment by a specified (or constant) period of time, hence the term *constant time delay*. The instruction continues until the student performs successfully without the prompt

Wolery, Ault, Gast, Doyle, and Griffen (1990) compared constant time delay and a system that provided the student with the least amount of prompting necessary for success. They reported student gains under both methods but found constant time delay to be more effective. Later, these same researchers (Wolery, Ault, Gast, Doyle, & Griffen, 1991) used constant time delay to teach domestic and vocational tasks. Interestingly, each student of a dyad was taught only part of the task. The authors reported that constant time delay was effective and that all students gained a substantial amount from the instruction of their partners—just through observation. Likewise, in a study to compare the effects of time delay and observational learning, Schoen and Sivil (1989) reported time delay to be effective and that considerable learning seemed to take place simply from the observation of instruction. Schuster, Stevens, and Doak (1990) used constant time delay to teach word definitions to students with mild disabilities. They also reported that some of the students maintained some generalization over time.

Goal instruction analysis (GIA) helps the teacher in evaluating the student's progress and in developing individual lesson plans in the appropriate amount of detail and needed assistance.

McDonnell (1987) compared constant time delay and systematic prompting to teach students with severe disabilities to make simple purchases. He found the constant time delay procedure to be more efficient. Later, McDonnell and Ferguson (1987) compared a time delay procedure with a decreasing prompt hierarchy to teach four teenagers with moderate mental retardation to successfully use an automated teller machine. Both procedures produced positive results, but they reported the time delay procedure to be more efficient.

Prompting by itself is a powerful tool that has been used in a variety of ways. For example, Chadsey-Rusch, Karlan, Riva, and Rusch (1984) used verbal prompts to teach work-oriented conversational skills to adults with mental retardation. With a similar group of adults, Karen et al. (1985) taught telephone communication skills by using a combination of visual and verbal prompts. Bannerman, Sheldon, and Sherman (1991) successfully, by using a combination of prompting and modeling with a variety of reinforcement techniques, taught adults with severe and profound mental retardation to respond to fire alarms and to safely exit their homes.

Another technique to help students with mental retardation find success is having the teacher, instructional assistant, volunteer, or a peer demonstrate (or model) a task. Modeling can be an effective way of helping a student master a GIA segment. Yoder and Forehand (1974) combined modeling with verbal cues in teaching students with and without mental retardation. They reported that, although either method was useful alone, the combination of the two was most effective in helping students acquire concepts. Goldstein and Mousetis (1989) successfully taught language skills to six young children with severe mental retardation by having students' peers model the skills. Also, prompting has been successfully used to teach simple first-aid skills (Marchand-Martella, Martella, Christensen, Azean, & Young, 1992) and independent living skills (Walls, Crist, Sienicki, & Grant, 1981). For most teaching situations, the GIA should be designed to gradually reduce the teacher's modeling role and to increase that of para-professionals and parents. When peer tutors are used, however, they must be carefully selected and trained so that the slower learner does not resent the peer who is modeling. To achieve maximum independence, modeling, like other forms of assistance, must be extinguished as quickly as possible.

Graduated Guidance

Ideally, assistance is built into the GIA in such a way that it can be given when the student needs it and gradually reduced or eliminated according to the student's individual prescription (Colozzi & Pollow, 1984). The following sequence has been shown to be successful: (a) offering direct assistance or graduated guidance, (b) advising or providing needed information (including that which might have been prematurely faded), (c) prompting or reminding the learner of information already given, and (d) encouraging but giving no actual assistance. Sometimes these components will be used in combination, rather than in sequence. Hourcade (1988) reported success in using both physical guidance and gestural prompts in a variety of tasks. Schloss, Alexander, Hornig, Parker, and Wright (1993) used verbal prompts, modeling, and physical guidance to teach students with mental retardation to prepare simple meals.

A student may be unable to perform some tasks without physical help, particularly if his or her mental retardation is severe/profound. When physical assistance is needed, the GIA will initially provide hands-on restraint and guidance in making necessary body movements, such as drawing, writing, cutting, and following directions. Although at first the teacher or therapist may need to provide virtually all of the effort, gradually the direct assistance is reduced and replaced with subtler forms of support that can be eventually withdrawn or faded out altogether. This process is referred to as *graduated guidance*. For example, when a task is first introduced, the teacher may have to place a guiding hand on the student's hand and encourage the needed movements with fairly firm pressure; however, gradually the pressure becomes gentler, then guidance is offered with no pressure, and finally subtler forms of assistance, such as prompting or supervising, will be all that need be used.

Supervision, Monitoring, and Independence

Independence in daily life and vocation is a common goal for the individual with mental retardation (La Greca, 1983; Langone & Burton, 1987; Siegel & Sleeter, 1991), yet all the limitations caused by mental retardation seem to contribute to its difficulty. The level of independence an individual can achieve is inversely proportional to the need for external supervision, and a student with mental retardation usually requires closer supervision to an older age than a child with no disability. All GIA procedures encourage individual independence by emphasizing instruction in natural surroundings and by allowing the student to experience the natural consequences of his or her actions.

The goal is to eventually find a satisfactory balance between necessary obedience (external control) and desired independence (internal control) that can be emphasized throughout a student's educational program. The ideal GIA should provide a sequence similar to the following: (a) supervision, in which an adult watches the student closely, possibly in a group with other students; (b) monitoring, in which the adult stays in the immediate area but avoids overt intervention; and (c) independence, in which the adult is able to withdraw and allow the student to perform for increasingly longer periods of time without supervision. A given GIA may involve these components and others, singly or in combination. As the process is repeated, the student eventually learns to perform a variety of tasks in an acceptable manner with increasing independence.

Courage, Self-Confidence, and Independence

Successful achievement of task goals goes beyond performing necessary movements or making appropriate responses; successful performance and independence require courage and self-confidence. On a simple level, a student may have the skills to walk a balance beam but may become frightened and unable to perform if the beam is raised a few inches. Similarly, students with mental retardation are often unwilling to take risks in academic areas (Baer, 1990; Perske, 1972), preferring to stay with routine mechanical functions, such as arithmetic computation, rather than expand to more practical but more difficult problem-solving activities. Thus, on the one hand, many students capable of employment can succeed in on-campus job placement where they feel familiar and comfortable but will be initially frightened by the prospect of doing similar work in an off-campus setting. On the other hand, working through prerequisite skills is about the only way for them to gain the necessary experience. In fact, Horner, Jones, and Williams (1985) demonstrated that students with mental retardation can and do generalize from classroom and other activities to more advanced experiences. Some, though not all, tend to fear the unknown and may become uneasy when faced with new areas of knowledge or experience; they must be guided carefully to avoid disabling fear, discouragement, or frustration.

Students with mental retardation, however, must experience and overcome some failure and frustration in order to achieve their potential independence, although it may be difficult for teachers and parents to watch this occur. Thus, an individual's prescriptions must include elements of risk taking and challenge. Each student must meet the unexpected and learn to cope with it. The extent of a person's courage or self-confidence is difficult to measure or describe in discrete terms, but the teacher must have the courage and discernment to incorporate challenging situations into the GIA to provide each student with a program that will enable that individual to achieve maximum growth.

Self-Management, Goal Setting, and Independence

Researchers have reported success in using various forms of self-management to promote independence in students with mental retardation, inside and outside the classroom. The GIA process gradually increases the amount of responsibility for behavior and performance placed on the student and decreases the responsibility of teachers, parents, and others. McCarl, Svbodny, and Beare (1991) reported increased productivity and on-task behavior when they used a self-recording technique with three highly distractible students with mild to moderate mental retardation. Allen, White, and Test (1992) likewise reported success when they instituted a picture/symbol form of self-monitoring of a variety of community-based educational tasks with a group of students with moderate to severe mental retardation.

Self-management techniques can be particularly valuable in preparing students with mental retardation for eventual independent living because self-monitoring should be an ongoing process, even when a teacher or supervisor cannot be present. Accordingly, Lovett and Haring (1989) used self-management successfully to improve the performance of adults with mental retardation on daily living skills. Lagomarsino, Hughes, and Rusch (1989) and Zohn and Bornstein (1980) reported moderate success with using several self-monitoring techniques to hold students with mental retardation increasingly responsible for quantity and quality of performance in employment settings. Cole and Gardner (1988) demonstrated that having students with mental retardation set simple goals had a positive effect on their performance on a number of tasks. Although they focussed on the students' performance on the tasks, learning to set personal goals is in itself a laudable achievement.

To guide students with mental retardation in learning to use self-monitoring techniques, the following sequence is recommended: (a) self-recording that involves plotting one's own work results as evaluated by others, (b) monitoring that depends on gradually increasing one's own self-evaluation, and (c) goal setting and self-teaching that encourage the student to select the skills and concepts he or she is to learn.

Proactivity and Independence

The ultimate goal for all students is proactivity, which involves recognizing, setting up, and solving practical life problems. This process involves special challenges in working with students with mental retardation. To be independent, a student must be aware of emerging problems in his or her life and take initiative in structuring priorities and finding solutions with as little external control or supervision as possible. In doing this, the student must use both acquired and inherited skills.

Mechanically performing tasks has little meaning if the student cannot use the skills proactively. For example, it makes little sense to teach a student how to perform even simple mathematical calculations if he or she cannot use those skills to solve practical problems when the need arises. Similarly, it is a hollow achievement if a student memorizes safety procedures that he or she cannot apply to everyday hazardous conditions. If the student is to become independent, he or she must have the skill, as well as the motivation, to perform and solve life problems largely unsupervised. These fundamental calculations are essential, however, as are learning activities in which teachers and others provide drill, practice, supervision, and motivation to the extent necessary. Naturally, some students continue to require assistance and full- or part-time supervision much longer than others, and their instruction and practice must never expose them to unsafe situations. Providing this type of individualized but effective instruction is one of the challenges of mental retardation.

An important feature of the DPE approach is that it reminds teachers, therapists, and parents that students must take increasing responsibility for their own behavior and achievement. Personal love and concern for a student with mental retardation may make it difficult to avoid "overcoaching" or to limit the number of treats or other rewards when such rewards are no longer necessary for reinforcement. But the person administering the child's prescription must keep in mind that, at every state of the educational process, the student must be increasingly prepared to eventually be employed, at which time praise and other reinforcements will not be given every time the individual exerts some effort or completes a task satisfactorily.

Level of Difficulty and Performance

To progress, a student must work with increasingly difficult materials and learn to complete increasingly complicated tasks. One easy way to increase task difficulty without overwhelming the student is to present increasingly difficult examples or problems of the same general type. For example, the student could be asked to perform the same process with increasingly advanced words, more difficult concepts, higher numbers, or more complicated instructions or problems. A teacher might use simple, familiar vocabulary words when a verbal task is first introduced, advancing to more difficult, unfamiliar words as the student becomes more proficient.

In task analysis, each segment selected must be matched against the teacher's best estimate of the student's current level of potential and achievement. The GIA diagnoses the student's learning ability and projects the level of difficulty that can be pursued. If the prescription is not ideally matched with ability level at the outset, necessary adjustments can be made because each prescription is regarded as tentative and subject to constant evaluation.

Degree of Mastery

The GIA involves a progressive sequence of abilities and actions designed to help a student in progressing from introductory phases of a skill or concept through the learning phases to a final stage of mastery that involves application, initiative, and proactivity, as shown in the Mastery section of Figure 7.1. Hewett (1967) suggested arranging educational tasks from an attention level to an achievement level. Although sometimes it will be appropriate to combine some phases or to teach them simultaneously, a student's mastery of every skill or concept should be diagnosed carefully to ensure maximum teaching efficiency.

Because degree of mastery is somewhat arbitrary, teachers must be flexible. A preset standard, such as "80% level of mastery" will invariably be too demanding for some students and some tasks but not sufficiently challenging for others. Graded-sequential tasks require greater mastery than other types because additional progress is dependent on a solid base of accuracy. In addition, tasks involving safety and survival require a high degree of mastery: Crossing a street without accident is not acceptable at 80% or even 95%. Thus, the accepted mastery level for a task must be determined according to the nature of the task itself, the urgency of the learning, and the way the individual task fits into a sequence of more difficult or meaningful accomplishments.

Grace and Sophistication

An aspect of mastery for many tasks is degree to which the student can complete the segments naturally, smoothly, and gracefully, with a minimum of errors or accidents. If individuals with mental retardation are to be accepted by society when they are adults, they must be competent in performing the tasks of everyday living, but they must also be *socially invisible:* Their speech and actions should not cause them to be conspicuous in a crowd. To promote elements of grace, fluency, and social sophistication, along with basic motions of a task, the teacher could have a student repeat a task already learned, concentrating on increased smoothness, greater tact, or what might be commonly called a "more normal performance." To make this a more deliberate part of the teaching process, a Grace column might be added to the GIA. In the early segments, it would be obvious from the notation "no" in the column that grace was not stressed; in subsequent segments, the teacher could indicate "some" as a reminder that this aspect should receive some attention. With subsequent instruction and repeated examples and practice, the student would gradually increase in confidence and competence, moving steadily toward a more graceful performance.

Most tasks to be mastered by a student with mental retardation will be presented through more than one age level. As the student matures and progresses, mastery of these repeated skills and concepts will be more complete. Often, the initial presentation just introduces a task; for example, the student may learn that people do certain things on a daily basis to make a living—they have a "job." As the concept is encountered at succeeding ages, the student learns to accept increasing responsibility to perform classroom and school duties—his or her "job." Eventually, the student may participate with a regular "job" in a supervised work experience program. Finally, the student is ready to have a real-world "job," finding employment and earning his or her own way.

Materials

Materials refers to much more than a mere list of the tangible objects to be used in the diagnosis/prescription. Each component must be *manipulatable*, meaning that, proceeding from left to right, manipulating (e.g., increasing, decreasing, discontinuing) each material makes the task increasingly difficult and sophisticated and increases the student's achievement level. For example, "weight" cannot be readily manipulated, but "light weight" can be gradually increased until the student is working with heavy objects. The achievement level of a task is significantly affected by the nature of the materials and by the size and number of objects necessary for it (Grieve, 1982). Ordinarily, the larger the number of objects involved in a task, the more difficult the task becomes. For example, if a student with mental retardation is sorting and classifying clothes into piles for washing, increasing the number of clothes or the number of piles makes the task more difficult.

Increasing the size of the objects involved in a task may increase or decrease the difficulty level. For tasks involving physical strength or endurance, it is easier for a student with mental retardation to work with small, lightweight objects than with large, heavy ones; increasing size increases the challenge for the student. If discrimination or eye-hand coordination are involved, however, smaller objects may increase difficulty; for example, a student may need to use a large pencil, crayon, or ball before working with a smaller one.

Multisensory Approaches

Another way of controlling the difficulty level of a task for a student with mental retardation is to teach some segments with multisensory procedures. If a student is having a problem recognizing numbers or letters, forming them from felt, sandpaper, or even cookie dough (Fernald, 1943) adds the tactile sense to the visual and auditory, thereby increasing the number of learning channels the student can employ to bridge the gap between a learned and an unlearned segment.

Mental imagery also allows the students to use a multichannel approach for retaining material that is taught. Surburg (1991) was successful in using mental imagery to prepare students with mental retardation for a motor task. Rose (1984) reported success in using a rehearsal strategy to prepare his students for oral reading. Greeson (1986) went a step farther and combined mental imagery with modeling for preschool children on a variety of tasks involving recall and paired associate learning; he was able to significantly improve their performance.

Memory

The learning of students with mental retardation is particularly impaired by poor long- and short-term memory. Although memory and learning are certainly not synonymous, memory is involved in every aspect of learning; thus, an individual with a poor memory is not likely to be an efficient learner. Because an individual with mental retardation has difficulty remembering information, directions, procedures, and concepts, the effects of the other deficits associated with the condition are magnified. Students can, therefore, be expected to have particular difficulty in solving long, complicated, and multistage tasks (Ellis & Allison, 1988; Hornstein & Mosley, 1987). In fact, if the memory problems could be compensated, most of the other deficiencies associated with mental retardation could be overcome with education.

Although the memory deficit cannot be cured, both long- and short-term memories of most students with mental retardation can be improved with carefully planned instruction and practice (Scruggs & Laufenberg, 1986; Watkins et al., 1982). Accordingly, all GIAs for a student with mental retardation should include gradually increasing memory components. Because of the complexity of the deficits involved with mental retardation, it is often difficult to discern whether a student's inability to perform a particular task is due to poor memory or to some other deficiency, such as poor comprehension or inadequate reasoning. This difficulty should not cause undue concern, however, because the GIA provides a means whereby memory, reasoning, and comprehension can all be strengthened simultaneously.

Task Stages

Multistage tasks often consist of a number of intermediate actions that must be completed by the student to accomplish mastery. If these steps can be isolated and taught separately, they are called *task stages.* For example, washing dishes, making a sandwich, and cleaning up a work space, though often considered to be single tasks, are really made up of several stages, each of which might be taught separately. A task stage is an act or small cluster of acts, usually in a series, performed by the student—not to be confused with GIA segments or steps, which are the procedures used by an instructor to teach a target task. In practice, answering a question is a multistage task. For example, answering a written question requires the respondent to decode and understand the question, formulate the response, and encode and write the response. This is one reason even a written checklist may impose an additional burden on an individual with mental retardation although written instructions are almost always helpful to others.

Number of Stages Involved in a Task

The number and nature of the stages into which a target task is broken can be manipulated to change difficulty and performance level. Generally, the more stages involved in a task, the more complex and difficult it will be (Crist, Walls, & Haught, 1984). For example, even asking a question can be a multistage task: hearing, understanding the question or instruction, ascertaining what is wanted, and finally taking the proper action. For the student with mental retardation, the normal complexity of multiple stages is compounded by the fact that the purpose and appropriate solution for the task are not obvious throughout all the stages as they might be to a student who does not have a disability. At each stage, the student must hear the question and evaluate it, formulate an answer, and respond. A teacher can easily forget to include some of the information the student needs to make an appropriate response at each stage or may overcompensate and provide more information at a given stage than the student can handle. For this reason, students should be given opportunities to master single-stage segments first. Later, the achievement level of a task may be increased by introducing segments of two or more stages.

Stage Relatedness

In addition to the number of stages involved in a task, the teacher needs to consider the extent to which the stages are interrelated. If the relationship is strong and obvious, when the student completes one stage, the next stage will be fairly apparent. If the stages are less closely related, however, the task will usually be more difficult. Thus, task difficulty and resulting student achievement can be increased by manipulating the relatedness of segment stages: generally teaching closely related stages initially, then moving to more loosely related, and finally to essentially unrelated stages. Segment stages can be related in several ways.

Content   The content of a multistage task is usually determined by the materials that will be used. For example, if the student is told, "Put the scissors on the table and get your pencil," three unrelated content elements—scissors, table, and pencil—are involved. Although these materials may be familiar to the student, their content or attributes are not related. Therefore, retrieving two crayons is more difficult than retrieving one, but it may be easier for a student with mental retardation to locate two crayons even, if they are different colors, than to locate one crayon and one pencil. In any event, diagnosis and prescription for students at this level of learning must address all of these variables.

Stage Settings   The difficulty of a task is increased for a student with mental retardation if the stages must be performed in different settings even though the stages may be similar in content. For example, the task "sweep the floors of these two rooms" calls for the same act to be performed in two different settings; this task necessitates several additional steps for the student. On the one hand, the student has to remember what to do after sweeping the first room; however, because the nature of the stages is closely related, completion of the first easily suggests the second. On the other hand, the student must close down operations in the first room and set them up in the second, and this task adds acts to the instruction. Thus, the change in setting increases the overall difficulty level of the task.

Stage Sequencing   Task stages that are dissimilar in many ways may be related because of sequencing: One stage may lead logically to another. For example, in the sequence "put these chairs on the table and then sweep under the table," the chairs must be removed to clear space for the sweeping, so the sequence should be fairly easy for a student to remember. Similarly, if a student is told to "read this paragraph and answer the questions on it," the sequence cannot really be confused because the student must read the paragraph before answering questions related to it. The logic in the sequence of the tasks provides a strong memory link for the student with mental retardation, who may have difficulty remembering unconnected groups of instructions.

Unrelated Task Stages   Task segments containing unrelated stages are usually more difficult for a student with mental retardation because they make greater demands on the student's memory and concentration. Sequences such as "close the door and bring me the pencil" and "water the flowers and get a bag of cement from the truck" can be mastered, but they should be presented after the student has had experience with more logically related sequencing.

Use of Compensatory Devices

Compensatory devices, such as walkers, wheelchairs, crutches, handrails, life jackets, written instructions, multiplication tables, calculators, and templates, may be used with students with mental retardation, but the decision to use them must be evaluated carefully. If a device such as a calculator, magnifier, hearing aid, printed instructions, or wheelchair is to be needed permanently, then teaching a student to use it properly might be a highly appropriate life goal, and the GIA must include the device as part of the learning process. If the contrivance is intended to be temporary, however, the GIA should call for a series of trials without the supporting device to reduce the child's dependence on it and to fade its use as soon as possible. Often, it takes several years of careful observation (diagnosis, prescription, and evaluation) to determine whether the device must be used permanently or is simply a means to an end. This decision could well be considered with each update of the age 25 projection. Bear in mind also that every year or two, the composition of the student's IEP team is likely to change. Therefore, some effort must be made to convey this information to each new IEP team (level-to-level curriculum planning in Chapter 3).

Time Considerations

Time parameters can be manipulated in several ways to increase a student's performance level and to provide direction for the GIA. In some instances, increasing the time allowed for task completion makes the task easier or less demanding. In other instances, decreasing the time actually increases the task difficulty by urging the student to work more rapidly.

Amount of Time Allotted to a Given Segment or Task

When the amount of time a student is given to complete a task is decreased, in most cases the task or segment becomes more difficult and requires a higher level of skill. Many individuals with mental retardation are limited in employment and other opportunities, not because they cannot perform necessary tasks, but because they perform them more slowly than other people. Students can be taught to think and act more quickly if the teacher has them repeat a GIA segment a number of times, gradually diminishing the time allowed. Manipulating time components is particularly effective when an upcoming segment is substantially more difficult than preceding segments, and the increased speed helps the student gather momentum for approaching the more difficult task. For example, gradually decreasing the time in which a student must perform an on-campus job helps the student gain the speed and confidence necessary to hold a similar or comparable job in the community.

For some skills and capabilities, the educational goal is to increase, rather than decrease, the amount of time on task—for example, increasing a student's attention span or lengthening the time the student persists at the task and deals effectively with distractions. When increasing time for a skill or behavior, the teacher must be careful to increase the substance of the task as well so that the student will not be merely slowing actions and reactions to fill time by taking increased time to do something that could be done much more quickly.

Latency

Latency is the amount of time that elapses between giving instructions and commencing the task. For children with mental retardation, task instructions are usually simple and concise, and the task begins immediately. But when the children become adults, they must be able to delay beginning a task when such a delay is necessary or appropriate. This delay is particularly important to vocational success. On the job, a worker will often be given a series of instructions that must be carried out at varying times, and a supervisor rarely has the time or patience to give new instructions each time the individual completes a small segment of a larger assignment. Teachers can help students become accustomed to delayed beginnings by incorporating the delay in the instructions for the task: "You may start when I snap my fingers"; "Start when the bell rings"; or "For tomorrow, you are to . . ." With such practice, the student gradually learns to begin a task at a designated time, rather than begin everything immediately after instructions have been given.

In contrast, if a student has trouble with procrastination and inattentiveness, the teacher will want to deliberately decrease the time between receiving the instructions and beginning the task.

Amount of Time That Elapses Between the Completion of the Task and the Reward or Evaluation

It is difficult for most young children to accept postponed gratification or reward; it is especially difficult for children with mental retardation. The teacher must carefully assess the individual child's ability to work effectively for a recognition or reward that is not immediate and then build that time component directly into the GIA. Once the initial GIA is set up as close to the child's individual threshold as possible, the length of time between task or segment completion and reward can be gradually increased. The goal is to prepare the student to participate in weekly performance evaluations at school and eventually to succeed on a job that will produce paychecks only once or twice a month.

Rewards and Reinforcements

The importance of constant support and reinforcement for students with mental retardation has been well established. The importance of independence, initiative, and proactivity for adults with mental retardation is acknowledged as well. To achieve optimum independence, an individual must learn to use knowledge and skills when specific rewards and reinforcements are not present. Although it is difficult for a teacher or parent to conclude an activity without praising the student or offering a reward, the educational procedures must be structured to help the students develop the ability to work and succeed with as little outside support as possible. Of course, one major life goal for individuals with mental retardation is independent living that includes full employment to the extent possible. Full-time or even part-time employment is also a primary goal that involves remuneration. Thus, the IEP team is challenged to delineate those activities needing temporary rewards from those in which tangible or monetary rewards are typically continued, such as in employment and self-regulation (Whitman, 1990).

The team should work toward the use of natural rewards or those that occur in real-life situations as a result of an individual's decisions and performance—those that accrue to others who have no disabilities. To accomplish this, the form and amount of reinforcement to be offered should be carefully selected and built into the GIA. In the diagnostic phase of the GIA, the teacher should evaluate the student's need for reinforcement, as well as the individual's customary response to various types and degrees of reward. During the prescriptive phase, the teacher should then outline a plan to help the student in learning self-evaluation of work, along with study and independent living skills. Initially, the GIA projects the point to which the student can be expected to perform a segment or subtask without specific reward. After that point is reached, the reward can be eliminated (Wolff, 1994). If the student seems unable to continue the task without the reward, the teacher should be flexible enough to restore it; however, because of the danger of overdependence on reinforcement, the teacher may want to experiment with manipulating other GIA components before doing so.

BASIC GIA MANEUVERS

Figure 7.2 represents a sample GIA involving only the basic GIA maneuvers. In forming the GIA, the teacher selects a target task from a student's IEP, which has been based on the student's life goals. Initially, it is best to select a simple task. The procedure begins at a level that the teacher is quite certain the student has already mastered, and the components—such as materials, assistance, reinforcement, and time constraints—are selected to ensure that optimum mastery levels will be attained. Components are manipulated one at a time to gradually increase the difficulty of the task and to build the level of performance. For example, increasingly difficult materials may be used as diminishing amounts of assistance are offered.

Figures 7.2, 7.3, and 7.4 are based on the target task of teaching a student to dive from a diving board into a swimming pool. This task was chosen because it is well

Evaluation Dates:

Segment Nos:	1	2	3	4	5	6	7	8	9	10	11	12	13	14	15	16	17	18
Components:																		
Side of Pool																		
Shallow Water		+																
Life Jacket On																		Off
Nose Plugs																No		
Modeling						No												
Teacher							Aide											
Repeated Instruction					—										No			
Repeat Back Instruction				No														
Prompting											—							
Encouragement														—				
Hand-on-Hand								Push									None	
Catcher in Pool																		
No Grace Required									+									
Feet First																		
Edible Reward (F)			No															
Verbal Praise (F)												V						
Pat on Back (F)										V								
Immediate Reward																		
No Time Required													Some					

FIGURE 7.2 Basic GIA Manipulations
Note: F = Fixed; V = Variable.

known and components can be easily understood, although the specific task is probably not appropriate for most students with mental retardation. It is also an excellent example of the reversion principle, discussed below. Moreover, it is an example of how a GIA can help the IEP team in detecting a goal or task that is inappropriate. The sample GIAs of other chapters use goals or tasks that are appropriately taught to students with mental retardation. Whether a primary task or a subtask is involved is not important at this point in the process.

Each segment—that is, all the components in a column—are combined to form a single test item; the GIA is not a checklist. For example, Segment 6 is the same as Segment 5—except that modeling is discontinued in Segment 6. The manipulation and fading of components are clearly evident in Figure 7.2. The components have been manipulated so that as the student's GIA moves from left to right, the demands on the student are increased in small but controllable increments: (1) the list of components makes up segment number 1; (2) in segment number 2 the student is found to be unafraid of water and is moved to the deeper end of the pool; (3) the edible reward is eliminated; (4) having the student repeat the instructions to the teacher is eliminated; (5) giving the student repeated instructions was eliminated; (6) the teacher stopped modeling the task; (7) the teacher turned the teaching of the task over to an aide; (8) the hand-on-hand jumping into the pool was eliminated; (9) the student was taught to jump in with less splash; (10) the pat on the back was reduced from fixed (F) to variable (V); (11) the aide used less prompting; (12) the verbal praise was reduced from fixed (F) to variable (V); (13) the student was helped to stop wasting time; (14) the teacher taught the aide to use less verbal encouragement; (15) repeated instructions were eliminated; (16) the nose plugs were removed; (17) physical assistance was eliminated; and (18) the life jacket was removed.

The column that lists the initial components is segment number 1 and is administered to the student as a test item just as numbers 2 to 18 are. Using the first column as testing segment number 1 also helps the teacher detect any component that is not easily manipulated.

Individualizing the GIA

Any person making even a casual examination of Figure 7.3 will likely disagree with the specific components selected, as well as with the way they were manipulated. This objection affirms the need for individually designed GIAs. The components, as well as the symbols used to designate how each component is to be manipulated, need to make sense only to the teacher or therapist until he or she needs to teach an aide or volunteer how to assist in teaching the student. The teacher, therapist, or parent must select and use those components with which he or she is comfortable.

Reversion Points

The casual inspection of Figure 7.2 suggests the need for the reversion principle, a simple but essential part of GIA—or any procedure for teaching students with mental retardation. Some components cannot be manipulated in small increments. For example, in Figure 7.2 the next logical manipulation of "side of the pool" is to move to the "1-m diving board." Diving boards less than 1 meter in height are rarely available. The student's initial experiences on the diving board can be extremely scary and challenging. Thus, the teacher may need to provide a less challenging situation by using a *reversion*. He or she does this by reverting back to some components that were previously eliminated. The requirements of other components are eased, and usually assistance is increased. This aid helps the student overcome the sharply increased demands of the component that cannot be manipulated in small increments. The same procedure can be used to help the student gather momentum to attempt a more difficult example or problem.

Another reversion will probably be necessary if the student were to master the "1-m diving board," the next logical manipulation being the "3-m diving board." Other examples are the student entering the water head first—any compromise between feet first and head first is likely to be painful. In some instances, turning the instruction over to an aide might also require a reversion.

It is important to realize that the reversion principle should not be applied in lockstep fashion. Moving the student from the 1-m to the 2-m diving board will require a reversion, but putting the life jacket back on the student at this height might inflict pain or injury. Reversion, like the other GIA principles, must never violate common sense or safety requirements.

To demonstrate the flexibility and capacity of the GIA, Figures 7.2 and 7.4 show a wide variety of GIA components, most of the components that could conceivably be used in such a task, whereas actual classroom GIAs use only the components that are appropriate to a specific student and one particular target task. Usually, increasing the number of components produces a more detailed GIA, with smaller learning increments; this specificity and depth generally increase with the severity of the child's mental retardation. The number of components used in a real-life GIA depends on the unique level, rate, and learning style of the student.

APPLYING GIA PROCEDURES IN THE CLASSROOM

Although it is necessary to understand the basic procedure in order to implement it, even in this simple example an excessive amount of time and effort would be necessary to locate the student's educational frontier on the target task if all steps were followed exactly as presented. Some students would progress through many segments before reaching the point of faltering and failing, a point that is necessary for the diagnosis to end and the prescription to begin. Figure 7.3 shows how a diagnostic procedure can be built in that is similar to the basal age procedure used in administering standardized tests. This technique (discussed in Sections 6 and 7, below) is called *checkpointing*. The following is a complete listing and description of the steps in the GIA procedure—including checkpointing.

1. Identify the Target Task

The target task is selected from the prioritized list of annual goals and short-term objectives on the student's IEP. The target task need not be remedial; it should be the next logical area of learning suggested by the IEP sequence.

2. Select a Subtask if Necessary

If it appears that the target task will require a good deal of instructional time, it may be divided into subtasks to be taught either separately or simultaneously. For example, if it appears that the target task of teaching a boy with mental retardation to dress himself will take a considerable amount of time, it may be best to make the donning of each article of clothing a separate subtask with its own GIA. Otherwise, the GIA for putting on the shirt may be complete, dormant, and in the way while teaching him to put on his trousers. If, however, he is to put on his socks each time he puts on his shoes, these two articles can be diagnosed and prescribed as one GIA. If it appears that the target task of teaching a student to tell time will require several months of instruction, a workable subtask would be teaching the student first to read the hour hand of the clock. The target task should not be extended too far into the future. The precision of the GIA makes it possible to discern whether the student is likely to master a target task more quickly or slowly than originally anticipated and thus whether the IEP team will need to adjust the student's overall goals. With a little experience, testing and teaching the GIA may show that the student was not really ready for the skills and concepts of the GIA.

3. Identify the Appropriate Entry-Level Skills

Once the target task and subtasks have been identified, the teacher should list prerequisite entry-level skills or concepts, including maturity, stamina, and intelligence. Identifying such prerequisite skills is essential in working with students with mental retardation. Failure to do so is comparable to expecting an average student to learn algebra without first mastering the multiplication tables. Because entry-level skills and concepts are not always obvious and because students with mental retardation learn very slowly, even experienced teachers sometimes attempt to teach tasks for which the prerequisite skills have not yet been mastered. As the GIA process helps in clarifying the nature and complexity of a task, these prerequisites become more apparent. The learning characteristics discussed in earlier chapters suggest some of the most important entry-level skills that should be considered. Teachers must remember that entry-level skills can be indirectly as well as directly related to the target task. Finally, the entry-level skills are classified to make certain all are considered and there is little need for undue concern about the classification of a given entry-level skill.

Directly Related Entry-Level Skills

Many skills are natural extensions of previously mastered skills and concepts; for example, when a child who has learned to count to 20 learns to count to 100, the new task very obviously builds upon the old. Often, the new subtasks extend the old but make it more complex. Thus, a student learns first to identify coins and then to make change. Entry levels may include understanding safety measures or comprehending the purpose and rules of a new game or sport. Because of the importance of entry-level skills and concepts, students working toward off-campus job placement must learn work-related skills in a closely supervised on-campus program where teachers are experienced in assessing deficiencies in prerequisite skills employers might be unaware of.

Indirectly Related Entry-Level Skills

Some entry-level skills may appear less directly related to a target task and still be important to accomplishing it. For example, to evaluate a collection of coins, a student must be able to add numbers as large as 25; otherwise, working with the quarter will be impossible. Similarly, if a student is being taught to tell time, an alert teacher will assess whether the student has a concept of what time is and how it is used and also whether the student is able to count by 5s.

A less obvious category of indirect entry-level skills includes *basic abilities*, such as requisite IQ or adequate levels of physiological and psychological maturity. Unlike the other forms of entry-level skills, these abilities cannot be improved by teaching. If the student is lacking in these areas, the IEP team will need to consider discarding the specified tasks or postponing them until the maturity occurs.

Often, when a student with mental retardation lacks these basic abilities, target tasks can still be taught by adjusting the communication level. All tasks must of necessity be presented on a level consistent with the student's ability to listen, read, understand, and follow oral or written directions. Often, a teacher must be creative in finding communication approaches that will compensate for the lack of intellectual or physical maturity. Careful evaluation of the entry-level skills reveals the need for creative approaches in communicating effectively with the student.

Evaluating entry-level skills also helps a teacher in establishing priorities in the student's curriculum and determining whether a task for which the student lacks the prerequisites is permanently or only temporarily inappropriate. If the IEP team must decide between equivalent target tasks, selection might be influenced by the adequacy of entry-level skills for the various options.

4. Treat the Entry-Level Skills if Necessary

If a student has partially mastered an entry-level skill or if the entry-level skill is not essential, a teacher may decide to teach the entry-level skill simultaneously with the target task. If the student's deficiency is serious or if the entry-level skill is particularly significant, however, then it must be taught immediately even if the target task or subtask must be set aside temporarily. The entry-level skill or concept may be diagnosed, prescribed, and taught as a subtask with its own GIA.

5. Select the GIA Components to Be Used

Selecting realistic and manipulatable GIA components is most crucial. Experience shows that if the components are manipulatable, the rest of a GIA more-or-less falls into place. Figure 7.1 provides a list of components and classes of components that can be used as a checklist for teachers beginning to use GIAs. These are only general suggestions, however; it is important to remember that every task will require that components be selected and adapted to fit the unique circumstances of the child and the target task. For some tasks, the size and number of materials may be the most important components; for others, the types of materials may be more significant. In the sample GIA, the height of the diving board is extremely important; in selecting reading materials, the size of the print will probably be crucial.

The sample GIA chart in Figure 7.4 demonstrates a workable format for writing a GIA. The horizontal rows show GIA components; the vertical columns show the task segments. Each horizontal row shows how one component was used initially, and then whenever that component is manipulated (e.g., altered, eliminated, reinstated), an appropriate notation is made in the appropriate column. "No" is written to indicate that the GIA component for that column has been eliminated, at least temporarily; "yes" is marked to show that the component—previously eliminated—is being reinstated. Other manipulations are indicated by more specific words or phrases: increase, decrease, or simply (+) or (–). A notation of "6 ft" might be used to indicate that the student is jumping into water 6-ft deep. A teacher should select only those components that can actually be manipulated. For example, all of the components listed in Figure 7.2 can be increased or decreased in a variety of ways; however, specific problems, examples, or dialogue would not make good components because a teacher cannot change them easily to alter the focus or the difficulty of the task. Sometimes teachers find it helpful to group components by classification—for example, placing components related to materials in one section of the chart, those related to mastery or to assistance in another.

6. Create and List the Appropriate Checkpoints

It is obvious from the casual examination of Figure 7.4 that administering all those segments as individual test items would take an inordinate amount of time. Therefore, GIA uses a procedure called *checkpointing*, which is nothing more than a basal/ceiling age procedure borrowed from standardized testing.

In testing, a student's basal age is the difficulty level on which the individual does not experience success on almost every question. In calculating scores, the student is given credit for all items below that basal level of difficulty. Similarly, checkpointing tests the student only on a sample of the GIA segments. After the first few goal or task segments are arranged in order of increasing difficulty, a diagnosis checkpoint is chosen arbitrarily by selecting every Nth (e.g., 3rd, 5th, 11th) segment. Rather than administer every segment in testing the student, the teacher uses only those segments (e.g., 3rd, 5th, 11th) designated as checkpoints.

In this manner, checkpointing diagnoses a student's current performance level on a target task so that the individual prescription can begin on that level. Time is not wasted presenting concepts and skills that the student has already learned, and material is not offered that the student will not be able to learn. Instruction should begin near a student's ceiling and progress forward. This tactic enables reviewing and reteaching of concepts immediately below the ceiling and then moving forward with the target concepts and tasks. The review provides a base upon which to build, as well as the momentum necessary to improve the student's performance.

Figure 7.1 lists components often included in GIA segments. Modifiers, such as *harder example, more grace, less time,* or simply *increase, decrease, more, less, heavier,* or *longer* can be added. Using a simple yes or no reinstates or discontinues the use of any component. Making an additional entry in any column simply modifies the last entry in that column. To demonstrate processes involved with GIA manipulation, examples and nonexamples are given.

7. Use Checkpointing to Diagnose the Student's Achievement Level on the Target Task

Checkpointing is an effective process of evaluation. Like finding the basal age on a test, the checkpointing procedure helps in locating a student's educational frontier without taking the time to test the student on GIA segments that can be easily performed. Just as students are given credit for the items below basal age on the test and no credit is given for sporadic correct answers above the ceiling age, the students' GIA maps out previous and resulting segments, but these segments are not administered in the diagnosis unless the student fails a succeeding segment. With experience, the teacher or therapist learns to establish checkpoints and to test students quickly. The nature of a student's success on each checkpoint helps in determining the number of components to be manipulated in forming the next checkpoint and the speed at which the checkpointing procedure will move. If a student does not appear to be significantly challenged at succeeding checkpoints, the procedure will move quickly. When the student begins to falter, checkpointing slows down because it is now evident that the student is getting closer to his or her present frontier.

The teacher or therapist begins the checkpointing procedure by selecting or formulating any GIA segment that is clearly between the student's basal and ceiling ages, as described in Sections 5 and 6. He or she manipulates the component in one of the columns to make the task segment slightly more difficult than the previous segment; all other components remain the same. If the student is successful in completing the segment, the teacher or therapist then manipulates a component in another column; again, the others remain constant. The teacher or therapist continues to manipulate components, one at a time, until the child is no longer consistently successful and it is evident that the ceiling age has been reached. By choosing which components are manipulated and how extensive the manipulation is, the diagnostician can control the rate at which the checkpointing process will occur.

The Checkpointing Process in Diagnosis

Figures 7.3 and 7.4 illustrate how a teacher used the checkpoints to locate a student's educational frontier. The student responded easily to Checkpoint A but began to falter on Checkpoint B, and failed on C. Checkpoint C located the student's approximate

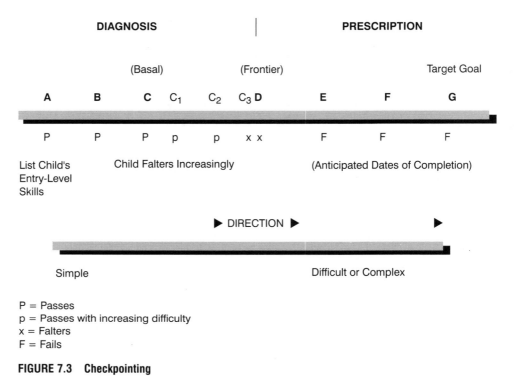

FIGURE 7.3   Checkpointing

basal age. At this point, the teacher simply retreats back to Checkpoint B and prescribes forward through Checkpoint C and beyond.

The teacher was able to discern that the student's educational frontier was somewhere between two highly defined checkpoints: B, which was passed, and C, which was failed. The GIA retreats to a point between the current checkpoint and the last point that was completed successfully and continues until the teacher is able to discern the most difficult task segment the student can master at the time. At this frontier, the diagnosis ends and the prescription and teaching can begin. The next GIA segment constitutes the student's first prescription. The transition between the testing and the teaching should be so smooth that a casual observer in the classroom would probably be unable to tell when the teacher stopped diagnosing and began prescribing. Although basals and ceilings are, to some extent, subjective, they are probably the most accurate system of any presently being used for determining where the instruction of a particular child should begin. The dates by which the teacher predicts the student will reach prescription Checkpoints D, E, and F are listed and used in evaluation. Figure 7.4 shows the complete GIA.

The complete GIA shows how the teacher administered all of the first segment as a single test item. This action is particularly important. First, it identifies any GIA component that is difficult to manipulate. After all, the teacher assumed that each component was essential. If the teacher finds that any of his or her components cannot be

Evaluation Dates:

Frontier → (column C)   Reversion → (column 17)   2/7 (D)   2/14 (E)   2/23 (F)

Segment Nos.:	2	A	4	5	B	B₁	B₂	B₃	C	11	12	13	D	15	16	17	18	19	E	21	22	23	24	F	26
Components:																									
Side of Pool																									
Shallow Water		+																							
Life Jacket On																Off									
Nose Plugs															No	Yes				No					
Modeling					No																				
Teacher					Aide									No		Teacher					Aide				
Repeated Instruction					−																				
Repeat Back Instruction		No																							No
Prompting									−				−						−						
Encouragement													−			+	−								
Hand-on-Hand									Push							None		No							
Catcher in Pool									+													+			
No Grace Required																									
Feet First																									
Edible Reward (F)		No																							
Verbal Praise (F)									Variable		∨												−		
Pat on Back (F)																								No	
Immediate Reward																									
No Time Required												Some													

FIGURE 7.4 GIA Diving

217

readily manipulated, it can be eliminated or changed. Because the entry level skills, the components, and the notations that show how each component is to be manipulated need to be meaningful only to the creator of the GIA, it is likely that some entries on the sample GIA do not make sense. In that event, they can be changed to suit the needs and intentions of the reader. Coloring alternate lines helps in tracking across a lengthy GIA. The GIAs should be in written form only until the teacher masters the process. Of course, it is possible to manipulate more than one component at any time. Doing so helps ensure that the prescription is moving as rapidly as it should. This is done in some of the sample GIAs at the ends of later chapters.

In Figure 7.4, a reversion was encountered in Segment 17 when the life jacket was removed. The life jacket must be either on or off; this dichotomy makes a component that cannot be manipulated in small increments. At that point, it was necessary to revert back to previously eliminated or manipulated components to help the student through the abrupt change.

Content and Accuracy of a Checkpoint

Because the GIA segments that serve as checkpoints are used throughout the DPE teaching sequence, they must be selected with care. If they are to be useful in designing detailed prescriptions for the students, all checkpoints must be described in terms of GIA components and must show not only the precise performance level and rate at which a student is progressing but also the specific circumstances and external support necessary to sustain that progress. For example, a realistic evaluation would go beyond stating that a student is ready for competitive employment to indicate whether the individual would need to work alone or with others, how much instruction and supervision would have to be given, how frequently praise or reward would be necessary, and what quality and quantity of work could realistically be expected.

Because GIAs must be accurate and detailed, the starting point must be as accurate as possible. Because checkpoints are the first GIA segments to be formulated, some preliminary or hypothetical experience with checkpointing is helpful in preparing a teacher to formulate, express, and interpret them with precision. For example, the following statement appears to be a logical checkpoint for the toilet training of a young boy with mental retardation: "Makes his toileting needs known." However, examination by an experienced teacher would indicate that a number of important questions are left unanswered, questions that involve a wide variety of entry levels: Does the child verbalize his needs, or does his face turn red with no verbalization? If he verbalizes, how does he do so? Does he volunteer the information, or must he be asked? Does he make his needs known consistently or just occasionally? Must his teacher be present, or will he indicate his needs to a parent or an instructional assistant? If conceptual distance is considered, weeks or even months of instruction would be necessary for a student to move from the lowest to the highest level of capability suggested by these questions. Because so much time is involved between these proficiency levels, accurate planning for detailed prescriptions and lesson plans could not occur if the checkpoint were as imprecise as the initial question.

8. Recheck the GIA Components and the Student's Entry-Level Skills

The GIA components must be reviewed periodically to determine whether the progress rate originally predicted for the student is accurate. If the student appears to be learning more rapidly than anticipated, some rudimentary components may be eliminated or speeded up; if the student appears to be learning more slowly than projected, additional support components may need to be sought. Because teachers sometimes tend to provide more assistance and supervision than students with mental retardation actually need, students may appear on the surface to be doing well when their success is largely due to assistance, prompting, advice, and reinforcement, rather than to solid mastery of skills and concepts. Thus, it is well to verify entry-level skills prior to beginning a target task, rather than merely assume they are due to a student's performance on other segments. Frequent checking may be necessary because entry-level deficiencies can become apparent after the teaching of a segment begins. For example, although the beginning stages of an arithmetic GIA might not require very much reading, later stages could demand more specialized reading skills. Therefore, a student's entry-level reading skills may appear to be sufficient as the GIA begins but prove inadequate as the teaching continues. When the student begins to falter, it may appear that the educational frontier in arithmetic is being approached when, in reality, arithmetic skills are adequate for the problems but a deficiency in entry-level reading skills is interfering with the student's ability to perform.

The acid test of education, of course, is whether the student can use the skills developed in the classroom in real-life situations. Thus, the teacher or therapist occasionally needs to have the student perform without assistance to check for initiative and independence. Also, it is important to observe each student in a practical situation to test whether the individual can recognize a solvable problem and use the acquired skills to find a solution to it.

9. Formulate the Detailed GIA Segments

Prescription begins at this step. Once the teacher or therapist has located the student's educational frontier, the student must succeed at every segment before going on to the next one. Each new segment is created by increasing, decreasing, eliminating, or otherwise altering one or more of the components from the previous segment to make slightly greater demands on the student. The number of components to be altered and the degree of manipulation must be adjusted to maximize the student's progress without being discouraging to the student.

A teacher or therapist would do well to sketch out several hypothetical GIAs before attempting to perform one on a student. A chart similar to that used in Figures 7.2 and 7.4 is useful for plotting both hypothetical and early actual GIAs until the maker has had enough practice to diagnose and prescribe a teaching procedure without preparing a written document first. The chapters in Part IV include many suggestions on how GIA applies to specific areas of learning.

Using a Component More than Once

Because components are used in combinations, a component can be used over and over, and a component that has been discontinued in some segments may be reinstated in others when a new combination necessitates it. For example, in the sample GIA, the life jacket might have been removed when the student was still at the level of jumping into the water from the side of the pool but reinstated the first few times that the student jumped from the 1-m diving board, had the student been especially nervous when the diving board became a task component.

Parallel Components

Two or more related components may be used simultaneously in a parallel situation. Whether the GIA is written or not, if it is planned carefully, each of the parallel components can be manipulated independent of the others. For example, in the sample GIA, three reinforcement components—tangible reward, verbal praise, and pat on the back—were used in a single segment. At the beginning, all three were used simultaneously; however, the tangible reward was soon dropped although the other reinforcements were continued.

Successive Components

In some instances, a component may succeed or replace an equivalent component. Had a different teacher designed the sample GIA, that individual might have preferred to use the pat on the back and the verbal praise at different times, rather than simultaneously. Because the pat on the back is the most rudimentary reinforcement, it probably would have been listed first in the column on the GIA where reinforcement was to be indicated; later, when the teacher was ready to make the change, the word *praise* would have been written in the square or cell just below *pat* in the same column; this would show that verbal praise would succeed the pat on the back. Two methods used simultaneously are given separate columns, as they are in the sample as written.

10. Set Project Completion Dates for Each Prescribed Checkpoint

When checkpointing is used in evaluating the GIA, the student's progress can be documented with great precision and the appropriateness of the rate at which the student is moving can be verified. Every Nth segment (e.g., 3rd, 6th, 10th) is arbitrarily selected as an evaluation checkpoint.

A systematized plan for instruction is developed as the prescription estimates the time a student will need to progress to each future checkpoint. Contingencies, such as the school's time requirements, class schedules, or the amount of emphasis the IEP team places on the target task, must be coordinated. A date is then written by each checkpoint; on the sample GIA in Figure 7.4, dates are recorded across the top. When the projected date arrives or after the student completes the checkpoint, the projected and actual performance rates can be compared. If a student arrives at checkpoints early, indicating that the instruction has been more efficient or the student more capable than anticipated, projections for future checkpoints may be adjusted accordingly. Possibly, the student's life goals can even be increased. In contrast, if the student is consistently later in arriving at checkpoints than anticipated, instructions, rate, or expectations may need to be reduced, or the task may need to be removed from the student's IEP or reduced in priority. Dates do not need to be exact, but they should be calculated carefully to provide satisfactory evaluative data. The age 25 projection should be used to provide guidelines in deciding when a student's life goals must be adjusted.

A FINAL NOTE

The most common mistake teachers are likely to make in learning how to use GIA procedures is that their components are not truly manipulatable. They have particular difficulty with the "materials" components. Remember, the "materials" components are not simply a list of the objects to be used. Each material must be in manipulatable form. For example, pencil, paper, book, and size are not readily manipulated. In place of these, try large pencil, wide-lined paper, simple book or story, and small numbers (of materials). To increase the difficulty and achievement level of the GIA, these can be gradually manipulated to small (regular size) pencil, narrow-lined paper, more difficult book or story, and larger number. A good test of how well the components are to manipulate occurs when the entire list of components is applied as a single test item in segment (checkpoint) number 1 (see segment number 1 of Figures 7.2 and 7.4—side of pool, shallow water, life jacket on, etc.).

SUMMARY

As discussed in this chapter, goal instructional analysis (GIA) is an important prerequisite to diagnostic-prescriptive teaching. Instruction is given for performing both a hypothetical and an actual GIA, including gradually adapting what is initially a written document into a largely unwritten diagnostic-prescriptive teaching procedure.

I also demonstrated how a teacher can use the GIA process to provide a detailed instructional road map that can be followed by parents, paraprofessional staff members, peer tutors, or others assisting with the education of students with mental retardation. Assessing entry-level skills and considering them during the planning process were stressed.

I showed how the GIA can provide detailed documentation of the performance and progress of a student with mental retardation because the data derived from the GIA projected plan certify both the level and the rate of a student's performance.

CHAPTER 8

Classroom Management and Discipline

Points to Study and Ponder

1. How likely are students with mental retardation to have behavioral problems? Why must this likelihood be decided on an individual basis?
2. Is there any relationship between life goal planning and classroom management?
3. What relationship exists between obedience and self-control?
4. How are self-reliance and making one's own decisions related?
5. How are proactivity and self-reliance related?
6. How can the age 25 projection be used to promote proactivity and self-reliance?
7. What are some precautions to exercise in using detention and suspensions to discipline students with mental retardation?
8. What is reality therapy, and how can it be used in the goal instruction analysis (GIA) procedures?
9. What is assertive discipline, and how can it be used in GIA procedures?
10. For what purposes might a teacher be sued for his or her activities in the classroom?

I f a classroom is to be a center of learning, it must be organized and managed well. The disciplinary aspects of classroom management are of particular concern to pre-service students and inexperienced teachers who tend to rank the treatment of behavioral problems high on lists of skills in which they feel personally inadequate. Moreover, many administrators contribute to the fears of new teachers by overemphasizing student control and discipline in preemployment interviews and in-service teacher evaluations. These concerns of administrators are not without justification because little positive learning occurs when students are out of control. Improving classroom management skills pays great dividends in the overall performance of students with mental retardation, as well as increases the teacher's personal satisfaction. Obviously, the more time a teacher spends on purely disciplinary matters, the less effective that teacher is in the more important aspects of teaching. Most disciplinary action distracts not only the student being disciplined but also other class members. Time is wasted that could have been spent teaching and learning. Correcting a chronic behavioral problem, however, might be the most important long-term IEP goal for a student—including one with mental retardation (Davidson et al., 1994). Davidson and his colleagues reported that the strongest predictor of aggressive behaviors in individuals with mental retardation in community-based settings is history of such past behavior. Chronic behavioral problems, if uncorrected, can disqualify a student from success in adult life regardless of his or her other accomplishments.

In this chapter, I show how the diagnostic/prescriptive techniques and other procedures can be used to teach individuals with mental retardation how to control and manage their own behavior and to make personal decisions. A secondary purpose is to help teachers and parents overcome any real or imaginary inadequacies they may perceive about their classroom management skills and to relieve some of the anxieties they may have about the disciplinary needs of students with mental retardation.

MENTAL RETARDATION AND THE INCIDENCE OF BEHAVIORAL PROBLEMS

In Chapter 1, I suggested that, on the one hand, students with mental retardation do not necessarily present serious disciplinary problems. On the other hand, some of these students are understandably difficult to handle, and their teachers must be prepared to deal with a wide range of behavioral problems. The concept of regional variation suggests that low-identification states tend to identify primarily students whose mental retardation is severe/profound. And the more severe and profound forms of mental retardation tend to result in a greater incidence of behavioral problems.

It appears that, as a group, students with mental retardation generally have a slightly higher than average incidence of behavioral problems (Reber, 1992; Russell & Forness, 1985). Their behavioral problems tend to be of a less serious nature, however, than those of individuals without mental retardation (Beier, 1964; Matson & Barnett, 1982). Vandever (1983) matched more than 1,000 students with and without mental retardation according to MA, gender, and eligibility for free or reduced-price school lunches. He discovered that students with mental retardation are no more likely to be suspended from school than other students. The school suspensions of students without mental retardation are more likely to be the result of offenses related to drugs and alcohol. He also found that the offenses of students without mental retardation tend to be more serious and disruptive (disobedience, indecent language, and disrespectful behavior). Lang and Kahn (1986) found that students with mental retardation are less involved in crime and delinquency than those with behavioral disorders and learning disabilities. Edgerton (1986) reported alcohol and drug abuse to be less serious problems among students with mental retardation than among other students. In general, it appears that students with mental retardation who have problems with the law tend to have committed less serious offenses. Ordinarily, these behavioral problems should not cause undue concern for their teachers because classes for students with severe/profound mental retardation usually have fewer students and because the teachers are likely to hire paid adult aides or assistants. In recent years, however, the courts in both England (Peagam, 1993) and the United States (*Hacienda La Puente School District of Los Angeles v. Honig*, 1992) have increasingly held that students with severe behavioral problems are disabled under the law. In these cases, the schools are barred from suspending or expelling these students.

PREVENTIVE MEASURES

Because a student with mental retardation spends so much more time with and in the care of parents and other family members than with school personnel, it is important that teachers use particular caution in the area of management and discipline. It is unfair for educators to employ any particular disciplinary measure (no matter how effective it may be) that the parents disapprove of or are unable to maintain. For this reason, educators must make special efforts to involve the student's parents at every stage of management and discipline. Level-to-level program planning is also necessary in management and discipline to ensure the student has a well-coordinated program that encourages him or her to become increasingly mature in decision making. Otherwise, the student is likely to leave school having been forced to conform to a variety of behavior-shaping techniques but with no sense of self-direction.

I stress preventive measures and techniques that help anticipate and head off most behavioral problems. I do not dwell unnecessarily on "disciplinary" techniques, most of which tend to be negative, even harsh, and should be used only as a last resort. Many disciplinary procedures do not treat—or even seek—the causes of a student's misbehavior, but rather deal only with the outward, observable signs of a behavioral problem. For example, a forgetful student often receives the same treatment as one who is deliberately disobedient. Many students and teachers, as well as parents, confuse the enforcement of discipline with teaching self-control and seek foolproof disciplinary techniques or "whips" to enforce unfailing obedience in all cases. The IEP team should identify and stress natural consequences of a student's actions and preventative measures wherever possible.

Preventive procedures are not likely to solve all behavioral problems among students with mental retardation. Sometimes a student will have developed some behavioral problems before being enrolled in the teacher's class. For these reasons, I discuss some direct treatment procedures to use while initiating long-range preventive programs and seeking the causes of a student's misbehavior. Many direct disciplinary measures tend to be aversive and are widely criticized (Meyer & Evans, 1989). In some instances, preventive measures may appear to work more slowly than direct measures, but they tend to promote intrinsic motivation, initiative, and self-control, rather than simply evoke responses to external influence and force. One effective preventive procedure is to gradually enable the student to foresee and deal with the natural consequences of his or her acts. To accomplish this, the instruction should take place in the home, at work, and in other natural settings wherever possible.

POSITIVE CONSIDERATIONS

Teachers of students with mental retardation have several positive things going for them. Discussing some of these positive considerations may help the teachers see that dealing with disciplinary problems is not as ominous as it may appear at first. For several reasons, the erroneous notion persists that people with mental retardation are likely to be dangerous—even delinquents and criminals. Although one might reasonably assume that more intelligent perpetrators of crime are more likely to avoid detection and conviction, it has been found that generally the mean IQ of persons convicted of felonies is somewhat below average. In fact, as early as 1934, Glueck and Glueck reported that a high percentage of persons arrested for crimes had mental retardation. In 1934, however, relatively few special school programs were available for students with mental retardation, and more recent studies—though not entirely encouraging— paint a more positive picture (Watanabe & Forgnone, 1990).

Small Classes

One advantage of teaching students with mental retardation is that the classes (except in mainstreamed situations) are usually smaller. In most instances, teachers of students with mental retardation should not expect to spend an excessive amount of time handling discipline problems. Realistically though, if a teacher had 25 to 35 such students in a single class, as is typically the case with nondisabled students, one would expect a generally chaotic situation. Most school districts compensate by limiting a self-contained class to no more than 8 to 12 students—although this number varies greatly from state to state.

Instructional Assistants

Another advantage of teaching students with mental retardation is that one or more instructional assistants or classroom aides are likely to be assigned to special classrooms. One reason that instructional assistants are needed in the education of students with mental retardation is to compensate for the great variety of problems and deficiencies intrinsic to mental retardation.

Attitudes of Students with Mental Retardation

In Chapter 2, I pointed out that most students with mental retardation generally tend to be trusting and obedient. They are likely to perceive the teacher as an authority figure—even on the first day of school. Of course, they still may test teachers and other adults, as other students do. For example, a student may talk out of turn or get out of her seat without permission to test the teacher's reaction, but these minor problems are not usually difficult to handle. Most students with mental retardation tend to be forgiving and unlikely to hold grudges—even on a "bad" day. Edgerton et al. (1984) and Sellin (1979) found that students with mental retardation have a generally positive outlook on life. Further, most students with mental retardation seem to love school and are likely to complain if school is canceled unexpectedly.

LIFE GOAL PLANNING AND CLASSROOM MANAGEMENT

Perhaps the most encouraging knowledge for teachers is that many discipline problems in any classroom can be greatly alleviated or eliminated by proper planning and teaching techniques. To put it another way, if a student is either bored or working at his or her frustration level, the teacher (or parent) can usually expect a continual barrage of disciplinary problems. The teacher can minimize the time spent on disciplinary matters if each student is learning valuable and practical skills and concepts presented at his or her unique level and rate of mastery. Walker (1993) reported that noncompliance is more likely to occur with individuals with mental retardation where instructions, lessons, and tasks are vague and indefinite. The life goals curriculum planning approach and the diagnostic-prescriptive teaching methods described throughout this book provide the means to overcome these program weaknesses. In this chapter, I also show how to use this planning approach and these methods directly in helping each student to achieve maximum independence and self-control.

The regional variability in identification practices greatly magnifies and intensifies the inherent range of ability a teacher may be called on to manage. In a practical sense, this variability means each teacher must be prepared to use a wide assortment and extent of management and disciplinary measures. Considered together, the inherent heterogeneity of mental retardation and the regional variation in identification practices make the need for a highly individualized life goal planning approach at least as significant in classroom management as in any other area. The planning and conducting of educational programs for each student with mental retardation must be done in light of this great range of ability.

THE QUEST FOR INDEPENDENT LIVING

Students—with mental retardation or without—must pass through several stages to become independent as adults: (a) being obedient, (b) being cooperative, (c) making good choices, (d) making sound decisions, and (e) exercising proactivity and initiative. These stages are not mutually exclusive. Even the more mature students with mental retardation will be involved in the early stages to some extent. Disciplinary procedures are limited primarily to the obedience stage.

Being Obedient

Obedience can be defined as meeting the expectations or demands of others. One of the first and most important things a child must learn in the classroom is to "play school" (sit down, be quiet, respect the rights of others, and perform as responsible adults direct). Neither the student nor the student's classmates are likely to learn very much until the student learns to be obedient to this extent. Also, some students whose mental retardation is severe/profound may not achieve an appreciable degree of independence and essentially must be obedient to others throughout their lives. The more severe the mental retardation, the more the individual will depend on others for direction and support. As a young student with mental retardation enters school, it is usually necessary to teach obedience for the individual's own safety and to establish and maintain an effective learning environment (Huguenin, 1993). Many students, however, including some with mental retardation, have been taught at home to be obedient and cooperative. The teacher can begin immediately to teach this type of student to accept responsibility for his or her own actions, independence, self-discipline, appropriate decision making, and proactivity. The educational program for such an individual must concentrate on helping him or her follow necessary prescribed rules and requirements of others. All people must learn to be sensitive and obedient to a variety of rules, regulations, of family members and employers. Therefore, at the same time a student with mental retardation is learning to make realistic personal decisions, that student must be introduced to an increasing number and variety of regulations he or she must obey.

Natural Consequences

Obedience, as used here, refers essentially to compliance with essential home, school, and societal laws, customs, mores, and the expectations of friends, employers, fellow employees, and a variety of other people. A word of caution is in order, however, for those who work in school settings with students with mental retardation. McDonnell

Periodic reevaluation of the age 25 projection suggests the extent to which an individual with mental retardation will live independently as an adult.

(1993) pointed to the ethical question of having one person enforce compliance on another and suggested that such interventions must be initiated with great care. Those involved must ensure that requiring obedience must be done carefully and only if doing so is an appropriate objective for the student. Equally important is the matter of determining how and to what extent compliance is essential for the student to eventually develop optimum independence and to make as many of his or her own decisions as possible. On the one hand, programmatical overemphasis on compliance tends to create and perpetuate dependence; on the other hand, an individual who runs amok, throws temper tantrums, and demonstrates little self-control is unlikely to experience any appreciable amount of independence as an adult.

Wehmeyer (1994) reported that students with mental retardation and—to somewhat of a lesser extent—those with learning and other disabilities have considerable difficulty perceiving the extent to which they are subject to external control. As a result, the students must learn to differentiate among laws, rules, mores, and customs to which they must conform and areas where they can choose what to do and how to act. Thus, the IEP team must determine the point at which the compliance aspects of the individual's program should be faded out in favor of self-regulation (Baer, 1990; Mithaug, 1993). Logically, the programs of self-regulation, decision making, and development of independence should be nonaversive and should be accomplished in the most natural settings (Turnbull & Turnbull, 1990). The age 25 projection may be used in helping the student's teacher and IEP team identify that student's educational frontier in the area of obedience, begin instruction at the correct level, and proceed toward optimum independence and self-direction.

Positive and Nonaversive Management Procedures

Nonaversive behavioral management procedures (essentially, those involving positive, as opposed to negative or punishment) have proved highly effective with students with mental retardation. Physical guidance/restraint may be necessary in some instances, particularly where the well-being of the individual or the safety of teachers and classmates is in jeopardy. Any degree of independent living or employment success, however, requires these measures to be diminished and replaced by positive procedures, self-control, and self-determination as soon as possible (Friman, 1990; Wehmeyer & Metzler, 1995). Non-aversive procedures have been used with success not only in reducing unacceptable social and other negative behaviors but also in teaching and encouraging positive behaviors. Miner (1991) used food as a reward to reduce self-stimulation in a 12-year-old male with severe mental retardation and visual impairment. Another effective, general procedure (often referred to as *differential reinforcement of other behaviors,* or DRO) draws attention away from negative behaviors and focuses on different, positive conduct. Donnellan and LaVigna (1986) used this procedure, manipulated other reinforcements, and controlled the offending stimulus in various ways as they successfully reduced several negative behaviors. Kennedy and Haring (1993) used DRO and a variation of DRO they described as escape DRO (termination of instruction is contingent on the omission of the negative behavior). They reported the combination DRO approach to be very effective in reducing problem conduct in three adolescents with severe disabilities. Matson and Keyes (1990) reported movement suppression to be effective in self-injurious and aggressive behavior when paired with either DRO or verbal reprimands. Two other procedures used for the same purposes are *time-out* (removing the individual from the problem stimulus or environment) and *overcorrection* (a retributive plan that requires the offending individual to make amends and return the situation to a better state than when the offense was committed). Tyson and Spooner (1991) reviewed the historical use of isolation (in-room) time-out, exclusion (out-of-room) time-out, prone restraint, in-seat restraint, standing restraint, mechanical restraint, and overcorrection in a residential institution. They reported that all had some positive results, but they also noted that some were extremely aversive. Even time-out procedures (like others that isolate or suspend participation and learning) are aversive to some extent (Costenbader & Reading-Brown, 1995). Foxx and Shapiro (1978) used a simple ribbon to mark the boundaries of a time-out area. This technique provided easy monitoring and less than complete isolation. In most instances, there is no real need to isolate the individual completely, and an area marked by a masking tape or a small room divider will usually work quite well.

Being Cooperative

Cooperation is generally a higher state of well-being than obedience. Cooperation expects the student to conform to group rules and expectations and to support common projects. Obedience and cooperation with other people are basic prerequisites to independent living, transition, and work experience. On the one hand, a person who never learns obedience is not likely to make sound choices or decisions. On the other hand, an individual (including one with mental retardation) who remains in the obedience stage is not likely to be very successful either. True independence is achieved by finding a healthy balance between doing as one pleases and being obedient where it is advantageous or necessary. Parents, teachers, and other IEP team members must help the students find this balance as accurately as possible.

Making Good Choices

Making choices means learning to select from the most appropriate of available alternatives. This stage is a step above being obedient and cooperative and is a prerequisite to making sound decisions. For our purposes, the available alternatives from which the student "chooses" are those the teacher or parent identifies, offers, monitors, and evaluates. The major goals of this stage are to make the individual aware that many situations offer a variety of alternatives and that his or her personal preferences are important. A good place to begin is to help the student become aware of his or her performance in behavioral and other classroom tasks and activities. Liberty and Paeth (1990) successfully encouraged students with severe and multiple disabilities to record their own performance data using mechanical and electronic counting devices, such as calculators.

Munk and Repp (1994) cited the use of several nonaversive procedures, together with student choice of task, to reduce problem behaviors. In the early stages of choice making, the student simply selects from two or more inevitable alternatives. The student usually must perform or experience both (or all) of the alternatives; he or she simply gets to choose which to do first. For example, the choices of work-play, reading-arithmetic, work-treats, and play-treats offer an opportunity for the student to indicate simple preferences and make simple choices where the consequences are not serious.

Making Sound Decisions

Decision making is an introductory form of problem solving. In another sense, it is advanced choice making. The difference between choices and decisions is mainly a matter of sophistication. Like a choice, a decision may be contrived to some extent, but a decision is followed by increasingly significant consequences, whereas a choice is not. Mahon and Bullock (1992) encouraged self-control by providing only instruction, encouragement, and verbal praise in helping adolescents with mild mental retardation make leisure-related choices and decisions. Early in the choice stage, the parent or teacher may allow the student to choose the order of two tasks or lessons. The choice involves no real decision because both alternatives must be accomplished; the only question is which one is to be accomplished first. As the child matures, the choices become decisions that are increasingly refined and that begin to offer meaningful options. One may allow a maturing student to determine not only which assignment to pursue first but also how long to spend on the first assignment. Such a choice has some of the consequential characteristics of a decision, but later the teacher insists that the delayed task also be completed. Furthermore, if the student spent a great deal of time on the first task, he or she must later make up the time on the second.

Teachers, parents, and other IEP team members must diagnose the decision-making ability of each student individually and prescribe and teach appropriate programs (Morris et al., 1993). Instruction in making good choices, judgment, and decisions can begin by having the student classify vicarious situations (e.g., pictures) of foods liked, foods not liked; foods good for the body, foods not good for the body; nice, not nice;

good manners, poor manners; safe, dangerous; fair, unfair; working, playing; productive, unproductive; working, not working; and earning money, spending money.

Group Participation

During each of the obedience-to-independence stages, individuals will likely participate in small groups with other students or with the whole class. The teacher occasionally may seek or contrive instances during which the students make decisions in groups—for example, "When should we start to clean up?" "What game should we play at recess today?" "When should we line up?" "Can we finish this before lunch?" and "What should we have for a treat today?" In pursuing group choices or decisions, the teacher should let each student participate so that everyone believes his or her opinion is valuable. The teacher should not let one or two students unduly influence each decision, but rather he or she can skillfully guide a discussion so that increasingly mature alternatives are selected by the group. Listening to each student and letting the more mature have slightly greater influence in the group decisions help less mature individuals make increasingly better choices.

The Teacher's Role in Student Choices and Decisions

The teacher must be careful to keep the instructive role in structuring the decision-making process in the proper perspective. He or she must learn to anticipate the quality of choices or decisions each child is likely to make in a given set of circumstances. Allowing a student to make whatever decisions he or she wants is not adequate. Throughout the process, the teacher must resist the urge to offer too much advice and assistance to some students but at the same time provide thoughtful guidance where it is actually needed by others. Some students find comfort in continuing familiar activities or stagnating at a level they have already mastered. Some students with mental retardation persist with some activities (e.g., playing with dolls, riding a stick horse, playing "cowboys and Indians") that do not promote growth and maturity. It is well for the teacher to work closely with the student's parents in helping the student find a reasonable compromise between immature but social-age behavior and CA-appropriate behavior that will enable the student to successfully enter the world of work.

As the teacher encourages the students individually and in groups to become as independent as possible by teaching them to make progressively meaningful choices and decisions, the teacher should carefully monitor his or her participation. The law holds the teacher, not the students, responsible for the conduct and safety of the class. The teacher must be careful not to offer a choice to either an individual or a group unless he or she is prepared to deal with the consequences. This is particularly important in disciplinary matters. Although it is a good procedure to have the members of the class participate in establishing class rules, the teacher is the one who must enforce them. The teacher will find that some classes of students tend to draft more stringent (or liberal) class rules and prescribe more severe consequences for breaking a rule than the teacher can enforce.

Exercising Proactivity and Initiative

Proactivity is the ability to identify, recognize, analyze, and solve problems in daily living. The need to develop an individual's initiative is demonstrated by the process of learning to make sound decisions and achieving the highest level of independence. The teacher will readily recognize that students with mental retardation have great difficulty achieving a high level of proactivity and initiative. They typically do not analyze and solve problems very well. Proactivity, however, is one of the most important components of independent living and must be a dominant and persistent goal of the educational program of every student with mental retardation. Of what value are a person's problem-solving skills if that individual cannot apply the skills in practical situations?

Proactivity is more than just a stage; it is the desired mastery level in every target task. To help each student with mental retardation achieve the highest degree of independent living possible, he or she must not only be able to solve practical problems but also recognize that a problem is at hand, analyze the problem, select the best solution from other alternatives, solve the problem, and apply the solution to the problem in everyday life. In other words, although decision making essentially teaches the student to solve problems identified by others, proactivity goes a step farther and teaches the student to identify and solve problems in real life.

Proactivity is admittedly difficult to teach in the school setting. The teacher is trying to teach students with mental retardation to exercise independent thinking and decision making, but at the same time is responsible for the safety and well-being of the students. In all early situations, the teacher plays a key role in deciding which alternatives to offer the student so that he or she can make choices or decisions. The school environment is not usually well-suited to allow students to experience and practice proactivity and independence. Typically, in the school setting, teachers and others not only identify for the students the problems they are likely to encounter but also formulate the solutions to the problems. Then they supervise the students to minimize their mistakes and even provide reinforcement necessary for motivation. As the students leave school, they suddenly find themselves having to do all this for themselves. This realization can be troublesome for any person, but for one with mental retardation, it can be devastating. Students with mental retardation are well known for the difficulty they have in transferring their training and dealing effectively with their environment. This is why it is necessary to teach self-control and personal decision making in the natural environment wherever possible.

Because the teacher cannot allow students with mental retardation to exercise complete freedom in decision making, the teacher can use three basic procedures in the classroom:

1. Emphasize proactivity as a goal in every classroom activity.
2. Operate the program for older students in the community wherever possible to minimize the problems of transfer and transition.
3. Encourage the parents to participate in the planning and operation of the program by giving the child appropriate problems to solve in the home.

DIAGNOSING A STUDENT'S INDEPENDENCE AND DECISION-MAKING ABILITIES

The age 25 projection (Figure 8.1) helps the teacher and IEP team visualize each student's progress toward the desired degree of internal control, independence, and decision-making ability the IEP team has set as a goal. Figure 8.1 deals essentially with criterion-referenced data, so the age 25 projection will not produce standardized scores. Using the projection, the teacher can establish plateaus and indicate arbitrary increments of performance. Moreover, the teacher should not expect early estimates of the student's ultimate performance to be unrealistically accurate. Unfailing accuracy is probably not possible but is approached through frequent reevaluations.

Goal instruction analysis (GIA) skills remind the teacher that these plateaus are more accurate if he or she perceives or describes them not only in terms of the student's performance but also with reference to what it takes (in terms of external motivation, time, and assistance) to get the student to achieve at that level. The age 25 projection helps the teacher and the IEP team in planning the student's overall program to achieve the maximum level of self-direction, control, and independence.

Debbie, whose case is depicted in Figure 8.1, is 14 years old and is partially integrated in regular classes. Her IEP team estimates that she will graduate in 4 years. With only 4 years of school remaining, she must achieve one fourth of her eventual school progress during each of the next 4 years.

Examples of plateaus for Debbie are "needs occasional prompt," "needs reminder when in a group," and "falters badly in new situations." At first, the teacher may want to plot these plateaus, but if the teacher has only a few students, he or she can remember how each student performs. The important thing is to keep each student moving toward the final goal.

This is a good example of how the age 25 projection can help in planning a realistic program. During each of Debbie's remaining school years, the IEP team should per-

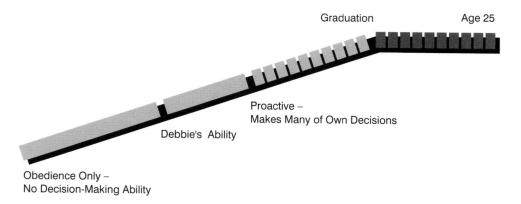

FIGURE 8.1   Age 25 Projection Showing a Student's Ability to Make Own Decisions

ceive a clearer picture of the level of self-control and independent living she is likely to achieve before she leaves school. If an annual evaluation shows that Debbie's progress toward self-control is greater than expected, the team may want to replace her expected or current participation in a sheltered workshop with a community-based work experience program, followed by full- or part-time employment and a more independent living style than they had previously projected for her. If Debbie proves to be less capable of independent living than the IEP team had anticipated, her educational goals and program can be adjusted accordingly.

GIA AND MAKING CHOICES AND DECISIONS

GIA helps in identifying the complete range of skills and concepts necessary for an individual to become as successful and self-supporting as possible—from the most rudimentary skills and concepts through those needed for independent living. Before instruction begins, however, the IEP team must place these skills and concepts on a prioritized continuum of increasing difficulty or mastery level, determine the individual's current level of mastery, and then launch instruction at that level. The IEP team must then pursue the individual's level of mastery on the continuum so that valuable time and teaching resources are not wasted on skills and concepts that the individual has already accomplished or that are too difficult. Such a pursuit is necessary because it is difficult for a student with mental retardation to determine and state whether or not he or she has already mastered the material. Many other students will complain about repeating previously learned material, but students with mental retardation rarely do so. Moreover, they are not likely to astonish the teacher with an unexpectedly high level of performance on the skills and concepts that were already covered.

GIA COMPONENTS IN DECISION MAKING AND INDEPENDENCE

Table 8.1 shows examples of the specific components the teacher might use in setting up a GIA in choice making, decision making, proactivity, and independence. The arrows suggest this sequence. Table 8.1 also shows the form and sequence in which each component might be manipulated to increase task difficulty and skill achievement level. Remember, the teacher must create his or her own components to fit the student, the teacher's teaching style, and the particular task. Bold type indicates key words or abbreviations that might be used if the manipulated components are being plotted.

The first component listed on each row of Table 8.1 (e.g., Few, Familiar, Obedience, Minor, Two) are examples of beginning components to be placed on each horizontal line of the GIA form. The terms and abbreviations that follow these components on each row suggest ways the components can be manipulated to increase the individual's level of decision making, self-direction, and independence. Abbreviations are usually (though not always) necessary because of limited space on the chart. *Manipulate* means to increase, decrease,

TABLE 8.1 Using GIA in Teaching Decision Making

Type of Component	Components: Form and/or Sequence of Progression
MATERIALS	
Number	Few ⟶ More ⟶ Many
Type	Familiar ⟶ Less ⟶ Unfamiliar
MASTERY	
Level	Obedience ⟶ Choice ⟶ Decision ⟶ Proactivity
Consequences	Minor ⟶ More serious ⟶ More serious
Alternatives	Two ⟶ Three ⟶ More
Source	Teacher only ⟶ With student consultation ⟶
	Increase (student consultation) ⟶ Student initiated
ASSISTANCE	
	Repeat Instructions ⟶ Shorter ⟶ None
Instructor	Teacher ⟶ Teacher and aide ⟶ Aide ⟶ Employer
Level	Explain Choices ⟶ Less ⟶ None
Type	Prompt ⟶ Less ⟶ Less ⟶ None
	Encourage ⟶ Less ⟶ None
TIME	
Make Choice	No Restraint ⟶ Quicker ⟶ Immediate choice
Experience the Consequences	Immediate ⟶ Delayed ⟶ Natural
REWARD	Immediate ⟶ Delayed ⟶ Natural

fade, eliminate, substitute for, introduce, re-introduce, and so forth. After the student begins to have success under the direction of the teacher, it may be possible to involve an aide or volunteer so that the teacher can work with other students. Later, when a particularly difficult segment is at hand, the teacher may have to become involved again (at least temporarily). The basic idea is to begin with the simplest choices and maximum assistance and gradually make the choices more meaningful and reduce all types of assistance until the individual is making significant decisions and is becoming increasingly responsible for his or her own behavior (Horner, Day, Sprague, O'Brien, & Heathfield, 1991).

Likewise, reinforcement components would logically progress from tangible to intangible, fixed to variable to intermittent to occasional, immediate to delayed, and extrinsic to intrinsic over a period of time. In setting up the GIA, the teacher must be able to manipulate the components in the column in which each component appears. For example, Teacher (in the Instructor row) means the teacher conducts the entire activity. Later, that row would show how the teacher could gradually turn over part and then most of the activity to an aide, to a volunteer, and eventually to an employer. Specific tasks the student will perform and specific instructions or dialogue that passes between the teacher and the student do not make good components because they cannot be manipulated. Components such as prompt, reward, and encourage, however, can be manipulated by gradually decreasing them until the student is as nearly on his or her own as possible.

Any GIA must be individually designed in consideration of the student and the task to be mastered. In each successive row on the GIA chart, the teacher manipulates the single component that he or she thinks will make the slightest increase in the difficulty and performance level of the task. Increasing the difficulty or complexity of the task expands the individual's level of mastery. The teacher should begin with a combination of components that ensures success; then the teacher can manipulate the components to increase difficulty (and, hence, the individual's level of mastery). The number of manipulations needed to achieve success will be different for each student. It may be well to review the GIA checkpointing procedure discussed in Chapter 7 in determining the student's present level of functioning or frontier.

This process should continue until the student completes his or her school program; thus, a myriad of intermediate steps and components are necessary to provide the instructional substance for that period of time. The teacher can use hundreds of specific choices and decisions from all aspects of the student's program to achieve the final goals. The other categories of components, such as teacher assistance, time considerations, and rewards, are roughly the same as with other GIAs.

As the student matures, the teacher can increase the task difficulty or mastery level of the choices in a number of ways:

1. **Number of alternatives in making choices.** Choosing from three or four alternatives (even three or four different treats) can be considerably more difficult than simply choosing between two.
2. **Complexity or difficulty of the alternatives.** In keeping with the increasing difficulty concept of the GIA, the teacher should present simple and uncomplicated choices before those that are either difficult or complex.
3. **Relative complexity or difficulty of the alternatives.** As the student learns to choose from among several more advanced alternatives, the teacher can begin to manipulate the relative differences among them—for example, choosing a difficult task in a preferred activity versus a simple assignment in a less preferred activity.
4. **Time requirements.** After the teacher has increased the time devoted to the choices, he or she can experiment with a long, preferred activity versus a shorter, less preferred one. The student then learns to determine how much

time to devote to each task, given that he or she must reach a certain level of performance or complete the amount of work the teacher—and later the student—determines. Each student can learn to postpone work on one project for a day or more but must complete the other under the teacher's guidance.

5. **Substance of the choices.** The teacher should progress to more meaningful choices as soon as possible—for example, healthful foods versus less healthful treats and reading or other preferred study activities to unscheduled time-out or game activities. Durand and Carr (1992) reported that time-out procedures are effective, but less so in the long run than using functional communication training (experience and instruction in behavioral self-control). Similarly, Haring and Kennedy (1990) found that, in a variety of tasks, DRO used in context with the task at hand is effective in reducing problem behavior and increasing performance, whereas time-out is ineffective. Interestingly, however, they reported that, in leisure activities, time-out is effective and DRO is ineffective. These experiences reinforce the notion that the teacher or IEP team must assess the child's reaction to reinforcement on an individual basis.

6. **Postponement of reward.** One of the most serious challenges in teaching initiative and independent living to students with mental retardation is helping them postpone rewards for the successful completion of a task. In most work situations in business or industry, no one pats each of the workers on the back and tells them how well they are doing as they complete each task. One advantage of the diagnostic/prescriptive approach is that the teacher can plan in advance how he or she will gradually introduce delayed, intrinsic rewards—eventually relying on those chosen, then designed by the student, and eventually reduced or eliminated. The other GIA components offer support to the student so that the loss of the reward is not too drastic.

7. **Consequences of a choice.** Although the choices usually placed before a young or immature child tend to be inconsequential, it is important that the choices be offered. At first, the teacher should select two classroom tasks that must be completed and let the child decide which of the two to do first, but present choices that do not have important or far-reaching consequences. The student gradually learns that alternatives have consequences and that the impact of some choices is more important than others—for example, the classroom animals will suffer if they are not fed and cared for promptly, and the room must be cleaned up before the class is dismissed.

8. **Student participation.** The teacher should increase the participation of each student in all stages of the GIA. For example, the child has a voice in the selection of the alternatives even if the teacher has to practically lay them out, select one, and explain to the student what he or she is to do. The important thing is to convince the student that his or her preference is of vital importance. They can also participate in the decisions on how long they will participate in a given activity. Ellis, Cress, and Spellman (1992) let adolescents with

moderate to severe mental retardation use timers and lap counters to success-fully exercise for a specified period of time.

SELF-EVALUATION

During the GIA process, the student must learn to evaluate his or her own work as early and as well as possible (Schloss et al., 1994). Teaching students with mental retardation to evaluate their own work is particularly difficult because they typically lack the essential entry-level skills, but it can be done to some extent. Each student must learn to balance the quality and quantity of his or her work and to judge how much time to devote to a pro-ject to achieve the desired quality. The teacher can begin by doing all the evaluation and recording and then teaching the student to help grade and record his or her own work.

Later, the teacher can help the student estimate how many problems he or she will be able to complete in a specified time. Students can also learn to predict how many problems they can get correct and then compare their estimates with their actual per-formance. This process helps them become aware of both the quality and quantity of their work. With every learning task, the teacher should let each student evaluate his or her own work as much as possible. A serious dilemma for individuals with mental retar-dation in contrived and real work situations is how to balance the quality and quantity of assigned tasks. Following one alternative may earn criticism for shoddy work, whereas following the other may result in low production. By the teacher offering guid-ance only as necessary, the student gradually learns that his or her opinions are valu-able and that self-evaluation is necessary and important.

CLASSROOM BEHAVIOR

A related goal of decision making is to help each student become increasingly responsi-ble for his or her own behavior. At first, the students must simply follow the teacher's rules and suffer the consequences he or she specifies for breaking them. As the stu-dents mature, the teacher can have them help formulate classroom rules. The teacher might also experiment with having the class determine consequences for breaking class rules, being careful to evaluate not only the rules themselves but also the repercussions for breaking them. Even students with mental retardation often suggest punishments that are severe or unusual. The consequences they select can prove to be unenforce-able, illegal, or simply embarrassing to the teacher. Therefore, all classroom rules and the consequences for breaking the rules are really the teacher's responsibility. A good working relationship with a student's parents or guardian suggests to the teacher the extent to which they prefer to be informed on the student's behavior. Long and Edwards (1994) suggested using a daily report card to communicate the student's status and progress on behavior and other school performance.

LEVEL, RATE, AND PROACTIVITY

All GIAs have three dimensions: level, rate, and proactivity. The rate at which a prescription progresses is as important as the level at which it begins. Obviously, some children will be quite independent and mature; others will need considerable support. The teacher must diagnose each student's need for structure and discipline, the ability to control emotions and behavior, and the level of reward or punishment that would be effective for him or her. For example, one student may respond favorably to verbal praise, whereas another may consider it unmanly and undesirable, or he may be unresponsive because of peer pressure. Individuals vary greatly in their progress toward self-direction and decision making, just as they do in academic and other areas. Many teachers are prone to either allow potential problems to build up until they explode or nip them in the bud so early that free expression is stifled. The GIA process helps the teacher in finding a reasonable, individual, and practical compromise between these two points.

Proactivity in management and discipline is the progress a student makes toward independent and successful living as an adult. Using the age 25 projection, each IEP team estimates the extent to which their student is likely to become independent while he or she is in school. It is extremely important that decision-planning and independence factors be considered with each new IEP. Early in a child's school career, these annual estimates are not likely to be highly accurate. Nevertheless, they should be carefully considered in the formulation of each student's annual IEP. Each year, the IEP team evaluates their student's progress to date and makes new plans to help foster his or her independence and decision-making capabilities. As the teacher reviews the progress of each student, estimates of that student's eventual self-control and independence levels will become increasingly accurate. It is not possible to predict with absolute accuracy, however, the extent to which a student with mental retardation will live independently, but the IEP team must base each student's educational program on the most accurate estimates. Some students will surprise the teacher and become either more or less independent than the teacher anticipated, but a fairly clear picture will develop if the teacher follows the age 25 projection for a number of years, particularly during the student's last few years of school. The teacher's task is to prepare each student for adult life as well as possible.

DIRECT TREATMENT TECHNIQUES

In this section, I give a brief description or flavor of some direct (but nonaversive) techniques that are particularly compatible with life goal curriculum planning and diagnostic/prescriptive procedures. These direct techniques can be used in extreme situations in which immediate corrective action is necessary or control must be maintained. In situations in which direct disciplinary techniques are needed, it is well to use those that help individual students increase their decision-making abilities and become increasingly responsible for their own actions. Many of today's popular disciplinary techniques tend to enforce conformity to classroom rules, treating symptoms of behavioral problems, rather than the underlying causes of those problems. An in-depth discussion of these techniques is beyond the scope of this book, but a brief description is provided so that the teacher can identify and study them in greater depth.

Often, a teacher of students with mental retardation may experience pressure to use a particular disciplinary procedure that has been adopted district- or schoolwide. In some instances, the adopted procedure is intended to be used with nondisabled and disabled students alike. For serious offenses, particularly those involving parent conferences, office referrals, or suspensions, most schools have adopted a standard referral/discipline policy. In such a situation, the teacher should become familiar with this policy and follow it. In most instances, however, the teacher will be given considerable latitude regarding the management/discipline procedures he or she may follow in the classroom.

One advantage to using standard, schoolwide procedures is that students will be better able to predict what is expected of them in future classes. For example, the teacher may want to expose a student with mental retardation to a particular discipline technique being used in the regular class program into which the student is being included. In this sense, the regular classroom serves as a type of natural setting. No single procedure will work with all students, however, especially with students with disabilities. Moreover, the effectiveness of any technique varies with the student, the teacher, and the situation. The membership of the student's IEP team will probably be relatively stable over time, and the team (particularly the parents) should be in a position to encourage each of the student's succession of teachers to recommend and evaluate an appropriate and practical system of procedures. In formulating his or her classroom management style, the teacher should select and use the most promising features of the recommended techniques.

Reality Therapy

Glasser's reality therapy (1965, 1969, 1984, 1986) has a number of strengths that recommend it for use with students with mental retardation. One salient strength is that it is a positive approach with the goal of helping each individual become responsible for his or her own acts. Reality therapy is very consistent with diagnostic/prescriptive teaching and is a gentle approach to classroom management unlikely to be misused. No harm is likely to come to a student if the teacher uses reality therapy without extensive training. However, the teacher should become as fully trained as possible with this or any other management techniques he or she plans to use.

Reality therapy was not designed specifically for students with mental retardation, so some modifications are necessary. Glasser's manuals are full of specific examples the teacher might encounter in various situations, including sample dialogues. The low language levels of most students with mental retardation might prevent them from understanding Glasser's questioning techniques. Further, they may be unable to analyze their own behavior, as well as that of the individuals in Glasser's examples, but with patience and experience, neither of these limitations should present serious problems. The teacher must realize that reality therapy, like any other approach, is no panacea and will not solve all management problems. And, as with any other approach, the teacher may have to take direct action to prevent one student from harming him- or herself or another student.

Glasser encourages individuals to make moral judgments about their actions and to commit to behavioral improvements in the future. Thus, the teacher asks, "Why is Billy's pen on your desk?" rather than, "Why did you steal Billy's pen?" Glasser does not permit a person to blame others for his or her behavior and points out that little is to be gained by blaming the environment. So, the teacher would ask, "What is wrong with taking someone else's property?" or "Why is it wrong to steal?" rather than tell the student, "It is just not right to steal," or, "You give Billy's pen back to him right now and don't ever do anything like that again." The teacher would ask, "What are you going to do about the situation?" rather than, "What made you do a thing like that?" or "Who put Billy's pen on your desk?" GIA procedures suggest ways to arrange these positive questions to help increase self-control and personal decision making. Glasser never uses the phrase "Don't let me catch you . . ." Proper behavior and responsibility for one's own acts are Glasser's goals, rather than encouraging denial or simply not getting caught.

Glasser's approach stresses the present and the future, rather than the past. He does not permit excuses for aberrant behavior and is not as interested in what caused an unsatisfactory situation as he is in how the person plans to improve in the future. Glasser repeatedly points out that mental hospitals are full of individuals who understand their problems but who have no commitment to improve. In using reality therapy, the teacher must treat each person as an individual whose opinions are very important.

Assertive Discipline

Assertive discipline, according to its originator (Canter, 1976) was designed for teachers who needed a "quick fix" to gain control in their classrooms. The basic philosophy of assertive discipline is to seize the initiative, take charge, and become the boss. As the name suggests, this procedure encourages the teacher to establish and maintain authority over the students, although it is essentially nonaversive. Potential behavioral problems are acknowledged and diffused in a number of ways.

Using assertive discipline, the teacher typically establishes a set of necessary rules that are clearly explained to the students. The penalties for breaking these rules are also stipulated so that the students are left with no excuses for their misbehavior. The penalties are arranged in a hierarchy that depends on the number and severity of the offenses. Such an arrangement might look something like this:

First offense	Warning
Second offense	Name written in a prominent place
Third offense	15 minutes' detention time after school

Fourth offense	30 minutes' detention time after school and the parents are called
Fifth offense	1 hour detention, principal notified, possible TPA (until parent appears) suspension
Subsequent offenses	TPA or specified-time suspension

The major strength of assertive discipline is that it is inexpensive and easy for both teachers and students to understand. It is popular and widely practiced. Its aim of helping the teacher maintain control of the class is commendable (Canter, 1992). Remember that the law holds the teacher responsible for the safety and conduct of his or her class. The teacher may use any part of assertive discipline with individual students who present difficult behavioral problems without getting other class members involved. Once a student's overt behavior is under control, the teacher can introduce a more positive program that encourages self-control—one that is more closely correlated to the student's overall curriculum goals.

One major weakness of assertive discipline is that its emphasis on external control treats only the overt symptoms of behavior. A second is that it deals only with discipline, and although it may reduce the amount of time the teacher spends on purely disciplinary measures, it does not necessarily promote a feeling of self-worth, nor does it usually support other parts of a student's program. Canter (1992) attempted to broaden the scope of assertive discipline to overcome these admitted weaknesses. Direct disciplinary techniques, however, such as reality therapy and assertive discipline, are recommended primarily as a last resort or as a temporary measure while the teacher establishes a more positive, long-lasting procedure.

Suspension

TPA suspensions dismiss the student from school until the parent comes to school for a conference. Suspensions ordinarily begin at the end of a school day, so unless the offense is particularly severe, resulting in immediate ejection from school, the student need not miss any classes. Although court decisions generally permit teachers, as well as administrators, to suspend a student from school, the teacher should not do so without first clearing such action with the school administration. In fact, anytime the consequences or punishment for violating the teacher's management program affects others outside his or her classroom, the teacher should obtain administrative approval. Often, however, a member of the school administration serves on the student's IEP team and is in a position to approve or disapprove the program at its inception.

Suspensions of any kind should be used as a last resort because they disrupt the student's school program. Suspensions are generally neither necessary nor effective with most students with mental retardation. Temporary removal from school, however, is sometimes necessary to prevent injury to the student or other members of the class. A suspension can also be strong encouragement for the parents to acknowledge that their child has a serious problem that warrants their attention. A teacher of students with mental retardation should not hesitate to insist on a temporary suspension if he or she has exhausted less severe remedies. Keep in mind that the law does not permit the suspension of any disabled student for longer than a specified period of time (typically, 3 to 10 days) without a formal hearing, so the teacher or other team members should check state and local regulations (*Adams Central School District No. 690 v. Deist,* 1983; *Honig v. Doe,* 1988).

Detention

It is legal in most states to punish students by detaining them when they would otherwise not be in school. Keeping capable students after the regular school day or detaining them in the same setting for an additional school year—for disciplinary reasons— may be an acceptable method of persuading them to stay on task during class time. It may work well with students who cause problems in class or fail to complete assignments. To a degree, it may encourage the students to become more responsible and teach them to spend their class time more profitably. Keeping students with mental retardation after school or preventing their promotion as a punishment is questionable, however, for several reasons. First, one can never be certain that a student with mental retardation will make the connection between the offense and the punishment, especially if much time elapses between the offense and the punishment. Second, unless the teacher supervises the detention, a student with mental retardation is not likely to make progress on lessons as other detained students do and may become even more of a behavioral problem. Because students with mental retardation are not typically advanced or promoted by their having fully met academic standards, preventing their promotion or graduation is also likely to be ineffective and inappropriate. Likewise, keeping a student with mental retardation after school for failure to maintain academic standards is usually unjustified. Such a punishment must not cause a student to miss transportation arrangements or meals. The teacher should also notify parents and obtain administrative approval before detaining a student.

Reinforcement and Reward

Initial GIA procedures often call for some type of reward or inducement—usually verbal praise or a pat on the back. It is generally recognized that external controls and reinforcements must be phased out or faded as soon as possible. In fact, it is best to use no reward beyond occasional praise and naturally occurring encouragement. For example, Brigham, Bakken, Scruggs, and Mastropieri (1992) used competition between groups to improve classroom behaviors. They reported that rewarding both teams and individuals is most effective. Fading out the rewards is intended to assist the students in generalizing and perpetuating the most favorable behaviors without forming a dependency on the overt reinforcements. This is particularly important with students with mental retardation because they usually need deliberate instruction and assistance to avoid becoming dependent on adults. Before adopting any program in which the teacher offers rewards for proper behavior or for positive accomplishments to individuals (and particularly to groups), it is well to determine whether the program is likely to make the students more dependent on the teacher and when (and by whom) the external controls will be phased out.

DPE TEACHING AND DISCIPLINE

Using any disciplinary measure or punishment with any student with mental retardation, the teacher must make sure that the student understands the reasons he or she is being punished. DPE teaching helps the teacher or IEP team discern which reinforcements or corrective measures are effective with a particular student. As with teaching the student to make good personal decisions, the program for that student must not dwell on punishment and external controls, but make the student increasingly responsible for his or her own actions. As a precaution, the teacher should avoid being alone in a classroom with a student, particularly an older one of the opposite sex.

LEGAL RELATIONSHIP AMONG TEACHERS, PARENTS, AND STUDENTS

A thorough discussion of educational law is beyond the scope of this book. It may be helpful, however, to present some legal principles that bear directly on the management of a class.

Litigation

All educators must recognize that the operation of any school is a legal process; everything that goes on in a school is either legal or illegal. There is no middle ground, although a given act may have to be resolved in court to determine whether it was, in fact, legal or illegal at the time it occurred. In education, the prospect of being sued is always present. A suit against a teacher is not likely to be successful, however, if the teacher is informed of his or her legal obligations and uses common sense.

In the following court cases, some teachers were found negligent, and others were exonerated. Using these court cases as a guide and considering the unique circumstances of teachers of students with mental retardation, the teacher should be able to avoid most of the potential legal problems. A legal relationship exists among teachers, parents, and students from the standpoint of the responsibilities teachers have in (a) providing a safe learning atmosphere, (b) protecting students from injury (*Honig v. Doe*, 1988), and (c) disciplining students (Yudof, Kirp, & Levin, 1992). Teachers who fail in these responsibilities may become adversely involved with the law in a number of ways, but space permits a discussion of only the more prominent of these.

Tort Liability

One way teachers become adversely involved with the law is to be sued over an injury to one of their students. Perhaps the most unpleasant part of teaching is the possibility of being sued "in tort." A *tort* is a legal wrong for which monetary damages can be collected, providing the suit is successful. A tort action typically involves a situation in which a student has been injured while under the care or supervision of a teacher. Depending on state laws, the parents of the child may sue to be reimbursed for their child's medical bills and for other expenses caused by the injury. In many cases, they seek punitive damages as well.

Merely being sued does not mean the person being sued must pay damages to anyone. Ordinarily, a teacher can be successfully sued for damages resulting from an act that occurred at school only if the court finds that the teacher was negligent. Before the teacher is required to pay monetary damages, a hearing must be held and the court must decide in favor of the party that sued the teacher. Just being taken to court, however, can be a traumatic event. Also, the teacher's professional life is always in jeopardy when his or her teaching skills are questioned in a courtroom. The courts have consistently held that a teacher cannot be held liable for an accident occurring to a student under the teacher's care, providing that the teacher was acting in a reasonably prudent and proper manner (Valente, 1987). One can well imagine that "a reasonably prudent and proper manner" as defined after the fact and in an air-conditioned courtroom might be somewhat different from what the teacher experienced in the classroom at the time—a further reminder of the need to maintain a margin of safety in such instances. The teacher is not the only school official usually named in this type of lawsuit. The individuals who instigate the lawsuit will usually sue the teacher, the principal, the school board, and anyone else who could possibly be involved and then collect damages from anyone who cannot provide a successful defense.

In some cases, the parents of a student may sue a teacher but not seek damages. If no injury has occurred, the parents may seek a court decision declaring that the teacher overstepped his or her authority. A good example is parental objection to class or school rules or punishments they consider to be unfair or excessive.

Proper Supervision

The courts have consistently held teachers responsible for proper supervision of students under their care. However, there are no conclusive rules to follow. The courts seem to rely heavily on the question of whether an injury to a student could have been reasonably anticipated and whether it could have been prevented by the teacher's presence. One important principle to follow, especially in the teaching of students with mental retardation, is to be where the students are. The teacher must not leave his or her students unsupervised if at all possible (*Collins v. School Board of Broward County,* 1985; *Honig v. Doe,* 1988; *Rodriguez v. Board of Education,* 1984).

Legal Aspects of Punishment

Another source of legal litigation between teachers and parents involves instances in which the teacher has punished a child in a manner the parents find excessive or unwarranted. If the child is injured as a result of the punishment, the parents (or the child) may seek damages. Often, however, the parents may merely seek a declaratory order from the court to force a change in policy that would rescind the authority of the teacher or other school officials over the child. The parents want reassurance from the courts that the offensive action will not recur, although they may ask the court to force the dismissal of the teacher.

In discussing punishment in the school, teachers must understand an important legal doctrine called *loco parentis.* Roughly translated and applied in practice, *loco parentis* means that while a child is in school, his or her teacher stands "in place of" that child's parents. Originally, loco parentis was interpreted quite literally: A child's teacher had virtually the same right to punish a child as did the parents. Over the years, however, the teacher's authority under the doctrine of loco parentis has gradually eroded. In an early case, the court applied the doctrine of loco parentis in ruling that a teacher did have the right to suspend (punish) a student for misbehavior that occurred in the classroom. The parents sought neither damages nor the teacher's dismissal, but merely asked the court for a writ forcing the teacher and the school to readmit the student (*State ex rel. Burfee v. Burton,* 1878). Although it is not a dead issue by any means, teachers today do not have nearly as much authority to punish a child or control the child's actions as they once had (*S-1 v. Turlington,* 1981).

Whether the courts have invoked the doctrine of loco parentis or not, they have consistently held that any punishment administered to a schoolchild must not be cruel or excessive and must be commensurate with the nature and gravity of the offense. The courts have also ruled that, in punishing a student, educators must consider the age, mentality, size, intent, and emotional maturity of the offender and ensure that the school official administering the punishment is not acting in anger or malice (*Shepard v. South Harrison R-II School District,* 1986).

Loco parentis is particularly important in administering corporal punishment. Although the U.S. Supreme Court has affirmed a lower court ruling (*Baker v. Owen,* 1975) that approved spanking, it is not a good method of classroom management and should never be used with students with mental retardation (Rose, 1989). Moreover, state or school districts may have restrictions on corporal punishment; if parents were to sue the teacher, charging that spanking their child was illegal, cruel, or excessive, the teacher might have to pursue the case far beyond local courts to get relief (*Fee v. Herndon,* 1990).

Emergency Procedures

A discussion of the legal relationship between parents and teachers understandably tends to produce an ominous feeling. It would be easy for the teacher to become discouraged, in light of all the potential legal pitfalls associated with teaching. Fortunately, most lawsuits like the ones discussed here could have been avoided had the teachers and other school officials exercised a minimum knowledge of educational law and a little common sense. Keep in mind, however, that the mere avoidance of legal liability is far from the extent of the teacher's responsibility in preventing accidents and in acting responsibly when accidents do occur. The teacher of students with mental retardation should be fully qualified in first aid and other emergency procedures. All teachers should be aware of their schools' policies on notifying parents and filling out accident reports when injuries occur. Teachers should make sure the children receive adequate instruction in potentially dangerous games and activities. Even a softball game can be extremely dangerous if the children are not properly instructed or supervised.

It is also important for every teacher of students with mental retardation to have complete emergency information for each of his or her students, including the names and phone numbers of parents or legal guardians and the name, office address, and phone number of the physician designated by the parents. The teacher also needs a statement signed by the parents or legal guardian, giving the teacher or other school officials permission to have the child transported to a licensed physician or hospital and to be treated in the event of a serious accident, illness, or other emergency. If an accident occurs in a classroom, the teacher may not have time to consult anyone in the school office. If parents fail or refuse to sign such a statement, the teacher should obtain from the principal or the school district's attorney the prescribed course of action to be taken in any emergency. The advantages of advance planning are obvious. The building principal should be informed of all nonroutine disciplinary measures, accidents, and any other unusual events that might prompt parental objection. In such matters, the principal is often the parent's first contact.

SUMMARY

In this chapter, I emphasized preventive management and disciplinary measures and also described some techniques and programs for direct intervention where necessary. I showed how to use life goal curriculum planning, DPE teaching, and GIA in classroom management and discipline. The following suggestions are recommended as the summary and implications of this chapter.

Use the DPE approach to make sure that, at all times during the school day, each student is engaged in some type of meaningful activity that leads however slowly but deliberately toward that student's life goals. One less obvious purpose of this is not a frantic drive for achievement, but rather to avoid times when students have nothing to do. When time is wasted, behavioral problems are more likely to occur.

Stress initiative and independence, even with young students with mental retardation. Help each student make as many of his or her life decisions as possible.

Counsel each student frequently and work out an individual plan to improve that student's decision-making ability and progress toward becoming as completely responsible for his or her own acts as possible. Because of the possibility of self-fulfilling prophecy or learned helplessness, be cautious in discussing a student's negative behaviors with parents or others in that student's presence.

Adjust to the heterogeneity of the class members. Set minimum standards where possible but do not hold all class members to the same standard of behavior. Experiment with having the class members suggest some general classroom rules but be sure they are justifiable and enforceable. Review the legal requirements of classroom management in this chapter. Do not do anything that may be illegal, no matter how effective it may be.

Remember that most students with mental retardation are capable of good behavior—or at least being mentally retarded does not necessarily result in poor behavior. Hold each student increasingly responsible for his or her own acts but be sure that each is capable of meeting the intensifying expectations.

Be positive in classroom management. Do not be vindictive in management and discipline. Do not resort to corporal punishment, even if it is permitted by your local or state laws and regulations. Never use physical force with a student unless it is necessary—for example, to prevent injury to that student, other students, or yourself.

Strive to make your classroom or home a pleasant learning environment and cultivate a genuine love for the students. Never yell or lose your composure if you can help it. If this is not possible, it may be well to look for another line of work. Make sure that instructional assistants and other adults in the classroom are aware of and are prepared to support your management procedures.

Allow students with mental retardation to enjoy a childhood and youth but do not lose sight of the fact that they will be adults and that the influence of school programs ends all too soon. Be consistent, firm, persistent, but loving with classroom expectations. Be prepared to overlook an occasional lapse of good behavior but do not allow an unacceptable behavior to build; you will have to abruptly crush it later.

Be as well prepared professionally as possible. If school experiences are to be profitable for students with mental retardation, they must rely heavily on the teacher and his or her programs.

Be as well prepared as possible for each school day. Have adequate lesson plans that not only cover the day's activities but also show where these activities fit into each child's long-range program. Arrive early enough to allow at least a few minutes in your classroom just to relax before the students arrive.

Decide in advance which direct disciplinary approach might work best with each student if such is needed. Never force a student (particularly a teenager) to confess before a group unless there is a compelling reason for doing so. Likewise, be careful about praising a teenager with other students present.

Work closely with each student's parents and IEP team in planning the student's management strategy. Consider what will happen to the student's behavior after he or she leaves school. Be careful not to join forces with a student against his or her parents. It may be necessary to support or comfort a student from an unsatisfactory home situation, but do not undermine the authority of the student's parents. Do not use disciplinary measures to which the parents would logically object unless you are prepared to justify the actions to the parent, which you may have occasion to do. Remember, the parents will usually find out about the incident.

part IV

Scope, Sequence, and Content of Curriculum

Curriculum Planning for Students with Severe/Profound Mental Retardation and Multiple Disabilities

Points to Study and Ponder

1. Why do students with severe/profound mental retardation need special consideration in curriculum planning?
2. What justification is there for considering students with severe mental retardation and profound mental retardation together?
3. What are *special health problems*, and how do they affect curriculum planning and teaching students with severe/profound mental retardation?
4. What is learned helplessness, and in what ways can it affect a student?
5. What does it mean to have a positive teacher attitude?
6. What is assistive technology, and how can it benefit students with severe/profound mental retardation?
7. How can an age 25 projection help the IEP team in deciding whether an assistive technology device is needed permanently or is simply a teaching tool to be phased out before the student finishes school?
8. What is sign language, and how is it used to teach students with mental retardation? Is it needed by these students permanently, or is it a teaching tool? Is there more than one sign language?
9. Why are self-help skills of particular significance in life goal curriculum planning for students with severe/profound mental retardation?
10. Why does this population need particular consideration in independent living, transition, employment, and leisure skills?

The major purpose of this chapter is to show how the life goal curriculum planning and DPE teaching procedures apply to students whose mental retardation is severe/profound. The skills, concepts, programs, and procedures discussed in this chapter are based on a number of important considerations:

1. Students who have severe/profound mental retardation are likely to have additional disabilities as well, and generally the potential for having these ancillary disabilities increases with the severity of mental retardation (Batshaw & Perret, 1992; Kennedy, 1930; Sirvis, 1988). These ancillary problems require teachers with special training and skills (Black, 1994). In the chapter, I show how to apply the principles and practices of the book to these students.
2. Most of the skills, concepts, programs, and procedures of this chapter are addressed to teaching individuals whose mental retardation is very severe or profound. The concept of *regional variation* (Chapter 1), however, reveals widespread and significant differences in defining severe and profound mental retardation.
3. Current practice discourages the early identification of the specific disabilities of young children, particularly those of preschool age (DeHaas-Warner, 1994; Rose & Smith, 1993; Volk & Stahlman, 1994). Also, mental retardation of the more serious or profound nature—especially when compounded by ancillary or multiple disabilities—is more obvious, pervasive, and easier to identify. Still, there is considerable confusion in the use of the terms *severe* and *profound*.
4. Current research practice tends to include both severe and profound mental retardation under the classifications of severe disabilities and developmental disabilities and to treat *severe* and *profound* as extensions along a continuum (Brimer, 1990; Poindexter & Bihm, 1994; Snell, 1993).
5. The skills and concepts of this chapter also serve as entry-level skills for those discussed in the other chapters of this part. If any student is unable to master the most fundamental skills and concepts of those chapters, the teacher or IEP team should use the vertical curriculum planning techniques of Chapter 3 and the features of this chapter to identify the student's learning frontier before proceeding.

TERMINOLOGY

Some investigators discern identifiable differences between severe and profound mental retardation, but in practice these differences need not be overriding. Because of the diagnostic/prescriptive procedures of this book and the indefinite use of the classifications severe and profound, it is not necessary to identify either the students or their instruction with a particular classification. These categories simply serve as general guidelines. In fact, most children without disabilities typically experience or master the skills and concepts of this book, but most do so at an early age and at home—or at least without deliberate or formal classroom instruction. Most children suffer no particular difficulty in doing so and develop normally without specific instruction. For example, Wehmeyer (1991) observed that students at risk for severe mental retardation exhibit repetitive motor behaviors topographically similar to those exhibited in typical infant development. For these reasons, a few developmental competencies—essentially, those that cannot be taught—are included to serve as guidelines to suggest when teachable skills and concepts can be taught. The basic idea is to identify, prioritize, and persistently reevaluate the life goals for these individuals and then to achieve those goals. Also, because of the huge discrepancy between these students' MAs and CAs, the IEP team must pay particular attention to age appropriateness (discussed later in this chapter).

The students addressed in this chapter are those whose mental retardation is the most extreme and limiting. Historically, the condition of these persons has been referred to as profound mental retardation (PMR) or custodial mental retardation (CMR). In this book, I describe this condition as severe/profound mental retardation with a reminder that the presence of ancillary or secondary disabilities is roughly proportional to the severity of the mental retardation.

Regional Variation

The concept of regional variation suggests that some states identify a much higher percentage of their student populations as having mental retardation than other states. The same is true of school districts within a given state. As a result, low-identification states and school districts tend to identify proportionately more students with severe/profound mental retardation. The efforts of some of these states appear to be concentrated primarily on this group. This focus means that an individual identified (and served) as severe/profound in one locality is likely to be perceived as mild/moderate in another area. Thus, in practice it is necessary to look beyond classifications and labels and to investigate the life goals and abilities of each student on an individual basis. Doing so is particularly crucial with the students and procedures described in this chapter.

Conceptual Distance

In any geographical area, the members of this population, by definition, are so far from normal development and achievement that they present some particularly perplexing learning/teaching problems. The notion of conceptual distance is especially significant to the students of this chapter. Even slight discrepancies between the present and the projected or desired performance levels of a student with severe/profound mental retardation may take months—even years—of intensive instruction and experience to overcome. The extreme heterogeneity of mental retardation implies that some students in the profound and multiple ranges will spend most of their school years mastering only the most basic skills and concepts. Thus, life goal curriculum planning for this group must be done with meticulous care, and their diagnostic/prescriptive teaching procedures must be especially precise and detailed (Hogg, 1983).

PREVALENCE OF SEVERE/PROFOUND MENTAL RETARDATION

Despite the current advances in medical science, the prevalence of students with severe/profound mental retardation seems to be increasing (Hallahan et al., 1986). Many children now survive a wide variety of prenatal, perinatal, and early childhood diseases and disorders that would have been fatal a few decades ago. Also, the gradual and encouraging reduction of some traditional causes of mental retardation, such as PKU, kernicterus, and hydrocephaly, are being offset by the increased prevalence of fetal alcohol syndrome (FAS), AIDS, and prenatal and postnatal substance abuse (Isbell & Barber, 1993). Gottwald and Thurman (1994) reported that prenatal cocaine use by mothers caused these mothers to pay less attention to their infants and that the infants themselves slept excessively and were distressed for significantly longer periods of time. Also, despite the uniformity one might expect in the rates at which the states identify their students with mental retardation, Hodgkinson (1989) reported that these students seem to be concentrated in larger cities and that the range and quality of available services varies from at least adequate to almost nonexistent.

With the passage of P.L. 94–142, the IDEA, and subsequent legislation, children with disabilities become the responsibility of the schools at increasingly early ages. Many young children (including many who have disabilities, but not mental retardation) lack the basic communication, social, motor, and other skills needed for eventual school success. Thus, curriculum planning for students with mental retardation and other disabilities must begin with the rudimentary, low-level skills and concepts discussed in this chapter.

HISTORICAL DEVELOPMENTS

Children with severe/profound mental retardation and multiple disabilities became the responsibility of the public schools only recently. By the time P.L. 94–142 became law in 1975, relatively few of these children had gained access to the public schools, and then primarily in larger cities. Most were in private schools and agencies, if they were in school programs at all. Many were in residential institutions where often they received little or no education or treatment; still others were kept at home. As a result, the development of methodology and functional curriculum planning for them are just now emerging. Further, because of these children's obvious and extreme learning difficulties and their tendency to have serious secondary disabilities, special methods, techniques, materials, and treatments for them have developed in a variety of disciplines. These disciplines include speech and language pathology, psychology, family and social science, physical education, physical therapy, occupational therapy, and recreation therapy. When children with severe/profound mental retardation came to the public schools, their curriculum was a loose conglomeration from the disciplines of physical and speech therapy, psychology, various treatment techniques, and terminology, in addition to education and special education.

The tendency to include students with mental retardation in regular classes varies greatly from one geographical area to another. Teachers of students with mental retardation, however, must be prepared to deal effectively with the students—even those with severe and profound mental retardation—in a variety of school settings. Typically, these teachers must also coordinate activities and schedules with one or more auxiliary specialists, who may work directly with the students or serve as consultants. In either event, it may be helpful to be familiar with some of the more common terms and procedures used by these specialists (see the Glossary).

WHY STUDENTS WITH SEVERE/PROFOUND MENTAL RETARDATION NEED SPECIAL CONSIDERATION

Conceptual distance suggests that students with severe/profound mental retardation make up an extremely heterogeneous group. They invariably manifest extreme and persistent deficiencies across the whole spectrum of human skills, concepts, and activities. Because of their extreme learning problems, it is easy for others, including parents and educators, to treat them as eternal children and lose sight of the fact that virtually all will become adults. Yet, even the predictable deficiencies of severe/profound mental retardation leave each individual with some ability upon which to build an educational program. The task for the teacher, parent, and other IEP team members is to pinpoint each student's achievement level on each of these abilities and to design programs that provide daily progress toward optimum success in adult life.

Another reason students with severe/profound mental retardation need special consideration is simply that they represent a low-incidence disability. This means that most of their preadult needs come from curriculum Area C—or those discussed in Chapter 3 that are not deliberately taught to students without mental retardation. Teachers and other IEP team members, however, are highly unlikely to have experienced Area C skills and concepts in school settings themselves. Thus, they tend to assign low priority to (or to be unaware of the need for) these vital skills, particularly in a school setting. In the initial phase of a classic study, Hudson (1960) surveyed teachers of students with severe/profound mental retardation as to the highest priority skills needed by these students. Even at that early date, the teachers came up with an impressive array of functional skills and concepts to be taught. In the final phase of the study, however, Hudson observed that, day after day, these same teachers hammered away at preschool- and kindergarten-level academics—even at the secondary level and as the students neared graduation.

The relative severity and predictability of the deficiencies have some important implications for these students:

• Their eventual achievement levels and life goals will be extremely limited.
• Their educational programs will consist largely of skills and concepts not taught to other students.

- They are likely to need a variety of highly specific teaching methods and techniques not commonly used with other students.
- Their learning environments must be specially planned and maintained.
- Their educational programs must be planned with particular care, and their IEPs and lesson plans must be much more detailed than for other students.

Special Health Problems and Medications

Students with severe/profound mental retardation are particularly vulnerable to all childhood diseases (West, Richardson, LeConte, Crimi, & Stuart, 1992) and complex medical health problems (Lehr, 1990). Lehr reported that the numbers of students with complex health problems are increasing. These difficulties are generally known as *special health care problems* (Urbano, 1991). Sirvis (1988) pointed out that this emerging group of individuals is sometimes referred to as *medically fragile* and that they have a wide variety of unique educational needs greatly intensified by their extreme medical needs. Not only do these problems tend to reduce the students' vitality and well-being, but their treatment also may cause frequent and prolonged absence from school. Also, the likelihood that a student is taking one or more medications is generally proportional to the severity of that student's mental retardation. Fortunately, a number of medications are quite effective in controlling seizures, the effects of cerebral palsy, and behavioral problems and in reducing the adverse consequences of some other secondary disabilities (Marcus, 1993; Rudrud & Striefel, 1981). Unfortunately, most of these medications have negative side effects, one of the most common being a significant reduction of the individual's cognitive and motor abilities and even disturbance of sleep patterns (Poindexter & Bihm, 1994). Teachers of this group of students must be prepared to manipulate gastrointestinal tubes and catheters and to administer the medications. Traditionally, these procedures have been reserved for nurses and other specially trained professionals.

Often, the complex medical and other health problems of students with severe/profound mental retardation require that they be transferred from desks, wheelchairs, mats, and special equipment designed to meet their unique needs. Obviously, teachers, parents, and others must be careful to avoid injury to themselves or the child in making these transfers. Injuring one's back while lifting or carrying a child can also result in injury to the child. Those responsible to lift or carry children should use slings and mechanical devices if available; however, these tend to be cumbersome. Common advice in such lifting is to keep the back straight and lift with the legs as much as possible. Also, a variety of lifting belts, braces, and other devices have been designed to provide support. Lifting a child is particularly hazardous because of the "reaching out" aspect. For this and other reasons, it is usually wise to make child transfers by using two or more adults.

Each of these special health conditions can create unusual problems for students with severe/profound mental retardation. Unlike the temporary health problems experienced by most other students, these conditions tend to be severe and chronic, and even though they may be treated in hospitals and elsewhere, they often persist to some extent throughout an individual's school years. Not only do the conditions place severe limitations on an individual's ability to function in the classroom, but also valuable teaching time is consumed while teachers and other school professionals treat the conditions themselves. Also, students with severe/profound mental retardation not only learn very slowly but also tend to forget rapidly and can be expected to lose more achievement ground over weekends and summer vacations than other students. Thus, their IEPs often call for extended school year (Katsiyannis, 1991), year-round, and summer school programs.

In dealing with this group of individuals and their unique needs, it is all too easy for teachers and others to overemphasize their chronic health problems and to conclude that no activities or instruction is possible. Even the term *medically fragile* is intimidating to some workers (Black, 1994). The IEP team must carefully assess the limitations imposed by the student's special health needs—with the advice of competent medical personnel where appropriate—so that the educational programs can provide the appropriate and needed physical and other activities. Given their unique needs, these students should be treated as normally as possible and in natural community settings (Graff & Ault, 1993; Hobbs, Perrin, Ireys, Moynihan, & Shayne, 1984). Graff and Ault also reminded professional workers not to overlook the expertise of the parents of such children.

Because of the many and varied health problems likely to be present in students whose mental retardation is severe/profound, their teachers must make a special effort to maintain a safe learning environment (Aronson, 1990; *Childress v. Madison County*, 1989). Odess and Margaliot (1994) declared that providing safe toys for this population was not only essential but also possible.

Interaction of Learning Characteristics

I described in Chapter 2 how the learning limitations imposed by mental retardation tend to interact with and compound each other. Nowhere is this phenomenon more apparent and significant than in working with children and youths whose mental retardation is severe/profound. Having diminished cognitive ability by itself greatly complicates and impairs the learning/teaching process. The addition of any additional mental, physical, health, or learning disability not only imposes its own limitations but also diminishes the means available to the teacher and the student to cope with the original problem. In this manner, each additional or secondary disability interacts with and makes every other learning problem more difficult to overcome.

The negative effects of the interaction among these learning characteristics can be offset to some extent by concentrating instruction on several learning characteristics in the same lesson. Every lesson should assist each student to become an increasingly efficient learner even though the improvement may be extremely slight.

TEACHING STUDENTS WITH SEVERE/PROFOUND MENTAL RETARDATION

The GIA procedures in Chapter 7 and other chapters in Part IV show how to overcome a number of teaching/learning situations and problems that are particularly difficult in severe/profound mental retardation. Some of the more perplexing of these problems and situations are discussed here. For those who teach students with severe/profound mental retardation full-time, Snell (1993) or Brimer (1990) is recommended.

Attainable versus Nonattainable Life Goals

Perhaps the most fundamental perspective needed in programs for students with severe/profound mental retardation is the balance between life goals that are possible for the student to eventually achieve and those that are not. This perspective is particularly difficult to realize for a variety of reasons with students whose mental retardation is severe/profound: (a) The eventual adult life status for these students tends to be one of dependence on others, but the level of independence each individual will achieve is difficult to predict; (b) the great disparity between their CAs and MAs can be obscure and deceiving; and (c) their extremely slow progress means that mastery of a single skill, concept, or goal may extend through several years and require the efforts of a succession of programs and teachers.

Another consideration in prioritizing life goals for students with severe/profound mental retardation is to determine whether or not a particular skill or concept will be developed to a practical point by the time the student leaves school. Everyone in mental retardation has seen teenagers—even those whose mental retardation is severe/profound—laboring away at preschool and early childhood activities that have little or no practical value at the students' achievable levels. Because the students in this population learn and progress so slowly, their life goals are not only extremely limited but also obscure. It takes an insightful IEP team and much long-term planning to strike the needed balance between an individual's eventual achievable and nonachievable life goals.

Learned Helplessness versus Independence

Those who work with students with mental retardation must learn to recognize and deal with learned helplessness, a condition in which individuals who are exposed to constant failure come to assume that they are not capable of acceptable performance (Maier & Seligman, 1976). Williams and Barber (1992) indicated that learned helplessness is largely an inability to recognize and negotiate internal and external loci of control. The authors pointed out that occasionally most people experience learned helplessness, which they characterize as a manifestation of passive behavior and blaming others for failures or shortcomings. Although students with severe/profound mental retardation are not as likely to verbalize or rationalize their behavior, they tend to give up easily or to refuse to attempt tasks that appear difficult or with which they are unfamiliar. Mulhauser (1993) recognized that although learned helplessness may be typical of students with multiple disabilities, she demonstrated that most individuals from this population can be trained to make acceptable choices with well-planned programs.

A related form of learned helplessness common in mental retardation is one in which individuals learn to depend on others to do things for them that they could do (or learn to do) for themselves (Grossman, 1991; Weisz, 1979). Learned helplessness causes a variety of instructional problems with students with severe/profound mental retardation because their many real limitations make it difficult to delineate those activities that are within the students' abilities and those that are too difficult. Thus, every diagnostic/prescriptive lesson must encourage the student to achieve a greater degree of decision-making ability, independence, and responsibility for his or her actions.

Chronological versus Mental Age Appropriateness

Age appropriateness at its best means providing materials and activities suited to a child's chronological age (Gardner et al., 1992; Hanline & Fox, 1993). Unfortunately, the more severe the mental retardation, the more difficult true age appropriateness is to achieve. In teaching students with severe/profound mental retardation, age appropriateness means much more than just careful selection of books and pictures. The entire learning environment for these students must be designed and carefully maintained to serve children and youths who are much younger mentally than they are chronologically. This ability group is comprised entirely of individuals who will become adults without a great many of the communication, social, transitional, and other skills they so desperately need. The social ages of students in this ability group typically lie somewhere between their MAs and CAs. Therefore, their lessons must be presented on a low cognitive level but be designed carefully to meet their life goal needs.

Immaturity, Student Preferences, and Working with Parents

Ultimately, children with severe/profound mental retardation tend to remain under the care, influence, and control of parents and other family members much longer than other children—often indefinitely. This situation has several important implications. First, the child is likely to have mastered many social skills at home—to some extent. Therefore, careful diagnosis is necessary to locate the child's frontier in social development. Also, the parents should be—and likely are—particularly involved in teaching these skills and concepts to their child. Therefore, time spent in cooperative efforts to help the parents teach, assist, and cope with their child's problems is particularly appropriate and beneficial.

The IEP team must also encourage and assist parents and other family members to use similar materials and procedures. Adapted/created/enhanced (ACE) stories (discussed in Chapter 10) are extremely helpful in this regard. Careful level-to-level planning is also particularly important to ensure that age-appropriateness goals are persistently followed as the student begins each new year.

Ideally, the personal preferences of every student should weigh heavily in the creation of that student's school program. The younger the students and the more severe their mental retardation, however, the less ability they will have to express personal preferences. The students discussed in this chapter also tend to manifest noticeably less physiological, sociological, and psychological maturity. Thus, it is usually very difficult to design an educational program—or even a single lesson—that balances such a student's interests and his or her needs. Students with severe/profound mental retardation may or may not prefer to be treated as younger children, but often they assume (or are assigned) roles as children younger than they really are. They often prefer to play with children younger than themselves. They may also choose picture books, stories, and other activities that are appropriate for younger children, although these materials are the only ones available that they can comprehend.

This immaturity presents some interesting challenges. Even though students with severe/profound mental retardation are immature, they vary greatly as individuals. The variations of immaturity have some serious implications for the learning/teaching process. The skills and concepts needed by an individual must be presented within the limitations imposed by the individual's unique level of immaturity. Teachers and parents must be careful not to expect a student to master a skill or concept his or her mind and body are not prepared to perform. At the same time, however, the teacher and the IEP team must encourage the student to mature and broaden his or her life interests as far as possible, usually a difficult task. For nonreaders, this must be done by locating and developing activities and materials that have low cognitive levels but that use pictures and themes appropriate to older boys and girls as well as adults. The IEP team must select with care the informational and recreational stories—such as ACE stories—to be read to nonreaders. These sources must be not only age appropriate but also presented on the proper language level. The same applies to videos and movies. Age 25 projections provide the team with an excellent means to persistently evaluate the student's progress and to determine the extent to which he or she will continue to depend on these sources and procedures as adults.

Appendix C provides an age/stage chart that illustrates normal development. It shows the approximate age that selected skills or abilities emerge in nondisabled children. The major purpose of the chart is to help teachers and other members of a student's IEP team reconcile the student's extremely low levels of maturity and achievement with his or her potential life goals. Because of the heterogeneity of students with mental retardation, it is not feasible to construct a developmental chart just for them. Like most developmental charts, Appendix C lists lower levels of maturity and skill toward the top of the chart and higher levels toward the bottom.

This chart must be used with great care. It is not always appropriate to compare the development of children who have mental retardation with that of children who do not have mental retardation. In addition, students with mental retardation tend to remain in some stages much longer than others. Used wisely, the chart can accomplish several purposes:

1. **It can help identify entry-level skills.** Once the teacher identifies a skill, concept, or life goal, the age/stage chart suggests some of the entry-level skills to be considered. Vertical curriculum planning (in this case, upward chaining) identifies fundamental skills, concepts, and prerequisite activities.

2. **It can help in planning the direction the skill, concept, activity, or target task should take.** Vertical curriculum planning (downward chaining) determines where a particular target task is likely to lead. Downward chaining helps in clarifying what additional skills are needed for the target task to eventually result in practical and appropriate achievements and abilities.

3. **It can indicate how horizontal (backward and forward) chaining identifies skills and concepts in other curriculum areas likely to be appropriate at the same level of development as the skills and concepts being considered.** Caution is essential here, however; a child whose mental retardation is severe/profound may be much more deficient in one curriculum area than another. For example, one such child may learn to walk at about the same age as other children but may never learn to speak at all. Others may develop fairly good communication skills but never be able to walk.

4. **It illustrates the notion of conceptual distance.** The chart should serve as a reminder of the tremendous disparity between the developmental rates of students with and without mental retardation. A typical child will typically pass through each of these stages within the indicated time period (e.g., 6 months). Students with severe/profound mental retardation always require more effort, resources, instruction, and maturity time to traverse the same conceptual distance.

Positive Learning Environment and Teacher Attitude

Perhaps the greatest single contribution a teacher can make to students with severe/profound mental retardation is to have a positive attitude and to establish a positive learning environment. Such an attitude requires that the teacher not become overwhelmed or discouraged by a student's extremely slow learning rate. A positive teacher is not intimidated by practical life goals that appear to be difficult to attain even though the goals are extremely limited, compared with those of other students. A positive teacher insists on teaching a student with mental retardation to perform a task, rather than to perform that task for him or her. For example, it may be simpler and more expedient to simply make the beds, particularly for older individuals, than to teach them to make the beds themselves. This philosophy tends to be shortsighted, however, and overlooks the importance of self-concept and independence. A positive teacher strongly stresses self-help skills for the students, such as being toilet trained and being able to feed and dress themselves. A positive teacher is never satisfied with a lower level of independent living than an individual may be capable of (Brown & Lehr, 1993). Wherever possible, it is better to toilet train students, rather than to diaper them, and to teach them to dress themselves, rather than to dress them.

Because of chronic and complex medical health problems, it is often necessary for a child with severe/profound mental retardation to learn to adapt and use a wheelchair, but a positive teacher will provide an optimum opportunity for the child to learn to walk if it is possible. The student's IEP team, in consultation with medical and other specialists, must carefully assess and monitor the nature, severity, and permanence of the medical or physical problem (e.g., cerebral palsy, hip deformity, clubfoot, muscular dystrophy) and decide whether or not the child can and should be taught to walk. Usually, such decisions can be made only after persistent trial and error and evaluation. Lehr and McDaid (1993) further asserted that these children should be educated in normal surroundings wherever possible; that is, their fragile health problems by themselves should not unduly influence their placement or learning environment.

A positive teacher knows that a high level of student obedience is necessary at an early age but that the ultimate goal is for the individual to be as independent and to make as many of his or her own life decisions as possible. Teachers of students whose mental retardation is severe/profound must be particularly careful to maintain a safe and comfortable learning environment. These students may be nonverbal even as adults, and it may be difficult for them to make their needs known. It may also be difficult for them to indicate preferences in activities or lessons. Typically, they are more dependent on parents, teachers, and others around them than any other students in the schools.

The following suggestions may be helpful in establishing and maintaining a satisfactory learning environment:

* Be alert for signs of anxiety and stress that are often caused by teachers, parents, and others whose expectations are too high and who design and present lessons and materials that are too demanding in terms of rate and level (Bredekamp, 1986).
* Be careful to avoid injury when lifting and carrying a student.
* Supervise students with severe/profound mental retardation very carefully so that they don't fall, choke, or become entangled in swings, toys, wheelchairs, and so on.
* Allow students whose mental retardation is severe/profound to make toy and play-thing selections for themselves wherever possible but encourage them to experiment with a variety of toys and leisure activities.
* Keep instructional toys and materials out of sight, except when familiarity, rather than novelty, is desired. Covering or hiding toys from view avoids distractions during periods of instruction.
* Toys, games, materials, and all other equipment must be free from lead-based paints, sharp or protruding parts, and pieces small enough to go into the mouth. When smaller objects are necessary for instruction, provide full-time, close supervision.
* Provide students whose mental retardation is severe/profound with some of their own equipment and toys in the classroom as soon as possible to develop a sense of self-worth and ownership and to develop cooperative play and sharing skills (Bredekamp, 1986).

- Make sure the students complete their own work, rather that allow peer tutors, volunteers, regular class teachers, or instructional assistants to complete the work for them.
- Make it a point to improve, rather than to indulge, a student's unacceptable behavior or poor performance.
- Make full-length mirrors available.
- Model acceptable behavior and verbalize activities to the students, also telling them what they are doing and why they are doing it. In such activities, adults must use clear language as nearly on the child's receptive level as possible.

PLANNING CURRICULUM

Diagnostic/prescriptive teaching procedures generally call for the skills and concepts from each student's prioritized life goals to be arranged in order of increasing difficulty or achievement level. In this way, the instruction for each student bypasses previously learned skills and concepts and moves to the instructional frontier that is unique to that student. These previously learned skills and concepts may need to be considered and diagnosed as entry-level skills for new skills and concepts to be covered. For these reasons, the later sections of this chapter briefly discuss the major headings and subtopics of the curriculum planning charts in the order they typically develop in children. The curriculum planning charts are found in Chapter 3. Some specific skills and concepts to be considered are included in Appendix D.

Some of the most important decisions the IEP team must make for a student with severe/profound mental retardation is the extent to which that student needs these low-level skills and concepts. It is important to remember that the lower a student functions, the less likely that student is to demonstrate complete mastery of any skill or concept. Therefore, the IEP team must identify the point at which the student should "move on" without such complete mastery. For example, most students with mental retardation will not outlive their need to improve listening comprehension skills. When (if) such a student reaches the ability level where reading (and eventually reading comprehension) is appropriate, instruction in both areas may be needed. Most skills, concepts, and procedures (e.g., toilet training, augmentative communication, ambulation, supported employment) discussed in this chapter may not be needed by students whose mental retardation is relatively less severe.

Curriculum for all students with mental retardation is concentrated on four basic components:

1. Teaching the students such fundamental-to-advanced skills and concepts, basic communication, social, and motor skills—called developmental learning
2. Teaching each student how to learn as efficiently and independently as possible, to become increasingly responsible for his or her own acts, and to make as many of his or her own life decisions as possible

3. Teaching the students needed skills and concepts they are unable to pursue independently
4. Teaching each individual how to compensate for those skills and concepts he or she is unable to master and to cope as well as possible in adult life without such mastery

With so many limiting deficiencies, one can readily see why the educational programs for a student with mental retardation need to be so carefully planned. The majority of the curriculum for students with severe/profound mental retardation consists of Area C skills and concepts (see Figure 3.1 in Chapter 3) that most children learn incidentally at home and, for the most part, before they start school. For example, toilet training for members of this population may persist to age 10 or beyond, thus occupying an inordinate amount of the time that becomes unavailable for teaching/learning other vitally needed skills and concepts.

Adaptations to the Curriculum Planning Chart

The skills, concepts, and target tasks for students with severe/profound mental retardation can be generally listed on the same curriculum planning chart as for other students with mental retardation. In using the curriculum planning charts of Chapter 3, however, there are two important considerations:

1. The same terms in the column headings may refer to different levels of achievement. Communication skills for a higher functioning student may be focused on tasks such as giving oral reports and participating in independent job interviews. For a student whose mental retardation is severe/profound, communication skills are likely to be a matter of making basic needs known and knowing where to seek needed assistance. Endurance for one such student may mean learning to run greater distances and play group games; for another student, endurance may be a matter of cardiopulmonary exercises as a means of survival.
2. Some subtopics in each column are particularly important to students whose mental retardation is severe/profound. Examples of these subtopics are self-help skills, making basic body movements, and augmented communications and speech alternatives. In any event, the IEP for each individual should concentrate on the prioritized skills and concepts that are the most practical and appropriate for that individual.

Age 25 Projection

The age 25 projection has special meaning in teaching students with severe/profound mental retardation. Because these students tend to remain much longer at rudimentary levels of development (compared with other students), their life goals must be planned, prioritized, and evaluated with particular care. Many such students use wheelchairs and are either unable to make their needs known or can do so only with help and difficulty. Even as they get older, these students are often unable to speak or walk. In working with such a student, the student's IEP team must not lose sight of the fact that teenagers (including students whose mental retardation is severe/profound) are at least halfway through school.

The IDEA requires that, at roughly age 14, every disabled student's life goals be identified. Plans must be formulated and adopted to help the student make the difficult transition from school life to adult life. Using the age 25 concept over a period of time, the student's IEP team can gain fairly accurate estimates of the eventual life status of even the student with the most profound mental retardation.

Goal Instructional Analysis (GIA)

GIA procedures are especially helpful in establishing efficient learning/teaching situations for students whose mental retardation is severe/profound. Their extremely slow progress makes highly detailed lesson planning necessary and beneficial. Fortunately, having fewer students in a typical class for these students makes additional time available for greater detail in planning. Generally, the more slowly the child learns, the greater the number of GIA components the teacher should use. In other words, teaching dressing skills to a child who will ultimately require 2 years to master putting on his or her shoes unassisted requires many detailed lesson plans. Using a large number and variety of GIA components allows the planning of even minute-by-minute procedures where necessary and reveals otherwise imperceptible achievement. Because such highly detailed lesson plans are not usually required by higher authority, they need to be committed to writing only as required by the teacher. With experience, the teacher should readily recognize instances in which more (or less) detailed lesson planning is necessary. Typically, teachers of students with mental retardation are already overburdened with paperwork.

Some initial components likely to be particularly applicable to students whose mental retardation is severe/profound are suggested in Figure 9.1. In most instances, the components listed suggest sequences that generally increase task difficulty and demand higher performance levels of the students (e.g., smooth to rough surface).

Using GIA components suggested by those listed in Figure 9.1 and others from Figure 7.1 of Chapter 7, the teacher can design specific learning/teaching segments appropriate for each student. Some representative target tasks in major areas of emphasis are suggested below and in Appendix D, together with some related subtasks. In most instances, the target tasks make good long-term and annual IEP goals (or those goals to be achieved in about a full school year). The subtasks are stated in more specific terms. Mastery of these subtasks contributes to the achievement of the long-term goal (or target task). Thus, the subtasks make good IEP short-term objectives. Short-term objectives should be as measurable or demonstrable as possible and may need to specify some definite increments of achievement, such as movements to be made, items to be counted, and amount of time a student persists with an activity.

MATERIALS
smooth to rough surface
soft to hard
light to heavy
easy to difficult

MASTERY
Makes movement
• rotary
• up and down
• side to side
• on command
• from various positions

ASSISTANCE
animated instructions
from story read by teacher
from story read by other adult
hand-on-hand
teacher-assisted movement
unison with teacher
unison with other students

ASSISTIVE TECHNOLOGY
alternative devices
• switches
• communication boards
• crutches
• wheelchair
• walkers

TIME CONSIDERATIONS
unlimited time to complete
unlimited time for each trial

TASK
easy to more difficult
simple to complex

MONITOR/SUPERVISE
one-on-one
close supervision to monitoring

REWARD
immediate to delayed reward
tangible to intangible reward

FIGURE 9.1 Suggested Components

It is often easier to formulate skills, concepts, and activities for a student with mental retardation in terms of what the program calls for, rather than what the student is expected to learn. One reason for this is the students' lack of verbal ability. Thus, the teaching/learning situations created as a result of the general, abbreviated IEP suggestions below may need to be stated as to what the student will perform. For example, "animated instructions" from the assistance components is stated as a teaching strategy, but a student may learn in a variety of areas by using animated (or pictured) instructions. Evaluation in these instances concentrates on how the student performs and improves where that strategy is used.

CURRICULUM PLANNING IN SPECIFIC SKILL AREAS

Each curriculum-planning or skill area in the following sections suggests some specific long-term goals, annual goals, and short-term objectives, specific skills, concepts, and target tasks of each column of the curriculum planning chart that are likely to be appropriate for an individual student. These are only representative, however, and those for a specific student must be identified or created on an individual basis.

Communication Skills

The high incidence of various communication problems in severe forms of mental retardation has been well established (Carduso-Martins, Mervis, & Mervis, 1985;

Assistive technology enables a student to learn by listening to recorded information.

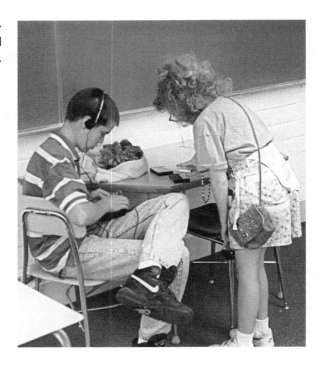

Kennedy, 1930). On leaving school and entering life as an adult, every student should be able to communicate as well as possible with other people. Therefore, the development and improvement of communications skills must be an ongoing part of the curriculum planning process for students whose mental retardation is severe/profound at every age level. Many school-age students with severe/profound mental retardation are in the lower developmental levels of speech and language—even learning to make audible sounds. In an extreme case, Rogow (1993) reported on a student with some rudimentary reading and writing skills in two languages but who did not initiate speech. For a student with severe/profound mental retardation, optimum communication skills might include a number of rudimentary skills and concepts that need not be taught to other students with mental retardation. Many of these students must be taught assistive technology and alternatives to speech.

The relative inability of students with severe/profound mental retardation to communicate well poses some crucial problems in the learning/teaching process. Most such students have predictable difficulties in both receptive and expressive language and speech. Most will not learn to write or spell well enough to use these communication skills effectively as adults. The fact that a student is unable to respond (or to respond accurately) to questions in either oral or written form can be an almost overwhelming limitation. Not only is it challenging to teach nonverbal students, but it also is particularly difficult to assess the extent of their achievement. Without speech (or at least some sort of expressive language), the student has difficulty asking questions and making his or her needs known. Yoder and Davies (1992) found that the utterances of students with developmentally delayed speech were more intelligible in routine than in nonroutine situations and where practical information was involved.

Using Assistive Technology

One of the most encouraging developments in recent years has been the advancement of technology and its application to the education of students with severe/profound mental retardation. Conceivably, some type of electronic or other device is available for teaching in almost every area of curriculum and at every age and ability level—including severe/profound mental retardation (Cook, 1995). Parents and teachers must be especially careful in using hand-held calculators, computers, and other electronic devices with students whose mental retardation is severe/profound. These devices have both advantages and disadvantages that are particularly significant in working with these students. For example, these devices can be highly motivating and interesting. They may also be the best or only means for these students to accomplish certain tasks. Programs are available to teach a wide variety of skills and concepts, and they can be particularly helpful in teaching communication skills. Some computers and other devices are interactive, allowing two-way communication with the student (Gandell & Laufer, 1993). Computers can also evaluate students' responses and adjust the rate and level at which the learning material is presented. Tremendous advancements in both hardware and software are occurring at an ever-increasing rate. Future advancements may overcome most or all of the disadvantages.

Some potential weaknesses in technology exist in several areas, including portability, obsolescence, compatibility, adaptability, and cost. To be truly practical, all skills and concepts learned at school must be applicable in real-life situations—situations in which computers and electronic devices may or may not be available. For example, even a student whose mental retardation is quite severe may learn to write letters with a computer program in which he or she simply "clicks" on a picture that describes the information to be conveyed or requested. The direct benefits of such a program are obvious wherever the individual's adult environment includes a similar computer, program, and printer. The individual may also need ongoing support to use the procedure, but then some degree of supervision is often available with severe forms of mental retardation. Of course, this procedure may teach the student communication skills that are independent of the computer and that can be applied orally or in rudimentary writing.

Only individual—and usually ongoing—evaluation can determine which students can and must learn to apply the skills and concepts mentally or with paper and pencil and which students will have similar devices available at home, in other classes, in other schools, in the workplace, or elsewhere in the community. Both modes of application are difficult because students with severe/profound mental retardation are known to have extreme difficulty in transfer of training (Hayes & Taplin, 1993) and because availability of the devices is often limited. Evaluation must affirm that the skills and concepts are meeting these criteria; otherwise, using any electronic device is questionable. The motivational element must also be carefully evaluated. These devices, like television, may be captivating and entertaining, but the student doesn't have to interact socially with either. Thus, it is easy to assume that a student is learning useful concepts when he or she is merely occupied—particularly with students who have motivational or behavioral problems. The teacher must constantly evaluate the student's ability to apply computer-taught communication, arithmetic, or other skills in practical situations. Of course, the purpose of using these devices in the first place may have been to exchange information with the student while his or her communication skills were developing. In any event, the teacher and IEP team must carefully weigh the advantages and disadvantages of using such teaching devices. Skills learned on such a device may, in fact, be splinter skills, no matter how captivating such a device may be.

Alternatives to Speech   In teaching students whose mental retardation is severe/profound, it is often necessary and beneficial to develop and use some alternative speech and communication techniques, such as signing and head pointers, sign boards, picture boards, switches, language boards, and other compensatory devices (Baumgart, 1990; Reichle, York, & Sigafoos, 1991; Silverman, 1989). In an exhaustive review of the literature, Silverman (1995) reported a variety of these devices to have been beneficial in many ways (improved behavioral and social skills, as well as ability to communicate) to individuals of all ages and with many different disabilities. It is difficult to predict which students will respond well to instruction and eventually develop satisfactory communication skills and which students will not (Reichle & Yoder, 1985). Therefore, some of these students need alternative and augmentative procedures only until they are able to communicate in conventional ways; others need to use these alternatives after they leave school. All types of augmentative communication tend to be slow, often cumbersome, and require the individuals to carry the devices with them. Some of these devices are limited in scope, and most of them make communication—especially dialogue—possible only with others skilled in their use. Because the devices tend to attract undue attention in social situations, most users require considerable training, experience, and encouragement before they will voluntarily use them in public.

Finally, instruction in their use consumes time and other resources that could be used to develop conventional language. Even the most rudimentary speech is likely to be more useful in the long run than considerable skill in using speech alternatives. One must not overlook, however, the need for permanent effective alternatives to speech where they are indicated (Fishman, 1987; Reichle et al., 1991). Snyder, Freeman-Lorentz, and McLaughlin (1994) demonstrated that students with mild/moderate mental retardation can be responsive to augmentative intervention procedures. These researchers used a variety of augmentative techniques to improve vocabulary learning rates and improved sentence selection for five children whose CAs ranged from 7 to 9.

The dilemma of the permanent need for augmentative communication presents the student's IEP team with another situation for which the age 25 projection might be used. During the early years, every nonverbal child is likely to profit from one or more alternatives to speech. As with other projections, however, a young child's communicative ability and style when he or she leaves school is difficult to predict. As the child matures, his or her eventual development of speech and resultant diminished need for augmentative procedures becomes more apparent.

Most of the communication skills and adaptations discussed here are prerequisites to communication skills discussed in Chapter 10. Many of the lower level skills, concepts, and target tasks of communication and language concept development discussed in that chapter are appropriate for these students. For example, an individual must be able to produce vocal sounds some time before he or she can utter intelligible words. Specific instruction in such rudimentary tasks as proper breathing, sucking, swallowing, and control of drooling may also be necessary. Lancioni, Brouwer, and Coninx (1992) noted that medical control of drooling was only moderately successful. They reported only limited success using electronic cuing timers to remind individuals whose mental retardation was severe/profound to wipe their faces at regular intervals.

Teachers, therapists, and parents must verbalize extensively with the students as they work with them using alternative procedures. Their receptive language always develops somewhat ahead of their expressive language. The language level of each child's instruction must be as nearly on that child's instructional level as possible. If the child is on the *go, come, stop, sit down* level, teachers and parents must adjust their language as near to that level as possible—at the same time regularly modeling a slightly higher level.

Manual Communication Manual communication has several forms, including sign language and finger spelling. Sign language was developed as a means of communication for people with severe hearing impairments and others who were unable to develop effective speech. It has become increasingly popular in teaching students with severe/profound mental retardation. Sign language is commonly used to reinforce spoken language and to facilitate communication while the student is learning to speak (Sensenig, Mazeika, & Topf, 1989). As such, the student is taught receptive signing to receive information and instruction. Many students with mental retardation can also learn to sign to express desires, to request help or information, and to give information. Some such students, like people with hearing impairments, must use signing as a primary substitute for oral communication.

The most common form of manual communication in mental retardation is American Sign Language, sometimes abbreviated as Ameslan. The major advantages of sign language are that it appears to be easier for some people to learn than spoken language and that it has a wide vocabulary. It is considered to be a complete language in that it has its own system of grammar and syntax. Ameslan is not necessarily based on English, and if used extensively, it imposes an additional language structure on the student. Further, Silverman (1995) pointed out that the lower the individual's mental age, the more time and effort are required for him or her to master each sign, a consideration that is significant to other types of manual communication as well. He also indicated that any type of manual communication requires a minimum amount of visual acuity, motoric ability, and coordination. Therefore, in mental retardation, signing is often used as a supportive procedure or vehicle for teaching speech, rather than as a substitute communication system. As such, signing is often limited to single words and concepts, such as go, stop, eat, sleep, run, toilet, and so forth, although some students may never develop effective oral speech.

Some finger spelling may also be helpful in mental retardation, especially with proper nouns and uncommon but necessary expressions. Manual communication is highly portable, compared with most technological devices, such as computers, switches, and sign boards. Of course, the principal disadvantage with any type of manual communication is that it can be used only to communicate with others skilled in its use (Doherty, Karlan, & Lloyd, 1982; Dunham, 1989). Moreover, spelling is particularly difficult for students with severe/profound mental retardation and multiple disabilities. A further consideration in adopting and adapting manual communication for students with severe/profound mental retardation is the extent to which a given sign is readily apparent, or iconic (Griffith & Robinson, 1980). For example, Gates and Edwards (1989) reported that students with mental retardation learned Amerind (American Indian Hand Language) signs more readily than Ameslan signs, apparently because the Amerind signs were more iconic or concrete. Thus, teachers and other IEP team members must continually evaluate each individual's progress and the continued merits of manual communication. Classroom activities should always be designed to give the child good reasons to use spoken language.

Social Skills

As in other curriculum areas, a large portion of the school time of a student with severe/profound mental retardation must be devoted to helping that student achieve a great many social and related skills that other children learn almost incidentally at home or elsewhere. Hamre-Nietupski, Nietupski, and Strathe (1992) reported that, generally, the more severe the mental retardation, the more strongly the involved parents tend to prefer programs that offer good sociological adjustment. Some of the highest life goal priorities for these students include self-help and grooming skills, meeting people, social awareness, citizenship, personality development, obedience, and making decisions. The long-term goals and short-term objectives identified here begin at low achievement levels, but instruction does not necessarily begin there. The student must be carefully diagnosed in each area to determine the point at which instruction should actually begin. Students with severe/profound mental retardation require much more extensive and intensive instruction in sociological—as well as other—areas to develop acceptable performance levels (Cheseldine & Jeffree, 1982).

Self-Help Skills

Social instruction for a student with severe/profound mental retardation is often characterized by functions and activities that must be performed regardless of the individual's ability to participate. For example, until an individual is able to perform these functions for him- or herself, others must bathe, wash, dress, and feed that individual and keep him or her free from unsafe and unsanitary conditions, offensive odors, exploitation, and abuse by others. This means that a student with severe/profound mental retardation may be rather passive at first, gradually learning to participate in and eventually perform as much of each function as possible.

This situation can be discouraging to the child's teacher who often prefers to provide instruction in areas of learning that are taught to other children. The IEP team must carefully consider these basic skills, whose mastery is essential to everything the individual will do—either as a child or later as an adult. To some people, self-help skills may seem mundane and of low priority, possibly because the skills are easily mastered as children by most people. For those who have not acquired these basic skills, however, they are of the highest priority.

A number of investigators have taught self-help skills by using specific procedures that fit well into the structure of GIA. McKelvey, Sisson, Van Hasselt, and Hersen (1992) used graduated (gradually faded) guidance to teach dressing skills to a child with profound mental retardation, blindness, deafness, and a seizure disorder. Freagon and Rotatori (1982) compared natural and contrived environments to teach a variety of self-help skills to group home residents and found the natural situations to be more effective.

Space does not permit an exhaustive list of social skills and concepts. Naturally, students with severe/profound mental retardation will vary greatly as to the time and effort each will require to complete a given skill or concept. Where self-help problems exist, however, they can have devastating effects on the individual. An individual who is not toilet trained will have virtually no chance for success in social, employment, independent living, or recreational situations regardless of achievements in all other areas. The same is true of the more abstract traits of honesty, dependability, and trustworthiness. In teaching these vital skills, the IEP team must not take anything for granted. For example, a few years ago, a U.S. senator criticized a colleague from the House of Representatives by declaring that most of the beneficiaries of some legislation the congressman was sponsoring would be people who were "not even toilet trained." The congressman's reply was direct and compelling: "Senator, if I had to choose between being toilet trained and learning to read, I would choose toilet training every time."

As a student with severe/profound mental retardation nears the age of leaving school, the potential level of his or her independence should become increasingly clear. In many instances, the individual will be able mainly to cooperate with other adults who take care of him or her; in other cases, the person may achieve considerable independence under varying degrees of supervision. The student must be taught obedience, initially with the goal of eventually stating preferences and making as many of his or her own life decisions as possible.

Social skills components are arranged in sequences that gradually but persistently increase the student's participation. Students with severe/profound mental retardation must progress as far as possible along a typical long-range sequence: mere awareness → passive participation → partial participation → full participation. The GIA components can also be manipulated to gradually shift control of activities and decision making from teacher to student. This can be done by listing *teacher* as an initial component (meaning the teacher is in full control) and *student* at the point on that component row where the student is able to participate to a greater extent. On a separate component row, *passive* can be listed as the initial component that is manipulated to *partial* and then to *full* to indicate the extent to which the student is expected to participate. For example, a student may be unable to lift his or her arm to operate a switch or other device. Thus, the teacher—or an instructional assistant—must provide all the energy to move the arm. As strength gradually develops in the arm, the participation of the student increases.

Some sample long- and short-term goals and objectives (target tasks and subtasks) in communication for students with severe/profound mental retardation are found in the other chapters of this unit and in Appendix D. These samples serve as guides in designing GIAs to meet the unique needs of individual students. The teacher must create a variety of GIA components and manipulate them to arrange the GIA segments in order of increasing difficulty and achievement levels.

Home and Family Skills

Family living skills are quite varied but usually include basic food selection, storage, preparation, sanitation, care of clothing, cleaning, dusting, and working with other family members. Home and family living skills also include all of the social and communication skills discussed above.

Independent Living Skills

Helping every individual with mental retardation be as independent as possible is a major educational goal and must be stressed at every age level. Unwittingly or otherwise, all of us probably encourage students with severe/profound mental retardation as they develop some forms of learned helplessness and overdependence. For example, we rightly insist on obedience from children while they are young, often punishing them for unacceptable behavior and rewarding or reinforcing behavior that is compliant—even subservient. It is particularly important, however, that enforcing compliance among this population be accomplished with nonaversive procedures (Berkman & Meyer, 1988; Tyson & Spooner, 1991; also see Chapter 8). It is admittedly difficult to identify the appropriate point at which to begin de-emphasizing obedience and to begin stressing independence—bearing in mind that obedience will be a vital, lifetime virtue for many students with severe/profound mental retardation. The development of independence and proactive skills must be emphasized throughout the individual's school career.

Leisure Activities Skills

The leisure/motor skills and activities column of the curriculum planning chart includes sensorimotor activities, basic body movements, balance, coordination, fine and gross motor skills, endurance, and physical education. Obviously, most of these skill areas could logically have been listed in other columns—for example, social, transition, and home and family. They are closely related to these areas as well as to each other, and learning activities can be designed to cover several of these areas in a single lesson. Some subdivisions and shorter term goals for these physical/motor activities likely to be appropriate for students with severe/profound mental retardation include such basic body movements as creeping, crawling, positioning, posture, sitting, standing, and walking.

For most students with severe/profound mental retardation, diagnosis/prescription in motor activities begins at the level of making basic body movements of the limbs and torso. In some instances, an individual may be unable to move his or her own limbs. In these cases, the limbs must be manipulated by other people to prevent atrophy of the muscles. For some students, these activities will occupy a considerable amount of time during each school day. Some electric and mechanical equipment, such as treadmills and motorized exercisers, is available to assist in the manipulation and exercise of the body limbs. Use of such equipment has certain risks, however, one of which is potential overexertion. It is advisable to obtain the necessary releases from the parents and the individual's physician before using this equipment in the school. Most hospitals now require a variety of release forms before placing a patient on this type of equipment. Like many learning/teaching activities for a student with severe/profound mental retardation, the physical/motor skills must be planned from a level of having the student participate and gradually developing the ability to perform as independently as possible. Some younger children with mild or moderate mental retardation may also need some of the rudimentary skills and concepts identified here.

Art, music, and recreation are also included in this section. Because students with mental retardation do not typically develop sufficient skill in art or music to perform in these activities, it is all too common to assign them a low priority. Students with mental retardation, however, like all other people, need to develop diversion and entertainment skills, so art and music might well be considered as part of leisure and recreation development. These students require extensive training, support, and exposure in order to develop recreational and leisure skills.

Transitional and Vocational Skills

Cognitive, social, and other problems cause severe limitations in a student's ability to obtain and succeed on a job. Nevertheless, many students with severe/profound mental retardation can be trained to perform a variety of remunerative tasks (Schepis, Reid, & Fitzgerald, 1987). The preparation for an optimum employment status or level of students with severe/profound mental retardation must be carefully and constantly evaluated. Most students with severe/profound mental retardation must rely heavily on sheltered, supported, and unpaid employment procedures. As the student gets older, the IEP team will be in a position to make increasingly accurate predictions of each student's eventual employment potential. Some students may eventually qualify for some type of gainful employment; others will work in a sheltered environment, at best. During the school years, it is difficult to determine the future employment status of a student and to offer that individual the type of appropriate transitional training and work experience he or she needs. It is all too easy to spend the student's valuable instructional time preparing him or her for a specific job or a high level of employment, for which he or she eventually fails to qualify. Black and Meyer (1993), however, reported generally positive attitudes of government workers, counselors, and supervisors toward videotape samples of employment training—even for those whose disabilities were quite severe.

The age 25 projection is very valuable in predicting the type and level of employment each student is likely to need. Following the principles of the age 25 projection, specific job skill training, job information, and preparation for employment should be delayed (possibly until the early teens) until the student's employment potential is relatively clear. During the student's early school years, it is probably best to concentrate

Communications
1. **Is aware of surroundings →**
   Transition—following instructions
Is increasingly aware of sounds
Interrupts activity to attend noise or command
Stops movement at noise or voice (starts,
     blinks, makes other eye movement)
Responds to own name → Social
Responds to teacher's voice

2. **Responds to stimuli from**
   surroundings → Social
Smiles with coaxing and modeling
Reaches for proffered toy or object → Leisure
Points to object on command → Arithmetic
Picks up indicated object on command
Yields "one" object on command → Arithmetic
Yields "two" objects on command →
     Arithmetic
Responds to "No" and "Hot" → Home

3. **Pays attention to teacher-selected**
   cues → Social
Makes eye contact with teacher, then with
     aide, volunteer, classmates
Pays selective attention to movements

Pays selective attention to classmates
Pays selective attention to pictures and
     picture books
Pays selective attention to teacher
Uses nomination (approximates by pointing,
     turning head or looking)
Attends to task with increasing "white" or
     controlled noise and other planned
     distractions
Works for increasing periods of time without
     disturbing others → Transition
Attends to story, activity, or lesson for increas-
     ing period of time

4. **Develops speaking apparatus →**
   Leisure—Motor → Social
Cries (may be random or purposeful)
Breathes deeply → Leisure (Endurance)
Breathes quietly
Breathes without laboring
Does breathing exercises—blows feathers,
     cotton balls, paper windmills
Imitates teacher-demonstrated tongue, lip, and
     jaw movements
Controls swallowing

FIGURE 9.2   Communications

on preemployment social, communications, and physical/motor skills. Other high-priority life goals for the younger students include getting along well with other people, accepting home and classroom duties and responsibilities, following directions, developing good work habits, using public transportation, acquiring minimum map-reading skills, and observing safety measures in a variety of community settings.

Avoiding serious adverse habits and social problems is also among the highest priority goals for any student, including those with severe/profound mental retardation. How employable is a person who is given to fighting, swearing, or nose picking or who throws a temper tantrum even just occasionally? Currently, the fast-food industry is an excellent source of employment and job training for students with mental retardation. A worker who is observed fussing with his or her hair or who has offensive body odor or a similar problem, however, is likely to cause customers to avoid that establishment—and possibly other units of the same regional chain. Such a student is functionally unemployable even if he or she has exemplary employment skills otherwise.

Keeps own nasal passages clear
Wipes own nose
Uses physical activities to build lung capacity
  necessary for proper breathing
Imitates head movements
Attempts to imitate facial expressions
Makes some purposeful facial expressions

5. **Develops visual tracking skills →
    Leisure—Motor**
Visually tracks horizontally
Visually tracks vertically
Visually tracks in circular pattern
Tracks with pencil between thick, wide-apart
  parallel lines
Tracks with pencil between thick, wide-apart,
  lines that are increasingly curved

6. **Develops visual perception skills →
    Leisure—Motor**
Makes visual search for indicated object
  or picture
Does dot-to-dot with shapes, letters, and
  numbers
Draws or approximates simple pictures
Feels object to help in identification
Generally recognizes left and right

Uses some symbolic play
Uses trial and error to solve simple situations,
  shape own environment

7. **Develops prewriting eye-hand
    coordination → Leisure—Motor**
Holds pencil, chalk correctly
Scribbles with large pencil
Copies simple designs with large pencil
Holds chalk correctly
Scribbles on chalkboard
Copies simple designs on chalkboard
Uses increasingly smaller writing instruments

8. **Improves listening skills (Social)**
Appears to begin listening and attending
Listens quietly while others relate events, tell
  stories, answer questions, etc.
Listens to short, simple story
Listens to stories of increasing length

9. **Identifies common sounds**
Identifies common sound (e.g., train)
  by pointing to picture or object
Identifies sounds of wind, music, car, fire
  engine, ambulance, police car, familiar
  animals, by pointing → Home and
  Family (Safety)

FIGURE 9.2   Continued

SAMPLE SKILLS, CONCEPTS, AND ACTIVITIES IN SPECIFIC CURRICULUM AREAS

In the area of communications, some skills, concepts, and activities that might be appropriate for a student with severe/profound mental retardation are shown in Figure 9.2. The list is not intended to be exhaustive, merely representative. Parentheses suggest that the skill, concept, or activity could logically be taught jointly with, followed by, or reinforced by skills, concepts, or activities from one or more other curriculum areas. Additional goals (skills and concepts) appropriate for students with severe/profound mental retardation and multiple disabilities can be found in other chapters of this part and in Appendix D. The major heading is a long-term or annual goal and is followed by several shorter term goals or objectives, each of which can be further subdivided if necessary. Any long-term goal or short-term objective (or its subdivisions) can be treated as a GIA target task or subtask if the student has difficulty mastering it.

SUMMARY

In this chapter, I discussed curriculum planning for students with severe/profound mental retardation and multiple disabilities. Children in this classification are more likely to be identified as having mental retardation than those whose mental retardation is less severe.

I emphasized that these children invariably have great difficulty—even in learning self-help skills. I also emphasized, however, that most of them do surprisingly well if they have good educational programs.

I outlined some considerations, procedures, and suggested sample goals to help these children become as independent as possible.

CHAPTER **10**

Communication Skills

283

Points to Study and Ponder

1. What is language? How does it differ from speech?
2. What is language concept development?
3. What are the differences between receptive and expressive language?
4. What is the giant word syndrome, and how does it apply to students with mental retardation?
5. What are locus and value concepts, and how are these concepts related to teaching arithmetic?
6. What are inclusive and exclusive statements, and why are these concepts important in teaching students with mental retardation?
7. What are consequential or conditional statements, and why are these concepts important in teaching students with mental retardation?
8. What are alternative statements?
9. What is an ACE story? Who usually writes the ACE story?
10. How can an ACE story be used to teach a skill or concept to a student before that student can read?

One of the most important things any person must learn to do is communicate with others. The free flow and interchange of ideas is central to the development of any society. Ordinarily, most members of a society communicate well enough to help perpetuate and advance the society. Unfortunately, any individual member of that society who does not communicate well is unable to take full advantage of the benefits available. Likewise, such a member is unable to participate and make as full a contribution as he or she would otherwise. The need for good communication extends into the home, school, church, employment, leisure activities, and all social situations. Good communication skills are vital for any degree of success in adult life.

AGE APPROPRIATENESS AND DEVELOPMENTAL LANGUAGE

In this chapter, I show that the development of communication skills is such that instruction must begin at an early age and continue throughout the student's school career. Good communication skills are so vital that they should be emphasized at all age levels. At no point will a child outgrow his or her need for these valuable skills, although even these skills must be prioritized as the child nears the age of graduation. Because communication is stressed throughout the school career of a student with mental retardation, it is particularly important to ensure that each skill and concept added to a student's curriculum is age appropriate. As a student with mental retardation learns communication skills that approximate his or her MA, it is easy for the IEP team to lose sight of the student's approaching graduation date (Karen et al., 1985). The instructional materials used to teach the communication skills that are prerequisite to reading, arithmetic, and social skills have direct or implied language levels, all of which must be age appropriate.

DEFINITIONS

Research has consistently shown that students with mental retardation have great difficulty developing good speech and communications skills (Hornstein, 1986; Kennedy, 1930; Merrill & Jackson, 1992; Scudder & Tremain, 1992). Karlin and Strazulla (1952) found a strong, positive relationship between the severity of mental retardation and the extent of language delay. They also reported that students with mental retardation lag farther behind their peers in speech and language development than in any other area. This chapter deals with the development of communication skills, particularly for students with mental retardation. To treat this topic in a nontechnical manner, it is necessary to use some practical definitions.

Carroll (1961) defined language as "a structured system of arbitrary vocal sounds and sequences of sound which is used in interpersonal communication and which rather exhaustively catalogs the things, events, and processes of human experience" (pp. 331–345). Since that time, a tendency has developed to use the term *language* as the complete communication process, as well as to use *language* and *communication* synonymously, as is done in this book. Both terms have come to include the total process by which an individual listens, speaks, thinks, reads, and writes in receiving and transmitting thoughts and ideas (Jordan, 1976; Thomas & Carmack, 1990). For our purposes, communication skills include communication support devices and nonverbal gestures, such as facial expressions and body language (Banbury & Hebert, 1992; Hobson, Ouston, & Lee, 1989; Marcell & Jett, 1985; McAlpine, Kendall & Singh, 1991). Interestingly, Thomas and Carmack (1990) even include a person's thoughts and ideas that are used in personal decision making as a type of language, which they call *intraindividual communication.* Students with mental retardation have difficulty in all areas of language and communication but do profit from well-designed instructional programs (Gottardo & Rubin, 1991; Rosenberg & Abbeduto, 1987).

Receptive Language

Receptive language is the process of receiving incoming communication that is mainly visual and auditory but that can include body language and other sources. In practice, receptive language may include some elements of nonverbal expression (e.g., pointing and other responsive actions) without which it is difficult to observe and measure a student's receptive vocabulary.

Expressive Language

Expressive language refers to the process of formulating ideas and expressing those ideas with appropriate speech, action, or both. The expressive language of students with mental retardation almost always lags considerably behind their receptive language. Furthermore, Abbeduto, Furman, and Davies (1989) reported that even these students' receptive language tends to be inferior to that of students without mental retardation who have equal MAs. Although most children can point to a picture representing the correct answer to a question before they are able to express their response verbally, this discrepancy is particularly evident in students with mental retardation.

Speech

The spoken form of expressive language is referred to as *speech.* It is initiated in the brain and requires precise coordination between the brain and neuromuscular organs to produce intelligible sounds needed for effective communication (Thomas & Carmack, 1990).

Language Concept Development (LCD)

Before and during the time children are learning to speak, they formulate ideas and perceptions that are essential to effective communication. This is known as *language concept development (LCD)* and is a prerequisite or entry-level skill to all other skills and concepts. It is particularly essential in teaching reading, writing, speaking, health, social studies, arithmetic, work and study habits, and other prevocational skills. A concept is built largely through experience. A student with mental retardation typically has great difficulty mastering abstract facts and concepts and learns more quickly those things he or she has had direct and well-planned experiences with (Hornstein, 1986; Watkins et al., 1982). Because all language is so abstract, it is advisable to introduce the prerequisite or entry-level concepts of a subject before introducing the subject itself.

It is difficult for a child, particularly one with mental retardation, to learn to interpret a particular passage of material before he or she has had some experience with or understands the concepts involved. For example, it is possible to teach a student with mental retardation to identify the word *zoo* on a flash card. But the student will remember the word much better if he or she has had experience with and already understands the concept of a zoo.

Likewise, it is difficult, if not impossible, to teach a student with mental retardation to tell time if he or she has not first mastered certain time concepts, such as the value of time, how time is used, the influence of time on people's lives, and so forth. Without first mastering the concept of a task, the task itself often becomes mere word-calling or rote memorizing. In teaching a group of young children to read, one teacher found that the children who had not tasted or tried any popcorn could not read the word *popcorn* after two weeks of instruction, whereas those who had eaten popcorn could identify the word after a day or two.

STRUCTURE OF LCD

It is not wise to delay the teaching of reading or arithmetic until all prerequisite language concepts are completely developed. Because of the obvious relationship between LCD and prereading and premath experiences, one might assume that only young children need instruction in LCD. Students with mental retardation, however, need LCD instruction (e.g., in listening skills) at all ages. Furthermore, it is difficult to decide when to begin teaching the reading, math, and other experiences for which the LCD activities were prerequisite.

Consider the stages a newborn infant goes through in developing communication skills. The infant's family and others use a great deal of verbal and often gestural language, as though the infant could understand (Duker & Van Lent, 1991). The language is usually limited to simple words and phrases. Likewise, the teacher should use low-level language with young, nonverbal children with mental retardation, anticipating that they will eventually understand and respond. The "Mmmm-mommy's big guy," and the "Come and see Grandpa" may appear at first to be doting behavior, but this type of dramatized language is necessary in demonstrating what communication is and why it is necessary. In other words, this is LCD for the child.

Teachers and other adults must give young children with mental retardation specific instructions, ask them questions, and carefully observe the response. At first, a child responds with nonverbal behavior. The child can always respond to "Which one is Grandpa?" or "Where is Daddy?" by pointing before he or she can respond verbally. This nonverbal compliance is usually described as *receptive language*. The persistent questioning accompanied by obvious, pleasant hints is probably how all of us learned to use language (Lahey, 1988).

A newborn learns to respond to visual stimuli in much the same way. The child's awareness of Mother coming into a room, reaching for a shiny toy, and learning that a bottle of milk is satisfying are all essential language concepts. Visual language is harder to observe, measure, and teach—especially with younger children. This difficulty is probably why students with mental retardation have particular difficulty learning to read—a task heavily dependent on visual cues. Because these students have difficulty mastering the essential entry-level skills, these skills often are overlooked.

Table 10.1 is an outline of the general sequence children go through in learning how to communicate with others. The sequence is composed of several developmental phases or elements, most of which are discussed separately (although they are not necessarily taught separately). These elements are closely related and not mutually exclusive. A major purpose of Table 10.1 is to help the teacher in identifying the elements that contribute to the student's language development and to make sure that no element is overlooked. Even a very young child with mental retardation engages in several phases within a given language activity. By the same token, older students still need review and further instruction in the introductory phases after they have progressed to higher levels of achievement. Each cell of Table 10.1 represents an element of LCD, and the table is followed by a general discussion of each element. Table 10.1 is not a chart to be filled out, but rather is intended to help the teacher in analyzing the individual elements that constitute the teaching of communication. To use common terminology, the elements are a mixture of human abilities and tasks to be performed.

Visual Abilities

Visual abilities may be classified in many ways. The classifications I use in this chapter include visual reception, perception, memory, comprehension, sorting, classification, ordering, sequencing, and closure. A brief explanation of the elements of the visual abilities listed in Table 10.1 follows.

Visual Reception

Visual reception is essentially the ability to see. The quality or sharpness of vision is known as *visual acuity*. *Visual reception* is the receiving of stimuli or communication

TABLE 10.1   Language Concept Development: Diagnosis/Prescription

Language Tasks and Levels of Achievement	Receptive Language		Expressive Language	
	Visual	**Auditory**	**Visual**	**Auditory**
Reception				
Perception				
Memory				
Comprehension				
Sorting				
Classifying				
Ordering				
Sequencing				
Closure				
General Description				
Refined Description				
Movement or Action				
Functional Communication				
Determine Purpose and Propose Title				
Predict and Anticipate				
Demonstrate and Apply				
Proactivity				

that radiates from a source, such as a light, object, or activity, toward the observer. Children obviously must have adequate vision if they are to do their best in school. Although preschool physical examinations, as well as those conducted by teachers and other school personnel, will uncover a great number of the visual problems of children, many problems remain undetected. The school nurse is usually available to do vision screening, but teachers should also do some general vision screening. The standard way to check general visual acuity is with a Snellen chart, which consists of letters arranged in progressively decreasing size. The Snellen chart can be used in the classroom, but students must have no opportunity to observe the chart beforehand. Several adapted versions of the Snellen are available for use with nonreaders. The most common of these is the Snellen E, which uses only the letter *E* to replace all the other letters on the standard Snellen. The *E*'s face different directions on the chart, however, and the nonreader has only to point in the direction the *E*'s face. Parents of children whose vision is less than 20/20 should be notified, but one must be careful not to unduly alarm parents by making too many referrals. It is advisable to check with parents to identify students who may have had glasses prescribed but who do not wear them.

Visual Perception

Visual perception is the ability to recognize and begin to organize visual input; it is the beginning of concept formation. Although visual reception is a function of the eye, visual perception takes place essentially in the brain. The exact location of faulty visual input is difficult to pinpoint, even for a specialist. Some indications of poor visual perception include difficulty in copying designs, figures, or letters, or reversals of any type. Unexplained inability to read, particularly with approaches that strongly stress visual skills, is also a significant indicator. But all of these skills require some motor ability; this requirement makes the exact problem more difficult to pinpoint.

Visual Memory

The ability to remember and recall visual stimuli is known as *visual memory.* This ability can be observed, tested, and strengthened in a number of ways:

Let the student observe some familiar objects for a short period of time and then cover them to see whether he or she can recall the objects.

Show an array of objects to a student and take one object away while the student is not looking. Then see whether he or she can name the missing object.

If the student is nonverbal, use a duplicate set of objects and let the student point out the missing object or element from the duplicate set.

If the lesson is too difficult, arrange the duplicate set in the same pattern as the one from which an object has been removed. The achievement level of the lesson may be increased by removing more than one object or by adding one or more objects.

Other helpful activities that increase a child's memory span are card games and the game Concentration, particularly if the teacher designs the games and other activities by using objects and symbols directly related to activities that satisfy the student's other IEP goals. A *symbol* is a representation of an actual object, such as a model, mock-up, or picture. The teacher should use color cards, numbers, letters, simple words, and other schoolwork symbols as soon as the student becomes sufficiently familiar with them. As early as possible, the teacher should begin to use more functional communication objects, examples, and activities, such as using the telephone, shopping, home living, and meeting transitional goals (Mire & Chisholm, 1990).

Visual Comprehension

Visual comprehension is the ability to understand and evaluate visual stimuli. It is easy for teachers of students with mental retardation to forget that all numbers, letters, and words are highly abstract. Further, most of these abstract symbols offer no hint as to their meaning. The letter *s* has a hissing sound by custom and usage, and a child must learn to identify it properly by rote and continued exposure. The language activity of most young children is largely limited to using labels or nouns. Normally, they accomplish this with few time constraints and great opportunity for repetition.

It may be best for the classroom teacher to consider visual perception, memory, and comprehension simultaneously. It is difficult to diagnose a student's ability in visual memory or comprehension until he or she is able to sort or describe objects and symbols—tasks that require all three skills plus auditory ability. Students must make some response to visual cues before one can evaluate how well they perceive or remember the cues. Early responses from students are likely to be pointing or following directions. Teachers must take every opportunity to use language on each student's level and encourage oral responses as soon as possible.

Visual Sorting

Visual sorting is the ability to arrange visual stimuli by general configuration or by attribute. The child first learns to put objects together that share obvious attributes, such as overall size, color, and shape. Achievement level is improved by increasing the number of objects and sorting categories. To avoid confusion for the students, objects and symbols intended to be similar must be precisely alike, and the others must be substantially different.

A color copier can be used where precision is needed in making pictures, letters, words, and other symbols look alike. Increasing achievement levels require less exactness in these details. Progress from simple sorting tasks to classification gradually lessens the need to make the stimulus objects exactly alike. A copier also has another significant function. Initially, students with mental retardation are likely to have difficulty switching from the teacher's hand-lettered flash cards to the words in their books, unless they are printed in the same font. A copier can enlarge letters and words from the students' reading materials to make flash cards in the same style of print.

The concepts of sorting and likeness-difference are closely related, and it may be well to teach them at the same time. Once the student has learned how to discriminate among objects and symbols visually, he or she can use these skills to approach likeness-difference. The teacher then can point out how the contents of one sorting pile or stack are different from another. Remember that difference is a much broader concept than likeness; few things are exactly like a given symbol or object, but an infinite number of things are different.

Visual Classification

Visual classification is somewhat more sophisticated than visual sorting; it consists of sorting by class, group, function, and other less obvious properties. Classification has many practical applications and can be quite complex as the bases of sorting become increasingly subtle, elusive, and implied. As a student's language ability increases, he or she is gradually able to associate two or more objects by assigning them to the same general class or group (e.g., dogs, cats, animals, letters, vowels, vegetables, shirts, clothes, hammers, scissors, tools). Other examples are good-bad foods; things that go in the kitchen, bathroom, laundry room, kitchen, and so on. At first, a child must be reminded of the bases for discrimination as the bases become increasingly subtle and sophisticated.

Subsequent classification tasks are made increasingly difficult by gradually making the differences less obvious. The tasks should also become more practical. A moderate classification task requires the student to select or classify objects according to utility or location. For example, "Which of these would we find in the _____ (kitchen, bathroom, farm, or zoo)?" or, "Which of these comes from _____ (plants, trees, or the store—later, a particular store)?" More advanced questions are, "Where would I find a _____?" and "Who would use a _____?" and "What is a _____ used for?"

Another fairly sophisticated classification task is matching letters or words written in different fonts. This concept teaches the student that a given letter has the same application whether it was written by the teacher, printed on a typewriter, or taken from a book. An even more advanced classification skill is matching and sorting uppercase and lowercase letters and differentiating between manuscript and cursive letters. This activity must be done with care. Students with mental retardation can be easily overwhelmed by the task of sorting a conglomeration of letters that differ by font and by manuscript-cursive and uppercase-lowercase presentations.

Visual Ordering

Visual ordering is classification by value or numerical relationships. In earlier classification tasks, the student assigned the objects to groups without regard to value. Plants, animals, letters, words, and tools were sorted without regard to value, rank, or sequence. Early sorting tasks required the student to sort similar objects by size and eventually by number, but differing values were not involved. The student must learn to deal with ordinal concepts (e.g., first, second) and eventually relative terms (e.g., *larger* and *smaller, many* and *few, expensive* and *inexpensive*). Related activities have the student rank several single objects from largest to smallest, tallest to shortest, or heavier to lighter and then rank groups of objects from most to least and so on. Instruction on these concepts assumes that the student has the potential to comprehend them in later reading and problem-solving activities and should be carefully diagnosed in terms of the student's life goals.

Visual Sequencing

Visual sequencing is closely related to visual ordering, except that it involves even more subtle cues. Eventually, the student must learn that some things have an order or sequence that is not necessarily related to attribute, general appearance, or value. For example, the third of three cartoon frames is no more valuable than the first or second, but all must be placed in the proper sequence to make a meaningful story. Likewise, each word in a sentence must be in its proper place to make sense, although there are no value discriminations. The ordinal concepts of first, second, third, and so on may be more closely related to sequencing than ordering because no actual values are necessarily involved.

Students must be constantly engaged in conversation as they develop these visual skills. Teachers and others must encourage them to describe what they are seeing and doing whenever possible. Having the students sit quietly and sort objects may help them in acquiring language concepts but is unlikely to encourage verbal language. The main problem with many published reading readiness materials is that they do not provide for much verbal interaction. Another persisting problem with such materials is that they are not usually age appropriate. Videotapes made by the teacher are very effective in teaching any type of visual sequencing.

Visual Closure

Visual closure is the ability to put visual images or perceptions together that belong together. Visual closure skills begin with discrimination and description and continue through sequencing. For example, a big ball and a black dog may go together because they were together in a story, picture, or event. Often, a visual closure task involves reassembling a whole whose parts have been separated by time or space. GIAs in visual closure include doing jigsaw and other puzzles; using blocks to duplicate prescribed patterns; unscrambling letters to make a word; unscrambling words to make a sentence; doing crossword and word search puzzles; spelling; and writing sentences, paragraphs, and stories. Puzzles for younger children should initially involve quite large puzzle parts that have been cut in logical places so that each piece contains an identifiable part of the puzzle picture.

Auditory Abilities

Auditory abilities may be classified in much the same way as visual abilities. The classifications I use in this chapter are auditory reception, perception, memory, comprehension, sorting and classification, ordering and sequencing, and closure. A brief explanation of the auditory abilities listed in Figure 10.1 follows.

Auditory Reception

The ability to hear is known as *auditory acuity* or *auditory reception*. It is advisable to have the school nurse check the students' hearing at least once each year if possible. Preschool physical examinations and in-school screening procedures uncover many hearing problems. Many will go undetected, however, or may develop after the examinations are conducted. Hearing problems can also be temporary—due to colds or ear wax impaction. Hearing problems in children may manifest themselves in a variety of subtle ways. A student with either a temporary or permanent hearing loss may appear to be mentally slow, lazy, distractible, irritable, or antisocial, so hearing should be checked frequently. This checking can be done by using informal screening procedures, such as whisper and conversation tests, at least part of which should be done with the student's back turned.

Poor auditory reception among young children often results in poor or delayed speech or articulation problems, voice problems, and stuttering. If these results occur, the teacher should enlist the services of a speech/language pathologist. These professionals (formerly called speech therapists) typically do not try to remediate speech problems as early as they once did. They have found that young children outgrow many of the articulation and other problems they formerly treated rather extensively. Also, instead of giving individual instruction in the proper production of speech sounds, a communication specialist usually prefers to give language lessons to the children in small groups or to help the teachers design and give this type of instruction.

Beyond screening the students' hearing, recommending further testing, and working with a communication specialist, a teacher can do little to correct the problem (Winitz, 1984). However, the teacher may help a student compensate to some extent for a hearing difficulty by giving preferential seating, by increasing proportionally the stimulation through other channels—tactual or visual—and by facing the child when speaking. The general rule for addressing a person who is hard of hearing is to speak distinctly in a normal tone and at a normal rate, without distorting lip movements and facial expressions. But in individual instruction, it may be necessary to emphasize the placement and movement of the lips, tongue, and teeth to show a student how to form sounds and words.

Auditory Perception

Auditory perception is the ability to form concepts from auditory cues. It is probably more difficult to delineate the abilities of students in auditory reception, perception, memory, and discrimination than with the visual counterparts. These differences can often be detected only by a specialist using more sophisticated equipment, such as the Pure Tone Audiometric Test or a technique called *tympanometry,* which evaluates the function of the inner ear. The tones a person hears in this test are presented with decreasing volume until the person is unable to hear them at all. This is an accurate indication of auditory reception or acuity. Perception, however, implies evaluation and response. If a student cannot make sense of the auditory stimuli, he or she is said to have an auditory perception problem. The teacher must be sure, however, that the auditory tasks are within the student's range. For a student who has the necessary auditory acuity, activities and procedures that might be helpful include listening to short sentences and stories, answering questions about the content, or listening and responding to various types of music in marches, rhythm bands, and dances.

Auditory Memory

Auditory memory is the ability to recognize and understand sounds. It is closely related to auditory perception, and it is difficult to test one without the other. A student must be able to perceive and remember auditory stimuli in order to respond in an appropriate manner. If the problem is one of memory, the student may hear instructions properly and begin to perform appropriate action, only to forget what he or she intended to do. Good auditory memory tasks include having the student repeat back single sounds, numbers, and words, and then simple sentences and phrases.

Auditory Comprehension

Auditory comprehension, like visual comprehension, is difficult to observe and measure unless the person makes some type of response. Making a response to auditory stimuli, however, also requires auditory perception, memory, and discrimination. Motivation and attention are also important to both visual and auditory memory. Often, a child has been allowed to pay little attention to significant auditory cues. Because everyone's hearing is continually bombarded with a stream of stimuli that vary in volume, tone, pitch, and significance, a student must learn to separate the background noise (the unimportant) from what is important and necessary for survival or appropriate action. Achievement levels may be raised in auditory comprehension by having the student respond to simple, increasingly complex instructions, as well as to school bells and timers.

The student must also learn to evaluate the volume, pitch, tone, and significance of sounds. For example, the loudest of several incoming sounds sometimes requires the most immediate action, and sometimes it does not. If a student's teacher or parent raises his or her voice, compliance is more essential. The command may be directed at someone else, however, possibly someone farther away. The beginning automobile driver reacts to every sounding horn but soon learns to respond, in an inexplicable way, only to that which applies to him or her. An athlete learns to hear the coach's instructions even over the screaming voices of hundreds of spectators. Each student in a classroom must learn to ignore those sounds that do not pertain to the immediate task; this ability is called *auditory discrimination*. Auditory discrimination is particularly important in a child's ability to speak and to read. Ordinarily, children must be able to discriminate speech sounds before they can produce the sounds appropriately, a prerequisite skill to learning to read. One may want to experiment with the student in a number of activities involving varying amounts of external auditory stimulation. Using recorded instructions played through earphones may help the student at first; then the student should gradually be exposed to more normal circumstances.

The teacher can often test the student while working on other activities. One of the best ways to diagnose the language abilities of students is to read to them. Reading a short passage from a story on the approximate language level of the students and asking questions can determine the auditory language level of each student and help in teaching all of these specific auditory language skills. Listening comprehension is a significant entry-level skill to both reading comprehension and math problem solving. Adapted/created/enhanced (ACE) stories are great for this purpose and teach a lesson or moral at the same time.

Auditory Sorting and Classification

Auditory sorting and classification are closely related abilities that enable a student to classify or sort auditory stimuli by attribute. Typically, the teacher presents the sounds and the student determines the attributes of the sounds, such as sameness and loudness. Common speech sounds may be classified in various ways: plosives, sibilants, nasals, voiced, unvoiced, and fricatives; but there is little merit in requiring students to memorize or apply these labels. Some speech sounds (e.g., the plosives) require closing the lips, stopping the breath, and then letting it go suddenly. Beyond that, the task for the student is to recognize common sounds (e.g., street sounds, animal sounds) and describe them. One way to do this is to have the student imitate or reproduce each sound; another way is to have the student tell whether two sounds are the same or different. It may also be helpful for students to describe sounds as loud, soft, pleasant, and musical. Recordings and pictures of sound sources can be beneficial, particularly for students with mental retardation. For example, the student is shown a picture of animals and then asked to make or identify the appropriate sounds. Recorded voices of the student's classmates can also be used in a variety of ways.

Auditory Ordering and Sequencing

Auditory ordering and sequencing are important abilities that help a person arrange sounds in meaningful ways. If a child is to learn to speak and read correctly, he or she must be able to produce the necessary sounds and then arrange them in an appropriate order to make meaningful words, thoughts, and sentences (Hoogeveen, Smeets, & Van der Houven, 1987). Engelmann (1967) suggested that auditory (as well as visual) order and sequencing skill development are prerequisites to the whole communication process. He hypothesized that culturally disadvantaged students (and presumably others) fail to learn that many activities are sequential in nature. Crawling, walking, speaking, reading, and all types of problem solving require adherence to a rigorous sequence. Another example of sequencing is having the student repeat back increasingly complex series of digits, sounds, sentences, and directions as they are pronounced to him or her.

Auditory Closure

Auditory closure is the skill of putting auditory cues or parts together that collectively make meaningful wholes. In a phonetic reading approach, a student learns to identify the sounds of letters that are later presented in combination to form words with sounding drills. Closure skills are essential in helping students put the parts together so that they can pronounce the word. The instructions for the Basic Concept Inventory suggest the following questioning technique: "I'm going to say a word, but I'm going to say it slowly, and I want you to tell me what the word is. For example, if I said 'rrr-oom,' what word is that? Or if I said 'mmm-ee,' what word is that?"

Other common words used in closure drills are *look, make, my, read, run, shoe, see, up,* and *food*. Achievement levels are raised by presenting more difficult words (e.g., *want, well, went, where, him, his*) and then introducing words having consonance blends in the initial position (e.g., *please, pretty, flower, sleep, green, blue, black, brown*). Extreme difficulty with this type of closure skill suggests that the student is likely to have difficulty with a phonetic approach to reading, and it may be well to try a more visual reading approach.

It is well to reserve the plosive sounds (*p, b, g, t, d*) for later presentation in auditory closure. Although these are usually easy for the child to produce in isolation, they are nevertheless difficult to use in closure drills, particularly in the initial position. Students have a strong tendency to attach an extraneous vowel sound (usually *uh*) to the preceding plosive sound. For example, the student will often say "tuh" for "t," so in the closure drill, the word *tin* becomes "tuh-i-n," rather than "t-i-n." Some students can overcome this difficulty if the teacher monitors the inconsistency and tries to correct it; for others, the problem is more severe. It is also helpful to have the student whisper the sound and then add the voice later.

GENERAL ELEMENTS OF LCD

The remaining language elements of Table 10.1 are generally more advanced, and their visual and auditory modes of communication are discussed together. They begin early in the student's experience, however, and are central to all other expressive and receptive, as well as visual and auditory, communication tasks and skills. These elements should be considered for inclusion in each student's IEP as soon as he or she is ready and after the teacher and other team members determine the extent to which that student will need and be able to master them.

General Description

A student must learn to identify complete wholes, such as intact objects and the major parts of a picture. Initially, the student can perform by pointing and later by taking other action—eventually with a verbal response. In a sense, general description is a manifestation of other visual and auditory abilities. The question "Where is Daddy?" requires the student to discriminate among all of the people and objects to which *Daddy* might apply. Displaying a series of pictures with simple but increasingly complex themes and greater numbers of subjects requires the student to "Show me the (man, boy, girl)" or "Which one is the (desk, table, ball, pencil)?"

Refined Description

As a child is learning to make general descriptions, he or she begins to add descriptors and detail to oral and written communication, such as stories. Like general description, refined description begins early in the child's language experience and includes reception, perception, memory, and other language tasks. The child is taught to deal with increasingly descriptive adjectives that denote number, color, and shape. Achievement level is increased by adding subtler descriptors and by increasing numbers and combinations of adjectives, such as *the big, black ball(s), the older boy, the mother,* and *the police officer.* Both general and refined descriptions combine receptive and expressive language with visual and auditory stimuli and responses.

Movement and action (including simple gerunds, participles, and infinitives) are a vital part of precise language. Students with mental retardation must also learn to use these language forms as well as possible (though not by name). It is important to diagnose and project each student's eventual needs and mastery of verbs and verb forms. A student with mental retardation could spend most of his or her school career on these concepts because they are very abstract and there is literally no end to them. Teachers must be careful not to overemphasize these verbs because, unfortunately, at no point does their inclusion in a student's IEP become obviously futile. The concepts of walking, running, sitting, jumping, playing, and working are all part of beginning language. For example, displaying the appropriate pictures, the teacher says, "Show me walking, playing, working." These concepts are then gradually incorporated into the student's IEP as the student can master them. Some infinitives (e.g., *to run, to walk, to build, to help*) are also necessary for students with mental retardation. These forms can be taught at the same time and in the same ways as simple gerunds.

FUNCTIONAL COMMUNICATION

The last four elements of Table 10.1 are the goals and practical purposes of teaching communication skills to students with mental retardation. All of the other elements must be considered according to how they contribute to the student's eventual ability to communicate. These final elements are actually the reason for all other language instruction. In other words, every skill and concept in the student's IEP should either be practical in itself or should lead to mastery, or at least competence, in solving practical life problems.

Moral, Purpose, and Title

Drawing implications and meaning from incoming stimuli is the major purpose of communication. The student must be able to perceive the reasons and utility of language (as well as other) activities. The student should understand and eventually express as well as possible what was learned, why it was learned, and how it is to be used. The student must experience the newly acquired skills and concepts in making decisions; in relating them to other skills, concepts, and activities; and in showing how they help the student in becoming a better person. Proposing a suitable title for a story may be somewhat obscure and formal for most students with mental retardation, but doing so assesses the student's ability to perceive the overall picture of a story or passage he or she has read or heard. Creating a title for even a short story demands the student's skills in perception, memory, description, classification, and sequencing.

Predict and Anticipate

A good way to test a student's communication ability is to see how well he or she gains information from a story, activity, or experience and projects logical effects. It helps the student see the consequences of his or her own acts and circumstances by relating them to those of story characters. This technique permits the parent or teacher to discuss a student's strengths, situation, problems, and weaknesses in a vicarious and nonthreatening manner. Predict and anticipate skills can be tested, discussed, and taught with the following questions: What will happen next? What will (character from the story) do now? What did he or she learn? What would you do now? and What do we learn from this experience?

Demonstrate and Apply

The teacher and other members of the IEP team must constantly evaluate their student's ability to use and apply newly acquired skills in solving practical problems. For the most part, these are classroom experiences contrived to be as real-life as possible. Some appropriate activities are playing cooperatively; lining up before recess; making personal choices; participating in team activities, discussions, and role playing; riding the school bus; using demonstrated materials and procedures; participating in playground activities and contrived classroom store. One main advantage of demonstrate and apply experiences is that they can be carefully controlled, evaluated, and redesigned where necessary.

Proactivity

Proactivity takes the student outside the classroom and into the home and community. This is the ultimate test of the student's ability to use newly acquired skills and concepts in solving his or her life-goal problems as independently as possible. Proactivity experiences are usually very effective and practical. Because they are conducted in the community—a setting that requires increased travel, supervision, and usually additional funding—they tend to be inefficient and time-consuming. Because these experiences are so functional and necessary, the students must be as well prepared for them as possible by balancing proactive experiences with preparatory demonstrate and apply activities of the classroom. For example, Dudley and Schatz (1985) recommended teaching functional communication skills to students with mental retardation to help them in making increasingly significant decisions about job preferences and other transitional experiences. Such instruction must be initiated early and conducted persistently as such students proceed through school. The instruction culminates with each student's participation in demonstrate/apply and finally proactive experiences.

DIAGNOSTIC/PRESCRIPTIVE TEACHING AND LCD

Students with mental retardation have a wide range of language abilities that need to be diagnosed to present their developing communication skills at the correct rate and level. This is done in successful diagnostic/prescriptive teaching primarily by arranging the skills, concepts, and tasks to be taught in order of increasing difficulty or projected student achievement level. The skills and concepts taught to a student with mental retardation must also increase in sophistication and practicality. The basic procedure is to arrange the skills, concepts, and activities in a tentative, sequential, individual curriculum, determine the student's achievement level in the sequence, and then begin to teach at that level.

The elements or phases of Table 10.1 are generally arranged in order of increasing difficulty, but they overlap a lot. Some of the later elements are obviously too difficult and sophisticated for a young student, yet an older student does not outgrow the need for increased skills in the earlier phases. The later elements are increasingly functional and practical and end with proactivity that places the student in real-life situations. Also, beginning with movement or action, the receptive and expressive, as well as visual and auditory, delineations begin to lose their identity. The elements of LCD are rarely taught in isolation. Receptive language and expressive language are used together by both the student and the teacher. A student's receptive language develops first and is used to elicit expressive language. In the meantime, the teacher uses expressive language to give explanations and instructions. Likewise, auditory and visual stimuli are given together.

Goal instruction analysis (GIA) in this area begins with simple and concrete objects, progresses to more complex and less common objects, expands to semiabstract models and pictures, and finally teaches abstract symbols, letters, numbers, words, and actions. At first, the student may be able to retrieve only a ball and only point to a girl or a dog in a picture (receptive language). With increasing experience and instruction, the student can advance to the *big* ball and the *black* dog and on to even subtler descriptors, such as the father, the nurse, the police officer, and the cook. During these experiences, verbal labels and descriptors are applied as soon as possible so that the student can name the objects as the teacher describes or points to them (expressive language).

The visual stimuli used in early LCD must be simple, familiar objects and pictures, preferably those the student encounters in everyday life. Pictures should relate as directly as possible to the reading and math materials the teacher plans to use later. The use of pictures of familiar objects (e.g., balls, pencils, crayons, trees, houses, people) is more practical than the use of geometrical shapes in teaching skills of discrimination and classification to young students with mental retardation. The GIA is augmented by using an array of GIA components beginning with maximum but decreasing assistance and reinforcement with simple but increasingly demanding materials, mastery, and independence.

MANIPULATION OF SCHOOL DEVICES

While a student is mastering the language concepts necessary for successful reading, math, and other IEP topics, he or she must also learn how to use common classroom devices. The introduction of classroom tools, such as pencils, crayons, brushes, books, rulers, and scissors, introduces a variety of language concepts and instructions on the use of these devices. These common classroom materials can be introduced in classification, ordering, and sequencing activities, and each device offers great opportunity for dialogue with each student.

PRECISE LANGUAGE

The home and neighborhood language a young child hears is often imprecise. In fact, few children are likely to use the same type or level of language at home that they encounter in schoolbooks. A reliance on slang words, contractions, idioms, and even profanity in the home is often sufficient for a child to communicate in the informal surroundings of the neighborhood but usually causes difficulty with the more precise language of the school setting (Adger, Wolfram, & Detwyler, 1993). The child's classmates, teachers, and textbooks not only discuss topics with which that student is unfamiliar but also describe these topics in unfamiliar language. Most children appear to have some difficulty in making the switch from informal, oral speech to the more formal language of education. This problem is more pronounced, however, among students with mental retardation, whose difficulties in transfer of training are well known (these are discussed in Chapter 2).

Bereiter and Engelmann (1966) identified the giant word syndrome. They maintain that many children, particularly those they described as "culturally deprived," develop language patterns around the home and neighborhood by speaking in "verbal explosions." These word clusters express a more or less complete thought that is understood only in that setting, rather than in the precise manner of putting words together to make meaningful thoughts or sentences. Most students with mental retardation also have great difficulty in this language area. For example, the student may tell an older brother to "cuditout," a nondescript clause that has the desired effect of influencing a brother to stop what he was doing. However, the student does not learn that his giant word is composed of three elements: *cut, it,* and *out.* These words not only make unique contributions to that particular expression but also have application in other sentences. Furthermore, it is unlikely that the expression "cut it out" will appear in any formal reading material.

Teachers, as well as parents and older siblings, often contribute unknowingly to this process when they either fail to point out the relevant cues of language or use imprecise language themselves and give the child an imperfect language model. Parents and others should be encouraged to refrain from continually correcting the grammar of their children because this correction might tend to inhibit speech. As the age passes at which "Me want a drink" becomes inappropriate, teachers and others should stress "I want a drink." Parents should also be cautioned not to inadvertently encourage their children to be nonverbal by responding to grunts and gestures indefinitely. One wise and experienced primary teacher of children with mental retardation delays the teaching of *please* and *thank you* until her students have learned to ask for help with basic needs. She asserts that the word *please,* particularly when used with appropriate gestures, can serve as a multipurpose crutch and delay the need for speech. The potential in working with parents and in enlisting their cooperation should not be underestimated. Children typically spend far more time at home than at school; thus, even limited work with parents can yield tremendous communication dividends.

Teachers of students with mental retardation (and others who learn slowly) must learn to take nothing for granted, particularly in the area of language development. It is a mistake to assume that a child will naturally learn to use words such as *know, guess, not, right, wrong, same,* and *different* with precision, although many children are able to do so. In addition to dialogues with the students, the teacher can do most of the diagnoses in this area with informal means, such as observing speech patterns (particularly in peer group interaction) or using "direction" games. These games amount essentially to following directions and commission tasks, such as "Show me the blue one," "Bring me the one that is not white," "Bring me the little white one," and "Bring me the little one that is not blue." The game can be enhanced by having the directions given from behind a screen. Each student should practice both giving and following directions on his or her language level.

Locus Concepts

Locus concepts are those that imply proximity or location. These concepts not only are valuable prerequisites to the teaching of reading but also must precede arithmetic instruction. These include *top, bottom, side, back, front, inside, outside, open, closed, high, low, over, under, near, beside,* and *by.*

Value Concepts

Words that imply value are prerequisite to reading, as well as to arithmetic. From the beginning, arithmetic depends on concepts of value, equality, and relationship (Nelson et al., 1991). Some specific concepts to be included here are *big, little, tall, short, many, few, wide, narrow, light, heavy, more, most, less, equal, equal to, part, all, some, none, nearly,* and *almost.* These concepts can be taught with the ordering and sequencing procedures discussed earlier.

Multiconcept Statements

Multiconcept statements are those that involve the use of two or more concepts in a single statement, thought, or sentence. The following are examples of multiconcept statements.

Inclusive Statements

Inclusive statements are those that combine two or more concepts or thoughts; for a young child, these are ordinarily limited to those involving the concepts and *too.* The concepts of *not only-but also* and *together with* do not ordinarily occur in the language or reading material for young children. In diagnosing and prescribing inclusive statements, a teacher may say, "I need the book and the pencil; bring me the ball and the bat; we will go swimming today and tomorrow." Inclusive statements include the concepts *all, many,* and *everybody.* Examples are "Give pencils to everyone" and "Bring me all of the hammers." Another example is a statement or question that has a dangling qualifier—for example "Go get all of the brooms with red handles" and "Bring me all of the pans that have lids."

Exclusive Statements

Exclusive statements are those that mention but exclude one or more objects, concepts, or thoughts. They are often difficult for students with mental retardation and most young children to comprehend and follow because they involve several previously unencountered language variations. One of these is called a *specific determiner.* Up to this point, the child in language development has been generally successful if he or she could merely get the essence or the general idea of a statement, question, or command. Now, for the first time, the child must pay close attention to each element or word because just one word (e.g., *not, but*) changes the entire meaning. Examples are, "Bring me the balls that are not rubber" and "You will not need your gym clothes today."

These statements are complicated further if the specific determiner is hidden in a contraction, such as *isn't, wasn't,* and *aren't.* In doing a GIA, the more obvious version needs to be tested or presented first. Another problem with exclusive statements is they often make rather definite demands or statements followed by exceptions. Thus, the student may commit the first part of the statement to memory (and may even be in the process of formulating effective action) when the exception is added, requiring him or her to go back and reevaluate the previous information and make a change in plans—for example, "Go get all of the steaks, except the ones that are still frozen."

Consequential or Conditional Statements

Conditional statements also involve specific determiners and are usually identified by *if* or *if-then* relationships. More complex or difficult qualifiers are *since, now, that,* and *unless.* Part of the problem is being unable to foresee that the consequences of their acts may lie in a language deficit. This is a good example of how two deficiencies may compound each other. The poor general language facility of a student with mental retardation is aggravated by the fact that most of the consequences are announced in conditional statements.

One must be careful in telling a student with mental retardation, "If you are tardy one more time, then you must stay after school." Such an admonition imposes heavy language demands on the student, who must evaluate both ends of the conditional statement, weigh the consequences against the conditions, and then retain the information until it is needed. One must not impose requirements on children that are beyond their language capabilities. For example, Miss Nelson told George, an 11-year-old boy with severe mental retardation, "If you hit anyone today, you will have to miss treats." During the next few days, she made it a point to observe George's hitting behavior. George really seemed to miss having treats at the end of each day, but he continued hitting others. At the close of school each day, she admonished George about hitting others and reminded him of the conditions for participating in the treats. George's receptive language was very poor, and Miss Nelson finally became convinced that he did not understand why he was being punished.

A GIA in this area could include games and activities involving conditional directions: "If you have a red circle, place it in the box"; "If it is your turn, you may ride the tricycle"; "If you are wearing a hat, you may take one step forward."

Alternative Statements

Alternative statements usually involve the concept of *or*. Alternative statements may also use polar opposites or require a student to make choices. Language requirements involving polar opposites can begin at a rather simple level: "Is it black or white?" "Is it big or little?" "Is it hot or cold?" Some tasks that are slightly more difficult include "Is it warm or cool?" "Is it yellow or orange?" "Is it red or maroon?" "Is it 5 o'clock or 5:15?" "Is it nearer 12 o'clock or 12:30?" "Which is larger, this one or that one?" "Which glass has more water, this one or that one?"

Following Instructions

All people must learn to follow instructions. Even self-employed adults must carefully interpret the needs and preferences of those to whom they offer goods and services. Students with mental retardation are often expected to heed the advice, direction, or needs of others. One of the first things one notices about students with mental retardation is that they have great difficulty in following instructions. Although this may be true, the IEP team must not assume that a student with mental retardation is either completely without this ability or necessarily at the same stage of development as other students. They must carefully diagnose each student to determine the individual achievement level. This can be done either formally by designing specific "following instructions" games and activities or informally by carefully formulating instructions for other activities in such a way that each student is able to comprehend and follow increasingly difficult instructions. The strong tendency among teachers is to give most group instructions at the level of the least capable students. At the same time, giving instructions to either groups or individuals at the level of the slowest students does not encourage higher functioning students to further develop their instruction-following skills.

WORKING WITH PARENTS

It is probably not possible to overemphasize the importance of working with parents in developing their child's communication skills. In a typical school week, a student spends less than 20% of his or her time in school, and as a result the influence of parents and siblings on the LCD of a student is tremendous. The parents not only can help in both the diagnosis and prescription of LCD but also should be encouraged to use the prescribed language levels with their child at home. By having frequent parent-teacher conferences and home visits, a teacher can encourage the parents to provide good language models for their child. The teacher should provide parents with pictures, stories, and books from school sources and, where necessary, help in performing their vital roles in developing their child's communication skills. The teacher should tactfully explain how parents often discourage language development in their child by too readily providing for his or her wants and needs or by doing the child's speaking.

DIAGNOSING LCD: FORMAL MEASURES

Several criterion-referenced measures and norm-referenced tests can be used to assess the LCD of students with mental retardation. Most of these tests are designed for use with students without mental retardation, so one must select them carefully. Even when a test is designed especially for students with mental retardation, the great range of ability in mental retardation means that a given test may be appropriate and helpful for one student and not for another. Most of the tests described below can be administered by a classroom teacher—often with relatively little training or practice. Most of the information obtained from these tests will be at the Diagnosis I and II levels (see Chapter 6 on DPE teaching). The data these tests provide must be further refined and validated to provide accurate diagnoses and to help in making appropriate prescriptions.

Peabody Picture Vocabulary Test (PPVT-R)

The revised Peabody Picture Vocabulary Text (PPVT-R; Dunn & Dunn, 1981) can be used to obtain a general assessment of a student's facility with receptive vocabulary that is helpful in initiating a meaningful prescription in communication. But having obtained the PPVT-R data, the teacher needs to do further testing to determine precisely what to teach and at which level to begin. The PPVT-R is often used as a quick intelligence test and does yield an IQ score of sorts. Its content and design are quite narrow and are limited to receptive vocabulary, however, so it should not be used in the place of an IQ test. A particular strength of the PPVT-R is that it demonstrates a creative format teachers can use in designing and using their own testing and teaching materials. It also illustrates the use of basal and ceiling ages that are used in diagnostic and prescriptive teaching.

The format of the PPVT-R is a series of pages, each containing four pictures. Each page has a stimulus word that describes one of the pictures—for example, "Show me—engineer." After the student understands the directions, the teacher simply pronounces the word *engineer* and the student responds by saying the number of the picture. Nonverbal students may simply point to the appropriate picture. The student must get eight consecutive items correct to establish a basal age, and testing continues until the student misses six in any eight consecutive items; this procedure establishes a ceiling age. Although the PPVT-R was standardized with nondisabled children, it may be used with students with mental retardation. Many children whose mental retardation is severe or profound will score below the scales in the manual. The age range of PPVT-R is from 2½ to about 18. This test can be administered and scored in under 20 minutes.

Vineland Adaptive Behavior Scale

The Vineland Adaptive Behavior Scale (Sparrow, Balla, & Cicchetti, 1984) is a good example of a developmental scale administered to a second-party respondent, rather than directly to the subject. It was designed for use with students with mental retardation of ages ranging from approximately 3 months to young adult. The Vineland is administered to a "significant other" (e.g., a parent or teacher) because its subject matter is designed for individuals with severe or profound mental retardation and, therefore, has very low language and achievement levels. The respondent must be a responsible adult who is asked to describe the individual's typical behavior in a given area, such as dressing, feeding, or toileting. The test administrator then decides whether the individual habitually performs the indicated task. It is permissible to use a different respondent for each category or subtest.

The items of the Vineland are arranged in the general categories of self-help general, self-help eating, self-help dressing, self-direction, occupation, communication, locomotion, and socialization. Although it was standardized on a relatively small number of nondisabled children, it has been extensively revised and refined for use with people with severe/profound mental retardation. It has been widely used with institutionalized populations.

Preschool Attainment Record (PAR)

In many respects, the Preschool Attainment Record (PAR; Doll, 1967) is similar to the longer Vineland. Both are good instruments to use with students with mental retardation whose abilities and achievement levels are extremely low. Information from standard IQ and achievement tests is quite academic and not very useful in planning educational programs for students whose mental retardation is severe or profound. The Vineland and the PAR are more useful because their content is more closely related to the skills and concepts ordinarily taught to students with severe or profound mental retardation. Information may also be obtained by observing and testing the student or by interviewing a reliable informant. The categories of the PAR include ambulation, manipulation, rapport, communication, responsibility, information, ideation, and creativity. It can be used with children from birth to those with MAs of about 7. PAR was designed for and standardized on a nondisabled population, but it is helpful with students with mental retardation as old as 10 or 11.

Basic Concept Inventory

This Basic Concept Inventory (Engelmann, 1967) is a unique criterion-referenced test used to measure the mastery of the language and prereading concepts a student needs to succeed in school. It can be administered and scored by a classroom teacher and can be used to test students with mental retardation from preschool to early teenage. The information from the Basic Concept Inventory is helpful in pinpointing meaningful prescriptive exercises in language. Because the test is not standardized, there is no need to follow the recommended testing procedures. The teacher may use the test items for diagnostic purposes in any manner—even for instruction. A severe weakness of this test is that it covers only a narrow and limited sample of language concepts. It is quite old, and the version in use was designed as a field edition. Nevertheless, it is still useful.

The tests described above share the several following additional strengths:

1. **They demonstrate general testing procedures.** The PPVT-R and the Vineland are standardized tests and require adherence to testing procedures specified by the authors. They yield standard scores, but the PAR and the Basic Concept Inventory do not.
2. **They can help the teacher get acquainted with the students in a testing situation.** With these published tests, the teacher can concentrate on the testing situation without being unduly concerned about the content of the test.
3. **They demonstrate the kinds of content teachers may want to include on their teacher-made tests.** Using the basic format of these tests, teachers can design a test for a student with mental retardation by using the carefully selected pictures, objects, questions, and tasks they have on hand and plan to use in teaching the concepts tested. Combining the information obtained from these tests with the data from teacher-made tests gives a fairly accurate estimate of a student's readiness for classroom activities.

LIFE GOALS AND LCD

Communication is a major area of curriculum planning for students with mental retardation. All students with mental retardation need continuing instruction in LCD. The skills, concepts, and activities listed in any column (communication, in this example) are generated as follows:

1. List the communication skills, concepts, and activities from the IEPs of one or more students that are roughly on the same performance levels.
2. List the communication skills that are related to or suggested by skills, concepts, and activities in other columns (horizontal planning).
3. Tentatively list the communication skills that are prerequisite to other communications skills, concepts, and activities to be taught in the future (vertical planning or forward chaining).
4. Tentatively list the communication skills that logically follow those already entered (vertical planning or backward chaining).
5. List in the other columns the skills, concepts, and activities that are suggested by and will be taught with the listed communication skills (horizontal planning).

One Example

Table 10.2 illustrates how curriculum planning is done. The table shows only part of the curriculum planning chart and includes only a representative sample of the entries that might be needed to make up this part of the curriculum. In addition to the communication skills column, Table 10.2 includes two other columns (Arithmetic and Health and Physical Education) selected at random. Any of the other four columns would serve the same purpose. Of course, all columns must be used in planning the total curriculum. The entries listed are a combination of skills, concepts, and activities reduced to single words and short phrases; they do not need to be grammatically parallel.

Table 10.2 shows part of the curriculum designed by Mrs. Salazar, an experienced teacher assigned to a combination primary and upper primary class of students with mild or moderate mental retardation. The class had six students—two girls and four boys. Before school started, she was able to meet with the parents of all of her students. Tom and Roger, both 7 years old, had been in the class for most of the previous year, and their IEPs were on file. Mrs. Salazar participated in the IEP team meetings in which the IEPs of these two boys were updated.

Charles, who had just turned 5, was new to the school and needed an initial IEP, although the IEP would ordinarily have been completed prior to making a placement in a special class.

Tom's parents tended to deny that he had any serious learning problems. Tom's father thought Tom was just a little bit slow, a problem that Tom would outgrow in time. But Tom's mother, who had worked with him more closely at home, thought he would probably need some special help in his school work. The parents had agreed to a trial placement in the special class as a compromise.

All three placement teams were headed by the school principal, who invited the parents to the meetings and worked out the meeting times and days. But the principal never attended or participated after the first meeting. The school psychologist and a speech/language pathologist were also on all three teams. Both had done some preliminary testing and had made their reports available to the team, but neither attended any of the IEP meetings. As is often the case, Mrs. Salazar and the boys' parents—particularly the mothers—worked out the details of the IEPs.

Age 25 Projection

Mrs. Salazar explained the age 25 projection to the parents of the three boys. She explained that, for students this young, the concept was less valuable in curriculum planning than it would be later. Because LCD is concentrated in the early school years, they agreed to use it as a guiding principle in later planning. Each team agreed to evaluate and monitor the boys' progress for the next year or 2 and to use the evaluations to make rough estimates of their eventual communication abilities. The parents of Tom and Roger, however, insisted that their children would eventually be able to communicate fairly well but would need considerable instruction to learn to do so.

TABLE 10.2   Curriculum Planning Chart Stressing Communication Skills

	Communication	Arithmetic	Health and P.E.

Preprimary to Primary Level	Audio and Visual:
	  reception
	  perception
	  memory
	  comprehension
	Own body parts
	
	Simple pictures
	Identifies familiar objects
	Makes basic sounds correctly
	Simple cut and paste
	Sort color cards (R,Y, and B)
	Follows simple
	  instructions (go, come, stop)
	Listens to stories
	Answers simple questions
	Repeats single words
	Memorizes own address
	Names of family members
	Identifies common sounds
	Repeats 3- or 4-word phrases
	Prewriting exercises
	Listens with slight distracting
	  noise
	Sings simple songs
	Uses names of classmates
		Simple pictures
		  Boy
		  Man
		  Girl
		  Woman
		  Big–little
		  Responds to own name
		
		Numbers in simple picture
		Aware of the clock
		More–less
		Simple counting
		Aware of calendar
		Top–bottom
		Rings on pegs
		Numbers in simple story
		  (two boys, two girls)
		Repeats one or two
		  numbers
		Matches by size
		Matches and sorts coins
		(P,N,D, and Q)
		Left–right
		Inclusive statements
		  (and, both, two)
			Washing hands
			Brushing teeth
			Exercise
			Walking
			Playground activity
			Manipulating crayons,
			  pencil, scissors
			Tall–short
			Introduction to water
			Skips rope
			Cup–spoon
			Fork, knife
			Simple grooming
			Simple hopscotch
			Wide balance beam
			Good diet
			Foods good for you
			Simple puzzles
			Rides tricycle
			Sorts pictures of foods

Upper Primary to Intermediate Level	Learning to write
	Knows address and phone
	Sorts names of classmates
	Sorts simple objects
	Repeats simple sentences
	Simple pictures
	  Identifies less familiar objects
	  Uses simple descriptors
	More complex instructions
	More difficult stories
	Identifies common consonant
	  sounds
	Identifies common, simple words
		Sorts printed numbers
		One-to-one correspondence
		Repeats 3 or more numbers
		Schedules by the clock
		Matches clock faces
		High–low, Tall–short
		Value of coins (P,N,D, and Q)
		Rote counts 1–10
		Orders by size
		Aware of money
		  value and use
		Introduce digital clock
			Brushes own teeth
			Manipulates
			  tape recorder
			Jumps rope
			Narrower balance beam
			Marches
			Catches large, soft ball
			Plays group games
			Plays relay-type games

Mrs. Salazar spent most of the first 2 or 3 weeks of school getting acquainted with her students by doing some preliminary testing, reading simple stories to them, and observing them in classroom and play activities. She also observed their reactions to some picture books she had made available to them. During this time, she made a tentative decision that these three boys were roughly on the same achievement levels—at least close enough that their IEPs could be achieved with a single curriculum outline. She also noted that their IEPs contained some common entries, although her GIA experience reminded her that each entry could describe a wide variety of mastery levels.

Charles's parents seemed to be happy with his placement, but they expressed doubt that he would ever be very successful in school—even in a special class. They seemed to have been unduly influenced by their family physician, who warned them that Charles's perinatal birth problems of prolonged labor and oxygen deprivation would likely result in his being "little more than a vegetable."

Roger's parents continued to have difficulty accepting his disability. Mrs. Salazar learned from other teachers that Roger's parents were socially prominent in the community and that they had enrolled him in several expensive preschool programs, all of which had eventually met with their disapproval. Tom's parents, like Roger's, were impatient to have him prepared for first grade, where he could learn to read, spell, and write like his older brothers and sisters had done.

As Mrs. Salazar got better acquainted with the three boys, she found that Tom was the slowest learner of the three, although his parents and the school psychologist's report suggested that his mental retardation was only moderate and he would likely need the special placement only temporarily. The other class members were older and were functioning on a higher level than these three boys.

IEP Meetings

The IEP committee meetings for all three boys were quite congenial, and the parents were cooperative, although Tom's and Roger's parents insisted on rigid academic programs to prepare them for reading and arithmetic. Roger's parents reminded Mrs. Salazar several times that they had expected Roger to be ready for first-grade class work by the time he was 6 years old and that they would insist on a regular first-grade placement by the next school year. She found the parents of both boys impatient with her suggestions that the IEPs include listening skills, learning to get along with the other class members, and awareness of time concepts. They preferred more advanced topics (e.g., reading readiness, counting to 100, telling time, learning to write), so these topics were entered on the curriculum planning chart, although they had to be rearranged later. The long-term objectives on the IEPs were expressed in general terms and provided overall guidelines agreed on by the parents. The details of curriculum planning and designing lesson plans and achieving the goals were left largely up to Mrs. Salazar.

CONSTRUCTING THE CURRICULUM PLANNING CHART

Table 10.2 shows the composite skills and concepts for all three boys. The table includes only a representative sample of the LCD entries Mrs. Salazar listed on the chart. Her experience with Tom's curriculum illustrates the basic steps needed for the others. The IEP for one student will usually suggest some skills and concepts that are appropriate and high priority for another student but that may have been overlooked by the second student's IEP committee.

Communication Skills from Tom's IEP

Mrs. Salazar entered all of Tom's long-term IEP objectives in the most appropriate columns on her curriculum planning chart. The IEP included the general concepts of developing oral language, reading readiness, counting to 100, and learning to write. These concepts proved to be far too difficult and had to be presented much later than the team had anticipated.

Oral Language

By the time she finished Tom's IEP, Mrs. Salazar knew that his oral language consisted of about five or six words, none of which were clearly pronounced. Therefore, she listed the following as entry level skills: makes basic sounds correctly, names own body parts, responds to own name, follows simple instructions, and repeats simple words. She planned to teach these in the near future and then proceed to the related LCD and other communication items.

Reading Readiness

Reading readiness proved to be a good example of an IEP element revealing many entry-level skills that need to be broken down into teachable components. Tom's problems with oral language suggested to Mrs. Salazar that he would not likely be ready for any formal reading activities for some time. So, she tentatively moved the reading readiness entry to the intermediate level.

Mrs. Salazar thought that one of the most important entry-level skills for reading was to develop listening skills and an awareness of books and their value. She initiated these skills by reading aloud to the students at least half an hour each day. She experimented with several books until she found some that all of her students seemed to understand and enjoy. After reading a simple statement from a story, Mrs. Salazar would ask each student a question on his or her language level. The responses of the other students helped Tom see that the books contained valuable information and also demonstrated the question-answer procedure. He was also able to observe the verbal interaction between the teacher and the other students. She would ask Tom the simplest question she could think of and help him answer by pointing to a picture of an object.

Counting to 100

It became clear that rote counting to 100 was also a task for a much later date. In fact, Tom could not count at all and had no awareness of number concepts. She moved rote counting to 10 to the intermediate level, with rote counting to 100 to follow later. Tom remained in Mrs. Salazar's class for the next 2 years, and he completed the entry-level skills for rote counting to 10 near the end of the second year.

Learning to Write

When Tom's parents suggested learning to write as an IEP skill, Mrs. Salazar suspected that the skill was also premature for Tom. Having little evidence that it would be too difficult for him, she made the entry. But after she worked with Tom for a short time, she obtained permission from Tom's mother to move learning to write to the upper primary level. They substituted prewriting activities that included several fine motor and eye-hand coordination activities, which she entered in the leisure column. Tom's mother also agreed that he needed to become aware of the concept of writing and that, without something to write about, writing would be a meaningless activity. They also decided to stress listening comprehension and oral speech as entry-level skills to writing. Later, Mrs. Salazar used a type of neurological impress procedure with her older students that stresses learning to write a word as the student is learning to identify it.

Communication Skills from Other Columns

Horizontal curriculum planning brings concepts at the student's achievement level from other columns. Because communication skills are basic to all other areas of the curriculum, entries in other columns suggest a myriad of needed communication activities at every age level. Combining the communication materials and activities with those of other columns helps in structuring the lessons to teach meaningful concepts, rather than to merely stress communication. For example, in selecting stories and pictures for listening comprehension and oral communication, Mrs. Salazar used pictures of foods and games from a health unit designed to help Tom achieve health and physical education goals. She also used objects and pictures of objects to illustrate number concepts from arithmetic. She read stories and used other activities that illustrated health and social skills. She also introduced her students to music by letting them march and participate in a rhythm band.

Arranging Prerequisite Skills

Vertical curriculum planning helps the teacher arrange the skills and concepts in order of increasing achievement level. It also helps the teacher identify prerequisite skills and concepts when the ones he or she has selected are too difficult or more advanced skills when they are needed. Every listing calls for an investigation of the necessary entry-level or prerequisite skills. All parts of the curriculum are tentative, especially as they apply to each student. Once the curriculum is tentatively completed, it is important to diagnose each student's achievement level and thus allow him or her to bypass or review previously mastered skills. It is also necessary to adjust the entries upward or downward as experience dictates. Some of the listed skills and concepts will be surprisingly more difficult for some students than others. Occasionally, every special education teacher encounters a situation in which one student does fairly well on a higher level task but falters on one that is ordinarily much more simple. For example, Mrs. Salazar successfully used sorting color cards as a prerequisite to teaching her students to name the colors on the cards. She found that one of her older students could identify the colors red, yellow, and blue but had great difficulty with all sorting tasks.

Future Communication Skills

Each listed skill or concept must be monitored, and projections should be made as to how it is likely to satisfy a student's life goals. If a skill is retained, plans must be made to teach the advanced and functional aspects of that skill. Listing the advanced levels of the skill or concept later in the student's program often involves level-to-level planning and the approval of the student's future teachers. The age 25 projection helps in evaluating whether each skill will be sufficiently mastered to be useful. Mrs. Salazar had to move many parts of Tom's curriculum to age levels for which she would not be responsible.

Horizontal Planning and Teaching

One way to greatly improve efficiency in teaching students with mental retardation is the use of horizontal planning. In the planning stages, skills and concepts listed in one column suggest activities to be listed in other columns. These related skills, concepts, and activities are taught simultaneously. This approach is particularly efficient in planning communication skills because they are involved in every other curriculum area. Horizontal teaching focuses lessons in listening, speaking, reading, writing, and following instructions on the skills and concepts of other areas. Mrs. Salazar consistently diagnosed and prescribed Tom's communication skills while she was working with him in other areas. The communication and language activities of younger schoolchildren usually have little or no intrinsic value and often show little relationship to the rest of a student's curriculum. This situation in regular education often occurs because of large class enrollments and the necessary dependence on textbooks dedicated to a single discipline. Special education offers some relief for this problem. With smaller class numbers, teachers are able to individually design and construct a greater part of each student's program and thus make horizontal teaching very feasible.

GIA AND COMMUNICATION

Some GIA components that can be used in diagnosing and prescribing communication skills and concepts are shown in Figure 10.1. These components are only suggested, and each communication target task requires its own array of components. Bold print indicates key words or abbreviations to be used if the manipulated components are being plotted. Some procedures, activities, and materials that might be used to encourage communication, related skills, and concepts are as follows:

Adapted/Created/Enhanced (ACE) Stories

One persistent problem imposed by mental retardation is impaired cognitive ability, an impairment that has a number of significant consequences. Among these consequences are serious deficits in reading performance, especially in reading comprehension. The reading comprehension skills of most teenagers with mental retardation are on primary levels, and as a result these students are unable to obtain practical information from books and other printed sources as their age-mates do. Books and stories suited to these teenagers' CAs are beyond their comprehension, and stories matched to their MAs tend to be childish, with little instructional value. When teachers use adapted/created/enhanced (ACE) stories, a student with mental retardation is able to gain information and master concepts long before he or she can read about those concepts. Information can be received and skills mastered even if the student never learns to read at all.

Reading an adapted/created/enhanced (ACE) story to a student with mental retardation helps the student with little or no reading ability master age-appropriate concepts.

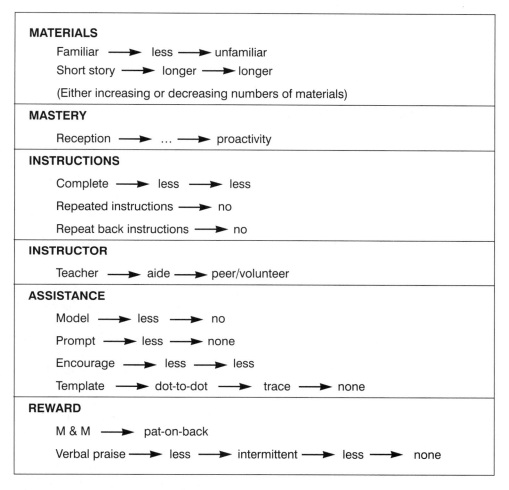

FIGURE 10.1 Language Concept Development: Diagnosis/Prescription

An *adapted story* borrows a theme, setting, or story line from an existing story. The topic may come from a television program or informational book, as well as a story. A *created story* is made up specifically to teach a particular lesson or concept. An *enhanced story* begins with an adapted or created story but changes or enhances it to teach a different lesson or concept. A story may be enhanced in many ways, including increasing or decreasing the language level, changing to a more age-appropriate story line, increasing the number or nature of the characters, and using more sophisticated adjectives and adverbs. A given story may undergo a series of enhancements, each teaching different related or unrelated concepts.

It is usually unnecessary to differentiate the terms *adapted, created,* and *enhanced,* except to recognize that (a) an adapted story usually acquires one or two elements of an existing story that originally had little or no application to students with mental retardation, (b) an enhanced story makes changes to a story that was intended to be appropriate for these students, and (c) a created story was originated by the teacher or parent and thus is more personalized to the specific student. ACE stories can be freely traded, but copyright laws must not be violated.

Uses for ACE Stories

The main purpose of ACE stories is that they be read to students with mental retardation to teach concepts these students are unable to read about themselves. They are equally beneficial, however, to other students whose reading is substantially below grade level. ACE stories are usually read to students by teachers and parents, but peer tutors and volunteers can be trained to read them as well. Eventually, some students may be able to read the stories for themselves or to other students with mental retardation. Some students are able to write stories, often with the aid of their teachers, parents, or other helpers.

ACE stories can be used for diagnosis as well as prescription. When a student reads all or part of a story, particularly one written on a practical theme, and answers some questions of varying difficulty, the individual's language and listening comprehension skills can be accurately assessed. The student's mastery of the content and lessons of the story will also be apparent. Through discussing the fictional characters of ACE stories, a teacher can help students rationally discuss social and other problems, and thus they learn how to handle such problems before or after these problems occur. Gersie and King (1990) reported success as they read, wrote, and listened to stories in rehabilitation and therapy with younger students, as well as with adults. ACE stories also show students the value of being able to read and write.

The stories may be of any length but need not be long. A story may consist of a single paragraph for younger students, or it may be longer to meet the needs of older or more capable students. The stories may be illustrated with pictures from magazines or elsewhere. In fact, a story could consist entirely or partly of pictures. The stories may be augmented as appropriate by using pictures, flannel boards, and models and by bringing to class some examples of objects relevant to the story line.

ACE stories are usually written and read by the student's teacher; with some direction, however, instructional assistants, volunteers, and peer tutors can create as well as read them. CA peers are usually enthusiastic and challenged by the task of identifying appropriate themes and lessons to form the basis for ACE stories. These peers can provide valuable insights into current, age-relevant problems. Students benefit most when peers, aides, and other volunteers who read the stories are carefully trained in questioning techniques.

Ways to Enhance a Story

Suppose a small group of 12- to 14-year-old students with mental retardation are in a transitional program where they are scheduled to begin on-campus work experience jobs. They must understand their job responsibilities and the importance of their relationships with their supervisors. The teacher or a parent might write a story or enhance an existing story about young people working at jobs and some of the problems they encounter. This or any other story may be altered in countless ways to make it appropriate for a different individual of any age, interest, and ability group.

If a computer is available, it is simple to make a copy of an existing ACE story and then to revise it as needed to teach a different lesson or to teach the same lesson to a different group. If a computer is not available, the original story can be copied and then enhanced by cutting and pasting and/or retyping. After these revisions, each story should be audiotaped for repeated use (Montague & Fonseca, 1993).

Message of the Story

Almost any social or problem situation can become the theme of an ACE story. Problems such as negative moods, offensive habits, and hurt feelings can be treated vicariously and impersonally with an ACE story or a series of stories. Other problems that can be dealt with effectively through stories include being offered a ride, candy, or drugs by a stranger; failing to put toys away; losing lunch money or other valuables; not knowing how much money things cost; not being invited to a party; finding a wallet or other valuable; not using deodorant; getting on the wrong bus; being taunted by a bully; getting injured; and being late for a job. The same basic story can be enhanced to teach several of these lessons to the same group.

To accomplish specific instructional goals for specific groups may involve changing various aspects of a story: the names and number of characters, the setting, the story line, and/or the message. The number of subjects (e.g., animals, objects) may need to be changed or the descriptors of those subjects (usually adjectives or names). For example, to teach different colors, sizes, and relationships, the small dog in one story may become large, black, red, playful, or mean in another—whichever is appropriate for the message that is planned for the students.

For older students, appropriate story settings may be dances, car races, and workplaces; appropriate themes include asking for a date, getting a job, living in an apartment, and being unable to perform an essential or desired task. The story about the young people on their new jobs could be altered so that the young people are moving into an apartment, changing to a new school, or any number of different situations. Using short stories with familiar themes and vocabulary that have been adapted to represent different problems or challenges is a good way to teach and encourage students with mental retardation to read.

Listening Comprehension and Language Development Through ACE Stories

Raising or lowering the language level of an existing story can make it appropriate for an individual or group different from the story's originally intended audience. To be appropriate, the language level of a story should fall somewhere between the receptive and expressive language abilities of the targeted student or group. Thus, a basic story devised to teach a lesson in courtesy to a group of transitional students can be used to teach the same lesson to a class of less capable students by lowering the language level.

Swinson and Ellis (1988) found that reading stories to young children with severe disabilities produces gains in verbal comprehension and verbal expression. Manipulating selected elements of ACE stories according to the prescriptions of the children in a group provides an excellent means of teaching a variety of listening and language skills. For example, a teacher can vary the length and difficulty of the story, the sophistication of the questions asked, and the amount of the story read between questions in order to diagnose and teach listening comprehension. Gradually increasing the levels of these DPE elements in successive stories helps increase the students' performance in these vital communication skills. Gearing the stories to the interest and comprehension levels of the students can also help increase listening skills.

Having been motivated by listening to stories read by others, some students begin to read the simpler stories for themselves. Even then, however, teachers should continue with the listening and communication skills instruction with increasingly difficult stories. Most students with mental retardation will continue reading considerably below grade level, yet they may make significant language gains from listening to ACE stories on their communication level. Other activities to encourage LCD and prereading skills include the following:

Have show and tell activities.
Describe pictures.
Use puppets.
Use a listening center.
Use a reading center.
Use ACE stories
      for listening activities.
      for reading.
Have children write their own library books.
Have children describe activities and events.
      Field trips
      Visits from resource persons
      Games
      Playground activities
Hold group discussions.
Use open-ended stories.
Tell sequential stories (each student contributes part).
Give oral reports.
Role-play.
Use questioning techniques, such as
      Why do we _____?
      Where do we get _____?
      What does a _____ do?
      What is a _____?

What is a _____ used for?
Sort pictures.
   Sequence pictures
   Action pictures
Put on a play.
Record a mock-up television screen.
Replay pictures of activities.
Use interactive videos.
Make color slide-sound presentations.
Show slides.
Show filmstrips.
Play records.
Use flash cards.
Use cassette tape recorders.
Record students' voices.
Record class activities.
Use ear phones with recorders.
Use a tachistoscope.
Follow instructional games.
Commission tasks.
Make and look at class picture albums.
Put together jigsaw and other puzzles.
Make storybooks from pictures.
Draw pictures of activities and experiences.
Learn simple songs.
Learn simple rhymes.
Play simple games.
Match colors.
Match objects.
Match pictures of objects.
Match letters.
Match numbers.
Use walkie-talkies.
Ride tricycles.
Roller-skate.
Jump rope.
Walk on balance beams.
Play ring toss.
Toss bean bags.
Play hopscotch.

Some specific LCD and reading skills and concepts are suggested in Appendix E. These skills and concepts might serve as appropriate long-term and annual goals in the IEPs of students with mental retardation.

SUMMARY

In this chapter, I emphasized the need to teach and encourage students with mental retardation to learn good communication skills. Language concept development (LCD) is the ability of an individual to form and evaluate basic perceptions and ideas. I also stressed the difficulty for a student with mental retardation to master essential skills without having first formed some basic perceptions about those essential skills.

This chapter provided a composite example showing the construction of a curriculum planning chart and a demonstration of how to select the chart entries from the IEPs of individual students. I showed how the student's IEP team can make tentative projections of that student's life goals and translate the goals into an effective IEP and a long-term curriculum. The resulting curriculum not only must meet the demands of the IDEA but also will keep the student at the peak of his or her learning ability.

The chapter covered how to write and use adapted/created/enhanced (ACE) stories to teach important lessons and concepts to students with mental retardation who may or may not be able to read.

CHAPTER 11

Reading, Writing, and Spelling

Points to Study and Ponder

1. What particular problems are students with mental retardation likely to encounter in learning to read?
2. What was the hornbook, and what did it have to do with the teaching of reading? Are any of its elements being used today?
3. What are the major strengths and weaknesses of the phonetic or phonic approach to teaching reading, especially for students with mental retardation?
4. What are the major strengths and weaknesses of the look-say approach to teaching reading, especially for students with mental retardation?
5. What are the major strengths and weaknesses of using basal readers to teach reading to students with mental retardation?
6. What are the basic elements of the author's recommended reading approach for students with mental retardation?
7. What is the relationship between language concept development (LCD) and reading?
8. What is the relationship between LCD and other skill areas?

n this chapter, I investigate the nature and importance of teaching reading, particularly as it relates to students with mental retardation. I discuss some specific problems teachers must often overcome in teaching reading to students with mental retardation. I also describe a plan to help in teaching this important skill and review the related skills of writing and spelling.

Smith (1968) suggested that learning to read is a notable accomplishment for anyone. Considering the complexities of learning to read, it is something of a miracle that anyone is able to do so, particularly anyone with a greatly diminished cognitive and language ability. Vacca, Vacca, and Gove (1987) declared that both reading and language ability are critical in mastering the complete process of reading. Kirk and Johnson (1951) stated that the reading capacity of students with mental retardation and the extent to which they should be taught to read can be determined only after an extensive diagnosis. The essential task of learning to read is the meaningful interpretation or decoding of words that are visual symbols and cues. The reader's goal should be to review systematically the symbols on a printed page and to perceive the same ideas, information, notions, and feelings the writer intended. As the image of the visual symbol is transmitted to the brain, it must be compared with other symbols previously experienced by the reader, who must then match it with the appropriate concept. The reader—even one who has mental retardation—must then take the appropriate action, which is usually to remember the concept and interpret what the writer meant to convey. The reader must do this with incredible speed, retaining the information for further use.

IMPORTANCE OF READING IN THE CURRICULUM

The ability to read is, without doubt, one of the most significant requirements for academic success. A child who reads poorly will almost certainly have difficulty in school, regardless of his or her other abilities. Even more important, a limited reading ability hampers a person throughout life and thus contributes to great disadvantages in vocational, family, and other life goal pursuits. These considerations are particularly significant in planning curriculum for students with mental retardation because these students rarely learn to read well. The very definition of mental retardation requires poor performance in adaptive behavior, whose central element is learning. In fact, a good reading program acts as a screening device for students incorrectly diagnosed as having mental retardation.

Although parents cannot always discern the other academic deficiencies of their child with mental retardation, they will usually recognize any lag in reading progress. Teachers often observe the anxiety of parents who want their child to learn to read at about the same CA as their other children. Occasionally, parents who recognize that their child has mental retardation insist that reading instruction for their child begin even earlier than for their other children. Beginning formal reading instruction before the child is ready, however, can be extremely frustrating for the child, as well as for the teacher.

Reading and Mental Retardation

Many question the feasibility of teaching reading to students with severe mental retardation. Although it is generally accepted that students with mental retardation experience serious difficulty in learning to read, their right to learn is widely accepted and is receiving increasing support from legislative bodies and the courts. The ability to read is so necessary that everyone should be given the greatest possible opportunity to learn to do so. Reading is a complex, highly abstract task, however, and learning to read is particularly difficult for students with mental retardation (Jenkinson, 1989; Merrill & Jackson, 1992; Merrill & Mar, 1987). Even so, reading should be—and is—an integral part of the IEP for most students with mental retardation. Further, each of these students must be considered to have at least some ability to learn to read. Cuvo and Klatt (1992) used three methods of teaching community-referenced sight words to students with mental retardation. They reported success with community-based instruction, as well as videotaped and flash card presentations in the classroom. Lalli and Browder (1993) compared the effectiveness and efficiency of stimulus fading, stimulus shaping, time delay, and a feedback-only procedure in teaching three adults with moderate developmental delays sight words. Their results showed no clear advantage for any one procedure. Thus, all three might be used with some confidence.

In most schools, learning to read is the major goal for the first 2 or 3 years. In fact, many consider this to be a major goal through all the elementary school years. Thereafter, teachers assume that the typical student has mastered the basics of reading and can use those reading abilities to master other skills and concepts. In any event, the reading material available for students with reading achievement levels below fifth or sixth grade typically has little value in transition, work experience, independent living, and other practical life skills. High-interest/low-vocabulary books with practical themes are available, but these must also be selected with care. This care is not crucial in regular education because students without disabilities reading at a third-grade level usually have 9 or more years of school remaining, which is usually adequate to remediate specific difficulties, develop reading comprehension, and apply proficient reading skills to the content areas of learning. If a student with mental retardation does achieve this level, however, it will ordinarily be later in his or her school career, when few years of instruction remain. Thus, teachers and other IEP team members must stress reading comprehension at every age level. Teachers of adolescents with mental retardation must recognize that terminal reading skills cannot be postponed. If the student demonstrates a limited capacity for sight words, the IEP team must carefully select those words that will optimum long-term utility. The specific sight words must be taken from the student's IEP that is based on his or her age 25 projection. Of course, the eventual reading achievement levels of younger children are not readily apparent, but as they get older and closer to graduation, the teacher will become increasingly aware of a great number of practical skills and concepts they need to (and can) master. The age 25 projection helps in establishing curricular priorities and in placing reading instruction within those priorities.

Age Appropriateness

In addition to having as much practical application as possible, the reading material for students with mental retardation must be age appropriate. Most teachers can affirm that most students, including those with mental retardation, are uninspired, even insulted, by reading and other instructional material designed for younger children. Even students whose mental retardation is severe/profound may reject childish illustrations, large-type print, and stories geared to the interest levels of younger students. Thus, parents and teachers must use examples, pictures, and reading material appropriate to the students' CAs, rather than MAs. Also, many of these books have a higher level of vocabulary than advertised.

Beyond the actual teaching of reading, it is important for the teacher and other members of the IEP team to help the student learn how to select his or her own reading material—particularly in recreational reading. For those who read well enough to read for leisure, they should be encouraged to read widely. This encouragement must be carefully balanced with the student's need to locate and choose his or her own reading matter. The student should become familiar with public libraries and other community resources so that he or she is encouraged to continue reading after leaving school. Broad community-based experiences are strongly recommended, and public libraries are an excellent source of functional information for the student in adult life.

Reading Problems and Inconsistencies

As if learning to read were not difficult enough, the beginning reader of English is confronted with a series of inconsistencies and conflicting instructions particularly inhibiting and confusing to a student with mental retardation. The teacher should be aware of these in designing the reading curriculum:

- Children usually learn to recite the oral alphabet in alphabetical order despite the fact that these symbols never make any sense in that order and have little practical utility until the children begin using a dictionary, telephone book, or encyclopedia. The oral alphabet is often available in children's books and songs at home and elsewhere, however, and it is easier to teach the sounds of the letters if the child already has a "name" or handle for the letter. Young children are often taught as many as five alphabets before they learn one of any real utility. In addition to the oral alphabet (the ABCs), four others are represented by manuscript and cursive writing in both upper- and lowercase. Teachers must use care in teaching manuscript and cursive alphabets and to present them in the sequence that they are prerequisite to reading and other instruction.

- English letters tend to be very inconsistent. For example, the letter *c* says 'k' as in *candy* and 's' as in *city*. It is best to evaluate the reading material to be used and present the most common use or sound for each letter in sounding drills and sight words; others should be saved until the student reads with confidence. The teacher can also present as sight vocabulary essential, nonphonetic words, such as *women, laugh, honest,* and *friend.*

- At first, teachers teach students to read orally, only to criticize the students later if they so much as move their lips. Teachers also teach students to read slowly and distinctly when they read orally, but later teachers expect the students to read much faster and to gain ideas from context clues and word clusters. Teachers and parents must move cautiously in altering concepts that have been deliberately taught.

- Teachers sometimes require students to memorize many reading rules, most of which are inhibiting, unnecessary, and fraught with exceptions (e.g., When two vowels go walking, the first does the talking; *i* before *e*, except after *c*). The reading program described later in the chapter eliminates all of these confusing rules.

TYPES OF READING INSTRUCTION

Reading instruction is of three traditional types. Teaching reading to students with mental retardation usually involves all three.

Developmental Reading

Developmental reading includes both the mechanics of reading and reading comprehension (Umans, 1966). Listening comprehension and general communication skills are vital entry-level skills to developmental reading. Students must ordinarily have some awareness of a concept before they can learn to read about that concept. Otherwise, learning to read is largely a rote exercise. Listening comprehension (and later, reading comprehension) must be stressed throughout the school career of a student with mental retardation, especially at the secondary level.

Adapted/created/enhanced (ACE) stories (discussed in Chapter 10) are excellent instruments to use in teaching listening comprehension and at the same time improve a student's general language skills and in teaching essential lessons and concepts the student's limited reading ability prevents him or her from reading about. As the student is learning to read, the ACE stories make excellent developmental reading material; they are functional and interesting because they are written expressly for the student and his or her peers.

The listening comprehension questions and discussions prompted by ACE and other specially selected and written stories stress content, as well as memory development and other prereading skills. Whenever possible, the students read and write about practical situations (e.g., what people do for a living, classroom rules of conduct, principles of good health, and similar concepts they are interested in and need to know about). When teaching spelling, punctuation, and sentence construction, teachers should use mostly familiar words and those that students will encounter in their reading material.

A developmental reading program typically occupies most of the elementary years and continues with daily instruction until the student becomes a proficient reader. The sequence should gradually progress from simple concepts and common words to more complex and practical themes and concepts. The primary emphasis in such a program is basic reading skills and fluency. Many schools and school districts adopt a single publisher's reading program and intend it to be used uniformly by all who teach reading. Teaching reading to students with mental retardation, however, often requires the teacher to design much of his or her own reading material and program. Teachers may also use their own reading material to augment the programs designed for students without disabilities; doing so takes advantage of the sequence of the regular program while adding the practical concepts needed by those with mental retardation.

Functional Reading

In functional reading, the major emphasis shifts from teaching reading to teaching the student to use his or her reading ability to obtain information necessary for solving problems in subject matter areas, in daily life, and in recreational reading. Students with mental retardation typically cannot maintain the same reading pace as their age-mates, and they fall progressively behind. At best, their reading proficiency is likely to remain at the primary and early intermediate levels even after they reach adolescence. So, functional reading must be initiated before they are competent readers—perhaps at approximately the same CA as their peers. Reading comprehension must be emphasized at every age level with students with mental retardation. This can be done by having the students learn words and read material that are intrinsically beneficial. Stories (e.g., ACE stories) can be used to teach moral and practical principles and use real people as examples while the student is learning to read. Parents and teachers must select stories and other reading material that are informative, interesting, and age appropriate. The identification and interpretation of emergency and survival words must be given high priority with all ability levels in mental retardation.

Remedial Reading

Remedial reading is appropriate for students who, despite reading instruction, still do not read with much success. Generally, most remedial reading instruction and programs are designed for older students with normal and above average IQs who are reading 2 or more years below grade level; thus, these programs are not always appropriate for students with mental retardation. Many of the stories and other reading material classified as remedial have themes as well as reading levels suitable for students with mental retardation. Some material used in community adult education and in teaching English as a second language (TESL) are also age appropriate, especially for older students with mental retardation.

Even though teaching reading to students with mental retardation might be difficult, the parents and teachers must not become discouraged or intimidated. Much evidence supports the fact that although most English dictionaries contain more than 50,000 entries, most people, including those with mental retardation, can communicate very effectively by mastering far fewer words than that. Allred (1977), reviewing several studies on this subject, concluded that approximately 90% of all written and spoken communication is conducted with fewer than 1,000 words. Many students with mental retardation learn to read quite effectively and to communicate fairly well in writing with very limited vocabularies when the words are carefully selected and prioritized.

DESIGNING AND EVALUATING THE READING PROGRAM

Each teacher of students with mental retardation must eventually design a reading program suited to his or her unique skills and preferences and to the needs of the students. Experience shows that no two such students learn exactly alike, and it is equally unlikely that any two teachers will teach reading (or any other subject, for that matter) with the same methods. In designing a reading program, however, it is best to take advantage of existing knowledge and technology; there is no need to start from scratch. The availability of such a wide variety of reading methods and techniques, each having its enthusiastic (sometimes passionate) proponents, indicates no single best way to teach reading to all students. These existing methods and techniques provide a fertile ground from which each teacher can adopt and adapt in designing his or her own reading program.

It may be comforting to know that the struggle to develop a foolproof reading program has consumed this entire century. Like the individual teacher, special educators in the United States have sought material and procedures that would help in teaching reading to all students, including those with mental retardation. This section provides some evaluative criteria and a brief review of some materials that have been used in the past; each had some strengths that might be incorporated into the reading program of an individual teacher.

How well does the approach correlate the teaching of language concept development, reading, writing, and spelling? Must writing and spelling be postponed until the student becomes a proficient reader?

How well does it combine the concepts of learning to read and reading to gain information?

Do the early reading materials have any strengths or implications for today's problem readers?

Does the reading material stress words and concepts a student with mental retardation is likely to need in daily life, particularly as an adult? If not, could it be adapted to do so?

Is the approach sufficiently flexible to accommodate the wide range of ability of students with mental retardation?

Would the approach be generally appropriate for students with mental retardation?

Does the approach involve a transition to traditional orthography and reading material?

Could the approach be used with one or two students with mental retardation in an integrated classroom?

Early Reading Approaches

In tracing the evolvement of reading instruction, it is helpful to note the weaknesses and strengths and to see how well each satisfies the evaluative criteria. The reading approaches discussed are arranged roughly in chronological order.

In the United States, the earliest method of teaching reading was undoubtedly the hornbook or slate approach. Although variations certainly existed, the procedure involved essentially recognizing the alphabet, followed by spelling of common words (e.g., *man, dog, book, boy, cat*), and was strongly characterized by rote memorization and recitation. The early McGuffey readers (McGuffey, 1909) followed essentially the same procedure. The relative success of this rote spelling or letter-by-letter approach is difficult to assess because comparative studies are almost nonexistent. Moderate success must have attended these efforts because it was common practice to retain in school only those students who showed considerable promise. The hornbook and McGuffey readers had little competition until the early 1900s. Gordon (1910) proposed teaching reading by using families of letters. He suggested that it made much more sense to teach words such as *cat, rat, sat* and *hit, pit, sit* in a given lesson than merely to select the words at random.

Before long, Gordon's system was refined somewhat by grouping words with the same initial consonant and medial sounds. For example, the words *bag, bat* and *bad* were taught together, as well as those proposed by Gordon. This procedure, in essence, comprised what became known as the *phonic* or *phonetic system* of teaching reading. Actually, the procedure was quite unrefined and did not call for the words to be sounded out—a natural consequence that developed somewhat later. During the 1920s and 1930s, the phonetic approach gradually lost popularity.

The year 1920 marked the end of two great events in American history. The Industrial Revolution, from roughly 1880 to 1920, together with World War I, from 1914 to 1918, provided great impetus to industrial technology that, in turn, required educated workers. Education came to be recognized as essential for everyone. Public support for education gradually gained acceptance, and compulsory attendance laws were enacted in every state. This turn of events resulted in not only greatly increased numbers of students flocking to the classrooms but also a shortage of well-trained teachers. The teacher shortage contributed to the downfall of the phonetic approach but probably would have had the same effect on any other procedure. Before 1920, few teachers had much more education or training than their average student was expected to receive. Furthermore, a teacher's training, even in teachers' colleges, usually amounted to more intensified instruction in subject matter areas, rather than in pedagogy. As a result, the schools were poorly prepared to cope with either the increasing numbers or the overwhelming range of ability evident in the students. Consequently, almost all current teaching procedures, but particularly the phonetic approach to reading instruction, came under fire in the professional journals and college classrooms.

These influences led to a heavy emphasis on the *look-say* or *sight method* of teaching reading, which depended heavily on the students' ability in auditory memory and discrimination. When a child encountered an unfamiliar word, the teacher simply pronounced it, repeating the word as often as necessary. The popularity of the look-say approach continued for the next two or three decades. Then, in 1955, Rudolf Flesch published his scathing indictment of the look-say method, which he held to be utter nonsense. At first, his plea seemed to influence professional educators very little, though it gained much popularity with the general public, particularly with parents who eventually applied great pressure on educators and publishers to emphasize phonetics more strongly.

In the meantime, Kirk (Hegge, Kirk, & Kirk, 1940, 1955, 1972) quietly published the results of several years of intensive investigation into the teaching of reading. Although he did not condemn the look-say method, he found it extremely difficult for many children, particularly those with lower IQs. His research showed that the rules accompanying reading instruction confuse and inhibit many students. He was particularly intrigued by the difficulty many students have in mastering the great variety of long and short sounds for each vowel. This interest led him to develop the Remedial Reading Drills, which were based on his *massed-differentiated-integrated method* of teaching reading.

Kirk suggested that a child's initial exposure to reading should involve mastering up to 150 sight words. Kirk's proposal, however, was designed for slow learners and other problem readers, not necessarily those with mental retardation. He referred to the identification of sight words as the *massed stage* that taught a child to recognize a word by total configuration or general appearance. The *differentiated stage* was characterized by word attack skills by which the child learned to "sound out" and eventually spell unfamiliar words. Kirk proposed merging the skills of the massed and differentiated stages in refining the child's reading ability in the *integrated stage*. This stage stressed comprehension and fluency as the child learned to read for information and pleasure. The child also learned how to use structural analysis and context clues.

The major contributions of the phonetic approaches are their systematic reduction of words into component parts. They also provide maximum correlation with spelling and writing. After a few weeks of instruction, most students can begin to write modest sentences on almost any simple theme. Students also learn to sound out unfamiliar words and to proceed independently. The weakness of phonetics is mainly that many words are nonphonetic and cannot be readily sounded out. The major strength and contribution of the sight-word approaches are that they must be used to teach these nonphonetic words. Grossen and Carnine (1993) maintained that phonetic approaches can be effective with a student with disability if they are well planned and evaluated. Teaching other words as sight words makes a consistent learning task for the student. Most students can remember an unfamiliar word after it is pronounced for them once or twice; this technique eliminates the need for extensive word attack procedures. Indeed, many students have learned to read very well without any instruction in phonetics. Further, many students have taught themselves to sound out new words, often not recognizing that they were actually doing so. A weakness of the look-say approach is that each new word must be learned essentially by rote. This can be a particular problem for students with mental retardation, who seem to have a limited capacity for sight words. Both the phonetic and sight-word approaches have their staunch advocates, however, and each has some elements that can be incorporated to varying degrees into a teacher's individualized reading program.

Initial Teaching Alphabet (ITA)

Many reading specialists have attempted to refine reading instruction by reforming or altering traditional orthography (manuscript and cursive writing). One of the most notable and widely publicized attempts was that of Sir James Pitman. In the early 1960s, he designed what he called the augmented Roman alphabet that eventually became known as the *initial teaching alphabet (ITA)*—a tremendous idea that arrived several centuries late (Mazurkiewicz & Tanzer, 1963). Had it been developed within 100 years or so of the invention of the printing press, the consistent ITA would probably have been widely accepted and might have prevented much of the anxiety and frustration that have traditionally plagued thousands of would-be readers. Of course, ITA, like any other procedures or material deviating from traditional orthography, must terminate with a transition to the type of print a student finds in other schoolbooks.

The ITA system involves 44 characters, essentially one for each common sound in the English language. Twenty-four letters of the alphabet are retained, so 20 new symbols have to be learned. Because ITA does not adapt very well to cursive writing, it is limited to manuscript print. ITA has no uppercase, however, and words that would ordinarily be capitalized are presented in bold print lowercase. What an advantage dealing with only one alphabet would be to students with mental retardation.

Pitman's use of a consistent one-symbol-per-sound and of each sound having only one symbol largely offsets most weaknesses of the phonetic method and the requirement of learning additional symbols. Using ITA, the student is able to learn more quickly and thereby gain the self-confidence so vital to becoming a fluent reader. Unfortunately, ITA also has several disadvantages: (a) Spelling, writing, and arithmetic must be effectively postponed until the student is a fairly proficient reader—and until after the necessary transitional period; (b) storybooks are available, but their use tends to solidify concepts that must be "untaught" later; and (c) valuable time is lost in the transitional period, and the difficulty in transition is particularly significant in a highly mobile population. For this reason, the adoption of ITA by an entire school district or even a school is questionable.

In light of the learning characteristics of students with mental retardation, however, the one-to-one correspondence of ITA symbols is very attractive; perhaps further research and experimentation will produce procedures for using ITA with students with mental retardation. Perhaps the greatest lesson teachers of students with mental retardation can learn from ITA is to systematically present only one sound of a given letter at a time. The internal consistency of ITA is an advantage not to be overlooked. The necessary transition from ITA to traditional orthography has been widely criticized, although the transitional period has been improved by initiating it earlier in the process. Further, the resemblance of ITA symbols to traditional orthography is relatively close, and the transition is not as difficult as it may appear.

Basal Readers

Without question, basal readers have been the most popular procedure for teaching developmental reading in the United States and most other countries. Because most students with severe/profound mental retardation receive their reading instruction in regular classes, the basal reader is the most popular approach for use with students with mental retardation as well. Even though the basal reader approach is not usually appropriate for students with mental retardation, often few alternatives are available for those who spend all or most of the school day in regular classes. Time requirements often prevent using several approaches in one classroom.

The advantages of the basal reader lie mainly in its relatively low cost and the suitability for use with large groups. Sometimes—especially at the primary level—a few students without disabilities read at about the same level as a student with mental retardation and can be placed in the same reading group. In these instances, however, it is well to evaluate the learning rates of the students because those with mental retardation, by definition, learn slowly and tend to fall increasingly behind their peers. Also, if these students without disabilities are teenagers, the appropriateness of a basal reader approach for them is also questionable.

A definite advantage of the basal reader approach is its popularity and teachers' familiarity with its use. Also, the publishers of basal readers usually provide a great deal of readiness and informal reading inventories and other evaluation materials. Basal readers have at least three potential disadvantages or weaknesses, particularly for students with mental retardation:

1. They are difficult to individualize. Attempts to individualize instruction must usually be limited to simply grouping the students and allowing some to proceed more rapidly than others.
2. Reading materials designed for students without disabilities almost always move too rapidly for most students with mental retardation. Ordinarily, new words are introduced too rapidly.
3. Basal readers typify the problems discussed earlier about materials that are neither age appropriate for most individuals with mental retardation nor intrinsically valuable at their reading levels.

The Edmark Reading Program

The Edmark Reading Program (Edmark Corporation, 1993) can be used with signing and is effective for students with language barriers. The later editions have greatly improved to include many more words that are functional to students with limited capacities for sight words. It features more than 400 of these functional words, from which the teacher may choose. The program emphasizes word meaning and involves no phonetic decoding. The program recommends a 5-step procedure: prereading, word recognition, direction books, picture-phrase cards, and storybooks. The program is relatively inexpensive and can be used with a few students with mental retardation in an integrated resource or regular class. It is currently available for the Apple II computer.

The Unit Approach

The unit approach provides an excellent foundation for a reading program. Using this approach, the teacher uses class discussions and other activities to teach meaningful skills and concepts from all areas of the curriculum. It has been popular in special classes for students with mental retardation and also in regular classes. Integrated classes offer an excellent opportunity to provide the varied levels of reading and other instruction needed by a wide range of students with cultural diversities and disabilities. For example, a young student's age 25 projection suggests the need for instruction in getting along with other people. The teacher selects and discusses stories that show how people relate to each other in positive and negative ways. (See "Story Enhancement," below.) For instructional efficiency, a creative teacher includes skills and concepts from other curricular areas in the basic unit.

One major strength of the unit approach is its flexibility. The teacher can quickly adapt a unit to a higher or lower level by selecting easier or more difficult reading and other material. He or she can also teach a unit to a group of students with differing achievement levels by having each student read and do assignments appropriate to individual needs and ability levels. Individual achievement levels suggest different assignments, mastery levels, and even different questions in class discussions. A carefully planned unit motivates the students whose needs and interests are considered in designing the basic unit.

Ironically, a potential weakness of the unit approach lies in its flexibility. Students do not share interests in the same topics or individual life goals. For example, age 25 projections of the students in a typical regular class at any level present a staggering challenge to the teacher. Under these circumstances, the educational program can evolve into a succession of units that may be interesting to students but that may not lead in a meaningful direction. Thus, the teacher must design each unit to maximize the achievement of each individual.

Story Enhancement

Often, it is difficult to find a story or a book that illustrates a particular point or teaches a specified lesson. The teacher can solve this problem by writing his or her own stories or by adapting existing stories to particular needs. These techniques can include either a section to insert into a story or a chapter to include in a book. The teacher could adapt almost any fictional story or book to illustrate the problems of getting along with other people, attending to personal hygiene, eating a proper diet, or finding and performing well on a job. ACE stories are a good example. It is not advisable to use this approach with classical or well-known books or stories, however, and teachers and others must not violate copyright laws under any circumstances.

Programmed Reading

Programmed instruction is obtainable in many subject areas, including reading. It is available in workbooks, as well as in computer programs. Its format typically follows a stepwise procedure of carefully planned (programmed) learning increments. Each step depends on the student's mastery of the preceding step. Before posing a new question or problem, a step (or frame) often discusses a new concept, offers explanatory material, and/or gives a worked example. Self-pacing, self-regulation, and immediate feedback are the main strengths of programmed instruction. The student can work at his or her own rate and review where necessary. Considerable drill and repetition are usually built into the procedure. Also, programmed readers can be used with one or two students in a class in which others are progressing more rapidly or working in larger groups. The major disadvantage of programmed instruction for students with mental retardation is that most programs do not include practical, life problems and situations within the reading levels these students will achieve. Most programs tend to be grade-level oriented, and the self-pacing provisions prevent these students from progressing beyond the primary levels. The general use of computer programs with students with mental retardation is discussed in Chapter 15.

Direct Instruction System for Teaching Arithmetic and Reading (DISTAR)

The DISTAR program, developed by Engelmann and Bruner (1988) for use with children with cultural differences, has also found some acceptance among teachers of students with mental retardation. Unlike other programmed instruction, DISTAR is programmed for the teacher, who is expected to follow explicit instructions on how to proceed and even what to say to the student when teaching reading. The authors strongly recommend that the teacher follow the suggested wording without deviation. Many teachers nevertheless provide their own variations to allow the sharper students to proceed more rapidly. The authors also recommend that no supplementary reading material be used. Teachers commonly violate this admonition too, apparently believing that departures or variations are sometimes necessary, particularly when working with students who learn very slowly.

This highly phonetic approach offers essentially one new concept with each lesson. Ordinarily, three or four students can be instructed at once. The program was obviously influenced by Gordon (1910) and Kirk (1958). The major strengths of DISTAR relate primarily to high student activity, positive (usually nonfood) reinforcement, and breaking down reading tasks into small, instructional increments. The early lessons teach phonetics well, and the cost is moderate.

DISTAR shares most of the advantages and disadvantages of other programmed instruction but has been especially criticized for its strong orientation to drill and oral recitation and its lack of creative and spontaneous communication. In the early lessons, students respond either individually or in unison to instructions or cues given by the teacher. Thus, DISTAR is an example of the problems mentioned earlier concerning age appropriateness and content. Relatively few words are presented in the early lessons that will be useful to most students with mental retardation once they become adults. Level II of DISTAR consists of stories that are at best innocuous and impractical and at worst inappropriate, weird, and even harmful. In a typical story, a young child gets trapped in a strange, creepy place and cannot escape without remembering secret words. In another, the child is covered with green spots and can get rid of them only by following special instructions. Such situations can be very threatening to young children probably having little appreciable positive influences.

A RECOMMENDED READING APPROACH

The vocabularies of the reading approaches discussed above all suffer from a common complaint: They are not very functional. The general approaches of all of them can be adapted, however, to meet regional, cultural, and individual needs. Sooner or later, every teacher of students with mental retardation must develop his or her own reading program. Because no single program meets the needs of all, that program must be sufficiently adaptable to meet the students' widely varying abilities and needs.

This section provides an outline to help in the development of such a program. Great flexibility is a strength of the outlined approach as it draws on the strengths of many specific programs developed over many years. In fact, the teacher must select his or her own methods and techniques, as well as the materials to place in the hands of the students. The teacher and other IEP team members must also decide on a tentative balance between sight-word vocabulary and word attack skills to be taught to each student. This balance must be reviewed and evaluated continually. Work attack skills can be very effective in helping a student with mental retardation recognize new words without assistance. Work attack skills, however, constitute a block of skills and knowledge that takes a considerable amount of time to master, yet they are of little or no value if not mastered in their entirety. Some students with mental retardation are unable to acquire a sight vocabulary beyond a few crucial emergency words. Unfortunately, the eventual sight-word capacity of an individual cannot be predicted with great precision during the time that developmental reading is being taught to that individual. Thus, teaching word attack skills to students whose mental retardation is severe/profound may consume valuable time that could have been better used in stressing survival words. Constant surveillance and evaluation seem to be the only way to avoid this situation. In some instances, the team may legitimately decide to postpone or even omit teaching phonetics.

The outline has four stages: A, B, C, and D. Stage C draws heavily from Kirk's massed-differentiated-integrated system and the Remedial Reading Drills, by Hegge et al. (1940, 1955, 1972). These drills are highly phonetic and have been used to help teach reading to several generations of students with mental retardation, but they were originally designed as a remedial reading program for students without disabilities. Kirk's analysis and approach to teaching word attack skills is the best available.

A. Language Concept Development (LCD)

Students with mental retardation must be carefully prepared for any reading program. A good place to start is with language concept development (LCD), as discussed in the preceding chapter. Some type of diagnostic/prescriptive procedure is essential to locate the starting point for each student and to ensure that each one masters the entry-level skills of reading. Demonstrating complete mastery of the entry level skills for any planned instruction, however, is asking a great deal of any student with mental retardation. Therefore, the timing of phasing out LCD and beginning to teach reading per se is never obvious. About the only way to make this decision is to de-emphasize the LCD program and to experiment periodically with some reading activities. Simply present some sight words to the student to see whether he or she can recognize and remember them. If the student can do so, continue with the reading instruction; if he or she falters or experiences more difficulty than anticipated, move the approach smoothly and unannounced back into the LCD program. It is important to avoid any fanfare or announcing the date the reading instruction is to begin. If the parents are active members of the IEP team, as they should be, they must be informed well in advance of the experimentations so that they do not become overly anxious. Otherwise, such an announcement may make it difficult to discontinue reading instruction if their child is not ready. This is good advice in teaching any student, but it is particularly desirable in working with students with mental retardation, who are older when they are ready for beginning reading instruction. By the time they are ready, both they and their parents are likely to be impatient for the process to begin. In any event, the student's need for LCD (e.g., listening comprehension) persists even as the actual reading instruction intensifies. The receptive vocabularies of students with mental retardation are almost always more advanced than their expressive vocabularies. This means they can understand, discuss, and learn more advanced concepts than they are able to read about.

B. Beginning Sight Words

The second stage of the recommended approach introduces beginning sight words. Some teachers may prefer to present word attack skills before teaching any sight words. In this event, Stages B and C may be interchanged, but it may be well to teach a few sight words before beginning the word attack skills. Selecting the sight words carefully makes it possible for the student to read and write simple sentences as the phonetic drills progress.

Many teachers regard learning the sounds of selected consonant letters a natural outgrowth of auditory closure in LCD. Some students with mental retardation seem unable to master auditory closure or blending syllables of words together to form the words. Without this vital closure skill, sounding drills are largely a waste of time, although the teacher may want to try teaching them together. Otherwise, it is best to concentrate on sight words.

This stage relates closely to Kirk's massed stage, in which the student learns to identify words by total configuration or general appearance and by repetition. At this stage, "reading" is little more than word calling, but the process continues until the student has accumulated a sight vocabulary of as many as 100 words. Many students with mental retardation seem to have a limited capacity for sight words, at least initially; that is, a student may make slow but steady progress up to a point, beyond which about as many words are lost in a week as are learned. About the only way to discern where and to

Reading instruction for adolescents with mental retardation should be functional and might include reading tasks from the individual's job.

what extent this is happening is to test (or spot-check) the student's entire sight list every few days. The student's limited capacity for sight words means that those words must be carefully selected from the first books and stories the student will read. Any words or phrases he or she is likely to encounter in work or other daily living activities should be added.

The students should learn to sound out the words that appear in the word attack drills; there is no need to teach them as sight vocabulary. In selecting sight words for a student, there is no need to avoid long words, such as *cafeteria, women, danger,* and *factory,* if the student will encounter them in early reading material or elsewhere. Words such as *cement, lime, gravel, shovel* or *flour, sugar, soda, salt, baking powder* may be related to a student's work experience or after-school job. If possible, all students should learn to spell and write their names, addresses, and phone numbers, most of which are nonphonetic. These words are grossly different in appearance from other words and will usually not be cause for concern. Ordinarily, the words to be avoided (or taught in time-separated lessons) are the ones that are similar in appearance, such as *there-three, he-here, were-where.* Also, teaching students with mental retardation to identify, write, or spell nonsense words and syllables is not recommended. For example, only the single consonants *d, f,* and *w* combine with __-i-sh to form real words, although the temptation is always to teach nonsense words, such as *bish, kish, and mish,* in order to complete word wheels, games, and other reading and spelling exercises.

C. Beginning Word Attack Skills

At about the same time the student is learning a basic group of sight words, recognition of the sounds of common consonants are presented from visual cues. The consonant sounds are presented in which they appear in the word attack material to be used. If flash cards are used for this purpose, they should have lowercase letters. Also, the letters on the flash cards must be of the same font or configuration as those in the words and drills and in books and stories the student will encounter later.

In the Remedial Reading Drills, the vowel sounds are systematically presented one per lesson. Kirk recommended carefully monitoring the students' pronunciation of the consonant sounds, particularly the plosives, in which young students have a tendency to add an unwarranted "uh" or "ah" sound. This usually occurs at the end of plosive sounds; thus, the sounds of "b," "k," and "p" become "buh," "kuh," and "puh." This unauthorized addition usually comes at the beginning of continuous sounds, so the consonants *m, n,* and *l* come out "uhm," "uhn," and "uhl." If uncorrected, this bad habit makes sounding and blending activities unduly difficult; for example, the student may have difficulty with the word *pin* if it is sounded "puh-i-uhn" instead of "p-i-n."

Stage C is characteristic of Kirk's differentiated stage, in which the student learns other word attack skills, including rhyming, alliteration, auditory and visual closure, and discrimination. The Remedial Reading Drills provide these activities. It is important to teach the drills in the order they are presented and that the student not be allowed to skip any of them.

The letters of each word should first be sounded separately and distinctly, rather than in combination—for example "s-a-t—sat" and "m-a-t—mat" rather than "s-at—sat," or "m-at—mat." Although sounding the words in this manner is a matter of preference and experience, Kirk's philosophy is that each letter consistently results in the same sound, regardless of its position in the word. This consistency also helps in developing spelling skills. Later, blends, diphthongs, and other combinations should be sounded as they are written—for example, "n-ai-l," "h-or-n," "s-old," "s-c-old," and "d-r-ank." In this way, the student learns to break down each word into its component parts and to sound out unfamiliar words. The last group of words in each drill is printed without spaces between the letters. The students should pronounce these as sight words but should sound out those they do not readily recognize.

D. Functional Reading Skills

This fourth stage is singularly important in the reading program. In the first three stages, the students learn primarily to recognize and manipulate words, but they are very little of terminal or practical value. Any student leaving school permanently at any point during the first three stages has only rudimentary, preparatory reading skills that by themselves have little utility. It is usually poor educational planning to assume that students with mental retardation will extend their reading skills much after school graduation, although it does happen. If annual IEP evaluations have included even cursory assessments of a student's progress on the age 25 projection, the teacher should be able to predict with increasing accuracy how well he or she will be able to read at graduation. If the students are still in the first three stages of the reading program with 3 or 4 years of school remaining, the teacher should probably de-emphasize developmental reading and concentrate on helping them survive in the world without being a good reader.

The functional stage helps the student add sight vocabulary, particularly irregular words not amenable to the phonetic approach. The student should learn to read silently and to read by phrases, rather than by single words. This stage also teaches the use of context clues in developing reading fluency and strongly emphasizes reading comprehension and proactivity. The primary purpose of reading instruction is to enable students to gain information from written sources and to communicate with other people as well as possible. This is why reading comprehension skills are strongly stressed. Also, listening comprehension skills must be taught continuously by reading to the students on a regular basis. Such reading from the content areas of the curriculum permits the teaching of concepts that are too advanced for the students to read for themselves.

Finally, teaching fairy tales and mythical stories to a student with mental retardation is certainly a matter of parent and teacher judgment but is a questionable use of his or her time. First, the key words in such stories are rarely practical or used anywhere other than in that particular story. Also, because a student with mental retardation learns to read when he or she is older than others, such stories are rarely age appropriate.

READING/LISTENING CENTERS

A classroom reading/listening center gives the students access to an ever-expanding variety of recreational and content materials. The center includes books and stories appropriate for the students in the current class. The cost of such a center is not great. All that's needed is a good tape recorder with multiple outlet capabilities, some tapes, and some space. The collection must cover a wide variety of topics and lessons but should not be cluttered by extraneous material. Most of the stories should be short, with only one story on each tape.

ACE stories can be placed in folders or covers with titles and pictures suggesting their content. The major purpose of producing ACE stories is to diagnose and develop a student's listening comprehension, but they also provide high-interest, low-vocabulary reading material with functional objectives. An ACE story is taped either when read to a group of students or at other times by a peer tutor or classroom volunteer. When taping before a group, it is a good idea to use a remote switch on the tape recorder to avoid taping unwanted periods of interruption or discussion. One great advantage of such a center is that a student using earphones can listen to a tape on a subject of individual interest without disturbing other students. The printed version of the book or story should also be available so that the student can follow along while listening to the taped version. Students must be encouraged to learn to read as soon as they are able. A student sometimes establishes an unhealthy dependence on the teacher-read and taped material.

Wherever possible, the students should be encouraged to compose their own stories. Mather and Lachowicz (1992) encouraged two or more students to collaborate on a single story. This procedure may be too difficult for most students with mental retardation, but it is possible with the teacher participating as necessary in composing the stories, filling in the "gaps," and doing most of the writing. Collaborated stories of this nature—even if they are mediocre—can be very popular because they are created or owned by the students. The stories written by older and more capable students may also make good reading material for the center. Individuals or groups of students can even cooperate in composing stories, dictating them to the teacher or other capable person who actually writes the stories as he or she edits the language level, grammar, and sequence. The center might also include picture books for younger children, as well as newspapers and magazines for older students.

SPELLING

Teaching spelling to students with mental retardation can be a particularly frustrating experience. First, it is about the most rote memory-oriented task the students face. They do not have enough time in school to learn to spell all the words others do, and it is difficult to prioritize the words to teach (Jenkinson, 1989). Teaching spelling to students with mental retardation, however, is possible. In fact, a number of signs are encouraging. Adequately written communication does not require as many words as one might expect. Rinsland (1945) discovered that about 25% of all written communication by children is accomplished with only 10 words, 60% with 100 words, and 76% with only a 300-word spelling vocabulary. Also, if a spelling program is prescribed in careful correlation with reading and writing, many students with mental retardation can learn to spell enough words well enough to communicate quite effectively. The best spelling list comes from the sight words used in teaching reading, although it is not necessary for students to be able to spell all of their sight vocabulary words. The students benefit from meaningful repetition by concentrating on the same words in listening, reading, spelling, and writing. Diaz, McLaughlin, and Williams (1990) reported success in teaching spelling by having the students copy the words in sentences. This procedure is particularly beneficial in the unit approach. Childs (1983) used a variety of rehearsal strategies to reinforce words from the spelling lists. The classroom listening/reading center might also include taped and written versions of a student's spelling lists.

Very few innovations or significant developments have occurred in spelling instruction over the last 100 years, except possibly the development of computers and other technological advancements. Most students today, including those with mental retardation, are taught to spell with some variation of this time-worn procedure:

1. Study the word.
2. Say the word.
3. Cover the word.

4. See the word.
5. Spell the word.
6. Check the word.
7. Write the word correctly.

Peer tutors and other volunteers usually work well in teaching spelling (Peach & Moore, 1990). Volunteers and other assistants must be carefully tutored in the procedure the teacher uses so that the students receive a consistent spelling program. Also, a number of computer programs are available to assist in teaching spelling (Harper, Mallette, & Moore, 1991; Stevens, Blackhurst, & Slaton, 1991). Computer software designed for students with mental retardation is not readily available, however, and the spelling words presented in such programs are not usually the ones the teacher would select otherwise.

DIAGNOSIS/PRESCRIPTION IN READING

The major purpose of educational diagnosis or testing is to determine what to teach next. There is little point in measuring skills and concepts not intended to be taught. Standardized reading tests may be used to gain a general idea of the achievement levels of a student with mental retardation. These tests, however, typically have none of these students in their normative samples. Diagnostic tests must be closely related to and used in conjunction with the long-term and annual goals of the student's IEP and the life goal curriculum planned for him or her. Most tests purchased from publishers are unable to evaluate these individual elements. Ordinarily, the student's teacher can provide a better, more practical testing procedure by observing and evaluating the student's progress through the individually designed communication and reading curriculum.

A major problem in using formal tests is that the content is usually designed for much younger students who, at any stage or grade level of reading, will have many more years of school ahead of them than do the students with mental retardation. This problem means that unless the teacher and other IEP team members actually plan to teach primary grade-level reading to teenagers with mental retardation, the tests will not be very helpful in either selecting the materials or establishing the level and rate of instruction. The lower grade levels of these tests do not include the practical concepts needed by students with mental retardation. Standardized tests, however, can remind the teacher of areas of learning he or she may have overlooked. Another advantage of standardized tests is their ready availability: Many school districts routinely administer reading achievement tests of one type or another to all students. Thus, the results of these tests are available, and without administering another test, the teacher can use the results to gain a general picture of each student's reading ability. By comparing the student's answer sheet to the test booklet, the teacher can also identify some of the student's specific reading problems.

Informal Diagnostic Procedures

Ekwall (1970, 1989) recognized three levels of reading achievement that are still recognized today:

1. **Free reading level.** The student can function adequately without teacher help. Comprehension should average 90%; word recognition should average 99%.
2. **Instructional reading level.** The student can function adequately with teacher guidance and yet be challenged to stimulate his or her reading growth. Comprehension should average 75%; word recognition should average 95%.
3. **Frustration level.** The student cannot function adequately. The student often shows signs of tension and discomfort. Vocalization is often present. Comprehension averages 50% or less; word recognition averages 90% or less.

Obviously, the skill levels suggested by Ekwall are somewhat subjective because the teacher must determine what constitutes "average 90%" comprehension by controlling the difficulty of comprehension questions. Likewise, the teacher must determine the level of word recognition skill as he or she selects the difficulty of the reading passages. Using Ekwall's three levels as suggested guidelines, however, the teacher should soon be able generally to recognize these three reading levels, although they will vary from one student to another.

Goal Instruction Analysis (GIA)

The GIA provides a highly specific method of diagnosing the student's reading abilities. GIA reveals not only the student's performance but also the type and extent of instruction and support needed by the student to maintain his or her measured level of difficulty. The analysis then suggests the next reading steps necessary and appropriate for the student and the approximate rate at which these steps should be presented. The analysis uses a sample of the reading material the teacher will use to teach this student once he or she locates the point at which to begin.

After the goal (or partial goal) has been selected, the GIA chart calls for a consideration and listing of the entry-level skills that are prerequisite to that goal. Often, a consideration of the entry level skills suggests that teaching that particular goal must be postponed. Occasionally, the significance of the entry-level skill is not apparent until its qualifying nature is observed in the diagnosis of the goal itself. In some instances, it may be necessary to teach the entry-level skill before continuing with the main goal, or it may be possible to teach it at the same time as the main goal.

One key to successful diagnostic testing is the arrangement of the testing tasks or items in order of increasing difficulty (increasing student performance expectations). The teacher introduces and maintains increasing difficulty by selecting the GIA components and the manner in which they are manipulated. For instructional purposes, the sample GIAs (as those listed below) may use more components than would be used in practice. In practice, one should use only the number and variety of components necessary, being careful not to lose precision by using too few.

Some GIA components of teaching a reading goal might include the following listed down the left side of the GIA chart:

Material
      Large print, then progressively smaller
      Familiar material, then less familiar to reading unfamiliar material
      Easy material, progressively more difficult
      Short, progressively longer stories
      Simple, progressively more complex
      Easy, but progressively more difficult questions
Mastery
      Simple, increasingly obscure, indirect descriptors in story
Rewards
      Fixed, then fixed ratio, then intermittent
      Combinations of M & M, verbal praise, pat on back
Assistance
      Complete instructions, repeated instructions
      Modeling, prompting, hand-on-hand, and tracing (in writing)
Time Considerations
      Constant time delay
      Gradually increase limit of time allotted to task
      Gradually increase time between task completion and evaluation or reward
Memory
      Slight, but gradually increasing demands
Supervision
      Teacher, then aide, then volunteer or peer tutor
      One-on-one (progress later to small group and total class)

Vertical Curriculum Planning

Table 11.1 shows how prescriptions may be developed and how a student may be expected to progress through a series of related prescriptions. The teacher can make entries as they occur, and the entries need not be grammatically parallel. The teacher who sketched out Table 11.1 began by listing some of the communication skills and concepts she planned to teach to two boys in her upper primary class. These two boys were new to her class, but working with them convinced her that they were of approximately equal ability and were the most capable students in the class. Her GIA, however, showed that both boys lacked the necessary entry-level skills for "Identifies three sight words." Therefore, she moved vertically on her curriculum planning chart to "Simple listening comprehension," where she planned to give them more experience with the three words in context. After doing this, she will have them progress vertically down the chart to more difficult skills and concepts—as soon as possible to the identification of sight words. Such vertical planning that includes either the primary or intermediate teachers and levels is called *level-to-level program planning.*

TABLE 11.1   Curriculum Planning Chart (Correlated with Arithmetic and Transitional Skills)

	Communication	Arithmetic	Transition
Preprimary to Primary Level	Prewriting exercises Inclusive statements Listening with slight distracting noise Sings simple songs Names of classmates Identifies common sounds Responds to simple pictures Answers easy questions	Teacher uses numbers in conversations Listens to stories having number concepts (and, both, two, etc.) Identifies numbers in picture	Follows simple instructions Recognizes own belongings Simple room duties Cuts and pastes
Upper Primary to Intermediate Level	Learning to write Knows address and phone Sorts names of classmates Simple listening comprehension Answers simple questions Repeats simple sentences High–low, Tall–short Identifies less familiar objects Uses simple descriptors More complex instructions More difficult stories Identifies common consonant sounds Identifies 3 sight words Classifies simple objects Retells simple story	Concept of today and tomorrow One-to-one correspondence Schedule by the clock Answers easy number questions Matches clock faces Value of coins (P,N,D, & Q) Rote count 1-10 Ordering by size Aware of money value/use Simple symbols of arithmetic Measures inches and feet Uses calendar effectively Concepts of left and right Counts by fives	Attends to tasks Manipulates common tools Sorts simple objects Participates in simple food preparation Good grooming Self-confidence Exercises for stamina Cleans up after self Dangers of drugs Stories about honesty Makes and keeps appointments
Intermediate Level	Addresses adults properly Identifies 12 sight words Learning to write More complex listening comprehension Follows simple written directions Identifies sounds of consonants Spells (writes) consonant sounds More complicated classification Repeats simple sentences Writes simple words Reads simple sentences Uses telephone correctly Recognizes danger and survival words Cursive writing Follows complex directions	Simple addition Counts to 100 Evaluate P, N, and D Tells time by the hour More difficult addition Measures for simple cooking North, south, east, west Writes numbers to 10 Evaluates money to $1.00	More room duties Stories on occupations Helps serve meals Washes dishes Dresses for occasion Public transportation —accompanied Makes simple wood objects Works on cooperative class projects Works in school lunchroom Cleans part of room

Horizontal Curriculum Planning

Table 11.1 also demonstrates horizontal curriculum planning by showing how these communication skills and concepts relate to the areas of arithmetic and transition. The Transition column of Table 11.1 was used to show how prevocational skills and concepts apply to younger as well as older students with mental retardation, but any of the other six curricular headings could have been selected at random to illustrate the same points. Some entries in the Transition column suggested reading and writing activities that were entered in the Communication column. For example, the teachers were aware that, without honesty, their students were unlikely to be employable, so they introduced stories about honesty that were read and discussed as part of their prereading instruction.

SUMMARY

I began this chapter with a review of the nature of reading and a description of some methods developed in the United States to teach reading to children. I covered a number of reading methods the teacher might draw from in developing his or her own reading program. I urged the teacher to use the age 25 projection to determine the extent to which he or she must stress reading to each student.

Also discussed were some specific problems teachers will likely encounter in teaching reading to students with mental retardation and some possible solutions to these problems. The diagnostic/prescriptive approach was recommended in teaching reading to students with mental retardation so that the reading program for them can be as efficient as possible.

I outlined the basic elements of a reading program and then discussed spelling and writing instruction for students with mental retardation and showed how these can be taught simultaneously with reading. Finally, I showed how to use GIA and curriculum planning skills and apply them to the representative areas of reading, writing, spelling, arithmetic, and transitional skills. I also provided a brief example of GIA and curriculum.

Social Skills

CHAPTER 12

Points to Study and Ponder

1. Why is proactivity of particular importance in the social curriculum of students with mental retardation?
2. What is a social disqualifier, and how does or should it influence life goal curriculum planning for students with mental retardation?
3. Can you identify any disqualifiers among self-help skills?
4. Is teaching social awareness a legitimate part of the curriculum for a student with mental retardation?
5. What are some particular problems that students with mental retardation are likely to have in establishing and maintaining personal friendships?
6. Why are social skills particularly important in transition and independent living?

ocial skills, along with transitional and communication skills, are at the heart of programs for individuals with mental retardation. Students must learn to get along with other people and to adjust to a wide variety of social situations. Social inadequacies, referred to by AAMR commissions as "impairments in adaptive behavior," can seriously limit an individual's opportunities in work situations, living arrangements, and leisure activities (Parent, Kregel, Metzler, & Twardzik, 1992). Traditionally, mental retardation has been defined largely in sociological terms (Grossman, 1977, 1983; Heber, 1961; Kanner, 1948; Luckasson et al., 1992). Because the term *adaptive behavior* is somewhat unclear and subject to practical criticism (Clausen, 1972; Westling, 1986), it is important to identify some specific social characteristics of individuals with mental retardation before designing specific instruction and activities.

In this chapter, I discuss some social concepts and skills most vital to a student's success in transition, employment, and independent living. Although social skills are interrelated and interactive, as well as closely related to most skills addressed throughout this book, they are grouped and classified so that they can be discussed. These skills are considered in relation to forming the student's annual and long-term curriculum goals. In addition, I demonstrate how to diagnose the student's abilities, readiness, and current performance levels and explain how to formulate specific prescriptions for teaching representative concepts and skills.

SOCIAL AND BEHAVIORAL CHARACTERISTICS

Children with mental retardation are likely to persist with childhood behaviors longer than other children. For example, they are likely to snatch the possessions of others at ages when most children realize this is not appropriate. As teenagers, they may play with children far younger than themselves; they tend to prefer childish games. Because of this slow development, other children may easily lose patience with children with mental retardation and often resort to taunting and ridicule.

The slow rate of social development of individuals with mental retardation sets them apart from other individuals with and without disabilities. McKinney and Forman (1982) indicated that classroom social problems of students with mental retardation tend to be more pronounced and observable than those of students with learning and emotional disabilities. Kidd (1979) and Zetlin and Murtaugh (1988) reported that students with mental retardation have difficulty making friends, making decisions, and otherwise coping with their environments. Kopp et al. (1992) found that preschool students with mental retardation showed significant deficiencies in social development.

Blacher (1982) found that the social-cognitive skill levels of students both with and without mental retardation are closely related to social age; because the social age of students with retardation is so far behind that of their age-peers, parents and teachers often have difficulty selecting learning activities and materials for them. Activities should be age appropriate even though a student may prefer activities that are more appropriate for younger students. Even students whose mental retardation is severe/profound go through individual, parallel, and group play sequences, and these phases must be considered as each student's educational program is designed.

CURRICULUM CONSIDERATIONS

Despite the number and severity of social problems characteristic of students with mental retardation, these students do master social skills in varying degrees if they are provided with well-planned programs suitable to their needs.

Selecting Appropriate Goals and Behaviors

The processes involved with diagnosing, prescribing, and teaching social skills are different from teaching skills in other areas in that social skills are involved with all aspects and phases of a person's life. High priority social skills need to be selected early in a student's life goal curriculum and then developed and stressed throughout the school experience. For example, Castles and Glass (1986) reported success using role playing to develop interpersonal problem-solving strategies in adults whose mental retardation was mild to moderate. They found the individuals' success was directly related to the severity of the retardation. Problem solving and other skills are developed continuously, so the IEP team does not need to evaluate frequently how much a student will be able to profit from an annual or long-term goal that has been only partially mastered.

Students' individual social interests and abilities need to be evaluated, and selected skills should be taught in social settings as similar as possible to the settings where interactions are likely to occur. To accomplish this, each student's teacher and IEP team should work closely with the parents, with group home parents, and with other postschool care providers to determine the skills that will be necessary for optimum independent living. Prospective employers, businesspeople, and other member of the community who will affect the eventual life of the individual may also be involved.

Stressing Proactivity

A major life goal for every individual with mental retardation is to be able to speak, act, and interact like others in society. A person with mental retardation should be "socially invisible"—he or she should not stand out in a crowd as being different from everyone else. To be able to do this, the student needs to learn when and how to say things that are appropriate. To become independent and proactive, the student must learn to recognize when a social decision is needed, to identify the choices available, to make the correct choice or reaction, and to cope with the result of the decision.

This ability to respond appropriately in social interactions is consistently ranked among the most crucial needs by parents and significant others in the lives of students with mental retardation. Variation in ranking of skills seems to be ability related, with parents of students with moderate disabilities rating functional life skills more highly, but parents of students with severe/profound disabilities favoring friendship and social relationship competencies (Brotherson et al., 1988; Hamre-Nietupski, Nietupski, & Strathe, 1992). Davies and Rogers (1985) reported that poor social development seems to be the greatest impairment to successful integration of adults with mental retardation who had formerly been hospitalized.

The area of social skills is one in which parents, teachers, friends, and caretakers usually find it most difficult to withdraw their direct support, supervision, and control. When a student has insufficient skills and may have to endure the consequences of a wrong choice, it is difficult to avoid intervening to protect the individual. Everyone needs to experience occasionally a poor performance, an awkward move, or a social mistake to learn how such problems occur and how to avoid them.

Most tasks involved in learning social concepts and skills should be treated as procedural-sequential tasks. They must be performed basically in their entirety from the outset, with control, advice, and supervision gradually reduced until the learner can function independently. The IEP team must emphasize proactivity throughout the social skills curriculum if maximum capability and independence are to be achieved.

Anticipating Vocational Pursuits

Lovett and Harris (1987b), who interviewed 48 older people with mild to moderate mental retardation, found that these individuals assigned highest priority to a combination of social and vocational skills. These areas overlap and reinforce each other, as found by Lignugaris/Kraft (1988), who observed that employees with mental retardation had fewer social interactions in their job settings than workers without mental retardation.

Anticipating Serious Social Problems

Such problems as dishonesty, cheating, lying, stealing (R. Williams, 1985), temper tantrums, and other serious behavioral problems (Everington & Luckasson, 1989) can disqualify a person with mental retardation from employment and independent living arrangements that might otherwise be available. These **disqualifiers** must be extinguished because even an occasional relapse may terminate an otherwise successful placement. Even a "simple" matter, such as tattling, which is common among students with mental retardation, can have adverse consequences. In designing a student's program, high priority must be given to avoiding and correcting these serious breakdowns in social function. Each student's situation must be diagnosed individually: The significance of each social deficit should be assessed, and the student's individualized program should be designed to correct the deficits that are likely to cause the greatest long-term difficulty.

Some inappropriate social behaviors may "disqualify" an otherwise capable individual from success in the workplace or other social situation and should be assigned high priority in curriculum planning.

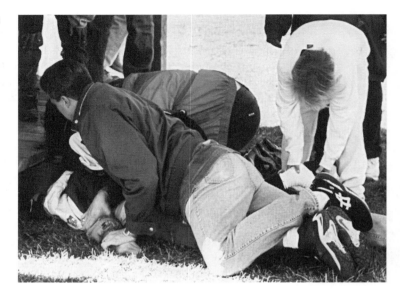

Involving Parents

From birth to age 18, children with mental retardation typically spend about 10 times as many hours under the supervision of parents and other members of their immediate family as they do in school or in school-sponsored activities. Thus, time devoted to supporting, assisting, and counseling with parents is generally time well spent. Many social skills the students must master can be taught most effectively in the home; parents become teachers and partners with teachers in providing instruction, practice, and monitoring of learning and change. Some skills are almost impossible to teach without the full cooperation of the family. Also, schoolteachers need to remember that the social concepts and behavior they teach the students will result in behavioral patterns the parents will have to deal with long after the school's responsibilities cease. Because the parents' responsibility for a student extends beyond the school's, the parents should be continually involved in the structuring, assessing, evaluating, and readjusting process.

School-based members of the IEP team should not underestimate the importance of home participation and family support, nor should they take it for granted. Teachers should encourage families to involve their children with mental retardation in all family activities, emphasizing family outings, vacations, holidays, and special occasions. Family members should be encouraged to communicate with their child in a variety of circumstances. For example, while riding in the family car, parents and siblings can help the child describe animals, scenery, crops, factories, businesses, or recreational facilities, noting such aspects as number, color, size, use, personal involvement, or future use. On family vacations or activities, parents can take photographs and make videotapes that can be reviewed later as the family discusses the sights and events that comprise their experience. Browning and Nave (1993) reported considerable success in using a prerecorded, interactive video program to teach social problem solving to students with mental retardation.

Aspects of daily living are more simply and naturally taught in the home setting. Family members should lovingly but persistently teach the child with mental retardation to dress and care for him- or herself as much as possible. Teachers and other members of the school staff can help the child's parents and siblings design and implement procedures that will be effective in helping the child. They can also help family members locate and obtain teaching materials appropriate to the child and the task. In addition, teachers can volunteer guidance and assistance for parents in providing good models of appropriate social behavior in the home.

Parents often fail to realize that these children need to be exposed to more, not fewer, social situations than other children if they are to be prepared for maximum independence later in life. Because it takes them longer to learn, they need additional opportunities to practice their developing skills. Members of the IEP team can help parents find a balance between their fear of exposing the child prematurely to encounters that may be threatening and the necessity of allowing adequate encounters for the child to learn appropriate patterns of behavior and response. Perske (1972) and Schloss et al. (1994) referred to this hesitance to participate in unfamiliar social situations as *dignity of risk.* Difficult as it may be for the parents, a child with mental retardation needs to be allowed to experience failure, even occasional taunting or ridicule, so that he or she will learn how to deal with it. Family members can gain important insights into a child's social needs and abilities by helping with class parties and field trips and by participating with the child in visits to stores, shops, and offices.

SELF-HELP SKILLS

Sometimes special educators have difficulty finding the point at which they should insist on the mature comportment that eventually will be prerequisite to a child's transitional and independent living skills. As special educators, they learn to tolerate aberrant behaviors as part of a disabling condition. Also, the stages of social development for the child with mental retardation roughly parallel those of a younger child, and it is sometimes easy to overlook the fact that a child who may be functioning socially like a very young child is actually nearing adulthood—a stage at which more advanced social functioning will be required. Students whose mental retardation is severe or profound typically need more intensified instruction than those who have a milder disability (Cheseldine & Jeffree, 1982).

It is important that the self-help skills basic to good grooming, meeting other people, and holding a job be given careful consideration as the curriculum is planned for students for whom independent living is a realistic goal (Reese & Snell, 1991). Even a slight developmental failure in such areas as eating, brushing teeth, bathing, washing, toileting, and dressing may disqualify a student from independent living opportunities, even if seemingly more advanced skills have been attained. For example, an individual's more visible social skills may be quite well developed, but a more basic deficiency, such as bad breath or body odor, can prevent the person from making friends and establishing other social relationships. Thus, diagnosis and prescription for instruction in a wide variety of social skills should be continued throughout the student's educational experience. Also, Dalrymple and Angrist (1988) pointed out that self-help skills should be taught in the most natural setting wherever possible.

Eating

All children need instruction in table manners and etiquette, but children with more severe forms of mental retardation may require basic instruction in merely feeding themselves independently (Sisson & Dixon, 1986; Stainback & Healy, 1982; Wolff, 1994). Those whose mental retardation is milder may be clearly able to feed themselves. This instruction in publicly acceptable eating practices can be given in a number of ways. Van Den Pol et al. (1981) successfully used classroom-based instruction to teach 3 male students (17 to 22 years old) how to order a meal, pay, eat, and leave the facility. The lunchroom at school can be used as an environment for teaching independent eating skills. With a little planning and creativity, the eating experience at school can be varied to simulate conditions found in the home, restaurants, cafeterias, and other places that the student might typically visit. The involvement of parents and family is particularly important (Dunklee, 1989). Although it may be difficult for the family when the child with mental retardation embarrasses other family members while eating in public places, the child needs more experience eating in public places, not less.

Dressing

Dressing oneself is another high priority self-help skill. Dressing is substantially more difficult than undressing. Although two of three adults with profound mental retardation studied by Diorio and Konarski (1984) were able to attain criterion for independent undressing, none reached criterion on dressing, even after more than 100 hours of training. Using oversized clothing, fading of guidance, and individualized reinforcement, however, Reese and Snell (1991) reported some success in teaching 3 children with severe disabilities to don and remove coats and jackets.

In addition to encouraging parents to train their children in selecting appropriate clothing and in dressing themselves, teachers should include specific instruction as part of the school curriculum. When students are preparing for physical activities, work experience, class recess, or other school activities, teachers can incorporate discussion of selecting clothing appropriate to weather conditions or to a specific activity. "Dress up" play for younger children provides a valuable opportunity to teach dressing skills. Rather than limit the activity to outlandish costumes, teachers should provide real-life clothing and teach the children such concepts as inside-outside and left-right, as well as skills such as manipulating buttons, snaps, and zippers (Bettison, 1986; Dixon & Saudargas, 1980; Honig, 1993).

MORE ADVANCED SOCIALIZATION SKILLS

For more capable students, attainable economic, vocational, and independent living success will involve social prerequisites beyond basic function. In planning individualized programs for such students, more advanced capabilities will need to be considered.

Developing Personality

Developing individual personality, along with a sense of identity, self-determination, and self-worth, is always important for students who are targeted for independent living (Wehmeyer & Mezler, 1995). Levy-Shiff, Kedem, and Sevillia (1990) found that adolescents with mental retardation have great difficulty developing a self-identity. They demonstrate both a unique personality profile and slower development than students of similar age who do not have mental retardation. Students with mental retardation also have more difficulty establishing a sense of physical self-image and in controlling their acts and behaviors. Widaman, Macmillan, Hemsley, and Balow (1992) proposed that helping students with mental retardation develop self-concept should be an important part of the curriculum. They also pointed out that the self-concepts of these students may vary greatly with gender and ethnicity.

Just the efforts of the IEP team and the student's own family can go a long way in helping the student develop a sense of him- or herself as a valued individual with physical and behavioral capabilities. As Levy-Shiff et al. (1990) pointed out, students with mental retardation often become jealous of family members who perform at higher levels than they do, particularly when younger siblings are involved. These problems have no single solution, and no activities or procedures will be effective with all families. Professionals from the school, however, can help the student's parents find ways of recognizing the achievements of each family member without drawing undue attention to the weaknesses of others.

Many activities can be adapted at both home and school. Young children and children with severe/profound mental retardation can gain a more accurate sense of self-image through the use of pictures. Group pictures of a child's family and school class can help the child identify him- or herself as an individual within a group. Individual pictures can be used to emphasize the uniqueness of the person and encourage the child to develop individual personality traits. Pictures can be used to represent ownership until the child becomes aware of his or her written name.

Parents can be encouraged to help their child develop a sense of self by allowing the child to have his or her own possessions: toys, books, his or her own room. Other family members should show respect for the child's ownership and control. The child can learn responsibility by caring for his or her own belongings; later, sharing these things can be an important step in developing social interactions. As well as possessions, the child with mental retardation should be given chores, along with all other members of the family. Occasionally, more complicated responsibilities should be assigned to teams of family members so that the child with mental retardation can share in the sense of accomplishment and the rewards of group contributions.

Introducing Moral Concepts

As part of the development of personality and self-image, children with mental retardation, like all children, must learn the difference between right and wrong. Right and wrong are abstract concepts with complex and sensitive implications. Unfortunately, not everyone defines right and wrong in the same way; and not everyone agrees on the extent to which a given social action might be "right" or "wrong" (Israely, 1985).

It is particularly important that parents be consulted when moral values are to be involved with teaching at a school. If students are taught moral values or procedures that do not agree with the parents' views, the parents will have to either live with or correct these values long after the school personnel are no longer involved in the student's life. IEP team members and parents should come to an agreement on high priority right-wrong concepts. Generally, an understanding of stealing and other acts of dishonesty incorporated into the law should be given highest priority if the student is expected to be a candidate for independent living or future employment. Next highest priority is usually given to actions and behaviors that parents and other team members agree are not socially acceptable, although they might not actually be illegal. Because these prioritized moral concepts add substantially to an already extensive school curriculum, parents should be encouraged to select concepts they will be responsible for teaching and monitoring themselves.

Promoting Social Awareness

Infants and young children generally remain close to home, where their social interactions are largely with their parents and siblings. As the children become older, their social life slowly expands to include the neighborhood, where they begin to make acquaintances and form friendships outside the immediate family circle. Thus, their social experience can be viewed in terms of a gradually expanding community, continually increasing in complexity as a greater number and variety of people become part of their lives.

Ordinarily, the school is the first place where any child must associate with large numbers of people outside of family and friends of his or her own choice. To promote awareness of classmates as other people, the teacher should help a child learn the names of classmates; snapshots or other pictures can be used to facilitate learning of names, as well as awareness of individuals and groups. Games that require students to identify their classmates by name are also effective. All children should learn to use appropriate words and behavior when introduced to others and to make introductions naturally, without stiffness or affectation.

Initial teaching of how to introduce and interact with others will concentrate on the student him- or herself and focus on making polite comments and performing acceptable behavior. A student who runs away from situations, hits others, or otherwise ignores what is considered decent behavior is not likely to be successful in independent living, employment, or other experiences involving social interaction (Mithaug, 1993). As soon as the student has gained confidence in knowing what to say and do, parents and teachers should shift emphasis to the student's awareness of other people and consideration of how his or her actions are likely to affect these people. Generally, obedience will precede self-control. The teacher or parent will need to assess a situation and guide the student in responding to it. Punishment for incorrect response should be avoided; as Marshall (1984) declared, punishment is completely incompatible with students learning to control their own behavior. As soon as possible, external control of behavior must shift to internal because the student will need to learn to make his or her own decisions in order to function well in society.

According to the concept of proactivity, the student with mental retardation should learn to recognize a social situation where a decision must be made, consider the alternatives, make an appropriate decision, and finally act on the decision—with as little supervision from others as possible. Ideally, the student will eventually learn to operate without any stated rules. Parents and teachers must work carefully and deliberately with the student to develop this capability without chaos. They must work from the premise that the student's behavior is considered acceptable until it has negative effects on someone else or results in poor-quality work. The following steps are suggested:

1. The student must abide by the rules set by the teacher or parent, who determines the consequences of any violation.
2. The student helps formulate the rules and the resulting consequences.
3. The student helps decide which rules he or she no longer needs.

Some students will require intermediate steps, but most students will be able to progress to the no-rules stage.

When a student encounters a problem or violates a former rule (or logically correct response), the teacher should provide a counseling session or role-play experience to explore ways to resolve the problem and prevent it from occurring again. Counseling with each other can help students become more aware of how their actions can affect other people. Similarly, group sessions in which students discuss social situations allow them to discuss their reactions openly and help them realize that everyone has similar problems. To allow students to hone and practice their skills, teachers and parents should plan experiences that simulate real-life social situations in surroundings similar to those in which the situations most likely occur.

ENCOUNTERS WITH SIGNIFICANT OTHERS

Typically, a person with mental retardation must learn to associate successfully with four general classes of persons, all of whom must be treated with respect: (a) employers, coworkers, and IEP team participants; (b) service providers, government officials, and businesspeople; (c) friends, roommates, and casual contacts; and (d) boy-girl and dating relationships. It is difficult to prioritize the groups to suggest a sequence for teaching.

Employers, Coworkers, and IEP Team Participants

Collectively and individually, employers, coworkers, and IEP team participants make significant decisions that will have far-reaching effects on the lives of individuals with mental retardation. Some may have chosen to work with or affect the lives of persons with mental retardation; many have no choice but must do so as part of their assigned duties. If one of these people is not pleased with a student's performance, that individual may be in a position to discharge the student, refuse a request, or deny the student admittance to an important or desired program. Butterworth and Strauch (1994) emphasized the close relationship between social competence and job success. They suggested task-related instruction designed to develop a strong relationship among the worker, the coworkers, and the employer.

Unfortunately, few of these people are likely to have had much experience with or training in the characteristics and needs of people with mental retardation, but they are more likely to have this training than those of the other classes. Fellow employees can represent equivocal challenges: They can be valuable sources of help and advice, or they can become informal supervisors—official or self-appointed. The worker needs to learn how to discern and evaluate the intentions of coworkers and associates. Therefore, students with mental retardation need specific training in recognizing the people who have influence over their lives and in treating them with appropriate consideration and respect. To prepare them to do this, either regular or special class teachers might invite representatives from this group, as well as officers of clubs and social and recreational organizations, to visit their classes and to explain to the students their positions and the services with which they are involved. Field trips to the police station, the fire station, city hall, and various businesses the students may encounter or in which the students might someday be employed can be extremely valuable experiences in preparing the students to interact with these people.

Service Providers, Government Officials, and Businesspeople

Although service providers, government officials, and businesspeople may or may not make decisions that seriously affect the lives of those with mental retardation, these people are usually more than just casual acquaintances. People who may exercise this kind of influence over a student's opportunities include police officers, fire fighters, and school administrators, along with other city, state, and government officials. Sadly, the most binding and consequential decisions may be made by those with the least knowledge and expertise—judges, attorneys, physicians, and administrators.

Business and professional people comprise a large group, most of whom offer a wide array of goods or services for a fee. The exchange of money for commodities purchased or services desired can present challenges for any individual. Often, purchases must be made in a hurried or crowded situation in which others may be waiting in line. The student with mental retardation must either learn to count out the desired money accurately and check his or her change or else arrange for assistance from a trusted companion. The student should not make payment with large bills in situations where exploitation is possible.

People with mental retardation experience a number of fears when dealing with professional people such as physicians, dentists, attorneys, and others who charge varying fees for their services. One valid fear is that the person with mental retardation will be charged thousands of dollars for the slightest service. Another fear is that the professional will be cold or difficult to approach. And the person is subject to the same fears of pain that many others experience when anticipating medical or dental procedures.

Friends, Roommates, and Casual Contacts

Making and preserving friendships is not easy for students with mental retardation. Zetlin and Murtaugh (1988) reported students with mild mental retardation have significantly fewer friendships than their peers without retardation. They further noted that the friendships of students with mental retardation tend to be less stable and of shorter duration than the friendships of their nondisabled peers. Because the school years are a valuable time for students to learn how to make and keep friends, school facilities should be used freely by teachers and parents to create opportunities for friendships to form. As with the development of other sociological skills, it is often necessary to take direct action in helping students with mental retardation establish friendships. Stainback and Stainback (1987) used a coaching procedure to facilitate the acquisition and maintenance of friendship skills.

Students with mental retardation need to be taught specific skills for meeting people and forming friendships. For example, they must be shown how to greet other people appropriately, particularly when it comes to shaking hands. Most people who are not disabled do not shake hands every time they meet someone, but individuals with mental retardation often consider shaking hands to be a requirement for every encounter. A safe approach is to teach the students to shake hands only if the other person offers his or her hand first. The students must also learn to address others respectfully and at an acceptable distance.

Placing students in proximity may not be sufficient. Students with mental retardation experience great difficulty making friends in either segregated or integrated classroom situations (Gottlib et al., 1975; Krauss, Seltzer, & Goodman, 1992). These findings are substantiated by Luftig (1988), who noted that even partially integrated students with mental retardation experience greater isolation and loneliness than their peers without retardation. He concluded that integration programs alone do not eliminate the social isolation that mental retardation provokes. Barber and Hupp (1993) found that adults with developmental disabilities who lived in small group homes had numbers of close relationships similar to those of adults in a nondisabled comparison group.

Taunting and teasing are persistent problems. Students with mental retardation must learn to discern the difference between friendly kidding and negative taunting, between a genuine offer of assistance or friendship and malicious baiting or teasing. They may have difficulty distinguishing between an honest mistake and a deliberate imposition; similarly, they may easily trust what appears to be a friendly gesture and not anticipate the possibility of abuse. To avoid embarrassing themselves and causing awkward situations, they also must learn to understand the difference between an offer of genuine friendship by peer tutors, classmates, volunteers, or others and the type of general kindness that offers service and consideration without inviting intimacy. The lack of social sensitivity and discernment may have one advantage: The students themselves do not feel social isolation as keenly as students without disabilities generally do. Rosen and Burchard (1990) found that adults with mental retardation whose social integration was ranked as very limited by nondisabled standards indicated they did not perceive themselves as socially isolated.

Individuals with mental retardation can easily exploit friendships and acquaintanceships unless they receive instruction in areas of consideration. Most teenagers without disabilities naturally sense when and how often it is appropriate to call their friends. But young people with mental retardation often irritate their friends and acquaintances by contacting them too often or at inconsiderate hours. Another impropriety is to ask casual acquaintances for their friendship. If they ask the wrong people to be their special friends, exploitation can easily occur.

The closest and stablest friendships for students with mental retardation are usually those with members of their families, including close relatives who may be living in the area. The makeup of such groups as school classes and recreational interest groups changes frequently, particularly during the secondary years; however, the relationship of the extended family generally changes little over time. Family members can also be important in obtaining eventual employment for the student with mental retardation. Hasazi et al. (1985) found that the majority of jobs held by 243 post-high school students with mental retardation were obtained through family members, as well as through friends. IEP teams must assess local conditions in selecting classes or combinations of classes that are most likely to be effective for the individual.

Boy-Girl and Dating Relationships

Dating and other kinds of relationships with those of the opposite sex require special consideration. The extent to which a student with mental retardation will be aware of or interested in the opposite sex is difficult to predict. For example, Williams and Asher (1992) indicated that students with mental retardation seem to understand the concept of loneliness and that the boys in their study reported more loneliness than peers with no mental retardation, whereas the girls did not. Obviously, the probability of dating (and marriage) is crucial; the possibility or likelihood suggests the need for substantial preparations, time, and resources. The mental retardation of some individuals is so severe that there really is no possibility of eventual marriage. Koller, Richardson, and Katz (1988) reported that none of the people they studied who had IQs less than 50 ever married. For those whose retardation is milder, however, marriage may be a possibility.

If a student's mental retardation is mild, it is important for parents, teachers, and other members of the IEP team who are forming the age 25 projection to consider the likelihood that the student will eventually marry and have a family and to adjust the student's life goals accordingly. The relative success of marriages by persons with mental retardation appears to be highly individualized. Koller et al. (1988) reported that marriages between individuals with mental retardation experience considerably more difficulties than marriages involving those who have no disabilities. Some investigators, however, report considerable success in marriages involving persons with mental retardation and defend their right to get married (Brantlinger, 1988; Maherali, 1989). In any event, the potential marriage in this population presents significant challenges to the members of IEP teams. The question of marriage is a good example of the need for continuing evaluation and periodic curriculum adjustments by the IEP team. If the age 25 projections suggest that the student is likely to eventually marry, extensive preparation and training in the skills and capabilities necessary for a marriage relationship must be a part of the student's educational program. Early in a student's life, an age 25 projection offers little evidence of the possibility of marriage, but over time such a likelihood becomes increasingly clear.

SOCIAL SENSITIVITIES AND PERCEPTIONS

Students with mental retardation need to develop social sensitivities that normally evolve naturally in the give-and-take of daily interaction. Teachers and parents need to be aware of differences in these students' perceptions and natural reactions to social situations so that teaching and experiences can be designed to compensate for some of the misperceptions and disabilities.

Developing Awareness of Others' Needs and Feelings

Students with mental retardation generally lack the ability to perceive a social situation from another person's point of view (Moffatt, Hanley-Maxwell, & Donnellan, 1995). Bradley and Meredith (1991) reported that students whose mental retardation they described as "educable" had particular difficulty in assuming the perspective of others and in understanding the meaning of friendship. They found the "perspective-taking" abilities of the students closely related to CA, seemingly because of a developmental lag, rather than a deficit. They suggested carefully planned assistance to help the students with their friendship problems. One way to encourage all people—including those who have disabilities—is to help them find ways to serve others. Many schools employ former students with mental retardation as classroom assistants. In an innovative activity, Everington and Stevenson (1994) successfully taught these students community living skills by engaging them in a shopping service for elderly people.

One reason why students with mental retardation do not develop the ability to take another person's perspective may be their inability to recognize the emotions that others exhibit. In separate studies, Hobson et al. (1989) and Xeromeritou (1992) found that students with mental retardation are less able than their MA peers to match pictures portraying various emotions with emotionally expressive voices. In a related study, Wilczenski (1991) reported that students with mental retardation are generally able to pose happiness and sadness but have great difficulty with other, more complicated emotions. Simply being in the company of other people does not automatically make students with mental retardation more aware of how their words and actions affect others, as would be the case with nondisabled students of comparable age. Further, these studies suggest that students with mental retardation may have to be carefully and deliberately taught how to role-play and visualize the perceptions of other people.

Students with mental retardation have difficulty perceiving and evaluating the attitudes of others. They tend not to understand how their actions affect their friends, family members, and even their employers. Blacher-Dixon and Simenosson (1981) discovered that individuals with mental retardation not only did poorly on perspective-taking (role-playing) tasks but also did not improve in a follow-up study a year later. Similarly, Park and Gaylord-Ross (1989) found the role-playing element of a social skills training program for teenagers with mental retardation largely ineffective. The purpose of the program was to train these youths for employment. Thus, role playing to develop social skills should be conducted and evaluated carefully.

Short et al. (1993) reported that students with mental retardation have greater difficulty perceiving humor. Thus, they must be taught to discern differences between friendly jokes and pranks and demeaning or potentially dangerous situations. The students need carefully planned instruction in using and interpreting body language, nuances, euphemisms, and subtleties of language to interpret the moods and emotions of others.

Although their perceptions of their own behavior and that of others may be different from those of most members of society, individuals with mental retardation must still learn to follow the "rules" of society. Such social negatives and disqualifiers as hitting, swearing, stealing, and behavioral outbursts must be eliminated. Then, practices such as taking turns and following acceptable social rules must be taught. Duncan and Canty-Lemke (1986) advised that adults respond to social and other errors made by people with mental retardation in the same way they would respond to the same behavior by any other member of society. Most people will not be as likely to make allowances for aberrant behavior as those who work with the person in school.

Overcoming Learned Helplessness

Students with mental retardation cannot ordinarily be held to the same standards of performance as their peers. For example, it may take intensive and extensive training to help these student overcome one or more of the disqualifiers discussed here—or learned helplessness, discussed in Chapters 2 and 9. Maier and Seligman (1976) described learned helplessness as a condition (or set of conditions) in which the individual consciously or subconsciously believes that outcomes or consequences are not affected or controlled by his or her actions. Further, learned helplessness seems to be much more common among students with mental retardation, compared with those with no disabilities (DeVellis & McCauley, 1979) and even compared with individuals with disabilities other than mental retardation (Williams & Barber, 1992). If not overcome early in life, learned helplessness can be fairly well set or intense by adolescence and can be a substantial impairment to establishing lasting friendships, as well as in employment and other social situations. On a positive note, Mulhauser (1993) found that well-planned programs can be effective in overcoming the effects of this phenomenon.

To apply and practice the social behavior they are learning, students with mental retardation must be encouraged to participate in parties, socials, and other recreational activities. Although most students with mental retardation are hesitant to participate in clubs or other social units, they should be given opportunities to attend athletic events, plays, dances, and various other activities generally planned primarily by the students, with teachers acting as advisors and chaperons. Although students with mental retardation may not choose to be involved in planning schoolwide activities, they should be urged to attend. They may feel freer to participate in planning their own social activities, but they will require a good deal of special instruction and assistance.

Preparing to Make Independent Decisions

Although decision making is discussed in detail in Chapter 8, it is considered here as well because most decisions involve social components and contexts. The ability to make decisions is dependent on self-control, which in turn is founded on obedience to the rules and laws of society. Obedience as a goal for students with mental retardation does not refer to fear of authority, but rather focuses on voluntary conformity with the common rules of society and respect for the rights of other people. Such conformity requires that the student learn the rules and expectations of society and exercise constraint in complying with them. Extensive training and experience may be necessary.

Because of the heterogeneity of mental retardation and the variation in individual conceptual distance, skills involved with decision making must be diagnosed and treated on an individual and ongoing basis. At no specific age level are all students able to make their own decisions and to manage their own affairs. The need for external motivation also varies with the individual. Parents, teachers, and other members of the IEP team must not assume that every student with mental retardation requires constant prodding and encouragement.

As students approach the age when they must be directly prepared for independent living, the IEP team must work with the parents in establishing the needed disciplinary boundaries and then in working out a plan to phase out external supports as soon as practical so that the students will not be dependent on others to an unhealthy degree. They must be careful that "obedience" is not stressed to the point that personal initiative and positive assertiveness are stifled beneath it.

Personal decision making is vital if a student is to eventually live as a member of a community. Davies and Rogers (1985) noted that many persons with mental retardation do not receive the training and experience necessary to make decisions that will be a part of their community life. Even personal decisions such as what to eat or wear, how to spend free time, and with whom to live are made less frequently by individuals with mental retardation living in group homes than by other adults who are part of a social community (Kishi et al., 1988).

Attitudes have varied toward the extent to which decision making can be expected in those with mental retardation. Whitman (1990) defined mental retardation as essentially a disorder in self-regulation that can be improved considerably through behavioral techniques. In contrast, Baer (1990) argued that Whitman overemphasized the self-regulatory deficits. But regardless of the extent of or emphasis on the inability to self-regulate, every person can be trained to make some personal choices and should be encouraged to state preferences and to make decisions whenever possible. Realon, Favell, and Lowerre (1990) demonstrated that even individuals whose disabilities are profound and multiple can make their own choices of leisure materials, and they interact more frequently when they are permitted to do so.

Using Assertiveness Appropriately

People with mental retardation typically do not stand up for themselves. They tend to let others speak in their behalf (Sigelman et al., 1981), but they can be taught to voice preferences on vocational and personal alternatives (Dudley, 1987; Lovett & Harris, 1987b). To make decisions and to achieve a successful transition from school to adult life, individuals with mental retardation must gain a degree of assertiveness, a need that is often overlooked (Fleming & Fleming, 1982). They must learn to say no politely—not only to drug dealers and potential abusers but also to door-to-door salespersons and telemarketers.

A student who is maturing must be given increasing opportunities to assert his or her own position and to take responsibility for the outcome. The student must learn to distinguish between the legitimate expectations of authority figures, such as peace officers, school officials, and employers, and the requests and demands of people who would take advantage of him or her. The DPE procedures of this and other chapters show how this kind of awareness can be developed.

Encouraging Religious Affiliation

Religious organizations and affiliations can be significant in helping the individual with mental retardation establish lasting friendships and develop acceptable social skills. The nature and extent of the contributions vary. Heifetz and Franklin (1982) reported that the 40 clergymen they surveyed were providing a wide range of support services to persons with mental retardation and their families. Riordan and Vasa (1991), however, surveyed 125 clergymen from a variety of religious denominations and found that most of them were aware of very few persons with disabilities in their congregations. The lack of awareness would seem to indicate that these religious leaders were providing little in the way of service or support to followers with disabilities. It appears that religious groups and agencies are generally overlooked as potential care providers and support bases for those with mental retardation—at least in many communities. Bersani and Heifetz (1985) reported that job satisfaction among direct-care workers in private community residences for adults with mental retardation is equal—if not superior—to that of workers in state-operated facilities.

Because of the nature of many religious beliefs, individuals and groups with strong religious convictions tend to be empathic and supportive, and religious groups generally sponsor wholesome activities. Weisner, Beizer, and Stolze (1991) reported that parents who classify themselves as "religious" seem to stress parental nurturance and show greater acceptance of their child's disability. To strengthen their own acceptance and to find opportunities to associate with supportive others, parents who have existing religious convictions are urged to maintain strong ties with the church, temple, or other institution of their choice.

In addition to providing personal support, churches typically offer spiritual and social activities in which a student with mental retardation can participate. With the encouragement of empathic spiritual leaders, the student's age-mates should be more understanding and accepting of disabling conditions than young people in the community at large. Thus, the student has increased opportunities to make friends and to learn to interact with a variety of people of differing ages and interests. Many churches co-sponsor such activities as Campfire Girls and Boys and Boy Scouts and Girl Scouts, all of which offer valuable opportunities for involvement and socialization for students with mental retardation. Another advantage is that religious organizations and groups are likely to continue both activities and personal support after educational services are completed.

Along with the indirect aid that comes from strengthening parents' personal convictions and facilitating the child's participation in social and service opportunities, churches and other religious organizations sometimes provide direct aid to children with disabilities and their families. Religious leaders are often in a position to find volunteers to provide care and services for persons with mental retardation and to help their family members cope with some of the problems caused by the disability. As the child becomes older, religious organizations, like many other service and social groups, can be instrumental in making initial contacts that result in successful employment. Many individuals with mental retardation find jobs through agencies and means that directly relate to traditional employment or special education (Clark & Kolstoe, 1990).

PROMOTING TRANSITIONAL SKILLS

A student with mental retardation who passes through the transition from school to employment is involved in three stages, all of which involve a variety of socialization skills. These experiences must be anticipated and provided for as instruction and support for the student are being planned. When these stages are used as GIA components, the student's employment preparation program can be designed in as much detail as the student's needs and characteristics require.

The first stage involves the student's status as a candidate for full-time employment. The student's status progresses in the following pattern: observer/trainee → helper → performer → leader. The student is in the *observer/trainee* period until he or she is sufficiently competent and mature to participate in an on-campus work experience program. During this time, the student participates in classroom and community experiences designed to teach the communication skills, social competencies, and other abilities that are prerequisite to entering the work experience program. During the period the student is considered a *helper,* he or she is assigned home and classroom chores and is involved in other activities that give experience in assuming responsibility, following instructions, and adapting to a variety of social and work situations. During the helper stage, the student works primarily under the constant supervision of a responsible adult. The student is given increasing responsibilities and is held increasingly accountable for completion of assigned tasks. In this manner, the student eventually reaches the *performer* stage, during which he or she is able to achieve and work with increasing independence. Becoming a *leader* involves a degree of supervisory responsibility over other workers. Although most students with mental retardation may be unlikely to assume positions of real leadership, they can be placed in charge of one or more workers of similar experience and capability. At every achievement level, the IEP team must maintain a balance between simple tasks done at a more advanced stage and more functional and complex tasks mastered at a lower stage.

The basic goal of the IEP team is to provide opportunities for the student to progress as far as possible. The student's status depends on the complexity of the tasks assigned, and the student may never be in a supervisory position in his or her eventual employment. Giving the student a brief experience in charge of others in a simple classroom task, however, helps the student in understanding and appreciating the role of supervisors in more complex real-world activities. At every age level, teachers should incorporate elements of this transitional preparation.

The second stage is a progression in the nature and quality of the work placement. Most students with mental retardation progress according to the following pattern: supported → unpaid → competitive employment. This sequence is discussed in detail in Chapter 14. All phases of the preparation program conducted on the school campus are sheltered in that they must be closely supervised. If additional close supervision is needed, sheltered employment can be applied at the necessary location and at any place in the sequence.

The third stage involves activities that occur in the setting designated for the work or transitional experience. The setting can be either on- or off-campus. Classroom activities, field trips, and other school-supervised experiences are considered "on-campus" even though they may take place in a variety of locations. All students, with and without mental retardation, are typically limited to on-campus settings until they are of legal age to participate in off-campus involvements—usually about the 16th year.

DIAGNOSIS/PRESCRIPTION/EVALUATION (DPE)

There is no "average" student with mental retardation. Students with this disability vary greatly in ability levels, potentials, and interests, as well as in age, gender, and physical capability. For this reason, procedures for diagnosing a student's needs, prescribing treatments, and evaluating results must be carefully adapted to the individual situation.

Informal Procedures

To make an informal diagnosis leading to prescription in the area of social choice for a child with mental retardation, a "What would you do?" procedure is effective. The choices the child is asked to make are generally arranged in order of increasing difficulty or complexity. Choices are recommended here for different levels, although some questions might be repeated as the child becomes more advanced—for example, "What would you do if a stranger offered you a ride?" Once these questions have been used to assess a basic level and some individual characteristics for the child, some time should be set aside each week for deliberate, well-planned training in social and ethical values.

Beginning Level
What would you do if
    someone pushed you down?
    someone took your ball (toy or other personal property)?
    someone called you a name?
    someone told a lie about you?
    someone said you didn't like him or her?
    someone said you took his candy?
    someone did not invite you to her birthday party?
    someone said, "I'll be your friend if you'll give me some candy"?
    a stranger offered you some candy?
    a stranger offered you a ride?
    someone started a fight with you?
    you wanted to go to a movie and your mother wouldn't let you?

Intermediate Level
What would you do if
    someone did not choose you for her team?
    a friend did not come to your party?
    a friend did not invite you to his party?
    someone called you "retarded"?
    a stranger offered you a ride?
    someone threatened to hit you?

someone challenged you to a fight?
someone kept you from using the rest room?
someone said he would beat you up if you didn't give him some money?

Miscellaneous
What would you do if
a friend was "cutting" school?
a friend was getting into trouble?
you did something you were not supposed to do?
you thought that others didn't like you?
you didn't feel well?
you had a toothache?
you saw an automobile accident?
you saw a building on fire?
you lost your job?

This procedure is similar to one proposed by Rosenthal-Malek and Yoshida (1994) in which they taught students with mental retardation self-interrogation. Using their techniques, the students learned to be proactive and ask themselves, "What would happen if I _____?" Continual diagnosis of a student's capabilities in social and ethical behavior occurs as a teacher or counselor observes the student in a series of situations in which decisions and choices must be made. For a young, immature student, the teacher should structure choice situations as preferences, rather than as choices among varying options. For example, the student might choose the book to be read to the class, the color he or she wishes to use in painting a picture, or whether to do arithmetic or reading first on a particular day. As the student matures, more significant decisions can be presented: whether to complete a project or get ready to meet the bus, whether to take an off-campus job rather than an on-campus position. Gradually, as the student gains experience, far-reaching decisions involving marriage, home, family, employment, and recreation can be introduced.

Individual Interviews/Counseling

One of the most effective means of performing a DPE in the areas of social, moral, and ethical training with students with mental retardation may be through a counseling interview. Stainback and Stainback (1987) suggested that counseling and coaching procedures should be conducted in a positive interaction style involving sharing, support, and opportunities for conflict resolution. The teacher or counselor should find ways of becoming very familiar with the social skills and maturity level of the student without prying into the student's personal life. If the student is inarticulate, appropriate advice and counsel may be based on observation of the student, rather than on the student's stated views and problems.

Several counseling approaches can be illustrated in techniques for handling the common but irritating and sometimes confusing matter of tattling. To help the student discern the fine line between tattling and personal responsibility, the teacher can create, adapt, or enhance (ACE) a story or incident involving the student in a tattling situation. After telling a story about a student faced with this problem, the teacher might ask, "Was Mary tattling when she told her mother about the stranger who offered to give Keeshia a ride home from school?" Or after elaborating a bit on an event that happened in the classroom recently, the teacher could ask, "Should Diego tell the teacher that Bart didn't help clean up after the activity?" Parents and teachers should encourage younger, more immature students to talk out their responses to situations involving problems such as tattling-citizenship.

When at all possible, a child with mental retardation should be encouraged to consult with his or her parents on personal and social problems because the teacher will not always be available. Personal counseling with members of the immediate family will be particularly appropriate in handling sensitive personal issues and problems, such as dating and boy-girl relationships as the child becomes more mature. Also, the home is usually the best place to deal with potentially troublesome situations, such as credit buying and dealing with door-to-door sales, that will occur as the child approaches independent living.

Puppetry

The social problems of children with mental retardation can often be effectively approached by using puppets. The "what would you do if" diagnostic procedure can be made more interesting and possibly less threatening for the children if puppets are asking the questions and reacting to some of the answers. Indirect counseling can be accomplished through puppetry as a child is invited to discuss a problem or an uncomfortable situation with a nonthreatening puppet. The actions and admonitions of puppets seem to appear more neutral to children—particularly children with mental retardation—than the advice and counsel of most adults. Puppets need not be elaborate or expensive. Effective puppets can be made from socks, gloves, or paper bags. Children often feel particularly close and comfortable with puppets they have made themselves.

Role Playing

Role playing can be used with or without puppets. Although the hypothetical situations involved in role playing are not as effective as real-life situations in teaching and counseling, the limitations of time and space often make role playing an effective means of discussing various problems and needs. Other techniques that have been used to help students get out their feelings and deal with them include ACE stories, play therapy, story writing, slide-sound shows, play writing, and picture stories. The ability of a student with mental retardation to benefit from these vicarious and indirect experiences, however, must be carefully evaluated on an individual basis. This characteristic appears to be closely related to the difficulty students with mental retardation have in recognizing and dealing effectively with the emotions and facial expressions of other people (Adams & Markham, 1991; Blacher-Dixon & Simeonsson, 1981; Park & Gaylord-Ross, 1989).

Goal Instruction Analysis (GIA)

GIA components can be compiled from a variety of sources. The GIA procedure organizes the components in a structured format in which they can be effectively adapted into diagnostic/prescriptive teaching. For example, Dixon and Saudargas (1980) used a combination of cueing and praise successfully in teaching toilet training. Similarly, Lancioni et al. (1992) used brief and flexible cues to reduce drooling in individuals with mental retardation. Many researchers, including Wolber, Carne, Collins-Montgomery, and Nelson (1987), used tangible and social reinforcements to teach tooth-brushing skills. The latter group reported that using a combination of both forms of reinforcement was more effective than using either alone. Reese and Snell (1991) reported success in using a combination of faded guidance, oversize garments, and individualized reinforcement to teach dressing skills to students with severe multiple disabilities.

More complex combinations are formed when more complicated and intangible behaviors are involved. La Greca (1983) combined modeling, coaching, and behavioral rehearsal to enhance interpersonal skills, social competence, occupational problem behavior, and length of employment with 12 individuals with mental retardation. In another employment situation, Martin and Morris (1980) employed visual feedback and ratio scheduling of pay to teach 5 workers with severe mental retardation the relationship between work and piece rate. Components with sample GIAs introduced in earlier chapters include modeling, cueing, encouraging, prompting, and reinforcement.

Specific Long-Term and Annual Goals

Appendix F identifies some specific skills and concepts that may serve as or suggest long-term and annual social goals appropriate for an individual with mental retardation. Although these are realistic goals, they must be carefully selected and prioritized, with other goals added as necessary. Most of the social skills, concepts, and activities listed in Appendix F could reasonably constitute long-term goals for one student with mental retardation and annual goals for another, depending on the student's individual abilities. Although most of these goals relate to those in the curricular areas of transition/vocation and communication, this relationship is not marked unless it is particularly significant.

Formal Procedures

As publishers—as well as authors, teachers, and therapists—attempt to prepare formal procedures for identifying and resolving social problems for students with mental retardation, these procedures' "average" is generally an achievement level too high or too low to meet the needs of a specific individual. Also, the pace recommended for presentation of published materials is either too fast or too slow for most students. Because the rate of presentation is fixed once the materials have been published, the level of the material is usually unsuitable as well.

Because of these weaknesses, the information derived from the testing procedures is usually too general to diagnose the varying needs of students with mental retardation, and most prescriptive and instructional materials available from publishers are too general to fit the students' specific needs. Chapter 6 introduces the DPE and explains how the imprecise data from formal testing procedures can be refined and enhanced to yield more accurate and usable information from which prescriptions may be formed. In addition, informal diagnostic/prescriptive procedures can be used to adapt some instructional materials for the needs of the individual, providing that materials have been carefully selected in the first place and that the general aspects do meet the basic needs of the student.

SUMMARY

In this chapter, I explained the need for a broad array of social skills for students with mental retardation. These skills are essential for every facet of their lives—in transition, independent and family living, leisure, and other environments.

I also stressed the particular importance of involving parents in the development of social skills for their children. Teachers and other school personnel are urged to help parents gain an understanding of the crucial needs for social skills.

Also emphasized was the need for self-help skills, cleanliness, and good grooming.

I also pointed out some of the unique problems students with mental retardation generally have in establishing long-term friendships and posed some possible solutions.

CHAPTER 13

Home and Independent Living

Points to Study and Ponder

1. Why are students with mental retardation likely to need special consideration in learning how to live independently as adults?
2. What independent living facilities are available to individuals with mental retardation in your area after they leave school?
3. What facilities and programs are available in your community to teach independent living skills (e.g., shopping, food preparation, laundry, home care) to individuals with mental retardation?
4. What is the relationship, if any, between regional variation (Chapter 1) and the necessity to teach independent living skills in the schools?
5. What is respite care, and why is it necessary?
6. Who are the intended recipients of respite care?
7. How could the age 25 projection help determine the sex education needs of an individual with mental retardation?

Students with mental retardation are unique in their need for specific instruction to live independently. Of course, other students may take some classes in parenting, family living, and even child rearing, but individuals with mental retardation are essentially the only students in school who need basic instruction and experience in being integrated into the community. They are about the only ones whose life goal curriculum must seriously consider preparations to live in a variety of living arrangements. These living arrangements constitute a hierarchy, described later in Figure 13.1. Because of this hierarchy, independent living skills are good examples of level-to-level curriculum planning wherein the skills are developed with increasing sophistication and achievement expectations as the student matures.

Individuals with mental retardation may eventually live in any of several arrangements—a regular home or apartment, a group home, a residential institution—and an individual's eventual placement is difficult to predict while he or she is in school. All types of government-operated residential institutions are unpopular today, but without a well-planned preparation program, an individual with mental retardation may not qualify for a more independent setting. One reason is that the opportunity to train a person in independent living is not usually available after the individual leaves school.

The purpose of this chapter is to identify some specific skills and concepts a person with mental retardation needs to become as independent as possible with respect to living arrangements. Like other chapters of this unit, it presents skills and concepts that relate most closely to independent living. It also covers some procedures and techniques appropriate in teaching those skills and concepts.

THE NEED FOR SPECIAL CONSIDERATION

Self-reliance and independent living require serious consideration for every person with mental retardation. Bice, Halpin, and Halpin (1986) investigated field independence and dependence among 80 children with mild mental retardation and 80 children without mental retardation (all between ages 8 and 13). The children without mental retardation, especially older white children, were more independent. Those with mild mental retardation, especially younger black children, were more dependent, showing that even those whose mental retardation is mild/moderate will ordinarily have considerable difficulty achieving complete independence after graduating from school. Edgerton, Bollinger, and Herr (1984) reevaluated 15 individuals with mild mental retardation whom they had studied in 1960–61. These individuals were making fairly good adjustments to adult life, but most still needed some assistance from social and other agencies.

Another reason that people with mental retardation need special consideration after graduation is poor and even fragile health. They typically suffer from a variety of mild to serious physical and medical ailments. Poor health appears to be roughly proportional to the extent of mental retardation. Asberg (1989) discovered that individuals with mental retardation had three times as many hospital visits and twice as many doctor visits as their CA peers during a 5-year period—although some of the variance appeared to be more closely related to their living arrangements than their disabilities.

A study by Fox and Westling (1986) of students with profound mental retardation revealed that over half used prescribed medications. Anticonvulsants, prescribed to 44.56% of the students, accounted for 74% of all medications.

Discussions throughout the book, especially the first five chapters, testify of the unique needs of students with mental retardation. All of these needs point out that they must be given special consideration if they are to succeed in adult life. They must have deliberate, well-planned instruction and experience in developing skills and concepts that others learn almost automatically—often at home or in other nonschool settings. These skills and concepts include developing self-worth and self-image; obeying rules, customs, and traditions; cultivating interests, hobbies, and leisure time activities; learning to handle emotions, accept blame, and settle grievances; and making as many of their own decisions as possible. They also need considerable assistance in safety, the selection of nutritious foods, the concept of diet, the need for proper rest and exercise, body cleanliness and sanitation, common communicable diseases (prevention and what to do if afflicted), the role of the physician and the dentist, how to tell if one is ill, how to report illness and accidents, how to know when to get help, and how to deal with harmful substances (alcohol, tobacco, drugs, prescription drugs, nonprescription drugs, and drugs prescribed for others).

Significantly, all of these needs are especially pertinent to independent living, but each must be individually diagnosed because students with mental retardation—even those to be found in any single classroom—vary greatly in the extent to which each has already mastered these skills and concepts and the rate at which instruction should proceed. These students also demonstrate great dissimilarity in how much progress each will make during his or her lifetime. Training and experience in independent living have a positive effect on the individual, however, and greatly improve his or her chances for success (Lozano, 1993). Williams and Cuvo (1986) reported considerable success in training 6 individuals with severe disabilities to maintain and make minor adjustments to their air conditioners, ranges, refrigerators, and other household appliances.

HORIZONTAL CURRICULUM PLANNING, AGE 25 PROJECTION, AND PROACTIVITY

Horizontal curriculum planning, the age 25 projection, and proactivity are important concepts for the IEP team to keep in mind as they plan for their student with mental retardation. Each is a useful tool in helping develop the best possible curriculum for that student.

Horizontal Curriculum Planning

The area of independent living is an excellent example of the need for horizontal curriculum planning where the skills are diagnosed and taught simultaneously with instructional activities from several other curriculum areas, particularly transition, communication, social skills, and arithmetic. Lovett and Harris (1987b) interviewed 48 adults with mild to moderate mental retardation who rated vocational and social skills as the ones they considered most important for successful community living, and these were followed by personal, academic, and leisure skills. Thus, the skills of virtually all other curriculum areas are necessary for and must be planned and maintained simultaneously with home and family living. The areas of socialization, transition, and communication skills are particularly important to the person's development of independent living skills.

Age 25 Projection

Wehman and Hill (1984) declared that approaches to enhance the integration of students into community activities should be based on specific goals and objectives specified in IEP. Procedures for carrying out a community integration placement also require assessment of community resources and progress to advertising the program and rewarding the community. The age 25 projection is an excellent procedure to help in predicting the type of living arrangement for which a person with mental retardation will eventually qualify. Later discussions of the various levels and types of living arrangements and the difficulties associated with each demonstrate why ongoing evaluation of the student's progress is so vital. One particularly perplexing challenge is that the student must usually prepare for one setting while living in another and that the decision of the person's placement is not ordinarily made until he or she leaves the school's protective and helpful environment. Further, even parents who will eventually seek out-of-home placements for their children are not very receptive to the idea while the children are young.

As with other areas of curriculum, the student's eventual abilities and independent living status must be carefully evaluated and predicted. Some skills and concepts of family and independent living can easily turn out to be *splinter skills,* or those that cannot be mastered sufficiently in school to be used in adult life. The IEP team can and must project with increasing precision into the student's independent living skills. The level of setting into which the student will eventually be placed has great implications for the related skills that student must master. For example, if a student's anticipated living arrangements require cooperative meal preparation, he or she must be able to contribute with little or no supervision. As the individual's living placement moves up the evaluation scheme in Figure 13.1, supervision generally decreases and the need for independent meal planning and other preparation skills increases.

Proactivity

Fettgather (1989) pointed out two curricula that are currently offered to students with mental retardation: one that promotes life skills, independence, and personal responsibility, and one that, though hidden, promotes dependence and immaturity. He declared that the former must be adopted. Students with mental retardation must be taught to be proactive in all settings, particularly group homes and other living arrangements.

They must learn to recognize their proper roles and take the initiative in fulfilling their obligations. They must be proactive in socialization, communication, and transitional skills. In each of these areas, a student with mental retardation must recognize that a problem is present, organize and analyze the problem, solve it, and use the solution. These skills cannot be taken for granted. For example, individuals with mental retardation often expect supervisors, friends, and others to pay for meals and entertainment as they often did in school programs. Their failure to buy their share of treats was noted by Sulzbacher, Haines, Peterson, and Swatman (1987).

PREPARATION FOR INDEPENDENT LIVING

It is not only popular but also wise to conduct the preparatory training for independent living and activity as much as possible in the community settings where the individual will live (Langone & Burton, 1987; Martin, Rusch, & Heal, 1982). It is difficult, however, for an individual to learn *how to live* in one living arrangement while actually living in another. To begin with, it is difficult to make the necessary arrangements; that is, trial apartments are not readily available for the individual to experience while he or she is living somewhere else. This means, in practice, much of the instruction for actual independent living must be simulated. Thus, in training the individual for independent living, the IEP team faces the challenge of balancing the necessary preparation in classrooms and other (contrived) settings with actual experience in the proposed or potential environment. Each setting has some advantages and disadvantages.

Community-based activities usually present some unique—usually not insurmountable—challenges, such as travel time and expenses, as well as supervision. Although on-campus sites usually offer the advantage of a ready supply of peer tutors and a more controlled atmosphere, community-based instruction can be particularly appropriate at the secondary level where consumer education, transition, work experience, and independent living skills need to be finalized. To meet these challenges, the teacher must make arrangements for and identify peer tutors, volunteers, and others to assist with the community-based activities. Teachers, volunteers, and others are reminded also that transporting school students in their private automobiles presents some liability problems that are not necessarily solved by the school district's commercial insurance. Because local conditions vary considerably and are regulated by the laws of each state, it is well to clear the supervisory, transportation, and liability aspects of off-campus programs with the responsible school and legal officials (Yudof et al., 1992). In any event, local conditions vary the needed balance between in-class and community-based preparation for independent living.

Another challenge is to help students with mental retardation transfer skills and concepts from one environment to another, such as from school to the community. Browning and White (1986) used interactive videos to teach independent living skills to teenagers with mental retardation. Birch (1994) reported success using videotaped role plays in promoting both health skills and social interactions among students with and without disabilities.

Transportation

Parents and teachers may easily overlook the fact that learning to ride a city bus is a fairly complicated task for a person with mental retardation (Burton & Bero, 1984). Skill in using public transportation, however, is highly significant because it is essential to independent living, as well as to employment and many other life situations. A number of skills must be taught in order to train a person with retardation to use bus service. The concept of heterogeneity in mental retardation points out the tremendous variation in student capability and experience: Some students will enter high school already capable of riding a municipal bus to a variety of destinations; some may never have ridden even a school bus.

Bus schedules are usually written in a format unfamiliar to the student. Some students with retardation will not be accustomed to identifying objects by number and will be confused by the numbering system, particularly when buses with different numbers may be going to the same destination. Because of this diversity, group instruction may be repetitious and inefficient for some and at the same time difficult for others. Ideally, diagnosis/prescription should be done on an individual basis. Because individualization is not always possible, Marchetti, Cecil, Graves, and Marchetti (1984) experimented with three approaches—classroom instruction, community instruction, and facility-grounds instruction—with 27 students whose retardation had been described as mild to severe. Although the facility-grounds (on-campus) group made the greatest gains, the researchers were sufficiently successful with all three treatment groups to warrant the conclusion that any of these methods can be used where it is most convenient. In an innovative procedure that might be used to correlate classroom and off-campus instruction, LaDuke and LaGrow (1984) used photographs of specific buses, boarding points, destinations, and bus numbers to teach bus travel to adults with "trainable" mental retardation. Their methods could be enhanced with videotaping procedures. The more severe the retardation, the less optimistic the prognosis of the individual becoming proficient in using bus transportation. Coon, Vogelsburg, and Williams (1981) taught a severely disabled 20-year-old woman to ride a bus but found that she had difficulty transferring the training to other environments.

Some GIA procedures and some suggested annual and long-term goal sequences related to bus transportation are presented later in this chapter and in Appendix G.

Self-Help Skills

All of the self-help skills discussed in the previous chapter are essential in independent living. Because the facilities for teaching independent living skills are not always available until a student is older, it may be well to emphasize self-help skills with younger students until they are fairly well mastered. The independent living skills per se can then be offered at the secondary level. Self-help skills are mentioned here because they are high-priority life goals for those with mental retardation. These skills can also be included in horizontal curriculum planning, and diagnosis/prescription can be combined with activities of almost all other areas, including social, transition, leisure, and communication, as well as in home and independent living. For example, acceptable personal appearance and good grooming are some of the most valuable assets of a person with mental retardation in any setting. The person who can present a pleasing personality and a pleasant appearance will usually find that he or she has great advantages in job-seeking opportunities, boy-girl relationships, and other social settings. With a well-planned curriculum, most of them can be taught to care for their bodies in such a manner as to appear neat, clean, and well-groomed. Even those whose mental retardation is severe/profound can be taught these essential skills.

Patterson (1984) used a home intervention approach designed to help parents teach young adults with mental retardation to develop good grooming, independent travel, and supermarket shopping skills. For younger students and less mature students with mental retardation, it may be necessary to begin at rudimentary levels—naming the parts of the body, discussing their functions, and using grooming aids, such as combs, brushes, hair sprays, and deodorants. As they mature and develop, diagnosis/prescription of these students must include such life goals as making proper selection of clothing, care and cleaning of clothing, clothing repair, keeping the body clean, and wearing clean underclothing. A full-length mirror mounted in the classroom helps everyone be constantly aware of personal appearance. One thoughtful teacher put this sign on the classroom mirror: "Would you hire this person?" It is also a good idea for the teacher to provide a good model by paying particular attention to his or her personal appearance.

Shopping Skills

Shopping for food, clothing, and other items constitutes a broad array of skills and concepts that are high priority for students with mental retardation. Being able to shop independently is obviously prerequisite to independent living. The type and level of a person's living arrangements are closely associated with the need and opportunity to do one's personal shopping. Shopping, budgeting, and consumer skills are discussed in greater detail in Chapter 16.

Food Preparation

Rimmer, Braddock, and Fujiura (1993) reported that obesity is more common among people with mental retardation than others and (unlike general health problems) seems to be inversely proportional to severity of mental retardation. They also noted that obesity is more of a problem among females than males and that people had lower incidence of obesity in residential than in community-based settings. Their findings imply that, in addition to general health counseling and planned physical activity, people with mental retardation also need instruction in the preparation of nutritious meals. Students with mental retardation should be able to prepare soups, sandwiches, and other simple foods regardless of their living arrangements. Such students often have great difficulty in preparing even simple meals not only because they lack the experience and motor abilities to do so but also because they cannot read and interpret recipes and other cooking directions. Further, the tremendous variation in age and ability of students with mental retardation compels teachers and parents to be creative in home, family, and other skills. Gines, Schweitzer, Queen-Autry, and Carthon (1990) reported success in using color-coded food photographs and meal code cards to teach these students to plan nutritionally balanced meals. Martin and Rusch (1987) employed a similar procedure they enhanced with a systematic withdrawal of instruction. Prerecorded videos may also be used to reinforce procedural-sequential tasks, including food preparation. Showing the videos with the sound off provides an opportunity to discuss the illustrated activity.

In evaluating a student's eventual status and ability to prepare meals, his or her IEP team must be particularly careful not to invest the student's valuable time in sophisticated meal preparation he or she will not be able to practice routinely in adult life. Schloss et al. (1993) taught students with mental retardation to prepare simple meals by using convenience foods, common procedures, and instructional techniques that included sight-word development and use of rebus symbols, together with graduated but diminishing verbal and other prompts. Browder, Hines, McCarthy, and Fees (1984) developed a procedure that stressed functional sight-word recognition needed to teach food preparation, laundry, and telephone skills.

Schuster (1988) discussed the costs involved in teaching cooking skills and pointed out that teaching individuals with mental retardation is far from an exact science and that they should be trained in natural settings wherever possible. Sarber, Halasz, Messmer, Bickett, and Lutzker (1983) taught menu planning and grocery shopping skills to a mother with mild mental retardation. They reported that, after training, the mother could plan 3 days of nutritious meals and could locate in a grocery store each item required for those meals. Nietupski, Welch, and Wacker (1983) taught 4 adults with moderate and severe mental retardation to use a pocket calculator and picture cue cards to figure state sales tax. Achieving success required a considerable time investment and thus showed that prioritizing is essential.

Laundry Skills

Doing their own laundry is another high-priority skill needed by students with mental retardation regardless of their eventual dependent/independent living status. Cuvo, Jacobi, and Sipko (1980) used praise and response contingent feedback to teach 5 young adults with mild and moderate mental retardation to sort garments to be laundered and to use a clothes washer and dryer. Although it is generally best to offer these and other home skills in most natural environments, some success is possible in teaching them in school settings. In an interesting study, Morrow and Bates (1987) trained 9 adolescents and young adults whose mental retardation was moderate and severe to use coin-operated washing machines. They used three types of materials: artificial (pictures), simulated (cardboard replicas), and natural (realistic). Most students increased their laundry performance with all three sets of school-based material, but generaliza-

The curriculum for an individual with mental retardation should be practical and community based.

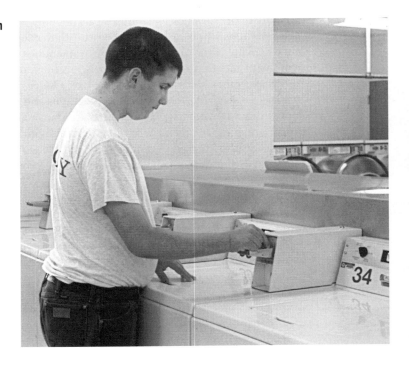

tion to community settings was limited. This study shows the importance of generalization, without which an activity is not functional. This instance was only an experiment to determine the functionality of a home or community activity simulated in a classroom. Instruction of this nature must be conducted in natural settings wherever possible. Earlier chapters have addressed the need for balance between classroom and community instruction. Ordinarily, it would not be difficult to take a group of students to a Laundromat so that the students could actually use coin-operated washers and dryers. Balance could be achieved by diagnosing and teaching entry-level or prerequisite skills and concepts (e.g., evaluating coins) in the classroom and conducting the culminating activity in its natural setting. It is also possible to permanently or temporarily install beds, ranges, microwaves, washers, and other appliances in the classroom or elsewhere on the school campus.

PLACEMENTS FOR INDEPENDENT LIVING

Without adequate training and experience, past generations of students with mental retardation were consigned to residential institutions or to watching television in the homes of relatives. In fact, much of the literature on independent living is focused on *deinstitutionalization,* or the transfer of residents of institutions to less-centralized facilities. Experience has shown, however, that many of these people lacked the necessary skills to live in and enjoy these community-based settings. Much of the criticism associated with the decentralized arrangements probably should have been directed toward the lack of ability, rather than toward the inadequacy of the newly designed facilities.

More recently, a great deal of attention has been given to the preparation of people with mental retardation for participation in independent living. For example, Brotherson et al. (1988) found that parents assigned highest priorities to preparation for successful future living arrangements for their children with mental retardation, together with socialization and employment skills. Some parents, however, have shown a reluctance to place their children with mental retardation in facilities outside the home despite the awareness that, in many instances, they must eventually do so. Bromley and Blacher (1989) surveyed 63 parents of children with severe disabilities in an effort to discover why the parents delayed placing their children outside the home. Their factor analyses revealed three main factors: guilt feelings, social support, and family relationships. This finding suggests that, as with other aspects of mental retardation, parents must be given increasing consideration and assistance in helping their children learn how to live independently. Lord and Pedlar (1991) reported an improvement in the quality of life for 13 of 18 individuals over a period of 4 years after deinstitutionalization. They identified four procedures they thought contributed to the individuals' success: planning and grouping people, leadership, community integration, and social networks. Although their work was with individuals transferring from institution to smaller facilities, the same procedures and assistance are logically needed by parents.

As one might expect, smaller living accommodations are generally preferred over larger facilities. Hemming (1986) pointed out that smaller living units are superior in most respects to larger facilities. Hemming's study surveyed 32 adults with mental retardation who had been transferred from large institutions to new, smaller units. They were tested 5.5 years after the transfer and demonstrated that they had retained or regained adaptive behavioral skills but had declined in psycholinguistic abilities. Barber and Hupp (1993) studied the development of friendship and found that adults with developmental disabilities living in small group homes and a nondisabled comparison group had similar numbers of close relationships, whereas disabled residents of large facilities had fewer close friends than either of the other two groups. Dudley (1988), however, found that some programs actually promoted relationships with neighbors, but others preferred to keep the role of neighbors to a minimum.

It is understandably difficult to predict the level of independent living each student with mental retardation will eventually achieve. Furthermore, once such a prediction is made, the best procedures to follow to prepare the student for that level are never obvious. One basic problem is that it is always difficult to prepare a student with mental retardation for a higher level of independent living while he or she is living in a lower level setting. The higher level setting almost always offers less supervision and support than such a student requires. Further, it is not usually feasible to place a younger student with mental retardation in an off-campus apartment or any other high-level setting. Thus, the actual experience must usually be delayed until the student is older. But by that time, the availability of school funds is almost at an end. Thus, the participation of teachers and other IEP team members must be efficiently planned and conducted. For these reasons, some have suggested it may be best to stress self-help skills over independent living in the earlier school years.

Supervision and Monitoring

One key indicator of independent living is the extent to which an individual must be supervised. Figure 13.1 lists a hierarchy of living arrangements available to people with mental retardation according to the supervisory needs of each setting. Each person is placed at the setting that appears to be most appropriate and for which funding is available. The costs to the person and the person's family generally increase sharply with each advancement. As the person works his or her way toward the top of the hierarchy, additional supervision and evaluation are needed, at least temporarily. The basic intent is for each person to work his or her way to as near the top of the hierarchy (to be as independent) as possible.

The dictionary definitions of *supervision* and *monitoring* overlap somewhat, but generally supervision refers to tighter controls with constant or frequent direct contact with each tenant. Monitoring is not as frequent and has less direct control. A supervisor is typically on the scene all or most of the time; (eventually, at least) a monitor may simply be available for consultation as needed. An important part of the role of either supervisor or monitor is to protect people with mental retardation from others who may exploit or otherwise take advantage of them.

There is some question about the relative independence an individual with mental retardation may experience in these facilities. For example, living with relatives may or may not offer much dependence, depending on the circumstances. It is also possible for some arrangements near the bottom of the hierarchy to offer considerable independence. Further, with some supervision and other assistance, any individual with mental retardation could live in a higher level of arrangement than he or she would otherwise. In any event, the IEP team should strive to place the individual as high on the hierarchy as possible.

FIGURE 13.1   A Hierarchy of Independent Living Facilities

Own home or condo, married or single
Rented home or condo, married or single
Rented own apartment, married or single
Shared, supported apartment, one
  or two others
Shared, supported apartment, several others
Living with parents or other relatives
Group home, partly supervised
Group home, supervised full-time
Community residential center
Residential institution

Training for Higher Level Living Arrangements

Generally, it takes a great deal of specific training for an individual to advance from one setting to the next higher level. The abilities of each individual to advance to the next higher level must be carefully diagnosed and plans made to assist and train the individual for such a move. For example, one young man demonstrated most of the skills necessary to be placed in a more independent setting. He had not learned to remain in one place, however, and had a strong tendency to wander. This had not been a serious problem in the more restrictive setting or in the classroom because there an aide would simply lead him back to his station. It is vital that those involved not lose sight of the training aspects of each placement. This type of training is second nature for teachers, but most service providers are not educators. It is all too easy to assume that because a person with mental retardation lacks decision-making ability, all their decisions must be made for him or her. In many instances, an individual is assigned to one of the group settings or living arrangements where the goals help the individual adjust to that type of setting, rather than prepare the person to function satisfactorily in a higher level setting that offers a more independent living style. Such a placement is unfortunate if the individual is really capable of achieving a higher level of living arrangement.

Another practical consideration is simply the availability of some living arrangements. Under the IDEA, parents of children with disabilities (as well as educators) become familiar with legal provisions requiring school programs to meet the needs of the children. While the children are in the public schools, special programs and placements must be made available to fit their needs, but after they leave school, private service providers and most other public agencies are under no such mandate. In practice, this means that the "significant others" in the lives of students with mental retardation must plan preparatory programs within community settings that are available—or might be available by the time they are needed. This is why parents must be encouraged to make early and ongoing preparations for their children. The tendency is to rely too heavily on available facilities, rather than make long-range plans to develop better facilities.

Residential Institutions and Group Homes

For younger children with mental retardation, greater emphasis is placed on helping their families keep them at home where they can attend public or private day schools (Vitello, Atthowe, & Cadwell, 1983). Another trend is to place younger children in foster homes or group homes where they also attend day schools with other children.

Residential institutions and group homes are considered simultaneously because they serve people with mental retardation of all ages and share several other attributes. Residential institutions and most group homes provide 24-hour care and may or may not provide educational programs within the facility itself. Most residential institutions gradually developed some educational programs from within, but these programs were subjected to severe criticism (Blatt & Kaplan, 1966; Lakin & Bruininks, 1985). For example, in most states, the educational programs in the institutional settings were the last to require their teachers to hold special credentials. Currently, most residential institutions send their residents of school age to nearby public day schools.

One difference between residential institutions and group homes is that residential facilities are typically much larger and are operated by state governments. Group homes are much smaller and are usually operated by private individuals or groups, although most of them depend heavily on state and federal funding. In recent years, a strong nationwide movement has aimed to disperse individuals with mental retardation to smaller, community-based facilities (Braddock & Fujiura, 1987). A large proportion of these individuals are being placed in group homes.

Typically, a group home provides two full-time "parents," rather than a number of attendants working in shifts as in the older institutions. Federal regulations, however, are beginning to require that the full-time "parents" be paid around the clock if they remain on the premises. This arrangement sharply increases costs and thus makes the per-child expenses greater. Similar regulations and practice limit the number of residents that can be maintained in a single facility; this also tends to increase costs. Naturally, smaller group homes generate smaller financial returns. Even with just two parents, the per-resident costs of operating group homes are often difficult to maintain, mainly because of the limited number of people with mental retardation who are placed in a single unit. As a result, many group home parents find it necessary to work at a job outside the facility during the day. This is significant for teachers and employers because it means no place for either younger or adult residents to go when they become ill at school or on the job. Nevertheless, the popularity of group homes seems to grow steadily.

The residential institution or school is usually considered a last resort as a placement because it provides the greatest isolation of an individual with mental retardation from his or her nondisabled peers. A few states have completely phased out their large, centralized, residential facilities, but despite the deinstitutionalization movement, most states still operate one or more residential institutions for this population. Whether all of these facilities will be phased out eventually remains to be seen. However, some individuals with profound mental retardation coupled with other disabilities will likely always need some type of constant, highly intensified care—possibly a residential setting. Group home service providers report that they turn away many applicants because their problems are too intense and require services the group homes are unable to deliver.

Except for the possible exception of these individuals with severe and multiple problems, the reports of deinstitutionalization appear to be generally favorable. Kregel et al. (1986) indicated that formerly institutionalized people with mental retardation surveyed were generally satisfied with their present situation and that most displayed some degree of competence in independent living skills. Although most seemed to be making a fairly good adjustment, only 20% felt any serious lack of money. It is noteworthy, however, that fewer than 25% responded to the questions personally.

Eastwood and Fisher (1988) compared the results of institutionalized and community-based facilities by observing matched samples of persons with mental retardation from each setting. One group that had been deinstitutionalized into community settings was matched with others who remained in the institution. Their assessment showed that the community-based clients surpassed those from the institution in social and cognitive skills (including reading/writing, quantitative, community orientation, leisure time, vocational, and social interaction) but, interestingly, not in daily living skills. Their examination of these school-related topics is a reminder that each individual of school age with mental retardation (regardless of the living arrangements) must have an IEP and is entitled to all other protections of the IDEA.

One traditional strength of residential institutions is that they gradually developed a wide array of services and professionals, such as speech and communication, occupational, physical, and recreational therapists. In addition, many institutions provided on-site medical, dental, and psychological services. Another advantage is that the residential institutions attracted great numbers of volunteers, a strength that group homes and decentralized facilities have found difficult to duplicate. A major challenge for the smaller facilities is to provide living accommodations for people with mental retardation while maintaining a satisfactory level of these essential services.

Some alternatives to residential settings, such as group homes, have been partly justified on the basis of reduced cost. Originally, it was thought that deinstitutionalization was more economical than residential institutions, and initially most of them actually were less expensive. Intagliata, Willer, and Cooley (1979) found group homes to be slightly less expensive than residential institutions. As these alternative programs have come under closer scrutiny from both public and private sources, however, costs have risen sharply, and there is growing evidence that group homes are not appreciably more cost effective than residential institutions—though quality of service rather than costs should be the determining factor.

The lower expenditures appear to have been due to reduction of services than less expensive operational costs. Once group home standards were imposed, their costs rose sharply. Bensberg and Smith (1984) found that, overall, group homes are at least as expensive as traditional institutions. Generally, group homes are still considered to be superior to residential institutions, but not simply because they are less expensive to operate. A study by Braddock, Hemp, and Howes in 1986 disclosed that the daily cost of maintaining an individual with mental retardation is over $100 in the United States. They also reported that the per diem contribution of the federal government is increasing while state governments' contribution is diminishing.

Community Residential Centers

Some communities have favored smaller, decentralized facilities, similar in many ways to the larger, residential institutions. They are still able to provide many auxiliary services of the centralized institution but are located closer to schools, churches, businesses, and other community facilities. Community residential centers vary greatly in size and level of services but are typically operated with public funds, though they may be private. The level of supervision is roughly equivalent to residential institutions. Like group homes, their cost effectiveness is closely related to the level of services they offer. Many students with mental retardation stay in these facilities until they achieve the necessary skills to live in group homes or higher level settings.

Apartments

It is difficult for many people—even those with average intelligence and skills—to maintain an apartment free of any external supervision, although most people eventually do so. Most people whose mental retardation is severe/profound require a great deal of supervision in their living arrangements throughout their lifetimes. Independent living, however, such as in an apartment, can be successful with adults whose mental retardation is mild or moderate. Foxx and Faw (1992) conducted an 8-year follow-up of 9 adults with mild to moderate mental retardation 8 years after training and reported that they had maintained most of the social and vocational skills of the training period.

Apartments are currently a popular living arrangement for mature individuals with mental retardation. In fact, apartment living offers about the most independent setting to which those whose mental retardation is most mild may aspire. Rosen and Burchard (1990) found that adults with mental retardation living in semi-independent apartments do not perceive themselves as socially isolated, although their actual social integration is very limited. However, even they have considerable difficulty maintaining themselves without some support. Salend and Giek (1988) interviewed 25 landlords who had rented apartments or rooms to individuals with mental retardation. Although 22 of the landlords indicated that they would rent to such individuals again, a significant number had experienced some problems because of poor independent living skills, extreme dependence on the landlord, or deviant behavior exhibited by the tenants. Some suggested that, where possible, it may be better to place adults in alternate blocks, rather than in an apartment complex or in adjoining apartments. In that way, they can then congregate if they want to without drawing undue attention to the group. Apartment living is quite expensive, and social service agencies are sometimes reluctant to provide the necessary financial assistance. Sometimes, however, these high-functioning people with mental retardation can provide part of their own on-the-job earnings. Monitoring can be adjusted so that some responsible adult may check up on each group occasionally or whenever incidental needs arise.

Living at Home with Parents and Others

A great many adults with mental retardation are currently living with their parents or other relatives. O'Brien (1993) pointed out that living at home can be a highly satisfactory arrangement and is often overlooked or rejected. Keeping these people at home is usually done at considerable social and financial sacrifice. Hodapp and Zigler (1993) reviewed the literature on this matter and concluded that society rewards out-of-home placement. In addition to the usual expenses, parents and other family members must provide for most services incidental to their children's disability. The parents are not compensated for most of these expenses, which can be enormous. Thus, financial incentives strongly favor placement in publicly supported facilities where family members may share part of the costs but are not usually required to do so—especially for adults.

The exact numbers of such persons living at home are difficult to determine because they are not necessarily identified as having mental retardation, as they might have been while they were of school age. Many parents are reluctant to place their sons or daughters in any setting outside the home (Bromley & Blacher, 1989). It is well to contact the parents of older students with mental retardation to determine their preferences. The training for students whose parents intend to keep them at home or to make future living arrangements for them with brothers, sisters, or other relatives should reflect those intentions. Keeping family members with mental retardation at home is not only a natural procedure but also has proved to be successful. Krauss et al. (1992) reported that the social support systems for these people living at home were extensive, diverse, and durable over time. Family members provided most of the social support. These authors also found males and those whose mental retardation was most severe to be at the greatest risk for social isolation. The findings reinforce the advisability of working closely in supporting parents and other family members. They also applauded the fact that adults with mental retardation were actively involved with other family members, a general and distinct weakness of all other living arrangements. The authors also noted, however, that the adults living at home tended to have fewer friends outside their social support network than those living in outside-the-home facilities.

Willer and Intagliata (1982) compared two residential alternatives—family care and group homes—for adults with mental retardation who had been deinstitutionalized. Those in the family care facilities were significantly more likely to improve their maladaptive behavior, but those in the group home settings were more likely to improve community living skills. These findings suggest that most parents need help in planning and maintaining good programs for their children who have left school. For example, teachers and other IEP team members can be of great assistance to the family in helping members learn to make friends and to broaden their social circles. Suggestions also include investigating churches, which usually sponsor a variety of social organizations and events. Adults with mental retardation tend to be largely unaware of these opportunities and are unlikely to initiate contact without some support. Individuals with mental retardation also have difficulty locating and participating in leisure activities. These activities provide many recreational opportunities, as well as the potential to make friends, and are essential in any setting, including the home. Wilhite, Reilly, and Teaff (1989) investigated the availability of recreational and leisure activities in group homes and other alternatives to residential placement and reported that, although these experiences were a part of residents' lives, funding was limited.

Respite Care

In long-term planning for individuals with mental retardation living at home or elsewhere, it is important to bear in mind that mental retardation doesn't simply "go away" with the passage of time. Likewise, the needs of family members are not likely to diminish over time. Wikler (1981) contended that although most literature concerning families concludes that an eventual adjustment takes place, stresses imposed by mental retardation tend to emerge and reemerge over time. One service that has been particularly effective in helping parents and others deal with these stresses is respite care. This is a service in which volunteers take individuals with mental retardation on periodic outings or provide overnight care to allow parents and other family members some freedom where continual care and supervision are needed (Cooley et al., 1989). Surprisingly, Salisbury (1990) discovered that biological mothers of children (ages birth to adult) with mild/moderate mental retardation were equally likely to use respite care as were mothers whose children had severe/profound mental retardation. This author also found a uniformly low level of use of respite care across groups and no significant difference between groups. This "time out" care is available through a number of organizations throughout the United States and Canada. The charge is usually nominal.

Own Home or Condominium

Considering the national trend to identify a diminishing population whose mental retardation is increasingly severe, it would seem unlikely that a person so identified would ever be able to own his or her own home. Mental retardation, however, occurs in rich families as well as poor. Also, the concept of regional variation proclaims that some high-identification states are still identifying some school-age individuals whose mental retardation is quite mild. Such an individual might conceivably inherit a home or condominium or be able to purchase one. Owning and managing a house are generally considered to require a higher level of independent living skills than a condominium because the latter is usually smaller and some of the usual homeowner's chores, such as lawn care and snow shoveling, are done by others on a contractual basis. Also, the condominium usually has a greater number of close neighbors who might be willing to offer advice or other types of support. The disadvantages of owning one's own home are the great number of complicated financial and other responsibilities that are not required in other settings. A basic approach for a student with mental retardation in such a situation is to teach him or her most of the independent living skills necessary for others plus those specific skills the person is likely to need. Beyond that, the student should be taught how to manage a home and to know how and from whom to get needed assistance. It is quite unlikely that such an individual would be able to purchase a home without the assistance of parents and other family members, who will also be available for continuing advice and support.

SAFETY

Another vital element in the preparation for independent living, employment, and other community-related activities is safety. Teaching safety is a very good example of horizontal curriculum planning. Safety awareness is an essential part of every facet of life and can always be taught with other topics or units and need never be taught in isolation. Home safety skills and concepts must be given high priority in curriculum planning because an individual will obviously not be successful in any aspect of life if he or she is unable to avoid accidents and injury.

Safety is usually taught quite incidentally in the schools; that is, few if any formal classes are offered, and safety is ordinarily taught as a by-product of other classes. Yet, diagnosing, prescribing, and teaching safety skills are good examples of the need to prioritize the curriculum of a student with mental retardation. There simply isn't time to teach all the safety skills the student needs to live independently. The student's IEP team could teach safety skills and procedures almost full-time and still not be assured that the student had achieved all of these essential competencies. Further, safety instruction is probably the most difficult area of all to test the student's proactivity by placing that student in real or contrived experiences where injury may occur if he or she lacks the skills in question. Safety awareness and practice, however, are essential to survive in every aspect of life, including all areas of the home or other living facility, travel, employment, recreation, business, and other parts of the community.

Significantly, home surroundings are the locale where a high percentage of accidents occur. An important element of safety at home and elsewhere is learning to deal with fire. A typical sequence for individuals with mental retardation is prevention of fire → escaping from burning buildings → reporting fires → putting out small fires. Wolinsky and Walker (1975) proposed a home safety checklist to be used with very young children with disabilities. Using such a checklist is an excellent procedure for every home, group home, and other facility serving individuals of all ages who have disabilities of any kind. Frequent use of the checklist makes an excellent tool for diagnosing each individual's safety awareness and skill and for diagnosing and concentrating on elements on which the individual shows deficiencies. Tymchuk, Hamada, Andron, and Anderson (1990) evaluated home safety assessment and training methodology for mothers with mental retardation. Although these authors reported some success, they noted that a considerable amount of training or support services is needed. Rae and Roll (1985) reported that implementing an intensive fire safety training program with institutionalized persons with profound mental retardation resulted in a significant decrease in mean evacuation time and gradual substitution of verbal for physical prompts.

By the time a child with mental retardation enters school, he or she must usually have learned to get around the neighborhood safely. Dealing with strangers and others who might abuse or exploit is one of the most important safety concepts to be taught to students with mental retardation of all ages. This part of the curriculum must be thoughtfully planned and conducted because these students must also be taught to rely on others for emergency and other assistance. Collins et al. (1992) provided a reminder that even adults with mental retardation tend to be gullible and must be taught to resist the lures of strangers. They recommended simple, generalized (or all-purpose) responses.

The curriculum must also include extensive diagnosis and instruction in crossing streets and activities that others learn incidentally at home or elsewhere. Vogelsburg and Rusch (1979) trained 3 young adults with severe mental retardation to cross the street at a partially controlled intersection. They reported that various instructional feedback was sufficient in teaching the approach and walk behaviors but that selective repeated practice was required to establish the "look" responses. Much of the safety instruction for children with mental retardation, however, must be conducted in the home and at school. Pattavina, Bergstrom, Marchand-Martella, and Martella (1992) taught a 12-year-old boy with severe disabilities to cross streets safely by using photographs with verbal rehearsal of appropriate street crossing, followed by community-based instruction. The skills were acquired, maintained at follow-up, and generalized to new streets. Wherever possible, safety instruction should be conducted in the natural setting. Marchetti, McCartney, Drain, Hooper, and Dix (1983) compared community-based and classroom instruction procedures to teach pedestrian skills to 18 adults who had mental retardation. They found the community training procedures to be superior because they resulted in significant improvement from pretest to posttest; however, they found little improvement in the classroom group.

As students with mental retardation find themselves in increasingly independent living facilities, the supervision gradually diminishes. As this occurs, the requirement to recognize emergencies and the need to summon help increase. Training and the opportunity to demonstrate competence must be available at every level. Spooner, Stem, and Test (1989) taught 3 adolescents with moderate mental retardation to (a) communicate an emergency (dial 911), (b) apply first aid for minor injuries, (c) apply a plastic bandage to a minor injury, and (d) apply first aid for choking. Marchand-Martella et al. (1992) compared two methods—social modeling and partial-sequential withdrawal—to teach 4 students (ages 6 to 12) with mental retardation or behavioral disorders to treat minor abrasions. Similar success was noted with both methods. Likewise, Bannerman et al. (1991) used prompting, modeling, and differential reinforcement to teach three nonverbal adults with severe to profound mental retardation to exit their group homes at the sound of the house fire alarm. All three learned to exit independently in less than 2 minutes in all or the majority of surprise fire drills.

The teacher must also fully recognize and be aware of his or her great responsibility for the safety and well-being of the students. Most lawsuits brought against teachers and school districts are the results of school accidents in which negligence (usually on the part of the teacher) is charged. Thus, the student's IEP team must carefully project, diagnose, and teach those safety skills and concepts the student is likely to need most. Some suggested specific long-term and annual goals are listed in Appendix G.

DIAGNOSIS

A person's accident proneness is difficult to measure. The topics covered in this chapter are unique in that no available formal testing procedures, tests, or scales are suitable for use with students with mental retardation. Thus, the teacher and other team members must rely on informal procedures, such as observation, oral questioning, videotaping, and demonstrations. For students whose mental retardation is mild/moderate, written, teacher-made tests can also be very effective, particularly if the test items are kept short and concise and if the true-false mode is used. It may be necessary to read the test to poor readers. Students can also be required to demonstrate or walk through proper health or safety procedures. Also, a "what would you do if . . ." procedure might also be used as an informal means of diagnosis, as well as discussion—for example, "What would you do if you were partway across the street when the light changed color?" "What would you do if your friend hurt his knee on the playground?" "What would you do if an electric tool gave you a shock?" "What would you do if you had to sneeze?" "What could you prepare for lunch today?" "What would you do if you woke up and your bedroom was filled with smoke?"

Goal Instruction Analysis (GIA)

A number of GIA components are particularly helpful and unique in diagnosing and teaching the long-term and annual goals of this chapter. These, together with general components used in other chapters and those especially appropriate to the circumstances, should be very effective. For example, Schuster, Gast, Wolery, and Guiltinan (1988) successfully employed a constant time-delay procedure to teach chained responses to adolescents with mental retardation. Briefly, *time delay* is a teaching procedure that allows the subject a uniform period of time to initiate or continue with succeeding parts of a task. These researchers evaluated the effectiveness of a 5-second time-delay procedure to teach three chained food-preparation behaviors to 4 adolescents with moderate mental retardation within a multiple probe design across behaviors. They reported that the skills were maintained over a 3-month period and generalized from school to home for subjects completing the generalization probe sessions. Later, Schuster and Griffen (1991) used a 5-second constant time delay procedure with recipe cards to teach drink preparation to 5 intermediate-age elementary students whose mental retardation they described as moderate. The procedure was effective in teaching all students how to complete the task, and a 12-month follow-up showed at least 81% accuracy.

The types of instructions and the extent to which they are given are mainstays in GIA. Martin and Rusch (1987) gradually withdrew instructional components and trainers after a previous study using picture recipe cards to teach 3 adults with mental retardation to prepare simple meals. In a similar study, Roberson, Gravel, Valcante, and Maurer (1992) used a series of pictures to teach several procedural-sequential tasks, including following a recipe. This technique provides varying levels of support and can be easily adapted to a wide variety of tasks. Miller and Test (1989) found both constant time delay and a most-to-least prompting strategy effective in teaching 4 young adults whose mental retardation they described as moderate to operate a washing machine and dryer. The constant time-delay procedure, however, was more efficient in terms of instructional time and number of instructional errors.

Sample GIA (Rides Municipal Bus Proactively)

Learning to ride a bus independently is essentially a procedural-sequential task. In other words, the task of riding the bus must be done in its entirety, rather than piecemeal. The IEP team considered this task to be high priority because it was needed for independent living, as well as for transitional and work experience. Willie, whose mental retardation is quite severe, was new to Ms. Petty's class but seemed capable and old enough to be placed on an off-campus job, the most appropriate of which required his ability to ride the city bus. However, he had never ridden even a school bus without prompting. Therefore, Ms. Petty decided she would diagnose Willie's bus-riding ability herself. She took an instructional aide along to be trained and to assume responsibility for Willie's training as soon as possible.

In sketching out the GIA, Ms. Petty planned to teach boarding and exiting skills as part of the overall task. As to GIA components, she decided that memory and time requirements could be incorporated with other components, such as aid and mastery. In aid or assistance, she planned a sequence of

Assistance
teacher conducted → aide → peer tutor
written checklist → shorter → none
verbal instructions → none
prompting → encouraging, phasing out both as soon as possible

Materials
picture of correct bus → none
specific bus → any city bus

Reward
verbal praise → less → none

Mastery
other student (friend) → any other student → alone

In written form, this GIA appears to be extremely simple—even unnecessary. In fact, the teacher had some previous experience with the GIA procedure, so she only sketched out for us the general sequence she followed. It took nearly 6 weeks, however, before Willie could catch and ride the bus by himself. Ms. Petty found that Willie had ridden the school bus only a few times, which provided less experience than she anticipated. The school bus picked Willie up at the curb in front of his home, and at school he left the bus with all other passengers. She found that he was reluctant to ride the city bus with the teacher's aide, so she went with him the first few times.

One practical problem she encountered was that the specific bus Willie was to ride to his home only passed a point a few blocks from the school every 30 minutes. However, this allowed time to practice leaving the classroom when directed and to find the bus stop by using a map that was soon not needed. In practice sessions, Willie would have missed the bus several times because he had difficulty matching the number on the bus with the one in the picture. Ms. Petty also found that Willie's practical map reading skills were more rudimentary than she anticipated. At first, he was unable to locate the bus stop using only the map without considerable prompting. This amounted to a minor reversion because without the picture of the bus or the map he could not continue without help. So she considered Willie's next checkpoint to be his frontier. From that point forward, she provided a combination of instruction and practice. For evaluation purposes, she projected that it would take about 3 weeks before Willie would agree to go with the aide—still with the indicated support—and that he would be able to meet and board the bus and ride home alone in an additional 3 weeks, but complete mastery took a little longer than that. She found that she had underestimated the time lost by the bus coming only every 30 minutes and that Willie would not recognize the correct bus as readily as she predicted. Another practical problem was that once Willie actually boarded the bus, the friend, aide, or the other student had to ride to Willie's home and then wait for the returning bus. After a few trials, however, they rode only part of that way, his mother met the bus, and the driver prompted him since the bus stop was several blocks from his home.

SCIENCE

Formal science instruction is not generally high on the priority list for students with mental retardation. Wielert and Sheldon (1984), however, lament the shortage of science teaching materials and procedures for students with mild/moderate mental retardation and argue that some science instruction would be helpful—especially if it is designed and conducted on an individual basis and focused on real-life situations. The dangers of alcohol and substance abuse, safety, grooming, food selection and preparation, health, and other home living skills should constitute most of the science curriculum for most students with mental retardation. Long-term life goals for a given individual might include discussions of flowers, trees, shrubs, vegetables, fruits, beneficial/harmful plants, weather, temperature, climate, seasons, helpful animals, and pets.

SEX EDUCATION

From birth to age 18, a child typically spends about 90% of his or her time with parents and other family members and only 10% in school-related activities. Further, the sex education needs of students with mental retardation vary greatly—particularly as to the age at which they need instruction. For these reasons, it may be well to consider that, for some aspects of a student's life, school personnel should not assume unwarranted responsibility. Doing so may develop attitudes and behaviors in a student that are unacceptable to the parents. Sex education is an excellent example of such an aspect. This development is particularly significant if the student has mental retardation because the parents must deal with any resultant problems on a long-term basis. Thus, the best procedure seems to be threefold: (a) long-term planning, (b) ongoing evaluation by the IEP team to determine the student's individual needs, and (c) seeking constant input from the parents—assuming that the parents choose to participate. Monitoring the student's sexual and other social needs should be part of the annual age 25 projections.

The teaching of sex education has always been controversial. Clark and Farley (1990) reviewed the controversy and the research as they apply to students with disabilities and offered four guidelines: (a) building self-esteem, (b) answering questions clearly and accurately, (c) avoiding threats and jokes, and (d) respecting children's privacy. The controversy can be avoided in most instances by encouraging and helping parents provide most of the instruction (Varnet, 1984). Teachers, nurses, and other school personnel can be invaluable resources to parents who will take the responsibility for teaching their children these and other vital social skills that are so essential for successful and independent living. For those parents who refuse or fail to take an active role in this part of their child's education, the IEP team is left to do its best without their help. However, the parents must be encouraged to approve or disapprove such plans as part of their child's IEP.

The life goal curriculum planning and diagnostic/prescriptive procedures of this book can be particularly helpful in teaching sex education because of its individual approach. Using these procedures, the student's parents, teachers, and other IEP team members can project the individual's eventual sex education needs with increasing accuracy as he or she matures and nears graduation. The student's prescription then addresses these needs as the prescription is evaluated on at least an annual basis. In this manner, the student is taught those concepts he or she needs, but the instruction does not initiate unacceptable actions or those that would cause needless problems for the parents and other family members. The minimum program for students with mental retardation should help them avoid sexual and other social abuse and exploitation.

ACE stories can be a valuable resource in treating these sensitive issues in a non-threatening but effective manner. ACE stories can address the problem indirectly by using story lines on any topic and at any language level. Hamre-Nietupski and Williams (1977) claimed success in using a model-test-teach design and a test-teach design in a sex education and social skills program to 20 students (ages 12 to 17) whose mental retardation they described as trainable.

SUMMARY

In this chapter, I stressed the need to prepare the individual with mental retardation to live as independently as possible in adult life. Home and family living may sound like skill clusters that can be mastered almost incidentally; however, living independently can be very complex.

I identified some major problems usually associated with the student living in apartments, group homes, and elsewhere and proposed some solutions to these problems. I also examined a hierarchy of living arrangements and showed how to evaluate them.

I also emphasized the need for respite care for individuals with mental retardation.

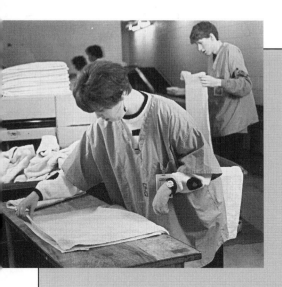

Transitional and Vocational Skills

Points to Study and Ponder

1. Why are students with mental retardation likely to need special consideration in learning how to find and keep suitable employment as adults?

2. How are independent living and successful employment related? Is either possible without the other?

3. What work experience programs are available to individuals with mental retardation in the high schools in your area?

4. What specific businesses and industries are available in your area in which individuals with mental retardation might find employment after they leave school?

5. If you teach—or otherwise work with—pre-high school students, what skills and concepts should you emphasize in preparing them for work experience and, later, for the world of competitive employment?

6. If you teach—or otherwise work with—high school students, what skills and concepts should their teachers emphasize now in preparing them for work experience and, later, for the world of competitive employment?

7. How can the age 25 projection help in determining the eventual employment needs of an individual with mental retardation?

8. Why is parent involvement particularly important in work experience and transition? Or is it less important than when their child was younger?

9. What are some problems and challenges that educators working with these students in special schools and classes might anticipate in preparing them for optimum employment success?

10. What are some problems and challenges educators working with these students in regular classes and inclusion programs might anticipate in preparing them for optimum employment success?

Society in the United States has traditionally placed a strong emphasis on the work ethic, an attitude that is reflected in its educational practices. Much effort of public and higher education is devoted to helping students qualify for suitable employment. Many other, more personal goals cannot be achieved or enjoyed without the self-satisfaction and peace of mind that come from making a genuine contribution to the family and to society and, of course, the financial resources that come from gainful employment.

The purpose of this chapter is to help parents, teachers, and other members of the student's IEP team in designing and maintaining effective programs in transition and work experience. The ultimate goal of these programs is to enable students with mental retardation to obtain and hold suitable jobs and to be as self-sustaining as possible.

This goal of satisfactory employment is particularly important in the education of children with mental retardation. This is why the central theme of any school plan or curriculum for students with mental retardation must relate closely to transitional and vocational skills (Elrod & Sorgenfrei, 1988). *Transition* in this context refers to the passage of a student with mental retardation from school-sponsored experiences to the postschool environment of employment and independent living. Clark and Kolstoe (1990) declared that "transition from school to adult living is a broad, life-career focus that parents, school personnel, and adult service agencies should have in developing transition programs" (p. 42). They also asserted that transition and independent living are inseparably related. Independent living is discussed in Chapter 13.

Most skills and concepts discussed throughout this book are concerned with improving capabilities that will eventually lead to employment. But the skills and concepts highlighted in this chapter relate most directly to the student's successful transition from the school to the workforce; they include finding job information, seeking and retaining a job, forming good work habits, following instructions, exercising self-control, and preparing for eventual employment through on-campus work experiences. Treatment in this and other chapters involves sample long-term, annual, and short-term IEP goals, along with some GIAs. A transition and employment preparation program for students with mental retardation must also consider communication and interpersonal-socialization skills.

CAREER EDUCATION

Professionals in the area of mental retardation currently define the term *career education* broadly enough to include virtually all preparation of individuals for the world of work. In this sense, career education includes helping students become aware of the necessity and rewards of working, in addition to teaching good work habits, career awareness, career exploration, job information, job simulation, and specific career preparation. Teachers of students at all age levels must become involved in career education. Because some career education is important for all individuals with mental retardation, the chapter covers preparation for all levels of employment, from work that is closely supervised and sheltered to work that is full and competitive. The term *career* is extended downward from the traditional application that implies the kind of profession or vocation for which a student with mental retardation rarely qualifies.

Importance of Parental Involvement

Parental involvement is an important component of a program that will provide a good prognosis for transition (Moon & Beale, 1984; Werching, Gaylord-Ross, & Gaylord-Ross, 1986). Parents of children with mental retardation are likely to be responsible for their children's welfare longer than most parents; thus, teachers need to consider and honor the parents' preferences regarding educational planning and goals. Studies have found that parents of children with disabilities express strong preferences for school programs that stress employment and other transitional skills (Brotherson et al., 1988; McDonnell, Wilcox, Boles, & Bellamy, 1985). In fact, McDonnell et al. (1985) reported that parents of children with mental retardation and other disabilities anticipated that their children would need extensive transition-type services up to 10 years after graduation. And predictably, transitional programs that involve parents have more success in meeting long-term goals for the children than programs that lack the parental component (McNair & Rusch, 1991; Retish, 1988).

Importance of Work Experience Training

Students with mental retardation are often unable to transfer training they have received at school to practical life situations; nowhere is this deficiency more evident than in the transition from school to adult life (Affleck, Edgar, Levine, & Kortering, 1990). Frank and Sitlington (1993) reported that only 20% of more than 300 high school graduates with mental retardation were making this adjustment successfully. Sitlington and Frank (1993) investigated the relationship of gender to employment success and reported no significant differences, except that males earned slightly more money.

One reason many current programs for students with mental retardation fail to meet the students' needs for transition to adulthood and eventual employment is that they tend to concentrate on academics, adjusting to levels appropriate for younger children (Edgar, 1988; Fettgather, 1989). Such programs often fail to recognize that it is difficult for students with mental retardation to achieve even a minimal level of functional literacy. Toch (1984) referred to the failure of students with low ability and disabilities as the dark side of a movement toward academic excellence. In contrast, Hasazi, Johnson, Hasazi, Gordon, and Hull (1989) reported that students with disabilities, including mental retardation, are more successful in transition if they are given specific work experience training. In fact, the training for work was shown to be more effective for students with disabilities than for students without. Also, Porter (1980) found that a well-planned program of vocational instruction has a positive effect on many junior high school students with mild mental retardation.

Importance of Social and Communication Skills

Social and communication skills are also important in the ability of a student with mental retardation to adjust effectively to adult life and eventual employment (Karen et al.,

1985; Mire & Chisholm, 1990; Roessler & Lewis, 1984). In transitional situations, the student will be placed in a wide variety of unfamiliar communication challenges and may need to use vocabulary and idioms that have not become familiar during the school experience. In the classroom, the teachers and other professionals may have placed their expectations at the student's current performance level. But in the transitional period, the student will need to respond to the expectations of employers, supervisors, and fellow employees, who are not likely to have had training or experience in assessing and adapting to a disability level. With specific and intensive training, many students with mental retardation can master the necessary skills for workplace communication. Chadsey-Rusch et al. (1984) reported success in teaching 3 adults with severe/profound mental retardation to ask essential questions in the employment setting.

Some of the most crucial transitional needs are in the area of interpersonal-socialization skills (Elksnin & Elksnin, 1991; Foss & Peterson, 1981; Fox, 1989; Greenspan & Schultz, 1981). Thus, in addition to communication skills, high curriculum priority must be assigned to reducing and eliminating disqualifying personal behaviors, such as temper tantrums, dishonesty, unkempt appearance, disobedience, hitting, and unsanitary habits. R. Williams (1985) pointed out that, to attain the greatest success, a child's parents must be closely involved here. She also identified the challenge of designing procedures to correct these serious social problems (e.g., stealing) while maintaining the child's privacy and dignity. Children must also learn less dramatic but socially acceptable behavior related directly to employability; for example, an individual to be employed in a restaurant must learn not to eat leftover food while cleaning up.

Life Goal Planning and Transition

Vocational goals projected for students with mental retardation are often unrealistic. This inaccuracy seems to stem partly from the general immaturity and inexperience of the students and partly from impractical goals that may be harbored by their parents and other members of their IEP teams. Usually, well-meaning parents and educators overestimate the student's eventual vocational abilities, but often the process reverses and they underestimate what the student will eventually be able to do.

Age 25 Projection, Proactivity, and Conceptual Distance

The age 25 projection offers the parents, teachers, and other members of the IEP team a means of reconciling differences between a student's real and assumed abilities. To implement the age 25 projection, the team must first review the long-term vocational IEP goals for the student, including all life goals the student is likely to complete while he or she is in school. Next, the team arranges annual goals as subdivisions of the long-term goals and thus projects which goals will be completed during each of the student's remaining school years. Finally, they arrange short-term goals as subdivisions of the annual goals.

Yearly review of this projection and evaluation of the status of the various goals help those responsible for the student's IEP in judging whether progress that is faster or slower than anticipated indicates the projections are built on incorrect assumptions about what the student will actually be able to attain. Accordingly, upward or downward adjustments may be made in the student's long-term goals.

This procedure is valuable because it almost forces parents and other team members to focus on the time that the student, needing to live essentially with the vocational skills and concepts achieved by that time, will leave school. During the student's early years, long-term life goals are understandably difficult to predict with accuracy. As the student reaches the teenage years, however, IEP team members using the age 25 projection should be able to envision the student's eventual life status with increasing precision. Burgess and Zhu (1990) indicated that realistic predictions for some students, particularly those whose mental retardation is severe/profound, must acknowledge that the individual may never be able to participate in competitive or paid employment. Such a determination must be made as early as possible in a student's life so that valuable time will not be wasted in attempting to prepare the student for vocational pursuits that can never be achieved.

If the IEP team continually evaluates the student's progress and predicts eventual status, including ability to perform as well as possible in adult settings of home, work, and community, the student's final school years can be used to refine practical problem-solving skills and to find compensations for those skills and concepts the student is unlikely to master (Cheney & Foss, 1984). Team members should use the concept of conceptual distance in predicting that the student's annual progress is likely to be commensurate with the progress of earlier years, with some allowance for spurts of growth that might occur with the added motivation of actually working in the community for the first time.

PLACEMENT IN SCHOOL

Chapter 5 presents detailed explanations of the strengths and weaknesses of regular and special class placement for students with mental retardation. This section reviews some of the more important considerations as they apply to transition. Of course, some settings are more conducive to effective work experience training and eventual transition than others, so if possible, consideration of these factors should be made before a student is in high school and his or her placement is already established. These decisions can best be made by the student's IEP team after it has evaluated local conditions. If decisions are not made early enough, the IEP team will have to work within placement parameters that have already been set.

When decisions regarding inclusion programs are being made, it is important to remember that mental retardation does not disappear with age and that, considering conceptual distance, the IEP team must anticipate that a student with mental retardation will fall progressively farther behind his or her peers. Hence, increased problems must be anticipated when the student reaches secondary level (Hasazi & Clark, 1988).

This progressive distance between students with retardation and their peers also increases the likelihood that a student with mental retardation will have considerable difficulty in obtaining and holding a job regardless of placement in regular or special classroom situations.

Lilly (1982) theorized that students whose mental retardation is educable (EMR, or presumably mild/moderate) share more characteristics with students who have no mental retardation than with students whose retardation is severer; he advocated placing them in a regular class curriculum, as did Reynolds (1989). Related to transition and future employment, potential advantages of mainstreaming for students with mental retardation include association with peers who represent superior communication and behavioral models (Stainback & Stainback, 1987).

This approach must be carefully evaluated, however (Brown et al., 1991). One employment-related complication occurs with the timing of graduation. Mainstreamed students with any disability usually graduate with their classmates at about age 17 or 18, an age at which a student with mental retardation is not ready to enter adult life, particularly to go into an independent job situation. Such a student could elect to remain in school until better prepared at age 21 or 22 but would be less likely to do so than a student in a special education program. In addition, the social modeling may not be as optimistic as planned. A number of social problems, such as dropping out, drug use, and delinquency, appear to have a strong correlation with low grades, low IQs, and low achievement levels (Cuellar & Cuellar, 1991; Rumberger, 1987; Walters & Kranzler, 1970). Low-achieving students, such as those with mental retardation, are likely to be placed in programs in which they are grouped with students who have a high incidence of these problems. In situations in which violence is increasing and discipline is decreasing, students with mental retardation who are mainstreamed with low-achieving classmates are likely to be exposed to negative, rather than positive, situations of interrelating and communicating with peers. Perhaps solutions for these social problems will soon be found, but the prospects do not appear to be favorable.

For good reason, P.L. 94–142 requires and the IDEA reinforces the need for a wide array of placements and service delivery patterns to serve school-age individuals with disabilities. Well-conceived special programs offer important strengths, particularly programs associated with individualized instruction and with transition and work experience needs. For example, it has taken many decades to develop work experience programs and vocation-centered curricula for students with mental retardation, even when necessary financial and other resources have been available (Brolin, 1989; Edgar, 1988, 1992). These programs have been developed primarily by specially trained teachers in conjunction with special classes. Special schools and classes are also criticized for the lack of role models for social and communication skills that students must develop to function effectively in the workforce and in society in general. However, these role models and associations can be provided in special facilities by peer tutors, recreation programs, and elsewhere in the community. It is noteworthy that the significant social contacts of an individual with mental retardation are not limited to CA peers—particularly after graduation. Work experience programs place students with mental retardation in real-life situations that provide interactions with people of all ages—employers, supervisors, fellow workers, and customers. Work experience programs, as well as significant field trips and community-based transitional programs, for students with mental retardation are not impossible to manage in regular class settings, but they do present some considerable challenges. For example, these students typically require much closer supervision than others. Also, it is difficult for a regular class teacher to manage the logistics (e.g., job location, insurance, transportation) while he or she is in charge of a large class of other students. The departmentalized format at the secondary level also tends to obscure the responsibility for work experience and transition, and it is essential that a specialist trained in mental retardation be available to operate the program and supervise the students on the job.

Regional variation and the nationwide trend to identify fewer and fewer students with mental retardation over time heavily affect transitional programs. Such students may begin mainstreaming having been identified as mentally retarded and provided with special services and then later change locations or schools and suddenly be without the assistance they previously needed in order to be successful. Many drop out. Even when students with mental retardation stay in school, regular class teachers rarely have the training, the insight, or the time to be able to offer the kind of program the students really need, particularly in the area of transition. Once students have been assigned to a mainstreamed or inclusion program, a knowledgeable teacher or transitional specialist should be assigned to track the progress of each student, identify the kinds of problems that might lead to dropping out, and institute an intervention program to give aid to these students and keep them in school (Kunisawa, 1988). This specialist must also contact each student who does drop out of school—particularly between school years or when a change of school building is necessary—and facilitate reentry whenever possible.

TRANSITIONAL COMPONENT OF PROGRAMS

Particularly at the secondary level, programs designed for students with mental retardation, whether mainstreamed programs or self-contained special education schools or classes, must emphasize transition and preparation for employment (Cobb & Hasazi, 1987; Edgar, 1987). As McDonnell, Hardman, and Hightower (1989) pointed out, high schools must expand their roles greatly to meet the transitional needs of students with severe disabilities. This is particularly true where students with mental retardation are concerned because their disabilities impose such severe and widely varying limitations on an individual's learning capabilities (Ohanian, 1990).

Because individuals with mental retardation typically have difficulties in competing with others in employment and with retaining their jobs, these aspects should be points of emphasis in their preparation programs. Thus, secondary vocational programs based on the work-release concept will probably not be successful. Instead, programs focused on the needs of students with mental retardation should include long-range planning by parents, along with most of the students' secondary teachers and administrators. Plans should be carefully written and adopted that will be eligible for school board and administrative approval and in conformity with legal requirements and guidelines.

Such plans should include provisions for curriculum collaboration, coordination with adult service agencies, financial support, transportation, and adequately trained professional personnel (Hasazi, 1985; McDonnell & Hardman, 1985; Stainback & Stainback, 1992). Although important, this type of extensive group planning may be difficult to actualize in behalf of a heterogeneous group of students who comprise roughly 1% of the student body, often less.

Assessing Personal Preferences

Students' personal preferences must be carefully considered. Depending on the severity of their mental retardation, many are not able to evaluate their own vocational interests and aptitudes. Thus, the extent to which individuals with mental retardation can speak for themselves and express realistic preferences must be carefully assessed (Stanovich & Stanovich, 1979). Because those whose retardation is mild/moderate can usually express vocational preferences to some extent or can be trained to do so, vocational interest inventories might be adapted for use with these students. Brookings and Bolton (1986) reported success in identifying vocational interests of persons with disabilities by using procedures that paralleled published vocational inventories. They recommended the United States Employment Service Interest Inventory (USES-II; United States Employment Service, n.d.) for vocational rehabilitation counseling with disabled adults. The USES-II could be adapted to assess the vocational interests of individuals with mental retardation if proper assistance were given to the responding individual. Clark and Kolstoe (1990) reviewed the use of vocational inventories with individuals with mental retardation, however, and reported none to be very satisfactory.

Perhaps the best use of formal interest inventories is to suggest lines of questioning and areas of possible interest to investigate with less formal procedures. Certainly, when the mental retardation is too severe for the individual to qualify for the vocations and trades described in most vocational interest inventories, special adaptations must be made. In addition to using an inventory with such a student, it is wise to consult with the student or a parent or with some other respondent who knows the student well. In this manner, the AAMD-Becker Reading-Free Vocational Interest Inventory or a current revision (Becker, 1987; Becker & Becker, 1983), originally intended for students with mild/moderate mental retardation, might be adapted for those whose disability is more severe. When Wilgosh and Barry (1990) used a third-party respondent procedure with parents of 29 students whose mental retardation they described as "trainable," they found greater correspondence between parent and teacher ratings than between inventory scores and ratings.

In addition to formal inventories, more informal, personal methods may be used to discern students' interests and desires. One procedure that has proved beneficial is to make a "photo album" of local businesses and industries that offer experience and employment to students with mental retardation. Videotapes showing aspects of the businesses, including the tasks involved in the available jobs, could also be used. These tapes could be played and replayed for discussion, with or without the sound.

Evaluation and education for students with mental retardation must focus on the highest level of employment the individual is likely to achieve in adult life.

Evaluating Skills

Capabilities as well as interests must also be assessed if career education is to be realistic. Most state divisions of rehabilitation or special education offer some assistance in work skills evaluation for older students with disabilities, including those with mental retardation. Evaluation centers sponsored by these agencies may offer both formal and informal procedures. For example, after receiving a battery of aptitude and interest inventories, the client may also be given a series of work samples typical of actual tasks performed in business and industry. If such an agency is not available, students may be placed in a variety of employment situations including on-campus and competitive off-campus examples, and their aptitudes as well as apparent preferences observed.

Considering Safety

One of the most important considerations in planning any curriculum for students with mental retardation is the safety of the individual. Safety is of obvious and special concern in transition because students in all phases of work experience and employment must travel and work in environments that become increasingly unprotected. Potentially dangerous objects, liquids, tools, and other materials must be available on the job and cannot be placed out of reach as in the home and classroom. Furthermore, as students gain work experience, increasing independence and decreasing supervision will be expected.

In addition to physical risks and hazards, the transition from school to independent living, work experience, and employment will result in a wider array of social situations that may be potentially hazardous to the student with mental retardation. The life goal planning for every student with mental retardation must consider the increasing risks of abuse and exploitation that come with the transitional experience.

WORK EXPERIENCE

The core of any transitional program is work experience that involves students directly in the world of work. Direct work experience is invaluable in helping students with mental retardation make the adjustment from school into the fullest employment they can handle. Technology and resources needed to establish effective work experience programs are becoming available (Meers, 1992).

A number of significant benefits to a work experience program go beyond merely gaining salable skills. Motivation is a life-long benefit: Students learn by working that work is necessary, that it must be done well, and that it can be rewarding. As work itself becomes meaningful, students also see meaning in the classroom learning and school-based activities that have led up to it. Additional benefits occur in socialization and acceptance: Students are viewed with new respect by friends and family members who see them working and possibly even earning money; friends may be envious of those who are able to do this during school time. A benefit often overlooked by educators is that of long-term cost effectiveness. Hill and Wehman (1983) reported that placing students with mental retardation—even those whose retardation is severe—in competitive employment represents a substantial saving of thousands of tax dollars.

On-Campus Work Experience

In a work experience program operated by the school, students are placed in a progression of work stations or jobs on school property. The first experiences take place on campus where students can be closely supervised. The progression is diagnosed and prescribed individually, beginning with prerequisite skills and concepts, advancing to career education, moving into classroom jobs, and finally culminating in campus jobs. Each situation is diagnosed in terms of safety and efficiency, and supervision is administered accordingly. When the situation permits, supervision is gradually relaxed, but tighter supervision is usually necessary when students move from one setting to another—for example, when students leave the classroom or immediate vicinity for the first time. Because of the nature of on-campus programs and the necessity of waiting until students reach the legal age for working off-campus, most students complete all phases and settings offered by the school. Both on-campus and off-campus phases of the work experience program must be carefully correlated with career education and other school-related activities, especially those that emphasize intrapersonal skills (Nietupski, Hamre-Nietupski, Welch, & Anderson, 1983).

Off-Campus Work Experience

As soon as students have reached the legal minimum age and are diagnosed as ready, they are moved to an off-campus work experience program. State and local laws vary, but typically the age is 15 or 16. Individual programs are diagnosed and prescribed, generally in the following sequence: sheltered → supported → unpaid or unsupported → competitive. At this phase of the work experience program, students may bypass one or more settings as appropriate to individual capabilities and needs. Off-campus work experience represents an abrupt and substantial increase in the demands made on the individual. For example, this experience may be the first in which the student is required to leave campus unsupervised, use public transportation, and report for work unsupervised. Such a broadened experience is based on a whole new set of entry-level skills that must be evaluated and taught where necessary. Chapter 7 contains several *reversion* procedures that are necessary in these instances to help the person through this type of abrupt task with components that cannot be manipulated in small increments.

Several kinds of work experience have been adopted by U.S. schools to assist students in making career decisions, gaining skills, and eventually finding employment after graduation. Some are more useful for students who do not have disabilities than for those who do. However, some elements of each of the most common programs have the potential to be beneficial for students with mental retardation.

Vocational Work Experience

Vocational work experience, patterned after traditional apprenticeships, places the student in a situation to be trained for a specific vocation or trade. This kind of program is not commonly used with students with mental retardation because such students rarely qualify for a vocation or trade per se. Such students may be employable as helpers in vocational or trade areas, however; with extensive training and experience, individuals with mental retardation can often perform beyond the general public's expectation in the world of work. Each student's IEP team must carefully weigh the student's characteristics and potentials to discern the advantages and disadvantages of investing the student's time in a specific business or area of employment.

Exploratory Work Experience

Exploratory work experience places the individual in a variety of job situations designed to assess the student's aptitudes, interests, and skills at the same time that valuable work training is being acquired. Such experiences can be structured on campus, where students can participate with a variety of supervisors and other employees in a succession of placements capable of being sheltered or otherwise controlled as needed. Students are generally rotated to a new placement every 6 to 8 weeks. Possible opportunities include placement under supervision of custodians and groundskeepers or work in cafeterias, snack bars, or messenger services. Supervisors may be hesitant at first to work with exploratory work experience students because each student's participation is transitory, and by the time the individual is well enough trained to contribute constructively, he or she is due for a transfer. Most school employees, however, are willing to help if they understand the nature of the students and the importance of meeting these work experience needs.

Off-campus sequences can also be structured; typically, a program consists of a series of stations in the community or a series combining school and community. Students are assigned to each station for a period of time and are rotated until each has experienced all of the stations; they usually receive school credit but no pay. During the experience, the students participate in a work orientation or career education class in which the teacher/coordinator counsels them individually and as a group, provides job instruction and information, and conducts discussions of the students' experiences on the various job placements. This type of transition into the community is particularly advantageous for students who are timid or students whose aptitudes, interests, and skills are particularly limited or in need of further evaluation.

Although it has many advantages, a program of this type is not without its difficulties. Schools may find it more difficult to persuade merchants and businesspeople to cooperate than to solicit the help of school employees. Yet, it is important that the number of placements be equal to or greater than the number of students in order to facilitate the rotation system. Another potential drawback concerns transportation. Students who must depend on school buses for transportation must have placements located close enough to walk either to the school or to their homes. As the students rotate through the stations, their transportation needs must be reevaluated with each change.

General Work Experience

Sometimes referred to as work practice, general work experience gives a student a thorough introduction to the world of work by assigning him or her to a job that will generally last at least a full semester, often a full school year. For this employment, a student will usually receive both school credit and some remuneration. This is the method most frequently used for students with mental retardation.

Each student's IEP team must work carefully in planning the most beneficial work experience for that individual by using the evaluative data compiled in the career education processes and in the earlier on-campus and off-campus work sequences. Careful evaluation is important because it is easy to underestimate or overestimate the abilities of a student with mental retardation. If abilities are in question, placements of shorter than the semester duration may be desired because they will result in a greater variety of work settings where the student may be observed and evaluated as well as receive job-specific training. This approach reduces the risk of observing and training the student exclusively in one or two limited fields that may later prove to be unsuitable. If the student's interests and abilities have been fairly accurately discerned, however, longer-term placements are desirable because they teach the student to maintain him-

or herself on a job, which is one of the major goals of a general work experience pro-gram. For such students, it is recommended that off-campus placements be established to last for the entire school year.

Sheltered Workshops

Some students, particularly those whose mental retardation is severe/profound, need a protective environment where they can learn to work in a competitive atmosphere. Sheltered workshops are work experience environments where the primary function is to provide experience, training, evaluation, and employment for individuals with dis-abilities, in contrast to placements in schools, businesses, and industries, where the pri-mary function is to create products or perform services, with the participation of per-sons with disabilities a minor aspect of the operation. Some sheltered workshops serve several disabilities; others focus on only one disability, such as mental retardation. School districts and public agencies may operate their own sheltered workshops or contract with privately owned and operated sheltered workshops for work-related ser-vices. Most sheltered workshops are financed partly through public or private funds and partly through contracts with business firms through which the workers provide certain services for a specified amount of money. Private workshops sometimes charge tuition, for which school funding can be used for participation by school-age students. When participants are no longer eligible for school subsidy, funding is generally obtained from parents or from other public or private sources. Most participants in sheltered workshops are older youths and adults.

Sheltered workshops operate under a variety of purposes and methodologies. An ideal sheltered workshop for students with mental retardation should include at least the following: (a) evaluation of client vocational skills, (b) general and specific training for employment, (c) remuneration for those unable to work elsewhere, (d) opportunity for recreation, (e) placement services for future employment, and (f) long-term employ-ment for those unable to move on to other job opportunities. Job placement in the com-munity, however, is almost always considered to be superior to retaining the individual in the sheltered workshop. Unfortunately, recreation, placement, and terminal employ-ment are often overlooked. Some workshops are reluctant to provide recreational facili-ties even though these are particularly important for school-age clients; although school funding is used for recreation for other students, those with mental retardation are often neglected. Placement and terminal employment are more significant for students with mental retardation than for those with other disabilities because students with mental retardation are more likely to need services for longer periods of time.

Although sheltered workshops are generally used only with students whose mental retardation is severe or profound, the workshop environment offers many important advantages to this population. The wide array of services and activities offered by the workshop enables students to bypass the other off-campus experiences that might be too difficult or competitive for them. In-depth evaluation of interests and of social and interpersonal skills can be provided, along with typical work samples and both general and specific employment training, because sheltered workshops employ personnel with the training and experience to accomplish these goals. The unity of purpose is another general strength of sheltered workshops: They can concentrate on evaluation, training, and employment needs of their clients, rather than on the production of goods and services. Work experience placements in industries, businesses, and public services cannot devote comparable time or personnel to students with mental retardation because the presence of the students is only superficial to the day-to-day workplace operation.

Although they offer these strengths, sheltered workshops have been subjected to increasing criticism (Ferguson & Ferguson, 1986; McCaughrin, Ellis, Rusch, & Heal, 1993). An inherent potential weakness of any sheltered workplace is its institutional environment. Students with disabilities tend to be segregated socially unless workshop supervisors make special efforts to provide social and recreational activities or to ensure that students attend activities elsewhere in the community. Another weakness stems from the financial dependency of the workshop on contracted work from business or industry. Despite the focus of the institution on helping students with disabilities, production pressure does tend to encourage retaining the best workers, who ironically are those most able to move on to work experience in a less sheltered environment. Also, experience and seasonal conditions show that it is difficult—though not impossible—to arrange for a reliable flow of contract work projects that are realistic and that provide the desired training for a workforce that is—or should be—constantly losing its best-trained members.

Until recently, most programs have not provided placement assistance for students who are ready to leave their training facilities. This lack has made it difficult for students to gainfully use the skills they have acquired. Clients who require terminal employment can sometimes be placed in such facilities as Good Will Industries, but those capable of holding outside jobs should be placed in suitable situations in business and industry.

FINANCIAL OPTIONS FOR WORK EXPERIENCE

One of the most popular ways to classify work experience placements is the extent to which the student is paid. Ordinarily, a student with mental retardation must progress through a sequence of unpaid or unsupported → supported → competitive work experiences. As one would suspect, some students are capable of advancing through this sequence more rapidly than others.

Unpaid or Unsupported Work Experience

Students usually begin their work experience in various arrangements under which they receive school credit but are not paid for the work. The term *unpaid* refers to this situation; *unsupported* means that the employer is not being paid to employ and/or train the student. On-campus work experience is usually unpaid, although students may receive some compensation if the school has funds available. For students with mental retardation, off-campus employers often think the students' low productivity does not warrant payment and that the training the students receive is enough compensation for what they contribute. Unsupported or unpaid employment jobs are usually in closely supervised settings where the student serves as a helper to a responsible adult; examples include safe, simple assembly line work, such as packing small fruit; assisting with custodial work; stocking grocery and other shelves; and assisting and cleaning in fast-food restaurants, bakeries, pet shops, garden centers/nurseries, schools, and so forth.

Supported Employment and Work Experience

Supported employment is a situation in which the student's parent, the school district, or another source is required to pay the employer to employ and train the student. In supported employment, the student may be paid some or all of the support funds or may not be paid at all. The funds often pay for an employment counselor to assess the client's abilities and interests, to help the client find a job, and to provide training, supervision, and other assistance to help the client assume the most suitable employment role for which he or she is capable. The number and type of specific job locations are endless and vary with the location, but usually they include all of those listed above for unpaid/unsupported employment—with increased responsibility and accompanying productivity. Hospitals have been a great source of work experience opportunities for students with mental retardation. They offer an almost unlimited variety of "helper" settings with gradually increasing responsibilities, including gift shops, casual to serious food preparation and service, groundskeeping, plumbing, cleaning, laundry service, and many others. Recent emphasis on sanitation has imposed a few limitations on the availability of hospital placements, but the opportunities appear to continue—particularly for students whose disabilities are not seriously limiting.

Supported employment may be an acceptable alternative to sheltered workshops, particularly for individuals whose mental retardation is relatively severe (Konig & Schalock, 1991; Sinnott-Oswald, Gliner, & Spencer, 1991). Test, Hinson, Kuel, and Solow (1993) interviewed 34 persons with developmental disabilities in supported employment and reported that the majority of them liked their jobs and would rather work in the community than in a workshop. The people also indicated that they were making friends on the job.

The employment counselor may also provide training and counseling to the employer regarding the nature of the disability, the capabilities of the trainee, remuneration for the student, and issues of tax and insurance. Supported employment usually occurs in the private sector, although government agencies may also participate. McCaughrin et al. (1993) reported that supported employment is quite cost-effective—in fact, more so than the sheltered workshop approach. Inge, Banks, Wehman, Hill, and Shafer (1988) compared individuals in sheltered workshops with those in competitive employment on a number of variables. They found that those in competitive employment made greater gains in advancement, fiscal responsibility, community integration, physical abilities, and social skills. In making similar comparisons of local conditions and facilities, IEP team members are cautioned to make sure that the competing groups are of equal ability; that is, to make valid comparisons, the individuals must be either randomly assigned to the competing facilities or shown otherwise to be of equal CA, IQ, and so forth. One might assume that, in using intact groups, the individuals already placed in competitive employment are likely to be superior to those in the sheltered workshops. It is likely that future developments will include the best elements of both sheltered and competitive work environments.

Competitive Employment

The ultimate work experience for an individual with mental retardation is competitive employment. This arrangement places the individual in gainful employment that is not directly influenced or supported by public or private charitable funds. The individual capable of doing so should go into competitive employment as soon as possible and soon graduate to a full-time job. The individual may still be a trainee and may also be a student. Students who can go into competitive employment before graduation can be visited and assisted by school personnel if necessary. Researchers are somewhat inconsistent on the prognosis for competitive employment for persons with mental retardation, but they agree that it should be encouraged whenever it is realistic. Wehman et al. (1985) found that the students they studied did quite well in competitive employment when they had been supplied with adequate training and experience. Heal, Copher, De Stefano, and Rusch (1989) were less optimistic about overall success but agreed that increasing individual training, supervision, and other services did increase the odds for a student. Goldberg, McClean, LaVigne, and Fratolillo (1990) affirmed that even doubtful competitive placements result in a higher quality of life for an individual with mental retardation than continuing sheltered or supported employment. Steere, Wood, Pancsofar, and Rucker (1993) maintained that vocational programs for students with severe disabilities can be successful if the programs are well designed and operated. Competitive work experience and employment opportunities are virtually unlimited and vary with local situations but include all those mentioned above for unpaid and sheltered employment. Care must always be exercised, however, to select jobs for students in safe work environments. Admittedly, after graduation a student may seek any type of employment he or she prefers, but practical and liability considerations should rule out unsafe situations selected by school officials.

SETTING UP THE WORK EXPERIENCE PROGRAM

In establishing a work experience program, several aspects must be considered. These aspects include meeting the necessary legal, financial, and insurance requirements; locating suitable job settings; and providing appropriate supervision and remuneration.

Legal Considerations

Any school program must conform with existing local, state, and federal laws and regulations. But such compliance is especially important when work experience programs will take individuals of school age into situations where they are likely to receive less supervision than they would on other school-sponsored activities. Most school districts have a business manager or another official who is responsible for securing the legal guidance necessary to operate school programs. Members of a student's IEP team should consult these officials and acquaint themselves with legal provisions and requirements. Teachers, work supervisors, and other program participants who are not specifically trained in the law should obtain all legal opinions and permissions in writing.

Safety is an important matter, legally as well as morally. Although the ultimate purpose of work experience programs is to enable the student to maintain employment and to travel independently to and from a job, the student must be given only the freedom of action he or she can handle without injury or harm. State laws usually provide some limitations as to placements that may be hazardous, such as truck or shipping docks, places where alcoholic beverages are involved, and settings where a student's moral development may be impaired.

The workload of a child is also restricted by law. Child labor legislation dictates the number of combined hours a child can spend between a job and school—in many places a total of 40 hours a week or less. School-age children who are not in school full-time will usually need valid work permits. State and local regulations may also mandate the amount of school credit that can be given for an out-of-school experience.

Financial Considerations

Operating a good work experience program does not usually require excessive expense. If the program is initiated as an alternative to part of an existing program, additional teacher time will probably not be necessary. Additional expenses for transportation, insurance, and supplies are generally minimal.

Insurance Requirements

The school official responsible for ensuring that the program operates in compliance with the law is usually also responsible for maintaining adequate insurance coverage. Ordinarily, both the school district and the employer will carry workmen's compensation insurance, but program developers should be sure this coverage is in place. It is usually beneficial to consider students as employees of the school district when they are working at unpaid jobs and to shift to the employers' workmen's compensation coverage when they begin to receive pay. Both school district and employer will usually carry liability insurance. It is strongly recommended that the teacher or supervisor of a work experience program have professional liability insurance as well.

The Jobs

Initial placement for students in work experience programs is often in jobs where they function as "helpers," rather than take the positions of full-time employees. Some students will remain indefinitely as helpers, but those who are capable should be given adequate opportunities and training to qualify for the highest employment level they have the ability to attain.

The most effective procedure for placing students appears to be the informal process of supervisor evaluating the interests, needs, and aptitudes of a given student, matching the student to a carefully evaluated job situation, and then making contact with the employer on an individual basis. The supervisor should discuss the nature and extent of a student's disabilities thoroughly with the employer. It is also important to consult closely with the parents in determining appropriate and beneficial placement for the student. Hasazi et al. (1985) reported that many students with mental retardation find employment through informal means. The researchers found that the majority of the 343 students they studied eventually found jobs mainly through their families and friends. This finding would suggest that involving parents and other family members in developing employment-related capabilities during the intermediate years is well worth the effort.

Overall attitudes of employers toward hiring individuals with disabilities have been positive, particularly in large enterprises. Sitlington and Easterday (1992) interviewed 84 employers and concluded that most had honorable motives for offering employment to students with mental retardation. After surveying Fortune 500 corporate executives, Levy, Jessop, Rimmerman, and Levy (1992) reported generally positive attitudes toward the employability of persons with severe disabilities. Craig and Boyd (1990) found that urban and rural employers had an approximately equal willingness to hire people with disabilities. They also indicated that proportionally more large employers than small employers had workers with disabilities and that public administration, transportation, and service industries than other industries were more likely to hire people with disabilities. Baumeister and Morris (1992) asserted that rural vocational programs can be effective when they are well planned with well-trained supervisors, administrators, and employers.

Work experience and possible eventual full-time employment for students with mental retardation have been found in a number of areas. In recent years, employers in the fast-food industry have trained and employed many students with mental retardation. Employers in other industries that have shown a general willingness to participate in work experience programs include hospitals, fruit packing companies, commercial and house cleaners, farms, and food processing firms. Students with mental retardation have been successful in job placements in which they have been assigned as helpers in offices, laundries, garages and gas stations, body and fender shops, kitchens, bakeries, hotels, rest homes, classrooms, hospitals, restaurants and cafes, paint shops, nurseries, factories, and mail rooms. These students have also been shown to be capable in assisting specialists such as painters, mechanics, custodians, carpenters, and beauticians.

With varying degrees of assistance and supervision, students with mental retardation have worked as "independent" sewing machine operators, elevator operators, vegetable peelers, dishwashers, stock clerks, assembly line workers, mail sorters, kick press operators, playground attendants, hospital orderly assistants, file clerks, messengers, photocopier operators, press cleaners, supply clerks, fruit pickers, buspersons, and collators.

In arranging job experience placements for students with mental retardation, it is important to consider the availability of transportation to and from job sites. Often, parents will consent to drive their child to and from work. Local bus service is available in many places, and some students with retardation are capable of using it. Some districts have been known to provide taxis when other means of transportation have not been available; other districts have used minibuses or vans. Supervisors should avoid assuming responsibility for transporting a student to and from a job. Such a practice is unwise from the standpoint of insurance, and in many places it is forbidden by law.

Supervision and Evaluation

Supervision is probably the most crucial aspect of the work experience program; programs without adequate supervision usually are not successful. The fact that an individual needs a work experience program is evidence that he or she is not ready to enter the job market without supervision.

It is important that the school work experience supervisor be able to locate additional jobs and consult with employers while the students are on the job. If a job is complex, the supervisor may need to work alongside for a few days until the student becomes accustomed to the routine. Thus, the purpose of the program is defeated by the flip-flop practice of some districts in which a supervisor teaches Class 1 in the morning while Class 2 works, and then teaches Class 2 in the afternoon while Class 1 is on the job.

Supervision/evaluation visits should be frequent, and ordinarily the employer does not need to be notified in advance every time. Experience has shown that employers are generally willing to cooperate with work experience programs in inverse proportion to the amount of paperwork they are required to do. Thus, the supervisor should fill out any necessary evaluation forms and checklists by questioning the employer, rather than leave forms for the employer to complete on his or her own time.

One major purpose of any work experience program is to expose the student to a variety of employers, fellow employees, and supervisory personnel. Each person is likely to adhere to a different management or supervisory style to which the student is supposed to become accustomed. Experience shows that work experience placements—like the world of work generally—tend to range from at least businesslike to unsympathetic or downright hostile places to work. Some employers, however, develop a paternalistic attitude toward a student employee with mental retardation, fearing that any negative comments will cause trouble for the student. Much has been said in earlier chapters of the need for nonaversive reinforcement in working with students with mental retardation. In an interesting survey of supported employment job coaches and supervisors, Helms and Moore (1993) reported great confusion and different interpretations as to what constituted nonaversive—as opposed to aversive—intervention for workers with disabilities. Understandably, in placing a student with a disability, the tendency is to favor situations in which the employer and supervisors are friendly and the atmosphere congenial—a work situation that may or may not reflect the real world. The school work experience supervisor or IEP team must carefully consider these possibilities in making the placements. Further, the work experience supervisor needs to ask specific, pointed questions. For example, "Does he get here on time?" invites a vague nod; "What time did he arrive at work today?" identifies a specific behavior. "How is she doing?" does not give the employer a clue about how to judge the student's performance. But, "How would you rate her last assignment?" or "Does the student's work performance merit a paid (though possibly below minimum wage) position?" focuses on a specific situation that can be described and discussed.

One aspect of evaluation often overlooked is the client's satisfaction. Dudley and Schatz (1985) demonstrated that even workers whose mental retardation is relatively severe can be interviewed and/or observed to identify and evaluate their contentment with the employment situation. Likewise, Moore, Agran, and Fodor-Davis (1989) used proactive self-management techniques, such as goal setting, self-instruction, and self-reinforcement, to improve the production rates of 4 workers with severe mental retardation.

Remuneration

Because students in a work experience program produce less per hour than regular employees, they usually receive less than the minimum hourly wage established by law. Permission for this lower wage must be obtained in writing from the appropriate state office, usually the state wage and hour or industrial relations agency. It is not possible to obtain blanket consent to waive the minimum wage for all participants in a program. Each student must be cleared individually by presenting appropriate documentation of the nature and extent of the disability.

Although the student is receiving school credit for the work assignment, providing financial compensation has many benefits as well. At the beginning of the work placement, the student will probably be producing less than is compensated by the employer's teaching and supervision; at this time, the student does not need to be paid. When production exceeds the employer's expenditure, however, the student should receive wages of some sort. Some programs consider a student on unpaid probation for the first 2 or 3 weeks—longer if the student's retardation is severe/profound. At the end of the probationary period, the placement is evaluated on the basis of the student's progress and the employer's needs, and the student is either paid, placed in another assignment, or kept on probation for a specified period.

To be fair to the employer, as well as to the student, it is necessary that performance standards be determined for the tasks involved and that the productivity of the student be evaluated and compensated accordingly. The performance standard should be roughly determined by the number of work units a worker with no disabilities is able to produce in 1 hour. If the student with mental retardation can produce one fourth as much in an hour as the average workers, he or she is paid one fourth the amount the average workers receive (Kolstoe & Frey, 1965; Schepis et al., 1987; Siegel & Sleeter, 1991). Kolstoe and Frey (1965) suggested that quality as well as quantity be included in the calculation and that breakage and needed supervision can be considered as well.

PROVIDING WORK EXPERIENCE AND TRANSITION AT ALL AGE LEVELS

Although most discussions of work experience and transition focus on the secondary or terminal phase, every work experience director knows that a student with mental retardation who is not exposed to vocation-related skills and concepts at every age level will not have a favorable prognosis for eventual employment (Moore, Agran, & McSweyn, 1990).

Instructions and Directions

In Chapter 8, I pointed out that obedience is usually an essential prerequisite for independence and general success in adult life for individuals with mental retardation. Beyond obedience, these individuals have difficulty following oral and written sequences, instructions, and directions and must be specifically taught to do so at every age level (Fujiki, & Brinton, 1993). Irvine, Erickson, Singer, and Stahlberg (1992) successfully used picture sequences and drawings to teach procedures essential to independent living. Agran et al. (1989) used a combination of picture cues, verbal prompts, and reinforcement to teach instruction-following skills. Commission tasks are an excellent technique to teach these valuable skills.

Primary and Intermediate Levels

Many significant transition-preparation skills must begin early and continue throughout the school years. For example, students can be prepared for physical aspects of employment by activities that foster eye-hand coordination and small and large muscle coordination and that develop physical strength and stamina. The following general work-related attitudes should be a continuing part of the diagnosis and prescription for every student: gaining an appreciation for work, knowing that people work for a living, mastering time concepts, and giving service to others. To prepare students for the social needs and demands of the workplace, early learning experiences can focus on developing good manners and grooming habits, respecting the rights and property of others, and getting along with others. To ensure that students develop the highest level of maturity they can for approaching the workplace, diagnosis and prescription can include skills that foster an increased attention span, build a sense of responsibility, develop good work habits, and enhance the student's poise and self-concept.

Specific activities can be included in school routine that will promote many of these attitudes, skills, and maturity factors in young children with mental retardation, both those in special classes and those integrated into classes of other students. For example, in one school the primary special class is responsible for the "milk project." Each day, children from the special education group call on each elementary teacher to take orders for lunchtime milk. After they return to their classroom, the children determine the number of containers of milk needed for the day and phone the order in to the central office. When the milk is delivered, the children count out the number of cartons for each classroom; then, using two red wagons, they deliver the milk orders. In addition to finding a practical use for counting, sorting, and arithmetic, the children experience responsibility and service as they participate in the project. As a particular bonus, they have become the envy of the other children in the school because they "get out of class," participate as special helpers, and get to pull a wagon in the halls.

At another school, the special education class took the assignment of caring for the flower bed surrounding the flagpole at the front of the school. Although a few plants had to be sacrificed during the first few weeks, the flower bed soon became the showplace of the school yard. Other service-oriented projects that have been successful in developing many work-related attitudes, skills, and concepts in children with mental retardation include gathering up playground equipment, performing messenger duties, taking lunch counts, reporting attendance, acting as row captains in classrooms, and cleaning up part of the playground. When children with mental retardation are integrated into regular classes, teachers need resist the temptation to assign such duties only to the brighter children who can be counted on to do the best work; teachers must realize that the children with mental retardation need the developmental aspects of these experiences.

Intermediate and Prevocational Levels

Vocational and other related in-school activities have been shown to be closely related to future employment, salary, and general transitional and postschool success even though the overall employment outlook for students with mental retardation is not necessarily entirely positive (Hasazi et al., 1985). Employment preparation activities appropriate for the intermediate and prevocational levels include incorporating career education, assessing individual interests, discovering how to find jobs, reading want ads, mastering specific home skills, and, of course, on-campus work experience.

During the intermediate and prevocational years, adolescents with mental retardation are sufficiently mature to perform a great number of job-related tasks but are too young to be legally placed off-campus in any type of employment status. These years are an excellent time to master replicated skills that can be transferred later to home and job situations. For example, in a community-based setting, Simmons and Flexer (1992) taught rest room cleaning skills that could later be used in independent living arrangements and in employment. Kohl and Stettner-Eaton (1985) successfully used fourth graders to teach cafeteria skills to students with severe disabilities.

Students at these levels can participate in jobs and activities that help them develop skills, attitudes, and behavior that will eventually be relevant to their employment capabilities: electing class officers, delivering mail and supplies, and checking out and repairing playground equipment. School service projects are beneficial; they can be done in groups if students are too immature to perform them on an individual, unsupervised basis. To develop positive attitudes and responsibility, McCuller, Salzburg, and Lignugaris/Kraft (1987) used a job initiative procedure that, although originally developed in a sheltered work environment, could be easily adapted to a classroom. They showed pictures of messy rooms, withering plants, and other situations in which jobs needed to be done and then described related situations to students with mental retardation. They found that 3 trainees who had severe mental retardation could recognize the needed task and proceed with decreasing assistance and prompting. Such a procedure could be enhanced by using Polaroid photographs of actual situations. Videotaping can also present a variety of social as well as work situations; discussions could be held as students are viewing the videos with the sound turned off.

Some preemployment skills for students with mental retardation can be developed in an industrial arts program, including manual dexterity, eye-hand coordination, production and assembly-line techniques, and ability to follow instructions. To promote these needed employment skills, a program must be included on a student's IEP, with provisions for ongoing evaluation. Cunningham (1988) reported that students with mental retardation he described as educable performed poorly on industrial arts tasks, compared with students with no disabilities and even those with learning disabilities. He concluded, however, that students with mental retardation can perform some tasks successfully. The tasks must be selected and prioritized carefully, and close instruction must be provided. Joyce and McFadden (1982) used industrial arts activities to introduce use of tools, woodworking techniques, basic measurement concepts, and safety procedures to students with disabilities—including mental retardation. Horton (1983) reported success in integrating a small group of "educable mentally retarded junior high students" into a standard industrial arts class by using direct instruction and simplified class procedures. If an integration procedure is to be used, however, extensive assistance, special instruction, and modification of class requirements should be anticipated because most students with mental retardation will flounder in industrial arts experiences much as they do in academic classes if they are not carefully monitored, with instruction adapted to their needs.

DIAGNOSING AND PRESCRIBING TRANSITIONAL GOALS

Because students with mental retardation are such a heterogeneous group, no single program is likely to be appropriate for all students in a class or school. Many students, particularly those whose retardation is severe/profound, may never qualify for unsupported employment. Although the unemployment rates among individuals with mental retardation are unacceptably high (Burgess & Zhu, 1990), many students are capable of eventual employment, and every effort should be made to identify and prepare these students. Because these students vary greatly in the abilities and interests they bring to the transitional program, DPE procedures should be used to evaluate each student's readiness for work experience. A student's IEP team should first tentatively identify potential life goals related to transition and work experience by using the age 25 projection and then use the DPE procedure to locate the student's present performance level on the projected track.

Goal Instructional Analysis (GIA)

The remaining sections of this chapter present some sample long-term life goals, annual goals, GIA components, and GIAs that might be helpful in planning a transitional and work experience program for a student with mental retardation. The arrows (→) link a stated goal to other areas of the curriculum that might be combined with it for efficient diagnosis, prescription, and instruction. Because social, communication, and transitional skills and concepts are so closely related that they are assumed to be linked, arrows have not been considered necessary. Any satisfactory communication or social skill will automatically enhance employment and vocational potential, and any employment experience or vocational setting will automatically reinforce and refine communication and social skills.

All of the rudimentary goals considered in this chapter are based on goals, skills, and concepts introduced in Chapter 9. Thus, a teacher or IEP participant may refer to Chapter 9 if a student's diagnosis shows that he or she is not ready for the long-term goals indicated below. An example of such adaptation is made with a life goal from Chapter 9—uses increasingly acceptable table manners—that is preparatory to eventual goals in a transitional program.

Uses increasingly acceptable table manners → Home → Leisure → Arithmetic
Avoids negative behaviors at table (sniffing, picking nose, slurping)
Uses napkin with increasing dependence and grace
Asks politely for food to be passed
Serves food to self
Cleans up after self at meal
Knows and follows lunchroom rules
Receives and passes food to others at meal
Uses bread as "pusher"
Helps set table
Locates own place at table

Horizontal curriculum planning links this long-term goal and its annual goals or subdivisions to all other areas of the curriculum—especially home and family (independent living), leisure (eating in the presence of others), and arithmetic (consumer skills). These goals, like almost all others, can be linked to communication, social, and transitional goals for efficient instruction; thus, they are not marked by arrows. Mastering these goals should prepare a student for the more advanced goals described in this and other chapters. If a student has difficulty with the goals expressed in this chapter, earlier goals can be reviewed and reassessed. Designations such as *knows, understands,* and similar verbs must be verified by the student by responding verbally, pointing, demonstrating, exercising proactivity, or other active means appropriate to the individual.

Sample GIA

After the students have gained a little experience with the GIA procedure, the class requirement to write out a complete GIA is relaxed. At this point, they report that if they can formulate an appropriate number of manipulatable components, the rest of a GIA is simple. The job sequence planned for Brad, for example, was supported → unpaid → competitive employment; the components for a sample GIA follow:

Assistance
Teacher obtained job → increasing independence on Brad's part
On-the-job supervision was close → gradually and virtually phased out

Mastery
Simple jobs → increasingly realistic and demanding
Working around familiar others → unfamiliar others → alone, when appropriate
Reinforcement

No remuneration (potential of pay in the future) → naturally occurring pay

The teacher did not indicate specific dates for completion because he thought they would be only of general assistance. He recognized, however, that Brad must make considerable, realistic progress each year if he was to attain his employment goals.

Appendix H includes some additional, specific skills and concepts that may serve as or suggest long-term and annual transitional and work experience goals appropriate for a student with mental retardation.

SUMMARY

In this chapter, I outlined the critical need of students with mental retardation for effective programs in work experience and transition. I provided evidence that, despite the limitations imposed by mental retardation, the individuals can be trained to become relatively self-sufficient.

I discussed some problems the students encounter in obtaining and holding suitable employment and also defined some problems the work experience supervisors face in organizing and maintaining the programs.

CHAPTER **15**

Practical Arithmetic

423

Points to Study and Ponder

1. What is consumer education, and how does it apply to students with mental retardation?
2. Why are students with mental retardation likely to need special consumer education?
3. What strengths or weaknesses are individuals with mental retardation likely to have that cause them to succeed or fail in arithmetic?
4. What are time concepts, and why are they difficult for a student with mental retardation to master?
5. What practical aspects of measurement are likely to be appropriate in the curriculum for an individual with mental retardation?
6. What practical aspects of money are likely to be appropriate in the curriculum for an individual with mental retardation?
7. What is estimation, and how does it apply to teaching arithmetic to students with mental retardation? Do you think estimation is a viable and practical procedure in teaching any students with mental retardation with whom you are acquainted?
8. Could some mastery of the concept of estimation be of any value to a student with mental retardation who is confronted in adult life with an arithmetic problem he or she is unable to solve?
9. How could the age 25 projection help in determining the arithmetic needs of an individual with mental retardation?
10. Do students with mental retardation need any special consideration in consumer education to be successful in adult life?
11. Under what conditions can computers and hand-held calculators be used to teach arithmetic and other concepts to students with mental retardation?

The purpose of this chapter is to help parents, teachers, and others in identifying appropriate arithmetic skills and concepts for students with mental retardation and to suggest strategies for teaching these skills. Arithmetic for students with mental retardation generally consists of number awareness, counting skills, fractional parts, and the fundamental arithmetic operations (addition, subtraction, multiplication, and division), along with such practical applications as time, measurement, money, and consumer skills. Many, if not most, students with mental retardation will not be able to do more complex operations like addition, subtraction, multiplication, and division of fractions or multiplication and division of whole numbers. Because of regional variation, however, the decision on whether to teach these skills must be made on an individual basis.

This chapter also covers the practicality and long-range potential of hand-held calculators and computers in teaching students with mental retardation. Some of the more rudimentary arithmetic concepts are discussed in Chapter 9. Some specific, long-term and annual arithmetic goals are suggested at the end of this chapter and in Appendix I.

ARITHMETIC SKILLS AND LIFE GOAL PLANNING

Mathematics is a highly organized, remarkably sequential discipline that increases in difficulty and complexity. Because students with mental retardation have poor cognitive skills, the abstract concepts and operations of mathematics will be difficult for them. Nagle (1993) found a very high positive correlation between WAIS-R (Wechsler, 1981) IQs and arithmetic achievement among students whose mental retardation he described as educable. Abbeduto and Nuccio (1991) reported students with mental retardation to have poorer number concepts than a group of their MA age peers. Also, Porter (1993) indicated that counting ability is closely correlated with MA. Baroody (1986) reported similar results but noted striking individual differences, suggesting an individual approach to arithmetic. These studies also emphasize the need to prioritize arithmetic skills in the curriculum for students with mental retardation.

Although there is much individual variation, many students with mental retardation have difficulty achieving beyond the third or fourth grade level, especially in problem solving (Bilsky & Judd, 1986). Experienced teachers have found that, because of the problem-solving deficiency, many adolescents with mental retardation are laboring through third- and fourth-grade arithmetic workbooks even though reading and arithmetic abilities at the fifth- and sixth-grade levels are generally considered to be minimal qualifications for functional literacy.

Mathematical concepts and skills are particularly difficult for a student who has mental retardation but are important to that student's achieving an acceptable level of independent living as an adult. Parents, teachers, and other IEP team members must be careful not to place arbitrary limitations on the student or to assume that the student will reach unrealistic goals. The IEP team should carefully monitor each student's progress in arithmetic according to a developmental approach until the student reaches adolescence. When the team estimates that the student has 3 or 4 years of school remaining, the program should probably shift to emphasize practical problems at the complexity level and in the social environments that student is most likely to experience in adult life.

In outlining the student's curriculum in arithmetic, the IEP team must consider the following:

Current and Potential Family

Team members must prepare for the day when the student with mental retardation will no longer be able to receive school-sponsored services. Family members typically assume some, if not all, responsibility at that point, and their attitudes and abilities must be considered in planning the student's program. The IEP team must also consider that some students with mental retardation are likely to marry and have families of their own, particularly in high-identification states. If the student with mental retardation is likely to be the head of a family, additional mathematical skills will need to be mastered so that the student will be able to assume complex family leadership roles.

Anticipated Level of Independent Living

Whether a person with mental retardation marries or not, a primary life goal should be to live as independently as possible in adult life. Independence is feasible, however, only to the extent that a person can effectively make personal decisions and solve practical problems. As in other areas of life goal curriculum planning, a student's IEP team members, with increasing input from the student, must choose mathematical skills and concepts in terms of the extent to which they anticipate the student will be living independently in adult life.

Consumer Education Needs

A person with mental retardation, like every other person, is a consumer of both goods and services. If he or she is to live independently, the life goal curriculum must include a strong component of consumer and family living skills. The individual must understand how to select goods and services that are appropriate and within his or her means and how to obtain and pay for them. Mathematical skills are essential to these aspects of a person's becoming a capable consumer. Thus, the IEP team will need to anticipate the person's potential adult lifestyle to effectively plan the mathematics component.

Employment

Full and suitable employment is an important goal for individuals with mental retardation who have the capability for it. If possible, individuals should have sufficient income to support themselves and any others who might be dependent on them. In addition, the sense of self-worth and self-confidence that comes from employment is especially important for an individual with mental retardation. Although the individual will not have to work full-time with mathematical concepts, almost every job requires some mathematical skill. IEP planning should consider the mathematical requirements involved with the types of employment that will probably be available to an individual.

Leisure Activities

Leisure activities are just as important and justifiable for a person with mental retardation as for any other person. His or her level of personal independence, however, will determine the availability of these activities. Leisure activities usually involve admissions, ticket purchase, travel, and other costs, all of which require mathematical skill. Planning of the mathematics component should include a student's interests and anticipated future desires for recreation and leisure.

LEARNING CHARACTERISTICS AND ARITHMETIC

The abstract but precise nature of mathematics, with its rigid sequence, unfamiliar terminology, and constant need for problem solving, challenges specific weak areas of students with mental retardation. A number of these students' learning characteristics make arithmetic particularly difficult (Parmar et al., 1994). A few are reviewed here, although they are discussed in greater detail in Chapter 2.

Generally Low Cognitive Levels

Students with mental retardation have a low level of general intellectual functioning. Limited cognitive ability impairs all learning but is often more detrimental in arithmetic than in any other subject—particularly if problem solving is involved (Bray et al., 1994). Spitz and Semchuck (1979) found that students with mental retardation tend to scan only a minimum of the available information when solving a problem. Similarly, Bilsky and Judd (1986) reported that the problem-solving abilities of adolescents with mental retardation are significantly inferior to those of much younger fourth graders without mental retardation even though the groups are equal in computational skills. They found that students with mental retardation have particular difficulty in discarding irrelevant material from an arithmetic problem and that they must be deliberately taught to do so. If students lack the ability to sort and process information in a problem, teaching computation is largely pointless. For example, a student might be given the following problem: "There are _____ chairs, _____ boys, and _____ girls in the room. How many children are there altogether?" A student with mental retardation usually tries to add the number of chairs in with the numbers of boys and girls. Although the student might compute the sum correctly, the answer would not accurately solve the problem.

A related deficiency is difficulty with problems that involve a series of stages or operations or that include several sources of necessary information. A student might be given this problem: "Would 2 dozen cookies be enough for 14 boys and 13 girls at a party?" The student with mental retardation would have difficulty because the problem involves several operations. The interrelationships of these operations are not readily apparent: (a) recognizing the practicality that each of the 14 boys and 13 girls would need a cookie, (b) adding 14 + 13, (c) recognizing that 2 dozen equals 24, and (d) recognizing that 24 cookies are insufficient to serve 27 people. Often, one problem will merge into another: How many more cookies are needed?

Transfer of Training

A student with mental retardation typically has great difficulty relating skills and concepts learned in one experience to other situations (Hayes & Taplin, 1993). For example, a student who learns to make a bed in the family living center at school may be unable to make one at home. A student who is able to count a number of coins may not be able to count the number of cans on a shelf; or a student who can identify half of an orange may not project this to identify half of an apple or banana.

Difficulty in Abstract Thinking and Reasoning

A student with mental retardation has great difficulty comprehending and working effectively with the highly abstract terms and concepts of mathematics, such as *add, subtract, equal, one, seven, zero, place holder, tens column, average, fraction,* and *percentage.* Learning the "foreign language" of arithmetic is a notable accomplishment for any child but is especially difficult for one with mental retardation, who will typically have poor language skills and particular difficulty with abstract symbols. Essential abstract terms and concepts must be introduced carefully as they are needed.

In an old but classic study, Cherkes (1975) pointed out that students with mental retardation and others with low IQs have particular difficulty following the rules of logic that are essential in mastering arithmetic. Logical processes are more abstract than the language used to describe them; like the terms, they must be introduced slowly, and comprehension and application must be monitored closely.

Limited Reading Ability

Cummins and Das (1980) pointed out that one of the most serious constraints on arithmetic achievement for students with mental retardation is their poor reading ability. The reading level of available instructional material for arithmetic is usually too difficult for a student with mental retardation—especially if the material is age appropriate and otherwise acceptable.

Other Characteristics

Students with mental retardation have a number of other learning characteristics that are particularly significant in arithmetic, including difficulty following instructions, poor comprehension, limited memory, and short attention span (Judd & Bilsky, 1989). Proactivity and practical problem solving introduce interpretive and classification skills that require extensive instruction and experience. For example, a student with mental retardation would have difficulty with this problem: "Bill spent _____ for milk, _____ for bread, _____ for other groceries, and _____ for rent. How much did he spend for food?"

WORKING WITH LEARNING CHARACTERISTICS

Regardless of the general classroom procedures, some formal instruction in arithmetic should be included in each school day—particularly for preadolescent students. The arithmetic concepts included in general study units and in other subject areas motivate the student in arithmetic, but ordinarily the concepts are inadequate to constitute a full arithmetic program.

Compensation versus Remediation

The dilemma of whether to compensate or remediate is acute in the area of arithmetic. Because compensatory measures and devices can become crutches for low-achieving students, many argue that compensation should not be used. Others suggest that if a student cannot succeed without the crutch, the obvious solution is to use the crutch. The decision must be made on an individual basis, involving such considerations as the preference and practices of the student's future teachers, the age of the student, the extent to which he or she has already used compensatory procedures or devices, and the IEP team's best estimate of the student's ultimate potential achievement level. Teachers and others who work with students with mental retardation must assess the individual student's ability in each characteristic and use that ability level as a base for planning the student's arithmetic program.

Relationships with Other Skill Areas

An additional consideration is that the student's arithmetic activities can help in improving other of the student's known deficiencies. For example, some terminology of arithmetic can be the subject of an ACE story. Information about clothing, food, and other consumer costs can be gleaned from a study of newspapers. Arithmetic lessons of gradually increasing length, practicality, and difficulty can increase the student's memory, attention span, and ability to read and follow instructions. Skills in other closely related areas that can be treated simultaneously include the social skills of dressing and good grooming, the consumer skills of selecting appropriate clothing and purchasing the clothing, and the home skills of cleaning and caring for the clothing.

BASIC CONTENT AREAS

In mathematics, as in every curriculum area, basic concepts must be assessed before the formal operations can be taught. After preliminaries, however, structure should not be a matter for undue concern. Preliminary skills and concepts may require several years or more for some children; afterward, the sequence becomes less obvious but should generally follow the notions of concrete to abstract, smaller numbers before larger numbers, or less striking differences before subtle ones for comparisons. Concepts involving money, measurement, and time should also be included at the appropriate stage. Numbers, counting, and number concepts must be used in other curriculum areas wherever possible. ACE and other stories should emphasize numbers and number concepts wherever possible.

Appendix I also lists some sample long-term and annual arithmetic goals. The student's IEP team must also monitor the student's progress carefully to determine the extent to which that student should be instructed in these operations. For example, as the student reaches adolescence, the team must predict his or her eventual ability to use multiplication and division in solving life problems before they struggle to teach these operations.

Preliminary Concepts and Skills

Teachers must carefully prepare the students with the underlying base of terminology, concepts, and relationships before attempting the fundamental operations of arithmetic—addition, subtraction, multiplication, division, and fractions. Chapter 10 covers some prearithmetic skills and concepts, as well as some activities that might be used to teach them.

Only careful deliberation by the IEP team can determine the extent to which each of these prearithmetic skills must be mastered before proceeding to formal instruction in arithmetic. It would be well for each teacher to generally plan out these preoperational concepts and sequences for the students he or she ordinarily teaches. The need for basic arithmetic concepts varies with the individual student and the extent to which each skill area is to be mastered. For example, counting 15 objects may be more difficult than rote counting to 100. The tasks must be arranged wherever possible so that each step builds upon the last.

Time Concepts

Most members of society are organized and regulated by the clock. Some members of minority groups, however, may be an exception of sorts. Nel (1993) reported that some minorities (notably native Americans) have different concepts of time. But even these differences emphasize the need to diagnose and prescribe the teaching of time concepts on a highly individualized basis. To be a successful member of a family and of society, a person with mental retardation in most segments of society must be able to tell time. Unfortunately, learning to tell time is one of the most difficult and abstract tasks young children have to learn. Not only is the process abstract, but it also involves conflicting and confusing terminology. A particular time of day can be expressed in several ways. For example, 2:15 may also be expressed as a quarter after 2, 15 after 2, quarter past 2, or a little after 2.

Digital watches and clocks have greatly simplified the task of telling time because they are easily read. A teacher might begin by using either a digital or traditional clock until the student has mastered one quite well and then introducing the other. It may also be helpful to display both clocks side by side. The concepts of A.M. and P.M. are highly abstract but must be mastered if the student is to use the skill of telling time to his or her advantage.

The measurement skill of telling time by itself has limited value. The student must also be aware of time concepts and time requirements. He or she must be aware that time passes, that it is valuable, and that a knowledge of time can be used to one's advantage. These more in-depth understandings are necessary if a student with mental retardation is to remain socially invisible (his or her condition is not obvious to everyone). The student's constantly being late or asking others what time it is attracts unnecessary attention.

If time is an ongoing part of the everyday conversation of a student with mental retardation, he or she gradually becomes aware that people do things according to time. A teacher should find frequent occasions for time-related comments: "It's time to go now," "You're late," "We will complete this in the afternoon," "The bus will be here in 5 minutes," "We will bake it for 10 more minutes." Some additional time concepts that should be both formally taught and included in daily conversations are listed in Appendix I.

Measurement

Like concepts of time, concepts of measurement must be correlated closely with language concept development. The student must be familiar with the concepts of top-bottom, more-less, all-some, cold-hot, high-low, tall-short, empty-full, big-little, as well as part, piece, some, several, many, all, and none. These concepts can then be used in teaching the more direct elements of measurement, such as teaspoon, tablespoon, cup, pint, quart, and gallon; ounce and pound; inch, foot, yard, and possibly mile; and degrees (temperature). Area and volume measurement should be taught only if the student's projected lifestyle seems to require them and if he or she has the prerequisite cognitive and number skills. The student must be able to manipulate common measuring devices, such as rulers, yardsticks, measuring cups, thermometers, and scales. Familiarity with these devices can usually be taught as the related concept is introduced. The teaching of measurement concepts must be focused toward practical considerations, such as cooking, sewing, budgeting, and others specifically related to home living and job skills.

Money

Concepts related to money can be extremely confusing to young children. Coins are the first and sometimes the only objects young children deal with that have a value other than one-to-one. For this reason, it may be well to use objects other than coins or bills to teach the fundamentals of counting. The experience of children with money varies greatly. Some children of low arithmetic achievement may exhibit a startling skill in the use of money. For children who have had considerable experience, money concepts can sometimes be used in teaching the fundamental operations.

Because children with mental retardation have difficulty with transfer of training, real money must be used wherever possible. Play money made of paper or plastic usually looks and feels unreal, and many students with mental retardation have trouble transferring skills obtained with play money to real coins and bills. Ten to 15 dollars in change is usually sufficient for teaching a child, not out of proportion to the cost of other instructional materials. And experience shows that losses are usually negligible.

PROACTIVITY IN TEACHING MATHEMATICS

The concept of proactivity offers a practical perspective for evaluating the merits of arithmetic instruction. For arithmetic instruction to be valuable in adult life, mastery must go considerably beyond solving problems designed by a teacher or a textbook.

Problem Solving

The ultimate goal of arithmetic instruction for a person with mental retardation is the same as the goal for any other person: the ability to successfully solve practical problems on that person's ability level (Gable, Evans, & Evans, 1993). To achieve this goal, problem solving, rather than rote memory or computation skills, must be emphasized at every age level. As a student with mental retardation reaches adolescence—when the more difficult mathematical concepts are logically taught—the IEP team must take particular care to assess his or her ability to use the concepts in recognizing, setting up, and solving practical life problems.

Unfortunately, story or thought problems are generally disliked by low-achieving students. Students with mental retardation have particular difficulty because such problems are abstract and generally involve a multistage format that requires memory and discrimination. Many teachers of low achievers tend to avoid problem-solving activities and practice because the students do not like them and because progress is understandably slow. Yet, practical problem solving must be stressed at every age, beginning at the primary level (Howell & Barnhart, 1992).

But if practical problem solving is not emphasized, serious questions arise about the merits of teaching fundamental arithmetic operations at all. Of what value is the ability to recite addition and subtraction facts and operations if the person cannot use these abilities to solve life's problems? The teenagers involved in a study by Bilsky and Judd (1986) illustrate the dilemma that occurs when a teacher places unrealistic emphasis on computational skills and assumes that problem-solving skills will automatically follow or be taught later by someone else. Bilsky and Judd found that most students with mental retardation are nearing graduation with computation skills about equal to those of their MA peers but that they were sorely deficient in problem-solving abilities.

The following is a suggested sequence for teaching proactive problem solving to students with mental retardation:

1. Identify a problem that exists in the classroom, home, job, store, and so forth.
2. State the problem.
3. Have the student state the problem.
4. Ask, "What does the problem want you to find out?" (Write it down.)
5. Ask, "What information do you have to work with?" (Write it down.)
6. Estimate the answer. (What would be a reasonable cost, length, weight, etc.?)
7. Repeat 3 and 4. (Optional)
8. Solve. (Ask the student what operation[s] are needed.)
9. Make sure the solution is in the appropriate units and that the units are understood.
10. Compare the answer to the estimate.
11. Use the obtained information in practical situations.

Estimation in Problem Solving

To use the information obtained from problem-solving experience, a student must be able to check his or her work independently and to recognize obviously inaccurate solutions (Gable et al., 1993). One means of giving the student this capability is by teaching estimation. Learning to estimate as an arithmetic tool might seem too difficult for students with mental retardation. Admittedly, estimating is highly abstract and therefore difficult to teach to any low-achieving student. If the student cannot estimate the solution to a practical problem with reasonable accuracy, however, it is doubtful whether he or she will be able to use the data derived from the "answer."

Estimating the solution to a mathematical problem helps in ensuring against a student's making a mistake that could easily result in ridicule or exploitation. In solving an arithmetic challenge, most students with mental retardation find it difficult to select the appropriate operation. Also, they have difficulty changing cents to dollars and cents and understanding and manipulating decimal points. Mistakes of this type almost always result in an absurd solution. If the student has the ability to anticipate the approximate amount of a debit or credit, he or she should be able to judge whether calculations have resulted in usable information. Although hand-held calculators (discussed below) may improve the student's computational ability, overall accuracy and practicality still depend on his or her ability to set up the problem, manipulate decimal points, and use the obtained information.

Making change is an important application of the ability to estimate. If a low-functioning student is unable to calculate change accurately in a realistic situation, the skill of estimation may help compensate because a student can detect major exploitation by making a rough estimate of the amount of change due from a purchase. A related compensatory skill is the ability to estimate the total cost of purchases and then offer an amount of money equal to or just slightly greater. A student with mental retardation can also be trained to judiciously consult parents and other family members or perhaps a trusted friend in determining the cost of an item.

Estimating can also be of great value in developing concepts of time and in creating awareness of time (e.g., "You may play for 10 minutes," "How long do you think it will take?" "How long will you be gone?"). A teacher might promote awareness of time by displaying clock faces that show the time certain things are to be done: the time for each child to go to therapy, to clean up, to get ready for lunch, or to catch the bus. If such methods make the child aware of the importance of learning to tell time, the skill can be taught much more easily.

Estimation must be a part of everyday conversation; highly motivating involvements, such as field trips and community-based activities, are good places to begin. Teachers, parents, and other family members must frequently raise practical questions about the student's environment. Many of the questions, particularly at first, are designed to create awareness and need not be answered. If a question is on the appropriate instructional level for a group of students, they may be asked to set up and solve the problem and thus demonstrate to the other students that such problems arise from time to time, that the problems have solutions, and that the solutions yield valuable information. Questions like the following may be asked routinely, timed to initiate appropriate instruction:

About how much do we usually pay for a loaf of bread?
About how much would we pay for two loaves of bread?
It was 10 o'clock when you started on this project. What time do you think it is now?
Bill is 57 inches tall. How tall do you think Amir is?
Before we look at this label, how much do you think this jacket costs?
What time do you go to speech?
About how much does a quart of milk cost?
What would you expect to pay for a quart of milk and a loaf of bread?
About how much would you pay for both the skirt and the blouse?
About how much will it cost for each of us to ride the city bus from school to the grocery store?
You worked a few more hours this week than last week when you earned $55. About how much did you earn this week?

This procedure also can be used to promote conversation and to encourage precise language. The language of measurement, as well as the skills and computations of arithmetic, should be included in many aspects of the lives and schooling of individuals with mental retardation, not limited to the period of time devoted to formal instruction in arithmetic. As the student works through a variety of practical problems, he or she gradually builds up a reservoir of information concerning common measurements and expected costs of everyday goods and services. This knowledge gained from experience can help in evaluating the accuracy of the answer to a problem.

CONSUMER EDUCATION

The most practical life problems in arithmetic for students with mental retardation relate to consumer education. Specifically, consumer education involves conserving money, budgeting, shopping, and obtaining essential services. In all areas of the curriculum, the IEP team of each student must project as accurately as possible that student's need for and eventual mastery of arithmetic concepts, but nowhere is this more evident than in consumer activities. Consumer experiences are laden with skills, concepts, and procedures that are extremely difficult and time-consuming to teach. And many of them are well beyond the mastery level of most students with mental retardation. The IEP team must determine what the student can be expected to learn with his or her limited abilities and resort to compensation for other skills that will be a part of the student's projected adult lifestyle. Most people with mental retardation require some supervision in all aspects of consumer education, but this varies greatly with the individual. Thus, the team must carefully determine the type and extent of instruction the school can and should provide.

Conserving Money

Although people with mental retardation typically earn much less than people without disabilities, most of them will have some income to care for. Ordinarily, people with mental retardation do not need to actually calculate such financial matters as savings accounts, bank charges, sales tax, payrolls, social security, federal and state taxes, and other payroll deductions, but they must understand the benefits and procedures to some extent. Most banks have customer service representatives who offer some assistance, but they usually are reluctant to assume major responsibilities for their depositors. Most of them offer some assistance in understanding bank statements and in working through other banking procedures. Because ownership is essentially shared, credit unions tend to be particularly helpful.

If the income of a person with mental retardation amounts to very much, he or she must be taught to keep savings in a safe place. Cuvo, Davis, and Gluck (1991) used a self-paced workbook to teach 20 young adults with mild disabilities to pay bills, use a savings account, and use money orders. Although many people with mental retardation can master the mechanics of writing checks, responsible banking involves complex procedures. Keeping an accurate ledger requires mathematical skills, as well as self-discipline. Reconciling a bank statement is difficult for most people, and it is a rare person with mental retardation who can do this without considerable assistance. The hardest part of such a reconciliation is recognizing, locating, and correcting a mistake—an extremely complex process.

An alternative to teaching the person with mental retardation about the traditional checking account is to teach the person with retardation to keep his or her money in a bank or credit union under an arrangement limited to deposits and cash withdrawals. If the person withdraws cash to meet immediate needs and writes no checks, each transaction gives an immediate and accurate balance of available funds. Transactions can be made either in person or by automatic teller machine (ATM), which accepts deposits and discloses balances. Shafer, Inge, and Hill (1986) taught a person whose mental retardation they described as moderate to use an ATM by using a task analytic approach. The "cash only" banking procedure offers relative security and requires minimum bookkeeping ability. The most obvious disadvantage is the inconvenience—especially if the bank or ATM is located some distance from the person's home.

Students can learn many of the principles of conserving money through a class bank—similar to a class store. Using real money is always more effective in teaching students with retardation than using imitation money. But if the class bank is likely to involve large sums, imitation coins and bills are advised.

Budgeting and Shopping

People with mental retardation, whose resources are usually very limited, must learn to budget for, locate, and select needed goods that are adequate and affordable (Williams & Ewing, 1991). Some of the most essential and valuable concepts in arithmetic relate to shopping; fortunately, students with mental retardation respond reasonably well to well-planned programs in this area.

Several researchers have reported some degree of success in teaching budgeting and shopping skills to students with mental retardation. LaCampagne and Cipani (1987) pointed out that an individual with mental retardation cannot be truly independent until he or she can earn, budget, and spend money wisely to meet expenses and to pay bills. Nietupski, Clancy, and Christiansen (1984) used a device with a series of pictures to prompt students with moderate disabilities to make purchases from a vending machine. Matson and Long (1986) taught 3 adults with mild/moderate mental retardation to generalize initial instruction to adaptive shopping and other community skills. Using performance feedback, social reinforcement, in vivo modeling, self-evaluation, and social and tangible reinforcement, they claimed that rapid and dramatic improvements occurred soon after treatment began.

As with most classroom activities, teachers of students with mental retardation must create and produce much, if not most, of the material they use in teaching arithmetic. Hang (1981) developed a calculation system (CHISANBOP) based on finger manipulation. Sandknop, Schuster, Wolery, and Cross (1992) created an innovative number line device that they used to teach their students to select the least expensive grocery items. A similar procedure by Irwin (1991) taught children with mental retardation to add by counting-on, and Paddock (1992) reported success in using ice-cream sticks to teach basic counting skills. McConkey and McEnvoy (1986) taught counting and other basic arithmetic skills by using a variety of teacher-made and other games. Gaule, Nietupski, and Certo (1985) taught 3 young adults with moderate/severe disabilities to use an adaptive shopping aid to prepare a grocery shopping list, locate and obtain items in a supermarket, and purchase those items.

Other consumer education skills and concepts that the IEP team may need to consider include reading street numbers, making mail order purchases, dealing with hospital and life insurance, handling money orders, and figuring sales tax. Sales tax charts may be obtained from a number of places, including stationery stores.

Much of the instruction related to budgeting and shopping can be initiated in the upper elementary grades and intensified during the junior high school years. When interest is high, students are receptive, and research has shown that generalization can be achieved. Bourbeau, Sowers, and Close (1986) found that students with mild/moderate mental retardation are able to generalize intensive in-class training in banking skills to community settings. Westling, Floyd, and Carr (1990) showed that students with mental retardation can learn valuable consumer skills in a variety of settings. Working in several department stores, they provided training and experience in shopping skills to students aged 13 to 21 whose mental retardation they described as moderate to profound. After studying operational behaviors, social behaviors, number of settings in which criterion performance was achieved, and number of sessions required to achieve criterion, they reported no significant differences between treatment (setting) groups.

If it is not possible or feasible to conduct the instruction in natural or community settings, a classroom store can be used to teach shopping skills with some sense of realism. At the least, such a contrived activity might bridge the generalization gap between basic or developmental skills and concepts (that are best taught in a classroom setting) and the culminating activities (that must somehow be applied in the naturally occurring environment). The store can be stocked with some items students would really be able to purchase. Boxes and cans representing other items may be emptied from the bottom to keep labels intact and to preserve the sense of realism. Class members can then fill and seal off the bottoms of these containers and use them for sorting and stocking shelves, as well as for estimating costs, contriving purchases, and making and checking change.

Students with mental retardation must be taught to set up and operate within simple budgets. For capable students, these skills can be introduced early with classroom instruction; they can be moved to appropriate community settings as the students mature. As in most phases of the educational program, the cooperation of parents and other family members is essential. Students who earn money in the home or neighborhood or who receive monetary allowances have a strong advantage in learning to operate a budget. Teachers may also use budgets for parties and other classroom activities to demonstrate budgeting procedures with the whole class or with small groups. Any budget instruction must emphasize the reality that expenditures cannot exceed income.

Most people have difficulty discerning between needed and wanted goods, but this distinction is especially difficult for students with mental retardation. Although it takes patience and some ingenuity, a teacher can use in-class discussions, role-playing situations, and ACE stories to help the students learn how to make these important decisions. In addition, members of the IEP team may want to offer their services to help the parents provide instruction and practical experience in this important area.

A related challenge is helping people with mental retardation deal with door-to-door vendors, telephone solicitors, and home shopping channels on television. It may be well to teach people with mental retardation to avoid buying anything from this type of solicitor. The items for sale are almost never on the person's budget—especially a person with mental retardation—and these transactions are difficult for them to track and pay for. Also, a person with mental retardation finds it difficult to evaluate items sold in this manner and does not know what to do if purchases are defective.

Obtaining Services

When people with mental retardation achieve a degree of independence, they need to obtain for themselves a number of services provided for people with mental retardation who live in more restrictive settings. They must be able to contact and work with such professionals as doctors, dentists, tax consultants, and attorneys. Teachers can invite professionals to make presentations to the class or to small groups. Also, arrangements might be made for small groups or individuals to visit the offices of these professionals to consult on hypothetical problems assigned for the class or on real problems related to their work or independent living.

Running a Household

Relatively few persons with mental retardation are likely to be sufficiently independent to buy their own homes, although such a purchase is not impossible, especially in high-identification states. This level of independence involves extremely difficult arithmetic skills and concepts, such as buying and selling property, mortgages, contracts, property tax, and car insurance. Household functions involving potential arithmetic implications that they are more likely to encounter include visiting eating establishments, using public transportation, and operating laundry facilities. Researchers have been successful in preparing students with mental retardation in many such areas.

CONTRIBUTIONS OF COMPUTERS AND CALCULATORS TO TEACHING

In the professional literature, the term *computer assisted instruction (CAI)* may refer to either of two procedures, both of which are in common use by teachers of children with and without mental retardation. Teachers may use computers to design, conduct, and evaluate programs for students (Iacono & Miller, 1989; Lin, Podell, & Rein, 1991), or the students may work directly on computers to master skills and concepts designed and presented on computer software programs (Ronau & Battista, 1988). Both types of programs are becoming increasingly available even as they increase in sophistication.

Teacher Use in Assessment and Planning

A variety of software programs have been designed to assess a student's abilities in a given subject and to present either a printout or a monitor display of the logical sequence of lessons for that student. Such a program evaluates the student's progress on each lesson and then presents the next. The program may have the facility to increase or decrease lesson difficulty and thereby regulate the rate of the student's achievement. These programs can be coupled with interactive videos that permit the student to respond to questions and problems posed by the program and to receive immediate feedback, along with further instructions and problems appropriate to the student's specific performance level. Thorkildsen and Hofmeister (1984) developed and tested this type of computer-controlled, interactive videodisc program with students whose mental retardation they described as severe. They reported that the program was easily learned and that it seemed to hold significant potential for the assessment, diagnosis, prescription, and instruction of such students.

Potential Strengths and Weaknesses of CAI

The only purpose of discussing the potential weaknesses and strengths of using technology in the classroom is to assist teachers, parents, and other members of IEP teams in evaluating its use for the student with mental retardation whose program is under consideration. Like any educational method or program, use of computers for planning and assessment by teachers must be carefully considered. The availability of technology, the skill with which it is used, and the purposes for its use must all be considered locally. Only then can the use of computers, hand-held calculators, and other technological devices be justified for use with a particular student. That such a device was found to be beneficial (or disadvantageous) in another location or with other groups of students should serve mainly as a basis for investigation. The use of technology has definite strengths and potentialities, but it is not a cure-all or long-term solution for the challenges and difficulties of teaching students with mental retardation.

Finally, technology is advancing at an incredible pace, and any potential weakness may be overcome in the future. I hope the two major concerns discussed here fall into this category. First, most current software tends to be highly academic, with few programs available in the practical aspects of curriculum, such as transition, work experience, and independent living. Second, whatever achievements accrue to a student with mental retardation must be transferable; that is, the student must be able to perform the mastered function, solve the confronting problem, or apply the acquired knowledge using available means and devices—and usually without supervision.

A student must be able to generalize or perform in practical settings those skills and concepts learned on a computer or other assistive device.

Some computer software allows a teacher to further program the lessons to suit the needs of individual students. In addition to this advantage in individualization, teachers' use of computers provides advantages in flexibility and in the broad scope of the presentations. Fitzgerald, Bauder, and Werner (1992) and Fuchs, Fuchs, and Hamlett (1992) pointed out that using computers for record keeping and standardized test scoring conserves the teacher's valuable time and thus allows more time for interacting directly with the students. Reiss (1992) used computer technology to assess the difficult case of an individual who had a dual diagnosis—mental retardation and mental illness. Computers have also been used extensively in research (Margalit, 1991; Pressman, 1986).

DIRECT USE OF COMPUTERS BY STUDENTS WITH MENTAL RETARDATION

Teachers are not the only individuals in the special education classroom who use computers. Having students with mental retardation work directly with computers is becoming very popular. Investigators have reported success using computers in mental retardation to increase vocabularies (Conners, 1990), spelling instruction (Dube, McDonald, McIlvane, & Mackay, 1991; Stevens et al., 1991), and art (Gerber, 1994); Browning and White (1986) used interactive video to teach interpersonal skills. Montague and Fonseca (1993) used computers to improve the story-writing skills of students with a variety of disabilities, and Vacc (1987) reported success in teaching letter-writing to students with mild mental retardation. Vacc's students wrote longer letters by using word processors, with no appreciable differences noted in overall quality, compared to handwritten letters.

Advantages of Having Students Work on Computers

Computers can be highly motivating—even captivating—for these students. Students with mental retardation have expressed favorable attitudes about direct computer use. Gardner and Bates (1991) interviewed 59 students whose mental retardation they described as educable. The majority of the students said they liked using computers and thought they learned more while using them. Because of this tendency to motivate, computers have been used effectively to increase the attention spans of students with mental retardation. Other advantages of computers include their capacity for individualization and their adaptability. Current software covers a wide variety of topics, including story writing and other subjects, and the diversity is likely to become even greater in the future (Storeygard, Simmons, Stumpf, & Pavloglou, 1993). Greenwood and Rieth (1994) pointed out that computer technology is developing rapidly and that any disadvantage may be overcome in the future.

Potential Weaknesses of Computers

Although computers have been shown to be motivating and versatile as instructional tools for students with mental retardation, it is important for educators—especially the members of a student's IEP team—to be aware of limitations and potential disadvantages as well. Iacono and Miller (1989) focused their investigations of computer use on the known limitations that mental retardation imposes on the students. They found some obvious advantages to computer use but cautioned that teachers must pay close attention to the learning characteristics of mental retardation when they decide how and how often to have their students work on the computer. For example, students with mental retardation typically have particular difficulty with transfer, generalization, and independent study, three characteristics that are essential in mastering a computer. Therefore, they might have some difficulty in working directly with the computer. Also relevant to the weaknesses in transfer and generalization is the fact that much computer software is written in a game-type format. Parents and teachers must be aware that even though such a program may teach a valuable skill, that skill may not be usable if the student cannot transfer it to another situation or relate it to the rest of his or her IEP or curriculum.

It is currently difficult to obtain software that is appropriate for use with students with mental retardation. Most available programs are highly academic and are too fast paced. Computer technology is advancing at an incredible rate, however, and functional programs may soon be readily available. In the meantime, it is possible for the teacher or parent to produce his or her own software designed expressly for an individual student. Whether one is purchasing software or designing it for teaching students with mental retardation, the most significant consideration of any method is whether the skills or concepts mastered at school can be used in practical settings. If real-life application cannot take place, the student is merely learning splinter skills. The most important consideration is not how well a student with mental retardation can learn to use a computer, but rather how well the student can use the computer-taught skills and concepts to solve life's practical problems. It is not uncommon to see students with mental retardation working diligently at programs that appear to bear little relationship to preparation for successful adult life.

Concerns about the weaknesses of computer use by students with mental retardation are not limited to the software. One serious concern is compatibility. Although students may enjoy using the computers and may learn some skills that are transferable and even a few that are practical, the real question is whether the students are achieving greater mastery of those skills than they would with more traditional methodology. Most of the literature cited in this chapter reports demonstrated progress of students using computers, but most of the investigations did not include control groups. Exceptions are expressly noted.

Lin et al. (1991) cast some doubts on the overall efficacy of computer use by students with mental retardation when these authors compared computer use to paper-and-pencil techniques for word recognition by using students with and without mental retardation. They found that the computer method produced faster response times but that the paper-and-pencil practice resulted in greater accuracy. Similarly, Baumgart and VanWalleghem (1987) compared a computer method to teacher-taught methods of teaching grocery sight words to 3 students with mental retardation by using an alternating treatment design. Their study indicated that, in a practical sense, using the computer was not really effective. Two of the students learned equally well with either method; the third learned only with the teacher-taught method. Ronau and Battista (1988) reported that even eighth graders without mental retardation found a computer version of a ratio and proportion activity to be significantly more difficult to learn than the paper-and-pencil version. Chen, Hsing, and Bernard-Opitz (1993) compared CAI and personal instruction with 4 young children with autism and reported the predictable motivation factor, but CAI did not affect their learning rates. Although these studies do not suggest that computer participation has no merit in teaching students with mental retardation, they do suggest that such activities must be carefully planned and evaluated.

In evaluating practicality of computer use, teachers need to remember that the goal of teaching any skills and concepts on a computer is that the student will eventually be able to set up and solve a problem. Experience shows that students with mental retardation typically require close and constant direction and prompting when working on computers. Thus, it is unlikely that a person with mental retardation will ultimately use a computer to solve practical problems or to provide useful information. Therefore, if a student with mental retardation is taught basic operations and principles with a computer, he or she must also be taught to apply the same principles with paper and pencil or other common means. To be realistic, evaluations of computer instruction must be conducted orally, with paper-and-pencil, or with whatever means the student with mental retardation is likely to have available after leaving school. The IEP team should monitor the student's level of computer independence and project the computer use that will likely take place in the student's independent adult life.

Problems with Computer Compatibility

A teacher who uses computers with students with mental retardation needs to be aware of potential problems with compatibility. Students with mental retardation are not able to learn multiple programs and to shift back and forth as easily as students without retardation. For example, when a student moves from elementary to junior high school, the computers at the new school may or may not be compatible with those on which skills have been initially learned. In some instances, computers are incompatible within the same school. Incompatibility problems may also arise because the computer that a student has at home is different from the computers at school. If the student has no computer at home, he or she has little opportunity for school-home cooperation. The compatibility problems are further complicated by obsolescence. It is difficult, if not impossible, to coordinate the necessary updating of software and hardware, either from one school or level to another or from school to home.

Although, on the surface, computers may seem an ideal way of providing highly motivating, individualized material for children with mental retardation, in many aspects using computers has not demonstrated clear superiority in terms of speed, accuracy, or some other advantage. In such cases, computer methods must be considered less desirable than paper-and-pencil procedures because of the significant cost, increased instructional time, and problems of incompatibility and transfer or generalization. The deciding factor seems to lie with an active, well-organized IEP team that can assess the student's achievement, needs, and abilities and project how well instruction in the use of computers is likely to benefit that student.

DIRECT USE OF HAND-HELD CALCULATORS BY STUDENTS WITH MENTAL RETARDATION

When May and Marozas (1989) surveyed 60 teachers of children with severe and multiple disabilities, the majority of the teachers reported they had students who used electronic devices in the classroom. The teachers found the devices to be generally beneficial, but they reported that the students had difficulty learning how to use them.

Hand-held calculators are obviously more readily available, more portable, less expensive, and easier to use than computers. They come in a variety of models and formats, yet they are not plagued with compatibility problems to the extent that computers are. They are not as motivating, however; they yield less information, and they are less versatile because most of them relate primarily to arithmetic problems. Both students and teachers, however, can become fascinated with them and overlook the weaknesses.

Calculators require a great deal of instructional time and effort if a student with mental retardation is to use one to solve practical problems. If a student is to advance beyond the simple addition and subtraction of whole numbers, he or she must be able to convert cents to dollars, to manipulate decimal points and place holders, and to use the information obtained. Frederick-Dugan, Test, and Varn (1991) claimed success in teaching 2 students (ages 18 and 20) whose mental retardation they described as moderate to use a hand-held calculator to make purchases. They reported some generalization to other purchase sites, with a satisfactory degree of retention over several weeks.

Calculators are invaluable in teaching students with mental retardation to estimate. A student can compare the initial estimate of a solution to a practical problem, such as the total amount of a purchase, to the computed solution using the calculator. The proximity of the two solutions gives the student working independently some assurance that he or she has accurate information on which to make a decision.

Of course, it is difficult to train any person, but particularly one with mental retardation, to carry a calculator and to use it independently in appropriate circumstances. Yet, when students are trained to do so, the calculator can be useful in solving real-life needs, as well as classroom problems.

DIAGNOSIS/PRESCRIPTION AND GIA

As in most other areas of curriculum for students with mental retardation, diagnosis/prescription in arithmetic must be done by informal means. Few norm-referenced tests are available in arithmetic, but most were not written for students with mental retardation and did not include these students in their normative samples.

Existing Tests

Some of these formal tests, such as the Key Math Test (Connolly, 1988), can be used for students with mental retardation, particularly with younger ones. Even the excellent Key Math Test, however, moves rapidly through a succession of representative arithmetic items, and the conceptual space between any two items testing the same topic (e.g., fractional parts) may require months—even years—of instruction for students with mental retardation. The arithmetic concepts tested by the Key Math Test are well designed and can be used by a teacher to check the sequencing of his or her informal arithmetic program. The same is true of the arithmetic sections of general achievement tests. Significantly, most practical concepts of consumer arithmetic emphasized in this chapter are not measured at all by formal tests.

Curriculum Integration

Instruction in arithmetic for students with mental retardation should be related as closely as possible to other curriculum areas, such as family living, communication, and transition. Emphasizing relationships helps in showing the students why arithmetic is important and how it is used in everyday life. Thus, prescriptions based in other curriculum areas should have arithmetical components to avoid having to teach number concepts as separate activities.

Goal Instruction Analysis (GIA)

Even though complete independence may not be possible, at least partial participation in consumer activity is likely to increase the student's self-respect, as well as his or her performance. Therefore, increasing student responsibility should be strongly emphasized, particularly from adolescence onward.

A written GIA can be very helpful in documenting student progress, but because the ultimate goal of GIA is to enhance overall instructional techniques, the procedures may be performed informally. It is often helpful to sketch out a GIA on occasions when diagnosis/prescription seems to have reached a dead end, but otherwise written outlines may be gradually phased out. When GIA procedures are not being used, it is beneficial to continue to use the number and variety of GIA components appropriate to the student and his or her long-term and annual goals. Experience shows that it is all too easy to revert back to a handful of general purpose components and to forego the great precision offered by the GIA.

SAMPLE LONG-TERM AND ANNUAL ARITHMETIC GOALS

Appendix I lists some arithmetic skills and concepts that are particularly significant to this chapter. As with other appendixes, GIA or other evaluative procedures may indicate that the lowest-level activities of Appendix I are too difficult for the individual, in which case the IEP team should refer to Appendixes C and D for more rudimentary skills and concepts. Likewise, the performance levels of some individuals may be superior to those listed.

In practice, of course, the long-term and annual goals for each student must be formulated on an individual basis. Many students with mental retardation need skills, concepts, and activities even more fundamental than those on the list. The sample long-term and annual goals include a combination of skills, concepts, and activities. Some of these goals cover considerably more conceptual distance than others. A given annual goal from the list may be an appropriate long-term goal for some students whose mental retardation is more severe. As with the sample skills and concepts of the other appendixes, a great deal of evaluation and prioritizing is necessary to design an acceptable, long-term, life goal curriculum for an individual with mental retardation.

Proactivity, estimation, and practical problem solving are stressed throughout the listing of arithmetic skills and concepts. Admittedly, these high-level skills are difficult for students with mental retardation. In this chapter, however, I discuss the inefficiency and pointlessness of teaching these individuals to make basic mathematical calculations (e.g., column addition) unless they are able to use these operations in solving life's practical problems. Further, proactivity suggests that they must be able to set up and solve practical problems largely without assistance if they are to live independently. Thus, it may be more beneficial to teach an individual with mental retardation to set up and solve a practical—but rudimentary—problem than to stress higher-level fundamental operations. The IEP team must also bear in mind that many such individuals will live in settings that offer considerable supervision.

SUMMARY

In this chapter, I discussed some of the specific limitations mental retardation imposes on an individual. I also suggested some procedures to use in diagnosing the arithmetic abilities of a student with mental retardation.

I then discussed some of the more functional arithmetic skills and concepts the student is likely to need to be successful in adult life.

In the chapter, I also discussed some of the strengths and precautions of using computers and other electronic devices in teaching arithmetic and other subjects to students with mental retardation. I suggested that, though very popular, computer programs must teach concepts that can demonstrate their usefulness away from computers and that are valuable in later life. Hand-held calculators and other electronic devices are usually much smaller and more portable, but their practicality must also be carefully assessed away from the classroom.

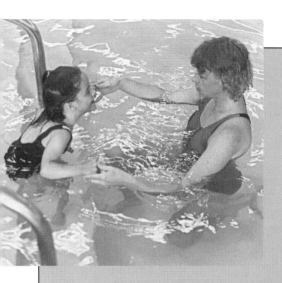

CHAPTER 16

Leisure, Recreation, Motor, Art, and Music Skills

Points to Study and Ponder

1. What leisure activities are available in your community for students with mental retardation after they leave school?
2. What relationship is there between the leisure activities offered in a typical school and those the student with mental retardation is likely to participate in after leaving school?
3. In your opinion, which is generally better preparation for individuals with mental retardation in adult life—team sports or individual activities?
4. How can leisure activities be used to develop decision-making skills with students with mental retardation?
5. To what extent should a student with mental retardation be permitted—or trained—to select his or her own leisure activities in school?
6. Do you think the advantages of the Special Olympics tend to outweigh the disadvantages? Do you think the Special Olympics should be continued?
7. What percentage of the school curriculum for a student with mental retardation should be devoted to art, music, and drama?
8. In an old but interesting study, Weston (1977) established a strong correlation between grades in physical education classes and the tendency to drop out of school before graduation. What do you think would be the findings of a similar study in your local high school(s)?
9. Do you believe that life goal curriculum planning and individual diagnosis and prescription are needed in leisure activities?

The purpose of this chapter is to provide a rationale and a procedure for identifying leisure skills and activities likely to be high priority for a given individual with mental retardation. The more rudimentary levels of physical, motor, and other leisure activities are discussed in greater detail in Chapter 9. In curriculum planning, leisure activities are closely related to social and independent living skills. The chapter also covers the need to follow good safety practices, especially in physical, motor, and recreational activities.

WELL-BEING, PHYSICAL CHARACTERISTICS, AND LEISURE ACTIVITIES

The great heterogeneity of mental retardation has many implications in planning leisure and motor activities. To begin with, individuals with mental retardation are known to have poorer general health than those with no disabilities (Asberg, 1989; West et al., 1992). Coulter (1993) discovered that epilepsy occurs much more often among students with mental retardation than it does in the general population. These students have also been found to be more accident prone (Dunne et al., 1993) than others and are more likely to indulge in compulsive, self-injurious behavior (King, 1993). Interestingly, Crandell and Roeser (1993) reported that these students are more likely to have excessive or impacted cerumen and that they also have a greater prevalence of prescription drug usage (Fox & Westling, 1986; Rimmer et al., 1993). More recently, Schupf, Ortiz, Kapell, Kiely, and Rudelli (1995) discovered that students with severe/profound mental retardation have a significantly higher prevalence of internal parasites than do those with mild/moderate mental retardation or no mental retardation. Chiappone and Libby (1972) and Kamon and Fujita (1994) found that these students also tend to have a wide variety of visual problems, compared with their peers.

Fox, Switzky, Rotatori, and Vitkus (1982) found that children with mental retardation tended to be overweight and the authors proposed a program of weight training. Others have used various procedures to control obesity and to improve the general health and well-being of individuals with mental retardation. Croce (1990) employed aerobic exercise and a controlled diet to improve the endurance and reduce obesity in 3 adults with severe mental retardation. Fox, Hartney, Rotatori, and Kurpiers (1985) reported the incidence of obesity in 337 children with mental retardation to be over 22%—much higher than among children without mental retardation. Interestingly, they also reported that the presence of obesity was not related significantly to race, gender, age, or level of mental retardation. Beasley (1982) demonstrated that adults with mental retardation could effectively be taught to jog and that this activity not only had a very favorable effect on their stamina and endurance but also improved their work performance.

Students with mental retardation compare more favorably with either their MA or CA peers in physical activities than they do in mental or academic tasks (see Chapter 2). For this reason, the huge range of ability imposed by mental retardation is probably not as apparent in the leisure, motor, and physical activities as in other areas. Nevertheless, some individuals, particularly those whose mental retardation is mild or moderate, have few, if any, noticeable limitations in either fine or gross motor abilities. As such, they have the physical ability at least to participate in a wide variety of leisure and recreational experiences. Others—generally those whose mental retardation is more severe or profound—will require lifetime assistance with their physical and recreational activities. This assistance may consist of help in making even the most modest body movements.

Even though students with mental retardation compare more favorably with their CA peers in physical and motor areas than in other areas of curriculum, no studies have shown them to be actually superior to their CA peers in motor activities. If such a study finds any group mean differences, it invariably shows students without mental retardation to be slightly to considerably superior. MacKay and Bankhead (1985) and Bankhead and MacKay (1982) found the prevalence of fine motor problems to be inversely proportional to intelligence. They reported that the abilities and performance levels of individuals with "subnormal" intelligence were notably inferior to those of "normal" and superior intelligence in task complexity, tracking, and reaction time. Likewise, Moon and Renzaglia (1982) reviewed the literature and concluded that people with mental retardation as a group are in serious need of well-planned fitness programs. This conclusion is significant because students with mental retardation and others who do poorly in physical and leisure activities are likely to be unwilling or unenthusiastic participants, especially in regular classes, where the competition is toughest.

With the trend to identify a progressively smaller percentage of the nation's schoolchildren as having mental retardation, we can anticipate that the identified students tend to have more severe mental retardation and generally have more physical limitations as well. This trend, together with mainstreaming or inclusion procedures, also means that many students who formerly would have been identified and served in some type of special education class are now being placed in regular classes, where some needed services tend to be less readily available. Thus, for these students in regular classes, the needed recreational services and instruction may have to be provided by resource teachers or in some other service delivery pattern.

LEISURE ACTIVITIES IN THE CURRICULUM

Leisure activities for students with mental retardation must not be overlooked. Individuals with disabilities need recreational development just as other individuals do, and these needs continue throughout an individual's life (Browder & Cooper, 1994). Dattilo and Schleien (1994) defined leisure for individuals with mental retardation to include recreation, free-time activities, and the freedom to choose activities. This chapter also includes art and music activities.

The major goal in presenting leisure skills to an individual with mental retardation is to help that individual enjoy life more fully. For several reasons, leisure activities for a student with mental retardation must be individually diagnosed and prescribed with particular care: (a) A student with mental retardation cannot learn all that other students master, (b) a tremendous number of skills and concepts must be deliberately planned and taught in mental retardation that other students learn incidentally at home or elsewhere, and (c) students with mental retardation constitute an extremely heterogeneous group (Vicari et al., 1992). Conceptual distance explains why even slight differences between the performance levels of two students or between the present and desired performance levels of an individual student are highly significant in terms of instructional time, effort, and other resources. Some students with mental retardation will eventually become quite independent with respect to leisure skills; others will be persistently dependent on others.

These three reasons help explain the considerable controversy about the extent to which leisure instruction and experience should be offered to students with mental retardation. There is no reason to assume that leisure activities are any less important in the lives of individuals with mental retardation than with others. Because students with mental retardation have limited time to master the many skills and concepts essential for successful adult living, the experiences offered by the school must be prioritized and planned with particular care. In making age 25 or other projections and evaluations, members of the IEP team must predict as accurately as possible the types of activities the individual is likely to participate in as an adult. Richardson, Katz, and Koller (1993) found that the social clusters of leisure activities among young adults with mental retardation varied considerably by gender and marital status and that all were somewhat isolated socially. Hamre-Nietupski, Krajewski, et al. (1992) proposed extending leisure activities for students with severe disabilities into summer.

PHYSICAL AND LEISURE SKILLS

The IDEA specified that needed physical education services, by themselves, are considered to be a justifiable part of a disabled student's IEP. Many students with mental retardation need supervised activities in both fine and gross motor activity to ensure that muscles do not atrophy. Certainly, the development and improvement of individual stamina are necessary to preserve life, as well as to enable a person to enjoy the quality of life that he or she might otherwise qualify for. In planning curriculum for students with mental retardation, however, some investigators have suggested that leisure and recreational instruction should be assigned relatively low priorities. For example, Lovett and Harris (1987a) reported that 73 "significant others" in the lives of adults with mental retardation rated vocational, social, and personal skills significantly more important than either academic or leisure skills. These two researchers (Lovett & Harris, 1987b) also interviewed 48 adults—whose mental retardation they described as mild to moderate—as to the skills they considered most important for successful community living. These adults rated vocational and social skills as most important, followed by personal, academic, and leisure skills, a ranking similar to that by the significant others questioned in the previous study.

Leisure activity is not without its advocates, however, who assume that such experience and instruction are equally as justifiable for people with mental retardation as for others (Hirst & Michaelis, 1983). McEnvoy and McConkey (1983) interviewed 67 mothers in Ireland about play for their children, aged 2 to 12 years, whose mental retardation ranged from moderate to severe. These mothers generally viewed play as important, enjoyable, and beneficial but declared their children's play to be passive and lacking in variety; this deficiency suggested a need for increased consideration both at home and at school. Thus, a major problem for the IEP team of any student with mental retardation is to determine the proportion of the valuable instruction time available to such a student that should be devoted to leisure and recreational activities when so much time is needed to develop good vocational, personal, social, and communication skills.

Benefits of Leisure and Physical Instruction

It is encouraging to note, however, that students with mental retardation can and do profit to some extent from instruction and experience in all areas of motor or physical activity. Holland (1987) noted that students whose mental retardation he described as educable performed more poorly on each of seven physical/motor tasks, but he also found that they were responsive to instruction. Distefano and Brunt (1982) studied uncertainty of movement and its relationship to gross motor activities among young children with mild mental retardation. They noted that uncertainty of movement increased reaction time and movement time significantly in a simple task of running, whereas no change in performance was noted for children with no mental retardation.

Hirst and Shelley (1989) found that children with mental retardation and even those with multiple disabilities can effectively participate in play activities and games, such as singles (isolated) play, rotation play, and associative play, but that the experience must be carefully structured for them. Nietupski and Svoboda (1982) demonstrated that even adults whose disabilities are severe can be taught fairly complicated games. Jeffree and Cheseldine (1984) reported that, with good planning and the use of programmed games, basic leisure skills acquired by adolescents with severe mental retardation significantly increased their level of activity and their interactions with classmates.

Training and participation in recreational activities result in a number of unexpected or subtle benefits. McConkey (1985) declared two widely held beliefs about recreational activities to be in conflict with available evidence: (a) that children with disabilities don't play and (b) that play is essentially a good way for children with disabilities to merely pass the time. He concluded that play can help these children learn. Marion (1979) suggested that leisure-time activities, such as gardening, hammering and nailing, and using puppets, are likely to aid in the development of socialization, attention span, and self-concept skills of students with mental retardation. Bedini, Bullock, and Driscoll (1993) tested a model leisure training program and reported positive changes in behaviors and attitudes indirectly related to the activity itself. Likewise, McGimsey and Favell (1988) reported that two daily periods of jogging and strenuous physical activities resulted in systematic reductions in problem behavior for most of their subjects who were severely aggressive, hyperactive young adults and institutionalized individuals with profound mental retardation. Rynders, Schleien, and Mustonen (1990) investigated an intensified, integrated camping experience for 3 children with and 5 children without severe disabilities. They reported that the campers with disabilities demonstrated improvements in targeted skills, the campers without disabilities increased their prosocial interaction bids, and staff attitudes improved.

Independence and Decision Making

To live independently, individuals with mental retardation must be able to select and choose their own recreational activities (Bullock & Mahon, 1992). Leisure activities also provide an excellent opportunity to develop the individual's ability to make his or her own choices and decisions (Bambara & Ager, 1992). The development of these decision-making skills has proved to be beneficial in other areas as well. Dattilo and Rusch (1985) found modest success in teaching individual decision making by allowing individuals with mental retardation to choose leisure activities in which they would participate. Later, Dattilo and St. Peter (1991) suggested that the activity program include elements of self-determination, leisure appreciation, self-awareness, decision making, social interaction, knowledge and use of leisure resources, and recreational participation. Many individuals with mental retardation have difficulty outgrowing the need for continuing guidance. Nietupski et al. (1986) successfully used diminishing reinforcement and prompting with 3 adolescents who were moderately/severely disabled to make a choice of leisure activity and then to sustain that activity for gradually longer periods of time with decreasing teacher supervision.

The tremendous heterogeneity in mental retardation makes the offering of such choices to groups of children difficult in most instances. That is because students with mental retardation should be encouraged to participate in age-appropriate activities while they are in school (Calhoun & Calhoun, 1993; Evans et al., 1995). At the same time, their educational programs must prepare them for their lives as adults. Because the activities they choose tend to be more appropriate for children younger than themselves, it is all too easy to provide them with a few activities available to large school groups and overlook the fact that each will soon be an adult with no one to organize even group—much less individual—activities. This means that the student's parents and other IEP team members must find an acceptable balance between age-appropriate, in-school recreation and curriculum designed to enable the student to seek out and participate in leisure activities in adult life. The team must not overlook either aspect of the student's education. It is well to consider the likelihood a given individual will go bowling, camping, or swimming on his or her own after leaving school. In many instances, such activities may serve that individual's current recreational needs but ignore his or her long-range needs. For example, swimming is an excellent and relatively inexpensive activity available year-round in most communities (Doremus, 1992). An obvious advantage of water activity is that (unlike team sports) it can be enjoyed by one's self or with any number of other people.

The student's IEP team must also plan a balance between spectator and participatory sports. They must assess the student's ability and interest in both types of activities. For example, where they are appropriate, team sports tend to be very competitive

The recreational preferences of individuals with mental retardation should be carefully evaluated and presented because team sports and large group playground activities are not usually popular in their adult lives.

in nature but help the individual develop his or her own strength, coordination, and endurance. Such activities help teach the concepts of cooperation, team play, sportsmanship, winning and losing gracefully, and following instructions. The IEP team, however, must evaluate the likelihood that a student with mental retardation will continue to participate in these group activities after leaving school. Where an older student's continued involvement in such an activity is possible, the team members should contact community, church, youth group, and other recreational leaders to enable and assist the student in making the necessary transition. As the student matures, all facets of the program should permit him or her to experience individual participation, similar to work experience and other transitional activities. Obviously, the parents must play key roles in this type of program. They and other team members must be available to provide guidance and encouragement where it is necessary.

The IEP team must also carefully consider the degree or severity of the student's mental retardation because it greatly influences the level of independence that student will eventually achieve. As a student approaches the end of his or her school career, the extent to which he or she will be dependent on others to organize and conduct recreational activities should become increasingly clear. In some instances, the program might concentrate on improving that student's behavior so that he or she can continue to participate in group activities organized and conducted by family, community, and church groups. The IEP team may need to investigate the availability of these groups and help the student become involved before he or she leaves school.

Special Olympics

The Special Olympics provides an excellent opportunity for a person with mental retardation to achieve a number of worthwhile goals (Hamel, 1992). This is a private organization designed to give students with mental retardation an opportunity to participate in athletic and other activities. In practice, the Special Olympics serves primarily those whose mental retardation is severe/profound. This focus allows them to participate and compete with others of similar ability. Horner, Williams, and Knobbe (1985) reported the retention of skills performed to be quite positive over time, depending on the students' opportunities to practice and perform. Ballard and Calhoun (1991) applauded the motivational aspects of the Special Olympics and maintained that a number of academic activities—including art, mathematics, independent living, reading, and health—can be integrated into preparation for the Olympics.

In recent years, however, the Special Olympics has become somewhat controversial. Klein, Gilman, and Zigler (1993) reported that experts in mental retardation and parents of Special Olympics participants generally viewed the program as highly beneficial, particularly in terms of social adjustment and life satisfaction. However, some of the experts pointed out the segregative aspects of the program, and parents noted a variety of administrative problems. Orelove, Wehman, and Wood (1982) cited publicity, increasing awareness, and the opportunities for students with mental retardation to train and participate as definite advantages. They also noted the segregative aspects of the program and argued that it was overly competitive. Possibly tongue-in-cheek, they suggested that the competitive elements might be relieved by inviting individuals without disabilities to compete. Indeed, almost overnight, the early promoters of the Special Olympics discovered that even individuals with milder forms of mental retardation ran away with virtually all of the competitive events. This predictable situation was largely due to the high correlation between the severity of mental retardation and the incidence of ancillary special health care and physical problems. These are the real causes of poor athletic ability—not mental retardation itself. More serious concerns were registered by Low and Sherrill (1988), who noted the compounding dangers of a number of health, nutrition-related, and medical problems, including congenital heart disorders and seizures. Even now, individuals relatively free of these ancillary problems dominate the competitions. This has necessitated the use of extensive time trials, with heats and events having few participants. Still, the Special Olympics provides a real opportunity for many students with severe forms of mental retardation to participate in a variety of events, win medals, and gain recognition that would otherwise be beyond their grasp. Given that individual events are limited to forestall the dangers of cardiac arrest and other serious problems, it seems a shame to consider discontinuing the program.

The continued existence of Special Olympics programs confirms the extreme and unique needs of individuals with mental retardation. Such special programs are not generally needed by those with other disabilities. They are sorely needed, however, by those with mental retardation and have proved beneficial in many ways. A student with mental retardation may actively participate in Special Olympics activities as long as he or she meets the guidelines of age and ability level. If the student does not qualify, he or she may participate either by observing or assisting. To participate in any way, however, the individual may need considerable encouragement, instruction, and assistance. The Special Olympics continues to provide a great variety of year-round activities and events in most communities.

ART, MUSIC, AND DRAMA

The fine arts must not be overlooked as areas of interest for students with mental retardation. Although these subjects do not appear to lead to employment and independent living, all individuals must be able to find suitable recreational activities. The extent to which these subjects are included in a student's curriculum should be left to the discretion of the IEP team.

Art

Every school subject has advocates who recommend that every student become proficient in that subject to some extent while in school—and not without good reason (Uhlin & DeChiara, 1984). For example, Frith and Mitchell (1983) declared that art is a justifiable means of expression and that art education should be an essential part of the mental retardation curriculum—at least for children whose mental retardation is mild. They further asserted that the students must be taught by teachers certified in both art and special education. Frost (1985) declared that art not only can be a means of expression but also may promote interaction with the environment and provide independence and relaxation. Students with disabilities may also be taught to appreciate the beauty of the artwork of others. Blandy (1993) suggested that community-based programs be established in libraries, museums, and senior citizen centers where people with disabilities may experience art of various forms. Lowenfield (1987) decried the isolation from the environment of students with all disabilities and asserted that this detachment may be overcome by self-expression through drawings, paintings, and sculptures. He further maintained that such sensory experiences tend to improve self-concept and to release inhibitions. Bridges (1986) agreed and stated that, despite their disabilities, students with mental retardation are capable of expressing their experiences and relationships with others through their artwork. Greeson and Vane (1986) tested the creative and incidental learning abilities of adolescents whose mental retardation they described as educable by using an imagery-based, associative learning pictorial elaboration task. Even though the control group consisted of peers matched on MA, the performance of the students with mental retardation was poorer than that of students without mental retardation, although both groups were able to generate some original ideas.

In providing art instruction and activity for students with mental retardation, it is important that others, such as teachers, volunteers, and peers, not do the artwork for the students. This "helping" happened to one male student with profound mental retardation but with no discernible artistic talent. During a recreational art class, a college student helped him produce some impressive artwork. School officials were later frustrated in their attempts to place the young man in a work-related transitional program. The parents objected, citing their son's apparent progress in art as evidence that he really didn't have mental retardation at all and that formal art instruction was more appropriate. It is also essential to provide an honest evaluation of a student's "artistic achievements." In a similar case, a 20-year-old man with profound mental retardation moved from a rural area to a larger school district. School officials of the larger district, noting the limited instructional time remaining, suggested their widely acclaimed transitional workshop, designed to evaluate the young man's abilities and to prepare him for employment and independent living. The parents, however, insisted that their son be placed in regular classes—especially art classes, where he could further develop his art talent. It eventually was revealed that the rural district, having no appropriate special education classes or services available, had placed the young man in regular classes, including an art class. Because he had been unable to comprehend what the other students were doing, the art teacher had let him use finger painting materials largely unsupervised. The local weekly newspaper had featured his work in an article that noted his profound limitations. At no time had anyone suggested that his work had any merit or showed any promise. In fact, an art specialist rated his work as "substandard preschool." The school officials in the new district had to admit, in response to the parents' challenge, that none of their artwork had ever been the subject of a special newspaper feature. Unable to prevail in their quest, the parents moved to another school district.

Music

The musical aptitude of individuals with mental retardation has been largely uninvestigated (Miller, 1991). All of the comparative studies in his review of literature, however, showed individuals to have less general musical ability and aptitude than either their CA or MA peers. Doxey and Wright (1990) reported a strong positive correlation between musical aptitude and cognitive ability or IQ, implying that people with mental retardation are likely to have relatively little musical aptitude. Nevertheless, music for students with mental retardation has been advocated for several reasons. For example, Caouette and Reid (1991) noted that playing music to children had several favorable effects even though they were not taught to read or perform music. The investigators played music, white noise, and pink noise (miscellaneous sounds designed to measure distractibility) to 13 adults with severe mental retardation during a cardiovascular fitness activity and reported that music was effective in encouraging greater and more continuous physical output, whereas white and pink noise were not. In a similar study, Starke and Wright (1986) reported that the introduction of music and the elimination of distractions were easily implemented and were cost-effective in reinforcing and promoting higher workshop productivity rates for the experimental groups.

It is unlikely that most students with mental retardation will participate extensively in playing musical instruments as adults. L. Williams (1985), however, noted that students with a variety of disabilities can learn to play musical instruments well enough to form musical ensembles and to participate for self-satisfaction.

Drama

Drama, like other arts, must be carefully diagnosed and prescribed. A student's IEP team has the responsibility to evaluate the student's aptitude and interest in drama and to evaluate the relative benefits of drama in that student's present school program. As with other art activities, the team must consider the spectator and participant aspects of theater and drama, as well as the current and future merits of such instruction. Then they must project the place that theatrical experiences are likely to play in the individual's adult life. Brown (1988) justified and encouraged the teaching of drama to children with severe disabilities by combining drama with sign language. She hypothesized that signing and participation in dramatic productions encourage creativity among children with mental retardation and other severe disabilities. Likewise, Warger (1985) proposed that creative drama can be adapted and made accessible to children with mental retardation and most other disabilities. McGookey (1992) reported the organization of a theatrical group in which actors portray people with disabilities and respond to questions in character. She suggested that class members with disabilities might organize a similar group.

CURRICULUM PLANNING

Part of the controversy over the extent to which leisure skills and experiences should be included in the curriculum for students with mental retardation can be resolved by offering these activities in conjunction with other parts of the curriculum. Horizontal curriculum planning (Chapter 3) suggests that recreational skills, such as calisthenics, marching, dancing, and running, where appropriate, can be combined with counting, measuring, shopping, and other mathematical activities, as well as with many social and communication skills. Ballard and Calhoun (1991) showed how Special Olympics activities were integrated with mathematics, reading, health, independent living, and art for secondary students with mild to moderate mental retardation.

Because of the priorities involved, it is particularly important to use the age 25 projection or some other long-range planning program to determine which leisure and recreational activities are likely to be helpful to a student with mental retardation in adult life. The age 25 projection will also help the IEP team in determining which leisure activities are within the student's interest and ability level. IEP teams must bear in mind that every student with mental retardation has some ability or talent in virtually all areas of curriculum, including art, music, and drama. Yet, mental retardation imposes on a student modest to severe limitations in these areas, just as it does in other domains. Thus, it becomes the duty of the student's parents and other team members to determine the extent to which these leisure skills should be taught. The overall goal must be to enable the student to be as independent as possible, and his or her active participation must not only be sought but also developed, as outlined above. The team must also find the balance between the passive, in-school recreational aspects of leisure and the instruction designed to help the student select and experience leisure activities either actively or passively as an adult. These team decisions are never easy.

The student's parents and other IEP team members must not lose sight of the fact that the student is entitled to some recreation. These activities are a substantial part of the educational programs for all students. Yet, the student must also be perceived as a future adult whose abilities in finding appropriate and satisfying recreation will be relatively limited, as with other areas of endeavor. Consideration of future adulthood and the need for recreation is equally relevant in contemplating the place of art, music, and drama in the curriculum of a student with mental retardation.

Placement

Physical education and other leisure classes are generally considered to be quite automatic selections for mainstreaming or inclusion programs for students with mental retardation. For example, Jambor and Gargiulio (1987) declared that the playground is a common denominator for all children and suggested that the process of play is a natural setting for knowing and understanding oneself and others. Wilhite et al. (1989) agreed and pointed out that recreational and leisure services are essential in any setting. Watkinson and Titus (1985) reviewed research on integrating students with mental retardation into physical education and found improvement not only in motor performance but also in improved self-concept and social interactions and the attitudes of others toward people with disabilities. It is essential, however, that curriculum and placement decisions be made carefully and always on an individual basis. It is particularly important for the team members to investigate local circumstances, rather than nationwide research with large groups. Some procedures might work reasonably well in one locality having a predominance of students with mild/moderate mental retardation but not in the local area where the mental retardation of the student under consideration is more severe or profound.

It is also essential for the team to consider all elements of the local situation. It should be particularly helpful to consider how well regular physical education and other leisure classes are serving those for whom they have been designed—both locally and in the nation as a whole. In an impressive effort to identify the causes of school dropouts, Weston (1977) reviewed school records of former students of a large high school district in California. None of the students were identified as disabled; in fact, all had taken and passed the California High School Proficiency Exam (CHSPE). She discovered that grades in physical education classes were the most reliable predictor of school dropout. She described the situation to be little short of phenomenal: If the PE grades were high, the students stayed in school; if low, they dropped out. So striking were her results that she interviewed as many students as she could locate. In this follow-up procedure, the students identified two elements of physical education classes that contributed to their decisions to drop out of school. One was the "dress down" requirement, mentioned by boys about as often as girls. The other was the persistent competition that required them to vie almost daily with others whose abilities they deemed to be superior. Craft (1994), however, reviewed several articles in the literature and concluded that students with mental retardation can be integrated into regular physical education if the programs are well planned to meet individual needs and if the teachers are carefully prepared.

One major criticism of otherwise excellent Special Olympics programs is that they isolate the participants from their peers. Regardless of the merits of such criticism, the same standard might be applied to other leisure activities. On the one hand, a student with mental retardation might justifiably participate in an activity designed for people without disabilities if he or she can do so successfully. On the other hand, if the student cannot produce acceptable music or art, that student's substandard performance might bring about undue and unwanted attention. Thus, the IEP team should evaluate the lasting personal benefits resulting from the student's mere participation in a school chorus that is striving for excellence. Atterbury (1984) cautioned that music classes typically make complex and stressful demands on students, even at the elementary level, and that educators responsible for mainstreaming students with mental retardation or learning disabilities should examine music programs carefully before deciding that they are appropriate mainstreaming environments. She also suggested that music teachers must be involved in mainstreaming decisions. Increasing the tolerance level of other people is a worthy goal but one that must be considered in light of possible exploitation or demeaning of the individual, or failure to use the student's time wisely. The team must also evaluate the extent to which any activity will contribute to that individual's ultimate success in adult life.

The placement or overall service delivery pattern for a student with mental retardation is ordinarily determined by the student's needs in other curriculum areas, such as social and communications skills, work experience, transition, and independent living. Leisure skills are not usually considered to be of sufficient importance to dominate placement decisions. Therefore, the student's IEP team must plan his or her leisure skill development in whatever educational setting was selected to meet the student's other needs.

Safety

Finally, in all leisure activities for which the atmosphere is likely to be somewhat more relaxed than that for other areas of curriculum, it is important to ensure that the learning environment is safe and that safety rules are established, understood, and followed. Aronson (1990) recommended that teachers and caregivers receive infant and child first-aid training. She pointed out that such training is more likely to be needed than CPR. CPR instruction and the Heimlich maneuver are also vital, however, because the events surrounding the need for these procedures are often life-threatening and demand instant reaction (Baker, 1990). Steege and Retish (1982) pointed out that teachers are often confronted with emergency situations and that they need first-aid training. They should also be informed about "good Samaritan" laws designed to protect persons in nonmedical professions who provide emergency first aid. Aides and volunteers should receive similar training.

In physical and recreational activities, students with limited understanding, as well as moderate to serious physical limitations, are often expected to essentially duplicate activities for more capable students. The use of bats, hard balls, and other recreational tools must be properly supervised. Handrails must be in place, and wheelchairs, crutches, and stairs must be stable and in good repair. Art and other leisure activities at every age level also involve a number of potentially harmful substances, such as various paints, thinners, and lacquers and devices, such as scissors, paper cutters, awls, punches, needles, pins, tacks, compasses, and razor-sharp art knives. Also, a number of beads, blocks, and other objects could be swallowed.

DIAGNOSIS/PRESCRIPTION AND GIA

Diagnosis/prescription in all of the leisure areas will usually be done with informal means. A few norm-referenced tests in physical education are available, but most did not include students with mental retardation in the normative samples. In any event, the judgment of the parents and other IEP team members should be sufficient, especially if they observe the individual over a substantial period of time. In the area of leisure, it is particularly important to use school time wisely when working with students with mental retardation. Usually, little school time remains once they learn to make wise choices and decisions and to manage their own affairs to any appreciable extent. Also, they have so much to learn away from school once they are old enough and mature enough to work and learn off-campus. Most of their social, transitional, and independent living skills must be culminated in community settings. Ellis et al. (1992) hypothesized that individuals with mental retardation are more likely to engage in physical activities if they are trained to self-manage their activities. These researchers taught adolescents with moderate and severe mental retardation to increase their performance and the time spent on exercise activities by using self-management techniques—adapted timers and lap counters. The students must also be taught to enter and exit campus safely.

Many GIA components in other chapters work well in designing a GIA in leisure activities. Every leisure activity requires a different design for each individual even though each GIA is similar in some respects to every other GIA. Some GIA components are unique to leisure activities or have been used in isolation or in combination by other investigators. For example, Colozzi and Pollow (1984) used a prompt fading sequence, fading of teacher presence, and verbal directions in teaching 5 elementary-age students with mental retardation to walk from the entrance of their school to the classroom. Surburg (1991) found that imagery practice (a type of mental rehearsal) facilitated the execution of the reaction time component of a motor task and sometimes facilitated performance of the movement time component of the motor task with 32 adolescents with mild mental retardation. Heitman and Justen (1982) suggested several elements, such as social reinforcement (praise) and speeding up performance, that serve very well as GIA components in leisure and recreational activities. Bernabe and Block (1994) modified the rules of a girls' softball league to enable a girl with moderate to severe disabilities to participate. The modifications included concessions depending on the girls' batting and on-base averages. Realon, Favell, and Dayvault (1988) adapted and used a variety of battery-operated leisure materials to make activation easier for 10 nonambulatory and nonverbal, institutionalized adults with profound mental retardation. Demonstration and instruction results supported use of the adapted materials as a cost-effective means of increasing the independent leisure activity engagements of such clients. When a teacher shares results of these adaptations and components with parents, they can use them with the child at home.

In most communities, a variety of volunteers are readily available who can be trained to assist with recreational, as well as other, activities for students with mental retardation. Webster (1987) used peer tutors in adapted PE and noted that, in addition to helping in the PE program, the tutors had a positive influence on the academic learning time (ALT) of 3 students with moderate to severe mental retardation. Additional GIA components are suggested here, in other chapters, and in Appendix J.

SAMPLE LONG-TERM AND ANNUAL LEISURE GOALS

Appendix J lists some leisure skills and concepts that are particularly significant to this chapter. As with the other appendixes, GIA or other evaluative procedures may indicate that the lowest-level activities of Appendix J are too difficult for the individual, in which case the IEP team should refer to Appendixes C and D for more rudimentary skills and concepts. Likewise, the performance levels of some individuals may be superior to those listed.

One major purpose of providing leisure activities to individuals with mental retardation is to enable them to find and enjoy suitable recreational, physical, and personally satisfying pursuits after graduation. IEP team members can do much to help them experiment with a variety of recreational activities. The team must plan carefully in providing recreational activities that are likely to be available in the individual's community after he or she leaves school. Because of the relatively large numbers of students in school classes, it seems almost necessary to provide a variety of team sports that will not be available to the individual in adult life. Add to this the necessity of assessing the individual's preferences for different recreational activities and encouraging him or her to experience a wide variety of entertainment possibilities, and the IEP team is faced with some real challenges.

SUMMARY

In this chapter, I discussed the place of leisure and fine art activities in the curriculum of students with mental retardation. I pointed out the need these students have for well-planned leisure programs and also suggested that, in some instances, these activities might consume an unjustifiable portion of the student's school time. I further suggested that this matter must be resolved by the student's IEP team.

I also reinforced the need for the student to become as independent as possible and showed how leisure activities are related to that goal. I also outlined some principles and procedures to follow in establishing and operating leisure activity programs.

Epilogue

This book presented life goal curriculum planning for students with mental retardation, together with a practical, diagnostic/prescriptive/evaluative teaching approach. It also introduced a simple but effective process, called the age 25 projection, that enables the IEP team to continually monitor the student's progress toward his or her life goals and make the necessary changes to the goals and the student's programs to achieve the adjusted goals. The major purpose of this coordinated approach is to enable the student with mental retardation to become as successful and self-sufficient as possible in adult life and live as independently as his or her personal abilities and circumstances permit. Regardless of the methods or location used in accomplishing this purpose, life goal curriculum planning and some type of individual diagnosis and prescription seem to be essential elements for any student's educational program—but particularly for those with mental retardation (Schloss et al., 1994).

The techniques and procedures of this book were developed to prepare teachers in any situation to deal more effectively with students with mental retardation, regardless of the educational setting or placement. Also identified are a considerable number and variety of problems to be solved and challenges to be met. Solutions were proposed for some of these, but some remain to be wrestled with in the future. If it is true that a future without challenges is a dull prospect, then the future of mental retardation is bright indeed. Some major challenges and unresolved issues are discussed here.

A CHANGING SOCIETY

One future puzzle for students with mental retardation and those who work with them to cope with is simply the vast societal changes that are occurring. Many of these societal changes are known, and no doubt many more will occur in the future. I identified several of the known changes that seem to be particularly timely and significant: advancing technology, the shifting responsibility for funding in mental retardation, and the longevity of life and its effect on individuals with mental retardation.

Advancing Technology

One intriguing and exciting change society is undergoing is the rapid advance of technology. Modern IEP teams must be alert to avoid having their student with mental retardation get lost in the swirl of rapidly advancing technology—a phenomenon that has potentially positive and negative elements. On the positive side, it is inevitable that the scientific community will continue to make encouraging improvements in computer hardware and software and other technological advances; these will make it possible to better accommodate the specific needs of students with mental retardation. It is equally likely that advancements will occur in other areas of assistive technology, such as communication boards and similar devices. For example, devices are now available that translate a selected picture/switch into spoken language. The nonverbal student need only select and press the picture/switch that describes the desired question, request, or response to a question. These devices will become increasingly functional but smaller and more simple to use. Inexpensive software easily converts computer documents into spoken English. Similar advancements specifically appropriate for students with mental retardation can be anticipated in other contrivances for classroom use.

On the precautionary side, the advancement of societal technology in general imposes sharp increases in the entry-level skills for employment in most businesses and industries. These increasing demands heavily affect students with mental retardation, whose educational qualifications are typically minimal. The advancement of technology is always accompanied by an increase of high-level jobs relating to the production, marketing, maintenance, and repair of electronic and other mechanisms, but these are also beyond the students' skill levels. In the meantime, the food and other service industries available in most communities are a great source of employment opportunities for students with mental retardation.

Shifting Responsibility for Funding

Another apparent trend is the shifting of responsibility for social and educational programs from the federal to the state and local levels. Congressional leaders are making a strong attempt to hold state legislatures increasingly responsible for the funding of these programs—presumably to reduce the effects of rapidly increasing federal financial deficits. Congressional leaders are also advocating legislation that would terminate the obligation for states to pay for unfunded mandates (programs required by but not paid for by the federal government). Neither the extent to which these policies will be realized nor their overall effect is easy to predict. Shifting responsibility among governmental bodies in this manner, however, always seems to result in considerable time delays before the newly responsible agencies provide the necessary funding. In any event, local IEP teams and the significant others who champion the cause of students with mental retardation must be alert to ensure these students do not get lost in the shuffle.

Longevity and Mental Retardation

Individuals with mental retardation are living longer than ever before, although few definitive studies have investigated this matter (Eyman, Call, & White, 1991). Encouragingly, however, there is increasing interest in older individuals with mental retardation, and it is expedient that school programs for this population focus clearly on preparing them for successful adult life (Krauss et al., 1992).

CHANGING EDUCATION

Education in the United States has never been static, but has always been subject to periodic, sweeping changes. Although most of these changes have improved the educational opportunities for most students, they often affect students with mental retardation in unforeseen and inauspicious ways. For example, about once in every decade, a new "excellence" movement appears that purports to take American education back to fundamentals or basics (Schrag, 1995). Who would criticize any serious attempt to ensure that students were properly grounded in the fundamental skills necessary to achieve maximum success in the academic world? Yet, these attempts are invariably accompanied by the reestablishment and enforcement of more rigorous standards to pass classes and earn diplomas—usually laudable for all students, except those with mental retardation (Palardy, 1998; Toch, 1984). Most students with mental retardation can be expected to perform poorly in—and profit little from—such strenuous, academically oriented course work. Currently, the great emphasis is on providing a non-academic, functional curriculum for this population (Clark, 1994; Hamre-Nietupski, Nietupski, & Strathe, 1992). Thus, IEP teams and special educators must evaluate any such local movements and how they are likely to affect students from this population.

CHANGING POPULATION IN MENTAL RETARDATION

In Chapter 1, I describe a situation in which a rapidly decreasing percentage of U.S. schoolchildren are being identified as having mental retardation. Some people may conclude that this is a positive sign and that students who previously would have been identified—and served in some way—as having mental retardation are progressing satisfactorily in regular classes without any special assistance. Identification rates in some states, however, are less than 0.4%, a rate that corresponds roughly to IQs of 50 and below (MacMillan, 1982). It is difficult to perceive how these students could be succeeding without a great deal of special assistance. In general, failure to be identified means not receiving special education services of any kind—even resource or consultative help. Considering the severe limitations imposed by mental retardation, one might conclude that students from this population are in greater need of school assistance than any other group. In terms of percentage, however, school officials in this country identify and serve almost four times as many children in learning disabilities as we do in mental retardation (*Sixteenth Annual Report to Congress*, 1994). Thus, we do not appear to have lost our inclination to offer special assistance to students with disabilities generally—only those with mental retardation. We simply must find some way to identify and serve those students who have been disfranchised from special education.

Also, the courts are currently inclined to require the schools to accept students with even the most severe learning, behavioral, and other disorders (*Big Beaver Falls Area School District v. Jackson*, 1993; *Oberti v. Board of Education of Borough of Clementon School District*, 1993; Strain, 1990). This means that teachers of both regular and special classes are expected to accommodate students whose disabilities are most severe and limiting (Osborne, 1994).

ACHIEVING EMPLOYMENT, FINANCIAL, AND SOCIAL INDEPENDENCE

I have tried to avoid the controversy of special versus regular class placement for students with mental retardation, the point being that whoever reads the book is not likely to be in a position to greatly affect the controversy on a national scale. The reader is more likely to have the responsibility to select and/or design a program for one individual with mental retardation and to be limited to programs and resources available locally. This responsibility is momentous in any event because members of this population face some substantial challenges in achieving an appreciable measure of self-determination and independence—either as students or later as adults (Wehmeyer & Metzler, 1995).

I point out that the trend toward educating students with mental retardation in regular classes is supported by hundreds of journal articles and conference presentations. It is somewhat troubling that most of this literature is preferential—surveys, questionnaires, and opinionaires. No comparative research studies demonstrate the ability of students from mainstream, integrated, or inclusion programs to obtain and hold jobs. Nevertheless, the sheer number of these articles and presentations indicates strong support for the practice among parents, teachers, administrators, and peers of students with mental retardation. Thus, the movement of educating students with mental retardation in regular elementary and secondary classes will no doubt continue into the foreseeable future. IEP teams must continue to evaluate locally available programs and to select, adapt, and/or design those that are most likely to help their student achieve optimum success in adult life. They must be particularly sensitive to the student's needs in preparing for employment, financial, and social independence.

Self-Determination

To be independent in adult life, it is essential for a person to make as many of his or her own decisions as possible and to be allowed the freedom to do so (Bannerman, Sheldon, Sherman, & Harchik, 1990). Chapter 8 contains an outline of a simple but long-range procedure to enable even individuals whose mental retardation is relatively severe to learn to make decisions and become increasingly responsible for their own behavior. Also, in several chapters, I promote a procedure—proactivity—that teaches the person to recognize and solve practical problems in everyday life. IEP teams must encourage proactivity and personal decision making to develop optimum independence.

Slow Learners

Chapter 1 covers the significance of a group of students, loosely identified as slow learners, in U.S. schools. These students are not usually considered by their local educators to have mental retardation. In fact, their collective IQs range from a lower limit that coincides with the upper limit of mental retardation (as locally defined) to roughly 80, 85, or as high as 90. Yet, regional variation, presented in the same chapter, shows that the slow learners relate to mental retardation in at least two important ways: (a) A highly significant number of students identified as slow learners in one state or region would qualify to be diagnosed and served as having mental retardation in many other states and regions, and (b) a student who fails to qualify for identification and service in mental retardation is almost invariably served in whatever programs are locally available to the slow learners. Although islands of excellence dot the land, the overall evaluations of these programs are not encouraging. A major portion of the dropouts, substance abuse, delinquency, and other serious social problems is centered on this group. Also, experience shows that (like students who have mental retardation) individuals from this population have great difficulty obtaining suitable employment (Ekstrom et al., 1986; Joekel, 1986). For this reason, and because students with mental retardation are frequently placed either full- or part-time in classes designed for slow learners, every effort must be made to improve the quality and functionality of their educational programs. These programs must include work experience and transition training. The task of the IEP team, however, is to evaluate this situation locally and to place the student in the available program that is most appropriate and likely to enable the student to achieve his or her highest priority life goals. These students cannot wait until classes for slow learners attain perfection.

Appendix A

Implications of the Degree of Severity of Mental Retardation

Generally, the greater the extent or severity of the mental retardation individuals have,

1. The more likely they are to be identified at some time during their lives as having mental retardation (*Fourteenth Annual Report to Congress*, 1992).
2. The more likely they are to be identified by their parents as having mental retardation. The parents of a child with severe mental retardation may even admit or insist that the child has mental retardation but may not use the term *mental retardation*.
3. The more slowly they will progress through the developmental stages of normal infancy and childhood.
4. The earlier they will be suspected as having mental retardation by others (relatives or neighbors).
5. The more obvious or unanimous the mental retardation diagnosis will be.
6. The less likely they are to be aware (or appear to be aware) of the extent to which they are different from others. But they are aware of their differences, and one should never discuss the deficiencies of individuals with mental retardation in their presence (Dudley, 1987; Stanovich & Stanovich, 1979).
7. The less creative they will be.
8. The more clearly and extensively they will manifest the learning and other deficiencies discussed in Chapter 2 and elsewhere throughout this book.
9. The more likely they are to appear to have mental retardation: Most individuals with mental retardation have no outward physical stigmata, though many do (Drew et al., 1992; Richardson et al., 1985).
10. The more likely they will be to manifest secondary disabilities, such as speech, motor, sensory, and health problems.
11. The more slowly they will learn (Watkins et al., 1982).
12. The greater will be the discrepancy between their chronological and social ages.
13. The more likely they are to manifest behavior and discipline problems.
14. The more skills, concepts, or tasks one can identify that they are unable to perform well—academically or otherwise.
15. The more difficult it is to obtain a satisfactory placement for them in a foster home on either a temporary or permanent basis (Drydyk et al., 1980; Sellin, 1979).

16. The more likely they are to be placed in a special class, special school, group home, or even a residential institution.
17. The less controversy will surround their special placement.
18. The smaller the expected student-to-teacher ratio in their classes.
19. The fewer community activities (parades, dances, and other social affairs) they will be interested in, especially if they must decide to go on their own.
20. The more nearly the number of girls with mental retardation will equal the number of boys with mental retardation. In the mild/moderate categories, the boys outnumber the girls by a wide margin (Richardson, Katz, & Koller, 1986).
21. The more likely they are to be using prescribed medication (Fox & Westling, 1986).
22. The less likely they are to be using illegal substances.
23. The more likely they are to require catheters, G-tubes, and other highly technological health and survival devices while they are in school.
24. The more likely their classrooms, playgrounds, or bus arrangements will use an instructional assistant.
25. The more likely they are to qualify for post-high school education and training programs, such as sheltered workshops.
26. The more auxiliary and support services they will need and the longer these needs will persist.
27. The less likely they are to be ambulatory.
28. The fewer clubs and other extracurricular activities they will be interested in.
29. The fewer and less significant the decisions they will be able to make in their own behalf.
30. The less independence they will achieve in terms of living arrangements and the more emphasis on deliberate instruction the school programs must provide.
31. The more closely their activities must be supervised by other people—even as adults.
32. The more ordinary citizen privileges and rights (e.g., voting, marriage) they will lose or choose not to exercise, especially if they are not assisted by others.
33. The more difficulty they will have obtaining and maintaining employment.
34. The less money they will earn during their lifetimes.
35. The less appropriate are the traditional teaching methods, techniques, and materials designed and developed for others—including other students with mental retardation.
36. The smaller the percentage of regular curriculum they can be expected to master or that is appropriate for them.
37. The greater the amount of their curriculum that must be designed especially for their particular age or ability group.
38. The greater the assistance they need in acquiring acceptable social grace and skill.
39. The more difficulty they will have in making friends and maintaining lasting friendships.

40. The greater the assistance they need in learning to communicate effectively and the more likely they are to require instruction in the use of language boards and other augmentative communication procedures.

41. The greater the amount of their curriculum that must be designed expressly and individually for them—toilet training, physical therapy, sanitation, grooming, transition, work experience, safety, and other self-help skills that are taken essentially for granted by other students.

42. The more detailed their educational programs must be.

Appendix B

Helps in Working with Parents

1. Be patient and empathic with parents. They are likely facing intense personal and practical challenges in coping with the mental retardation of their child.
2. Be particularly sensitive to the needs of nontraditional (foster, surrogate) parents and guardians. Their collective needs vary tremendously.
3. Initiate a cooperative team effort between yourself and the child's parents. Assume a major—even dominant—role in keeping it going.
4. Discuss the child's progress with both parents whenever possible.
5. Never discuss a child's weaknesses or behavioral problems in the child's presence without carefully considering the effect that doing so may have on him or her.
6. Do not argue or become defensive if a parent manifests a negative attitude.
7. Try to support the actions and policies of your school board and administration. Avoid the precarious situation of taking sides with the parents against the administration. Counsel with administrators about insupportable decisions.
8. Be cautious in using educational and psychological terms with parents. Try to communicate with them on their own language level.
9. Work closely with colleagues to overcome any stigma that may be attached to children with mental retardation in your school.
10. Work with administrators so that the parents can be assured of a supportive, cooperative, team effort in finding the best program for their child. Expensive, disruptive court action can usually be avoided.
11. Be particularly careful with sensitive information. Do not gossip or share such information with parents of other children—or even with other teachers who are not involved with the child.
12. Be prepared to work amicably with parents who may never become fully cooperative.
13. Be tactfully persistent in encouraging the parents to obtain the most appropriate educational program for their child.
14. Use hypothetical examples to help parents avoid negative reactions to their child's condition—possibly a case study of overprotection or overexposure. Demonstrate the nature of the problem, but assure the parents that the example does not involve anyone in their school or community. Never use actual situations that the parent might recognize or discuss one child's problems or progress with another child's parent.
15. Do not get discouraged if the parents do not honor your requests or respond to your encouragement.

16. Explain that the purpose of the school, its personnel, and its programs is to support the parents.

17. Help the parents understand that the home and family life they provide for their son or daughter is more important in the long run than any school program.

18. Become familiar with the provisions of the IDEA and similar legislation and learn how they are interpreted in your school district. Help parents understand their rights under this law; it is generally better that they learn from school officials than from outside sources.

19. Respect the rights of the parents. Recognize their ultimate responsibility to secure their child's rights and to provide for their child's welfare.

20. Remember that parents will have varied and intense reactions to their child's mental retardation. Do not assume that all parents will react in the same predictable patterns, but be prepared to recognize and empathize with the patterns when they do occur.

21. Use persistent, consistent, gentle persuasion in helping parents understand mental retardation and cope with its effects.

22. Keep a personal file of the child's unique medical needs and problems, in addition to the information officially on file in the school office. Know whom to call in an emergency involving the child.

23. Be thorough in handling busing and other transportation arrangements for the child.

24. Work closely with the parents with any medication the child will need during school.

25. Work to ensure a safe learning environment for all students. Occasionally, review the legal requirements for parent-teacher relationships.

26. Review the management techniques described in Chapter 8, particularly those that involve the necessity of keeping parents apprised of their child's progress in school. Don't give the parents a legitimate reason to complain.

27. Work closely with parents in disciplinary decisions.

28. Encourage parents to join positive parent groups and to take advantage of respite care and similar services.

29. Make parents aware of the assistance their child received in completing schoolwork and craft projects that are taken home. If they are unaware that the child was given help, they may form unrealistic expectations for future projects.

30. Be positive but honest with the parents. Don't give them inflated estimates of their child's ability or achievement level. Expectations formed on an unrealistic base may result in frustrations and conflicts. Parents need accurate assessments in order to make proper decisions on matters that affect the life of their child.

31. Do not apologize for your inexperience or lack of training. Although arrogance will be offensive to the parents, undue humility may cause them to lose confidence in the program or the school.

32. Be careful in the way you handle sensitive information. Parents have a legal and personal right to any information the school may have regarding their child, but

they have no right to information regarding other children. This often becomes an issue when another child with a similar disability is placed in a program or is given special consideration for which their child does not qualify.

33. Try to establish a daily communication arrangement, such as a daily note—especially for young children.

34. Provide time before and after school to work with parents who are unable to attend conferences during regular school hours.

35. Consider all placements tentative. Most parents will cooperate if they realize that decisions are not final and that they can initiate change.

36. Demonstrate the child's progress to the parents with the GIA approach described in Chapter 7. This procedure helps parents understand not only the details of the child's performance but also the specific efforts and resources needed to reach and maintain that level of achievement.

37. Help parents of teenagers consider possible future living arrangements so that school facilities and programs may be used to prepare the child for maximum independence and effectiveness.

38. Help parents consider their child's future as an adult by using the age 25 projection concept.

39. Discuss the child's likely work experience and other transition needs early and consistently throughout the child's school experience.

40. Do not confront or accuse the parents if they do not follow through with a commitment.

41. Encourage both parents to work with their child in the classroom, at least once in a while. Encourage the child's family members to become involved as much as possible.

42. Enlist the parents' cooperation in developing their child's ability to make decisions and in guiding the child toward eventual independence and self-sufficiency.

Appendix C

Developmental (Age/Stage) Chart

Table C.1 is an age/stage chart of normal child development. It is included to help parents, teachers, and other members of the IEP team plan individual curriculum for students who are very young and/or who have serious developmental disabilities, such as severe mental retardation. Most of the skills, concepts, and activities depicted by the chart are developmental in nature, and little can be done to enhance or encourage them. A child with mental retardation or other serious disability is very likely to lag considerably behind the growth rate indicated by the chart but will usually progress in roughly the same sequence and at a generally predictable—but individual—rate.

The purpose of Table C.1 is to suggest the sequence of growth and development within which the age-appropriate skills and concepts of curriculum and instruction for an individual child might be planned and conducted.

TABLE C.1

Range	Communication and Cognition	Social, Motor, and Other
Birth to 3 Months	Makes undifferentiated cry Makes differentiated cry (2 months) Makes random noises (reflexive) • Coos and gurgles • Single syllables Stops movement to sound Stops movement to movement Some startle response Widens and shifts eyes Smiles reflexively Gazes, attending begins Maintains gaze at point where object disappears Follows (tracks) object swinging on a string (1 mo.) Follows (tracks) moving person (2 mo.) Recognizes bottle or breast Coos and chuckles, may laugh aloud	Sucks strongly Blows bubbles Raises head slightly—prone position (1 mo.) Clenches fist • Grasps some objects Moves arms and legs randomly Resists unpleasant sensations like wet towel on face (1 mo.) Holds head erect shakily in sitting position (2 mo.) Lifts head and chest lying on stomach Improves head control Grasps offered (nearby) object Seems to enjoy play
4 to 6 Months	Begins babbling (by 4th month) • Has some pitch and inflection Reacts to offered bottle Responds to others' voices Turns head toward sound Babbles for 2 or 3 seconds (by 6th mo.)	Passes object hand to hand Has some eye-hand coordination Begins to track moving object Supports head fairly well Shows some curiosity Directs grasp visually Sits with little support Rolls from back to stomach Passes object from hand to mouth
7 to 9 Months	Likes sound of own voice Imitates speech sounds and intonations of others Looks at named object, person Makes wide variety of sounds Points to named person Points to own named body part Reacts positively to "No" Tries to imitate facial expressions Produces most vowel sounds Shouts (non-cry) to attract attention Says "mama" and "dada"	Turns familiar object right-side up Takes object out of box Is usually shy around other people Seems to recognize others Sits on floor without support Pulls self to standing position Holds own feeding bottle Crawls on stomach Seems to explore Sits unsupported, changes position without falling Plays with more than one toy Unwraps simple package

TABLE C.1 Continued

Range	Communication and Cognition	Social, Motor, and Other
10 to 12 Months	Ends babbling as jargon (barely begins recognizable speech) Vocalizes to self in mirror Jabbers during play Utters first word at 10 to 20 months (Warning if none by 2 years) Relates word with object • Gives named toy Obeys simple command Gestures wants and needs (Some vocalization too) Says several words Holds up hands to be picked up Sees some cause and effect (tips over stacks of blocks) Says 3 or 4 words	Reacts to emotions of others Holds large pencil or crayon Stands unsupported Scribbles and makes marks Raises self up onto "all fours" Crawls on "all fours" Plays (rolls) ball with others Takes a few aided steps Drinks from cup Pulls self to standing position Takes few independent steps Picks up object with pincers grasp Yields toy on request Marks on paper with pencil or crayon
12 to 18 Months	Imitates adult speech roughly • Vocalizes with gestures Says up to 10 words (by 18 mo.) Says 1- to 3-word expression—"Yes—do" or "Want more milk." Recognizes picture of familiar object Uses up to 12 nouns Claims toys as own Uses plan to avoid obstacles Uses "plan" to obtain toy Shows interest in pictures Tries some trial-and-error activities Vocalizes—voice up and down—sounds like conversation Begins self-feeding	Stands and walks some unsupported Interacts with other children Throws ball or object Closes door
18 to 24 Months	Says up to 6 or 7 words Uses 2-word meaningful phrases (Protests "no bed") ("Love Mommy") Uses 50 to 200 words Indicates verbal toilet, other needs Engages in some symbolic play Engages in some dialog or two-way conversation Likes to be read to	Plays mostly by self Begins fast walk and run Uses, prefers pull toy Kicks a large beach or playground ball Climbs stairs (places each foot on each step) Runs or trots awkwardly Helps dress self Turns pages of book—poorly Imitates housework

TABLE C.1 Continued

Range	Communication and Cognition	Social, Motor, and Other
18 to 24 Months	Asks for common object by name Applies name to object Applies name to picture of simple or familiar object Turns picture right-side up Makes some mental plans for activity	
2 to 2.5 Years	Substitution and omission speech problems appear Asks simple questions Answers simple "what" and "where" questions Uses concept of "all" Attends to 5- to 10-minute story, answers simple questions Comprehends up to 500 words Completes 2 simple, related commissions	Parallel play emerges Jumps off small stool or step Walks down stairs one step at a time with some help Walks up stairs one foot on each step with some help Builds a tower of up to 5 blocks Can copy vertical lines Catches large, soft playground ball Feeds self, but may make mess
2.5 to 3 Years	Speech is 80% intelligible Asks questions Uses plurals Uses some contractions Uses some pronouns Uses some past tense Answers "who," "why," and "where" questions Asks for information Sorts simple, familiar objects Uses sentences up to 4 words Verbalizes toilet needs	Has some interest in cooperative play Catches small ball like volleyball Walks down stairs one step at a time largely unaided Walks up stairs one foot on each step largely unaided Balances on one foot for several seconds Makes rough copies of horizontal line and circle Is essentially toilet trained Opens door
3 to 3.5 Years	Comprehends up to 1,200 words Completes 2 unrelated commissions Uses up to 800 words Asserts some independence	Begins associative play Uses one object to represent another Makes rough copy of square Rides tricycle Catches soft, large, thrown ball

TABLE C.1 Continued

Range	Communication and Cognition	Social, Motor, and Other
3.5 to 4 Years	Infantile speech largely overcome Asks "how," "where," "why" questions Matches a few common colors Completes 3 simple commissions Knows which of 2 events was first Can relate fairly complicated event or story Answers "what if" questions Sustains fairly long conversation Uses mostly correct grammar in short sentences Knows own age Knows own last name Correctly points out 6 colors	Plays in small groups Draws man with no arms, legs Does simple cut–paste with help Prefers some playmates to others Balances on one foot for short time Rides tricycle Throws ball over head Washes hands unassisted
4 to 4.5 Years	Speech is essentially intelligible Comprehends 2,500 to 2,800 words Can sort pictures of same object Takes some pride in own work Can sort objects of similar size Is very imaginative Can relate long story Can tell main idea of fairly complicated story	Develops strong attachments and friendships Has cooperative play well established Draws identifiable man, includes most parts Does cut-and-paste activity well
4.5 to 5 Years	Can classify broad categories—the boys, the horses, the animals Comprehends 13,000 words Explains similarities and differences Recognizes own printed name Selects penny, nickel, dime on command	Abides by established game rules Can reproduce circle, triangle, square quite well Does beginning writing exercises Can dress self with essentially no help Zips zippers, fastens buttons, ties own shoelaces Cuts food with knife
5.5 to 5 Years	Is aware of others' speech errors Uses some slang Uses irregular comparatives—good, better, best Understands, estimates time intervals	Plays intently and for long periods of time Likes stunts Likes table games Invents simple games with rule structure

Source: This chart is drawn primarily from the author's experience, with some verification and assistance from Dr. Bonnie Lucido and the Michigan Project Find, Michigan Department of Education, P.O. Box 30008, Lansing, MI 48909.

Appendix D

Curricular Skills and Concepts for Students with Severe/Profound Mental Retardation

Communication Skills and Concepts

1. Produces vocal sounds
Makes random, seemingly purposeless sounds
Produces simple (guttural or babbling) sounds
Makes reflexive noises—coos, gurgles

2. Produces imitated, unintelligible speech sounds
Uses lallation and babbling
Jabbers—as during play
Uses echolalia, with increasing accuracy
Imitates simple vocal (guttural or babbling) sounds, single syllables
Imitates animal sounds
Imitates names of some classmates
Produces increasing number of cued sounds with increasing clarity
Uses noncrying voice to attract attention
Produces vowel sounds
Uses increasingly appropriate level of voice loudness
Uses intonation

3. Produces imitated, largely intelligible speech sounds
Imitates speech sounds (phonemes) on command
Imitates names of some classmates → Social

Imitates single, simple words
Defers imitation

4. Identifies beginning language stimuli (LCD) on verbal command
Points to above-waist body parts (nose, mouth, ear) → Home (Health and Safety)
Points to below-waist body parts (elbow, stomach, leg, foot) → Home (Health and Safety)
Points to article of clothing on command → Social
Points to family members on command → Social
Points to classmates on command → Social

5. Identifies more advanced language stimuli (LCD) by pointing → Social
Identifies (decodes) family members by pointing to their pictures
Identifies picture of self from single picture
Identifies self from picture of family group
Identifies self from pictures of few, then several classmates
Identifies pictures of teacher, aide, classmates, school nurse, principal
Identifies one color by pointing
Identifies increasing number of colors by pointing
Points to "big" object or "big one" in picture → Arithmetic
Points to increasingly subtle objects, cues, and so on in picture books

6.   Does 5 (above) while

Voicing an approximation of the verbal command

Voicing the verbal command with increasing
   clarity

7.   Does 5 (above) but by

Approximating the name as the body part or
   person is pointed to

Pronouncing with increasing clarity the name
   as the body part or person is pointed to

8.   Uses picture board as alternative to speech

Points to simple object pictured on picture
   board on command

Points to variety of objects pictured on picture
   board on command

Points to action word pictured on picture board
   on command

Points to needed object or service pictured on
   picture board

Answers simple question by pointing to answer
   pictured on picture board

Asks simple question by pointing to answer pictured on picture board

**9.   Uses appropriate switch(es) as alternative
   to speech → All areas**

Uses switch(es) activated by finger, hand, head,
   leg, foot

Uses switch(es) to activate computer or other
   electronic device

Uses switch(es) and accompanying device to
   answer simple, increasingly difficult, meaningful questions

Uses switch(es) and accompanying device(s) to
   complete appropriate class work

**10.   Uses gestures as alternative to speech →
   Leisure → Social (e.g., toilet training)**

Imitates (mimics) facial expressions

Uses facial expression to indicate urgency and
   status

Uses gestures to communicate needs

Uses gestures with imitated speech

Gestures needs

**11.   Uses signing as alternative to speech →
   Leisure → Social**

Uses signs with pictured objects

Uses signs in unison with teacher or aide

Signs simple words

Signs toileting needs

Uses signs to communicate other needs

Uses signs to answer simple questions

Uses signs to ask simple questions

Uses signs to carry on simple, increasingly
   meaningful conversation

12.   Imitates speech

Imitates speech sound on command

Imitates sounds of cue letters

Imitates (approximates) sound of teacher-pro-
   nounced words

Imitates teacher's name

Makes undifferentiated oral response to oral
   question

Makes undifferentiated sounds

Imitates two-word phrase

Imitates two-word command or sentence

Imitates three-word phrase, command,
   or sentence

**13.   Associates different presentations
   of same object or person →
   Arithmetic → Social**

Matches object with spoken name or label

Matches simple object with picture of object

Matches word with familiar object, animal, or
   person

Matches word with picture of familiar object,
   animal, or person

Matches line drawing with picture of same
   object, animal, or person

Matches picture with written names of object,
   gradually imitating names verbally

Matches spoken word with action picture (walk,
   sit, stand, run, jump, play)

Matches written word with action picture (walk,
   sit, stand, run, jump, play)

14. Classifies (or sorts) objects, animals, or persons → Arithmetic → Social

Sorts simple objects by using templates or shaped receptacles

Uses stackable plastic containers for sorting and classification tasks

Sorts familiar objects into two or more categories

Sorts pictures of familiar objects into two or more categories

Sorts pictures of common animals into two or more categories (e.g., dogs vs. cats)

Sorts pictures of familiar persons into two or more categories

Sorts pictures of persons by gender

Sorts pictures of familiar animals into two or more general categories (e.g., collies vs. bulldogs)

Classifies classmates by gender by leading them into proper group

Classifies pictures of classmates by gender

Classifies pictures of people into categories of adults and children

Lines up classmates by color of items of clothing worn by each

Sorts common objects, animals, or persons, gradually imitating names

Sorts written numbers

Sorts written words

Sorts two, then more printed survival words

Sorts words that begin with same sound

Gains word familiarity by matching and sorting

Sorts any of the above by using the same-different concept

15. Orders objects, animals, or persons → Arithmetic

Sorts objects into categories of large and small

Sorts objects into categories of tall and short

Arranges familiar objects by size

Arranges pictures of familiar objects by size

Arranges pictures of people by size or height

Lines up classmates by height (from tallest to shortest and vice versa)

16. Verbally sequences numbers and words → Arithmetic

Repeats one orally presented number

Repeats two, then increasing number of orally presented numbers in sequence

Repeats one orally presented word

Repeats two, then increasing numbers of orally presented words in sequence

Repeats orally presented two-word phrase, command, instruction, or sentence

Repeats orally presented sentence of three words or more

17. Learns to identify common colors → Home (Safety)

Points to one, then increasing number of colors on command

Matches two color cards

Sorts three, then increasing number of colors, gradually imitating, then pronouncing the names

Names one, then increasing number of colors verbally

18. Says meaningful words → Social → Leisure (Motor)

Says own name

Says names of family members

Says name of teacher

Says names of classmates

Responds to simple question with single word

Uses I, me, he, her

Uses simple verbs—walk, jump, run → Arithmetic → Leisure

Uses increasing number of common words—mostly nouns

19. Uses speech to obtain information and service → Social

Answers simple questions

Imitates (or mimics) asking simple questions

Asks simple questions

Asks verbally for needed assistance (with sign or gesture)

Asks verbally for needed assistance (without sign or gesture)

Initiates one-word request

Verbally makes food, water, and other basic needs known (with sign or gesture)

Verbally makes food, water, and other basic needs known (without sign or gesture)

20. Develops concept of self → Social → Arithmetic

Responds to own picture

Finds own chair or place at table by his or her picture posted thereon

Begins to claim objects as own

Sits at "own place" at table (without picture)

Uses *I, me, mine* verbally

Social Skills and Concepts

1. Becomes fully totally toilet-trained → Communication

Gestures when wet or soiled

Maintains dryness for increasing periods of time

Maintains unsoiled condition for increasing lengths of time

Makes toileting needs known (gesture, signing, verbal)

Sits on toilet for increasing lengths of time

Sits on toilet backward to avoid falling

Uses urinal

Sits on toilet as others do

Establishes toilet schedule

Lowers, removes necessary clothing

Cleans self after toilet (toilet paper, medicated wipes)

Flushes toilet

Goes to toilet unattended

Replaces clothing after toilet

Replaces underclothing

Toilets self with increasing independence

Uses sanitary napkins

2. Accepts being fed with increasing grace and decreasing mess → Leisure (Fine motor)

Opens mouth to accept food

Reaches for bottle when offered

Takes all offered food on spoon or fork

Sucks through a straw

Controls drooling

Swallows before speaking

Swallows between bites

Swallows quietly

Chews celery, apples, and other crisp foods quietly and without choking

Chews food adequately

Chews with lips closed

Chews without mess

3. Begins to feed self → Leisure (Fine motor)

Holds bottle with both hands

Holds cup with both hands

Holds cup with one hand with increasing skill

Holds spoon, knife, and fork properly

Uses spoon with increasing independence and grace

Uses fork with increasing independence and grace

Uses knife with increasing independence and grace

Eats with small bites

4. Feeds self with some assistance → Leisure (Fine motor) → Home

Feeds self finger foods

Pours liquid in own glass

Refills own cup

Serves self desired amount of food with decreasing waste

Unwraps packaged foods

Eats with increasing neatness and lack of mess

**5.   Selects own food → Leisure (Fine motor) →
       Communication → Home (Health)**

Indicates preference of foods by pointing
Indicates preference of foods by signing
Classifies foods by pictures into preferred/not
    preferred
Serves self from platters of food passed around
    table
Classifies pictures of foods into good/not good
    (nutritious)
Classifies pictures of foods into food groups

**6.   Uses increasingly good table manners →
       Home (Independent Living)**

Avoids negative behaviors at table (sniffing,
    blowing nose, picking nose, slurping)
Uses napkin with increasing dependence and
    grace
Asks politely for food to be passed
Serves food to self
Cleans up after self after meal
Uses napkin with increasing dependence and
    grace
Knows and follows lunchroom rules
Receives, passes food to others at meal
Uses bread as "pusher"
Helps set table
Locates own place at table

**7.   Understands and uses rules of
       sanitation and cleanliness →
       Safety → Transition → Home
       (Health, Safety)**

Changes underclothing daily
Uses handkerchief properly
Understands dangers of coughing and sneezing
Recognizes need to wash and bathe
Recognizes need to keep clothing clean
Washes hands before meal
Understands bathroom safety (electrical appli-
    ances, curlers, dryers, blowers, heaters, and
    so forth should never be located in bathroom)
Understands basic cleanliness and sanitation
Selects and uses own sanitary napkin

**8.   Develops an awareness of good grooming →
       Transition → Home (Independent Living)**

Classifies pictures of people into well-groomed
    and poorly groomed categories
Classifies pictures of self taken in well-groomed
    and poorly groomed situations
Recognizes pictures of well-groomed people
Asks for needed help in grooming
Checks over self for grooming before leaving
    home

**9.   Develops ability to care for
       own skin → Home (Health)**

Participates in applying facial creams and makeup
Applies body powder
Applies own facial creams
Applies own makeup
Cares for own skin
Uses facial and other cosmetics appropriately,
    particularly so as not to draw unfavorable
    attention
Washes own face
Washes own hands
Locates towel, washcloth, soap

**10.   Bathes, showers self with
       increasing independence →
       Home (Independent Living)**

Recognizes need to wash hands and shower
Locates towel, washcloth, soap, shampoo, rinse
Tests water temperature and indicates needed
    adjustment
Turns water on
Turns water off
Regulates water temperature unaided
Soaps own body
Rinses own body
Takes sitz bath with decreasing assistance
Takes sitz bath without assistance
Takes tub bath independently
Cleans (washes, showers, bathes, rinses, and
    dries) all parts of own body
Takes shower independently
Takes bath independently

11. Is increasingly aware of possibility of offensive body odor → All areas

Uses deodorant effectively

Changes underclothing daily

Showers or bathes daily

Washes hands and face regularly

Dresses appropriately (e.g., gym clothes) for strenuous activity

Showers after strenuous activity

Shaves under own arms

12. Learns to care for own hair → All areas

Classifies pictures of neat/unkempt hair

Classifies pictures of self with neat/unkempt hair

Combs, brushes, and picks own hair

Becomes aware of hairstyles with pictures, discussions

Selects own hairstyle with decreasing assistance

Keeps hair neat in selected style

Braids, curls own hair

Grooms (shampoos, rinses, washes, brushes, combs, braids, picks, sets, and curls) own hair

Shaves and trims beard

13. Cares for own nails → All areas

Becomes aware of need for clean, well-kept nails (pictures, discussions)

Recognizes when own nails need attention

Cleans own nails

Clips and files own nails

14. Cares for own teeth with decreasing assistance → Home (Health)

Cooperates while other person brushes his or her teeth

Assists by obtaining own toothpaste and toothbrush

Brushes own teeth with hand-on-hand assistance

Becomes increasingly aware of need for oral hygiene

Is aware of possibility and causes of bad breath

Brushes and flosses own teeth

Knows necessity and use of mouthwash

Uses own toothbrush

Uses own toothpaste

15. Dresses self with increasing independence → Home (Independent Living)

Lies, sits, or stands passively when being dressed

Cooperates when being dressed

Manipulates Velcro fasteners

Understands concepts of front and back

Understands concepts of on and off

Understands concepts of top and bottom

Operates buttons

Operates snaps

Operates zippers

Puts on own socks

Puts on designated item of clothing on command

Initiates putting on needed item of clothing

Puts on own belt

Puts on own shoes or boots

Laces own shoes

Operates safety pins

Takes off and puts on designated item of clothing on command

Ties own shoelaces

16. Obtains own clothing for dressing

Recognizes own clothing

Retrieves own clothes from drawer, hook, closet

Selects and lays out own clothes

Selects own clothing from among that of others

Selects pictures of clothing appropriate for given weather conditions

Selects pictures of clothing appropriate for differing social situations

17. Cares for own clothing

Picks up designated article of clothing on command

Picks up own clothes

Puts own clothes back in closet or on shelf with increasing neatness and accuracy

Hangs one item, eventually all of own clothing on hook or hanger

Polishes own shoes

Recognizes when clothing needs repair

Recognizes when clothing needs cleaning

Recognizes offensive odor in clothing

Asks for help in cleaning and repairing clothing

Sorts clothes into laundering groups

Irons own clothing with decreasing help

18. Selects and buys own clothing with increasing independence → Arithmetic (Consumer)

Classifies various articles of clothing (e.g., shoes vs. shirts, skirts vs. blouses)

Classifies various articles of clothing (e.g., types of shoes, types of skirts)

Classifies pictures of various articles of clothing (e.g., shoes vs. shirts, skirts vs. blouses)

Classifies pictures of various articles of clothing (e.g., types of shoes, types of skirts)

Classifies various articles of clothing by color

Classifies pictures of various articles of clothing by color

Participates in field trip to clothing store

Helps select and buy own clothing

Selects own clothing with help (contrived to actual)

Buys own clothing independently

19. Develops necessary obedience → All areas

Recognizes teacher's authority

Begins and ends play on command

Comes to activity on command

Learns to stay in assigned area

Obeys rules and requests of teachers and others of obvious authority

Recognizes authority figures (pictures, classifying)

Recognizes need for authority figures (ACE stories, discussions)

Recognizes authority and duties of aide, principal, bus driver, bus aide, police officer, doctor, nurse

Remains quiet when requested

Remains quiet while being read to

Repeats back stated rules—both before and when crisis occurs

Stays with group as on walking trip or playground

Exercises self-control in practical or contrived situation

Follows home rules

Helps make class rules

20. Makes increasingly independent decisions → All areas

Knows whom to ask for help in decision making

Asks for needed help in making decisions

Makes simple, inconsequential choices

Learns to accept consequences of choice between two alternatives

Makes choice between two increasingly meaningful alternatives

Learns consequences of own behavior

Makes simple, inconsequential, but increasingly consequential decisions

Selects own work to be done from two immediate and unavoidable alternatives

Charts own achievement marks after teacher or aide grades work

Corrects own work

Learns to grade and record own performance

Develops pride in own performance

21. Develops personality and awareness of self → Communication

Responds to own name

Recognizes own picture

Classifies pictures of facial expressions by mood

Imitates facial expressions from pictures

Imitates facial expression of teacher, aide, or volunteer

Interprets feelings and moods of others

Gets needed attention and assistance in appropriate manner

Smiles when stimulated

Discusses own preferences, likes, and dislikes for treats, foods, TV programs, books, games, friends, hobbies, movies, spectator sports, and so forth

Evaluates own class work in retrospect with increasing accuracy and self-confidence

Knows where to get help and advice in socially upsetting situations

Deals with change (schedules, friends, living arrangements, instructional aide instead of teacher, room duties, methods of performing duties, job placement) → Transition

Recognizes difference between good-humored teasing and demeaning behavior

Recognizes potentially dangerous social situations (e.g., ride invitation) → Safety

Understands own weaknesses and develops ideas as to how to cope or overcome

22. Perceives self in expanding social community → Transition

Recognizes own home

Recognizes picture of own home

Recognizes picture of own neighborhood

Recognizes picture of own school

Recognizes pictures of major public buildings

23. Develops individual honesty, dependability, and trustworthiness → All areas

Understands and practices the concept of honesty

Understands the concept of cheating

Understands the concept of lying

Understands the concept of trust

Understands the concept of stealing

Understands the concepts of fair/unfair

Accepts increasing responsibility for own actions

Makes increasing quantity and quality of own decisions

24. Shows increasing awareness of other people → Communication → Leisure

Clings to mother

Clings to or shows preference for some adults

Interacts with other children

Interacts with others outside special education placement

Knows difference between contacting friends and being "under foot"

Knows how often and what days and times to call friends

Knows how to call on friends

Makes some purposeful facial expressions

Plays "dress up" cooperatively

Plays "dress up" in parallel

Plays "dress up" independently

Plays cooperatively

Plays "dress up" alone, increasing to include others

Plays games following simple rules

Plays group games requiring taking turns (hopscotch, jump rope)

Plays in isolation

Plays in parallel

Plays taking turns with toys

Plays with one other age-mate

Plays with toy sharing

Plays, tolerating age-mate taking toy

Puts toys away

Recognizes moods and feelings from pictures

Respects the rights of others

Stops hurting age-mate on command (without restraint)

Understands how own behavior can cause loss of friendship

Understands how own behavior can disturb others

Yields toy belonging to another

25. Shows increasing respect for rights of others → All areas

Asks for toy rather than taking it

Avoids negative interpersonal behaviors (e.g., hitting, biting, kicking, swearing, pushing) for increasing periods of time without being reminded

Does not hit or hurt age-mates in play

Follows stated rules with increasingly less reminding

Follows subtle social rules

Gets along increasingly well with classmates and others

Helps another person with simple task on command

Helps classmate clean mess or spill

Understands concept of helping others

Helps others with wheelchairs, opening doors, cleaning up after activity, classroom improvement projects, school projects, community projects (on command, request, voluntarily)

Knows difference between tattling and responsible citizenship

Learns to accept group choice between activity alternatives

Observes simple game rules

Performs own home duties

Performs variety of classroom duties (may be contrived, if necessary)

Raises hand (approximates hand-raising) for permission turn

Recognizes unjust and unfair situations

Takes turn

Uses good audience manners (sits quietly, claps or applauds only when others do, eats quietly when permitted, comes on time, goes to bathroom before performance begins, excuses self when finding seat, stays until performance is over)

Waits for turn without being restrained, told, or reminded

26. Shows increasing ability and finesse in meeting people

Makes eye contact when meeting another person

Role-plays a variety of practical problems in meeting people

Says appropriate things to people with increasing skill and tact

Knows how to welcome or announce classroom guest

Knows when to shake hands (a safe way is only when another offers hand)

Leisure/Motor Skills and Concepts

1. Controls physical movements of eyes and tongue → Communication → Social

Sticks out tongue to imitate

Exercises and manipulates tongue

Blinks both eyes at same time

Blinks each eye

Blinks eyes alternately

Blinks eyes for yes/no, where necessary

Does tracking exercises

2. Moves head with decreasing assistance → Communication → Social

Moves head reflexively toward noise

Moves head up and down (nods)

Raises head from supine, prone positions

Rotates head (clockwise, counterclockwise)

Tilts head from side to side

Holds head steady

Moves head on command (up and down, left to right) with increasing precision

Uses pointer attached to head harness

Nods head for yes

Shakes head for no

3. Manipulates fingers and hands with increasing dexterity → All areas

Flexes and extends fingers

Grasps proffered toy or object

Moves fingers individually

Wiggles finger, thumb

Grasps hand of another person

Grasps object of convenient size

Grasps with either hand

Imitates fingerplays

Does increasingly difficult fingerplays with increasing coordination

Feels and explores with hands

Feels and explores with hands in thin gloves

Makes "hot dog" of clay

Releases object on command

Releases object for own purposes

Releases person's hand

Squeezes ball of cotton

Squeezes soft rubber ball of convenient size (on command, repeatedly, for strength gain)

Squeezes water from wet rag

4. Improves eye-hand coordination and fine motor dexterity (generally more gross activity first) → All areas

Builds tower with colored blocks

Builds tower with convenient-size blocks

Carries objects on tray

Combs hair

Drives peg into pegboard

Establishes or indicates handedness

Exercises with prewriting and writing activities

Finger paints

Does art exercises to increase eye-hand coordination and fine motor dexterity

Makes spiral circles between two wide-apart, increasingly narrow lines

Makes spiral circles of random size

Moves objects on table

Opens and closes simple containers

Peels potato, orange

Picks up jackstraws

Picks up object on command

Reaches for object out of reach

Reaches for proffered toy or object

Retrieves object without putting it in mouth

Shakes object

Ties knots

Transfers object from hand to hand on command

Turns pages of large, then smaller book

Unwraps wrapped food, candy, packages

Uses constructional toys (blocks, erector, Tinkertoys, Lincoln Logs, Legos)

Uses crafts to develop eye-hand coordination

Stacks objects with large tweezers

Uses pincers movement to grasp objects of decreasing size

Uses pincers movement out of immediate sight (behind back, over head, in perception bag or box, under table)

5. Moves arms with decreasing assistance → Communication → Social

Flexes and extends arms from lying, sitting, standing positions

Lifts arms bending and not bending elbows

Lifts arms without help (from supine, prone, sitting, standing positions)

Sustains uplifted arms without help for increasing periods of time

Lifts gradually increasing weights with arms

Moves hands in different motions—to midline and back, across midline and back, extended/close to body, back and forth, up and down, circular—in various starting positions and with increasing independence

Uses nomination (points to body parts, familiar people)

Claps hands at arms' length

Holds large object with both hands momentarily

Holds large object with both hands for increasingly longer time

6. Moves feet and toes with decreasing assistance

Flexes toes

Flexes and extends foot in supine position

Flexes and extends foot while leg is propped in elevated position

Flexes and extends foot while leg is propped at knee

7. Manipulates legs with decreasing assistance

Lifts leg from on-back position with decreasing assistance

Lifts leg with decreasing assistance from prone position

Lifts leg with decreasing assistance from prone position and leg propped at knee

Lifts leg with decreasing assistance from sitting position (using pulley arrangement where necessary)

Lifts leg with decreasing assistance from standing position

Lifts leg with gradually increasing weights

8. Moves torso with decreasing assistance

Rolls completely over to left, right with decreasing assistance

Rolls completely over with, then without support

Rolls partly to left, right with decreasing assistance

Rotates upper torso from standing position

9. Moves whole body in place with decreasing assistance

Kneels from standing position with decreasing assistance

Lies down from standing position with decreasing assistance

Pulls self from kneeling to sitting position with, then without support

Pulls self from kneeling to standing position with, then without support

Pulls self from sitting to kneeling position with, then without support

Raises up on elbows from prone position with decreasing assistance

Rises on "all fours" from prone position with decreasing assistance

Sits from standing position with decreasing assistance

Sits independently in chair

Stands alone on command

Stands alone voluntarily

Stands with help for increasing periods of time

Stands without help for increasing periods of time

Stands from kneeling position with decreasing assistance

Stands from sitting position on bed with decreasing assistance

Stands from sitting position with decreasing assistance

Turns around while standing

Sits, stands, and walks with increasing grace and good posture

10. Increases body balance and endurance with decreasing assistance and prompting

Runs, gradually increasing distance

Jogs, gradually increasing distance

Does increasing number of sit-ups

Does jumping jacks and other exercises with, without music

Does simple, but gradually increasingly difficult calisthenics and exercises

Lifts increasingly heavy weights

Balances on one foot for gradually increasing period of time

Balances on feet alternately for gradually increasing period of time

Balances on feet alternately with eyes closed for gradually increasing period of time

Jumps rope individually and in group

Understands and demonstrates need for building body endurance

Understands meaning of physical fitness

Swims increasing distance

11. Does prewalking locomotion with decreasing assistance

Crawls on hands and knees with decreasing assistance

Creeps on elbows with decreasing assistance

Cruises with increasing coordination and purpose

Picks up object from floor without falling

12. Walks with increasing grace and speed and decreasing assistance

Toddles

Avoids objects when walking

Walks without tripping

Walks up and down stairs with, then without assistance

Climbs stairs with increasing skill and grace

13. Performs individual, physical/recreational activity with increasing grace and decreasing assistance

Catches rolled ball from sitting position with decreasing assistance (ball rolled directly to child, gradually requiring child to move to catch ball)

Catches thrown ball of decreasing size and softness (gradually requiring greater effort and movement on part of recipient)

Catches, throws ball of generally decreasing size and softness (balloon, beach ball, volleyball, soccer ball, tetherball, kick ball, basketball, softball—probably not baseball)

Participates in general water play

Swims

Initiates own physical and recreational activities with decreasing assistance

Operates own wheelchair with increasing purpose, grace, coordination, and endurance

Prepares for Special Olympics event (preparation can be very motivating)

Participates in Special Olympics events

Roller-skates

14. Performs group, physical/recreational activity with increasing grace and decreasing assistance

Plays kick ball

Plays hopscotch

Jumps rope with group

Performs activities in unison

15. Performs simple, increasingly practical art activities → Communication → Most other areas

Identifies light and dark colors

Identifies common colors

Identifies increasing number of colors

Knows how colors appear in nature

Does fine motor and eye-hand tasks and activities with increasing skill and coordination as outlined above

Manipulates simple art devices (large, increasingly small brush, chalk, scissors, crayons)

Scribbles with chalk, crayon, pencil

Does simple cut-and-paste activities

Cuts and folds paper to match or copy displayed cut and/or fold

Cuts out paper doll and dresses with paper clothing (both male and female) → Health

Uses scissors in increasingly demanding activities

Draws simple stick figures

Draws simple face with increasing detail

Draws increasingly lifelike person

Draws or approximates simple pictures

Finger paints

Draws picture of simple but increasingly meaningful and detailed event (field trip, story, movie, video)

Makes holiday decorations and presents with increasing independence

Manipulates clay (pinch, squeeze, roll, stack, punch)

Uses clay to make simple but increasingly meaningful shapes and objects

Uses crayons to color—stays within the lines of object of increasing detail and decreasing size

Uses crayons, pencil, chalk freehand to make increasingly detailed objects or projects

Appendix E

Communication Skills and Concepts

Appendix E lists some communication skills and concepts that are particularly significant in Chapters 10 and 11. These skills and concepts are only representative and are not intended to be a complete curriculum for any individual. They are included to help the IEP team in designing a unique sequence of prioritized life goals appropriate for the individual in question. In some instances, the numbered headings might serve as long-term goals, the subheadings as annual goals; in other instances (particularly for individuals whose mental retardation is more severe), the numbered headings might be converted into annual goals, the subheadings into short-term objectives. If GIA or other evaluative procedures indicate that the lowest-level activities of Appendix E are too difficult for the individual, the IEP team should refer to Appendixes C and D for more rudimentary skills and concepts.

Generally, the skills and concepts are presented in order of increasing difficulty, but grouping by topic means that some topics are much more extensive and cover more conceptual distance than others. At the same time, some of the subskills necessary to master a given topic may be (or could have been) listed under several topics; otherwise, some subtopics

would be repeated frequently. Obviously, no two IEP teams could be expected to include the same topics and subtopics—or to use the same sequences—as in these appendixes. The arrows (→) in Appendixes D through J suggest other curricular areas in which horizontal curriculum planning is particularly appropriate. Communication skills, however, are extremely vital in all other areas of curriculum; thus, the use of horizontal curriculum planning arrows is limited in this appendix.

Primarily for brevity, all of the appendixes use terms like *uses, demonstrates, explains, tells,* and other verbs to describe actions to be taken by students with mental retardation. Teachers and other members of the IEP team must carefully evaluate and apply such terms to individuals with great care. The achievement levels and learning rates of individual students vary tremendously. Thus, the performance expectations and demands made of each student must be commensurate with the individual needs and abilities of each.

All of the appendixes emphasize proactivity and optimum development of independent living skills. Thus, practical problem solving and functional application are assumed for each listed skill and concept.

1. *Makes personal needs known*

Initiates one-word request

Asks simple questions

Asks verbally for needed assistance

States own name and address

2. *Attends to story, task for increasing periods of time*

Makes eye contact with teacher, then aide, volunteer, classmates

Tracks horizontally, vertically

Looks at picture books with increasing persistence

Attends to task with increasing "white" or controlled noise and other distraction

Works for increasing periods of time without disturbing others

3. *Uses oral communication with increasing functionality → All areas*

Says "please" and "thank you" appropriately

Imitates use of telephone

Uses pronouns—*I, me, mine*

Uses some past tense

Uses some plurals

Uses possessives other than *mine*

Uses up to a dozen words—mostly nouns

Engages in two-way conversation

Answers telephone

Answers questions about story, event, field trip

Develops sense of humor

Interprets preferences stated by others in class meeting or class

Uses word endings (e.g., *-ing, -ed*)

Makes simple, increasingly sophisticated announcements to class

Participates in simple, small group discussion

Retells story with increasingly greater detail

Relates events of recent past (e.g., this morning, yesterday, last week)

Speaks with increasingly correct grammar

Understands loud and soft, pleasant and unpleasant sounds

Understands need to be truthful and the consequences of telling falsehoods

Understands personal rights

Understands voice loudness

Whispers simple response

Generally recognizes left and right

Uses increasingly appropriate level of voice loudness

Uses plurals in speech and writing

Uses pronouns *I, me, he, her*

Gives simple, but increasingly complex, directions to others

Uses left and right in following classroom directions → Transition

Uses left and right in giving classroom directions to classmates

Uses north, south, east, and west in following, giving classroom directions

4. *Uses increasingly sophisticated, functional, inclusive statements → Transition*

Uses *and, all, all of them, everyone, some, most*

5. *Uses increasingly sophisticated, functional, conditional, alternative statements → Transition → Arithmetic*

Uses *if, when, when the bell rings, after, before, not until, some, several, many, either*

Plays conditional statement games—for example, Simon Says, Follow the Leader, Do As I Do

Follows conditional instructions

6. *Uses increasingly sophisticated, functional, alternative statements*

Uses *or, else, other*

7. *Uses increasingly sophisticated, functional, exclusive statements → Transition*

Uses *not, none, only, neither*

8. *Uses increasingly sophisticated, functional locus statements*

Uses *before, between, next to, near, over, above, under, around, on, in, out*

Participates in locus games and activities— *before, between, next to, near*

Lines up, placing one student *between, before, after, behind, in front of* another

9. *Answers increasingly difficult questions*

Answers simple question by nodding, pointing

Answers increasingly difficult questions from picture or picture book

Answers simple question—answer imbedded in short, simple sentence, passage, story

Answers increasingly difficult questions about material read aloud by parents and other family members

Answers questions on increasingly longer teacher-read story or event, field trip

Answers simple "where" and "when" questions

Responds to simple question with single word

Answers questions of increasing length

Answers increasingly difficult oral questions during a group discussion

Answers questions involving inclusive, exclusive, alternative, locus questions

10. *Gains increasing amount of information by listening to story*

Listens (attends) to increasingly longer sentence, passage, story

Identifies main idea of story with increasing length, sophistication

Identifies time, place, and setting of teacher-read story

Listens quietly while others relate events, tell stories, answer questions, and so forth

Listens to short, simple story

Recalls people, names, animals, objects, events where answer is directly mentioned in teacher-read book or story

Predicts ending of a partially read story

Relates general idea of teacher-read story of increasing length and sophistication

Recognizes past, present, and future tense in teacher-read stories

Relates general idea of viewed video or movie

Relates main idea of television program

Recalls people, names, animals, objects, events where answer is only indirectly mentioned in book or story

Tells moral, lesson to be learned from story, tape, or movie

Recognizes past, present, and future tenses in stories

Predicts what will transpire in future (e.g., this afternoon, tomorrow)

Identifies increasingly difficult causal relationships

11. *Uses increasingly sophisticated descriptors*

Matches pictures with names, gradually imitating names

Points to increasingly subtle objects, cues in picture books

Matches simple words with object or picture

Matches simple object to picture of object

Points to "big" object or "big one" → Arithmetic

Matches picture and correct object, word

Uses descriptors—large-small, number, color— with objects, models, pictures, stories, events, field trips

Describes objects, pictures, events with increasingly greater detail

Describes characters, events, moods from simple story

Uses increasingly subtle descriptors (e.g., number, color, size) in answering questions about a read story

12. *Understands, uses increasingly sophisticated verbs → Leisure → Transition*

Uses simple verbs—*walk, jump, run, sit, jump, play, stand*

Relates simple verbs with physical action

Performs eye-hand, fine motor, and gross motor tasks

13. Understands, uses sequencing →
Arithmetic → Leisure

Participates in short-term memory games
Repeats back single word on command
Repeats back increasing numbers of numbers, letters, words
Uses left to right progression
Repeats back two-word phrase, command, instruction, or sentence
Repeats three-word sentence
Uses increasingly long-term memory
Arranges simple, increasingly difficult cartoon frames in proper sequence to make story or thought
Relates simple, increasingly sophisticated event

14. Gains word, concept familiarity
by matching, sorting

Sorts two colors
Sorts common objects, gradually imitating names of the objects
Sorts letters, numbers, words
Sorts pictures of common objects, gradually imitating names
Sorts three colors
Sorts two lowercase letters (*t* and *s*?)
Sorts three printed survival words
Sorts objects in pictures by size → Arithmetic
Sorts words that begin with same sound
Sorts words that end with same sound
Uses same-different concept
Identifies object to perform orally indicated function
Lines up classmates by color of items of clothing worn by each
Lines up classmates by height → Arithmetic
Sorts tools (or pictures of tools) by occupation

15. Gains word, concept familiarity
by classifying

Classifies pictures of classmates by boys and girls
Sorts pictures of people by age
Sorts letters by vowels and consonants

Sorts pictures of animals into classes
Classifies classmates by boys and girls by leading them into proper group
Classifies pictures of tasks by appropriate location
Classifies foods (or pictures of foods) by food groups

16. Begins prereading, word-attack activities

Discriminates, sorts letters—common consonants first, then vowels
Identifies sounds of letters, common consonants first, then vowels
"Spells" sounds of common, consonant letters
Begins auditory closure drills
Does rhyming skills
Spells simple, phonetic words
Spells simple, irregular sight words
Does sounding drills

17. Begins using sight words
of beginning reading

Identifies picture of self from single picture, from picture of several family members, from pictures of few, then several classmates
Identifies (decodes) family members by pointing, in person, from pictures
Identifies pictures of teacher, aide, classmates, school nurse, principal
Knows teacher's name
Knows names of classmates
States verbally the names of objects, movements, events from picture books
Identifies and uses increasing number of words having increasing difficulty
Identifies simple, then more difficult words from near-future reading material
Initiates reading process—for pleasure and information
Reads with decreasing vocalization and lip movement
Uses word endings (e.g., *-ing*, *-ed*)
Identifies and uses increasing number of words of increasing difficulty

18. Identifies and uses emergency words with increasing sophistication

Beware of Dog
Deep Water
Do Not Enter
Emergency
Emergency Exit
Fallout Shelter
Fire Escape
Fire
Fire Extinguisher
High Voltage
Do Not Play In or Around
Flammable
First Aid
Poison
Not for Internal Use
Keep Out
Police
No Smoking
No Swimming
No Trespassing
Walk
Don't Walk
Danger

19. Identifies and uses survival words with increasing sophistication

Exit
Bus Station
Bus Stop
Closed
Open
Employees Only
Ladies
Gentlemen
Men
Women
Boys
Girls
Office
Nurse
Doctor
Dentist

No Loitering
Out of Order
Post Office
Private
Use Other Door
Wet Paint
Rest Rooms

20. Uses reading increasingly to gain high-priority information → All Areas

Learns to gain information from picture books
Checks out appropriate movies from library
Checks out appropriate reading or picture books from library
Checks out appropriate videos from library
Finds each of a list of common names in phone book
Finds family name in telephone book
Matches can and packaging labels with contents
Matches can and packaging labels with verbal descriptions
Gains simple but increasingly sophisticated and practical information from newspaper
Reads books at home
Reads for pleasure
Reads increasingly difficult and practical material
Uses telephone to gain needed information
Finds simple, increasingly difficult words in dictionary
Follows simple, increasingly complex written directions
Gains assistance from context clues
Uses maps, bus schedules for mobility → Transition → Social
Reads, understands reading material specific to job → Transition → Social

21. Masters beginning writing

Holds pencil, chalk correctly
Uses chalk and pencil erasers
Uses increasingly smaller writing instruments

Traces between thick, wide-apart, parallel
  lines
Traces between thick, wide-apart lines that are
  increasingly curved
Copies vertical, horizontal, and diagonal lines
Does dot-to-dot with line drawings, letters, and
  numbers
Draws or approximates simple pictures
Forms beginning letters and numbers
Reads simple words
Copies letters and numbers
Begins using lowercase letters
Copies letters from chalkboard to paper on desk
  with increasing accuracy
Begins to use uppercase letters
Begins writing simple words
Copies simple words, then short sentences
  from chalkboard to paper with increasing
  accuracy

22. *Uses writing for increasingly functional purposes → Leisure (Motor)*

Copies simple words from chalkboard to paper
  on desk with increasing accuracy
Writes own name on chalkboard, paper
Remembers and writes short sequence of let-
  ters, numbers, words
Writes names of family members
Writes names of classmates and teacher
Writes notes to friends, relatives, pen pals
Writes own name, address, phone number
Can take short message over telephone
Writes short message
Writes short, increasingly meaningful sentences
Writes, speaks with increasingly correct grammar
Writes short description of events with increas-
  ing detail and sophistication
Writes increasingly longer, more accurate
  reports

Appendix F

Social Skills and Concepts

Appendix F lists some social skills and concepts that are particularly significant in Chapter 12. These skills and concepts are only representative and are not intended to be a complete curriculum for any individual. They are included to help the IEP team in designing a unique sequence of prioritized life goals appropriate for the individual in question. In some instances, the numbered headings might serve as long-term goals, the subheadings as annual goals; in other instances (particularly for individuals whose mental retardation is more severe), the numbered headings might be converted into annual goals, the subheadings into short-term objectives. If GIA or other evaluative procedures indicate that the lowest-level activities of Appendix F are too difficult for the individual, the IEP team should refer to Appendixes C and D for more rudimentary skills and concepts.

Generally, the skills and concepts are presented in order of increasing difficulty, but grouping by topic means that some topics are much more extensive and cover more conceptual distance than others. At the same time, some of the subskills necessary to master a given topic may be (or could have been) listed under several topics; otherwise, some subtopics would be repeated frequently. Obviously, no two IEP teams could be expected to include the same topics and subtopics—or to use the same sequences—as in these appendixes.

Some of the skills and concepts of this appendix are very rudimentary; others are beyond the ability level of a given individual. Also, some subskill listings include some concepts that must be separated for diagnosis and instruction.

1. Develops good personality traits and mental health

Describes own hobbies and interests verbally

Reads or listens to stories and answers simple but increasingly difficult questions about honesty, fairness, cheating, dealing with change, and personal limitations

Helps another person with simple task on command

Knows when and with whom to share feelings

Knows how and when to keep confidences

Answers simple questions about accepting criticism

Deals/copes with change (schedules, friends, living arrangements, instructional aide instead of teacher, room duties, methods of performing duties, job placement)

Answers simple questions about courtesy, honesty, fairness, cheating

Describes own feelings to appropriate others

Understands own weaknesses and develops ideas about how to cope or overcome

Answers simple questions about dependability, promptness, thrift, industry, cooperation, kindness, helping others, getting along well on a job

Appears in public attracting less and less attention to self

Answers simple questions about crime, delinquency, substance abuse

Develops sense of humor

Acts in leadership role with decreasing help from teacher and others

2. Uses increasingly acceptable manners

Listens to, reads stories and answers simple but increasingly difficult questions about kindness, courtesy, using good manners

Avoids negative or offensive social behavior— belching and other offensive sounds, swearing, picking nose, interrupting others

Does not criticize others unfairly

Listens patiently while others talk

Knows when to shake hands (a safe way is only when another offers hand)

Uses *Miss, Mrs.,* and *Mr.* correctly and in right instances

3. Plays independently, in parallel, cooperatively

Plays in isolation

Plays "dress up" alone, increasing to include others

Plays games following simple rules

Plays taking turns with toys → Arithmetic → Leisure

Plays with one other age-mate

Plays with toy sharing

Plays, tolerating age-mate taking toy

Puts toys away

Takes turns (Arithmetic/Leisure)

Yields toy belonging to another

4. Cooperates, plays, works increasingly well with others → Leisure → Transition

Expresses own wants, needs without crying or whining

Gets along increasingly well with classmates and others

Answers increasingly difficult and functional questions about overcoming teasing and taunting, using self-control

Discusses differences among people (height, weight, color of hair and skin, profiles)

Plays group games requiring taking turns— hopscotch, jump rope

Recognizes increasingly subtle differences between tattling and group responsibility and responsible citizenship

Respects rights of others

Accepts criticism increasingly well

5. Increases skill and knowledge of social awareness

Answers increasingly subtle and difficult questions about home and family duties and roles

Listens to, reads stories and answers simple but increasingly difficult questions about getting along well with others

Answers simple questions about treating others fairly

Understands, discusses unjust and unfair situations

Imitates facial expression from picture

Imitates facial expression of teacher, aide, or volunteer

Interprets feelings and moods of others

Recognizes emotions, moods, and feelings demonstrated in pictures

States how story character should react to theme situation

Understands how own behavior can disturb others

Understands personal rights

Understands rights and preferences of friends
Understands concept of gossip

6. Associates with other people with increasing tact and skill → All other areas

Makes eye contact when addressed by teacher, aide, volunteer, classmates
Knows how to deal with strangers with increasing awareness → Home
Makes eye contact when meeting another person
Knows how to welcome or announce classroom guest
Answers simple questions about dealing with strangers
Recognizes and avoids gullibility
Says appropriate things to people with increasing skill and tact

7. Learns, demonstrates good citizenship

Describes own home duties
Develops good work habits
Works on assignments, projects with several other people
Completes his or her "share" of classroom duties
Participates in group activities
Participates in patriotic parade, service
Takes good care of property of others
Serves as class officer or teacher's helper
Participates, helps plan class party, meeting, election
Performs variety of classroom duties (may be contrived, if necessary)
Role-plays situations related to family roles, duties, and responsibilities

8. Serves, helps other people

Answers increasingly difficult and functional questions about how to help others
Participates in birthday and other parties honoring others
Makes simple present or card for family member or classmate
Helps classmate clean mess or spill

Helps others (on command, request, voluntarily) with wheelchairs, opening doors, cleaning up after activity, classroom improvement projects, school projects, community projects
Acts as little, then big brother/sister

9. Makes and maintains friendships

Listens to, reads stories and answers questions about friendships
Does not hit or hurt age-mates in play
Explains how own behavior can cause loss of friendship
Explains how right/wrong actions affect others
Knows when and with whom to share feelings
Knows difference between contacting friends and being "under foot"
Knows how often and what days and times to call friends
Knows how to call on friends at their homes
Knows to whom own name and address can be entrusted
Knows where to get help and advice in socially upsetting situations
Recognizes unwholesome social pressure

10. Understands, establishes good opposite-sex relationships → Leisure

Listens to, reads and answers questions about opposite-sex relationships
Avoids socially unacceptable or offensive behavior with opposite sex—for example, language, touching
Role-plays asking for date
Discusses customs and responsibilities of dating
Knows how to ask for date
Knows how to tactfully accept or reject request for date
Accepts refusal of date request

11. Understands, discusses duties and responsibilities of community helpers

Tells what duties family members perform on the job
Explains good citizenship, patriotism with increasing sophistication

States duties and functions of adults (doctors, nurses, farmer, housewife, custodian, groundskeeper, librarian, garbage collector, clerks, bank tellers)

States duty and responsibility of employer and foreman → Transition

12. Is increasingly aware of community projects and events

Listens to, reads stories and answers simple questions about family roles, duties, and responsibilities; patriotism; citizenship

Participates and reports on special family birthdays, outings, movies, videos, holidays (Christmas, Easter, Thanksgiving, Valentine's Day, Armed Forces Day)

Attends civic, sports, musical, recreational, artistic event → Leisure

Participates in project to benefit school—tree and flower planting, clean playground or hall

Participates in project to benefit community

Visits city council meeting, courtroom

Withstands pressure to do unacceptable acts

Participates in Boy Scouts, Girl Scouts, and similar organizations → Leisure

Uses good audience manners—sits quietly, claps or applauds only when others do, eats quietly when permitted, comes on time, goes to bathroom before performance begins, excuses self when finding seat, stays until performance is over

13. Expresses own preferences in preparation for making own decisions → All other areas

Discusses own preferences, likes, and dislikes for treats, foods, television programs, books, games, friends, hobbies, movies, spectator sports

Discusses personal preferences, likes, and dislikes of classmates with them

Discusses own preferences relating to school assignments and activities

14. Learns, practices obedience in preparation for making own personal decisions

Begins and starts play on command

Comes to activity on command

Remains quiet when requested

Remains quiet during class activities

Stays in designated play area

Stays with group on walking trip or playground

Repeats back class rules—both before and when crisis occurs

Follows conditional instructions—*if, when, after, before:* Simon Says, Follow the Leader, Do As I Do (Transition/Communication)

Follows home rules

Follows increasingly subtle social rules

Follows, explains concepts of leader/follower, helper

Helps make class rules

Recognizes, increasingly, difference between obedience and gullibility

Learns to stay in assigned area

Obeys rules and requests of teachers and others of obvious authority

Observes class rules of increasing sophistication

Observes simple game rules

Raises hand (approximates hand-raising) for permission, turn

Recognizes authority figures and duties of aide, principal, bus driver, bus aide, police officer, doctor, nurse

Understands concepts of helper, follower, leader

Waits without being restrained, told, or reminded

15. Records own classroom, other performance

Charts own achievement marks after teacher or aide grades work

Compares estimated with actual performance with teacher

Completes own checklist of day's activities and accomplishments with decreasing help and supervision

16. Evaluates own classroom, other performance

Answers simple but increasingly difficult questions about grading, evaluations, honesty, independent work

Overcomes aggressive and negative interpersonal behaviors—for example, hitting, biting, kicking, swearing, pushing—without being reminded for increasing periods of time

Corrects and grades own work

Corrects own work and charts own marks

Develops pride in own performance

Admits poor work

Admits social mistake

Admits fault in fight or argument

Evaluates own behavior, class work, job performance in retrospect with increasing accuracy and self-confidence

17. Chooses among alternatives proffered by the teacher

Makes simple, initially inconsequential but increasingly consequential choices

Accepts group choice between two alternatives

Exercises self-control in practical or contrived situation

Selects own work to be done from two immediate and unavoidable alternatives

Accepts consequences of choice between two alternatives

Accepts increasing responsibility for own actions

Makes increasingly consequential choices about sequence of duties, classroom tasks

Selects own work to be done from two unavoidable alternatives—one being delayed for short but increasingly longer periods of time

18. Helps select, formulate own learning objectives

Makes increasingly consequential choices

Helps select own on-campus work experience station

Asks for needed help in making decisions

Engages in critical thinking exercises on appropriate level with increasing sophistication

Estimates own abilities—for example, time to do assignment, run a track lap, complete a puzzle

Helps formulate class rules

Uses trial and error to solve simple situations, evaluate own progress

Develops increasing self-concept, decision-making ability, independence

19. Improves own grooming and personal appearance

Controls drooling

Classifies pictures of people into well-groomed and poorly groomed categories

Applies body powder, facial creams, makeup

Selects, applies, removes own jewelry

Buys own clothing independently

Cares for own skin

Checks self over before leaving home (Home)

Grooms—shampoos, rinses, washes, brushes, combs, braids, picks, sets, and curls—own hair

Polishes own shoes

Shaves own arms, legs, face

Trims own beard and mustache

Uses deodorant

Uses electrical appliances (shavers, curlers, hair dryers, blowers—independently and in bedroom) (Home)

Uses facial and other cosmetics appropriately, particularly so as not to draw unfavorable attention (progression—from unfavorable idea to being attractive)

Uses perfumes appropriately

20. Develops increasingly acceptable hygiene

Applies and uses own sanitary napkin

Brushes and flosses own teeth with decreasing assistance

Changes own underclothes daily

Is aware of possibility of bad breath

Is aware of possibility of offensive body odor
Knows need for mouthwash
Uses deodorant effectively
Uses own toothbrush
Washes own hands before meal

21. *Keeps own body neat and clean →*
Social → Transition
Cares for own nails
Wipes own nose with increasing independence
Recognizes need to keep body clean
Selects correct water temperature
Washes own face
Washes own hands
Takes shower or tub bath independently
Cleans (washes, showers, bathes, rinses, dries)
all parts of own body
Cleans own ears
Locates towel, washcloth, soap, shampoo, rinse
Dries self after bath or shower
Rinses own body
Showers after PE or other strenuous activity
Demonstrates bathroom safety—electrical
appliances, curlers, hair dryers, blowers,
heaters should never be used in bathroom

22. *Dresses self with increasing independence*
Cooperates when being dressed or assisted by
another
Recognizes own clothing
Understands front and back, inside out, on-off,
top and bottom
Dons own underclothing
Initiates putting on designated item of clothing
Laces own shoes (Home)
Manipulates Velcro fasteners
Operates buttons, snaps, zippers
Uses safety pins when needed
Picks up own clothes
Puts on belt, boots, coat, skirt, dress, trousers
on command
Puts on own socks
Puts on own pullover sweater, undershirt
Puts on own shoes

Puts on own underclothing
Puts on own zip or button sweater
Puts own clothes back in closet or on shelf with
increasing neatness and accuracy
Resnaps, zips underclothing
Retrieves own clothes from drawer, hook, closet
Selects and lays out own clothes
Selects own clothing (with help, contrived, from
catalog, field trip, actual)
Selects own clothing from among items belong-
ing to others
Takes off designated item of clothing on com-
mand
Ties own shoelaces
Understands clothing style
Dresses appropriately for different occasions
with decreasing assistance and supervision

23. *Feeds self with increasing independence*
Asks politely for food to be passed
Avoids negative and offensive behaviors at
table—sniffing, blowing nose, picking nose,
slurping, gurgling noises
Chews celery and other crisp foods quietly and
with mouth closed
Chews silently, lips closed, without mess
Cleans up table after snack
Develops good table manners—closing lips
while chewing, not playing with or exchang-
ing food, keeping food on plate, holding
utensils correctly, chewing quietly, talking
quietly
Eats with increasing neatness
Eats with small bites
Feeds self finger foods
Holds cup with one hand with increasing
dependence and grace
Holds knife, fork, and spoon properly
Knows and follows lunchroom rules
Locates own place at table
Uses spoon with increasing dependence and
grace
Passes foods to other
Pours liquid in own glass

Uses knife and fork to cut increasingly difficult meats and other foods

Refills own cup

Chooses own foods

Serves food to self

Serves self desired amount of food with no waste

Sits at own place at table

Swallows quietly between bites, before speaking

Uses fork with increasing dependence and grace

Uses increasingly good table manners

Uses napkin with increasing dependence and grace

Appendix G

Home and Independent Living Skills and Concepts

Appendix G lists some home and independent living skills and concepts that are particularly significant in Chapter 13. As with other appendixes, GIA or other evaluative procedures may indicate that the lowest-level activities of Appendix G are too difficult for the individual, in which case the IEP team should refer to Appendixes C and D for more rudimentary skills and concepts. Likewise, the performance levels of some individuals may be superior to those listed. Chapter 13 contains descriptions of some additional activities for such students.

Safety skills are intentionally and strongly stressed in Appendix G and must be emphasized in all home, school, and community activities. Any otherwise satisfactory activity or situation is unjustified if it is likely to result in an injury. Even though the listing of safety skills and concepts is extensive, it is not intended to be complete. As with all of the appendixes, a great deal of evaluation and prioritizing is necessary to design an acceptable, long-term, life goal curriculum for an individual with mental retardation.

1. Cleans bathroom
Wipes countertops
Understands, explains cleaning and disinfecting agents with increasing sophistication
Cleans and disinfects toilet bowl

Cleans around toilet bowl
Cleans bathroom floor
Cleans bathroom sink
Cleans mirror
Cleans shower and tub

2. Makes own bed with increasing independence
Observes, helps in bed making at school
Inserts pillows into cases
Uses, installs pillows, flat sheets, fitted sheets, blankets, spreads

3. Cleans living room
Selects, uses proper amounts of cleaning agents
Understands cleaning, waxing, dusting agents of increasing sophistication
Wipes off table
Cleans and dusts furniture
Cleans windows
Vacuums and cleans sofa and other overstuffed furniture
Vacuums floors
Vacuums overstuff furniture

4. Cleans, maintains kitchen → Transition
Cleans countertops
Cleans kitchen sink
Cleans microwave oven

Cleans refrigerator

Cleans stovetop, oven safely

Knows dangers of grease spills and splatters

Cleans mixers, blenders, other electric appliances safely

Knows function of and can use common kitchen implements properly and safely—for example, mixer, oven, microwave oven, refrigerator, freezer, blender, toaster, timer, pan covers, splatter covers

Understands need for sanitation in kitchen

Uses common kitchen implements properly and safely—for example, various sizes and types of spoons, spatulas, servers, measuring devices

Knows how to summon help for fires and other emergencies → Communication

6.   Washes dishes with increasing independence and proactivity → Transition

Sorts, classifies plates, saucers, dishes, cups, glasses, silverware

Washes, dries silverware, dishes, plates by hand

Scrubs, washes pots, pans

Adds dishwashing detergent in proper place, amount

Loads, unloads dishwasher—plates, cups, glasses, silverware in proper places

Operates dishwasher—cycles, temperatures

Unloads dishwasher correctly and stores dishes correctly, without breakage

Uses cleaning agents safely

7.   Understands, manages utilities

Helps maintain utilities in monitored living situation

Changes light bulbs safely

Explains 1-900 telephone numbers and their sometimes hidden charges

Explains rudiments of how electricity, natural gas work

Explains utilities—electricity, gas, telephone, water, garbage collection, cable television—and how these bills are paid

8.   Cares for own living quarters, apartment

Empties wastebasket

Cares for, empties garbage can

Mows lawn and disposes of clippings

Rakes leaves in yard

Recognizes trash bins and dumpsters

Shovels snow to clear walks, stairs

Arranges for repairs when necessary

9.   Cares for own clothing → Arithmetic

Identifies articles of clothing

Sorts clothes into washing categories—whites, fast colors, other colors

Washes simple but increasingly difficult clothes

Operates clothes washer—cycle, capacity, temperature settings

Adds appropriate soap or detergent, bleach in correct amount

Recognizes, hand washes delicate, other clothes when needed

Operates clothes dryer—estimates, sets needed time, temperature settings

Sorts, stores own clothes back in closet or on shelf with increasing neatness and accuracy

Irons clothes of increasing difficulty

Makes simple stitch repairs

Operates sewing machine safely

Sews on increasingly smaller, more difficult buttons

Uses sewing machine to make simple repairs

Discusses clothing style with parents, classmates

Helps select, buy own clothing

10.   Selects, buys nutritious foods → Arithmetic → Transition

Classifies pictures of materials into "to eat" and "not to eat" categories

Classifies foods into categories—fruits, vegetables, meats, dairy, sweets and desserts

Classifies pictures of foods into "good for you" and "not good for you" categories

Estimates, takes amount of food for own use with decreasing waste

Reads simple but increasingly sophisticated food labels

Sorts pictures of foods into categories appropriate for breakfast, lunch, dinner

Estimates, serves amount of food that makes up a serving with decreasing waste

Explains about ills of excessive fats, calories, sugars

Explains names of common foods

Explains what different stores carry

Explains where different foods are located in particular store

Explains where different foods can be purchased economically

Explains generally about food poisoning

Plans, selects foods

Plans simple menu of increasing sophistication

Recognizes materials that are not for eating

Selects most nutritious foods from vending machine

Sets table of increasing variety of types and shapes

Stores, rearranges foods in refrigerator

Sets table with increasing neatness and completeness

Understands, explains vitamins, minerals

11. Prepares simple, increasingly sophisticated foods → Transition

Safely thaws frozen foods

Unwraps food

Prepares cold cereals

Uses toaster to make toast

Makes simple but increasingly sophisticated sandwich

Cooks foods with pictured cookbook

Follows simple but increasingly difficult directions

Follows video in food preparation

Prepares assembly foods—tacos, sandwiches

Knows how to set, clear table with increasing skill and decreasing assistance

Makes simple but increasingly sophisticated meal of precooked foods

Prepares increasing variety of hot cereals—instant, quick, and regular oatmeal, wheat, rice

Prepares foods from mixes—Jello, cake, biscuits, soup, gravy

Prepares frozen foods—bread, rolls, tortillas, pizza, ice cream, yogurt, fruit juices

Prepares frozen foods with increasing skill

Prepares increasing portion of meal unassisted

Prepares instant foods—potato flakes

Prepares simple but increasingly sophisticated canned foods—vegetables, fruits

Prepares simple but increasingly sophisticated canned, premixed foods

Prepares simple but increasingly sophisticated drinks from mix

Prepares simple but increasingly sophisticated meat dishes—hamburgers, hot dogs, steaks, chops, stews

Helps cook complete meal

Reads and follows simple but increasingly sophisticated recipes

Selects and buys appropriate foods with decreasing assistance

Serves increasingly complex foods and meals to others with increasing skill

Makes simple but complete meal

Stores leftover food safely

12. Understands, practices good hygiene with increasing independence and proactivity → Social → Transition

Knows basic body parts

Changes underclothing daily

Covers mouth when coughing or sneezing

Develops hobbies involving physical movement and exercise

Explains body maturing processes

Explains, practices good posture

Explains need for good body health

Explains how to use handkerchief

Explains need to eat nutritious foods

Explains need to maintain proper body weight

Cleans own body independently

Explains basically what germs are and how they spread

Explains dangers of medicines in medicine chest

Explains dangers of taking medications prescribed for others

Explains function of basic body parts

Explains generally how diseases and parasites spread—blowing nose, sharing handkerchiefs, combs, brushes, toothbrushes, coughing, toileting

Explains how and where to get help with medications

Explains how to contact community health facilities and personnel

Explains need to wear clothing of proper weight—clothing catalogs, field trips

Handles own medication insofar as possible

Recognizes common illnesses—cold, flu, diarrhea, sore throat

Explains, demonstrates need for adequate rest

Explains, demonstrates need for good dental care

Explains, demonstrates need for regular, proper exercise

Explains, demonstrates use of dental care material and equipment—toothbrush, toothpaste, dental floss

Explains, demonstrates use of deodorant

Explains, demonstrates use of nail clippers, file

13. Understands, explains legal and illegal use of drugs, medications

Listens to, reads stories and answers questions about substance abuse

Explains dangers, penalties of illegal drug use, abuse

Explains dangers of using alcohol

Explains dangers of using tobacco

Explains difference between prescription and nonprescription drugs

Explains where community health facilities and personnel are located—hospital, own doctor's office, own dentist's office, public health nurse

Uses basic first-aid materials—bandages, antibiotic ointments

Uses medications under supervision

Uses rotating medication tray or box

14. Explains, practices good general safety procedures → Transition

Listens to, reads stories and answers questions about general safety practices

Responds to "No" and "Hot"

Explains basic concepts of safety

Keeps objects out of mouth

Explains rudiments of cleanliness, sanitation in variety of situations

Explains how to prevent spread of disease

Administers simple first aid

Communicates increasingly well and understands safety words

Deals correctly and safely with strangers—events involving car/candy, improper touching, undressing

Does not crowd or push in lines

Explains need for first aid

Explains dangers of hot things—boiling water, stoves, ovens, tubs, showers

Explains dangers and avoidance of lightning

Uses own observations of weather to select clothing

Explains how to answer telephone when home alone

Explains how to deal with strangers

Explains own name, address, phone number and knows to whom such information can be entrusted

Explains what to do if locked out of home or apartment

Participates in class and group safety discussions—"What would you do if . . . ," "Where would you get help for . . . "

Explains survival and emergency words of increasing difficulty, sophistication

15. Explains, practices proper conduct in emergencies

Listens to, reads stories and answers questions on how to handle emergencies

Arranges materials in hallways, basements, attics, stairways for safety and convenience

Explains dangers of playing with matches

Explains dangers of stairs

Explains dangers of taking medication of others

Explains dangers of taking overdose of medication

Converses with police officer, fire fighter in classroom

Follows escape route from posted map of building

Explains how to get help when ill or lost (911)

Explains sounds of approaching thunderstorm

Explains where to get help in emergencies—injury, fire, theft, glass breakage, flood, earthquake, live wires, gas leaks, water hazards

Operates electric home-cleaning appliances safely

Participates in fire drills—home, classroom, community

Pours liquids, granules, powders safely and without spilling; recognizes and understands fire and other emergency alarms

Recognizes common danger smells (smoke, gasoline, natural gas)

Recognizes common danger sounds (car horn, audible walk-wait, sirens, fire alarms—home, school, community)

Recognizes emergency situations (injury, fire, theft, glass breakage, flood, earthquake, live wires, gas leaks, water hazards)

Recognizes smell of natural gas

Stays with group in classroom, hallways, playground, gym

Explains, uses 911 number

Explains, uses fire escapes and escape routes—home, classroom, school

Explains, uses safe procedures in bathroom—young children/water, electric appliances not operated in bathroom or around water

Explains danger of escaping natural gas

Explains danger of bare electrical wires

Explains danger of uncovered electrical outlets, bare wires

Explains how matches work and uses them safely

Explains when and why additional help may be needed in emergencies

Uses keys and locks correctly and safely

Uses safe procedures in and around water—tub, shower, flooded basement

Uses sharp and pointed instruments safely—pencils, knives, scissors, pins, needles, compasses

Uses telephone to report fire

Verbally reports fire

16. Explains, practices safety relating to mobility → Transition → Leisure → Social

Knows what to do if lost

States dangers of playing in the street

Understands dangers of playing around railroad tracks, yards

Uses safe procedures in and around water (pool, river, lake, beach)

Crosses street only at intersections

Crosses streets safely with decreasing help and supervision

Uses handrails on stairs

Obeys nonelectric traffic signs

Obeys police officer directing traffic

Obeys traffic lights

Operates tricycle safely—mock traffic situations on playground, gym, classroom

Operates wheelchair safely—own, when helping others

Reads, understands traffic words, symbols, directions—wait; walk; don't walk; no pedestrians; pedestrians only; stop, go; red, green, amber colors; bicycle lane

Recognizes uniformed police officer

Recognizes, uses crosswalks

Rides bicycle safely

Explains, demonstrates bus safety

Explains, uses designated bicycle lanes

Explains dangers of jaywalking

Explains that police officer's direction takes precedence over traffic lights

Walks, jogs safely
Walks to and from school safely

17. *Explains, practices safety relating to water skills → Leisure → Social*

Assesses water depth at pool and explains personal limits

Explains necessity of boat safety, life jackets, following instructions, staying seated
Stays close to side of pool, shore
Explains necessity and use of life jackets in pool, boating
Walks to recreational activities in groups
Uses "buddy system"

Appendix H

Transitional Skills and Concepts

Appendix H lists some transitional skills and concepts that are particularly significant in Chapter 14. As with the other appendixes, GIA or other evaluative procedures may indicate that the lowest-level activities of Appendix H are too difficult for the individual, in which case the IEP team should refer to Appendixes C and D for more rudimentary skills and concepts. Likewise, the performance levels of some individuals may be superior to those listed. Chapter 14 contains descriptions of some additional activities for such students.

Social skills and concepts are extremely important in preparing an individual with mental retardation for the world of work and are strongly stressed in this appendix. Communication skills are also particularly important in helping an individual make the transition from school to work. Thus, these skills and concepts should be included in each individual's horizontal curriculum planning. Also, transitional skills are so vital to an individual's ability to live independently that it is often necessary to stress a particular skill in more than one work experience setting. As with the other appendixes, a great deal of evaluation and prioritizing is necessary to design an acceptable, long-term, life goal curriculum for an individual with mental retardation.

In Appendix H, as with the other appendixes, common verbs (e.g., *explains*) are used to suggest mastery and demonstration of a skill or concept on the appropriate level for the individual student. Many students with mental retardation are nonverbal, and the communication levels of most others are somewhat to considerably impaired.

Social Skills and Concepts That Relate Particularly to Transition

1. Respects rights of others
Recognizes written names of others
Recognizes spoken names of others
Sorts written names of others
Helps with group service projects

2. Is proactive in acceptable personal appearance → Home (Sanitation)
Bathes regularly
Washes hands and face regularly
Changes underclothing regularly
Dresses appropriately
Knows, explains sanitation

3. Respects property of others
Shares at all ages
Associates names of owners and property

Sorts property as "mine and _____"
Role-plays property issues

4. Respects space of others
→ Leisure → Home
Shakes hands only when appropriate
Stands 2 to 3 feet from conversing person
Maintains eye contact

5. Accepts criticism on job with increasing grace
Role-plays criticism situations
Accepts criticism at home
Accepts criticism in classroom

6. Copes with failure and disappointment → Leisure → Social
Evaluates own work with increasing independence
Responds to stories read about criticism

7. Obeys instructions on job → Leisure
Repeats back simple, increasingly difficult instructions
Recognizes concept of in charge
Obeys in classroom
Obeys at home
Follows simple, increasingly difficult oral instructions
Follows simple, increasingly difficult written instructions

8. Understands personnel relationships on job
Can explain owner, boss, foreman, employer, employee, supervisor
Can role-play relationships

9. Works when others not present
Has increasingly good work habits
Plays individual games
Works independently on on-campus job

10. Works with others present → Leisure
Works on group projects

Can take charge of group projects
Follows instructions for group project

11. Is completely honest → All areas
Correctly answers questions on honesty
- From listened-to story
- From story he or she read
- From classroom activity
- From contrived activity
- From community situation
- From job situation

12. Meets other people well
Family members
Classmates
Other workers and employees
Employers
Customers

Career Education and Preparation for Work Experience

1. Knows, explains what is proper to say to other people
Family members
Classmates
Other workers and employees
Employers
Customers

2. Can find own on-campus job
With unsupervised suggestions
In contrived (teacher arranged) interview

3. Understands concept of work
Explains why people work
Explains concept of income
Answers questions about work from stories

4. Indicates work experience and vocational preferences
Vocally
By pointing to picture of job or business

By discussing videotape of variety of jobs
Prior to actual experience on job
After some experience on job

5. Has adequate job information

Names several jobs he or she likes or would like
  to try
Tells what tasks are involved in preferred jobs
Tells where jobs are located
Describes solution to job transportation problem
Tells what work habits are necessary for pre-
  ferred jobs

6. Follows instructions with increasing skill and accuracy → All areas

Simple, in games
In group games
Group projects
From teacher
From classmates
With, without map
From teacher or other from behind screen
Written, oral
Increasing length, complexity

7. Understands time concepts → Arithmetic

Understands need to be on time
Compares clock, clock diagram to be on time
Tells time to nearest half hour
Tells time accurately
Uses stop watch
Uses time clock
Starts, stops promptly without perseveration
Understands wasting time

8. Reads well enough to perform on job

Basic reading
Survival words
Labels relating to job
Simple, increasingly difficult directions

9. Evaluates own work → All areas

Classroom tasks
Home tasks
Group tasks and projects

On-campus job
Off-campus job
Competitive job

10. Evaluates own work on competitive job → Social (decision making)

With school supervisor
In contrived interview with employer
In employer-initiated interview
In proactive interview with employer

11. Understands wages → Arithmetic

Works for wages in class activity
Spends wages in class store
Computes simple, increasingly difficult wage
  problem
Experiences piecework in classroom activity
Compares wages with expenditures in class
  activity
Explains where wages come from

12. Completes series of work assignments

Completes simple, increasingly difficult tasks
Completes variety of one, two, three commission tasks
Makes simple, increasingly complex projects of
  paper, leather, other materials

13. Practices safety → All areas → All levels of work experience and employment

Liquids, poisons, paints, cleaners
Procedures
Simple hand tools
More advanced hand tools
Simple power tools
Uses protective clothing and devices
  • Hot pads
  • Rubber gloves
  • Goggles and other eye protectors
  • Gloves
  • Steel-toed shoes
  • Shop aprons

14. Understands, effectively avoids all kinds of abuse, exploitation

Physical
Sexual
Financial
Sociological
Taunting and teasing
Stigma

15. Increasingly understands own abilities, limitations

Estimates time needed for a task or project
Reviews own work with teacher
Records own grades
Grades own work with decreasing assistance
Participates in own age 25 projection, where appropriate

16. Understands why attendance is important in work experience and employment

Defines or discusses *tardy, late, absent*
Tells why absence reduces pay
Tells why absence may result in loss of job
Tells why tardiness may result in loss of job—even with an excuse
Understands balance between being ill and missing work
Understands effect of communicable diseases

17. Names or discusses products produced by various local businesses, industries

Family business
Community businesses
His or her workplace

18. Serves as assistant in school

His or her teacher
Other teacher in school
Teacher in other school
Other school official

19. Participates in job interview for off-campus job

Mock or contrived
Teacher arranged
Teacher present
Alone

20. Knows sources of jobs

Family members
Friends
Newspapers
Personal, neighborhood flyers
Teachers
Returns to class after graduation for assistance with specific problems

21. Works in wood shop with increasing success

Makes simple, increasingly complex projects of wood
Makes simple, increasingly complex wood projects from plan/drawing
Correctly uses paint, brushes, sandpaper
Explains, uses different types of paint, other finishes
Correctly uses wood shop hand tools
Correctly uses simple, increasingly complex power tools

22. Works in metal shop with increasing success

Makes simple, increasingly complex projects of metal
Makes simple, increasingly complex metal projects from plan/drawing
Correctly uses paint, brushes, emery cloth
Correctly uses metal shop hand tools
Correctly uses simple, increasingly complex power tools

Off-Campus Work Experience

1. Can find own on-campus job

With unsupervised suggestions
In contrived (teacher-arranged) interview

2. *Participates in variety of exploratory work experiences with increasing independence*

With increasing/decreasing number of other workers

With decreasing supervision

With modest, increasing pay

With decreasing dependence in transportation

3. *Participates in variety of unpaid/supported work experiences with increasing independence*

With increasing/decreasing number of other workers

With decreasing supervision

With modest, increasing pay

With decreasing dependence in transportation

4. *Participates in variety of competitive work experiences with increasing independence*

With increasing/decreasing number of other workers

With decreasing supervision

With modest, increasing pay

With decreasing dependence in transportation

With increasing independence in finding own transportation

5. *Develops good work habits*

Role plays

- Honesty
- Promptness
- Hard work
- Helping others, cooperation

6. *Proactively recognizes work to be done*

His or her messy workspace

Picture of messy workspace

Picture of messy room

Video of messy room

Objects to be assembled

View of messy room

7. *Understands work responsibilities*

Rest periods

Various duties among workers

Cleaning up after self and group

Works without disturbing others

Respects older, more experienced workers

Does his or her share of unpleasant tasks

Performs classroom chores without prompting

8. *Participates in increasingly higher-level work experiences*

On campus

Unpaid/supported

Competitive

Full-time employment

9. *Participates in increasingly higher-level work in sheltered workshop*

Evaluation

Sorting

Work tryouts

Work samples

Assembly line

Unpaid/supported

Competitive, as possible

Full-time employment, as possible

Transportation

1. *Rides school bus with increasing independence → Social → Home*

Boarding and exiting

Locating boarding and exiting locations

Riding without aide

Knows what to do if he or she misses bus

2. *Locates boarding and exiting locations*

With still pictures

With videotaped model

From landmarks

From special, simplified map

From common map

3. Rides municipal bus with increasing independence

Boarding and exiting
Locating boarding and exiting locations
Riding without aide
From landmarks
From map
Knows what to do if he or she misses bus

4. Uses maps effectively

Locates object in classroom by using map
Locates object in school setting by using
   map
Locates object in community by using map
  • In group
  • Alone

5. Understands directional terms → Arithmetic

Up, down, forward, back
East, west, north, south

6. Operates elevator

Locates proper floor
Manipulates controls
Understands emergency procedures

7. Pays proper bus fare

Makes or obtains exact change
  • From picture
  • With help from trusted other
  • Uses pass correctly

Appendix I

Arithmetic Skills and Concepts

Appendix I lists some arithmetic skills and concepts that are particularly significant in Chapter 15. As with the other appendixes, GIA or other evaluative procedures may indicate that the lowest-level activities of Appendix I are too difficult for the individual, in which case the IEP team should refer to Appendixes C and D for more rudimentary skills and concepts. Likewise, the performance levels of some individuals may be superior to those listed. Chapter 15 contains a description of some additional activities for such students.

In practice, the long-term and annual goals for each student must be formulated on an individual basis. Many students with mental retardation need skills, concepts, and activities even more fundamental than those on the list. The long-term and annual goals listed here include a combination of skills, concepts, and activities. Some of these goals cover considerably more conceptual distance than others. A given annual goal from the list may be an appropriate long-term goal for some students whose mental retardation is more severe. As with the sample skills and concepts of the other appendixes, a great deal of evaluation and prioritizing is necessary to design an acceptable, long-term, life goal curriculum for an individual with mental retardation.

Proactivity, estimation, and practical problem solving are stressed throughout the listing of arithmetic skills and concepts. Admittedly, these high-level skills are difficult for students with mental retardation. Chapter 15, however, contains a discussion of the inefficiency and pointlessness of teaching these individuals to make basic mathematical calculations (e.g., column addition) unless they are able to use these operations in solving life's practical problems. Further, proactivity suggests that they must be able to set up and solve practical problems largely without assistance if they are to live independently. Thus, it may be more beneficial to teach an individual with mental retardation to set up and solve a practical—but rudimentary—problem than to stress higher level fundamental operations. The IEP team must also bear in mind that many such individuals will live in settings that offer considerable supervision.

1. Uses estimation and proactivity throughout arithmetic

Solves teacher-created practical arithmetic problems involving number concepts, one-to-one correspondence, size, height, weight, time, money, and measurement at each stage of development

Estimates or approximates a reasonable answer to teacher-created practical arithmetic problems involving number concepts, one-to-one correspondence, size, height, weight, time, money, and measurement at each stage of development

Uses (or tells how he or she will use) the information from teacher-created practical arithmetic problems involving number concepts, one-to-one correspondence, size, height, weight, time, money, and measurement in everyday life

Sets up, solves own practical arithmetic problems involving number concepts, one-to-one correspondence, size, height, weight, time, money, and measurement at each stage of development

Estimates or approximates reasonable answers to self-created practical arithmetic problems involving number concepts, one-to-one correspondence, size, height, weight, time, money, and measurement at each stage of development

2.   Is aware of general number concepts

Listens to or reads ACE and other stories especially written to include number concepts—big-little, tall-short, more-less, bigger-littler, taller-shorter

Rote counts to increasingly higher numbers

Uses one-to-one correspondence

Listens, responds to stories and discussions on concepts of many, most, all, none, part

Counts increasingly higher numbers of objects

Can tell which of two is bigger, taller, more, less

Understands pair, dozen

Writes symbols of whole numbers

Explains, uses arithmetic concepts—both, all, and, larger/bigger/smaller, taller/shorter, more than, less than, more/less, same/different

Explains concepts of long/short, some/none, all, many, fast/slow, go/stop, in order, near/far, thick/thin, full/empty

Explains concepts of none and nothing

Explains concept of zero

Plays locus games—in lining up, places one classmate between, before, after, behind, in front of—another classmate

Uses concepts of enough and not enough

Uses numbers in games and other classroom activities

3.   Performs rudimentary number operations

Counts 1, 2, then increasingly larger number of objects

Counts increasingly larger number of pictures of objects

Rote counts up to 5, then larger numbers

Uses one-to-one correspondence

Uses teacher-made grid to count objects

Uses egg carton to count a dozen

4.   Sorts, matches, classifies, sequences number-related objects

Sorts by alike-different

Sorts objects into increasing numbers of categories

Sorts printed numbers into categories

Matches numbers of objects with printed numbers

Sorts by more-less, many-few

Arranges objects in order by general size

Arranges pictures of objects in order of increasing height

Matches number of needed pencils, papers, crayons with number of classmates

Matches number of needed treats, napkins, drinks, places, spoons with number of people to be served

Classifies variety of common objects by type, size, number, value, weight, use

Arranges increasingly large number of objects in order from smallest number to largest number

Arranges increasingly large, written numbers in order from smallest to largest

Arranges written amounts of money by value

Sequences three or more objects by general size

Repeats 2-, 3-, 4-number sequence

5. Masters simple addition

Listens, responds to stories with adding or putting together

Discusses mixing or putting together

Relates rote counting to adding

Discusses concept of one more

Adds $1 + 1$

Adds 1 + other numbers to sum of 5

Adds $2 + 2$

Adds sums to 6, 8, 10

Adds increasingly larger sums

Uses, writes $(+)$

Works increasingly through concrete → semi-abstract → abstract concepts

Memorizes addition facts with increasingly larger sums

Solves practical problems appropriate to each instructional level

6. Is aware of time concepts → Transition → Social

Meets schedules with class members

Listens, responds to ACE and other stories involving time

Is aware of morning, afternoon, evening, night, noon

Is aware of today, yesterday, tomorrow

Explains that people do things according to time

Discusses times to go places with class

Discusses times for individual appointments

Discusses being on-time, late, early, and their consequences

Leaves for lunch, recess, therapy by comparing printed clock face on desk with classroom clock or watch

Meets deadlines by comparing drawn or pictured clock faces with classroom clock or watch

Responds appropriately to time concepts—mealtime, class change, other events

Uses time concepts in solving practical, life problems

7. Is aware of the passage of time → Transition → Home → Social

Is aware of concept of _____ more minutes

Is aware of indefinite times—now, later, soon, earlier, before

Is aware of time divisions—minute, hour, day, week, month, season

Listens, responds to stories, discussions on about an hour, a few minutes

Estimates time to complete project or activity

Explains concept of days in the week, month

Explains—on appropriate level—concepts of morning, noon, afternoon, evening, tonight, night, day, today, tomorrow, yesterday, and days of the week

Explains concepts of on-time, late, early → Transition

Explains days of week

Predicts what will transpire in future—this afternoon, tomorrow

Relates events of recent past—this morning, yesterday, last week

Responds to timer set by teacher or aide

Sets own timer to meet deadlines—to establish time concepts rather than use of timers

8. Understands age, aging on appropriate level

Knows ages of brothers and sisters

Knows ages of classmates

Knows, tells own age, birthdate

Arranges (lines up) classmates by age

Knows own and other house, telephone numbers

9. Is aware of clocks, watches → Transition → Home

Has some knowledge of fractional parts

Copies, matches drawn clock faces

Understands that clocks and watches yield information

Matches numbers of different color, size, font

Compares drawn, actual clock to meet activity

Copies (draws) clock faces

Explains that clocks vary in size, shape

Uses clock to meet scheduled activity
Explains A.M. and P.M.
Is aware of digital clocks and watches
Identifies face clock
Identifies parts of clock

10. Uses fractional parts according to ability level

Explains concept of one fourth in measurement
Explains concept of one half
Explains concept of one half in measurement
Uses fractional parts of a number of objects
Uses simple fractional parts of a whole
Uses simple but increasingly difficult fractional parts

11. Tells time → Transition → Home → Social

Recognizes numbers to 60
Explains that quarter means one fourth
Tells time to hour by hour hand
Explains that clock hands move in one direction
Explains that big hand shows minutes
Explains need for increasing precision
Explains quarter to, after, and half-past (use local terms)
Explains minutes shown by minute hand
Explains before and after
Tells approximate hour by hour hand
Tells hour and minute
Uses time-telling ability to solve practical problems
Tells time to nearest half-hour

12. Tells time with digital clocks, watches

Tells time with traditional clock as 3:15
Writes "3:15"
Identifies digital clock
Reads digital clock, watch
Matches time drawn on traditional, digital clocks
Draws digital clock to match traditional clock
Uses digital clock, watch to meet schedules

Matches pictures or drawings of face and digital clocks showing the same, then different times of day
Tells time with digital clock or watch
Tells time with either face clock or watch

13. Masters simple subtraction

Explains left (remaining), still there
Explains take, taken away, less, fewer
Listens to stories and answers questions about subtraction
Manipulates various numbers of objects in subtraction tasks
Can accurately count small, increasingly larger number of objects
Can count remaining objects
Solves $3 - 1$, $5 - 3$, and similar subtractions
Memorizes subtraction facts to appropriate level
Uses, writes $(-)$
Uses subtraction to solve practical problems at each level

14. Understands money-related concepts

Listens to, reads stories about shopping, prices, why we have to pay, what we must pay for, how change works
Explains money and its close relationship to honesty
Explains that money cannot be left "out"
Explains what money is used for
Explains, uses concept of money, worth, equals, dozen, first, second, third
Goes shopping with parents, living-unit supervisor
Pays for family, class, living-unit purchases

15. Understands use of coins

Matches coin with picture of coin
Matches coin with simulated coin
Matches equivalent amounts of money—actual coins, pictures of coins
Matches equivalent values of coins—5 P = 1 N, 2 N = 1 D, 10 P = 1 D
Matches increasingly larger coins with their symbol amounts

Matches increasingly larger coins with their
written amounts

Matches learned numbers with numbers of
clock that likely will be different color, size,
font

Explains uses of coins

Matches dollar bill with equivalents in coins

16. Sorts, matches, classifies, sequences coins

Sorts increasing categories of coins—P-N, N-D,
S-D, P-Q, N-Q, D-Q

Sorts two, eventually all common coins—penny,
then nickel, dime, quarter, half-dollar, dollar

States which of two coins has larger value—P,
N, D, Q, H

Arranges coins in order of increasing value
where coins are in consecutive value—P-N-
D, or N-D-Q

Arranges coins in order of increasing value
where coins are not in consecutive value—P-
D-Q, or N-Q-H

Arranges increasing number of coins by value

17. Evaluates coins

States which of two coins has larger value—P,
N, D, Q, H

Evaluates value of single coins—P, N, D, Q, H,
D

States value of various combinations of two different coins—P + N, N + D

Evaluates coins—two each of P, N, D, Q, H

Evaluates combinations of coins having increasing total value

Explains equivalent amounts written with $ and ¢

Estimates value of small but increasingly larger
number of coin combinations

18. Deals with, makes change according to ability level → Transition → Home → Social

Has fairly good addition and subtraction skills

Estimates approximate change from purchase
with increasingly large amounts of money

Approximates making change to avoid being
shortchanged

Counts out change beginning with amount of
purchase

Makes change for small purchase

Sells goods and makes change from class store

Uses simple cash register

19. Is aware of ordinal numbers → Transition → Home → Social → Communication (Reading)

Listens, responds to stories, discussions using
ordinal numbers

Is aware of and understands taking turns

Understands before, after, next

Understands progression, order, sequence

Listens to and discusses sequences of events

20. Understands temperature-related measurements

Explains the temperature-related concepts hot-
cold, warm, cool, sunny

Generally understands degrees of temperature

Relates temperature to clothing, other needs

Reads, uses thermometer

Relates temperature to time of day, seasons

21. Understands prioritized, linear measurements → Home → Transition

Listens, responds to ACE, other stories having
measurement-related concepts

Manipulates ruler, yardstick, scales, measuring
cup

Discusses, uses inch, foot, yard

Understands common fractional parts

Participates with classmates in measurement-
related activity

Uses maps on ability level

Explains the concept of width

Uses estimation in introductory measurement

Uses yardstick, ruler, measuring tape (clothing),
retractable tape (shop work)

Explains concept of length

Measures height of classmate in inches

Measures height of classmate in feet and inches

Measures own height in inches

Measures own height in feet and inches
Arranges objects in order by height
Explains concept of height
Lines up classmates by height—from tallest to shortest and vice versa

22. Explains, works with concept of weight

Arranges objects in order by weight
Compares own weight to growth chart
Weighs self on bathroom scale
Uses concepts of ounce, pound
Records own, classmates' height and weight on growth chart

23. Explains, uses concept of volume

Explains empty-full, teaspoon, tablespoon, cup, pint, quart, gallon
Explains concept of full/half-full in measurement
Measures sand, water in teaspoon, tablespoon, cup, pint, quart, gallon

24. Understands, uses basic money concepts → Social → Transition → Home

Can count substantial number of ordinary objects
Explains that money has value, utility
Understands that money is essential
Listens, responds to ACE, other stories involving money
Has fairly good addition concept, skills
Understands that money value transcends one-to-one
Identifies penny, nickel, dime, quarter, half-dollar, dollar bill
Knows value in cents of each common coin
Compares values—5 pennies = 1 nickel
Evaluates (finds value of) few, increasing number of like coins
Evaluates (finds value of) few, increasing number of different coins

Uses similar procedure with 1-, 5-, 10-, 20-dollar bills

25. Uses coins and bills to make purchases of increasing value

Has fairly good subtraction concept, skills
Uses small coins to purchase goods from class store
Can make change with small coins
Sorts 1-5, 5-10, 1-10 bill combinations
Uses bill changer to obtain necessary change (not just for vending machines)
Uses coins, bills in vending machines

26. Conserves own money

Listens, responds to ACE, other stories involving thrift, saving, spending
Discusses concepts of saving, spending
Has piggy, other types of banks at home
Knows, tells how commercial banks operate
Uses class bank and keeps track of funds
Knows advantages of direct deposit, withdrawal at bank
Can operate ATM
Can explain several ways to conserve own money
Has actual experience conserving own funds
Knows, uses simple, adequate budgeting procedures
Discusses needs, methods of saving money with parents, supervisor
Discusses means of buying clothing, foods economically
Discusses where to get help with monetary matters and problems
Explains generally what saving is and why it is necessary
Explains how to save money
Knows businesspeople who can be trusted
Saves part of own earnings
Knows, explains sources of supporting funds for persons with disabilities

Knows, explains SSI
Explains generally what insurance is
Explains generally what retirement means
Explains generally what social security is

27. Practices good consumer skills

Operates imaginary, then real own budget
Uses newspaper, other means to learn merchandise costs, prices, value
Knows where to locate needed consumer items
Learns to estimate reasonable or expected costs
Can make or evaluate change
Proffers appropriate amount, avoids rip-off
Understands problems of door-to-door sales
Understands pitfalls of borrowing money
Participates in class shopping activities
Tells price of grocery, other items by reading shelf label
Understands taxes, other hidden costs
Knows approximate costs of common services
Can use hand-held calculator to own advantage
Checks with family member or other trusted person before making solicited purchases
Discusses why materials in stores cannot be placed in pockets
Estimates the approximate cost of common services, such as having tooth pulled or filled, having someone help with income tax returns, doctor's office call
Explains checkout procedures in various stores
Explains concepts of debts and obligations
Explains concepts of bills, late payment penalties, interest, finance charges
Explains concepts of borrowing, time payment, lay away, savings accounts, checking accounts
Explains fraud
Explains *sale* and other consumer terms, such as *discount*
Explains how to handle, shop for fragile objects, material

Explains pitfalls of buying over telephone
Explains pitfalls of "free" offers and buying by mail
Tells cheapest cost per unit of weight or measurement by reading shelf labels bearing such information

28. Makes, uses own menus, budgets, shopping lists according to ability levels

Uses own lunch ticket in lunchroom
Helps budget for birthday, class, or other party
Helps make out family, class, group home shopping list
Pays for own lunch at lunchroom
Explains increasingly complicated menu
Helps make family or group menu
Helps make out family, class, group home shopping list
Arranges pictures of common foods in order of increasing cost
Checks with family member or other trusted person before making large purchases
Compares price and quality among different stores
Compares price and quality within one store—among different brands
Helps make out grocery list
Helps with family budget
Makes a budget for the day's lunch
Tells amount to be paid and change for the day's lunch

29. Buys own food with increasing skill and accuracy

Estimates approximate cost of common foods
Estimates approximate cost of increasingly less common but necessary foods
Gains information about food costs from newspaper
Uses manufacturers' coupons to buy needed foods

30. Buys own clothing with increasing skill and accuracy

Explains clothing sizes
Explains hosiery sizes
Explains shoe sizes

Tries on shoes for proper fit
Tells price of clothing, other items by reading shelf labels
Shops, compares price with quality

Appendix J

Leisure (Motor, Recreational, Music, and Art) Skills and Concepts

Appendix J lists some leisure skills and concepts that are particularly significant in Chapter 16. As with the other appendixes, GIA or other evaluative procedures may indicate that the lowest-level activities of Appendix J are too difficult for the individual, in which case the IEP team should refer to Appendixes C and D for more rudimentary skills and concepts. Likewise, the performance levels of some individuals may be superior to those listed. Chapter 16 contains descriptions of some additional activities for such students.

One major purpose of providing leisure activities to individuals with mental retardation is to enable them to find and enjoy suitable recreational, physical, and personally satisfying pursuits after graduation. IEP team members can do much to help them experiment with a variety of recreational activities. The team must plan carefully in providing recreational activities that are likely to be available in the individual's community after he or she leaves school. Because of the relatively large numbers of students in school classes, it seems almost necessary to provide a variety of team sports that will not be available to the individual in adult life. Add to this the necessity of assessing the individual's preferences for different recreational activities and encouraging him or her to experi-

ence a wide variety of entertainment possibilities, and the IEP team is faced with some real challenges.

Motor and Recreational Skills and Concepts

1. Negotiates stairs
Walks on level surface
Walks up stairs with increasing independence
Walks down stairs with increasing independence
Walks up and down stairs, placing each foot on alternate step
Walks up and down stairs with decreasing use of handrail

2. Participates in physical recreation activities individually and with group and family → Transition → Home
Rides school, public bus with increasing independence
Uses landmarks—to locate stops—with increasing skill
Participates in individual YMCA and YWCA physical activities of appropriate age
Experiences wide variety of recreational activities likely to be available after graduation

Establishes preference for different recreational activities

Participates in school social activities

Participates in community-operated physical activities for appropriate age-group

Participates in church-sponsored physical activities for appropriate age-group

Participates in activities designed for people with disabilities when appropriate

Participates in group games using ball of generally decreasing size and softness—balloon, beach ball, volleyball, soccer ball, tetherball, kick ball, basketball, softball

Participates in relay races

Performs activities in unison

3.   Attends high school, college, other community spectator sporting events

Scans newspaper, other sources of recreational activities

Watches baseball, football, soccer, basketball games

4.   Sets up own exercise program

Walks independently for increasing time and distance

Jogs independently for increasing time and distance

Does calisthenics

Goes bowling independently

Rides tricycle, scooter with increasing grace, coordination, endurance

Rides bicycle with training wheels

Rides bicycle with increasing grace, coordination, endurance

Roller-skates—traditional and in-line skates

Does aerobics—with and without music

Entertains self with variety of recreational activities

5.   Develops good water skills

Puts face, then head underwater

Jumps off side of pool—feet first, head first—when safe

Jumps off low diving board

Bobs in shallow, increasingly deep water

Dog paddles

Swims

6.   Participates in family, group, individual essentially nonphysical recreational activities → Communication → Social

Experiences outdoor activities, such as picnics, camping, fishing, swimming, horseback riding, with family and classmates

Develops good audience skills

Has personal pets to care for at home and at school

Participates in community organizations for appropriate age-group

Participates in church-sponsored activities for appropriate age-group

Participates in club formed among classmates at school

Participates in school social activities

Participates in YMCA and YWCA activities of appropriate age

Visits zoo, botanical garden, arboretum, farm, pet store

Learns a variety of recreational table games while in school
- Jacks
- Chinese and traditional checkers
- Card games

Music Skills and Concepts

1.   Listens to music for entertainment

Listens to music during rest period

Listens to music during study and work—for example, during art activities

Recognizes music previously heard

Knows when playing or listening to music is not appropriate—too loud, otherwise offensive to others

Listens to increasing variety of music

Attends plays, concerts, community activities

Chooses own music effectively
Discusses how music can affect moods
Participates in simple, increasingly complex
  dances
Plays instrument in school band or orchestra
Operates radio
Operates tape recorder and boom box
Manipulates earphones
Uses earphones for private listening

2.   Participates in class and family singing → Communication → Social

Claps, marches to music
Participates in rhythm band
Plays guitar or other instrument for own enjoy-
  ment
Plays guitar or other instrument in small group
  or combo
Participates in school choral group

3.   Watches television selectively for entertainment → Communication → Social

Operates television set
Discusses how television can be entertaining
  and educational
Locates various channels, programs
Watches television individually and with group
Interprets television schedule
Matches television schedule with favorite pro-
  grams
Watches television and videos with increasing
  selectivity

Art Skills and Concepts

1.   Puts picture puzzle together

Uses puzzle with pieces portraying complete
  objects
Reproduces puzzle on duplicated picture
Uses puzzle with pieces portraying parts of
  common objects—human body, car, chair
Uses puzzle with large, simple objects
Uses puzzle with pieces of decreasing size

Uses puzzle with pictures of meaningful
  objects, tasks

2.   Increases gross motor coordination → Transition

Works with clay, play putty
Manipulates pages of large, increasingly small
  book
Manipulates introductory art tools
Uses large tongs to manipulate objects

3.   Increases physical endurance → Transition

Rides tricycle, bicycle
Walks increasing distances
Lifts light, increasingly heavy weights
Jumps rope—alone and in group

4.   Increases fine motor coordination → Transition

Works with clay, puttylike materials
Builds towers with blocks
Sorts large, increasingly small objects into piles
Uses large plastic pliers to move object
Uses large, increasingly small tweezers to move
  small object

5.   Combines physical activity with hobbies

Collects coins, stamps, rocks, flowers, sports
  cards
Collects items of personal interest
Does needlework, knitting, other crafts →
  Home

6.   Selects, participates in both individual and group activities → Communication → Social

Understands, discusses need for rules, taking
  turns
Understands, discusses fairness, sportsmanship,
  honesty
Participates in activities chosen by others
Makes suggestions for group activities
Participates in group activities without anger or
  complaint
Helps select game or activity for group

7. Uses pencils, chalk, crayons

Holds pencil, crayon correctly
Uses large primary pencil
Uses increasingly small (normal) pencil
Draws between two bold, parallel lines
Draws spiral circles of random, increasingly
    specified size
Draws circles between two lines

8. Knows, discusses, follows safety rules →
Home (Safety)

Understands dangers of swallowing small
    objects
Participates in leisure activities safely
Uses sewing needles of generally decreasing size

9. Sews practical and creative objects →
Home → Transition

Uses safety pins
Uses scissors of increasingly smaller size and
    with increasing independence
Uses scissors to cut on lines of decreasing width
Uses sewing needles of increasingly smaller
    size and with increasing independence
Makes simple stitches
Sews simple seams
Sews on large, increasingly small buttons

10. Uses scissors for cutting paper

Uses large, easily manipulated, then more diffi-
    cult scissors

Cuts between two bold, widely separated,
    straight lines
Cuts between two bold lines with increasingly
    sharp curves
Cuts along single wide, increasingly narrow
    bold lines
Copies horizontal lines
Copies vertical lines
Copies lines with increasingly sharp angles and
    curves

11. Uses introductory art materials

Manipulates clay—pinches, rolls, squeezes
Sorts increasing variety of colored cards
Identifies primary colors
Finger paints
Uses construction paper of different colors
Uses variety of textures
Uses water colors
Uses variety of art media
Creates simple, increasingly complex pictures

12. Understands, uses colors

Identifies common colors
Sorts colors into increasing number of classifi-
    cations
Knows how colors appear in nature
Uses colors for practical purposes, such as traf-
    fic lights and signs

Glossary

abduction Moving away from the midline of the body. This sometimes refers to separating or spreading fingers and toes or extending the arms so that the arms are at maximum distance from the torso.

adapted/created/enhanced (ACE) story A story with a carefully planned concept, moral, or lesson a teacher writes and reads to a student with mental retardation; it enables that student with little or no reading ability to master the concept, moral, or lesson.

adduction Movement toward the body midline; moving the arms closer to the torso.

age 25 projection A curriculum planning procedure wherein the IEP team predicts the status of an individual with mental retardation at his or her age 25. Annual achievement evaluations enable the team to adjust and prioritize that individual's life goals.

age appropriate A curriculum planning concept (essential in mental retardation) that requires the inclusion of skills, concepts, and experiences as commensurate as possible with the individual's chronological and sociological ages.

assistive technology Electronic or mechanical devices, such as computers, hand-held calculators, and picture boards, that an individual with mental retardation may use to solve practical problems and to communicate with other persons.

ataxia Impairment of muscular coordination, balance, and control; inability to walk or walk gracefully or to perform smooth operations of the hands and fingers, such as writing. Ataxia is common in cerebral palsy.

athetosis Involuntary, wavelike movement of the limbs, caused by brain injury. Movements are often, but not always, rhythmic and appear to be beyond internal control. These movements interfere with voluntary movements. Athetosis is common in cerebral palsy.

babbling Making unintelligible and indiscriminate sounds. Making such sounds is an obvious prerequisite of speech. Some children with severe/profound mental retardation will need some stimulation and encouragement to make any audible sound at all.

basal age A concept or procedure, borrowed from standardized testing, that suggests the point at which individual instruction should begin. (See *ceiling age*)

ceiling age A concept or procedure, borrowed from standardized testing, that suggests the level above which individual instruction is too difficult for a given student. (See *basal age*)

compression The moving of body parts closer together (or the reducing of space between them) to improve their function or performance. An example is reducing the space between two vertebrae. This should be done only under the direction of a knowledgeable specialist.

conceptual distance A concept suggesting that the measurable distance (interval or space) between the achievement and proposed instructional levels of a student with mental retardation must be considered in terms of the time, effort, money, and other resources needed to close or accommodate the interval.

curriculum planning (horizontal) Planning and providing a variety of instruction and experiences at the approximate level of difficulty a student has demonstrated that he or she can master. Incorporating curricular elements from several columns of the curriculum chart for maximum teaching efficiency.

curriculum planning (level-to-level) Planning the educational curriculum and program of an individual with mental retardation with the individual's future teachers; especially crucial where a building change is involved.

curriculum planning (life goal) A systematic procedure for curriculum planning and instruction designed to enable a student with mental retardation to achieve his or her long-term life goals.

curriculum planning (vertical) Locating the approximate level of difficulty a student can master.

disqualifier An inappropriate social trait or peculiarity (e.g., throwing a temper tantrum) that is so offensive as to "disqualify" an otherwise qualified individual from achieving success in employment or independent living.

employment—competitive Employment of individuals with mental retardation that is free of external financial and other support.

employment—sheltered Employment of individuals with mental retardation that is closely controlled, as in a sheltered workshop.

employment—supported A job situation in which external funds and other support are given to an employee with a disability, the employer, or both. The situation is usually temporary, but necessary to sustain the employee on the job.

epilepsy A neurological disorder that causes varying and unpredictable brain emissions. The major problems for the affected individual are seizures (See *seizures*) and absence from school. Some medications relieve the seizuring problems to varying degrees but usually reduce vitality and alertness as a side effect.

extension The moving of a limb to its extreme open or straight position, also unflexing the fist. It is the opposite of flexion. Extension movements are extremely important to individuals with severe/profound mental retardation, some of whom will be unable to move a limb at all; other individuals may have some movement, but not sufficiently complete or resolute to be useful.

fixate To stare or focus the eyes on another person or object. To every child, fixation is or was at one time a necessary accomplishment. Prior to fixation, use of the eyes was largely uncontrolled, or at least random. Many students with severe/profound mental retardation—even some in their teens—will not have developed the ability to fixate for an appreciable period of time or to gain useful perceptions or information. Fixation is a prerequisite to paying attention, imitation, following instructions, and other elements of teaching-learning relationships.

flexion A bending movement of a limb, thereby decreasing the angle between the component parts. It is the opposite of extension. An example is touching the left shoulder with the left hand.

goal instruction analysis (GIA) A systematic procedure for curriculum planning and instruction that analyzes the act of teaching a skill or concept, rather than focuses on the individual tasks the student is expected to perform. GIA shows the individual student's progress and current status on his or her long-term life curriculum goals.

heterogeneity A concept suggesting that despite their individual, generally low, flat achievement profiles, groups of students with mental retardation are extremely heterogeneous, especially in view of conceptual distance. (See *conceptual distance*)

hyperextension The extending of a limb beyond its normal extreme position or normal range of motion—usually 180 degrees. Knees and elbows are usually less than functional if they cannot be extended to about 180 degrees. Extending these limbs beyond this point usually tends to make them less functional.

individualized educational program (IEP) A requirement of P.L. 94–142 (reinforced and enhanced by P.L. 101–476) that the educational program of every individual who has a qualifying disability must be commensurate with that individual's needs and abilities. These laws also require that the program be designed and supervised by a qualified committee (the IEP team) comprised of the individual's parents or guardian and qualified professional workers and that the individual be educated in the least restrictive environment.

infantile speech Delayed or poorly executed speech or that which is similar to speech of younger children. Infantile speech is considered to be superior to jargon in that infantile speech begins to include discernible, though poorly formed, words. A child may persist in infantile speech even after he or she can form fairly complex sentences and thoughts.

jargon Unintelligible speech. Jargon is considered to be superior to babbling in that jargon usually involves more sounds and eventually appears to be meaningful to the child.

kinetic sense The sense or awareness of movement of the body or limbs. An example is the Sister Kenny notion of "think here." The receptors that carry these sensations to the brain are called *proprioceptors*.

learned helplessness A condition (common in mental retardation) in which students perceive that their status and success are beyond their control or influence.

least restrictive environment (LRE) The classroom or educational setting that offers maximum social exposure to students without disabilities. Also, a current concept or practice that places students with mental retardation in such a setting.

mainstreaming → integration → inclusion A service delivery pattern sequence that has historically held regular class teachers increasingly responsible for the education of students with mental retardation.

midline An imaginary reference line drawn down the center of the body. The midline is important not only as a point of reference but also because many individuals with severe/profound mental retardation have great difficulty moving arms and even legs past the body midline.

modeling An instructional procedure wherein the teacher, instructional assistant, peer tutor, or another student models desired instructional behavior for a student.

occupational therapist A specialist trained to help a person develop fine (and some gross) motor control and visual motor abilities. This specialist helps a person learn to perform body movements commonly required by the person's environment, such as movements required by work, play, and self-help skills.

parent An individual's biological mother or father, but may also include the individual's foster parents or guardian. May refer herein to an adult who has legal custody of a person with mental retardation.

perseveration A characteristic (common in mental retardation) where an individual persists at an inappropriate task—or at an appropriate task to a point where the task is no longer appropriate.

phoneme The smallest sound—often the sound of a single letter. Phonemes are particularly important in the programs of individuals with severe/profound mental retardation because it is often difficult to get these individuals to produce single sounds and to learn to use them in words, and a great deal of time and effort (and detailed planning) is required to enable them to do so.

phonology The study of the sounds of language. (See *phoneme*) Careful, individual analysis is needed to help individuals with severe/profound mental retardation learn to produce and use the individual sounds in the order that is most suitable for each student.

physical therapist A specialist who teaches a person to make body movements. An essential specialist with many individuals with severe/profound mental retardation, a physical therapist may be a consultant to a teacher or work directly with the children.

positioning Placing a person in various positions that will promote good posture. Positioning sometimes requires adaptive equipment. Examples: (a) placing a child so that the head is in the middle of the midline and (b) using a backboard to help a child to stand straight.

prioritizing Arranging the life goals of a student with mental retardation in the order of their greatest functional priority.

proactivity A planning/instructional concept that teaches an individual with mental retardation to recognize, confront, set up, and solve a practical problem independently and to use the information derived therefrom.

psychomotor seizure A type of seizure in which the person performs a variety of behaviors, such as smacking the lips, walking, running, or repetitive speech. Unlike other seizures, the person usually does not lose consciousness or awareness.

random behavior Involuntary movements of the body or limbs. May be rhythmic and/or without purpose. This behavior may involve self-abuse and seems to be more internally controllable than athetosis. Examples are biting, hand-waving, rocking, and nodding.

reflexive Pertaining to body reflexes—actions that do not require thought, deliberation, perception, or neural response beyond the spinal or midbrain levels. Examples are breathing, sucking, heartbeat, smiling, and eye blinks. Often, therapy involves practice, repetition, and combining of activities to help the person improve and develop reflexive actions that are voluntary and to push internal control to the midbrain or cortical levels.

regional variation A phenomenon that demonstrates the extremely divergent rates at which different states identify and serve students with mental retardation from among their school-age populations.

rotation A twisting or rolling motion of the torso or limbs. An example is twisting the upper torso to the extreme left or right, usually from a sitting or standing position.

seizure A sudden, often violent attack often caused by epilepsy or neuralgia. The more serious seizures are called *grand mal,* during which the person usually loses consciousness and often has jerky movements of the whole body. The movements are usually random and may or may not be rhythmic. Less serious forms are called *petit mal,* during which the person usually does not lose consciousness. Petit mal seizures may be momentary and/or frequent and often cause the person to stumble, stare, blink, or lose awareness.

semantics The part of language or linguistics that deals with meaning, usually word meaning. For our purposes, stressing the meaning or function of a word or phrase, possibly opposed (or in addition) to word identification.

significant other A person who makes significant decisions and/or provides services that affect the life of an individual with mental retardation.

spasticity A condition caused by abnormally high muscle tension that results in loss of muscle control. Examples are uncontrollable body movements, often writhing, slurred speech, and extreme difficulty walking, writing, and speaking with an unsuccessful attempt at control. Spasticity is common in cerebral palsy.

stereotypical behavior Nonmeaningful rocking, swaying, or limb movement common in severe/profound mental retardation and not usually associated with cerebral palsy.

syntax Having to do with sentence construction. For our purposes, syntax refers to a child's ability to put two and then more words together to make a meaningful expression.

transition A high-priority life goal in mental retardation that enables the student to make the transformation (or *transition*) from school to optimum success in adult life.

work experience A school-sponsored activity that places students with mental retardation and other disabilities in increasingly demanding, unsupported, and realistic work situations.

References

Abbeduto, L., Furman, L., & Davies, B. (1989). Relation between the receptive language and mental age of persons with mental retardation. *American Journal on Mental Retardation, 93*(5), 535–543.

Abbeduto, L., & Nuccio, J. B. (1991). Relation between receptive language and cognitive maturity in persons with mental retardation. *American Journal on Mental Retardation, 96*(2), 143–149.

Abramowicz, H. K., & Richardson, S. (1975). Epidemiology of severe mental retardation in children: Community studies. *Education and Training in Mental Retardation, 80*, 18–39.

Adams, K., & Markham, R. (1991). Recognition of affective facial expressions by children and adolescents with and without mental retardation. *American Journal on Mental Retardation, 96*(1), 21–28.

Adams Central School District No. 690 v. Deist, 334 N.W. 2d. 775 (Neb., 1983).

Adger, C. T., Wolfram, W., & Detwyler, J. (1993). Language differences: A new approach for special educators. *Teaching Exceptional Children, 26*(1), 44–47.

Affleck, G. G. (1980). Physicians' attitudes toward discretionary medical treatment of Down's syndrome infants. *Mental Retardation, 18*(2), 79–81.

Affleck, J. Q., Edgar, E., Levine, P., & Kortering, L. (1990). Postschool status of students classified as mildly mentally retarded, learning disabled, or non-handicapped: Does it get better with time? *Education and Training in Mental Retardation, 25*(4), 315–324.

Affleck, J. Q., Madge, S., Adams, A., & Lowenbraun, S. (1988). Integrated classroom versus resource model: Academic viability and effectiveness. *Exceptional Children, 54*(4), 339–348.

Agran, M., Fodor-Davis, J., Moore, S., & Deer, M. (1989). The application of a self-management program on instruction-following skills. *Journal of the Association for Persons with Severe Handicaps (JASH), 14*(2), 147–154.

Allen, C. P., White, J., & Test, D. W. (1992). Using a picture/symbol form for self-monitoring within a community-based training program. *Teaching Exceptional Children, 24*(2), 54–56.

Allen, D. A., & Hudd, S. H. (1987). Are we professionalizing parents? Weighing the benefits and pitfalls. *Education and Training in Mental Retardation, 25*(3), 133–139.

Allred, R. A. (1977). *Spelling: The application of research findings.* Washington, DC: National Education Association.

Anastasi, A. (1988). *Psychological testing* (6th ed.). New York: Macmillan.

Aronson, S. S. (1990). Ask Dr. Sue. *Child Care Information Exchange, 76*, 23–24.

Artiles, A. J., & Trent, S. C. (1994). Overrepresentation of minority students in special education: A continuing debate. *Journal of Special Education, 27*(4), 410–437.

Asberg, K. H. (1989). The need for medical care among mentally retarded adults. A five-year follow-up and comparison with a general population of the same age. *British Journal of Mental Subnormality, 35*(68), 50–57.

Atterbury, B. W. (1984). Mainstreaming into music class: A note of caution. *Principal, 64*(1), 41–44.

Ault, M. J., Gast, D. L., Wolery, M., & Doyle, P. M. (1992). Data collection and graphing method for teaching chained tasks with the constant time delay procedure. *Teaching Exceptional Children, 24*(2), 28–33.

Baer, D. M. (1990). Why choose self-regulation as the focal analysis of retardation? *American Journal on Mental Retardation, 94*(4), 363–364.

533

Baker v. Owen, 395 F. Supp. 294 (M.D. N.C. 1975).

Baker, S. (1990). When an emergency happens. *Vocational Education Journal, 65*(2), 21.

Ballard, J. K., & Calhoun, M. L. (1991). Special Olympics: Opportunities to learn. *Teaching Exceptional Children, 24*(1), 20–23.

Bambara, L. M., & Ager, C. (1992). Using self-scheduling to promote self-directed leisure activity in home and community settings. *Journal of the Association for Persons with Severe Handicaps (JASH), 17*(2), 67–76.

Banbury, M. M., & Hebert, C. R. (1992). Do you see what I mean? Body language in classroom interactions. *Teaching Exceptional Children, 24*(2), 34–38.

Bankhead, I., & MacKay, D. N. (1982). Fine-motor performance in subjects of subnormal, normal, and superior intelligence: Reaction time and task complexity. *Journal of Mental Deficiency Research, 26*(2), 73–89.

Bannerman, D. J., Sheldon, J. B., & Sherman, J. A. (1991). Teaching adults with severe and profound retardation to exit their homes upon hearing the fire alarm. *Journal of Applied Behavior Analysis, 24*(3), 571–577.

Bannerman, D. J., Sheldon, J. B., Sherman, J. A., & Harchik, A. E. (1990). Balancing the right to habilitation with the right to personal liberties: The rights of people with developmental disabilities to eat too many doughnuts and take a nap. *Journal of Applied Behavior Analysis, 23*(1), 79–89.

Bansberg, B., & Sklare, J. (1986). *Career Decision Diagnostic Assessment user's guide.* Longmont, CO: Illinois Counseling Research.

Barber, D., & Hupp, S. C. (1993). A comparison of friendship patterns of individuals with developmental disabilities. *Education and Training in Mental Retardation, 28*(1), 13–22.

Barnett, W. S. (1986). Definition and classification of mental retardation: A reply to Zigler, Balla, & Hodapp. *Education and Training in Mental Retardation, 91*(2), 111–116.

Baroody, A. J. (1986). Counting ability of moderately and mildly handicapped children. *Education and Training of the Mentally Retarded, 21*(4), 289–300.

Baroody, A. J. (1987). Problem size and mentally retarded children's judgment of commutativity. *Education and Training in Mental Retardation, 91*(4), 439–442.

Batshaw, M. L., & Perret, Y. (1992). *Children with disabilities: A medical primer* (3rd ed.). Baltimore: Brookes.

Batshaw, M. L., Perret, Y., & Trachenberg, S. W. (1992). Caring and coping: The family of a child with disabilities. In M. L. Batshaw & Y. Perret, *Children with disabilities: A medical primer* (3rd ed., pp. 563–578). Baltimore: Brookes.

Baumeister, A. A., & Brooks, P. H. (1981). Cognitive deficits in mental retardation. In J. M. Kauffman & D. P. Hallahan (Eds.), *Handbook of special education* (pp. 87–107). Englewood Cliffs, NJ: Prentice-Hall.

Baumeister, M., & Morris, R. K. (1992). Rural delivery model for vocational education. *Teaching Exceptional Children, 24*(4), 40–43.

Baumgart, D. (1990). *Augmentative and alternative communication systems for persons with moderate and severe disabilities.* Baltimore: Brookes.

Baumgart, D., & VanWalleghem, J. (1987). Teaching sight words: A comparison between computer-assisted and teacher-taught methods. *Education and Training in Mental Retardation, 22*(1), 56–65.

Beasley, C. R. (1982). Effects of a jogging program on cardiovascular fitness and work performance of mentally retarded adults. *Education and Training in Mental Retardation, 86*(6), 609–613.

Beck, J., Broers, J., Hogue, E., Shipstead, J., & Knowlton, E. (1994). Strategies for functional community-based instruction and inclusion for children with mental retardation. *Teaching Exceptional Children, 26*(2), 44–48.

Becker, R. L. (1987). The Reading-Free Vocational Interest Inventory: A typology of vocational clusters. *Mental Retardation, 25*(3), 171–179.

Becker, R. L., & Becker, E. Z. (1983). Revision of the Reading-Free Vocational Interest Inventory. *Mental Retardation, 21*(4), 144–149.

Bedini, L. A., Bullock, C. C., & Driscoll, L. B. (1993). The effects of leisure education on factors contributing to the successful transition of students with mental retardation from school to adult life. *Therapeutic Recreation Journal, 27*(2), 70–82.

Behrmann, J. (1993). Including everyone. *Executive Educator, 15*(12), 16–20.

Beier, D. C. (1964). Behavioral disturbances in the mentally retarded. In H. A. Stevens & R. Heber (Eds.), *Mental retardation: A review of research* (pp. 453–487). Chicago: University of Chicago Press.

Benda, C. E. (1954). Psychopathology of childhood. In L. Carmichael (Ed.), *Manual of child psychology* (2nd ed., pp. 1115–1161). New York: Wiley.

Bensberg, G. J., & Smith, J. J. (1984). Comparative costs of public residential and community residential facilities for the mentally retarded. *Education and Training in Mental Retardation, 19*(1), 45–48.

Bereiter, C., & Engelmann, S. (1966). *Teaching disadvantaged children in the preschool.* Englewood Cliffs, NJ: Prentice-Hall.

Berger, R. S., & Reid, D. K. (1989). Differences that make a difference: Comparisons of metacomponential functioning and knowledge base among groups of high and low IQ learning disabled, mildly mentally retarded, and normally achieving adults. *Journal of Learning Disabilities, 22*(7), 422–429.

Berk, R. A., Bridges, W. P., & Shih, A. (1981, February). Does IQ really matter? A study of the use of IQ scores for the tracking of mentally retarded students. *American Sociological Review, 46,* 58–71.

Berkman, K. A., & Meyer, L. H. (1988). Alternative strategies and multiple outcomes in the remediation of severe self-injury: Going "all out" nonaversively. *Journal of the Association for Persons with Severe Handicaps (JASH), 13*(2), 76–86.

Bernabe, E. A., & Block, M. E. (1994). Modifying rules of a regular girls softball league to facilitate the inclusion of a child with severe disabilities. *Journal of the Association for Persons with Severe Handicaps (JASH), 19*(1), 24–31.

Bersani, H. A., Jr., & Heifetz, L. J. (1985). Perceived stress and satisfaction of direct-care staff members in community residences for mentally retarded adults. *American Journal of Mental Deficiency, 90*(3), 289–295.

Bettison, S. (1986). Behavioral aspects of toilet training for retarded persons. *International Review of Research in Special Education, 14,* 319–350.

Bialer, I., & Cromwell, R. (1965). Failure as motivation with mentally retarded children. *American Journal of Mental Deficiency, 69,* 680–684.

Bice, T. R., Halpin, G., & Halpin, G. (1986). A comparison of the cognitive styles of typical and mildly retarded children with educational recommendations. *Education and Training of the Mentally Retarded, 21*(2), 93–97.

Big Beaver Falls Area School Dist. v. Jackson, 624 A.2d 806 (Penn. Cmwlth., 1993).

Billingsley, F. F. (1993). Reader response: In my dreams: A response to some current trends in education. *Journal of the Association for Persons with Severe Handicaps (JASH), 18*(1), 61–63.

Bilsky, L. H., & Judd, T. (1986). Sources of difficulty in the solution of verbal arithmetic problems by mentally retarded and nonretarded individuals. *Education and Training in Mental Retardation, 90*(4), 395–402.

Birch, D. A. (1994). Utilizing role plays to develop health skills and promote social interaction between special education and non-special education students. *Journal of Health Education, 25*(3), 181–182.

Blacher, J. (1982). Assessing social cognition in young mentally retarded and nonretarded children. *Education and Training in Mental Retardation, 86*(5), 473–484.

Blacher, J., Nihira, K., & Meyers, C. E. (1987). Characteristics of home environment of families with mentally retarded children: Comparison across levels of retardation. *Education and Training in Mental Retardation, 91*(4), 313–320.

Blacher-Dixon, J., & Simeonsson, R. J. (1981). Perspective-taking by mentally retarded children: One-year follow-up. *Education and Training in Mental Retardation, 85*(6), 648–651.

Black, J. W., & Meyer, L. H. (1993). But . . . is it really work? Social validity of employment training for persons with very severe disabilities. *American Journal on Mental Retardation, 96*(5), 463–474.

Black, S. (1994). Will they break? *Executive Educator, 16*(5), 27, 30–32.

Blackbourn, V. A., & Blackbourn, J. M. (1993). An adolescent with moderate mental disabilities tutors a 1st-grade, nondisabled child. *Teaching Exceptional Children, 25*(4), 56–61.

Blackman, L. S., & Heintz, P. (1966). The mentally retarded. *Review of Educational Research, 36*(1), 5–36.

Blandy, D. (1993). Community-based lifelong learning in art for adults with mental retardation: A rationale, conceptual foundation, and supportive environments. *Studies in Art Education, 34*(3), 167–175.

Blankenship, C. S. (1986). Using curriculum-based assessment data to make instructional decisions. *Exceptional Children, 52*(3), 233–238.

Blatt, B. (1961). Toward a more acceptable terminology in mental retardation. *Training School Bulletin, 58*(2), 47–51.

Blatt, B., & Kaplan, B. (1966). *Christmas in purgatory.* Boston: Allyn & Bacon.

Blumberg, L. (1991). On display: Your child is being humiliated. *Exceptional Parent, 21*(7), 25–30.

Boggs, E., Dybwad, G., & Taylor, S. (1994). Historical perspectives on the definition of mental retardation. *Mental Retardation, 32*(1), 69–72.

Booney, V. H., Blixt, S., & Ellis, R. (1981). Stability of the WISC-R for a sample of exceptional children. *Journal of Clinical Psychology, 37*(2), 397–399.

Bourbeau, P. E., Sowers, J., & Close, D. W. (1986). An experimental analysis of generalization of banking skills from classroom to bank settings in the community. *Education and Training in Mental Retardation, 21*(2), 98–107.

Braddock, D., & Fujiura, G. (1987). State government financial effort in mental retardation. *American Journal on Mental Retardation, 91*(5), 450–459.

Braddock, D., Hemp, R., & Howes, R. (1986). Direct costs of institutional care in the United States. *Mental Retardation, 24*(1), 9–17.

Bradley, L. J., & Meredith, R. C. (1991). Interpersonal development: A study with children classified as educable mentally retarded. *Education and Training in Mental Retardation, 26*(2), 130–141.

Bradley, V. J., & Agosta, J. M. (1985). Keeping your child at home: The case for family support. *Exceptional Parent, 15*(7), 512–520.

Brady, M. P., Lineham, S. A., Campbell, P. C., & Nielsen, W. L. (1992). *Education and Training in Mental Retardation and Developmental Disabilities, 27*(4), 354–366.

Brady, M. P., McDougall, D., & Dennis, H. F. (1989). The schools, the courts, and the integration of students with severe handicaps. *Journal of Special Education, 23*(1), 43–58.

Brantlinger, E. A. (1988). Teachers' perceptions of the parenting abilities of their secondary students with mild mental retardation. *Remedial and Special Education (RASE), 9*(4), 31–43.

Bray, N. W., Saarnio, D. A., & Hawk, L. W. (1994). Context for understanding intellectual and developmental differences in strategy competencies. *American Journal on Mental Retardation, 99*(1), 44–49.

Bray, N. W., Turner, L. A., & Hersch, R. E. (1985). Developmental progressions and regressions in the selective remembering strategies of EMR individuals. *Education and Training in Mental Retardation, 90*(2), 198–205.

Bredekamp, S. (Ed.). (1986). *Developmentally appropriate practice in early childhood programs serving children from birth through age 8.* Washington, DC: National Association for the Education of Young Children.

Bridges, B. R. (1986). Images, imagination, creativity, and the TMR. *Art Education, 39*(1), 12–13.

Brigance, A. H. (1983). *Brigance Diagnostic Comprehensive Inventory of Basic Skills.* North Billerica, MA: Curriculum Associates.

Brigham, F. J., Bakken, J. P., Scruggs, T. E., & Mastropieri, M. A. (1992). Cooperative behavior management: Strategies for promoting a positive classroom environment. *Education and Training in Mental Retardation, 27*(1), 3–12.

Brimer, R. W. (1990). *Students with severe disabilities: Current perspectives and practices.* Mountain View, CA: Mayfield.

Brolin, D. E. (1989). *Life-centered career education: A competency-based approach* (3rd ed.). Reston, VA: Council for Exceptional Children.

Brolin, D. E. (1992). *Life Centered Career Education (LCCE) curriculum program.* Reston, VA: Council for Exceptional Children.

Bromley, B., & Blacher, J. (1989). Factors delaying out-of-home placement of children with severe handicaps. *American Journal on Mental Retardation, 94*(3), 284–291.

Brookings, J. B., & Bolton, B. (1986). Vocational interest dimensions of adult handicapped persons. *Measurement and Evaluation in Counseling and Development, 18*(4), 168–175.

Brotherson, M. J., Turnbull, A. P., Bronicki, G. J., Houghton, J., Roeder-Gordon, C., Summers, J. A., & Turnbull, H. R., III. (1988). Transition into adulthood: Parental planning for sons and daughters with disabilities. *Education and Training in Mental Retardation, 23*(2), 165–174.

Browder, D. M. (1991). *Assessment of individuals with severe disabilities: An applied behavior approach to life skills assessment* (2nd ed.). Baltimore: Brookes.

Browder, D. M., & Cooper, K. J. (1994). Inclusion of older adults with mental retardation in leisure opportunities. *Mental Retardation, 32*(2), 91–99.

Browder, D. M., Hines, C., McCarthy, L. J., & Fees, J. (1984). A treatment package for increasing sight word recognition for use in daily living skills. *Education and Training in Mental Retardation, 19*(3), 191–200.

Brown, F., & Lehr, D. H. (1993). Making activities meaningful for students with severe multiple disabilities. *Teaching Exceptional Children, 25*(4), 12–16.

Brown, L., Schwarz, P., Udvari-Solner, A., Kampschroer, E. F., Johnson, F., Jorgenson, J., & Gruenewald, L. (1991). How much time should students with severe intellectual disabilities spend in regular education classrooms and elsewhere? *Journal of the Association for Persons with Severe Handicaps (JASH), 16*(1), 39–47.

Brown, L. F., Branston, M. B., Hamre-Nietupski, S. M., Pumpian, I., Certo, N., & Gruenewald, L. (1979). A strategy for developing chronological-age-appropriate and functional curricular content for severely handicapped adolescents and young adults. *Journal of Special Education, 13*(1), 81–90.

Brown, V. (1988). Integrating drama and sign language. *Teaching Exceptional Children, 21*(1), 4–8.

Browning, P., & Nave, G. (1993). Teaching social problem solving to learners with mild disabilities. *Education and Training in Mental Retardation, 28*(4), 309–317.

Browning, P., & White, W. (1986). Teaching life enhancement skills with interactive video-based curricula. *Education and Training of the Mentally Retarded, 21*(4), 236–244.

Bruininks, R., Thurlow, M. L., & Ysseldyke, J. E. (1992). Assessing the right outcomes: Prospects for improving education for youth with disabilities. *Education and Training in Mental Retardation, 27*(2), 93–100.

Bruininks, R. H. (1974). Physical and motor development of retarded persons. In N. R. Ellis (Ed.), *International review of research in mental retardation* (pp. 209–261). New York: Academic Press.

Bullock, C. C., & Mahon, M. J. (1992). Decision making in leisure: Empowerment for people with mental retardation. *Journal of Physical Education, Recreation and Dance, 63*(8), 36–40.

Burack, J. A., & Zigler, E. (1990). Intentional and incidental memory in organically mentally retarded, familial retarded, and nonretarded individuals. *American Journal on Mental Retardation, 94*(5), 532–540.

Burgess, C., & Zhu, G. (1990). Should *all* mentally challenged people work? *Personnel, 67*(1), 20–22.

Burton, L., & Bero, F. (1984). Is career education really being taught? *Academic Therapy, 19*(4), 389–395.

Burton, T. A. (1981). Deciding what to teach the severely/profoundly retarded student: A teacher responsibility. *Education and Training of the Mentally Retarded, 19*(1), 74–79.

Bushweller, K. (1994). Turning our backs on boys. *American School Board Journal, 181*(5), 20–25.

Butterworth J., Jr., & Strauch, J. D. (1994). The relationship between social competence and success in the competitive work place for persons with mental retardation. *Education and Training in Mental Retardation and Developmental Disabilities, 29*(2), 118–133.

Calhoun, M. L., & Calhoun, L. G. (1993). Age-appropriate activities: Effects on the social perception of adults with mental retardation. *Education and Training in Mental Retardation, 28*(2), 143–148.

Canter, L. (1976). *Assertive discipline: A take-charge approach for today's educator.* Los Angeles: Lee Canter & Associates.

Canter, L. (1992). *Assertive discipline.* Port Chester, NY: National Professional Resources.

Caouette, M., & Reid, G. (1991). Influence of auditory stimulation on the physical work output of adults who are severely retarded. *Education and Training in Mental Retardation, 26*(1), 43–52.

Carduso-Martins, C., Mervis, C. B., & Mervis, C. A. (1985). Early vocabulary by children with Down syndrome. *Education and Training in Mental Retardation, 90,* 177–184.

Carlson, S. (1985). "Appropriate" school programs: Legal vs. educational approaches. *Exceptional Parent, 15*(5), 23–30.

Carney, R. N., Levin, M. E., & Levin, J. R. (1993). Mnemonic strategies: Instructional techniques worth remembering. *Teaching Exceptional Children, 25*(4), 24–30.

Carr, M. N. (1993). A mother's thoughts on inclusion. *Journal of Learning Disabilities, 26*(9), 590–592.

Carroll, J. B. (1961). Language development in children. In S. Saporta (Ed.), *Psycholinguistics: A book of readings* (pp. 331–345). New York: Holt, Rinehart & Winston.

Cartwright, G. P., & Cartwright, C. A. (1978). Definitions and classification approaches. In J. T. Neisworth & R. M. Smith (Eds.), *Retardation: Issues, assessment, and intervention.* New York: McGraw-Hill.

Cassidy, V. M., & Stanton, J. E. (1959). *An investigation of factors involved in the educational placement of mentally retarded children: A study of differences between children in special and regular classes in Ohio* (U.S. Office of Education Cooperative

Research Program, Project No. 043). Columbus: Ohio State University.

Castles, E. E., & Glass, C. R. (1986). Training in social and interpersonal problem-solving skills for mildly and moderately mentally retarded adults. *American Journal on Mental Retardation, 91*(1), 35–42.

Cegelka, W. J. (1978). Competencies of persons responsible for the classification of mentally retarded individuals. *Exceptional Children, 35*(1), 26–31.

Chadsey-Rusch, J. (1992). Toward defining and measuring social skills in employment settings. *American Journal on Mental Retardation, 96*(4), 405–418.

Chadsey-Rusch, J., Karlan, G. R., Riva, M. T., & Rusch, F. R. (1984). Competitive employment: Teaching conversational skills to adults who are mentally retarded. *American Journal on Mental Retardation, 22*(5), 218–225.

Chen, S., Hsing, A., & Bernard-Opitz, V. (1993). Comparison of personal and computer-assisted instruction for children with autism. *Mental Retardation, 31*(6), 368–376.

Cheney, D., & Foss, G. (1984). An examination of the social behavior of mentally retarded workers. *Education and Training of the Mentally Retarded, 20,* 216–221.

Cherkes, M. G. (1975). Effect of chronological age and mental age on the understanding of rules of logic. *Education and Training in Mental Retardation, 88*(2), 208–216.

Cheseldine, S. E., & Jeffree, D. M. (1982). Mentally handicapped adolescents: A survey of abilities. *Special Education: Forward Trends, 9*(1), 19–23.

Chiappone, A., & Libby, B. (1972). Visual problems of the educable mentally retarded. *Education and Training of the Mentally Retarded, 7*(4), 173–175.

Childress v. Madison County, 777 S.W.2d 1 (Tenn. App. 1989).

Childs, R. E. (1983). Teaching rehearsal strategies for spelling to mentally retarded children. *Education and Training of the Mentally Retarded, 18*(4), 318–320.

Clark, E. M., & Farley, J. W. (1990). Sex education for young children with special needs. *Preventing School Failure, 34*(2), 21–22.

Clark, G. M. (1994). Is a functional curriculum approach compatible with an inclusive education model? *Teaching Exceptional Children, 26*(2), 36–39.

Clark, G. M., & Kolstoe, O. P. (1990). *Career development and transition education for adolescents with disabilities.* Boston: Allyn & Bacon.

Clausen, J. A. (1972). The continuing problem of defining mental retardation. *Journal of Special Education, 6,* 97–106.

Cobb, B., & Hasazi, S. B. (1987). School-age transition services: Options for adolescents with mild handicaps. *Career Development for Exceptional Individuals, 10*(1), 15–23.

Cobb, H. B., Elliott, R. N., Powers, A. R., & Voltz, D. (1989). Generic versus categorical special education teacher preparation. *Teacher Education and Special Education, 12*(1–2), 19–26.

Cole, P. G., & Gardner, J. (1988). Effects of goal-setting on the discrimination learning of children who are retarded and children who are nonretarded. *Education and Training in Mental Retardation, 23*(3), 192–201.

Collins v. School Board of Broward County, 471 So.2d 560 (Fla., App. 4th Dist., 1985).

Collins, B. C., Schuster, J., & Nelson, C. M. (1992). Teaching a generalized response to the lures of strangers to adults with severe handicaps. *Exceptionality: A Research Journal, 3*(2), 67–80.

Collins, M. D., & Cheek, E. H. (1984). Quelling the myths about diagnostic-prescriptive reading instruction. *Momentum, 15*(4), 10–13.

Colozzi, G., & Pollow, R. (1984). Teaching independent walking skills to mentally retarded children in a public school. *Education and Training in Mental Retardation, 19*(2), 97–101.

Conners, F. A. (1990). Aptitude by treatment interactions in computer-assisted word learning by mentally retarded students. *American Journal on Mental Retardation, 94*(4), 387–397.

Connolly, A. J. (1988). *The Key Math Test—Revised.* Circle Pines, MN: American Guidance Service.

Cook, A. M. (1995). *Assistive technologies: Principles and practice.* St. Louis: C. V. Mosby.

Cooley, C. H. (1962). *Social organization: A study of the larger mind.* New York: Schocken Books.

Cooley, E. A., Singer, G. H., & Irvin, L. K. (1989). Volunteers as part of family support services for families of developmentally disabled members. *Education and Training in Mental Retardation, 24*(3), 207–218.

Coon, M. E., Vogelsburg, T., & Williams, W. (1981). Effects of classroom public transportation instruction on generalization to the natural environment. *Journal of the Association for the Severely Handicapped (JASH), 6*(2), 46–53.

Corbett, J. (1994). Special language and political correctness. *British Journal of Special Education, 21*(1), 17–19.

Costenbader, V., & Reading-Brown, M. (1995). Isolation timeout with students with emotional disturbance. *Exceptional Children, 61*(4), 353–363.

Coulter, D. L. (1993). Epilepsy and mental retardation: An overview. *American Journal on Mental Retardation, 98,* 1–11.

Cowen, P. A. (1938). Special class vs. grade groups for subnormal pupils. *School and Society, 48,* 27–28.

Craft, D. H. (Ed.). (1994). Inclusion: Physical education for all. *Journal of Physical Education, Recreation and Dance, 65*(1), 23–55.

Craig, D. E., & Boyd, W. E. (1990). Characteristics of employers of handicapped individuals. *American Journal on Mental Retardation, 95*(1), 40–43.

Crandell, C. C., & Roeser, R. J. (1993). Incidence of excessive/impacted cerumen in individuals with mental retardation: A longitudinal investigation. *American Journal on Mental Retardation, 97*(5), 568–574.

Crist, K., Walls, R., & Haught, P. (1984). Degrees of specificity in task analysis. *American Journal on Mental Retardation, 89*(1), 67–74.

Croce, R. V. (1990). Effects of exercise and diet on body composition and cardiovascular fitness in adults with severe mental retardation. *Education and Training in Mental Retardation, 25*(2), 176–187.

Cronis, T. G., Smith, G. J., Garnett, J., & Forgnone, C. (1986). Mild mental retardation: Implications for an ecological curriculum. *Journal of Research and Development in Education, 19*(3), 72–76.

Crosby, K. G. (1972). Attention and distractibility in mentally retarded and intellectually average children. *Education and Training in Mental Retardation, 77*(1), 46–53.

Cuellar, A., & Cuellar, M. (1991). Winners' and losers' circles: Conceptions of social and school-based factors affecting student achievement. *Journal of Educational Issues of Language Minority Students, 9,* 115–136.

Cummins, J. P., & Das, J. P. (1980). Cognitive processing, academic achievement, and WISC-R performance in EMR children. *Journal of Consulting and Clinical Psychology, 48*(6), 777–779.

Cunningham, S. (1988). Performance comparisons of learning disabled, nonhandicapped, and educable mentally retarded students on selected industrial arts tasks. *Journal of Industrial Teacher Education, 25*(3), 49–55.

Cuvo, A. J., Davis, P., & Gluck, M. S. (1991). Cumulative and interspersal task sequencing in self-paced training for persons with mild handicaps. *Mental Retardation, 29*(6), 335–342.

Cuvo, A. J., Jacobi, L., & Sipko, R. (1980). Teaching laundry skills to mentally retarded students. *Education and Training of the Mentally Retarded, 16*(1), 54–64.

Cuvo, A. J., & Klatt, K. P. (1992). Effects of community-based, videotape, and flash card instruction of community-referenced sight words on students with mental retardation. *Journal of Applied Behavior Analysis, 25*(2), 499–512.

Cuvo, A. J., & Riva, M. T. (1980). Generalization and transfer between comprehension and production: A comparison of retarded and nonretarded persons. *Journal of Applied Behavior Analysis, 13*(2), 315–331.

Dalrymple, N. J., & Angrist, M. H. (1988). Toilet training a sixteen-year-old with autism in a natural setting. *British Journal of Mental Subnormality, 34*(6–7), 117–130.

D'Amato, E., & Yoshida, R. K. (1991). Parental needs: An educational life cycle perspective. *Journal of Early Intervention, 15*(3), 246–254.

Dattilo, J., & Rusch, F. R. (1985). Effects of choice on leisure participation for persons with severe handicaps. *Journal of the Association for Persons with Severe Handicaps (JASH), 10*(4), 194–199.

Dattilo, J., & St. Peter, S. (1991). A model for including leisure education in transition services for young adults with mental retardation. *Education and Training in Mental Retardation, 26*(4), 420–432.

Dattilo, J., & Schleien, S. J. (1994). Understanding leisure services for individuals with mental retardation. *Mental Retardation, 32*(1), 53–59.

Davidson, P. W., Cain, N. N., Sloane-Reeves, J. E., Speybroech, A. V., Segal, J., Gutkin, J., Quijano, L. E., Kramer, B. M., Porter, B., Shohan, I., & Goldstein, E. (1994). Characteristics of community-based individuals with mental retardation and aggressive behavioral disorders. *American Journal on Mental Retardation, 98*(6), 704–716.

Davies, R. R., & Rogers, E. S. (1985). Social skills training with persons who are mentally retarded. *Mental Retardation, 23*(4), 186–196.

Dean, A. V., Salend, S. J., & Taylor, L. (1993). Multicultural education: A challenge for special educators. *Teaching Exceptional Children, 26*(1), 40–43.

DeHaas-Warner, S. (1994). The role of child care professionals in placement and programming decisions for preschoolers with special needs in community-based settings. *Young Children, 49*(5), 76–78.

Deneau, G. (1985). Another viewpoint on estimating expected grade achievement. *Directive Teacher, 7*(1), 4–7.

DeVellis, R. F., & McCauley, C. (1979). Perception of contingency and mental retardation. *Journal of Autism and Developmental Disorders, 9*(3), 261–270.

Dever, R. B. (1990). Defining mental retardation from an instructional perspective. *Mental Retardation, 28*(3), 147–153.

Diamond, K. E. (1994). Parents who have a child with a disability. *Childhood Education, 70*(3), 168–170.

Diaz, N. D., McLaughlin, T. F., & Williams, R. L. (1990). The effects of practicing words in sentences on generalization of spelling to written work with mildly mentally handicapped students. *Psychology in the Schools, 27*(4), 347–353.

Diorio, M. S., & Konarski, E. A., Jr. (1984). Evaluation of a method for teaching dressing skills to profoundly mentally retarded persons. *Education and Training in Mental Retardation, 89*(3), 307–309.

Distefano, E. A., & Brunt, D. (1982). Mentally retarded and normal children's performance on gross motor reaction- and movement-time tasks with varying degrees of uncertainty of movement. *Perceptual and Motor Skills, 55*(3), 1235–1238.

Dixon, J. W., & Saudargas, R. A. (1980). Toilet training, cueing, praise, and self-cleaning in the treatment of classroom encopresis: A case study. *Journal of School Psychology, 18*(2), 135–140.

Doherty, J. E., Karlan, G., & Lloyd, L. (1982). *Establishing the transparency of two gestural systems by mentally retarded adults.* Paper presented at the Annual Meeting of the American Speech-Language-Hearing Association, Toronto.

Doll, E. (1941). Definition of mental deficiency. *Training School Bulletin, 37*, 163–164.

Doll, E. (1946). Practical implications of endogenous-exogenous classification of mental defectives. *Education and Training in Mental Retardation, 50,* 503.

Doll, E. (1967). *Preschool Attainment Record.* Circle Pines, MN: American Guidance Service.

Donnellan, A. M., & LaVigna, G. W. (1986). Nonaversive control of socially stigmatizing behaviors. *Pointer, 30*(4), 25–31.

Doremus, W. A. (1992). Developmental aquatics: Assessment and instructional programming. *Teaching Exceptional Children, 24*(4), 6–10.

Downing, J. (1987). Conversational skills training: Teaching adolescents with mental retardation to be verbally assertive. *American Journal on Mental Retardation, 25*(4), 147–155.

Doxey, C., & Wright, C. (1990). An exploratory study of children's music ability. *Early Childhood Research Quarterly, 5*(3), 425–440.

Drash, P. W., & Raver, S. A. (1987). Total habilitation: A concept whose time has come—Reactions to four responses. *Mental Retardation, 25*(2), 87–89.

Drew, C. J., Logan, D. R., & Hardman, M. L. (1992). *Mental retardation: A life cycle approach* (5th ed.). Englewood Cliffs, NJ: Merrill/Prentice Hall.

Drydyk, J., Mendeville, B., & Bender, L. (1980). Foster parenting a retarded child. *Children Today, 9*(4), 10, 24–25.

Dube, W. V., McDonald, S. J., McIlvane, W. J., & Mackay, H. A. (1991). Constructed-response matching to sample and spelling instruction. *Journal of Applied Behavior Analysis, 24*(2), 305–317.

Dubow, E. F., & Luster, T. (1990). Adjustment of children born to teenage mothers: The contribution of risk and protective factors. *Journal of Marriage and the Family, 52*(2), 393–404.

Dudley, J. R. (1987). Speaking for themselves: People who are labeled as mentally retarded. *Social Work, 32*(1), 80–82.

Dudley, J. R. (1988). Discovering the community living arrangements-neighborhood equation. *Mental Retardation, 26*(1), 25–32.

Dudley, J. R. (1991). Increasing our understanding of divorced fathers who have infrequent contact with their children. *Family Relations, 40*(3), 279–285.

Dudley, J. R., & Schatz, M. S. (1985). The missing link in evaluating sheltered workshop programs: The clients' input. *Mental Retardation, 23*(5), 235–240.

Duker, P. C., & Van Lent, C. (1991). Inducing variability in communicative gestures used by severely retarded individuals. *Journal of Applied Behavior Analysis, 24*(2), 379–386.

Dulaney, C. L., & Ellis, N. R. (1994). Automatized responding and cognitive inertia in individuals with mental retardation. *American Journal on Mental Retardation, 99*(1), 8–18.

Duncan, D., & Canty-Lemke, J. (1986). Learning appropriate social and sexual behavior: The role of society. *Exceptional Parent, 16*(3), 24–26.

Dunham, J. K. (1989). The transparency of manual signs in a linguistic and an environmental nonlinguistic context. *Augmentative and Alternative Communication, 5*, 214–225.

Dunklee, N. R. (1989). Toilet training Carl. *Exceptional Parent, 19*(5), 36–40.

Dunn, L. M. (1963). *Exceptional children in the schools.* New York: Holt, Rinehart & Winston.

Dunn, L. M., & Capobianco, R. J. (1956). *Studies of reading and arithmetic in mentally retarded boys.* Lafayette, IN: Purdue University, Society for Research in Child Development.

Dunn, L. M., & Dunn, L. M. (1981). *The Peabody Picture Vocabulary Test—Revised.* Circle Pines, MN: American Guidance Service.

Dunn, L. M., & Markwardt, F. C. (1970). *The Peabody Individual Achievement Test.* Circle Pines, MN: American Guidance Service.

Dunne, R. G., Asher, K. N., & Rivara, F. P. (1993). Injuries in young people with developmental disabilities: Comparative investigation from the 1988 National Health Interview Survey. *Mental Retardation, 31*(2), 83–88.

Durand, V. M., & Carr, E. G. (1992). An analysis of maintenance following functional communication training. *Journal of Applied Behavior Analysis, 25*(4), 777–794.

Dyson, L., & Fewell, R. R. (1986). Stress and adaptation in parents of young handicapped and nonhandicapped children: A comparative study. *Journal of the Division for Early Childhood, 10*(1), 25–35.

Eastwood, E. A., & Fisher, G. A. (1988). Skills acquisition among matched samples of institutionalized and community-based persons with mental retardation. *American Journal on Mental Retardation, 93*(1), 75–83.

Eden-Piercy, G. V. S., Blacher, J. B., & Eyman, R. K. (1986). Exploring parents' reactions to their young child with severe handicaps. *Mental Retardation, 24*(5), 285–291.

Edgar, E. (1987). Secondary programs in special education: Are many of them justifiable? *Exceptional Children, 53*(6), 555–561.

Edgar, E. (1988). Employment as an outcome for mildly handicapped students: Current status and future directions. *Focus on Exceptional Children, 2*(1), 1–8.

Edgar, E. (1992). Secondary options for students with mild intellectual disabilities: Facing the issue of tracking. *Education and Training in Mental Retardation, 27*(2), 101–111.

Edgerton, R. B. (1967). *The cloak of competence: Stigma in the lives of mentally retarded.* Berkeley: University of California Press.

Edgerton, R. B. (1986). Alcohol and drug use by mentally retarded adults. *Education and Training in Mental Retardation, 90*(6), 602–609.

Edgerton, R. B., Bollinger, M., & Herr, B. (1984). The cloak of competence: After two decades. *Education and Training in Mental Retardation, 88*(4), 345–351.

Edmark Corporation. (1993). *Edmark Reading Program* (Levels 1 and 2). Bellevue, WA: Author.

Ehlers, W. H., Krishef, C. H., & Prothero, J. C. (1977). *An introduction to mental retardation: A programmed text* (2nd ed.). Columbus, OH: Merrill.

Eichinger, J., & Woltman, S. (1993). Integration strategies for learners with severe multiple disabilities. *Teaching Exceptional Children, 26*(1), 18–21.

Ekstrom, R., Goertz, M., Pollack, J., & Rock, D. (1986). Who drops out of high school and why? Findings from a national study. *Teachers College Record, 87*(3), 356–373.

Ekwall, E. E. (1970). *Locating and correcting reading difficulties.* Englewood Cliffs, NJ: Merrill/Prentice Hall.

Ekwall, E. E. (1989). *Locating and correcting reading difficulties* (5th ed.). Englewood Cliffs, NJ: Merrill/Prentice Hall.

Elksnin, N., & Elksnin, L. K. (1991). Facilitating the vocational success of students with mild handicaps: The need for job-related social skills training. *Journal for Vocational Special Needs Education, 13*(2), 5–11.

Ellis, A. K., Mackey, J. A., & Glenn, A. D. (1988). *The school curriculum.* Boston: Allyn & Bacon.

Ellis, D. N., Cress, P. J., & Spellman, C. R. (1992). Using timers and lap counters to promote self-management of independent exercise in adolescents with mental retardation. *Education and Training in Mental Retardation, 27*(1), 51–59.

Ellis, N. R., & Allison, P. (1988). Memory for frequency of occurrence in retarded and nonretarded persons. *Intelligence, 12*(1), 61–75.

Ellis, N. R., Deacon, J. R., Harris, L. A., Poor, A., Angers, D., Diorio, M. S., Watkins, R. S., Boyd, B. D., & Cavalier, A. R. (1982). Learning, memory, and transfer in profoundly, severely, and moderately mentally retarded persons. *Education and Training in Mental Retardation, 87*(2), 186–196.

Ellis, N. R., & Dulaney, C. L. (1991). Further evidence for cognitive inertia of persons with mental retardation. *American Journal on Mental Retardation, 95*(6), 613–621.

Elovitz, G. P., & Salvia, J. (1982). Attractiveness as a biasing factor in the judgments of school psychologists. *Journal of School Psychology, 20*(4), 339–345.

Elrod, G. F., & Sorgenfrei, T. B. (1988). Toward an appropriate assessment model for adolescents who are mildly handicapped: Let's not forget transition. *Career Development for Exceptional Individuals, 11*(2), 92–98.

Engelmann, S. (1967). *The Basic Concept Inventory* (teacher's manual, pupil's test, and scoring booklet). Chicago: Follett.

Engelmann, S., & Bruner, E. (1988). *Reading mastery I (resource kit): Distar reading.* Chicago: Science Research Associates.

Epstein, M. H., Polloway, E. A., Patton, J. R., & Foley, R. (1989). Mild retardation: Student characteristics and services. *Education and Training in Mental Retardation, 24*(1), 7–16.

Erickson, M., & Upshur, C. C. (1989). Caretaking burden and social support: Comparison of mothers of infants with and without disabilities. *American Journal on Mental Retardation, 94*(3), 250–258.

Evans, D. W., Hodapp, R. M., & Zigler, E. (1995). Mental and chronological age as predictors of age-appropriate leisure activity in children with mental retardation. *Mental Retardation, 33*(2), 120–127.

Everington, C., & Luckasson, R. (1989). Addressing the needs of the criminal defendant with mental retardation: The special educator as a resource to the criminal justice system. *Education and Training in Mental Retardation, 24*(3), 193–200.

Everington, C., & Stevenson, T. (1994). A giving experience: Using community service to promote community living skills and integration for individuals with severe disabilities. *Teaching Exceptional Children, 26*(3), 56–59.

Eyman, R. K., Call, T. L., & White, J. F. (1991). Life expectancy of persons with Down syndrome. *American Journal on Mental Retardation, 95*(6), 603–612.

Ezell, H. K., & Goldstein, H. (1991). Comparison of idiom comprehension of normal children and children with mental retardation. *Journal of Speech and Hearing Research, 34*(4), 812–819.

Farber, B. (1959). Effects of a severely mentally retarded child on family integration [Special issue]. *Monographs of the Society for Research in Child Development, 24*(2).

Farley, J. W. (1986). An analysis of written dialogue of educable mentally retarded writers. *Education and Training of the Mentally Retarded, 21*(3), 181–191.

Featherstone, D. R., Cundick, B., & Jensen, L. C. (1992). Differences in school behavior and achievement between children from intact, reconstituted, and single-parent families. *Adolescence, 27*(105), 1–12.

Fee v. Herndon, 900 F.2d 804 (5th Cir. 1990).

Ferguson, B., & McDonnell, J. (1991). A comparison of serial and concurrent sequencing strategies in teaching generalized grocery item location to students with moderate handicaps. *Education and Training in Mental Retardation, 26*(3), 292–304.

Ferguson, D. L., & Baumgart, D. (1991). Partial participation revisited. *Journal of the Association for Persons with Severe Handicaps (JASH), 16*(4), 218–227.

Ferguson, D. L., & Ferguson, P. M. (1986). The new victors: A progressive policy analysis of work reform for people with very severe handicaps. *Mental Retardation, 24*(6), 331–338.

Fernald, G. M. (1943). *Remedial techniques in basic school subjects.* New York: McGraw-Hill.

Ferraro v. Board of Education, 14 A.D.2d 815, 221 N.Y.S 2d 279 (1961).

Fettgather, R. (1989). "Be an adult!": A hidden curriculum in life skills instruction for retarded students? *Lifelong Learning, 12*(5), 4–5.

Fine, M. (1991). *Framing dropouts: Notes on the politics of an urban public high school.* Albany: State University of New York Press.

Fishman, I. (1987). *Electronic communication aids: Selection and use.* Boston: College-Hill.

Fitzgerald, G. E., Bauder, D. K., & Werner, J. G. (1992). Authoring CAI lessons: Teachers as developers. *Teaching Exceptional Children, 24*(2), 15–21.

Fleming, E. R., & Fleming, D. D. (1982). Social skill training for educable mentally retarded children. *Education and Training of the Mentally Retarded, 17*(1), 44–50.

Flesch, R. (1955). *Why Johnnie can't read—and what you can do about it.* New York: Harper & Row.

Fletcher, D., & Abood, K. (1988). An analysis on the readability of product warning labels: Implications for curriculum development for persons with moderate and severe mental retardation. *Educating and Training in Mental Retardation, 23*(3), 224–227.

Ford, D. Y. (1992). Determinants of underachievement as perceived by gifted, above-average, and average black students. *Roeper Review, 14*(3), 130–136.

Forness, S. R. (1985). Effects of public policy at the state level: California's impact on MR, LD, and ED categories. *Remedial & Special Education, 6*(3), 36–43.

Forness, S. R., & Kavale, K. A. (1993). Strategies to improve basic learning and memory deficits in mental retardation: A meta-analysis of experimental studies. *Education and Training in Mental Retardation, 28*(2), 99–110.

Foss, G., & Peterson, S. (1981). Social-interpersonal skills relevant to job tenure for mentally retarded adults. *Mental Retardation, 19*(3), 103–106.

Fourteenth annual report to Congress on the implementation of the Individuals with Disabilities Education Act. (1992). Washington, DC: U.S. Department of Education.

Fox, L. (1989). Stimulus generalization of skills and persons with profound mental handicaps. *Education and Training in Mental Retardation, 24*(3), 219–229.

Fox, L., & Westling, D. (1986). The prevalence of students who are profoundly mentally handicapped receiving medication in a school district. *Education and Training of the Mentally Retarded, 21,* 205–210.

Fox, R., Switzky, H., Rotatori, A. F., & Vitkus, P. (1982). Successful weight loss techniques with mentally retarded children and youth. *Exceptional Children, 49*(3), 238–244.

Fox, R. A., Hartney, C., Rotatori, A. F., & Kurpiers, E. M. (1985). Incidence of obesity among retarded children. *Education and Training of the Mentally Retarded, 20*(3), 175–181.

Foxx, R. M., & Faw, G. D. (1992). An eight-year follow-up of three social skills training studies. *Mental Retardation, 30*(2), 63–66.

Foxx, R. M., & Foxx, C. L. (1986). A demonstration of a successful parent-conducted remedial reading program. *Journal of Special Education Technology, 7*(3), 47–53.

Foxx, R. M., & Shapiro, S. T. (1978). The timeout ribbon: A nonexclusionary timeout procedure. *Journal of Applied Behavior Analysis, 11*(1), 125–136.

Frandsen, A. N. (1950). The Wechsler-Bellevue Intelligence Scale and high school achievement. *Journal of Applied Psychology, 34,* 406–411.

Frank, A. R. (1983). Formulating long-term goals and short-term objectives for individual education programs. *Education and Training of the Mentally Retarded, 18*(2), 144–147.

Frank, A. R., & Sitlington, P. L. (1993). Graduates with mental disabilities: The story three years later. *Education and Training in Mental Retardation, 28*(1), 30–37.

Frankenberger, W., & Fronzaglio, K. (1991). States' definitions and procedures for identifying children with mental retardation: Comparison over nine years. *Mental Retardation, 29*(6), 315–321.

Frazeur, H. A., & Hoakley, Z. P. (1947). Significance of psychological test results of exogenous and endogenous children. *Education and Training in Mental Retardation, 51*(3), 384–388.

Freagon, S., & Rotatori, A. F. (1982). Comparing natural and artificial environments in training self-care skills to group home residents. *Journal of the Association for the Severely Handicapped (JASH), 7*(3), 73–86.

Frederick-Dugan, A., Test, D. W., & Varn, L. (1991). Acquisition and generalization of purchasing skills using a calculator by students who are mentally retarded. *Education and Training in Mental Retardation, 26*(4), 381–387.

Fredericks, H. D., Baldwin, V. L., Hanson, W., & Fontana, P. (1972). Structure your volunteers. *Education and Training of the Mentally Retarded, 7*(1), 26–31.

Friend, M., & Cook, L. (1993). Inclusion. *Instructor, 103*(4), 52–56.

Friman, P. C. (1990). Nonaversive treatment of high-rate disruption: Child and provider effects. *Exceptional Children, 57*(1), 64–69.

Frith, G. H., & Mitchell, J. W. (1983). Art education for mildly retarded students: A significant component of the special education curriculum. *Education and Training of the Mentally Retarded, 18*(2), 138–141.

Frost, J. (1985). *Exceptional art/exceptional children.* Omaha, NE: Special Literature Press.

Fuchs, D., & Fuchs, L. S. (1994). Inclusive schools movement and the radicalization of special education reform. *Exceptional Children, 60*(4), 294–309.

Fuchs, D., Fuchs, L. S., Dailey, A. M., & Power, M. H. (1985). The effect of examiners' personal familiarity and professional experience on handicapped children's test performance. *Journal of Educational Research, 78*(3), 141–146.

Fuchs, L. S., Fuchs, D., & Hamlett, C. L. (1992). Computer applications to facilitate curriculum-based measurement. *Teaching Exceptional Children, 24*(4), 58–60.

Fujiki, M., & Brinton, B. (1993). Comprehension monitoring skills of adults with mental retardation. *Research in Developmental Disabilities, 14*(5), 409–421.

Gable, R. A., Evans, S. S., & Evans, W. H. (1993). It's not over until you examine your answer. *Teaching Exceptional Children, 25*(2), 61–62.

Gallivan-Fenlon, A. (1994). Integrated transdisciplinary teams. *Teaching Exceptional Children, 26*(3), 16–20.

Galston, W. A. (1993). Causes of declining well-being among U.S. children. *Aspen Institute Quarterly, 5*(1), 52–77.

Gandell, T. S., & Laufer, D. (1993). Developing a telecommunications curriculum for students with physical disabilities. *Teaching Exceptional Children, 25*(2), 26–28.

Garcia, S. B., & Malkin, D. H. (1993). Toward defining programs and services for culturally and linguistically diverse learners in special education. *Teaching Exceptional Children, 26*(1), 52–58.

Gardner, J. E., & Bates, P. (1991). Attitudes and attributions on use of microcomputers in school by students who are mentally handicapped. *Education and Training in Mental Retardation, 26*(1), 98–107.

Gardner, J. E., Taber-Brown, F. M., & Wissick, C. A. (1992). Selecting age-appropriate software for adolescents and adults with developmental disabilities. *Teaching Exceptional Children, 24*(3), 60–63.

Gardner, J. F. (1988). *Toward supported employment: A process guide for planned change.* Baltimore: Brookes.

Gargiulio, R. M., & Sulick, J. A. (1978). Moral judgment in retarded and nonretarded school-age children. *Journal of Psychology, 99,* 23–26.

Gast, D. L., Doyle, P. M., Wolery, M., Ault, M. J., & Baklatz, J. L. (1991). Acquisition of incidental information during small group instruction. *Education and Treatment of Children, 14*(1), 1–18.

Gast, D. L., Doyle, P. M., Wolery, M., Ault, M. J., & Farmer, J. A. (1991). Assessing the acquisition of incidental information by secondary-age students with mental retardation: Comparison of response-prompting strategies. *American Journal on Mental Retardation, 96*(1), 63–80.

Gates, G. E., & Edwards, R. P. (1989). Acquisition of American Sign Language versus Amerind signs in a mentally handicapped sample. *Journal of Communication Disorders, 22*(6), 423–435.

Gaule, K., Nietupski, J., & Certo, N. (1985). Teaching supermarket shopping skills using an adaptive shopping list. *Education and Training of the Mentally Retarded, 20*(1), 53–59.

Gaventa, B. (1990). Respite care: An opportunity for the religious community. *Exceptional Parent, 20*(4), 22–24, 26.

Gerber, B. L. (1994). Beyond drill & practice: Using the computer for creative decision making. *Preventing School Failure, 38*(2), 25–30.

Gersie, A., & King, N. (1990). *Story making in education and therapy.* Stockholm, Sweden: Stockholm Institute of Education Press.

Giek, K. A. (1992). Monitoring student progress through efficient record keeping. *Teaching Exceptional Children, 24*(3), 22–26.

Gines, D. J., Schweitzer, J. R., Queen-Autry, T., & Carthon, P. (1990). Use of color-coded food photographs for meal planning by adults with mental retardation. *Mental Retardation, 28*(3), 189–190.

Glasser, W. (1965). *Reality therapy.* New York: Harper & Row.

Glasser, W. (1969). *Schools without failure.* New York: Harper & Row.

Glasser, W. (1984). *Control theory.* New York: Harper & Row.

Glasser, W. (1986). *Control theory in the classroom.* New York: Harper & Row.

Glidden, L. M., Valliere, V. N., & Herbert, S. L. (1988). Adopted children with mental retardation: Positive family impact. *Mental Retardation, 26*(3), 119–125.

Glueck, S., & Glueck, E. T. (1934). *One thousand juvenile delinquents.* Cambridge, MA: Harvard University Press.

Goldberg, R. T., McClean, M. M., LaVigne, R., & Fratolillo, J. (1990). Transition of persons with developmental disability from extended sheltered employment to competitive employment. *Mental Retardation, 28*(5), 299–304.

Goldstein, H., Moss, J. W., & Jordan, L. J. (1965). *The efficacy of special class training on the development of mentally retarded children* (Cooperative

Research Project No. 619). Washington, DC: U.S. Office of Education.

Goldstein, H., & Mousetis, L. (1989). Generalized language learning by children with severe mental retardation: Effects of peers' expressive modeling. *Journal of Applied Behavior Analysis, 22*(3), 245–259.

Gordon, E. K. (1910). *The Gordon readers teachers manual.* Boston: D. C. Heath.

Gottardo, A., & Rubin, H. (1991). Language analysis skills of children with mental retardation. *Mental Retardation, 29*(5), 269–274.

Gottlieb, J. (1981). Mainstreaming: Fulfilling the promise? *Education and Training in Mental Retardation, 86*(2), 115–126.

Gottlieb, J., Gampel, D. H., & Budoff, M. (1975). Classroom behavior of retarded children before and after integration into regular classes. *Journal of Special Education, 9*(3), 308–315.

Gottwald, S. R., & Thurman, S. K. (1994). The effects of prenatal cocaine exposure on mother-infant interaction and infant arousal in the newborn period. *Topics in Early Childhood Special Education, 14*(2), 217–231.

Graff, J. C., & Ault, M. M. (1993). Guidelines for working with students having special health care needs. *Journal of School Health, 63*(8), 335–338.

Green, K. (1994). Careers in special education. *Occupational Outlook Quarterly, 37*(4), 2–17.

Greenspan, S., & Granfield, J. M. (1992). Reconsidering the construct of mental retardation: Implications of a model of social competence. *American Journal on Mental Retardation, 96*(4), 442–453.

Greenspan, S., & Shultz, B. (1981). Why mentally retarded adults lose their jobs: Social competence as a factor in work adjustment. *Applied Research in Mental Retardation, 2,* 23–38.

Greenwood, C. R., & Rieth, H. J. (1994). Current dimensions of technology-based assessment in special education. *Exceptional Children, 61*(2), 105–113.

Greeson, L. E. (1986). Modeling and mental imagery use by multiply handicapped and learning disabled preschool children. *Psychology in the Schools, 23*(1), 82–87.

Greeson, L. E., & Vane, R. J. (1986). Imagery-based elaboration as an index of EMR children's creativity and incidental associative learning. *Education and Training of the Mentally Retarded, 21*(3), 174–180.

Gresham, F. M. (1982). Misguided mainstreaming: The case for social skills training with handicapped children. *Exceptional Children, 48*(5), 422–433.

Grieve, R. (1982). Mentally retarded children's abilities in the process of comparison. *American Journal on Mental Retardation, 87*(2), 180–185.

Griffen, A. K., Wolery, M., & Schuster, J. W. (1992). Triadic instruction of chained food preparation responses: Acquisition and observational learning. *Journal of Applied Behavior Analysis, 25*(1), 193–204.

Griffith, P. L., & Robinson, J. H. (1980). Influence of iconicity and phonological similarity on sign learning by mentally retarded children. *American Journal on Mental Deficiency, 85*(3), 291–298.

Groff, M. G., & Linden, K. W. (1982). The WISC-R factor score profiles of cultural-familial mentally retarded and nonretarded youth. *Education and Training in Mental Retardation, 87*(2), 147–152.

Gronlund, N. E. (1990). *Measurement and evaluation in teaching* (6th ed.). New York: Macmillan.

Grossen, B., & Carnine, D. (1993). Phonics instruction: Comparing research and practice. *Teaching Exceptional Children, 25*(2), 22–25.

Grossman, H. (1991). Multicultural classroom management. *Contemporary Education, 52*(3), 161–166.

Grossman, H. J. (Ed.). (1977). *Classification in mental retardation.* Washington, DC: American Association on Mental Deficiency.

Grossman, H. J. (Ed.). (1983). *Classification in mental retardation.* Washington, DC: American Association on Mental Deficiency.

Gupta, S. (1990). The influence of early protein energy malnutrition on subsequent behavior and intellectual performance. *Canadian Home Economics Journal, 40*(1), 16–20.

Haas, D. (1993). Inclusion is happening in the classroom. *Children Today, 22*(3), 34–35.

Hacienda La Puente School District of Los Angeles v. Honig, 976 F.2d 487 (1992).

Hallahan, D. P., & Kaufman, J. M. (1986). *Exceptional children: Introduction to special education.* Englewood Cliffs, NJ: Prentice-Hall.

Hallahan, D. P., Keller, C. E., & Ball, D. W. (1986). A comparison of prevalence rate variability from state to state for each of the categories of special education. *Remedial and Special Education, 7*(2), 8–14.

Hamel, R. (1992). Getting into the game: New opportunities for athletes with disabilities. *Physician and Sportsmedicine, 20*(11), 121–122, 124, 126–129.

Hamre-Nietupski, S., Krajewski, L., Riehle, R., Sensor, K., Nietupski, J., Moravec, J., McDonald, J., & Cantine-Stull, P. (1992). Enhancing integration during the summer: Combined educational and community recreation options for students with severe disabilities. *Education and Training in Mental Retardation, 27*(1), 68–74.

Hamre-Nietupski, S., Nietupski, J., & Strathe, M. (1992). Functional life skills, academic skills, and friendship development: What do parents of students with moderate/severe/profound disabilities value? *Journal of the Association for Persons with Severe Handicaps (JASH), 17*(1), 53–58.

Hamre-Nietupski, S., & Williams, W. (1977). Implementation of selected sex education and social skills to severely handicapped students. *Education and Training of the Mentally Retarded, 12*(4), 364–372.

Handen, B. L., Feldman, R. S., & Honigman, A. (1987). Comparison of parent and teacher assessments of developmentally delayed children's behavior. *Exceptional Children, 54*(2), 137–144.

Hang, Y. (1981). *The complete book of CHISANBOP: Original finger calculation method.* New York: Van Nostrand Reinhold.

Hanline, M. F. (1993). Inclusion of preschoolers with profound disabilities: An analysis of children's interactions. *Journal of the Association for Persons with Severe Handicaps (JASH), 18*(1), 28–35.

Hanline, M. F., & Fox, L. (1993). Learning within the context of play: Providing typical early childhood experiences for children with severe disabilities. *Journal of the Association for Persons with Severe Handicaps (JASH), 18*(2), 121–129.

Hanrahan, J., Goodman, W., & Rapagna, S. (1990). Preparing mentally retarded students for mainstreaming: Priorities of regular class and special school teachers. *American Journal on Mental Retardation, 94*(5), 470–474.

Haring, K., Farron-Davis, F., Goets, L., Karasoff, P., & Sailor, W. (1992). LRE and the placement of students with severe disabilities. *Journal of the Association for Persons with Severe Handicaps (JASH), 17*(3), 145–153.

Haring, T. G., & Kennedy, C. H. (1990). Contextual control of problem behavior in students with severe disabilities. *Journal of Applied Behavior Analysis, 23*(2), 235–243.

Harper, G. F., Mallette, B., & Moore, J. (1991). Peer-mediated instruction: Teaching spelling to primary school children with mild disabilities. *Journal of Reading, Writing, and Learning Disabilities International, 7*(2), 137–151.

Harry, B. (1992). *Cultural diversity, families, and the special education system: Communication and empowerment.* New York: Teachers College Press.

Harry, B., Torguson, C., Katkavich, J., & Guerrero, M. (1993). Crossing social class and cultural barriers in working with families: Implications for teacher training. *Teaching Exceptional Children, 26*(1), 48–51.

Hartshorne, T. S., & Boomer, L. W. (1993). Privacy of school records: What every special education teacher should know. *Teaching Exceptional Children, 25*(4), 32–35.

Hasazi, S. B. (1985). Facilitating transition from high school: Policies and practices. *American Rehabilitation, 11*(3), 9–11, 16.

Hasazi, S. B., & Clark, G. M. (1988). Vocational preparation for high school students labeled mentally retarded: Employment as a graduation goal. *Mental Retardation, 26*(6), 343–349.

Hasazi, S. B., Gordon, L. R., Roe, C. A., Hull, M., Finck, K., & Salembier, G. (1985). A statewide follow-up on post high school employment and residential status of students labeled "mentally retarded." *Education and Training of the Mentally Retarded, 20*(4), 222–234.

Hasazi, S. B., Johnson, R. E., Hasazi, J. E., Gordon, L. R., & Hull, M. (1989). Employment of youth with and without handicaps following high school: Outcomes and correlates. *Journal of Special Education, 23*(3), 243–255.

Hayes, B. K., & Taplin, J. E. (1993). Development of conceptual knowledge in children with mental retardation. *American Journal on Mental Retardation, 98*(2), 293–303.

Heal, L. W., Copher, J. I., De Stefano, L., & Rusch, F. (1989). A comparison of successful and unsuccessful placements of secondary students with mental handicaps into competitive employment. *Career Development for Exceptional Individuals, 12*(2), 167–177.

Heber, R. F. (1961). *A manual on terminology and classification in mental retardation* (rev. ed.). Washington, DC: American Association on Mental Deficiency.

Hegge, T. G., Kirk, S. A., & Kirk, W. D. (1940). *Remedial reading drills.* Ann Arbor, MI: Wahr.

Hegge, T. G., Kirk, S. A., & Kirk, W. D. (1955). *Remedial reading drills.* Ann Arbor, MI: Wahr.

Hegge, T. G., Kirk, S. A., & Kirk, W. D. (1972). *Remedial reading drills.* Ann Arbor, MI: Wahr.

Heifetz, L. J., & Franklin, D. C. (1982). Nature and sources of the clergy's involvement with mentally retarded persons and their families. *Education and Training in Mental Retardation, 87*(1), 56–63.

Heitman, R. J., & Justen, J. E., III. (1982). Effects of social reinforcement on motor performance of trainable retarded students on speed and persistence tasks. *Perceptual and Motor Skills, 54*(2), 391–394.

Helms, B. J., & Moore, S. C. (1993). Perceptions of aversiveness by supported employment supervisors and job coaches. *Education and Training in Mental Retardation, 28*(3), 212–219.

Hemming, H. (1986). Follow-up of adults with mental retardation transferred from large institutions to new small units. *Mental Retardation, 24*(4), 229–235.

Henderson, W. (1993). Handicapism: A barrier to the successful education of children of all abilities. *Equity and Choice, 2*(9), 59–60.

Herman, S. E., & Thompson, L. (1995). Families' perceptions of their resources for caring for children with developmental disabilities. *Mental Retardation, 33*(2), 73–83.

Herr, S. S. (1984). The Phillip Becker case resolved: A chance for habilitation. *Mental Retardation, 22*(1), 30–35.

Hewes, A., Holt, M., Meranski, S., & Snell, J. (1924). Mental age and school attainment of 1,007 retarded children in Massachusetts. *Journal of Educational Psychology, 15*(5), 207–301.

Hewett, F. (1967). Educational engineering with emotionally disturbed children. *Exceptional Children, 33*(7), 459–470.

Hill, M., & Wehman, P. (1983). Cost-benefit analysis of placing moderately and severely handicapped individuals into competitive employment. *Journal of the Association for Persons with Severe Handicaps (JASH), 8*(1), 30–38.

Hilton, A., & Henderson, C. J. (1993). Parent involvement: A best practice or forgotten practice? *Educa-*

tion and Training in Mental Retardation, 28(3), 199–211.

Hirst, C. C., & Michaelis, E. (1983). *Retarded kids need to play.* New York: Leisure Press.

Hirst, C. C., & Shelley, E. Y. (1989). They too should play. *Teaching Exceptional Children, 21*(4), 26–28.

Hobbs, N., Perrin, J. M., Ireys, H. T., Moynihan, L. C., & Shayne, M. W. (1984). Chronically ill children in America. *Rehabilitation Literature, 45,* 206–213.

Hobson, R. P., Ouston, J., & Lee, A. (1989). Recognition of emotion by mentally retarded adolescents and young adults. *American Journal on Mental Retardation, 93*(4), 434–443.

Hodapp, R. M., & Zigler, E. (1986). Reply to Barnett's comments on the definition and classification of mental retardation. *Education and Training in Mental Retardation, 91*(2), 117–119.

Hodapp, R. M., & Zigler, E. (1993). Comparison of families of children with mental retardation and families of children without mental retardation. *Mental Retardation, 31*(2), 75–77.

Hodgkinson, H. L. (1989). *The same client: The demographics of education and service delivery systems.* Washington, DC: Institute for Educational Leadership.

Hogg, J. (1983). Sensory and social reinforcement of head-turning in a profoundly retarded multiply handicapped child. *British Journal of Clinical Psychology, 22*(1), 33–40.

Holland, B. V. (1987). Fundamental motor skills of non-handicapped and educable mentally impaired students. *Education and Training of the Mentally Retarded, 22*(3), 192–204.

Honig v. Doe, 108 S.Ct. 592 (1988).

Honig, A. S. (1993). Toilet learning. *Day Care & Early Education, 21*(1), 6–9.

Hoogeveen, F. R., Smeets, P. M., & Van der Houven, J. E. (1987). Establishing letter-sound correspondences in children classified as trainable mentally retarded. *Education and Training in Mental Retardation, 22*(2), 77–84.

Horner, R., Williams, J., & Knobbe, C. (1985). The effect of "opportunity to perform" on the maintenance of skills learned by high school students with severe handicaps: Brief report. *Journal of the Association for Persons with Severe Handicaps (JASH), 10*(3), 172–175.

Horner, R. H., Day, H. M., Sprague, J. R., O'Brien, M., & Heathfield, L. T. (1991). Interspersed requests: A nonaversive procedure for reducing aggression and self-injury during instruction. *Journal of Applied Behavior Analysis, 24*(2), 265–278.

Horner, R. H., Jones, D. N., & Williams, J. A. (1985). A functional approach to teaching generalized street crossing. *Journal of the Association for Persons with Severe Handicaps (JASH), 10*(2), 71–78.

Horner, R. H., Williams, J. A., & Stevely, J. D. (1987). Acquisition of generalized telephone use by students with moderate and severe mental retardation. *Research in Developmental Disabilities, 8*(2), 229–247.

Hornstein, H. (1986). Dichotic listening task performance of mildly mentally retarded and nonretarded individuals. *American Journal on Mental Retardation, 90*(5), 573–578.

Hornstein, H. A., & Mosley, J. L. (1987). Iconic memory deficit of mildly mentally retarded individuals. *Education and Training in Mental Retardation, 91*(4), 415–421.

Horton, S. (1983). Delivering industrial arts instruction to mildly handicapped learners. *Career Development for Exceptional Individuals, 6*(2), 85–92.

Hourcade, J. (1988). Effectiveness of gestural and physical guidance prompts as a function of type of task. *Education and Training in Mental Retardation, 23*(1), 38–42.

Houser, R., & Seligman, M. (1991). A comparison of stress and coping by fathers of adolescents with mental retardation and fathers of adolescents without mental retardation. *Research in Developmental Disabilities, 12*(3), 251–260.

Howell, S. C., & Barnhart, R. S. (1992). Teaching word problem solving at the primary level. *Teaching Exceptional Children, 24*(2), 44–46.

Hoy, W. K., & Miskel, C. G. (1991). *Educational administration: Theory, research, and practice* (4th ed.). New York: McGraw-Hill.

Huberty, T. J., Koller, J. R., & Ten Brink, T. D. (1980). Adaptive behavior in the definition of mental retardation. *Exceptional Children, 46*(4), 256–261.

Hudson, M. (1960). Exploration of classroom procedures for teaching trainable retarded children. *Exceptional Children, 27,* 224–229.

Huefner, D. S. (1994). The mainstreaming cases: Tensions and trends for school administrators. *Educational Administration Quarterly, 30*(1), 27–55.

Huguenin, N. H. (1993). Reducing chronic noncompliance in an individual with severe mental retardation to facilitate community integration. *Mental Retardation, 31*(5), 332–339.

Hutt, M. L., & Gibby, R. G. (1979). *The mentally retarded child: Development, training, and education* (4th ed.). Boston: Allyn & Bacon.

Hyde, D. (1990). School-parent collaboration results in academic achievement. *NASSP Bulletin, 76*(543), 39–42.

Iacono, T. A., & Miller, J. F. (1989). Can microcomputers be used to teach communication skills to students with mental retadation? *Education and Training in Mental Retardation, 24*(1), 32–44.

Idstein, P. (1993). Swimming against the mainstream. *Phi Delta Kappan, 75*(4), 336–340.

Inge, K. J., Banks, P. D., Wehman, P., Hill, J. W., & Shafer, M. S. (1988). Quality of life for individuals who are labeled mentally retarded: Evaluating competitive employment versus sheltered workshop employment. *Education and Training in Mental Retardation, 23*(2), 97–104.

Intagliata, J. C., Willer, B. S., & Cooley, F. B. (1979). Cost comparison of institutional and community based alternatives for mentally retarded persons. *Mental Retardation, 17*(3), 154–155.

Irvine, A. B., Erickson, A. M., Singer, G. H. S., & Stahlberg, D. (1992). A coordinated program to transfer self-management skills from school to home. *Education and Training in Mental Retardation, 27*(3), 241–254.

Irwin, K. C. (1991). Teaching children with Down syndrome to add by counting-on. *Education and Treatment of Children, 14*(2), 128–141.

Isbell, R. A., & Barber, W. H. (1993). Fetal alcohol syndrome and alcohol-related birth defects: Implications and assurance for quality of life. *British Columbia Journal of Special Education, 17*(3), 261–274.

Israely, Y. (1985). The moral development of mentally retarded children: Review of the literature. *Journal of Moral Education, 14*(1), 33–42.

Jambor, T., & Gargiulio, R. (1987). The playground: A social entity for mainstreaming. *Journal of Physical Education, Recreation & Dance, 58*(8), 18–23.

Jastak, J. F., & Jastak, S. R. (1965). *Wide Range Achievement Test.* Wilmington, DE: Guidance Associates.

Jeffree, D. M., & Cheseldine, S. E. (1984). Programmed leisure intervention and the interaction patterns of severely mentally retarded adolescents:

A pilot study. *Education and Training in Mental Retardation, 88*(6), 619–624.

Jenkinson, J. C. (1989). Word recognition and the nature of reading difficulty in children with an intellectual disability: A review. *International Journal of Disability, Development and Education, 36*(1), 39–56.

Joekel, R. (1986). Students at risk! *President's Newsletter. Phi Delta Kappa, 5*(1), 1.

Jones, L. A., & Moe, R. (1980). College education for mentally retarded adults. *Mental Retardation, 18*(2), 59–62.

Jordan, T. E. (1976). *The mentally retarded* (4th ed.). Columbus, OH: Merrill.

Joyce, D., & McFadden, L. (1982). Adaptive industrial arts: Meeting the needs of the handicapped. *Education and Training in Mental Retardation, 17*(4), 337–339.

Judd, T. P., & Bilsky, L. H. (1989). Comprehension and memory in the solution of verbal arithmetic problems by mentally retarded and nonretarded individuals. *Journal of Educational Psychology, 81*(4), 541–546.

Kail, R. (1992). General slowing of information processing by persons with mental retardation. *American Journal on Mental Retardation, 97*(3), 333–341.

Kamhi, A. G. (1981). Developmental vs. difference theories of mental retardation: A new look. *Education and Training in Mental Retardation, 86*(1), 1–7.

Kamon, T., & Fujita, T. P. (1994). Visual scanning patterns of adolescents with mental retardation during tracing and copying tasks. *American Journal on Mental Retardation, 98*(6), 766–775.

Kanner, L. (1948). Feeblemindedness: Absolute, relative, and apparent. *Nervous Child, 7*, 365–397.

Karen, R. L., Austin-Smith, S., & Creasy, D. (1985). Teaching telephone-answering skills to mentally retarded adults. *American Journal on Mental Retardation, 89*(6), 595–609.

Karlin, I., & Strazulla, M. (1952). Speech and language problems of mentally deficient children. *Journal of Speech and Hearing Disorders, 17*, 286–294.

Katsiyannis, A. (1991). Extended school year policies: An established necessity. *Remedial and Special Education, 12*(1), 24–28.

Kavale, K. A., & Forness, S. R. (1985). The historical foundation of learning disabilities: A quantitative synthesis assessing the validity of Strauss and Werner's exogenous versus endogenous distinction of mental retardation. *Remedial and Special Education (RASE), 6*(5), 18–24.

Keirn, W. C. (1971). Shopping parents: Patient problems or professional problem? *Mental Retardation, 9*(4), 6–7.

Kelly, E. M. (1949). Educational implications in the public school special class of the endogenous-exogenous classification. *Education and Training in Mental Retardation, 54*(2), 207–211.

Kelly, M. B., & Heffner, H. E. (1988). The role of attention in the elimination of chronic, life-threatening vomiting. *Journal of Mental Deficiency Research, 32*, 425–431.

Kennedy, C. H., & Haring, T. G. (1993). Combining reward and escape DRO to reduce the problem behavior of students with severe disabilities. *Journal of the Association for Persons with Severe Handicaps (JASH), 18*(2), 85–92.

Kennedy, L. (1930). *Studies in the speech of the feebleminded.* Unpublished doctoral dissertation, University of Wisconsin.

Kidd, J. W. (1979). An open letter to the Committee on Terminology and Classification of A.A.M.D. from the Committee on Definition and Terminology of CEC-MR Mental Retardation. *Education and Training of the Mentally Retarded, 14*, 74–76.

Kilpatrick, J. (1987). The medical metaphor. *Focus on Learning Problems in Mathematics, 9*(4), 1–13.

King, B. J. (1993). Self-injury by people with mental retardation: A compulsive behavior hypothesis. *American Journal on Mental Retardation, 98*(1), 93–112.

Kirk, S. A. (1958). *Early education of the mentally retarded: An experimental study.* Urbana: University of Illinois Press.

Kirk, S. A. (1964). Research in education. In H. A. Stevens & R. Heber (Eds.), *Mental retardation: A review of research* (pp. 57–99). Chicago: University of Chicago Press.

Kirk, S. A., & Gallagher, J. J. (1993). *Educating exceptional children* (7th ed.). Boston: Houghton Mifflin.

Kirk, S. A., & Johnson, G. O. (1951). *Educating the retarded child.* Cambridge, MA: Riverside Press.

Kirkham, M. A. (1993). Two-year follow-up of skills training with mothers of children with disabilities. *American Journal on Mental Retardation, 97*(5), 509–520.

Kishi, G., Teelucksingh, B., Zollers, N., Park-Lee, S., & Meyer, L. (1988). Daily decision making in community residences: A social comparison of adults with and without mental retardation. *American Journal on Mental Retardation, 92*(5), 430–435.

Klassen, R. (1994). Research: What does it say about mainstreaming? *Education Canada, 34*(2), 27–35.

Klein, T., Gilman, E., & Zigler, E. (1993). Special Olympics: An evaluation by professionals and parents. *Mental Retardation, 31*(1), 15–23.

Kohl, F. L., & Stettner-Eaton, B. A. (1985). Fourth graders as trainers of cafeteria skills to severely handicapped students. *Education and Training of the Mentally Retarded, 20*(1), 60–68.

Koller, H., Richardson, S., & Katz, M. (1988). Marriage in a young adult mentally retarded population. *Journal of Mental Deficiency Research, 32*(2), 93–102.

Kolstoe, O. P., & Frey, R. M. (1965). *A high school work-study program for mentally subnormal students.* Carbondale: Southern Illinois University Press.

Konig, A., & Schalock, R. L. (1991). Supported employment: Equal opportunities for severely disabled men and women. *International Labour Review, 130*(1), 21–37.

Kopp, C. B., Baker, B. L., & Brown, K. W. (1992). Social skills and their correlates: Preschoolers with developmental delays. *American Journal on Mental Retardation, 96*(4), 357–366.

Koury, M., & Browder, D. M. (1986). The use of delay to teach sight words by peer tutors classified as moderately mentally retarded. *Education and Training in Mental Retardation, 21*(4), 252–258.

Kozleski, E. B., & Jackson, L. (1993). Taylor's story: Full inclusion in her neighborhood elementary school. *Exceptionality: A Research Journal, 4*(3), 153–175.

Krauss, M. W. (1993). Child-related and parenting stress: Similarities and differences between mothers and fathers of children with disabilities. *American Journal on Mental Retardation, 97*(4), 393–404.

Krauss, M. W., Seltzer, M. M., & Goodman, S. J. (1992). Social support networks of adults with mental retardation who live at home. *American Journal on Mental Retardation, 96*(4), 432–441.

Kregel, J., Wehman, P., Seyfarth, J., & Marshall, K. (1986). Community integration of young adults with mental retardation: Transition from school to adulthood. *Education and Training of the Mentally Retarded, 21*(1), 35–42.

Kreitler, S., & Kreitler, H. (1990). Cognitive antecedents of imitativeness and persistence in chil-

dren with mental retardation. *American Journal on Mental Retardation, 95*(3), 342–355.

Krupski, A. (1979). Are retarded children more distractible? *Education and Training in Mental Retardation, 84*(1), 1–10.

Kunisawa, B. N. (1988). A nation in crisis: The dropout dilemma. *NEA Today (Issues '88), 6*(6), 61–65.

LaCampagne, J., & Cipani, E. (1987). Training adults with mental retardation to pay bills. *Mental Retardation, 25*(5), 293–303.

LaDuke, R. O., & LaGrow, S. J. (1984). Photo-bus-route-map: An intervention to produce independence in bus travel for mentally retarded adults. *Mental Retardation and Learning Disability Bulletin, 12*(2), 71–75.

Lagomarsino, T. R., Hughes, C., & Rusch, F. R. (1989). Utilizing self-management to teach independence on the job. *Education and Training in Mental Retardation, 24*(2), 139–149.

La Greca, A. M. (1983). Facilitating the vocational-interpersonal skills of mentally retarded individuals. *Education and Training in Mental Retardation, 88*(3), 270–278.

Lahey, M. (1988). *Language disorders and language development.* New York: Macmillan.

Lakin, K. C., & Bruininks, R. H. (1985). Challenges to advocates of social integration of developmentally disabled persons. In K. C. Lakin & R. H. Bruininks, *Strategies for achieving community integration of developmentally disabled citizens* (pp. 313–330). Baltimore: Brookes.

Lalli, J. S., & Browder, D. M. (1993). Comparison of sight word training procedures with validation of the most practical procedure in teaching reading for daily living. *Research in Developmental Disabilities, 14*(2), 107–127.

Lancioni, G. E., Brouwer, J. A., & Coninx, F. (1992). Automatic cueing strategies to reduce drooling in people with mental handicap. *International Journal of Rehabilitation Research, 15*(4), 341–344.

Lang, R. E., & Kahn, J. V. (1986). Teacher estimates of handicapped student crime victimization and delinquency. *Journal of Special Education, 20*(3), 359–365.

Langone, J., & Burton, T. (1987). Teaching adaptive behavior skills to moderately and severely handicapped individuals: Best practices for facilitating independent living. *Journal of Special Education, 21*(1), 149–161.

Lanier, N. J., & Chesnut, B. H. (1990). Train me now or pay me later. *British Columbia Journal of Special Education, 14*(3), 241–245.

Lawlis, G., & Roesel, R. (1983). Divorce in families of genetically handicapped/mentally retarded individuals. *American Journal on Mental Retardation, 11*(1), 45–50.

Lee, V. E. (1993). Educational choice: The stratifying effects of selecting schools and courses. *Educational Policy, 7*(2), 125–148.

Lee, V. E., Burkham, D. T., Zimiles, H., & Ladewski, B. (1994). Family structure and its effect on behavioral and emotional problems in young adolescents. *Journal of Research on Adolescence, 4*(3), 405–437.

Lehr, D. (1985). Effects of opportunities to practice on learning among students with severe handicaps. *Education and Training of the Mentally Retarded, 20*(4), 268–274.

Lehr, D. H. (1990). Providing education to students with complex health care needs. *Focus on Exceptional Children, 22*(7), 1–12.

Lehr, D. H., & McDaid, P. (1993). Opening the door further: Integrating students with complex health care needs. *Focus on Exceptional Children, 25*(6), 1–7.

Leinbach, M. D., & Fagot, B. I. (1991). Attractiveness in young children: Sex-differentiated reactions of adults. *Sex Roles: A Journal of Research, 25*(5–6), 269–284.

Leland, H. (1972). Mental retardation and adaptive behavior. *Journal of Special Education, 6*(1), 71–80.

Lennon, R. T. (1950). The relation between intelligence and achievement test results for a group of communities. *Journal of Educational Psychology, 41*(5), 301–308.

Lerner, J., Lowenthal, B., & Lerner, S. (1995). *Attention deficit disorders.* Pacific Grove, CA: Brooks/Cole.

Levy, J. M., Jessop, D. J., Rimmerman, A., & Levy, P. (1992). Attitudes of Fortune 500 corporate executives toward the employability of persons with severe disabilities: A national survey. *Mental Retardation, 30*(2), 67–75.

Levy-Shiff, R., Kedem, P. E., & Sevillia, Z. (1990). Identity in mentally retarded adolescents. *American Journal on Mental Retardation, 94*(5), 541–549.

Liberty, K. A., & Paeth, M. A. (1990). Self-recording for students with severe and multiple handicaps. *Teaching Exceptional Children, 22*(3), 73–75.

Lignugaris/Kraft, B. (1988). Social-vocational skills of workers with and without mental retardation in two community employment sites. *Mental Retardation, 76*(5), 297–305.

Lillie, T. (1993). A harder thing than triumph: Roles of fathers of children with disabilities. *Mental Retardation, 31*(6), 438–443.

Lilly, M. S. (1982). Toward a unitary concept of mental retardation. *Education and Treatment of Children, 5*(4), 379–387.

Lim, L. H. F., & Browder, D. M. (1994). Multicultural life skills assessment of individuals with severe disabilities. *Journal of the Association for Persons with Severe Handicaps (JASH), 19*(2), 130–138.

Lin, A., Podell, D. M., & Rein, N. (1991). The effects of CAI on word recognition in mildly mentally handicapped and nonhandicapped learners. *Journal of Special Education Technology, 11*(1), 16–25.

Lindsey, J. D., & Armstrong, S. W. (1984). Performance of EMR and learning-disabled students on the Brigace, Peabody, and Wide Range Achievement Tests. *Education and Training in Mental Retardation, 89*(2), 197–201.

Lindsey, J. D., & Stewart, D. W. (1989). The guardian minority: Siblings of children with mental retardation. *Education and Training in Mental Retardation, 24*(4), 291–296.

Link, M. P. (1991). Is integration really the least restrictive environment? *Teaching Exceptional Children, 23*(4), 63–64.

Lombard, R. C., & Hazelkorn, M. N. (1993). It takes two: Mainstreaming is easier when special educators and vocational teachers team up. *Vocational Education Journal, 68*(8), 32–33.

Long, N., & Edwards, M. (1994). The use of a daily report card to address children's school behavior problems. *Contemporary Education, 65*(3), 152–155.

Lord, J., & Pedlar, A. (1991). Life in the community: Four years after the closure of an institution. *Mental Retardation, 29*(4), 213–221.

Lovett, D. L., & Haring, K. A. (1989). The effects of self-management training on the daily living of adults with mental retardation. *Education and Training in Mental Retardation, 24*(4), 306–323.

Lovett, D. L., & Harris, M. B. (1987a). Identification of important community living skills for adults with mental retardation. *Rehabilitation Counseling Bulletin, 31*(1), 34–41.

Lovett, D. L., & Harris, M. B. (1987b). Important skills for adults with mental retardation: The client's point of view. *Mental Retardation, 25*(6), 351–356.

Low, L. J., & Sherrill, C. (1988). Sports medicine concerns in Special Olympics. *Palaestra,* pp. 56–57, 60–61.

Lowenfield, V. (1987). Therapeutic aspects of art education. *American Journal of Art Therapy, 25*(4), 111–146.

Lozano, B. (1993). Independent living: Relation among training, skills, and success. *American Journal on Mental Retardation, 98*(2), 249–262.

Luchow, J. P., Crowl, T. K., & Kahn, J. P. (1985). Learned helplessness: Perceived effects of ability and effort on academic performance among EH and LD/EH children. *Journal of Learning Disabilities, 18*(8), 470–474.

Luckasson, R., Coulter, D., Polloway, E., Reiss, S., Schalock, R., Snell, M., Spitalnik, D., & Stark, J. (1992). *Mental retardation: Definition, classification, and systems of support* (9th ed.). Washington, DC: American Association on Mental Retardation.

Luftig, R. L. (1988). Assessment of the perceived school loneliness and isolation of mentally retarded and non-retarded students. *American Journal on Mental Retardation, 92*(5), 472–475.

Lunenburg, F. C., & Ornstein, A. C. (1991). *Educational administration: Concepts and practices.* Belmont, CA: Wadsworth.

Lynch, E. C., & Staloch, N. H. (1988). Parental perceptions of physicians' communication in the informing process. *Mental Retardation, 26*(2), 77–81.

MacKay, D. N., & Bankhead, I. (1985). Fine-motor performance in subjects of subnormal, normal, and superior intelligence IV task complexity and tracking. *Australia and New Zealand Journal of Developmental Disabilities, 11*(3), 143–150.

MacMillan, D. L. (1982). *Mental retardation in school and society* (2nd ed.). Boston: Little, Brown.

MacMillan, D. L., Gresham, F. M., & Siperstein, G. N. (1993). Conceptual and psychometric concerns about the 1992 AAMR definition of mental retardation. *American Journal on Mental Retardation, 98*(3), 325–335.

Maheady, L., Sacca, M. K., & Harper, G. F. (1987). Classwide student tutoring teams: The effects of peer-mediated instruction on the academic performance of secondary mainstreamed students. *Journal of Special Education, 21*(3), 107–121.

Maherali, Z. (1989). Parenting rights of the mentally handicapped. *British Columbia Journal of Special Education, 13*(3), 235–252.

Mahon, M. J., & Bullock, C. C. (1992). Teaching adolescents with mild mental retardation to make decisions in leisure through the use of self-control techniques. *Therapeutic Recreation Journal, 26*(1), 9–26.

Maier, S. F., & Seligman, M. E. P. (1976). Learned helplessness: Theory and evidence. *Journal of Experimental Psychology, 105*(1), 3–46.

Marcell, M. M., & Jett, D. A. (1985). Identification of vocally expressed emotions by mentally retarded and nonretarded individuals. *American Journal on Mental Retardation, 89*(3), 537–545.

Marchand-Martella, N., Martella, R., Christensen, A., Azean, M., & Young, K. R. (1992). Teaching a first-aid skill to students with disabilities using two training programs. *Education and Treatment of Children, 15*(1), 15–31.

Marchetti, A. G., Cecil, C. E., Graves, J., & Marchetti, D. C. (1984). Public transportation instruction: Comparison of classroom instruction, community instruction, and facility-grounds instruction. *Mental Retardation, 22*(3), 128–136.

Marchetti, A. G., McCartney, J. R., Drain, S., Hooper, M., & Dix, J. (1983). Pedestrian skills training for mentally retarded adults: Comparison of training in two settings. *Mental Retardation, 21*(3), 107–110.

Marcus, J. C. (1993). Control of epilepsy in a mentally retarded population: Lack of correlation with IQ, neurological status, and electroencephalogram. *American Journal on Mental Retardation, 98,* 47–51.

Margalit, M. (1991). Promoting classroom adjustment and social skills for students with mental retardation within an experimental and control group design and reflections. *Exceptionality: A Research Journal, 2*(4), 195–204, 231–235.

Marion, R. L. (1979). Leisure time activities for trainable mentally retarded adolescents. *Teaching Exceptional Children, 11*(4), 158–160.

Marozas, D. S., May, D. C., & Lehman, L. C. (1980). Incidence and prevalence: Confusion in need of clarification. *Mental Retardation, 18*(5), 229–230.

Marshall, J. D. (1984). Punishment and moral education. *Journal of Moral Education, 13*(2), 83–89.

Martin, A. S., & Morris, J. L. (1980). Training a work ethic in severely mentally retarded workers: Providing a context for the maintenance of skill performance. *Mental Retardation, 18*(2), 67–71.

Martin, E. W. (1994). Inclusion: Rhetoric and reality. *Exceptional Parent, 24*(1), 39–42.

Martin, J. E., & Rusch, F. R. (1987). Use of the partial-sequential withdrawal design to assess maintenance of mentally retarded adults' acquired meal preparation skills. *Research in Developmental Disabilities, 8*(3), 389–399.

Martin, J. E., Rusch, F. R., & Heal, L. W. (1982). Teaching community survival skills to mentally retarded adults: A review and analysis. *Journal of Special Education, 16*(3), 243–267.

Mather, N., & Lachowicz, B. L. (1992). Shared writing: An instructional approach for reluctant writers. *Teaching Exceptional Children, 25*(1), 26–30.

Matson, J., & Barnett, R. (1982). *Psychopathology in the mentally retarded.* New York: Grune & Stratton.

Matson, J. L., & Keyes, J. B. (1990). A comparison of DRO to movement suppression time-out and DRO with two self-injurious and aggressive mentally retarded adults. *Research in Developmental Disabilities, 11*(1), 111–120.

Matson, J. L., & Long, S. (1986). Teaching computation/shopping skills to mentally retarded adults. *American Journal on Mental Retardation, 91*(1), 98–101.

May, D. C., & Marozas, D. S. (1989). Electronic devices in the classroom: Are they effective? *DPH Journal, 10*(2), 88–93.

Mazurkiewicz, A. J., & Tanzer, H. J. (1963). *Early-to-Read: i/t/a program.* New York: Initial Teaching Alphabet.

McAlpine, C., Kendall, K. A., & Singh, N. N. (1991). Recognition of facial expressions of emotion by persons with mental retardation. *American Journal on Mental Retardation, 96*(1), 29–36.

McCarl, J. J., Svobodny, L., & Beare, P. (1991). Self-recording in a classroom for students with mild to moderate mental handicaps: Effects on productivity and on-task behavior. *Education and Training in Mental Retardation, 26*(1), 79–88.

McCarthy, M. M. (1981). Education for the handicapped: Lawyers and judges will decide what your schools can and can't do for students. *American School Board Journal, 168*(7), 24–25.

McCartney, J. (1987). Mentally retarded and nonretarded subjects' long-term recognition memory. *American Journal on Mental Retardation, 92*(3), 312–317.

McCaughrin, W. B., Ellis, W. K., Rusch, F., R., & Heal, L. (1993). Cost-effectiveness of supported employment. *Mental Retardation, 31*(1), 41–48.

McConkey, R. (1985). Changing beliefs about play and handicapped children. *Early Child Development and Care, 19*(1–2), 79–94.

McConkey, R., & McEnvoy, J. (1986). Games for learning to count. *British Journal of Special Education, 13*(2), 59–62.

McCrea, L. (1990). A comparison between the perceptions of special educators and employers: What factors are critical for job success? *Career Development for Exceptional Individuals, 14*(2), 121–129.

McCrea, L. D. (1993). Frequency of job skills appearing on individualized plans of students with moderate retardation. *Education and Training in Mental Retardation, 28*(2), 179–185.

McCuller, G. L., Salzburg, C. L., & Lignugaris/Kraft, B. (1987). Producing generalized job initiative in severely mentally retarded sheltered workers. *Journal of Applied Behavior Analysis, 21*(4), 413–420.

McDermott, S. W., & Altekruse, J. M. (1994). Dynamic model for preventing mental retardation in the population: The importance of poverty and deprivation. *Research in Developmental Disabilities, 15*(1), 49–65.

McDonald, A., Carlson, K., Palmer, D., & Slay, T. (1983). Special education and medicine: A survey of physicians. *Journal of Learning Disabilities, 16*(2), 93–94.

McDonnell, A. P. (1993). Ethical considerations in teaching compliance to individuals with mental retardation. *Education and Training in Mental Retardation, 28*(1), 3–12.

McDonnell, J. (1987). The effects of time delay and increasing prompt hierarchy strategies on the acquisition of purchasing skills by students with severe handicaps. *Journal of the Association for Persons with Severe Handicaps (JASH), 12*(3), 227–236.

McDonnell, J., & Ferguson, B. (1987). A comparison of time delay and decreasing prompt hierarchy strategies in teaching banking skills to students with moderate handicaps. *Journal of Applied Behavior Analysis, 22*(1), 85–91.

McDonnell, J., & Hardman, M. (1985). Planning the transition of severely handicapped youth from school to adult services: A framework for high school programs. *Education and Training of the Mentally Retarded, 21*(4), 275–286.

McDonnell, J., Hardman, M., & Hightower, J. (1989). Employment preparation for high school students with severe handicaps. *Mental Retardation, 27*(6), 396–405.

McDonnell, J., & Laughlin, B. (1989). A comparison of backward and concurrent chaining strategies in teaching community skills. *Education and Training in Mental Retardation, 24*(3), 230–238.

McDonnell, J., Wilcox, B., Boles, S., & Bellamy, T. (1985). Transition issues facing youth with severe disabilities: Parents' perspective. *Journal of the Association for Persons with Severe Handicaps (JASH), 10*(1), 61–65.

McEnvoy, J., & McConkey, R. (1983). Play activities of mentally handicapped children at home and mothers' perception of play. *International Journal of Rehabilitation Research, 6*(2), 143–151.

McGimsey, J. F., & Favell, J. E. (1988). The effects of increased physical exercise on disruptive behavior in retarded persons. *Journal of Autism and Developmental Disorders, 18*(2), 167–179.

McGookey, K. (1992). Drama, disability, and your classroom. *Teaching Exceptional Children, 24*(2), 12–14.

McGuffey, W. H. (1909). *McGuffey's eclectic primer* (rev. ed.). New York: American Book.

McHale, S. M., Sloan, J., & Simeonsson, R. J. (1986). Sibling relationships of children with autistic, mentally retarded, and nonhandicapped brothers and sisters. *Journal of Autism and Developmental Disorders, 16*(4), 399–413.

McKelvey, J. L., Sisson, L. A., Van Hasselt, V. B., & Hersen, M. (1992). An approach to teaching self-dressing to a child with dual sensory impairment. *Teaching Exceptional Children, 25*(1), 12–15.

McKenzie, R. G., & Houk, C. S. (1993). Across the great divide: Transition from elementary to secondary settings for students with mild disabilities. *Teaching Exceptional Children, 25*(2), 16–20.

McKinney, J. D., & Forman, S. G. (1982). Classroom behavior patterns of EMH, LD, and EH students. *Journal of School Psychology, 21*(4), 271–279.

McNair, J., & Rusch, F. R. (1991). Parent involvement in transition programs. *Mental Retardation, 29*(2), 93–101.

Meers, G. D. (1992). Getting ready for the next century: Vocational preparation of students with disabilities. *Teaching Exceptional Children, 24*(4), 36–39.

Melnyk, L., & Das, J. P. (1992). Measurement of attention deficit: Correspondence between rating scales and tests of sustained and selective attention. *American Journal on Mental Retardation, 96*(6), 599–606.

Mercer, J. R. (1973). IQ: The lethal label. *Education Digest, 38*(5), 17–20.

Merrill, E. (1985). Differences in semantic processing speed of mentally retarded and nonretarded persons. *American Journal on Mental Retardation, 90*(1), 71–80.

Merrill, E., & Jackson, T. S. (1992). Sentence processing by adolescents with and without mental retardation. *American Journal on Mental Retardation, 97*(3), 342–350.

Merrill, E., & Mar, H. C. (1987). Differences between mentally retarded and nonretarded persons' efficiency of auditory sentence processing. *Education and Training in Mental Retardation, 91*(4), 406.

Merrill, E. C., & Peacock, M. (1993). Allocation of attention and task difficulty. *American Journal on Mental Retardation, 98*(5), 588–593.

Meyen, E. L. (1968). The education of the mentally retarded: A systematic error in curriculum development. *Education and Training of the Mentally Retarded, 3*(3), 164–168.

Meyer, L. H., & Evans, I. M. (1989). *Nonaversive intervention for behavior problems: A manual for home and community.* Baltimore: Brookes.

Michaelis, C. T. (1981). Home and school partnerships. *Exceptional Parent, 11*(3), 12.

Miller, L. K. (1991). Assessment of musical aptitude in people with mental disabilities. *Mental Retardation, 29*(4), 175–183.

Miller, U. C., & Test, D. W. (1989). A comparison of constant time delay and most-to-least prompting in teaching laundry skills to students with moderate retardation. *Education and Training in Mental Retardation, 24*(4), 363–370.

Miner, D. (1991). Using nonaversive techniques to reduce self-stimulatory hand-mouthing in a visually impaired and severely retarded student. *Review, 22*(4), 185–194.

Mire, S. P., & Chisholm, R. W. (1990). Functional communication goals for adolescents and adults who are severely and moderately mentally handicapped. *Language, Speech, and Hearing Services in Schools, 21*(1), 57–58.

Mithaug, D. E. (1993). *Self-regulation theory: How optimal adjustment maximizes gain.* New York: Praeger.

Moffatt, C. W., Hanley-Maxwell, C., & Donnellan, A. M. (1995). Discrimination of emotion, affective perspective-taking, and empathy in individuals with mental retardation. *Education and Training in Mental Retardation and Developmental Disabilities, 30*(1), 76–85.

Montague, M., & Fonseca, F. (1993). Using computers to improve story writing. *Teaching Exceptional Children, 25*(4), 46–49.

Moon, M. S., & Beale, A. V. (1984). Vocational training and employment: Guidelines for parents. *Exceptional Parent, 14*(8), 35–38.

Moon, M. S., & Renzaglia, A. (1982). Physical fitness and the mentally retarded: A critical review of the literature. *Journal of Special Education, 16*(3), 269–287.

Moore, S. C., Agran, M., & Fodor-Davis, J. (1989). Using self-management strategies to increase the production rates of workers with severe handicaps. *Education and Training in Mental Retardation, 24*(4), 324–332.

Moore, S. C., Agran, M., & McSweyn, C. A. (1990). Career education: Are we starting early enough? *Career Development for Exceptional Individuals, 13*(2), 129–134.

Morris, C. D., Niederbuhl, J., & Mahr, J. (1993). Determining the capability of individuals with mental retardation to give informed consent. *American Journal on Mental Retardation, 98*(2), 263–272.

Morrison, G. M., Laughlin, J., Smith, D., Ollansky, E., & Moore, B. (1992). Preferences for sources of social support of Hispanic male adolescents with mild learning handicaps. *Education and Training in Mental Retardation, 27*(2), 132–144.

Morrow, S. A., & Bates, P. E. (1987). The effectiveness of three sets of school-based instructional materials and community training on the acquisition and generalization of community laundry skills by students with severe handicaps. *Research in Developmental Disabilities, 8*(1), 113–136.

Morton, R. F., & Hebel, J. R. (1978). *A study guide to epidemiology and biostatistics.* Baltimore: University Park Press.

Mosley, J. (1985). High-speed memory scanning task performance of mildly mentally retarded and nonretarded individuals. *American Journal on Mental Retardation, 90*(1), 81–91.

Mosley, J. L. (1978). Integration: The need for a systematic evaluation of the socio-adaptive aspect.

Education and Training of the Mentally Retarded, 13(1), 4–8.

Mulhauser, M. B. (1993). *An experimental study of the impact of contingency awareness on expressive communicative initiations of students with profound multiple disabilities (learned helplessness).* Unpublished doctoral dissertation, Kent State University, Kent, OH.

Munk, D. D., & Repp, A. C. (1994). The relationship between instructional variables and problem behavior: A review. *Exceptional Children, 60*(5), 390–401.

Myers, B. A. (1989). Misleading clues in the diagnosis of mental retardation and infantile autism in the preschool child. *Mental Retardation, 27*(2), 85–90.

Nagle, R. J. (1993). The relationship between the WAIS-R and academic achievement among EMR adolescents. *Psychology in the Schools, 30*(1), 37–39.

National Center for Educational Statistics. (1988). *Annual report.* Washington, DC: U.S. Department of Education.

Nel, J. (1993). Preventing school failure: The Native American child. *Preventing School Failure, 37*(3), 19–24.

Nelson, R. B., Cummings, J., & Boltman, H. (1991). Teaching basic concepts to students who are educable mentally handicapped. *Teaching Exceptional Children, 23*(2), 12–15.

Nickles, J. L., Cronis, T. G., Justen, J. E., III, & Smith, G. J. (1992). Individualized education programs: A comparison of students with BD, LD, and MMR. *Intervention in School and Clinic, 28*(1), 41–44.

Nietupski, J., Clancy, P., & Christiansen, C. (1984). Acquisition, maintenance, and generalization of vending machine purchasing skills by moderately handicapped students. *Education and Training of the Mentally Retarded, 19*(2), 91–96.

Nietupski, J., Hamre-Nietupski, S., Green, K., Varnum-Teeter, K., Twedt, B., LePera, D., Scebold, K., & Hanrahan, M. (1986). Self-initiated and sustained leisure activity participation by students with moderate/severe handicaps. *Education and Training of the Mentally Retarded, 20*(4), 259–264.

Nietupski, J., & Svoboda, R. (1982). Teaching a cooperative leisure skill to severely handicapped adults. *Education and Training of the Mentally Retarded, 17*(1), 38–43.

Nietupski, J., Welch, J., & Wacker, D. (1983). Acquisition, maintenance, and transfer of grocery item purchasing skills by moderately and severely handicapped students. *Education and Training of the Mentally Retarded, 18*(4), 279–286.

Nietupski, J. A., Hamre-Nietupski, S., Welch, J., & Anderson, R. J. (1983). Establishing and maintaining vocational training sites for moderately and severely handicapped students: Strategies for community/vocational trainers. *Education and Training of the Mentally Retarded, 18*(2), 169–175.

Nixon, C. D., & Singer, G. H. (1993). Group cognitive-behavioral treatment for excessive parental self-blame and guilt. *American Journal on Mental Retardation, 97*(6), 665–672.

Nugent, P. M., & Mosley, J. L. (1987). Mentally retarded and nonretarded individuals' attention allocation and capacity. *Education and Training in Mental Retardation, 91*(6), 598–605.

Oberti v. Board of Education of Borough of Clementon School District, 995 F.2d. 1204 (3rd Cir. 1993).

O'Brien, J. (1993). Down stairs that are never your own: Supporting people with developmental disabilities in their own homes. *Mental Retardation, 32*(1), 1–6.

Odess, B., & Margaliot, S. (1994). Creating appropriate toys for children with multiple handicaps. *Review, 26*(1), 35–38.

Ohanian, S. (1990). P.L. 94–142: Mainstream or quicksand? *Phi Delta Kappan, 72*(3), 217–222.

Orelove, F. P., & Sobsey, D. (1991). *Educating children with multiple disabilities: A transdisciplinary approach* (2nd ed.). Baltimore: Brookes.

Orelove, F. P., Wehman, P., & Wood, J. (1982). An evaluative review of Special Olympics: Implications for community integration. *Education and Training of the Mentally Retarded, 17*(5), 325–329.

Orfield, G., & Ashkinaze, C. (1991). *The closing door: Conservative policy and Black opportunity.* Chicago: University of Chicago Press.

Osborne, A. G., Jr. (1994). The IDEA's least restrictive environment mandate: Legal implications. *Exceptional Children, 61*(1), 6–14.

Ottenbacher, K., & Cooper, H. (1982). *The effect of special class placement on the social adjustment of mentally retarded children.* Washington, DC: U.S. Department of Education.

Otto, W., McMenemy, R. A., & Smith, R. J. (1973). *Corrective and remedial teaching.* Boston: Houghton Mifflin.

Paddock, C. (1992). Ice-cream stick math. *Teaching Exceptional Children, 24*(2), 50–51.

Palardy, J. M. (1988). Back-to-basics revisited and reanalyzed. *Teacher Educator, 24*(2), 2–6.

Palo Alto Reading Program: Sequential steps in reading. (1973). New York: Harcourt Brace Jovanovich.

Parent, W. S., Kregel, J., Metzler, H. M. D., & Twardzik, G. (1992). Social integration in the workplace: An analysis of the interaction activities of workers with mental retardation and their co-workers. *Education and Training in Mental Retardation, 27*(1), 28–38.

Park, H. S., & Gaylord-Ross, R. (1989). A problem-solving approach to social skills training in employment settings with mentally retarded youth. *Journal of Applied Behavior Analysis, 22*(4), 373–380.

Parmar, R. S., Cawley, J. F., & Miller, J. H. (1994). Differences between students with learning disabilities and students with mild retardation. *Exceptional Children, 60*(6), 549–563.

Pattavina, S., Bergstrom, T., Marchand-Martella, N. E., & Martella, R. C. (1992). Moving on: Learning to cross streets independently. *Teaching Exceptional Children, 25*(1), 32–35.

Patterson, I. (1984). Parents teach self-help at home. *Special Education: Forward Trends, 11*(2), 25–26.

Patton, J., & Jones, E. (1994). Definitional perspective. In M. Beirne-Smith, J. R. Patton, & R. Ittenbach, *Mental retardation* (4th ed., pp. 56–98). Englewood Cliffs, NJ: Merrill/Prentice Hall.

Peabody Rebus Reading Program. (1966). Minneapolis, MN: American Guidance Service.

Peach, W., & Moore, L. (1990). Peer tutoring to increase spelling scores of the mildly mentally handicapped. *Journal of Instructional Psychology, 17*(1), 43–45.

Peagam, E. (1993). Who cares about control? *British Journal of Special Education, 20*(3), 100–102.

Pearman, E. L., Barnhart, M. W., Huang, A. M., & Mellboom, C. (1992). Educating all students in school: Attitudes and beliefs about inclusion. *Education and Training in Mental Retardation, 27*(2), 176–182.

Peng, S., & Takai, R. (1983). High school dropouts: Descriptive information from high school and beyond. *National Center for Education Statistics Bulletin, 1*(9), 1–9.

Perske, R. (1972). The dignity of risk and the mentally retarded. *Mental Retardation, 10*(1), 24–27.

Poindexter, A. R., & Bihm, E. M. (1994). Incidence of short-sleep patterns in institutionalized individuals with profound mental retardation. *American Journal on Mental Retardation, 98*(6), 776–780.

Polloway, E. A., & Smith, J. D., Jr. (1983). Changes in mild mental retardation: Population, programs, and perspectives. *Exceptional Children, 50*(2), 149–159.

Porter, J. (1993). What do pupils with severe learning difficulties understand about counting? *British Journal of Special Education, 20*(2), 72–75.

Porter, M. E. (1980). Effect of vocational instruction on academic achievement. *Exceptional Children, 46*(6), 463–464.

Powers, D. A. (1979). Mainstreaming EMR pupils at the secondary level: A consideration of the issues. *High School Journal, 63*(3), 155–159.

Powers, L. E., Singer, G. H., Stevens, T., & Sowers, J. (1992). Behavioral parent training in home and community generalization settings. *Education and Training in Mental Retardation, 27*(1), 13–27.

Pressman, H. (1986). Computers can make a difference. *Exceptional Parent, 16*(6), 14–16, 18–20.

Pruess, J. B., Fewell, R. R., & Bennett, F. C. (1989). Vitamin therapy and children with Down's syndrome: A review of research. *Exceptional Children, 55*(4), 336–341.

Pudlas, K. A. (1993). Integration: Students and teachers at risk? *British Columbia Journal of Special Education, 17*(1), 54–61.

Rae, R., & Roll, D. (1985). Fire safety training with adults who are profoundly mentally retarded. *Mental Retardation, 23*(1), 26–30.

Realon, R. E., Favell, J. E., & Dayvault, K. A. (1988). Evaluating the use of adapted leisure materials on the engagement of persons who are profoundly, multiply handicapped. *Education and Training in Mental Retardation, 23*(3), 228–237.

Realon, R. E., Favell, J. E., & Lowerre, A. (1990). The effects of making choices on engagement levels with persons who are profoundly multiply handicapped. *Education and Training in Mental Retardation, 25*(3), 299–305.

Reber, M. (1992). Dual diagnosis: Psychiatric disorders and mental retardation. In M. Batshaw & Y. M. Perret (Eds.), *Children with disabilities: A medical primer* (3rd ed., pp. 421–440). Baltimore: Brookes.

Reese, G. M., & Snell, M. E. (1991). Putting on and removing coats and jackets: The acquisition and maintenance of skills by children with severe multiple disabilities. *Education and Training in Mental Retardation, 26*(4), 398–410.

Reichle, J., & Yoder, D. E. (1985). Communication board use in severely handicapped learners. *Language, Speech, and Hearing Services in the Schools, 16*(3), 146–157.

Reichle, J., York, J., & Sigafoos, J. (1991). *Implementing augmentative and alternative communication: Strategies for learners with severe disabilities.* Baltimore: Brookes.

Reiss, S. (1992). Assessment of a man with a dual diagnosis. *Mental Retardation, 30*(1), 1–6.

Reiss, S., Levitan, G., & Szyszko, J. (1980). Emotional disturbance and mental retardation: Diagnostic overshadowing. *Education and Training in Mental Retardation, 86*(6), 567–574.

Repetto, J. B., White, W. J., & Snauwaert, D. T. (1990). Individualized transitional plans (ITP): A national perspective. *Career Development for Exceptional Individuals, 13*(2), 109–119.

Retish, P. (1982). Mainstreaming in the secondary schools: What price? *Journal for Special Educators, 18*(2), 46–48.

Retish, P. P. (1988). Expectations and special needs students. *Special Services in the Schools, 4*(3–4), 159–162.

Reynolds, M. C. (1989). A historical perspective: The delivery of special education to mildly disabled and at-risk students. *Remedial and Special Education (RASE), 10*(6), 7–11.

Richardson, S. A. (1989). Issues in the definition of mental retardation and the representativeness of studies. *Research in Developmental Disabilities, 10*(3), 285–294.

Richardson, S. A., Katz, M., & Koller, H. (1986). Sex differences in number of children administratively classified as mildly mentally retarded: An epidemiological review. *American Journal of Mental Deficiency, 91*(3), 250–256.

Richardson, S. A., Katz, M., & Koller, H. (1993). Patterns of leisure activities of young adults with mild mental retardation. *American Journal on Mental Retardation, 97*(4), 431–442.

Richardson, S. A., Koller, H., & Katz, M. (1985). Appearance and mental retardation: Some first steps in the development and application of a measure. *American Journal on Mental Retardation, 89*(5), 475–484.

Rimmer, J. H., Braddock, D., & Fujiura, G. (1993). Prevalence of obesity in adults with mental retardation: Implications for health promotion and disease prevention. *Mental Retardation, 31*(2), 105–110.

Rinsland, H. D. (1945). *A basic vocabulary of elementary school children.* New York: Macmillan.

Riordan, J., & Vasa, S. F. (1991). Accommodations for and participation of persons with disabilities in religious practice. *Education and Training in Mental Retardation, 26*(2), 151–155.

Roberson, W. H., Gravel, J. S., Valcante, G. C., & Maurer, R. G. (1992). Using a picture task analysis to teach students with multiple disabilities. *Teaching Exceptional Children, 24*(4), 12–15.

Roberts, G. I., & Samuels, M. T. (1993). Handwriting remediation: A comparison of computer-based and traditional approaches. *Journal of Educational Research, 87*(2), 118–125.

Robinson, N. M., & Robinson, H. B. (1976). *The mentally retarded child* (2nd ed.). New York: McGraw-Hill.

Rodriguez v. Board of Education, City of New York, 480 N.Y. 2d 901 (A.D. 2d Dept. 1984).

Roesel, R., & Lawlis, G. F. (1983). Divorce in families of genetically handicapped/mentally retarded individuals. *American Journal of Family Therapy, 11*(1), 45–50.

Roessler, R. T., & Lewis, F. D. (1984). Conversation skill training with mentally retarded and learning disabled sheltered workshop clients. *Rehabilitation Counseling Bulletin, 27*(3), 161–171.

Rogow, S. M. (1993). Language development in a nonvocal child. *British Columbia Journal of Special Education, 17*(3), 201–208.

Ronau, R. N., & Battista, M. T. (1988). Microcomputer versus paper-and-pencil testing of student errors in ratio and proportion. *Journal of Computers in Mathematics and Science Teaching, 7*(3), 33–38.

Ronnau, J., & Poertner, J. (1993). Identification and use of strengths: A family system approach. *Children Today, 22*(2), 20–23.

Rose, D. F., & Smith, B. J. (1993). Preschool mainstreaming: Attitude barriers and strategies for addressing them. *Young Children, 48*(4), 59–62.

Rose, T. L. (1984). The effects of previewing on mentally retarded learners' oral reading. *Education and Training of the Mentally Retarded, 19*(1), 49–53.

Rose, T. L. (1989). Corporal punishment with mildly handicapped students: Five years later. *Remedial and Special Education (RASE), 10*(1), 43–52.

Rosen, J. W., & Burchard, S. N. (1990). Community activities and social support networks: A social comparison of adults with and adults without mental retardation. *Education and Training in Mental Retardation, 25*(2), 193–204.

Rosen, L. (1955). Selected aspects in the development of the mother's understanding of her mentally retarded child. *Education and Training in Mental Retardation, 59,* 522.

Rosen, M. (1994). Empowerment: A two-edged sword. *Mental Retardation, 32*(1), 73–74.

Rosenberg, S., & Abbeduto, L. (1987). Indicators of linguistic competence in the peer group conversational behavior of mildly retarded adults. *Applied Psycholinguistics, 8*(1), 19–32.

Rosenthal, J. A., Groze, V., & Aguilar, G. D. (1991). Adoption outcomes for children with handicaps. *Child Welfare, 70*(6), 623–636.

Rosenthal-Malek, A. L., & Yoshida, R. K. (1994). The effects of metacognitive strategy training on the acquisition and generalization of social skills. *Education and Training in Mental Retardation and Developmental Disabilities, 29*(1), 213–221.

Rosenzweig, M. R. (1981). Neural bases of intelligence and training. *Journal of Special Education, 15*(2), 105–123.

Ross, M., & Salvia, J. (1975). Attractiveness as a biasing factor in teacher judgments. *Education and Training in Mental Retardation, 80*(1), 96–98.

Rudrud, E., & Striefel, S. (1981). Eight to twelve hertz occipital EEG training with moderate and severely retarded epileptic individuals. *Australian Journal of Developmental Disabilities, 7*(4), 173–179.

Rumberger, R. W. (1987). High school dropouts: A review of issues and evidence. *Review of Educational Research, 57*(2), 101–122.

Russell, A. T., & Forness, S. R. (1985). Behavioral disturbance in mentally retarded children in TMR and EMR classrooms. *Education and Training in Mental Retardation, 89*(4), 338–344.

Russell, T. (1984). Respite care: A means of rest and recuperation for parents of retarded individuals. *Pointer, 28*(3), 4–7.

Rynders, J. E., Schleien, S. J., & Mustonen, T. (1990). Integrating children with severe disabilities for intensified outdoor education: Focus on feasibility. *Mental Retardation, 28*(1), 7–14.

S-1 v. Turlington, 635 F2d 342 (5th Cir. 1981).

Salend, S. J., & Giek, K. A. (1988). Independent living arrangements for individuals with mental retardation: The landlords' perspective. *Mental Retardation, 26*(2), 89–92.

Salisbury, C. L. (1990). Characteristics of users and nonusers of respite care. *Mental Retardation, 28*(5), 291–297.

Salvia, J., & Ysseldyke, J. (1991). *Assessment in special education and remedial education* (5th ed.). Boston: Houghton Mifflin.

Sandknop, P. A., Schuster, J. W., Wolery, M., & Cross, D. P. (1992). The use of an adaptive device to teach students with moderate mental retardation to select lower-priced grocery items. *Education and Training in Mental Retardation, 27*(3), 219–229.

Sarber, R. E., Halasz, M. M., Messmer, M. C., Bickett, A. D., & Lutzker, J. R. (1983). Teaching menu planning and grocery shopping skills to a mentally retarded mother. *Mental Retardation, 20*(3), 101–106.

Scandary, J. (1981). What every teacher should know about due process hearings. *Teaching Exceptional Children, 13*(3), 92–96.

Schepis, M. M., Reid, D. H., & Fitzgerald, J. R. (1987). Group instruction with profoundly mentally retarded persons: Acquisition, generalization, and maintenance of a remunerative work skill. *Journal of Applied Behavior and Analysis, 20*(1), 97–105.

Schloss, P. J., Alexander, N., Hornig, E., Parker, K., & Wright, B. (1993). Teaching meal preparation vocabulary and procedures to individuals with mental retardation. *Teaching Exceptional Children, 25*(3), 7–12.

Schloss, P. J., Alper, S., & Jayne, D. (1994). Self-determination for persons with disabilities: Choice, risk, and dignity. *Exceptional Children, 60*(3), 215–225.

Schmitz, S. (1992). Three strikes and you're out: Academic failure and the children of public housing. *Journal of Education, 174*(3), 41–54.

Schoen, S. F., & Sivil, E. O. (1989). A comparison of procedures in teaching self-help skills: Increasing assistance, time delay, and observational learning. *Journal of Autism and Developmental Disorders, 19*(1), 57–72.

Schrag, F. (1995). *Back to basics: Fundamental educational questions reexamined.* San Francisco: Jossey-Bass.

Schultz, E. E., Jr. (1983). Depth of processing by mentally retarded and MA-matched nonretarded indi-

viduals. *Education and Training in Mental Retardation, 88*(3), 307–313.

Schupf, N., Ortiz, M., Kapell, D., Kiely, M., & Rudelli, R. D. (1995). Prevalence of intestinal parasite infections among individuals with developmental disabilities. *Mental Retardation, 33*(2), 84–89.

Schuster, J. W. (1988). Cooking instruction with persons labeled mentally retarded: A review of literature. *Education and Training in Mental Retardation, 23*(1), 43–50.

Schuster, J. W., Gast, D. L., Wolery, M., & Guiltinan, S. (1988). The effectiveness of a constant time-delay procedure to teach chained responses to adolescents with mental retardation. *Journal of Applied Behavior Analysis, 20*(2), 169–178.

Schuster, J. W., & Griffen, A. K. (1991). Using constant time delay to teach recipe-following skills. *Education and Training in Mental Retardation, 26*(4), 411–419.

Schuster, J. W., Stevens, K. B., & Doak, P. K. (1990). Using constant time delay to teach word definitions. *Journal of Special Education, 24*(3), 306–318.

Scott, M. S., & Greenfield, D. B. (1992). A comparison of normally achieving, learning disabled, and mildly retarded students on a taxonomic information task. *Learning Disabilities Research and Practice, 7*(2), 59–67.

Scrimshaw, N. S. (1993). Early supplementary feeding and cognition: A retrospective comment. *Monographs of the Society for Research in Child Development, 58*(7), 111–115.

Scruggs, T. E., & Laufenberg, R. (1986). Transformational mnemonic strategies for retarded learners. *Education and Training of the Mentally Retarded, 20*(3), 165–173.

Scudder, R. R., & Tremain, D. H. (1992). Repair behaviors of children with and without mental retardation. *Mental Retardation, 30*(5), 277–282.

Seifer, R., Clark, G., & Sameroff, A. J. (1991). Positive effects of interaction coaching on infants with developmental disabilities and their mothers. *American Journal on Mental Retardation, 96*(1), 1–11.

Seligman, M. (1993). Group work with parents of children with disabilities. *Journal for Specialists in Group Work, 18*(3), 115–126.

Sellin, D. F. (1979). *Mental retardation: Nature, needs, and advocacy.* Boston: Allyn & Bacon.

Sensenig, L. D., Mazeika, E. J., & Topf, B. (1989). Sign language facilitation of reading with students classified as trainable mentally handicapped. *Education and Training in Mental Retardation, 24*(2), 121–125.

Seventh annual report to Congress on the implementation of the Individuals with Disabilities Education Act. (1985). Washington, DC: U.S. Department of Education.

Seyfarth, J., Hill, J. W., Orelove, F., McMillan, J., & Wehman, P. (1987). Factors influencing parents' vocational aspirations for their children with mental retardation. *American Journal on Mental Retardation, 25*(6), 357–362.

Shafer, M. S., Inge, K. J., & Hill, J. (1986). Acquisition, generalization, and maintenance of automated banking skills. *Education and Training in Mental Retardation, 20*(4), 265–272.

Shepard v. South Harrison R-II School District, 718 S.W.2d 195 (Mo. App. 1986).

Shepard, L. A., Smith, M. L., & Vojir, C. P. (1983). Characteristics of pupils identified as learning disabled. *American Educational Research Journal, 20*(3), 309–331.

Short, E. J., Basili, L. A., & Schatschneider, C. W. (1993). Analysis of humor skills among elementary school students: Comparisons of children with and without intellectual handicaps. *American Journal on Mental Retardation, 98*(1), 63–73.

Siegel, S., & Sleeter, C. E. (1991). Transforming transition: Next stages for the school-to-work transition movement. *Career Development for Exceptional Individuals, 14*(1), 27–39.

Sigelman, C. K., Budd, E. C., Spanhel, C. L., & Schoenrock, C. J. (1981). When in doubt, say yes: Acquiescence in interviews with mentally retarded persons. *Mental Retardation, 19*(2), 53.

Sigelman, C. K., Winer, J. L., & Schroenrock, C. J. (1982). The responsiveness of mentally retarded persons to questions. *Education and Training of the Mentally Retarded, 17*(2), 120–124.

Silverman, F. H. (1989). *Communication for the speechless: An introduction to augmentative communication for the severely communicatively impaired* (2nd ed.). Englewood Cliffs, NJ: Prentice-Hall.

Silverman, F. H. (1995). *Communication for the speechless* (3rd ed.). Needham Heights, MA: Allyn & Bacon.

Simmons, T. J., & Flexer, R. W. (1992). Community-based job training for persons with mental retardation: An acquisition and performance replication. *Education and Training in Mental Retardation, 27*(3), 261–272.

Sinnott-Oswald, M., Gliner, J. A., & Spencer, K. (1991). Supported and sheltered employment: Quality of life issues among workers with disabilities. *Education and Training in Mental Retardation, 26*(4), 388–397.

Siperstein, G. N., Wolraich, M. L., & Reed, D. (1994). Professionals' prognoses for individuals with mental retardation: Search for consensus within interdisciplinary settings. *American Journal on Mental Retardation, 98*(4), 519–526.

Sirvis, B. (1988). Students with special health care needs. *Teaching Exceptional Children, 20*(4), 40–44.

Sisson, L., & Dixon, M. J. (1986). Improving mealtime behaviors of a multi-handicapped child using behavior therapy techniques. *Journal of Visual Impairment and Blindness, 80*, 855–858.

Sitlington, P. L., & Easterday, J. R. (1992). An analysis of employer incentive rankings relative to the employment of persons with mental retardation. *Education and Training in Mental Retardation, 27*(1), 75–80.

Sitlington, P. L., & Frank, A. R. (1993). Success as an adult: Does gender make a difference for graduates with mental disabilities? *Career Development for Exceptional Individuals, 16*(2), 171–182.

Sixteenth annual report to Congress on the implementation of the Individuals with Disabilities Education Act. (1994). Washington, DC: U.S. Department of Education.

Skodak, M., & Skeels, H. (1949). A final follow-up study of one hundred adopted children. *Journal of Genetic Psychology, 75*, 85–125.

Sluyter, G. V. (1982). Continuing education in mental retardation: A survey of leadership personnel. *Mental Retardation, 20*(4), 176–178.

Smith, C. (1989). *From wonder to wisdom: Using stories to help children grow.* New York: New American Library.

Smith, D. J. (1994). The revised AAMR definition of mental retardation and developmental disabilities. *Education and Training in Mental Retardation and Developmental Disabilities, 29*(1), 179–183.

Smith, J. D. (1981). Down's syndrome, amniocentesis, and abortion: Prevention or elimination? *Mental Retardation, 19*(1), 8–11.

Smith, R. M. (1968). *Clinical teaching: Methods of instruction for the retarded.* New York: McGraw-Hill.

Smith, T. E. C., & Dowdy, C. (1992). Future-based assessment and intervention for students with mental retardation. *Education and Training in Mental Retardation, 27*(3), 255–260.

Smith, T. E. C., & Hilton, A. (1994). Program design for students with mental retardation. *Education and Training in Mental Retardation and Developmental Disabilities, 29*(1), 3–8.

Snell, M. E. (Ed.). (1993). *Instruction of students with severe disabilities* (4th ed.). Englewood Cliffs, NJ: Merrill/Prentice Hall.

Snell, M. E., & Drake, G. P., Jr. (1994). Replacing cascades with supported education. *Journal of Special Education, 27*(4), 393–409.

Snell, M. E., Lewis, A. P., & Houghton, A. (1989). Acquisition and maintenance of toothbrushing skills by students with cerebral palsy and mental retardation. *Journal of the Association for Persons with Severe Handicaps, 14*(3), 216–226.

Snyder, T. L., Freeman-Lorentz, K., & McLaughlin, T. F. (1994). The effects of augmentative communication on vocabulary acquisition with primary-age students with disabilities. *British Columbia Journal of Special Education, 18*(1), 14–23.

Soraci, S. A., Jr., Deckner, C. W., Baumeister, A. A., & Carlin, M. T. (1990). Attentional functioning and relational learning. *American Journal on Mental Retardation, 95*(3), 304–315.

Sparrow, S. S., Balla, D. A., & Cicchetti, D. V. (1984). *Vineland Adaptive Behavior Scale* (A revision of the Vineland Social Maturity Scale, by Edgar A. Doll). Circle Pines, MN: American Guidance Service.

Spitz, H. (1945). Hospitalism: A follow-up report on investigation described in Volume I, 1945. In O. Fenichel (Ed.), *The psychological study of the child* (Vol. 2, pp. 113–117). New York: International Universities Press.

Spitz, H. H. (1981). A note on general intelligence and the MA deviation concept. *Intelligence, 5*(1), 77–83.

Spitz, H. H. (1983). Intratest and intertest reliability and stability of the WISC, WISC-R, and WAIS full-scale IQs in a mentally retarded population. *Journal of Special Education, 17*(1), 69–80.

Spitz, H. H., & Semchuck, M. T. (1979). Measuring the use of a principle by retarded adolescents and non-retarded children on a redundancy series test. *Education and Training in Mental Retardation, 83*(6), 556–560.

Spooner, F., Stem, B., & Test, D. W. (1989). Teaching first-aid skills to adolescents who are moderately mentally handicapped. *Education and Training in Mental Retardation, 24*(4), 341–351.

Stafford, S. H., & Green, V. P. (1993). Facilitating preschool mainstreaming: Classroom strategies and teacher attitude. *Early Child Development and Care, 91*(1), 93–98.

Stainback, S. B., & Healy, H. A. (1982). *Teaching eating skills.* Springfield, IL: Charles C Thomas.

Stainback, W., & Stainback, S. (1987). Facilitating friendships. *Education and Training in Mental Retardation, 22*(1), 18–25.

Stainback, W., & Stainback, S. (1992). *Controversial issues confronting special education: Divergent perspectives.* Needham Heights, MA: Allyn & Bacon.

Stancliff, R. J. (1995). Assessing opportunities for choice-making: A comparison of self- and staff reports. *American Journal on Mental Retardation, 99*(4), 418–429.

Stanovich, K. E., & Stanovich, P. J. (1979). Speaking for themselves: A bibliography of writings by mentally handicapped individuals. *Mental Retardation, 17*(2), 83–86.

Starke, M. C., & Wright, J. (1986). Improving the work performance of mentally retarded clients in a sheltered workshop. *British Columbia Journal of Special Education, 10*(4), 359–365.

State ex rel. Burfee v. Burton, 45 Wis., 30 Am. Rep. 706 (1878).

Staub, D., & Hunt, P. (1993). The effects of social interaction training on high school peer tutors of schoolmates with severe disabilities. *Exceptional Children, 60*(1), 41–57.

Steadham, C. I. (1993). Role of professional nurses in the field of developmental disabilities. *Mental Retardation, 31*(3), 179–181.

Steege, M., & Retish, P. (1982). Special education teachers' role in emergency treatment of students. *Education and Training of the Mentally Retarded, 17*(5), 330–332.

Steere, D. E., Wood, R., Pancsofar, E. L., & Rucker, R. E. (1993). Vocational training for secondary-level students with severe disabilities. *Teaching Exceptional Children, 25*(4), 7–11.

Stein, J. (1963). Motor function and physical fitness of the mentally retarded: A critical review. *Rehabilitation Literature, 24*, 230–242.

Stephens, B., & McLaughlin, J. A. (1974). Two-year gains in reasoning by retarded and nonretarded persons. *Education and Training in Mental Retardation, 79*(2), 116–126.

Stevens, K. B., Blackhurst, A. E., & Slaton, D. B. (1991). Teaching memorized spelling with a microcomputer: Time delay and computer-assisted instruction. *Journal of Applied Behavior Analysis, 24*(1), 153–160.

Stile, S. W., & Pettibone, T. J. (1980). Training and certification of administrators in special education. *Exceptional Children, 46*(7), 530–533.

Stoffregen, T. A., Baldwin, C., & Flynn, S. (1993). Noticing of unexpected events by adults with and without mental retardation. *American Journal on Mental Retardation, 98*(2), 273–284.

Storey, K. (1993). A proposal for assessing integration. *Education and Training in Mental Retardation, 28*(4), 279–287.

Storey, K., & Mank, D. M. (1989). Vocational education of students with moderate and severe disabilities: Implications for service delivery and teacher preparation. *Career Development for Exceptional Individuals, 12*(1), 11–24.

Storeygard, J., Simmons, R., Stumpf, M., & Pavloglou, E. (1993). Making computers work for students with special needs. *Teaching Exceptional Children, 26*(1), 22–24.

Strain, P. S. (1990). LRE for preschool children with handicaps: What we know, what we should be doing. *Journal of Early Intervention, 14*(4), 291–296.

Sulzbacher, S., Haines, R., Peterson, S. L., & Swatman, F. M. (1987). Encourage appropriate coffee break behavior. *Teaching Exceptional Children, 19*(2), 8–12.

Surburg, P. R. (1991). Preparation process facilitation of a motor task through imagery practice with adolescents who have mental retardation. *American Journal on Mental Retardation, 95*(4), 428–434.

Swanson, B. M., & Willis, D. J. (1979). *Understanding exceptional children and youth: An introduction to special education.* Chicago: Rand McNally.

Swinson, J., & Ellis, C. (1988). Telling stories to encourage language. *British Journal of Special Education, 15*(4), 169–171.

Taylor, R. L. (1980). Use of the AAMD classification system: A review of recent research. *American Journal on Mental Retardation, 85*(2), 116–119.

Terman, L. (1916). *The measurement of intelligence.* Boston: Houghton Mifflin.

Test, D. W., Hinson, K. B., Kuel, P., & Solow, J. (1993). Job satisfaction of persons in supported employment. *Education and Training in Mental Retardation, 28*(1), 38–46.

Thinesen, P. J., & Bryan, A. J. (1981). The use of sequential pictorial cues in the initiation and maintenance of grooming behaviors with mentally retarded adults. *Mental Retardation, 19*(5), 247–250.

Thirteenth annual report to Congress on the implementation of the Individuals with Disabilities Education Act. (1991). Washington, DC: U.S. Department of Education.

Thomas, P. J., & Carmack, F. F. (1990). *Speech and language: Detecting and correcting special needs.* Boston: Allyn & Bacon.

Thorkildsen, R., & Hofmeister, A. (1984). Interactive video authoring of instruction for the mentally handicapped. *Exceptional Education Quarterly, 4*(4), 57–73.

Tiemann, K. A. (1991). The Baby Doe case: A technique to address values, deviance, and handicaps. *Teaching Sociology, 19*(1), 79–81.

Tirapelle, L., & Cipani, E. (1992). Developing functional requesting: Acquisition, durability, and generalization of effects. *Exceptional Children, 58*(3), 260–269.

Toch, T. (1984). The dark side of the excellence movement. *Phi Delta Kappan, 60*, 173–176.

Tomporowski, P. D., & Allison, P. (1988). Sustained attention of adults with mental retardation. *American Journal on Mental Retardation, 92*(6), 525–530.

Tomporowski, P. D., & Tinsley, V. (1994). Effects of target probability and memory demands on the vigilance of adults with and without mental retardation. *American Journal on Mental Retardation, 98*(6), 688–703.

Tredgold, A. F. (1937). *A textbook of mental deficiency* (6th ed.). Baltimore: William Wood.

Turnbull, A. P., & Turnbull, H. R., III. (1990). A tale about lifestyle changes: Comments on "toward a technology of 'nonaversive' behavioral support." *Journal of the Association for Persons with Severe Handicaps (JASH), 15*(3), 142–144.

Turnbull, A. P., Turnbull, H. R., III., Shank, M., & Leal, D. (1995). *Exceptional lives.* Englewood Cliffs, NJ: Merrill/Prentice-Hall.

Turney, A. H. (1931). Intelligence, motivation, and achievement. *Journal of Educational Psychology, 22*(6), 426–434.

Tyler, L. (1990). Communicating about people with disabilities: Does the language we use make a difference? *Bulletin of the Association for Business Communication, 53*(3), 65–67.

Tymchuk, A., Hamada, D., Andron, L., & Anderson, S. (1990). Home safety training with mothers who are mentally retarded. *Education and Training in Mental Retardation, 25*(2), 142–149.

Tyson, M. E., & Spooner, F. (1991). A retrospective evaluation of behavioral programming in an institutional setting. *Education and Training in Mental Retardation, 26*(2), 179–189.

Uhlin, D. M., & DeChiara, E. (1984). *Art for exceptional children.* Dubuque, IA: Wm. C. Brown.

Umans, S. (1966). *Designs for reading programs.* New York: Columbia University.

United States Employment Service. (n.d.). *United States Employment Service Interest Inventory (USES-II).* Washington, DC: Author.

Urbano, M. T. (1991). *The child with special health care needs in the preschool setting.* San Diego, CA: Singular.

Utley, C. A., Lowitzer, A. C., & Baumeister, A. A. (1987). A comparison of the AAMD's definition, eligibility criteria, and classification schemes with state departments of education guidelines. *Education and Training in Mental Retardation, 22,* 35–43.

Vacc, N. N. (1987). Word processor versus handwriting: A comparative study of writing samples produced by mildly mentally handicapped students. *Exceptional Children, 54*(2), 156–165.

Vacca, J. L., Vacca, R. T., & Gove, M. K. (1987). *Reading and learning to read.* Boston: Little, Brown.

Valente, W. D. (1987). *Law in the schools.* Englewood Cliffs, NJ: Merrill/Prentice Hall.

Van Den Pol, R. A., Iwata, B. A., Ivancic, M. T., Page, T. J., Neef, N. A., & Whitley, F. P. (1981). Teaching the handicapped to eat in public places: Acquisition, generalization, and maintenance of restaurant skills. *Journal of Applied Behavior Analysis, 14*(1), 61–69.

Vandercook, T., York, J., & Forest, M. (1989). The McGill Action Planning System (MAPS): A strategy for building the vision. *Journal of the Association for Persons with Severe Handicaps (JASH), 14*(3), 205–215.

Vandever, T. R. (1983). Comparison of suspensions of EMR and non-retarded students. *Education and Training in Mental Retardation, 87*(4), 430–434.

Varnet, T. (1984). Sex education and the disabled. *Exceptional Parent, 14*(4), 43–46.

Vicari, S., Albertini, G., & Caltagirone, C. (1992). Cognitive profiles in adolescents with mental retardation. *Journal of Intellectual Disabilities Research, 36,* 415–423.

Vitello, S. J. (1978). Involuntary sterilization: Recent developments. *Mental Retardation, 16*(6), 405–409.

Vitello, S. J., Atthowe, J. M., Jr., & Cadwell, J. (1983). Determinants of placement of institutionalized mentally retarded persons. *Education and Training in Mental Retardation, 87*(5), 539–545.

Vockell, E. L., & Asher, J. W. (1995). *Educational research* (2nd ed.). Englewood Cliffs, NJ: Prentice-Hall.

Vogelsburg, R. T., & Rusch, F. R. (1979). Training severely handicapped students to cross partially controlled intersections. *AAESPH Review, 4*(3), 264–273.

Volk, D., & Stahlman, J. (1994). "I think everybody is afraid of the unknown": Early childhood teachers prepare for mainstreaming. *Day Care & Early Education, 21*(3), 13–17.

Voltz, D. L., & Damiano-Lantz, M. (1993). Developing ownership in learning. *Teaching Exceptional Children, 25*(4), 18–22.

Walker, D. K., Singer, J. D., Palfrey, J. S., Orza, M., Wenger, M., & Butler, J. A. (1988). Who leaves and who stays in special education: A 2-year follow-up study. *Exceptional Children, 54*(5), 393–402.

Walker, R. G. (1993). Noncompliant behavior of people with mental retardation. *Research in Developmental Disabilities, 14*(2), 87–105.

Walls, R. T., Crist, K., Sienicki, D. A., & Grant, L. (1981). Prompting sequences in teaching independent living skills. *Mental Retardation, 19*(5), 243–246.

Walters, H., & Kranzler, G. D. (1970). Early identification of the school dropout. *School Counselor, 18*(2), 97–104.

Ward, M. J., & Halloran, W. J. (1989). Transition to uncertainty: Status of many school leavers with severe disabilities. *Career Development for Exceptional Individuals, 12*(2), 71–81.

Warger, C. L. (1985). Making creative drama accessible to handicapped children. *Teaching Exceptional Children, 17*(4), 288–293.

Warren, S. A. (1987). Response to Drash, Raver, and Murrin: Can we cure mental retardation. *Mental Retardation, 25*(2), 75–78.

Warren, S. F., & Abbeduto, L. (1992). The relation of communication and language development to mental retardation. *American Journal on Mental Retardation, 97*(2), 125–130.

Wassermann, S. (1992). Serious play in the classroom: How messing around can win you the Nobel Prize. *Childhood Education, 68*(3), 133–139.

Watanabe, A. K., & Forgnone, C. (1990). The mentally handicapped juvenile offender: A call for transition. *Journal of Correctional Education, 41*(1), 20–24.

Waterman, B. B. (1994). Assessing children for the presence of a disability. *News Digest, 4*(1), 1–25.

Watkins, R. S., Boyd, B. D., & Cavalier, A. R. (1982). Learning, memory, and transfer in profoundly, severely, and moderately mentally retarded persons. *American Journal on Mental Retardation, 87*(2), 186–196.

Watkinson, E. J., & Titus, J. A. (1985). Integrating the mentally handicapped in physical activity: A review and discussion. *Canadian Journal for Exceptional Children, 2*(2), 48–53.

Weathers, C. (1983). Effects of nutritional supplementation on IQ and certain other variables associated with Down syndrome. *Education and Training in Mental Retardation, 88*(2), 214–217.

Weber, J.-L., & Stoneman, Z. (1986). Parental nonparticipation in program planning for mentally retarded children: An empirical investigation. *Applied Resarch in Mental Retardation, 7*(3), 359–369.

Webster, G. E. (1987). Influence of peer tutors upon academic learning time: Physical education of mentally handicapped students. *Journal of Teaching in Physical Education, 6*(4), 393–403.

Wechsler, D. (1981). *The Wechsler Adult Intelligence Scale—Revised (WAIS-R).* San Antonio, TX: Psychological Corporation.

Wechsler, D. (1991). *The Wechsler Intelligence Scale for Children—Third Edition—WISC-III.* San Antonio, TX: Psychological Corporation.

Wehman, P., & Hill, J. (1984). Integrating severely handicapped students in community activities. *Teaching Exceptional Children, 16*(2), 142–145.

Wehman, P., Hill, M., Hill, J., Brooke, V., Pendleton, P., & Britt, C. (1985). Competitive employment for persons with mental retardation: A follow-up six years later. *Mental Retardation, 23*(6), 274–281.

Wehmeyer, M. L. (1991). Typical and atypical repetitive motor behaviors in young children at risk for severe mental retardation. *American Journal on Mental Retardation, 96*(1), 53–62.

Wehmeyer, M. L. (1994). Perceptions of self-determination and psychological empowerment of adolescents with mental retardation. *Education and Training in Mental Retardation and Developmental Disabilities, 29*(1), 9–21.

Wehmeyer, M. L., & Metzler, C. A. (1995). How self-determined are people with mental retardation? The National Consumer Survey. *Mental Retardation, 33*(2), 111–119.

Weisner, T. S., Beizer, L., & Stolze, L. (1991). Religion and families of children with developmental delays. *American Journal on Mental Retardation, 95*(6), 647–662.

Weisz, J. R. (1979). Perceived control and learned helplessness among mentally retarded and nonretarded children: A developmental analysis. *Developmental Psychology, 15*(3), 311–319.

Werching, A., Gaylord-Ross, C., & Gaylord-Ross, R. (1986). Implementing a community-based vocational training model: A process for systems change. *Education and Training of the Mentally Retarded, 20*(2), 130–137.

Wesson, C. L. (1992). Using curriculum-based measurement to create instructional groups. *Preventing School Failure, 36*(2), 17–20.

West, M. A., Richardson, M., LeConte, J., Crimi, C., & Stuart, S. (1992). Identification of developmental disabilities and health problems among individuals under child protective services. *Mental Retardation, 30*(4), 221–225.

Westling, D. L. (1986). *Introduction to mental retardation.* Englewood Cliffs, NJ: Prentice-Hall.

Westling, D. L., Floyd, J., & Carr, D. (1990). Effect of single setting versus multiple setting training on learning to shop in a department store. *American Journal on Mental Retardation, 94*(6), 616–624.

Westling, D. L., & Fox, L. (1995). *Teaching students with severe disabilities.* Englewood Cliffs, NJ: Merrill/Prentice-Hall.

Weston, S. T. (1977). *The California High School Proficiency Examination: The decision of students about school enrollment after passing the CHSPE.* Unpublished doctoral dissertation, Brigham Young University, Provo, UT.

Whiteley, J. H., Zaparniuk, J., & Asmundson, G. (1987). Mentally retarded adolescents' breadth of attention and short-term memory processes during matching-to-sample discriminations. *Education and Training in Mental Retardation, 92*(2), 207–212.

Whitman, T. L. (1990). Self-regulation and mental retardation. *American Journal on Mental Retardation, 94*(4), 347–362.

Widaman, K. F., Macmillan, D. F., Hemsley, R. E., & Balow, I. H. (1992). Differences in adolescents' self-concept as a function of academic level, ethnicity, and gender. *American Journal on Mental Retardation, 96*(4), 387–403.

Wielert, J. S., & Sheldon, D. S. (1984). Make science accessible to all your students. *Science Teacher, 51*(4), 56–58.

Wikler, L. (1981). Chronic stresses of families of mentally retarded children. *Family Relations, 30*, 281–288.

Wilczenski, F. L. (1991). Facial emotional expressions of adults with mental retardation. *Education and Training in Mental Retardation, 26*(3), 319–324.

Wilczenski, F. L. (1994). Changes in attitudes toward mainstreaming among undergraduate education students. *Educational Research Quarterly, 17*(1), 5–17.

Wilgosh, L., & Barry, M. (1990). Assessment of vocational interests of TMH students. *British Columbia Journal of Special Education, 14*(2), 133–136.

Wilhite, B., Reilly, L., & Teaff, D. (1989). Recreation and leisure services and residential alternatives for persons with developmental disabilities. *Education and Training in Mental Retardation, 24*(4), 333–340.

Willer, B., & Intagliata, J. (1982). Comparison of family-care and group homes as alternatives to institutions. *Education and Training in Mental Retardation, 86*(6), 588–595.

Williams, G. A., & Asher, S. R. (1992). Assessment of loneliness at school among children with mild mental retardation. *American Journal on Mental Retardation, 96*(4), 373–385.

Williams, G. E., & Cuvo, A. J. (1986). Training apartment upkeep skills to rehabilitation clients: A comparison of task analytic strategies. *Journal of Applied Behavior Analysis, 19*(1), 39–51.

Williams, L. D. (1985). A band that exceeds all expectations. *Music Educators Journal, 71*(6), 26–29.

Williams, M. V., & Barber, W. H. (1992). The relationship of locus of control and learned helplessness in special education students. *British Columbia Journal of Special Education, 16*(1), 1–12.

Williams, R. D., & Ewing, S. (1991). Consumer roulette: The shopping patterns of mentally retarded persons. *Mental Retardation, 19*(4), 145–149.

Williams, R. L. M. (1985). Children's stealing: A review of theft-control procedures for parents and teachers. *Remedial and Special Education, 6*(2), 17–23.

Wilson, J., Blacher, J., & Baker, B. (1989). Siblings of children with severe handicaps. *Mental Retardation, 27*(3), 167–173.

Winitz, H. (1984). *Treating articulatory disorders.* Baltimore: University Park Press.

Wisniewski, L., & Alper, S. (1994). Including students with severe disabilities in general education settings. *Remedial and Special Education (RASE), 15*(1), 4–13.

Wixson, K. K. (1991). Diagnostic teaching (assessment). *Reading Teacher, 44*(6), 420–422.

Wodrich, D. L., & Barry, C. T. (1991). A survey of school psychologists' practices for identifying mentally retarded students. *Psychology in the Schools, 28*(2), 165–170.

Wolber, G., Carne, W., Collins-Montgomery, P., & Nelson, A. (1987). Tangible reinforcement plus social reinforcement versus social reinforcement alone in acquisition of toothbrushing skills. *Mental Retardation, 25*(5), 275–279.

Wolery, M., Ault, M. J., Gast, D. L., Doyle, P. M., & Griffen, A. K. (1990). Comparison of constant time delay and the system of least prompts in teaching chained tasks. *Education and Training in Mental Retardation, 25*(3), 243–257.

Wolery, M., Ault, M. J., Gast, D. L., Doyle, P. M., & Griffen, A. K. (1991). Teaching chained tasks in dyads: Acquisition of target and observational behaviors. *Journal of Special Education, 25*(2), 198–220.

Wolff, R. P. (1994). Management of behavioral feeding problems in young children. *Infants and Young Children, 7*(1), 14–23.

Wolinsky, G. F., & Walker, S. (1975). A home safety inventory for parents of preschool handicapped children teaching. *Exceptional Children, 7*(3), 82–86.

Wolraich, M. L., & Siperstein, G. N. (1983). Assessing professionals' prognostic impressions of mental retardation. *Mental Retardation, 20*(1), 8–12.

Wolraich, M. L., & Siperstein, G. N. (1986). Physicians' and other professionals' expectations and prognoses for mentally retarded individuals. *Education and Training in Mental Retardation, 91*(3), 244–249.

Wood, T. A., & Flynt, S. W. (1991). Maternal reaction to diagnosis of mental retardation: A retrospective study. *British Columbia Journal of Special Education, 15*(2), 137–145.

Wood, W. R. (1981). *Educational concerns among handicapped and non-handicapped students, their parents, and teachers.* Unpublished doctoral dissertation, Brigham Young University, Provo, UT.

Wright, C. W., & Schuster, J. W. (1994). Accepting specific versus functional student responses when training chained tasks. *Education and Training in Mental Retardation and Developmental Disabilities, 29*(1), 43–56.

Xeromeritou, A. (1992). The ability to encode facial and emotional expressions by educable mentally retarded and nonretarded children. *Journal of Psychology, 126*(5), 571–584.

Yanok, J. (1988). Individualized instruction: A GOOD approach. *Academic Therapy, 24*(2), 163–167.

Yanok, J., & Derubertis, D. (1989). Comparative study of parental participation in regular and special education programs. *Exceptional Children, 56*(3), 195–199.

Yoder, P., & Forehand, R. (1974). Effects of modeling and verbal cues upon concept acquisition of nonretarded and retarded children. *Education and Training in Mental Retardation, 78*(5), 566–570.

Yoder, P. J., & Davies, B. (1992). Greater intelligibility in verbal routines with young children with developmental delays. *Applied Psycholinguistics, 13*(1), 77–91.

York, J., Vandercook, T., Macdonald, C., Heise-Neff, C., & Caughey, E. (1991). Feedback about integrating middle-school students with severe disabilities in general education classes. *Exceptional Children, 58*(3), 244–258.

Ysseldyke, J. E., & Algozzine, B. (1982). *Critical issues in special and remedial education.* Boston: Houghton Mifflin.

Yudof, M. G., Kirp, D. L., & Levin, B. (1992). *Educational policy and the law* (3rd ed.). St. Paul, MN: West.

Zeaman, D., & House, B. J. (1963). The role of attention in retardate discrimination learning. In N. R. Ellis (Ed.), *Handbook of mental deficiency: Psychological theory and research* (pp. 159–223). Hillsdale, NJ: Erlbaum.

Zetlin, A. G., & Bilsky, L. H. (1980). Reasoning by trainable mentally retarded and young nonretarded individuals. *Journal of Mental Deficiency Research, 24*(1), 65–71.

Zetlin, A. G., & Murtaugh, M. (1988). Friendship patterns of mildly learning handicapped and nonhandicapped high school students. *American Journal on Mental Retardation, 92*(5), 447–454.

Zetlin, A. G., & Murtaugh, M. (1990). Whatever happened to borderline IQs? *American Journal on Mental Retardation, 94*(5), 447–454.

Zigler, E. (1973). The retarded child as a whole person. In D. K. Routh (Ed.), *The experimental psychology of mental retardation* (pp. 267–273). Hawthorne, NY: Aldine.

Zigler, E., Balla, D. A., & Hodapp, R. (1984). On the definition and classification of mental retardation. *Education and Training in Mental Retardation, 89*(3), 215–230.

Zigler, E., & Hodapp, R. M. (1986). *Understanding mental retardation.* Cambridge, UK: Cambridge University Press.

Zimiles, H., & Lee, V. E. (1991). Adolescent family structure and educational progress. *Developmental Psychology, 27*(2), 314–320.

Zohn, C. J., & Bornstein, P. H. (1980). Self-monitoring of work performance with mentally retarded adults: Effects upon work productivity, work quality, and on-task behavior. *Mental Retardation, 18*(1), 19–25.

Author Index

Subject Index